AMERICAN SCARE

AMERICAN SCARE

Florida's Hidden Cold War
on Black and Queer Lives

ROBERT W. FIESELER

DUTTON

DUTTON
An imprint of Penguin Random House LLC
1745 Broadway, New York, NY 10019
penguinrandomhouse.com

Images on pages 1, 6, 21, 28, 35, 46, 58, 66, 77, 84, 95, 125, 139, 148, 160,
168, 177, 179, 188, 203, 212, 220, 229, 241, 250, 258, 279, 286, 298,
311, 318, 336, and 340 are courtesy of Florida Memory.

Images on pages 9, 113, 118, 121, 269, and 327 are courtesy of Art Copleston Papers.

LIBRARY OF CONGRESS CATALOGING-IN-PUBLICATION DATA

Names: Fieseler, Robert W., author.
Title: American scare: Florida's hidden cold war on
Black and queer lives / Robert W. Fieseler.
Description: New York, NY: Dutton, [2025] |
Includes bibliographical references and index.
Identifiers: LCCN 2024062027 (print) | LCCN 2024062028 (ebook) |
ISBN 9780593183953 (hardcover) | ISBN 9780593183977 (ebook)
Subjects: LCSH: Florida. Legislature. Legislative Investigation Committee. |
National Association for the Advancement of Colored People. | African
Americans—Florida—History. | Homosexuality—Florida—History. |
Communism—Florida—History. | Florida—Politics and government—1951–
Classification: LCC F316.2 .F42 2025 (print) | LCC F316.2 (ebook) |
DDC 305.8009759—dc23/eng/20250228
LC record available at https://lccn.loc.gov/2024062027
LC ebook record available at https://lccn.loc.gov/2024062028

Printed in the United States of America
1st Printing

The authorized representative in the EU for product safety and compliance is
Penguin Random House Ireland, Morrison Chambers,
32 Nassau Street, Dublin D02 YH68, Ireland,
https://eu-contact.penguin.ie.

To Art Copleston,

who entrusted me with his life;

and to Bonnie Stark,

who entrusted me with her life's work.

Whatever

returns from oblivion returns

to find a voice.

—Louise Glück, *The Wild Iris*

Contents

ACT V CRASH LANDING

Storm Chasing

September 2021

IT'S AS IF the forces of justice and karma break and break upon the shores of Florida. From the swords of colonizers to the whips of overseers to the dynamite of Klansmen to the attack dogs of police, the land has acted as a New World Eden for strivers with oppressive dreams. It's a place where power plays beyond ordinary rules and where some folks get away with everything.

It was September 4, 2021. Hurricane Ida, a Category 4 storm, had made landfall several days prior. In the trunk of my rental van was sufficient evidence, twenty-some bankers boxes of historical documents, to deliver to what I believed would be a mortal reckoning on Florida and its past. I knew I had to get these materials across state lines even if that meant hiding them in my storm-ravaged city.

Hurricane Ida walloped the Gulf Coast on August 29, and it downed the power lines to my hometown of New Orleans, which sweltered without electricity in the peak of midsummer. I was in Chicago when the storm alerts hit my phone, and I had to book a hotel reservation on the fly in northern Mississippi for my husband and our two kittens, who immediately evacuated our house. Ordinarily, I'd have hopped a flight to join my displaced family. But my husband assured me from a Red Roof Inn that he was fine and the kitties settled, and I'd made a promise to someone in Tallahassee, Florida. It was an unusual promise (a spiritual boon for a historian in my position), a promise that I'd willingly accept a gift, that I'd take something unique off someone else's hands. And on that promise hinged an entire history at risk of vanishing.

I couldn't forget what Bonnie Stark, the first Johns Committee scholar, told me when we spoke that first time via video chat two weeks prior: "There are maybe twenty boxes of the papers. And I have them. Because the gentleman for the legislature who was overseeing the release of the papers, he came to appreciate how hard I was working, and when they finally transferred everything to the Florida Archives, he gave me the hard copies. And I've lugged these around forever. Right now, they're in my office at work."

Bonnie Stark possessed something that shouldn't exist. She held the secret second set of the complete records of the Florida Legislative Investigation Committee (FLIC), also called the Johns Committee—a forgotten cabal of gerrymandered white legislators that went after Black and queer citizens in the mid-twentieth century at the height of anti-Communist hysteria. In the Johns Committee's path of destruction lay the freedoms of the masterminds of Florida desegregation, plus the lives and careers of more than thirty preeminent scholars, at least seventy-one teachers, and as many as five hundred college students, whose persecution led all the way to the steps of the state supreme court and the U.S. Supreme Court. The crusades of these Florida men and their nearly decade-long reign had all but vanished from the American story, the records sealed and then censored upon release. Names of victims were deleted by agents of the state who never had to say sorry. After all, why say sorry to a ghost?

The State of Florida, Governor Ron DeSantis's Florida, labored under the belief that it possessed the only surviving copies of FLIC records under lock and key. In a land of supposed sunshine laws, state authorities hid their histories in plain sight in the Soviet pillbox–like structure of the Florida State Archives, where the establishment could monitor who accessed them and obstruct the curious few with burdensome procedures and policies. "When you get power in Florida," state senator Lauren Book forewarned me, "you can use it to pick on any-one." In a Gulf borderland where administrations become regimes on a dime, people out of power tend to get hurt.

I knew I had to move this cargo out of Florida before state authorities caught wind of what Bonnie Stark had stashed and how I planned to use it. Within the official State Archives, I was permitted to review only one redacted page per one folder at a time, while sitting in one specific seat that directly faced the desks of watching bureaucrats, who could snatch things away on impulse. With all the files at my disposal, documents could be analyzed and cross-referenced from first page to last. Duplicates could be compared, instead of culled, with redaction mistakes noted and leveraged to recover knowledge. De-censorship would be possible. Power had lynched history, but by an unforeseeable twist, it could be restored. Then we, the people, might finally sit with the story they didn't want us to read.

On September 4, I loaded up box after box in the parking lot of Bonnie Stark's legal office. She had kept the records to herself for nearly thirty years, to the point that it shocked her mentor to learn of them, and then she entrusted them to a veritable stranger. What did that feel like for her? I detected relief in her eyes as she watched them leave her sight. Later, I worked up the courage to ask her. "I remember thinking I have to help him," she said. "I felt a kinship to you, that we shared a common appreciation for the importance." I peeled out of Florida's capital city. Who am I to inherit such a quest, I asked myself, such a gift as this life's work? And to what extent did my whiteness or my maleness or my middle-class upbringing somehow set me up to receive a lucky break out of a clear blue sky? How am I different from any other outsider who appropriates a people's history and then explains it back to them without shame?

Overwhelmed with impostor syndrome, I thought about turning around as I neared the tip of the Panhandle. As I crossed a bridge above a bay, my questions spun in the other direction. Aren't any Floridians besides Bonnie Stark even curious why, once a decade, an anti-queer or anti-Black movement will sprout from their soil, flourish, and spread its seeds across America in a panic that inevitably claims that tough action will save innocent whites from a moral hellscape? Why, to privilege a sunshine dream, are generation after generation of Florida strongmen allowed to escape culpability? How could one peninsula be such a pressure point for the American body politic, such a wavemaker for the nerves?

I possessed a hefty part of the answer in the back seat of my van. Although Florida didn't invent the American Scare, the strain of fear sown by the Johns Committee blooms first here before heading elsewhere. Yet I was still in Florida's jurisdiction, and I had the wildest thought that Governor DeSantis himself would be waiting at the border in his duck boots and blue fleece vest—standing with hand outstretched before a highway blockade. But nothing ridiculous like that happened.

I exhaled a short breath regardless as I passed the inverse "Welcome to Florida" signage and crossed state lines. Hours later, I entered the balmy cover of New Orleans, a metropolitan region asleep in shadowy quiet. Streetlights stretched overhead like the arms of sheltering saints. As I arrived at my shotgun house, neighbors sat gossiping and clinking beers on a nearby stoop. They rose to high-five and greet me with their storm stories.

Politely declining offers of help, I off-loaded the boxes by candlelight into my living room, which looked unfamiliar in the yellow glow. Then I blew out the lights, one by one, like a man from another time. The history they tried to kill has survived, I affirmed as I waited for my eyes to adjust. And someone in authority miscalculated terribly, I realized as I looked over the trove of evidence. You can't half kill the truth. Not in America, where it'll only play dead, go dormant for years, and resurface to tell its story of being buried. "No lie can live forever," preached the Reverend Dr. Martin Luther King Jr. in his final Sunday sermon before a nobody shot him in Memphis.

We are a nation where self-evident truth outlives power, and not even pharaohs can carry their lies with them when they close their eyes to meet the same eternal rest as paupers. I tried to grab a few hours' rest before heading north to reunite with my displaced family. In my dreams, a man with no face redacted the Constitution in the name of public safety.

INTRODUCTION

I.

Race

November 13, 1961
(Box 2, Mississippi Papers, FBI Records)

THERE WAS LITTLE a white man couldn't do in the name of the law in Florida, especially when exercising his duties through an appointed or elected position, especially when he wore a uniform or an insignia. High in a conference room of the Di Lido Hotel, an eleven-story tower overlooking Miami Beach, these white men met in secret. Intelligence agents from ten southern states in still-segregated America, they gathered pursuant to orders from their governors and legislatures for the purpose of defending, in their own language, "our own States' rights against any and all enemies."

More than five years since Virginia senator Harry F. Byrd's call for "massive resistance" in Dixieland toward the second U.S. Supreme Court *Brown v. Board of Education* ruling for public schools to integrate "with all deliberate speed," these were the lawmen and watchmen holding the line against federal overreach.

Through brute force and legal chicanery, states like Louisiana, North Carolina, and Tennessee had mostly held back the tide of intermixing. Florida, with just five desegregated school districts (out of sixty-seven) into the 1960 school year, accommodated so-called integration mongers among the least, with only hard-liners like Alabama and Mississippi beating it out for full boasting rights: zero desegregated schools. Florida lawmen in particular understood that the best way to be above the law was to be a legal white knight and/or an extralegal enforcer. For example, a white official could close down public pools rather than permit a court-ordered integration and face no backlash. This was a great oversight in American jurisprudence: a condition of lawlessness within the law, through which southern whites could not be penalized when the law, from state constitutions on downward, existed chiefly to advantage them over others.

The law of the South could contort in knots to avoid white guilt. Agents of "law and order" exploited these situational loopholes with no small swagger. For centuries, with a few decades of federally enforced exceptions during Reconstruction, the racial status quo of the South reigned as a near-feudal fiefdom of white dominion. Into the early 1960s, Black men were still expected to step in the gutter and avert their eyes whenever a white woman passed on the sidewalk. No Black man, not even a Black convict speaking to a white convict in a prison yard, could safely address a white man without calling him "mister." In Florida courtrooms, Black citizens were commonly called "darky" by prosecutors, and the official anthem of the State of Florida, "Old Folks at Home," hailed "darkies" of the "old plantation" at diplomatic meetings and gubernatorial inaugurations.

"Racial agitation" largely sprang from the rare circumstance in which a so-called uppity Black denied genuflection to a low-status white, who then rallied a mob to restore essential order. At its zenith, the law of Florida could best be represented by whatever a white sheriff, elected through voter suppression in Black-majority counties, told a browbeaten Black man in an isolated room as that man etched an X signature upon a confession already typewritten. Between 1924 and 1941, if the Black "confessee" was convicted of a capital crime in the

State of Florida, the white county sheriff who compelled that confession received the honor (and public relations windfall) of throwing the switch at the ritual electrocution.

But by November 1961, these white leaders, defenders of the segregated order, felt themselves besieged. National sentiment was slowly shifting, with Freedom Riders on Greyhounds testing interstate travel, southern universities being desegregated by court order, Blacks conducting "wade-ins" at beaches, and Dr. Martin Luther King Jr. becoming a well-known figure. White lawmen from Florida and Georgia expressed a need for a new forum "in order to better exchange information between the Southern States, which outside forces are now attacking." Some forty lawmen answered the call to come to Miami Beach for a three-day summit. Most brought along their white wives, who spent afternoons browsing boutiques. Some wives hauled their kids along.

Meanwhile, on Cape Canaveral farther up the coast, NASA was propelling Florida's newfound status as a cultural and scientific gem. In the spirit of these times, southern agents fancied themselves as a bit like the astronauts: exemplars and defenders of the American Man. "The Magic City, the Tropical Playland of the world," wrote famed University of Florida geography professor Sigismond Diettrich of this 1950s metropolis. "The Mecca of millionaires striving for health-giving sunshine, palms and tropical skies, the blue waters teeming with marine life, the white sandy beaches teeming with sun bronzed humanity. . . . This is Miami, more a dream and an idea than a stark reality."

Here at the Di Lido Hotel, a 329-room modernist wonder built by architect Morris Lapidus, assembled heads of southern sovereignty commissions, chiefs of "state FBIs," representatives of state legislative committees on un-American subversion, and generals of major police forces. All led on-the-ground resistances, some known to the wider public and some clandestine within state and county borders. All traveled to Miami in their official capacities. Few would turn down an invitation to a table such as this one, set by the likes of the Florida Legislative Investigation Committee (FLIC) and its power broker: Florida state senator Charley Johns, although Charley knew not to show his face at the confab, lest he be pulled into intrigue himself.

Democrat Charley Johns, attendees knew, was leading the so-called anti-Communist purge in his home state as chairman of an independent committee that, through open hearings and secret interrogations, aimed to shed light on Reds trying to integrate schools, foster chaos, and pervert the American family.

Post–federal Red Scare, southern populists like Charley had adapted the term *Communist* to mean a white race traitor or a nonwhite challenger to the "southern way of life" (defined by historian Charles Reagan Wilson as a racial dog whistle that "encouraged white southerners to invest enormous meaning in the southern identity," reinforced by "belief in the moral superiority of white southerners surrounded by allegedly savage Black people"). FLIC agents bandied the C-term cavalierly to give their social agendas the semblance of a national security emergency. They in truth possessed none of the competencies needed to spot a single legitimate Soviet agent, though it was hard to parse if they hid awareness of this insufficiency or convinced themselves the opposite through their own ego-stroking. "Not strong, not open," Remus J. Strickland, chief investigator for the FLIC, later admitted of Communism in Florida without additional self-analysis. "Hard to detect."

Shrewdly, Charley Johns preferred to do his harshest work through proxies, and so he dispatched from the state capital of Tallahassee an intermediary: Florida house representative Richard O. Mitchell. Promptly at nine o'clock in the morning on Monday, November 13, in a conference room with a view of the Atlantic, the convention of investigators began. Host Remus Strickland of the FLIC called the meeting to order. Emphasizing the highly confidential nature of what was about to be shared, Strickland welcomed into their hushed chamber Florida assistant attorney general George R. Georgieff, special prosecutor for "all crimes of subversion" in the Sunshine State. Georgieff briefed the room on Florida's "Cuban problem," relative to the hundreds of Cuban refugees fleeing the Castro regime and flooding Miami. Forebodingly, he estimated that at least 10 percent of those who landed in the United States were Communists planted by Castro for subversive purposes—part of the notorious "Red" plan to hasten a Cold War victory for the Soviet Union.

Next, Lieutenant H. A. Poole of the Georgia Bureau of Investigation, a state spy division modeled on J. Edgar Hoover's Federal Bureau of Investigation, reported on the southern racial situation. Priming the group, Poole stated how "we southern states cannot rely on the FBI to exchange any information with us on agitative groups." The assertion met with knowing nods. With federal intelligence untrustworthy, Poole stressed the "importance of keeping the information furnished by one state to another confidential."

Hitting his stride, Poole categorized the Southern Christian Leadership Conference, a Black minister–based organization in the forefront of the Black civil rights movement, as a subversive organization. Poole named its leader, Dr. Martin Luther King Jr., as a driving force of racial agitation, a walking terror who fundraised for Communist-affiliated teachers running radical workshops, such as the Highlander Folk School in Monteagle, Tennessee, where the lawbreaker Rosa Parks received training. Poole cited Communist agitators as the true menace behind that summer's interstate Freedom Rider bus fiasco—a challenge of the federal Interstate Commerce Commission's prohibition of segregation in interstate bus travel that ended in a blazing Greyhound on an Alabama roadside and a beatdown at the hands of a chain-wielding white mob in Birmingham—"as well as most all other racial agitation carried on." To shouts of agreement and "Hear! Hear!" Lieutenant Poole closed by declaring Dr. Martin Luther King Jr. "the most dangerous agitator running loose today."

Representatives of other segregated states followed Poole with similar reports of unrest compounded by federal interference. Gwin Cole, investigator for the Mississippi Highway Patrol, proudly discussed how Freedom Riders near the state capital of Jackson were manhandled "from the time they were arrested in Mississippi until they were convicted and made bond or were imprisoned." Present in the room, Brigadier General T. B. Birdsong, who led the arresting charge against the offenders, beamed proudly. Howard Chandler of the Arkansas State Police, representing the state where President Eisenhower had called in federal troops to escort the Little Rock Nine Black students integrating Central High School in 1957, spoke with optimism of white vigilante Minute Men in Arkansas, Georgia, Louisiana, and southern Illinois organizing "to resist the Communists, should they take over." A confidential Mississippi State Sovereignty Commission report noted

Remus J. Strickland

the room's support for the Minute Men network: "It would not be any trouble for them to get armed."

Last to speak, convention host Remus J. Strickland rose to touch on a groundbreaking subject in southern law enforcement. Strickland had recently concluded an investigation, he shared, into homosexual perverts teaching in Florida schools and colleges, which resulted in at least 140 teachers and 15 professors being fired for moral lapses. This homosexual "purge," as it was called by Florida lawmakers as well as the few homosexual activists in existence in the United States, had never been more popular among Florida parents, who largely viewed homosexuals as insidious devils and godless Communists keen to tempt their children into an underworld of sex criminality. Strickland described how Florida agents "revoked a sex pervert's teachers license to teach in Florida for life" and promised lists of fired sex deviates to his fellow colleagues, lest those former teachers be so shameless as to reapply for licensure in other states. Many in the room had never heard the taboo of homosexuality discussed so openly before or presented as an attack on southern society on par with Dr. King. Those in the conference room applauded Strickland's savvy.

The totality of the day's presentations sent a resounding message: Blacks, Cubans, Communists, and homosexuals, aligning treasonously behind federal rights and privileges, constituted a societal infestation. This unholy cabal of subversives intended to annihilate the almighty "southern way of life." The United States, attendees believed, was en route to collapse from within, like Weimar Germany. The irony that they themselves were conspiring to subvert the U.S. government, while projecting that claim upon their enemies, escaped them. Strickland adjourned the day's conference for drinks in the hotel cabana and a dip in the Di Lido's Olympic-size pool, where more was discussed in earnest while wives sunbathed.

After recovering from their hangovers, the lawmen reconvened late the following afternoon, November 14, to adopt the bylaws of a new alliance: the Southern Association of Intelligence Agents. Unanimously, they signed their names to an alternate group "Constitution" that promised to "always be on alert and ready to take proper action against any person or persons who propose to overthrow our form of government." With their founding documents passed, the confederation elected officers. Lieutenant H. A. Poole of the Georgia Bureau of Investigation was named president for his demonstrated expertise on racial topics. Conference host Remus J. Strickland was elevated as the group's executive director for the deep impression he'd made concerning the sex pervert crisis.

The interstate alliance agreed to meet again that upcoming June in Hot Springs, Arkansas, a popular southern spa town. Group president Poole, cautioning confidentiality in all matters going forward, praised attendees for their productivity. In celebration, Strickland hosted a soiree that night for the agents and their wives at Café Le Can Can in a nearby tower. They dined on broiled young squab chicken followed by a showstopping dessert called Chantilly Wedge Fantasia. By special instruction of state senator Charley Johns, all charges were "paid the same evening by Mr. Dick Mitchell," the Florida state house representative attending to the group's needs. Taxpayers of the Sunshine State (including the Black integrationists they pilloried) footed the bill through their contributions to the state treasury. Members of the Southern Association of Intelligence Agents had already begun the practice of passing confidential reports, but now their back-channeling was authorized and official.

The Louisiana Bureau of Criminal Identification and Information gave Strickland a lead on an integrationist preacher who had been run out of Baton Rouge and was now pastor of a Congregational church in Daytona Beach. Strickland had already mailed the Mississippi Sovereignty Commission an educational blacklist naming all teachers suspended on suspicion of homosexuality from Florida schools. As supplementary intel, Strickland provided for reference to all signatory members of the Southern Association of Intelligence Agents a hush-hush list of known racial organizations "either Communist altogether, Communist-front, or heavily Communist infiltrated." Since the U.S. Supreme Court had struck down federal sedition laws, which made it hard to prosecute agitators, Strickland implored his fellow investigators to "expose and let the public itself destroy the movements as they are brought out into the open" through public hearings.

Even after unfavorable coverage in northern media concerning wanton violence toward the Freedom Riders, state agents like Strickland argued that the battle for order could be won in a wider court of publicity by disgracing the presumed guilty. As the sun set behind the Di Lido Hotel and the distant city, throwing long shadows toward the crystal blues of the Gulf Stream and the first emerging stars, the men toasted each other and their powers of solidarity. "On behalf of my wife and myself, I wish to express to you and Mrs. Strickland my thanks for your most gracious hospitality," gushed President H. A. Poole in a letter to Strickland. President Poole wrote separately to Florida state senator Charley Johns, in a gesture playing up to Strickland's boss, "Mr. R. J. Strickland, your chief investigator, exerted every effort possible to make our visit to your state a pleasure." Despite all the overtones of secrecy, *The New York Times* sniffed out the covert meeting in Miami within six days. The headline announced: "Security Bureau Formed in South."

Facing an onslaught of questions from the media as well as pressure from FBI director J. Edgar Hoover, President H. A. Poole petitioned association members to excise the word *intelligence* from their group name, which provoked Strickland to vent: "I do not bend to the whims of news publications or news reporters and do not give a tinker's damn about what they print." In a mollifying gesture, the alliance rebranded as the Southern States Investigator's Association. Across the South and beyond, many such gatherings were taking place. Hoover couldn't discover them all. As the region's "first line of defense," white officers locking arms in defiance, the association planned to meet again that June at the Arkansas Hot Springs and heed the cry of Dixie, lest she vanish.

II.

Sex

Art Copleston, circa 1959

January 20, 1959
(Box 7, Copleston Papers)

THEY CAME FOR him in accounting class when he was taking his final exam. When the metal doors flew open and banged, the clatter echoed throughout the seats of Matherly Hall. He didn't think to look up, at first. The exam was half his grade, and he didn't have seconds to spare. Maybe a late student, he told himself.

Then came the squeak of boots above the scribble of pencils, the smell of leather and gunmetal over that of paper and erasers. Feet trudged up to University of Florida (UF) accounting professor James F. Moore, seated on the lecture hall dais. "Art Copleston," a voice ordered. "There," Professor Moore answered softly. It was the resignation in the voice—ordinarily, the booming projection of a proud academic—that provoked the twenty-six-year-old college sophomore to finally, reluctantly, peer up from his desk.

Before his professor, three men in powder-blue uniforms stood in

matching sheriff's hats with holstered pistols. Two were already looking in his direction, just as other students in the room were lifting and
turning their faces toward him. Copleston looked pleadingly at his
professor, but Professor Moore wouldn't quite meet his eye. Why
wasn't a public educator yelling, "What the hell's going on?" or even
asking for IDs as law enforcement swarmed the room? There was nowhere to run from where he was seated—in the middle of the lecture
hall, away from an exit. Perhaps he shouldn't have come today, he
thought, but then he'd have automatically failed the course. Though he
had no criminal record, though he was an honorably discharged U.S.
Air Force veteran attending university on the G.I. Bill, Art Copleston
was fast becoming a regular target of these humiliations.

Copleston knew to drop his pencil, rise from his chair, and put his
hands in the air. Tan and trim with a crew cut, blue-eyed and baby-
faced, he must have looked elfishly handsome despite his obvious
panic. The officers in blue waved him forward, hands resting on side-
arms as if Copleston posed a danger to public safety. He recognized
none of these men on sight, but uniform insignias suggested Florida
state highway patrolmen. "It was pointed out to me that if you took
them out of their classroom, there was the benefit of shock," noted Officer John Tileston, the campus agent who stage-managed these arrests. The class observed passively as an officer clapped a hand on
Copleston's shoulder. They led him past the lecture hall dais and out
an exit and shoved him into an idling squad car. This was years before
Miranda rights came into being. Though Copleston wasn't declared to
be under arrest, he knew that resisting the officers would have forced a
scuffle and made his classmates presume his guilt. Besides, resisting
could have provoked the officers into making a verbal accusation: one
terrible word starting with a q, a word people ordinarily hissed, a word
bullies called him on the playground as a child, a word that would
mean he had to transfer to an out-of-state school.

It was a crisp, sunny day in Gainesville that January, with countless
students lounging in cardigans on the sprawling mid-Florida campus
of green lawns, concrete archways, and Spanish moss draped over tall
pine trees. "The physical factors of Florida's geography have hardly
changed, if any, since Ponce de Leon discovered the land and gave its
mellifluous name 'Terra Florida' in 1513," wrote University of Florida

geography department chairman and famed Florida scholar Sigismond Diettrich, "yet their meaning to man and their effects upon human life have undergone tremendous transformations." In the front seat of the car, the officers lit up and said little. Smoke drifted over Copleston's back seat. There was little to do but watch his fellow students out the window.

More than twelve thousand strapping youths like himself had enrolled at the University of Florida that fall, a new record. UF also, contentiously, had just accepted its first Black student into the law school in spite of Florida's policy of interposition, an attempt to bypass federal law through assigned seating policies that placed stated segregation powers above the U.S. Supreme Court's *Brown v. Board of Education* decisions. (Interposition was, of course, among the South's oldest political tricks, a ploy dating back to the 1798 Virginia Resolutions that George Washington rebuked as "unlawful.") At a campus panel the prior year, the dean of the College of Education, J. B. White, joined three other professors stating that they have no "moral obligation" to push for integration. These delay tactics failed when the UF law school dean rejected interposition as an illegal evasion and insisted on abiding by the U.S. Supreme Court's *Brown* directives, lest his law school lose accreditation. As a partial result, the Florida campus became a hotbed for stealth activities of state law enforcement.

In February 1958, J. B. Matthews, an American ex-Communist turned informant for the House Un-American Activities Committee (HUAC), and former senator Joseph McCarthy testified before Charley Johns on the alleged ties between Communism and the National Association for the Advancement of Colored People (NAACP). While Matthews was more motivational speaker than legal witness, his anti-Communist rhetoric, although tangential to Chairman Charley Johns's case, primed the public.

That June, Chairman Charley Johns turned his eye toward the school in Gainesville. As the Florida Legislative Investigation Committee chairman, he was endowed with extrajudicial powers to root out illegal subversion. From the border with Georgia at the St. Marys River across the Panhandle and down the peninsula into the Key West surf, every inch of the Sunshine State constituted Charley's investigatory turf. Charley already was disdainful of academics, as he'd attended the University of Florida for only two months as a younger man but never graduated. Wanting to marry his high school sweetheart, he'd dropped out of classes to join the railroad—hiding the decision from his mother for months. Charley eventually worked his way up to the position of railroad engineer on the deluxe *Orange Blossom Special*, which ran from New York City to Miami, but attached a "Jim Crow car" for Blacks who rode the southern leg.

Now sniffing out Communists closer to his alma mater, Charley Johns recalled a former UF professor named John H. Reynolds, who in 1953 refused to answer questions from the HUAC in Washington, D.C., during the so-called federal Red Scare:

Q: "Are you now a member of the Communist Party?"
A: "I refuse to answer that. . . ."
Q: "Have you ever been a member of the Communist Party?"
A: "I refuse to answer that also."

Federal legislators subpoenaed Professor Reynolds on suspicion of his being part of a "Red cell" of students interested in Communism at Harvard in the 1940s. Within hours of his stand in Washington, D.C., Reynolds was suspended by the UF president and called to appear before a faculty board. Rather than face another kangaroo committee, he resigned from his tenured job.

But Reynolds continued to live and socialize in Gainesville and advocate for "Pink" integration policies among friends, a fact that irked his enemies. In this era, "Pink" school integrationists were theorized to be turncoats in league with (or at least susceptible to) "Red" Soviets. Some five years later, legislators and state agents remained determined to catch the proverbial "Commie that got away." Charley Johns sent chief investigator Remus Strickland to Gainesville that summer in hopes of unearthing the elusive Soviet sympathizers infiltrating academia. UF president J. Wayne Reitz in turn offered free use of his campus police officer John Tileston—a handsome, married twenty-three-year-old Korean War veteran—for the undercover operation. "The Johns Committee wanted me to work with them about finding all the queers and the Communists on campus," affirmed Tileston.

Since teachers in public universities like John H. Reynolds operated in loco parentis, alone with students for hours in classrooms, Charley Johns and Strickland believed that they were positioned to challenge Florida's cultural stability. Charley had already promised to use his constitutional powers to fire any teacher with the gall to be a member of an organization with plans to kill segregation: the NAACP. "It is my understanding, and this is purely hearsay," Charley told a legislative session, "that the NAACP is attempting to organize on the University of Florida campus, and the [federal] Un-American Activities Committee has said that there's a number of known Communists that belong to this organization." Recognizing Strickland's presence on campus, the student newspaper, the *Alligator*, initially speculated that Strickland was "trying to pinpoint 'information' that some professors at the University of Florida have advocated racial integration."

Remus J. Strickland was a Tallahassee policeman drafted into covert "legislative enforcement" by Charley Johns. "Strick," as Charley lovingly called him, had previously worked with the state to investigate potential Communist collaboration within the NAACP during the Tallahassee bus boycott of 1956—a protest of Tallahassee's segregated bus system that culminated in the repeal of the city's segregated seating ordinance. (The same day as that repeal, however, Tallahassee officials implemented "assigned seating" for Blacks and whites on buses, sorted by race, which made victory essentially Pyrrhic for Black freedom activists.) Strickland's tactics in that prolonged campaign included arresting civil rights demonstrators who traveled in volunteer car pools as "common carriers," aka unlicensed taxis. Strickland's tenacity in pursuing a civil rights organization that Charley firmly believed to be a Soviet front had won him the admiration of the state's most powerful legislator—and an exclusive job.

By the first week of June 1958, confidential FLIC informants staked out John Reynolds's home and began assembling files on the cavalcade of artists and professors who visited the residence. Among those observed and tailed to their next locations were University of Florida professor of education David Lane and botany professor Ernest Ford, tagged as one of the worst "Pinks" of the Gainesville area. Both men were now indelibly on the lists of Remus Strickland and Charley Johns.

By August 18, Chairman Charley Johns subpoenaed all faculty

records and employment application records held by UF president Reitz, and Reitz complied expeditiously. An adept backroom dealer, Charley maintained a close relationship with the UF president. As a state senator, he was on the Florida committee that determined budgetary appropriations for UF, and as a result, he frequently wrote President Reitz with odd requests and expected results. He even had special permission to park in Reitz's driveway at the Presidential Home for an easier walk to Florida Field during Gator home football games.

But when the hunt for Communists came up with nil throughout the fall of 1958, Strickland faced mounting pressure from boss Charley, who'd tied his political fortunes so closely to FLIC that everyone knew it as the Johns Committee. Charley Johns needed Strickland to justify FLIC's budget of $75,000 for a "State FBI" by producing something, anything, concrete in the area of subversive activities before the funds ran dry. The Johns Committee had recently canceled open hearings and declared itself "hamstrung" by the NAACP. Several times, Senator Charley Johns reminded Strickland that their committee possessed all the authority of the legislature to enter university spaces without warrants and detain citizens at undisclosed locations, subpoena witnesses, take sworn testimony, edit witness statements, gather evidence, administer loyalty oaths, employ secret informants, examine academic transcripts and class assignments, and even acquire student medical histories. Strickland was also immune from liability, and should any lawsuits be brought against his actions, the Florida attorney general would be compelled to represent him.

The John Reynolds stakeout in Gainesville bore surprising fruit, revealing associations between the disgraced former professor and his friends at the Gainesville Little Theatre, a small troupe of amateur players loosely associated with the University of Florida. Within that local dramatic circle, investigators were stunned to discover a brimming underworld of homosexuals. Locals like Arthur "Hoyle" Wyman, owner of an off-campus gay party estate called the Chicken Ranch, rubbed shoulders and perhaps more with tenured faculty on the university payroll, including one department head named Sigismond Diettrich. Quickly sizing up the local arts scene, Strickland and his agents extended their spying campaign to locations where homosexuals like Wyman and his roommate Lonnie Rhoden frequented, including the Chicken Ranch and a near-campus bar called the Burger House.

Conferring with Alachua County sheriff Joe Crevasse, who had jurisdiction over Gainesville, Strickland began an entrapment operation in Gainesville's notorious cruising center: the men's restroom in the basement of the Alachua county courthouse. Sheriff Crevasse agreed to keep that public bathroom, a convenient stroll from campus, open after dark, and the prospect proved tantalizing to a swath of men seeking anonymous encounters, their exhilaration converting to horror and confusion when state agents like Strickland or Tileston approached.

By that September 27, Charley Johns chaired an emergency meeting with Strickland and Florida State Board of Control chairman James J. Love (boss of UF president J. Wayne Reitz) in the courthouse directly above said bathroom after touring the facilities. Though their meeting lacked a quorum of committee members and therefore was unofficial when Charley gaveled it to order, its decisions were binding. Charley Johns briefed three of the state's educational leaders on "homosexual activities" at the university. As stated in the meeting minutes, "Members of the Board of Control agreed to direct Dr. J. Wayne Reitz, President of the University, to instruct the campus police chief to cooperate fully." The minutes continued: "Members of the Board of Control present promised that Dr. Reitz would not send down any word of this matter at all," lest the intended targets, including those in the basement below, scatter when they sensed a trap.

Charley Johns enjoined Strickland to pursue these homosexual leads even though FLIC's operating statute did not permit committee investigators to search for sex criminals per se, only organizations "advocating violence or a course of conduct which would constitute a violation of the laws of Florida." Florida law, nevertheless, remained crystal clear that the "abominable and detestable crime against nature" was a felony offense punishable by up to twenty years in prison. The Florida Supreme Court had upheld such sodomy convictions as recently as 1954. Moreover, the Florida State Board of Education could revoke teaching certificates for infractions involving "moral turpitude," which gave Strickland some breathing room.

By his October 1958 progress report, Strickland boasted that he'd uncovered a "considerable homosexual operation" meriting a formal expansion of their legislative focus. Attempting to reverse engineer a rationale for why a Communist hunt started turning up queers, as they called their targets, Charley Johns challenged his committee members to establish a causal link between homosexuality and political subversion. (In actuality, Florida homosexuals abided by southern codes of "mutual discretion" and thus remained apolitical and non-self-identifying, believing the relief of their urge to be more verb than noun, more play behavior than personal trait. "Prejudice will fade away all alone if we don't make things worse by fighting it," a gay man from Dixie famously told the editors of the Los Angeles–based queer magazine *One*.)

MEN IN BLUE drove Art Copleston off the campus toward the Manor Motel, a whites-only motor court on the edge of town popular with tailgater families during whites-only football season. It was mostly empty during the winter months, barring the occasional traveling salesman. They rode together for about twenty minutes, during which time Copleston wondered how a college undergrad like himself got caught up in a state spying operation. He strained to recall when he hit the silk of their web. It must have been when Officer John Tileston spotted him laughing with friends that past summer at the Burger House.

The Burger House was a "3.2 bar," a college tavern permitted to serve only beer with a 3.2 percent alcohol content, which in theory prevented younger drinkers from becoming disinhibited and engaging in erotic debauchery. In an era when most homosexuals lived euphemistically as "bachelors," the Burger House was a known "guy bar," a "bohemian" establishment, a low-lighted locale where Copleston circulated in his element. Closeted gays whispered that it was a "fairyland." As he lived within what he called easy "boom-boom" distance, in the Thomas Hall dorms across the street, Copleston, a wiry weight lifter, was wont to prowl for a tight-waisted companion who might accept an invitation back to his quarters, where they'd mutually review male "physique magazines." It was only at the last minute, face-to-face, that

Copleston would utter the inevitable code word—*Gay?*—to avoid misunderstandings. Just being cognizant of this term placed him at the vanguard of Florida sexuality.

Unleashing this illicit twist of a pleasant word from his lips, Copleston knew, made him more naked than naked—every time, placing not only his desire but his future in the coy hands of a stranger. The best-case scenario meant instant consummation. The worst-case scenario meant falling down a social abyss: being exposed and expelled, then disowned by all relations, then forever unemployable, then suicidal, drunk, and homeless.

Copleston chatted up a cute prospect near the bar's front door, where the line formed for the jukebox, when a classmate approached. "There's a guy sitting at the bar who's been watching you a long time," the fella whispered. "And, by the way," he continued, "I hear there's some sort of strange investigation going on. . . ." Copleston turned to his left and became leveled in the fixed glare of a comb-slick man he later learned to be a campus policeman. Officer Tileston, at the Burger House tailing Hoyle Wyman and Lonnie from the Chicken Ranch, quickly made Art Copleston his new pursuit.

One by one, familiar faces from the Burger House were taken out of classes by men in powder-blue uniforms. Several admitted to their homosexuality and were expelled, Copleston recalled. Tileston later explained that several, during repeated interrogations at the campus police station, gave up Copleston as a fellow queer. The Q-word always stopped Copleston, a military veteran, short. It was an ugly word, a fighting word, a killing word even—an unconscionable slur even if true, felt Copleston, an attack on his character and his name.

The men in blue marched Copleston from the squad car into a cleared-out room at the Manor Motel, its blinds drawn. It was about 10:15 a.m., and Copleston sat at a long table across from a group of middle-aged men in gray suits. None shook his hand. "I'm Mark Hawes," a man spoke in introduction. Hawes was a "barrel-chested, gravel-voiced ex-Marine," a six-one Aryan bruiser. "I'm counsel for the Florida Legislative Investigation Committee. This gentleman here is Senator Randolph Hodges, from Cedar Key." Twenty-six-year-old undergraduate Art Copleston now sat before an elected official.

"How are you?" Senator Hodges asked.

"How are you, Senator?" Copleston responded, attempting politeness. What's a senator got to do with me? he wondered.

"He's a member of our committee. And I think you already know . . . ," Hawes began to say before Copleston caught the face of his pursuer and interrupted, "How are you, Mr. Tileston?"

ACT I.

Launch

CHAPTER 1

Call Me Charley

Charley Johns,
circa 1954

January 1, 1955
(Clerk of the House Papers, University of Florida Archives)

ACTING GOVERNOR OF Florida Charles "Charley" Johns, future founder of the Johns Committee, paused to admire his portrait in his last hours in the Executive Mansion. It was New Year's Day 1955. In the gilded frame floated a face he liked: soft and sensible, warm and white. It was a regular guy's face, indisputably the face of a man whose chief hobby was working (as he liked to say), a face his gubernatorial campaign claimed "All Florida Needs" before, it turned out, all of Florida *didn't* quite need him in that capacity when he lost the primary to finish out the rest of his executive term.

Indeed, the very political party that Charley Johns had bled for throughout his entire career expected him to swallow his pride and reassume his old seat in the Florida state senate, where he stumped for the "Pork Chopper" faction of conservative Democrats. Worse, in that May 1954 primary, state Democrats passed him over for a "Lamb Chopper" rival, Senator LeRoy Collins. That very night, silk-stocking LeRoy Collins rested next door to the Executive Mansion in the Grove Mansion, the ancestral estate of his ultra-wealthy and ultra-connected wife. Technically, acting governor Charley Johns had already turned over the keys to the state mansion to governor-elect LeRoy Collins that New Year's Eve. Most of the Johnses' family possessions had been packed up and carted home, and the acting governor was living out of suitcases.

That upcoming Tuesday morning, January 4, Charley would be expected to don Florida's traditional morning dress suit of tailcoat, top hat, and striped pants and meet LeRoy Collins, who'd wear the same outfit, at the doors of the Executive Mansion. As duty demanded, Charley would escort Collins to the steps of the state capitol. Charley planned to plaster on a smile to preserve order and legitimize the Democratic Party's peaceful transfer of power. But in the days before, he seethed.

He twirled his chain watch rhythmically around his finger, an old habit from his railroad-conducting days that calmed his nerves whenever he gamed out his future. What happened to Charley Johns? Who had done it to him? And, most important, how could Charley Johns regain his power?

Around Charley, the Executive Mansion exhibited signs of disrepair. Wallpaper peeled in places, and the rugs were threadbare. Completed in 1907, Florida's fourteen-room Georgian-style manse was a testament to the South's post-Reconstruction longing for the antebellum era. Florida men raised the Executive Mansion as a tribute to one-party rule, when the 1885 state constitution was relatively new and the Black vote was being actively subdued. In its very language, the Florida constitution of 1885 prohibited interracial marriage and made school segregation mandatory, while creating the option for a poll tax to disqualify poor voters. A precursor and an inspiration for the Mississippi constitution of 1890, the South Carolina constitution of 1895, the Louisiana constitution of 1898, and many others, the Florida constitution of 1885 pioneered a model for Black disenfranchisement and codified a slavery-lite system that greased its wheel on the exploitation of segregated Black labor.

The cream-colored Executive Mansion, designed to give white governors a home-field advantage over visiting heads of state, embodied these tropes. In its half century of use, the mansion at 700 North Adams had housed fifteen of Florida's finest families. But its glory had faded so badly by the mid-twentieth century that Governor Fuller Warren, serving from 1949 to 1953, nicknamed it the "State Shack."

Charley Johns harbored a fear deep in his gut that the history surrounding him would disappear into an abyss, as went the way of all things in the Everglades State, including the very nickname itself. Still, the Executive Mansion held personal memories. It represented the first real home for the Johns family in Florida's capital city of Tallahassee. Charley Johns, during all his years in the Florida state senate prior to ascending to the governorship, hadn't wanted his wife, Thelma, or his school-age daughter, MarkleyAnn, to move if the transplantation would be temporary. By constitutional mandate, the Florida state senate met in session just sixty days every two years, so Senator Charley Johns served out most of his terms in his hometown of Starke, a rural train depot town of fewer than two thousand residents in the upper middle of the Florida plateau—lake country at a remove from the coast.

As a young legislator on Capitol Hill, Charley scraped out a semi-bachelor's existence and rented a small room, he remembered, across the street from LeRoy Collins's Grove Mansion. Early on, state attorneys flagged elected representative Charley Johns for what was called *two-jobbing*, working for the executive branch while simultaneously serving in the legislature. Evidently, Senator Charley Johns had been earning $200 per month as a state motor vehicle tag inspector in blatant violation of the separation of powers. Around that same time, Charley let slip on the senate floor that he'd worked for the Dade County Hialeah dog track in the summer of 1937, right when the senate debated gambling regulations. "I worked so hard at the track I didn't want to go back last year," Charley explained, as if exhaustion was the only reason that he wasn't still employed by gambling interests. Revelations like these, however, couldn't do lasting harm to Charley, as he was considered charming enough to skate free, so long as he provoked laughs by saying the quiet parts of his tomfoolery loudly. Charley's tame look and mode of dress, often described as that of a Baptist deacon, frequently got him out of jams. When caught as a two-jobber, Charley Johns was permitted by senate leadership to resign his inspector post and continue in the senate without suspension or censure.

Charley—a white landowning college dropout in a state whose founders were white landowning males without college pedigrees—benefited personally from the strictures of the 1885 constitution, drafted when Florida was an agricultural hinterland of fewer than 400,000 citizens, a frontier state barely stitched together by a network of schooners and steam trains. Nearly fifty years later, that same Reconstruction-era constitution reigned supreme, compelling counties and municipalities to appeal to Tallahassee for all but the most routine of needs. The state's sixty-day legislative sessions every two years were madcap affairs clogged with local petitions, which received automatic yes votes unless legislators noticed and objected.

The capitol was routinely filled beyond capacity. New wings under construction were full of dirt, dust, and noise as representatives crammed into committee rooms the size of closets or met with constituents at office desks in hallways. Locals hawked circus peanuts in the atrium as tourists knocked into state senators. Constitutional rules prevented the printing of legislative bills before legislators voted, so the reading aloud of a bill was often the only chance for legislators to make a yea or nay decision. Within this free-for-all, almost any pork barrel expenditure could be slipped into a larger bill, the prevailing philosophy for bill passage being what the Florida Supreme Court called "Enact in haste, repent at leisure." Pet projects deemed too audacious for ordinary hours could be passed on what legislators decreed as "pet bill night," when every representative could sponsor a bill to sail through to the governor's desk with no questions asked.

Six feet tall, with clear blue eyes and an aw-shucks grin, Senator Charley Johns navigated these all-day and sometimes all-night sessions with skill. He spoke with a mellifluous accent and cultivated a bumpkin persona that hid a calculating mind. "You can't resist liking him," remarked an unidentified rival in the Florida senate. "I have a hard time reminding myself that I hate him."

In the Florida state senate, Charley was known to keep his word, although he also rarely gave it plainly, instead hedging bets with under-the-breath qualifiers, crafty escape hatches, and verbal bob and weaves. For example, voicing support for the coeducation of male and female college students after World War II, he said, "I was for making the University of Florida a co-educational school during this emergency, and if I do not change my mind, I will support co-education for our colleges." He was for the issue, and so long as he stays for the issue, he's still for the issue—well, unless he doesn't continue being for the issue, and then he's against the issue. As a traditionalist Democrat, Charley became known for playing the rules of government to his advantage, ensuring he and his supporters benefited. "Out of all the members of the senate, he probably did more for individual constituents," recalled a fellow legislator. "And I'm not talking about big things. I'm talking about little things." After all, was it his fault that he and his friends benefited from laws and decrees, as written?

Between 1890 and 1954, Florida's population exploded from 400,000 to about 3.5 million. By around 1950, when Gallup polled U.S. citizens on where they would most like a winter vacation, Florida and California topped the list. Lured by modern air-conditioning, crystal-blue waters, and towering palmettos, military veterans in droves returned to the state that housed their subtropical training camps during wartime. Simultaneously, Florida powered into economic relevance. By the 1955–56 season, Florida was producing a third of the world's citrus. Simultaneously, from 1954 to 1960, the rate of growth in Florida manufacturing surpassed that of any other state.

Everything grew in Florida: tomatoes, sweet corn, beans, cities, defense spending, families, fantasies. Cherubic babies cropped up everywhere as a result of all the newlywed lovemaking. As missile research commenced in earnest off Cape Canaveral, a coastal expanse that soared in per capita income, an influx of defense capital and PhDs made Florida the scientific envy of the planet. It seemed that every American home wanted a taste of Florida's frozen concentrated orange juice and every major writer had a Key West pied-à-terre.

Yet Florida's legislative boundaries were still largely based on 1885 county maps, when the majority of the state population resided in the northernmost reaches close to Georgia. Although the Florida constitution provided for reapportionment of the legislature every ten years, no reapportionment occurred for four decades following ratification. No one could make the Democratic Party act because the North Florida power faction benefited from the setup, and Democrats remained the only real option on the ballot because they promised and delivered segregation with each election. Then in 1925, in response to a census that showed South Florida as having a majority of the state population for the first time, the Florida senate agreed to expand from 32 to 38 seats and, by a "gentleman's agreement," gave South Florida the six new districts. This steamrollering on the part of North Florida legislators meant that South Florida, despite its higher population, would have just 16 seats to North Florida's 22. No attempt was made to reapportion any segment of North Florida, critiqued South Florida senator E. J. Etheredge, who voted nay as part of the minority Democratic faction.

An enthusiastic young legislator named Charley Johns helped the reapportionment bill sail through the Florida house. Through such maneuvering, Florida officially deviated from population-based representation—the basis of most democratic systems. By the 1940s, antique district boundaries created a form of extreme geographic gerrymandering called malapportionment, through which the state legislative vote failed to be allocated equally among voters regardless of where they lived. As South Florida grew unimpeded throughout the 1950s, voting malapportionment became most pronounced in Miami's Dade County, which now held more citizens than the entire state in 1900. Yet 500,000 Dade County residents still elected just one state senator. Meanwhile, 20,000 some-odd voters in Bradford and Union Counties could elect and reelect one Charley Johns to the same upper chamber. Blessed be.

Rather than address this systemic flaw, Charley and his allies coordinated to preserve it. North Florida representatives loved how voting rolls within their districts were limited to friends and neighbors, and it therefore mattered little to them, from a bird's-eye view, if representatives chose their voters and not the other way around. Working together, Charley and company created a twenty-man North Florida voting bloc nicknamed the Pork Choppers, or the Pork Chop Gang. "They took a blood oath on all major issues," recalled a South Florida senator named Ed Price. "If one North Florida senator asked for the support of the Pork Choppers, he would get it." Pork Choppers cast themselves as underdog populists fighting aristocratic Lamb Choppers, à la former Yankees moving to South Florida. The blood oath to white rule, of which Senator Price spoke, may not have been figurative. According to several sources, including a former clerk of the house, a Charley Johns–led loyalty ceremony took place in 1955 at a fishing camp off the Aucilla River called Nutall Rise, a Tallahassee-adjacent property owned by a fellow state senator.

As the lines of power happened to be etched in the soil by the North Florida founders, all Pork Choppers needed to do to increase their control of the legislature by the early 1940s was declare candidacy and stand still in a navy-blue blazer. By the 1953 session, Pork Chopper Democrats held the voting majorities in both the Florida house and the Florida senate while representing districts with less than 15 percent of the state population. Thus every Florida senate president from 1947 to 1965 turned out to be a Pork Chopper. In this highly engineered scenario, Pork Chopper senate presidents became the conduit through which passed all state legislation.

CHAPTER 2

The Flour-Sack Boy

A young man fishing in North Florida, circa 1959

February 27, 1905 (*Bonnie Stark Files*)

WHEN CHARLES EUGENE "Charley" Johns first caught sight of the world at the family home on February 27, 1905, he was well positioned for greatness: heir to one of the founding ancestral lines of Bradford County. Charley's grandfather served in the state legislature in 1887 following Florida's "Redemption" of white authority, and his father, Everett, a Nassau County chief deputy sheriff, seemed on the same path to power until he was denied by tragedy, dying in the line of duty when Charley was an infant and his older brother, Everett "Markley" Johns, only ten years old. Deprived of a breadwinner, Charley's family of four stared poverty in the face, but they were looked after by Starke chapters of Masons and Elks, fraternal organizations of which Everett Johns had been a member.

Growing up, Charley watched his mother struggle to make ends meet. She sewed his underwear out of the spare cloth from flour sacks, and he often walked around barefoot. Whenever he'd go down to the Tom Sawyer–style swimming hole by the creek, he'd hide behind the bushes to undress for fear that other boys would see his skivvies and tease him. This fear of his being discovered as such a nothing, of his family being revealed as destitute in a manner so close to his core, proved traumatic for him. (This painful memory, recounted in Charley's many retellings of his childhood, skims over the fact that young Charley was present at the swimming hole and not excluded from the fun.)

As a youngster who delivered the neighborhood groceries for pocket money, Charley led a rather quaint life in a remote town where, paradoxically, trains frequently passed, the train being both a romantic and an economic engine for the young man. Charley liked to stop and listen to the train whistles, as if they were church bells. Starke also contained a long-standing faction of the Ku Klux Klan, but reputedly neither Everett nor Markley nor Charley, when the time came, joined its ranks.

Older brother Markley attended the University of Florida College of Law in nearby Gainesville and graduated with high honors in 1915. "He was not but 19 when he graduated law school and passed the bar," recalled Charley. "He had to be twenty-one to start practicing . . . [so] he got made twenty-one by the law." Indeed, the Johns family possessed the power to legally change Markley's age, a feat that should have been impossible. After a respectable career as an attorney, Markley decided to continue the Johns family legacy of public service. He ran successfully for the state senate in 1928.

Markley's colleagues elevated him to president pro tem for the senate's 1931 session and then crowned him senate president-designate for the next session. Markley stood at the ready to preside over the state's upper chamber. But at only thirty-five, he collapsed with pneumonia. When Markley Johns perished on January 6, 1933, twenty-six-year-old Charley lamented what might have been for his brother. "I just loved Markley more than anything in the world," recalled Charley. "When he died, it tore me up. I vowed right then to become Senate President—for Markley." It's revealing that Charley never matured into Charles, not even after he became the patriarch of the family after Markley's death. As a business owner, on the campaign trail, Charley would forever use his nickname, as if he never left boyhood.

As it happened, Charley stood in an enviable position to inherent his older brother's mantle. Popular from his days as a baseball and basketball player at Bradford High School, Charley had grown from an enthusiastic boy into his own. After graduating from high school in 1923, he quickly dropped out of college and forged ahead with a career on the railroad—a way to earn money that locals understood and respected—and the pursuit of his sweetheart, Thelma, nicknamed Ted. Jim Crow was firmly entrenched in the Florida railroad industry, with Florida being the first state to mandate segregated train cars in 1887, and Charley rose through the ranks there.

Like many natural-born leaders, Charley had the memory of an elephant. "He had a memory for names and faces like I've never . . ." said his son Jerome Johns. "He could remember people, where he met them, when he met them." A year after Markley's death, Bradford County voters elected Charley Johns to the Florida house of representatives for the 1935 session. Theirs was in part a sympathy vote, yet the *Miami Herald* trumpeted the election:

> Another Johns is coming to Tallahassee from Bradford County. This time it is Charley E. Johns, younger brother of a former popular senator. . . . He is one of the few legislators who was not afraid to fight back against the demands of the Florida Education Association for more money. . . . Mr. Johns is one of that younger group of officials who promises to make history in this session. Not yet 30.

Charley arrived as a freshman legislator in time to cast a vote in a unanimous Florida house resolution to make "Old Folks at Home," an 1851 plantation melody celebrating the Suwannee River's southerly flow through the Panhandle to the Gulf, the official state anthem. Popularized by white minstrel performers (in blackface for comedic effect), the song glorified the "longing" of whites for a bygone time. "Oh, darkies, how my heart grows weary," the lyrics went, "far from de old folks at home!" Two years later, local voters elevated Charley to the Florida state senate. Plainspoken Charley now held his brother's old seat in Florida's upper chamber, and access to senatorial clout proved lucrative. Campaign ads for Charley often touted his quid pro quo credentials: "Remember What Charley Johns Has Done for Us."

Tiring of the dirt roads that tested the tires of his Model T coupe,

Charley supported legislation that paved roads and highways throughout Bradford County. Charley also championed increasing benefits to
widows of Confederate veterans and a pay raise for teachers in segregated schools. Naturally, Charley used his elected office to increase the
earnings of private holdings such as the Charley E. Johns Insurance
Agency. Charley's Starke Ice Corporation, likewise, secured a handshake deal to provide all the ice for University of Florida football
games. "It was a big job," agreed Charley in retrospect. "We would
start at two o'clock in the morning and go over there with a crusher on
the back of one of the trucks."

The very same year he became a state senator, Charley leapfrogged
over several candidates in a seniority-driven system to earn a conductor post with the Seaboard company. A king of the rails, he commanded all aboard the segregated coastal passenger train the *Orange
Blossom Special*, where Black porters in crisp white uniforms famously
served Caucasian passengers in elegant sleeper cars and sun lounges
from New York City to Miami. Black passengers, typically housed in
a Jim Crow car that hooked up to the *Orange Blossom Special* at
Washington, D.C., rode as veritable steerage behind the coal-fired engine so as to be supervised by Florida conductors like Charley, who by
statute were "invested with all the powers, duties and responsibilities
of police officers" to ensure proper division according to "the race to
which such passenger belongs." Thus was Charley the trainman rendered a member of segregated law enforcement. He got a taste of total
authority and liked it.

Charley's only political misstep occurred in 1940, when he ran for
a U.S. congressional seat in Washington, D.C., against incumbent
Democrat R. A. "Lex" Green. Announcing his candidacy for Florida's
second federal district, Charley neglected to requalify for the state legislature, thereby playing without insurance. Lex Green also hailed
from Starke, which meant that he and Charley drew from the same
batch of voters. The race exposed Charley as having little legislative
experience, while Green touted major projects completed with federal
funds such as the new Starke city hall. Almost as fast as Charley had
declared himself a congressional candidate, he was out of the race.
Charley was trounced so badly that he would excise this campaign

from his biography, either implying or claiming to serve in Florida's upper house uninterrupted from his freshman term to retirement: "Elected to State Senate in 1936, reelected since."

It remains unclear why thirty-five-year-old Charley Johns did not enter military service during World War II. Indeed, he received his draft card from the Bradford County draft board on October 16, 1940. Perhaps Charley's engineering work with the Seaboard Air Line Railroad, which he listed in the employer slot of his draft card, qualified as an "essential trade" and spared him the brutalities of combat. Perhaps someone on high decided that his ability to keep American trains running on time constituted a national service. Was it Charley's fault that he'd once more chosen the right line of work?

Charley prospered during wartime and consolidated power relationships. On the personal front, Charley and Ted Johns welcomed a baby girl into the world named MarkleyAnn—the "Markley" portion of the name in honor of his brother. In 1944, Charley sprinted out the gate to announce his candidacy for his old seat. "I promise when you elect me your senator, I will show no partiality," Charley said in a prepared statement, as if the election had already occurred. He ran unopposed. According to the *Tallahassee Democrat*, incumbent senator Hal Maines passed on his chance to qualify as a candidate for reelection because of traditional agreements "which permit the membership to rotate among the counties." Afterward, despite Senator Maines's understanding about county rotations, Charley held on to the 15th District senate seat through multiple future elections, mostly running as a lock without Democratic opposition.

In 1951, Charley Johns served as president pro tem of the state's upper house, just as his brother had twenty years prior. Charley rallied that session to honor the memory of Markley by voting to hang his brother's portrait in the senate chamber beside past senate presidents. Two years later, Charley fulfilled his promise to Markley by being unanimously elected president of the Senate, or so his résumé would claim. Charley was, in fact, preselected by nineteen fellow Pork Choppers at a secret caucus in April 1951 after jockeying in a small skirmish with Senator N. Ray Carroll of Kissimmee for the position. Charley's title officially became senate president-designate until his swearing in at the start of the 1953 session.

As the anointed, Charley Johns began to do a curious thing in his public appearances: speaking of himself in the third person, as if his political persona now needed an intermediary. "He is no more for the sales tax than Charley Johns," said Charley of a governor who'd signed a sales tax into law. Charley could grandstand while banking on a political logic that allowed Pork Choppers to have it both ways at once: striking a noble chord while practicing amoral realpolitik. That January 1953, thirty days before the session commenced, senate-president-designate Charley Johns collapsed in Starke during a Masonic ritual. He awoke in an oxygen tent. Doctors at first suspected a heart attack. Wondering if he was cursed to die young, like his brother and father before him, Charley bemoaned that he "was going to let Markley down."

As Charley lay in the hospital, the new Florida governor, Dan Mc-Carty, packed up the family car and drove to the Executive Mansion. As a Lamb Chopper candidate, McCarty had advocated for full reapportionment to enfranchise his South Florida constituents. "I am in the people's corner, and I am ready for the opening bell," he promised in his announcement speech. A chain-smoking, Kennedy-esque figure who advocated for "clean, efficient, and progressive government," Mc-Carty threatened to place a wedge through Florida's Pork Chopper base of working-class whites. Elected resoundingly at forty years old, this energetic reformer pledged to champion business interests over the traditional spoils system.

In a hurry to enact his agenda, Governor McCarty worked round the clock. After dusk, he oft hosted a series of open houses at the Executive Mansion to charm legislators. These get-togethers evolved into late-night meetings between Pork Choppers, the governor, and the governor's confidant, Senator LeRoy Collins, who conveniently lived next door to the Executive Mansion. The Collins and McCarty families developed such close ties that they shipped over catered leftovers from each other's gatherings several times a week.

Dan McCarty paid a price for the workload. Within six weeks of his inauguration, he suffered a health catastrophe, going into cardiac arrest and nearly dropping dead. His condition, although temporary, created a constitutional crisis. There was little stipulated in writing about how to proceed if a sitting governor remained alive but incapacitated. As the supposed next-in-line successor to the governor, Charley Johns was relieved when McCarty's presumed heart attack was swiftly downgraded to a gallbladder issue, an ailment that caused him to lose more than forty pounds throughout 1953. Senate-president-designate Charley Johns responded to the governor's emergency by declaring that he would act responsibly should the worst occur. Charley told the *Miami Herald*, "I would feel in my heart that it is Dan's administration. I supported him all the way." As the Associated Press reported on March 2, 1953, Charley stated that if called to finish McCarty's term, he would feel obligated to carry on McCarty's policies with McCarty's appointees.

On April 6, Charley Johns took the oath of senate president at the joint opening session of the Legislature. "A sentimental quest will have a storybook ending," rhapsodized the *Fort Lauderdale News*. Starke's *Bradford County Telegraph* hailed the man for "achieving a goal that has been uppermost in his mind . . . to carry out the responsibility that was to have been his brother's." Charley's swearing-in occurred with his mother, wife, and children in attendance. Veteran legislators who knew and loved Markley Johns wept as Charley stood in the office of the senate president and posed with twin portraits of himself and his brother.

In Markley's name, Charley had accomplished a political goal that had consumed more than eighteen years of his life. He now intended to dedicate his remaining years to his own sizable ambitions. After the capitol ceremony, the family held an "informal reception" at the Tallahassee Country Club. An orchestra played as Charley and Ted Johns led the first dance in a moment that, to the room, felt like a coronation.

CHAPTER 3

Acting Governor

Charley Johns, with portraits of himself and brother, Markley Johns

March 1953 (*State of Florida Archives*)

FOLLOWING HIS CARDIAC arrest, Governor Dan McCarty ran Florida's executive branch in a weakened state from a bedroom of the Executive Mansion. McCarty's lieutenant, Senator LeRoy Collins, opposed several of senate president Charley Johns's proposed bills that session, including a complex initiative to rotate horse racing dates at Miami racetracks, which Governor McCarty vetoed and called a "dangerous experiment." Concurrently, McCarty questioned the renewal of several big policies with the Charley E. Johns Insurance Agency, saying, "I don't consider it good policy for any state agency to do business with any public official." The senate president began to suspect that Governor McCarty might be sincere in his opposition to patronage politics. What might come next, Charley wondered, his insurance contract with the state prison? Thus Charley decided to seek more leverage.

Inspired by the much-publicized hearings of the House Un-American Activities Committee in Washington, D.C., Charley sponsored a bill to establish a Florida "joint legislative committee to investigate criminal and subversive activities." As outlined, this eight-member committee would be authorized to conduct investigations when the legislature was out of session; possess subpoena power; hire staff with a $50,000 appropriation; and hold witnesses in contempt with the fixed penalty of one year in jail, plus a $1,000 fine per offense. The committee would be entitled to conscript state, county, and local law enforcement and empowered to make recommendations to the governor to assist the executive branch in its enforcement of state law. In effect, Charley Johns's proposed legislative committee would absorb executive powers and perform judicial functions.

Introducing his bill late on a Friday afternoon in May 1953, senate president Charley called his proposed measure a "God-fearing piece of legislation" fit for "a God-fearing state." Acrimonious debate ensued. Senator LeRoy Collins accused the senate president of trying to form a "snake committee" to "grovel around in the rocks attacking unsuspecting people." Charley countered that his bill's opponents were "apostles of the status quo, defenders of thieves" and claimed it would be a good idea for a so-called snake committee to "crawl in the grass and weed out this crime." After three days of debate, the scales tipped against Charley's bill when four lawmakers who'd promised votes to him rose to switch their support. "I don't want to see innocent people get hurt," declared Senator Irlo Bronson of Kissimmee. The bill failed on the senate floor by a vote of 19 to 17. In response, the senate president plotted.

During the 1953 legislative session, the question of gubernatorial succession took on increasing urgency. An ailing Governor McCarty, defying medical odds with a complex recovery, called on the legislature to debate and pass one of two potential bills that would change the emergency succession plan for his office. Given the legislature's malapportionment and flagrant corruption within Charley's Pork Chopper faction, a number of officials expressed privately that it would be undemocratic for even temporary custodianship of McCarty's seat to be held by Charley Johns. The bills proposed to take succession away from the senate president and give it to either a lieutenant governor or the Florida secretary of state.

The Florida state house passed the two succession bills with supermajorities. Governor McCarty proposed giving Charley Johns the final say in the direction of this constitutional change, as both men had been recently ill, and the move was designed to safeguard democratic norms. As president of the senate, Charley Johns understood that any bill required his say-so to receive a vote in the chamber. He issued no public statements, knowing none were needed. He rejected both options.

Why alter a duty of an office that senate presidents, like himself, had fulfilled since time immemorial? Per usual, it hardly mattered to Charley if he behaved capriciously, so long as he had the backing of a rule that permitted him to do so legally. Additionally, in a deeply internalized way, Charley could not overcome the self-image of being the poor boy in the flour-sack underwear behind the bushes. The idea of someone taking something promised to him or implying he was some leftover figurehead out of the past made him feel emasculated and provoked his attack.

With days left in the 1953 legislative session, Charley Johns sent the proposed lieutenant governor succession bill to two senate committees for consideration and sent the proposed secretary of state bill to three committees for the same purpose. Proficient in parliamentary procedure, Charley understood that every one of these committees had to independently discuss, amend, and/or recommend said bills before they could be introduced, debated, and voted upon by the full chamber. Thus were all of them strangled in red tape. On June 5, 1953, in accordance with the legislature's long-celebrated sine die closing ceremony, the sergeant at arms for each Florida chamber dropped a handkerchief from opposite ends of the capitol rotunda at the same moment, and house speaker Farris Bryant and senate president Charley simultaneously banged their gavels. Never before had the drop of a handkerchief carried so much weight for Florida's future. The 1953 session was complete, and little now stood between Charley and the Executive Mansion besides one faltering heartbeat.

Governor Dan McCarty's health took another turn that September. After several weeks in the hospital, he had a second heart attack and died on Monday, September 28, 1953. His body was placed in the capitol rotunda, where thousands filed past to pay their respects. At six p.m. on September 29, not an hour after pallbearers carried McCarty's body from the capitol atrium, Charles E. "Charley" Johns stood in the senate chamber for his public swearing-in as the new governor. Standing beside Charley, his twenty-five-year-old son, Jerome Johns, opened a Bible to the 23rd psalm, which read, "The Lord is my shepherd; I shall not want." Resting his left hand on the Bible, Charley Johns recited the governor's oath before Florida Supreme Court justice John E. Mathews of Jacksonville, a close friend who understood North Florida values.

As he waited for Dan McCarty's widow and her three children to vacate the Executive Mansion, Charley Johns took up residence in a nearby hotel. Dining on breakfasts of eggs and California melon, Charley Johns permanently entered third-person status in his habits of speech, as if gaining the capacity to neutrally advocate for himself. The *Miami News* even printed an explainer for readers—"Like many other politicians, Johns frequently uses the third person in talking about himself"—feeling the clarification necessary. "Charley Johns is for economy," Charley Johns stated. "I tell you one thing. Charley Johns is against bookies." When asked if he felt that he could carry out McCarty's program with McCarty loyalists, Charley Johns mimed that he couldn't hear the question and then blustered, "Why it got so in Tallahassee that people were asking if Charley Johns was going to run the state government or McCarty people."

The Florida Supreme Court speedily ruled against Pork Chopper Democrats clamoring to call their beloved leader "Governor Charley Johns" and affirmed "acting governor" as his proper title. When McCarty's widow left the Executive Mansion in mid-October, the Johns family took possession. Moving Ted and MarkleyAnn into the mansion felt like arriving at a promised land. Charley marveled at seeing his wife and daughter strolling up the historic walkway before the mansion's Ionic columns, lounging near the garden pool, and serving guests from the silver Battleship Florida punch bowl adorned with his state's great seal.

Despite previous assurances made by Charley that he would govern as a steward of "Dan's administration," the acting governor demanded the resignations of seventeen McCarty appointees, including the Game and Freshwater Fish commissioner, who'd declined new policies with the Charley E. Johns Insurance Agency. "If I don't have men in there that I have confidence in, I want them out," Charley told *The Tampa Tribune*. When the McCarty appointees refused to resign, acting governor Charley Johns fired them on charges ranging from incompetency to neglect of duty.

Under Charley, the spoils system returned in earnest. He threatened to refuse to sign paychecks for University of Florida personnel unless he had the ability to "look over" the school's incoming president. Separately, Charley called state road commissioner Richard Simpson into a meeting with two executives from a Florida engineering firm. "The acting governor told me the engineers were friends of his," Simpson explained to the *Tampa Times*. Charley demanded that Simpson cancel a road contract awarded to an out-of-state firm and hand the contract to his friends, although their bid was $100,000 higher.

Meanwhile, the Florida Supreme Court ruled on another constitutional matter: Acting governor Charley Johns was eligible to run in the special election of May 1954, whereby voters would formally elect the person to finish out the final two years of McCarty's term. Now sanctioned as a candidate, Charley was positioned to run perceptually as an incumbent. His campaign capitalized with the slogan: "Let's KEEP Charley Johns Our Governor." The Florida Supreme Court left open the possibility that acting governor Charley Johns might also be eligible to run in the 1956 gubernatorial election for the next full term. If he just kept winning, Charley would become the first governor under Florida's 1885 constitution to succeed himself.

While riding a tide of public approval built on profligate spending, particularly on roadbuilding, Charley Johns stumbled on a fundamental issue: segregation. His misstep came as a surprise to segregationist allies, who'd perceived Charley as staunchly in their corner. Though the Florida Supreme Court declared the Democratic Party's whites-only primary to be unconstitutional in 1945, then-senator Charley Johns had supported a bill barring Black participation in state primaries in 1947. Additionally, although Charley Johns claimed to oppose the Florida Ku Klux Klan, then-senate president pro tem Charley Johns had voted against a 1951 bill that called for the unmasking of the Klansmen and an end to cross burning. White citizens of Florida lynched no fewer than 315 Black citizens between the years 1877 and

1950, which made Florida a capital of racial terror. Intimidation still reigned.

With the *Brown v. Board of Education* case landing on the U.S. Supreme Court docket in 1953, racial tensions surged. Florida represented one of only four states with zero net school integration and the most populous state with a complete "dual school" system, in which white and Black children were forbidden to be educated together even in private schools. As *Atlantic* contributor and outspoken segregationist Herbert Ravenel Sass voiced in the widely circulated pamphlet "Mixed Schools and Mixed Blood," fear of mandated mixed-race schooling triggered deeper white concerns of teenage "miscegenation," or interracial coupling. "Not all kinds of racial discrimination are evil," wrote Sass, "unless we are prepared to affirm that our forefathers blundered in 'keeping the breed pure.'" Miscegenation, in former slave states, remained an arrestable offense categorized as a form of adultery or fornication.

Some of the most horrific racial violence in the South overlapped with Markley and Charley Johns's tenure in public service. In 1920, a white mob killed four Black men and razed an entire section of the town of Ocoee, Florida, when Black residents attempted to vote. In 1923, a racially motivated massacre struck the village of Rosewood, with at least six Black residents murdered during a white siege; the town was subsequently abandoned, and people can still visit its ruins. In 1951, the first president of the Florida NAACP, a Black teacher named Harry T. Moore, dared to challenge a white sheriff. On Christmas Eve 1951 in Mims, Florida, when assassins knew he would be home for the religious holiday, more than twenty sticks of dynamite exploded beneath Moore's front porch. The explosion left Moore and his wife, Harriette, severely burned and at death's door. The local hospital refused to treat Blacks, and so Harry T. Moore perished shortly after a long ambulance ride to a neighboring county. Florida newspapers whitewashed the story by misleadingly reporting the man's death as more or less by evisceration instead of prolonged suffering. Meanwhile, unlit dynamite left on the steps of Miami High School and the Dade County courthouse served as warnings against so-called racial progress. Around that time, Virgil D. Hawkins, the son of a Lake County minister in northern Florida, became the first Black man to apply to the University of Florida law school. After being rejected by reason of his race, Hawkins sued for admission to the state's flagship legal institution, but his case was sidelined in the Florida Supreme Court. He slept beneath houses and pretended to divorce his wife lest they both end up like the Moores.

Brown v. Board of Education, handed down on May 17, 1954, caught acting governor Charley Johns off balance by declaring unequivocally and unanimously that "separate educational facilities are inherently unequal." On the day of the *Brown* ruling, referred to as "Black Monday" in the South, the acting governor was on the campaign trail in Palm Beach County attempting to appeal to moderate South Florida voters. According to the *Miami Herald*, Charley gave the impression of being at a "brief loss here." Conspicuously, he avoided mention of the *Brown* decision in stump speeches. After conferring with an advisor, Charley called a special press conference, where he read aloud from a telegram sent from his office to the Florida attorney general: "Please make exhaustive study of the ruling." When asked the direct question "Are you going to permit Negroes to attend school with White children?" the acting governor answered, "I will withhold making a statement."

Perhaps fatally for a man in the heat of a campaign, Charley's rival LeRoy Collins found resounding words for *Brown*: "We should call together the best brains in our state to study the situation and meet it calmly and properly." In spite of continual missteps, Charley won the first round of the Democratic primary. Nonetheless, he failed to receive 50 percent of the vote, which forced a runoff election against his sole remaining Democratic opponent: former McCarty lieutenant LeRoy Collins.

Their widely televised debate that May 13, broadcast live from Miami, made LeRoy Collins a national name. Holding back a smirk, Senator Collins began their debate with a backhanded remark by thanking the acting governor for showing up. Collins then pulled out a copy of the early edition of the *Miami Herald*. Chuckling, he read aloud from a Johns campaign ad declaring Charley to be the resounding winner of the night's debate. The Johns campaign, headquartered in Starke and perhaps unaware that Miami newspapers printed an early edition that was distributed around eight o'clock the night before, had mistakenly taken out an ad intended for the next day and humiliated their champion.

After Collins's opening salvo, the acting governor sat silent on live airtime. "Earthshaking," recalled Clifford Herrell, a Miami Springs politician working for the Collins campaign. "I'll never forget Charley Johns's look on his face." Attempting to recover after several flubs and false starts, Charley claimed to know nothing about the ad: "That's not Charley Johns, and the citizens of Florida know that's not Charley Johns." Disoriented in the minutes that followed, Charley periodically shuffled through large stacks of paper to gather his answers as if he were unstudied. Collins closed out the evening by criticizing Charley's opposition to the 1951 bill to unmask the Florida Ku Klux Klan. As time ran out and the moderator made closing remarks, the acting governor attempted to talk over the host.

In a desperate final push, Charley complained that he'd tried to get Collins "to run on his own record, to get off the coattails of Charley Johns." Voters disagreed. There was a massive turnout that May 24, and Senator LeRoy Collins trounced the acting governor. It was the most unequivocally democratic election Charley had faced in his career, with the outcome determined by a popular vote instead of by a gerrymandered district count, and his bid went down in flames more publicly than did his 1940 congressional campaign. Governor-elect Collins announced plans to hold hearings in the senate chamber with all former McCarty appointees spuriously fired by the acting governor. All, Charley suspected, would likely squeal about backroom dealings under "Spoilsman Johns," as the *Tampa Tribune* nicknamed him, or maybe even bring attention to the way that Charley may have used official powers to steer contracts to his businesses.

Having purloined and lost a governorship, Charley now desperately needed a political windfall to survive the stigma of being walloped. In Boca Raton, at the annual meeting of the Southern Governors' Conference, the acting governor opened with a speech calling for an amendment to the U.S. Constitution to preserve segregated schools. Simultaneously, he declared yet another battlefront. Charley, who'd favored creating a state legislative investigation committee in 1953, again trumpeted crime and corruption as "our most serious problem." Outlining an agenda for the 1955 session, Charley stated, "I plan now to introduce and fight for legislation to create a state FBI next spring; I think a force of 12 to 15 trained investigators . . . with the authority to step into any situation any place in the state is the answer." An unfolding scandal helped him.

With exemplary political timing, a homosexual Eastern Airlines flight attendant named William T. Simpson was murdered in Miami on August 2, 1954. Simpson had been out cruising for the weekend in his Chevrolet convertible when he picked up a nineteen-year-old hitchhiker named Charles Lawrence along Biscayne Boulevard. Simpson and Lawrence were closely tailed by Lawrence's friend, twenty-year-old Lewis Richard Killen. When Simpson and Lawrence pulled off U.S. Highway 1 onto a secluded road known as "Lover's Lane," Killen approached Simpson's car with the intent to "roll" him, extorting money at gunpoint. But before Killen could reach the convertible, Lawrence shot Simpson point-blank in the torso with a .22-caliber pistol. Simpson staggered from the vehicle, and the assailants bludgeoned the man together. They tossed him into the starlit bay, where he bled out into the water.

Simpson's murder and the subsequent trial, for which Lawrence and Killen received only manslaughter convictions when they claimed self-defense against an "unnatural sex act," led to an anti-homosexual panic. Florida's anti-queer legacy ran deep. In 1842, Florida was the first U.S. state to pass its own law (rather than simply adopting British common law) to make sodomy a capital offense, for which anyone found guilty "shall suffer death." Florida's antebellum law remained on the books until 1868, when the Reconstruction government reduced the sodomy penalty to twenty years in prison with hard labor for the renamed "abominable and detestable crime against nature." By the 1950s, almost anyone convicted of a "crime against nature" in Florida became sorted as a "Grade 1" felon and handed off to the state road board. As chain gang labor, homosexual convicts could be utilized to pave new turnpikes and satiate the desires of fellow prisoners who might otherwise revolt over zoo cage–like sleeping quarters and slop-bucket meals. Moreover, through accounting sorcery, the roadside sweat of homosexual felons could qualify as an "in-kind contribution" from the state for matching federal highway grants.

Simpson's murder and the prosecution of two "teenage Miami

boys" for what seemed a righteous act made Pork Choppers delirious with anger, as many sympathized with the killers. "Pervert Colony Uncovered . . . ," blasted the *Miami News*. Police estimated "a colony of some 500 male homosexuals," "perverts," and "sexual psychopaths" in their fair city. Unempirical estimates jumped to more than 8,000 homosexuals, as the local press editorialized. "So many downtown bars cater to these people that the area in which they operate has been nicknamed Powder Puff Lane," the *Herald* reported breathlessly. Prompted by the uproar, Mayor Abe Aronovitz gave his city manager an ultimatum: Clean up the "crackpots and perverts" situation or be fired. Subsequently, at least thirty-five "males who act mighty like girls" were rounded up at Miami Beach, and at least nineteen "suspected perverts" were picked up in a series of raids on "suspected hangouts." Alerted to the crisis, acting governor Charley Johns appointed a Miami attorney to coordinate with law enforcement in driving out the queers. In a letter to the Miami mayor, Charley clarified his move "to cooperate with you and your office in the eradication and control of sex deviates."

Through several "tough on crime" maneuvers, Charley repositioned his brand to recover some face in the last days of his administration. At a cost of $4,000 to taxpayers, the acting governor commissioned the printing of 7,500 copies of a propaganda booklet touting the accomplishments of the Johns administration, including $100 million in state expenditures to build 2,700 miles of roads. The last official act of Charley's outgoing Florida Turnpike Authority was acknowledging a debt to the state road department of more than $2.5 million. As Charley-appointed commissioners resigned en masse on January 3, governor-elect Collins announced that he would, as his first official act, reinstate the wrongly fired McCarty appointees.

At ten o'clock in the morning on Tuesday, January 4, acting governor Charley Johns met governor-elect LeRoy Collins in front of the Executive Mansion. The morning was bright and clear. "The governor's orders," a Johns aide explained to the press, "are to make it as smooth a transition as possible." Smiling continuously, wary of ever being caught in a scowl, Charley sounded a conciliatory note in his farewell address at the capitol: "Perhaps this will be my last opportunity to speak publicly before personal and political friends and foes."

As LeRoy Collins walked to the inaugural platform to take the oath, Charley said in a stage whisper, "Roy, I've left a little present for you. You'll find a headache powder in the desk drawer." A band then played the state anthem, "Old Folks at Home," to mark the occasion. It was one of Charley's favorite songs, but it pained him to hear it played for his nemesis.

For perhaps the rest of his life, Charley Johns would miss the power and gravitas of living in the old mansion. By and large, building engineers agreed that Florida governors had outgrown their first house, just as Florida voters, Charley feared, might someday outgrow the Pork Choppers. This was a leftover building for leftover men. The Governor's Mansion lacked a worthy reception hall, and the dining room table comfortably sat just twelve guests, which made every state dinner a buffet affair. In its place would rise a new residence for a new first family in what was becoming a New Florida.

By the end of January, plans for a new state mansion, modeled on Andrew Jackson's Hermitage, were quietly approved, and Governor Collins informed his cabinet that he favored construction on the present site. The mansion's original contents were auctioned to subsidize the demolition of the structure, and Collins expressed hopes that several handpicked materials could be salvaged, in order that the new dwelling would possess a little "atmosphere of the old." By August, they were digging for time capsules in cornerstones and tearing down the old girl.

CHAPTER 4

Oaths of Office

*Governor-elect LeRoy
Collins and acting
governor Charley Johns*

May 1956
(*Clerk of the House Papers, NAACP Papers, Box 4*)

RETURNING TO THE Florida state senate, Charley Johns made good on his anti-crime proposals by sponsoring Senate Bill 227 to create a "joint legislative committee to investigate subversive and criminal activities." Charley Johns's proposed committee would have broad powers to investigate any potential state crime.

Yet, in a reality check for the returning senator of the 15th District, the newly installed Pork Chopper senate president W. Turner Davis opposed the measure. Charley also sponsored a "red hunting" bill to compel all state employees to report membership in "subversive or un-American" organizations. "It's just to keep Communists out of our state government," Charley explained to reporters. Both measures failed. Bitterly, Charley then watched LeRoy Collins become "the first man in Florida's political history to win the governorship in the first primary" for the 1956 gubernatorial election. The man stole Charley's crown by succeeding himself.

More challenges to the "way of life" brewed. On May 26, 1956, not six months after Rosa Parks sparked a massive boycott against segregated transit in Montgomery, Alabama, two Black female students, Wilhelmina Jakes and Carrie Patterson from Florida Agricultural and Mechanical University (FAMU), boarded a city bus in Tallahassee. They sat in the only vacant seats, which happened to be in the white section, and refused to move. Police arrived. Jakes and Patterson were arrested, charged with inciting a riot, and released on bond. The next day, a cross was set aflame in their front yard. Word spread, and on May 29, a consortium of FAMU students, local ministers, and NAACP leaders voted unanimously to begin a community-wide boycott of city buses until Black riders received equal access to seating. Protesters formed an Inter-Civic Council, led by local minister and president of the Tallahassee branch of the NAACP Reverend C. K. Steele. To ensure that Black protesters who relied on public transit could continue to get to work, the Inter-Civic Council organized a volunteer carpool system.

During the months of protest that followed from May through December, Tallahassee's transit company hemorrhaged money from the absence of Black riders and reported to city government that they could soon go bankrupt. On June 4 and 5, city commissioners refused the demand of "full integration" of the bus franchise and canceled routes through two redlined Black areas of town. As another method of counterpressure, Detective Sergeant Remus J. Strickland of the Tallahassee Police Department (and future chief investigator of the Johns Committee) staked out the busiest carpool pickup locations and began arresting the volunteer drivers on charges of operating illegal taxis. Strickland later admitted that he had no knowledge of payments made in money for the carpool, but that didn't stop him from citing more than twenty of the volunteer drivers for lacking proper "hire tags" on their vehicles.

To pursue these charges, Tallahassee authorities hired a thirty-one-year-old white lawyer out of Tampa named Mark R. Hawes as special city prosecutor. In court, Hawes charmed city judge John Rudd with his pluck. In a ruling that threatened to end the boycott without concessions, Judge Rudd called on "Divine Guidance to arrive at a just decision" and then found the volunteer drivers guilty of operating an illegal transportation system. He sentenced them to $500 in fines each or sixty days in prison. To keep the drivers out of jail, the Inter-Civic Council raised some $11,000 to pay the fines. Forced to disband the carpool, Reverend C. K. Steele urged the protesters to endure: "The war is not over; we are still walking."

Almost concurrently in Miami, Black parents formed battle lines to push for integrated schooling. On June 12, 1956, a contingent of six Black parents with school-age children led by Miami NAACP president Father Theodore Gibson filed a federal suit against the school board of Dade County. This small group of plaintiffs, on behalf of their children, called out Florida's dual-school system as operating in violation of *Brown*. Father Gibson's son, Theodore Jr., was a junior high student slated to attend segregated Booker T. Washington High. Theodore Jr. wished to attend white Coral Gables High, a better-equipped school. As noted in the suit, Gibson's son "made application to a pillar school for reassignment," but "applications were denied." Determined to afford his son opportunities that he was never allowed, Father Gibson sued "As Next Friend" for his son and put his life and reputation at risk by appending his own surname to the legal action: *Gibson v. Board of Public Instruction of Dade County.*

Black residents at opposite ends of the state bucked the "southern way of life" through civic action and the courts. Nonetheless, Governor Collins remained undeterred in his approach of peaceable rhetoric and firm measures to preserve segregation. That July 1956, within days of the *Gibson v. Board of Public Instruction of Dade County* filing to integrate schools, Collins called a special session of the legislature to pass a pupil assignment law for the "management of the public schools at the local level." Modeled on a 1955 North Carolina law and skillfully crafted so as to not run afoul of *Brown*, Florida's pupil assignment law never once utilized the word *race*. Rather, white school superintendents became sanctioned to consider "available facilities" while assigning student slots based on appropriateness. Thus the dual-school system was preserved, as it always had been in Florida, one student at a time.

Once in the special session, however, an irate Florida legislature largely departed from Collins's moderating stances. With Senator Charley Johns's support, the Florida senate passed a resolution condemning the U.S. Supreme Court for its usurpation of state sovereignty. Stridently, the Florida House moved to consider an "interposition" resolution—parroting verbiage passed by former Confederate states from Alabama to Virginia—to assert Florida's state constitutional powers above the federal judiciary. Collins, wary of reprisals from President Eisenhower amid the deluge of federal lawsuits, sounded the alarm with allies on the floors of both chambers to halt its passage. It was a true emergency moment.

In this bedlam, as legislators furiously debated interposition, Senators Charley Johns, John Rawls, and Dewey Johnson quietly sponsored a bill for a chamber vote. The proposed Senate Bill 38 called for the establishment of a Florida Legislative Investigation Committee, a bicameral body to investigate organizations "advocating violence or a cause of conduct which would constitute a violation of the laws of Florida." Unable to acquire and keep power democratically, Charley once again sought to self-generate power by unprecedented but legal means. Although Senate Bill 38 (SB-38) did not specify the NAACP or the Inter-Civic Council as its targets, as Charley anticipated repercussions for naming either group, Senator Dewey Johnson admitted to reporters that he could think of "no other group the bill would fit."

As written, SB-38 handed a small legislative faction authorization to investigate any potential infringement of the state legal code—absorbing the fact-finding powers of the executive branch. On July 25, the Senate passed SB-38 by a resounding 28 to 7. With the threat of Black skin touching white on crowded Tallahassee buses and in Miami classrooms, Senator Charley Johns at last got his committee to investigate subversive crime. The next day, in a breach of protocol, six state senators who'd voted nay to SB-38 were permitted to switch their votes to yes. Swiftly, without committee recommendation, a Florida Legislative Investigation Committee bill was brought before a turbulent house floor, and it passed by a two-thirds margin.

As the final minutes of the special session ticked by, Governor Collins succeeded in deadlocking the interposition resolution on the house floor. However, in open rebellion, the house leadership refused to adjourn their chamber through sine die. Governor Collins took the unprecedented but constitutionally authorized step of adjourning the legislature by governor's proclamation. It was a "history-making move," according to the *Tallahassee Democrat*, a measure of last resort that Pork Choppers called a "low blow." Collins ending the session by diktat all but killed any hopes to pass an interposition resolution in 1956.

Rather than personally weigh in on the FLIC act, which passed with veto-proof supermajorities, a weary Governor Collins allowed Senate Bill 38 to become law without his signature. Collins explained his passive sanction in a late August news release:

> I regard the matter as one for the legislature's determination and do not feel I should exercise my executive authority either to approve or veto the bill. I am confident, too, that the members of the Committee will recognize their responsibility to all the people of Florida and not abuse the broad powers granted them.

The first meeting of the Florida Legislative Investigation Committee, held in the state capitol on September 11, 1956, was perfunctory and tame—with fewer than ten people stuffed into a small committee room. New members limited their focus to start-up parliamentary business. Although he'd helped form the group by sponsoring its legislation, Senator Charley Johns didn't show. He passed along his "proxy vote" to Senator Rawls via handwritten note on Charley E. Johns & Sons Insurance stationery. "I have a Director meeting of Presidential Ins. Co.," Charley wrote, "and I will be unable to be present." By prioritizing one of his many businesses over a state obligation, Charley sent a mild ego check to his peers—giving notice that his time was in demand.

Proxy voting was standard operating procedure for Florida senators. It allowed legislators, who held seats on up to eight committees per session, to register their obligatory "attendance" at simultaneous meetings by way of signed notes, much like hall passes, without being present. "A terrible system," opined Florida legislator Clifford "Cliff" Herrell. "Too late, they changed it so that there had to be a majority of warm bodies." Proxies counted for quorum, such that a committee chairman could potentially hold a meeting and vote on measures while sitting in a room by himself, so long as he had enough slips. A freshman senator once met alone with Charley Johns for a meeting of the senate insurance committee. "Where are the other six members?" asked the freshman. "They're all here," Charley answered, pulling six ballots from his pocket.

Thus did Charley, absent that September day, miss a minor skirmish resulting in Representative Henry Land, a Pork Chopper from Orange County, being elected the first committee chairman. With its leader chosen, FLIC voted unanimously to "secure all information available in other states and in Washington, D.C., relative to the National Association for the Advancement of Colored People." Representative Cliff Herrell, the only moderating voice Governor Collins managed to slip onto FLIC, didn't contest the measure. Herrell was a 240-pound bulldog of a South Floridian, a "big city Pork Chopper" who often voted with the rural majority. "He doesn't believe in fighting power," criticized the *Miami Herald*, "he tries to use it." Further brainstorming with the group, Senator Dewey Johnson suggested the need for possible secret meetings in executive session going forward: "We will have to hear some complaints in private, or we won't get the witnesses to testify." Senator Johnson proposed that FLIC should operate "like the Un-American Activities Committee of the American Congress."

At FLIC's second meeting, on October 10, 1956, Chairman Henry Land reported that he'd obtained copies of the House Un-American Activities Committee (HUAC) procedural rule book to help with the drafting of FLIC bylaws. After consulting with Florida attorney general Richard Ervin, Chairman Land confirmed that FLIC members would be "immune from what they do or say" within liberally construed bounds "so as to allow the Committee to accomplish its purpose." The Florida attorney general also avowed that he would be compelled to represent any FLIC member "being sued for damages growing out of the functions and actions of the Committee."

Defining itself as "neither an accusing (grand jury) nor a trial (petit jury) body," FLIC adopted bylaws to recognize its statutory right to subpoena witnesses; hold any witness in contempt "if a witness refuses to answer a question"; and to prevent any witness from reading a prepared statement not first submitted to the FLIC chairman to "determine its relevancy." Resolving that no information concerning FLIC should be released to the public except by the chairman, groundwork was laid to limit civil and judicial protections for future FLIC witnesses. Chairman Land confessed that he feared having open hearings might "lead to big headlines," which could mar covert investigations, and indicated his preference for closed meetings, which the public could not monitor or influence.

FLIC agreed to hire professional staff. Tallahassee detective Remus Strickland and special city prosecutor Mark Hawes, the team that charged and prosecuted twenty-one Black drivers in the Tallahassee carpool cases, were hired as investigator and attorney for the Florida Legislative Investigation Committee, respectively, and welcomed aboard. A formidable solicitor with Pork Chopper aspirations, Hawes applied to become FLIC's chief counsel to stop Communism in its tracks. As stated in his cover letter, he viewed the position not as a job but as "an opportunity to serve the Legislature and the people." Sensing a true believer on their hands, FLIC agreed to pay the chief counsel a part-time salary of $11,000 —a higher wage than almost every full-time lawyer working for the state in 1957, save the attorney general himself.

Off in the background during the committee's initial plays, Senator Charley Johns was again late to another FLIC meeting that November and entirely absent from one in December. As if sitting on the fence, Charley expressed that he'd heard objections to the way state funds were being spent "or feared some might be made." He voiced his wish that the Florida public be informed why only $15,000 of the $50,000 state appropriation for FLIC had yet to be spoken for in the budget. This was a textbook example of Charley having it both ways in the press. He asked in the same breath: Exactly how much are you spending, and why aren't you spending it faster? In response to Charley's sniping from the wings, Chief Counsel Mark Hawes confirmed that a FLIC investigation into the NAACP "general situation" as well as the Tallahassee bus boycott was "beginning to roll."

FLIC investigator Remus Strickland sent a confidential memorandum to all Florida police chiefs requesting the financial records of

every current or closed bank account of the NAACP within their juris-
dictions. Thus was the power of FLIC magisterially flexed over all
state law enforcement, who were compelled by statute to reply. The
growing stature of FLIC made Florida an anti-subversion trendsetter,
with HUAC mimicry and anti-NAACP ideology becoming pro forma
throughout the South. In late June and early July 1956, Alabama's attorney general obtained a court order to bar the NAACP from their
state, and South Carolina's legislature created a nine-member investigation committee to look into so-called Pink integrationists at
universities. By late 1957, Texas, Arkansas, Georgia, Louisiana, North
Carolina, and Virginia all created similar inquisitorial groups—
miniature HUACs and FBIs hell-bent on impeding threats to the "way
of life."

Steps from the capitol, the bus boycott in Tallahassee reached a crisis pitch. With the volunteer carpools kaput due to Hawes and Strickland, Black leaders of the flagging Inter-Civic Council took a sizable
risk. On December 24, 1956, at loggerheads with city authorities following months of civic action, Reverend C. K. Steele and other frontline figures all boarded Tallahassee buses together. Contending that
the recent federal *Browder v. Gayle* ruling (which ended the Montgomery bus boycott in a victory for Black riders) also applied to Florida, they climbed the steps and sat in the white-reserved sections.
Local Black layfolk, watching their ministers place themselves in
harm's way, followed their lead in an act of mass revolt, while deputy
sheriffs scampered to recover a fifty-pound stash of TNT hidden by
white supremacists to "preserve peaceful relations." The very next evening, Christmas Day, sixteen sticks of dynamite destroyed the parson-
age of the Bethel Baptist Church in Birmingham, Alabama—nearly
killing its Black minister, Reverend Fred L. Shuttlesworth, and his
family. The night after in Montgomery, two integrated buses were
fired upon with bird shot and .22-caliber bullets. No one could identify the culprits.

In Miami on January 3, 1957, a U.S. district judge ruled in favor of
local bus plaintiffs, making a similar case to the Tallahassee bus boy-
cotters. In an oral opinion, the judge pronounced, "I have no hesitation
in saying that these segregation laws (pertaining to buses) are unconstitutional and hence unenforceable." In a panic to avoid Miami's fate,

Tallahassee repealed its segregated seating ordinance posthaste. Concurrently, city commissioners passed an "assigned seating" ordinance. It was the transit equivalent of a pupil assignment law, endowing each bus driver with the authority to sort human beings into separate sections one rider at a time.

After breaking for the holidays, FLIC set their first open hearing dates for February 1957 in Tallahassee. The committee gave Chief Attorney Mark Hawes broad authority to subpoena more than twenty NAACP officials, Inter-Civic Council leaders, and bus protesters. In state capitol room 50 on February 5, Chairman Land called the inaugural hearing to order. Chief Counsel Mark Hawes took the floor. A virile father of five (soon to be six), Hawes had served in the U.S. Marine Corps and sustained injuries at Iwo Jima. He was keen to prove "corruption" and "barratry"—a crime in which lawyers persuade clients to stir up litigation for profit—among Black lawbreakers challenging the way of life he'd fought for. Hawes let loose an opening barrage against the first witness: would-be University of Florida law school integrationist Virgil Hawkins. Hawkins, described by the *Miami News* as the "Daytona Beach Negro who has waged an eight-year fight to gain admittance to the University of Florida law school," took the stand and testified to not remembering whole meetings or conversations from his nearly decade-long campaign for an equal education.

Other witnesses took Hawkins's cue and played out the clock by citing frequent memory lapses. Senator Charley Johns joined the proceedings in time to hear testimony from Horace Hill, Virgil Hawkins's NAACP-appointed lawyer, who couldn't recall how he was paid to represent Hawkins; how he got hired for the job; or to what extent he took direction from the NAACP Legal Defense Fund attorney Thurgood Marshall. As the Associated Press described, committee members became "obviously nettled by repeated answers of 'I don't remember.'"

In a research coup that Chairman Land characterized as "sheer luck," Mark Hawes revealed that FLIC had obtained sensitive documents and correspondence between Virgil Hawkins, his lawyer Horace Hill, and an NAACP Legal Defense Fund attorney named Robert

L. Carter. Despite the fact that such communications were protected from review by attorney-client privilege, Mark Hawes forged ahead and read aloud from what appeared to be stolen work papers—materials not shared by the NAACP in any context of legal discovery with FLIC. "If the copies are authentic . . . and Carter didn't give them to the committee," Horace Hill said later, "somebody must have sneaked into my office and got them."

Tempers spiked during a particularly circular give-and-take between the lawyers Hawes and Hill, when Hill maintained that a letter supposedly between him and Carter, submitted by Hawes as FLIC evidence, wasn't actually signed by him. Hill suggested the possibility that he either didn't write the note or didn't send it. With Mark Hawes being expertly stonewalled, Senator Charley Johns leapt into the exchange.

JOHNS: Isn't this witness an attorney?
MR. HAWES: Yes, sir, he is an attorney.
JOHNS: Well, he should realize that he is fast perjuring himself, and the penalties for such perjury.
HILL: That is why I am trying to be exact, sir.

It was a rare headline-grabbing exchange for the day. Sensing his moment, Charley leveraged the back-and-forth to ask a showstopping question as the witness was about to leave: "Have you ever been or are you now a member of the Communist Party?"

This legalistic inquiry, as much as it was a request for information, had been sharpened by Wisconsin senator Joseph McCarthy during the federal Red Scare into a weapon of character annihilation. Being asked these particular words, in this runic order, in 1957 placed a citizen under immediate suspicion as a potential violator of the social order and a traitor to the nation. No decent person would face such an attack, common sense dictated.

It was the first major instance that a committee member used the loaded words to expose an enemy—and Charley Johns was the one who spoke them. Flummoxed and insulted, Horace Hill stumbled in his answer, which Charley imperiously dismissed.

HILL: I never had been and never—I am not now and I never
  intend to be. I say that in all sincerity and honesty to you,
  Mr. Johns.
JOHNS: That is all.

The exchange provoked silence in state capitol room 50. Otherwise
bored by long hours of evasive testimony, committee member John
Rawls at one point slipped off his shoes in the hearing room. Purportedly, Rawls knew how to take a nap with his eyes open. When Chairman Land finally called recess, according to the *Tallahassee Democrat*,
Senator Rawls couldn't find his shoes and "almost had to go home
barefooted." It was a practical joke played on him by fellow committee
members, who also faded in and out of attention.

Behind the scenes, FLIC members hankered to make a muscular
statement by moving to hold a resistant witness or two in contempt,
but the Florida attorney general dashed their hopes in a letter to Mark
Hawes. "I can find no provision of law which authorizes the Committee to directly cite the refusing witness for contempt," the attorney
general advised. To render punishment, FLIC would need a full vote of
the sitting legislature to confirm each and every contempt citation, and
no penalty could last beyond sine die. Since the 1957 session wouldn't
begin until April, FLIC found its hands tied in the face of witness
insubordination—able to make menacing threats, but unable to make
good on any of them.

Mark Hawes declared that he saw no reason for the Tallahassee
hearings to continue. Chairman Land hastily scheduled a new round
of NAACP hearings to begin in Miami, the site of the *Gibson v. Board
of Public Instruction of Dade County* lawsuit, on Monday, February
25, 1957. To catch witnesses off balance, no FLIC subpoenas had been
issued to "any NAACP members in the Miami area" until that Saturday, February 23. Then in near unison, process servers delivered
twenty-five court orders to twenty-five NAACP leaders and Black locals to appear at ten a.m. that Monday at the county court. FLIC knew
precisely who to subpoena because they'd already acquired Florida
NAACP leadership rolls, as well as records of leaders in other NAACP
state organizations, through the attorney general of Texas.

The Miami NAACP witnesses, explained Chairman Land, were of

particular interest to FLIC due to their "bringing suits to integrate the schools in Dade County." Many of these private citizens in the cross-hairs scrambled to make the FLIC hearing at the appointed time. Some reportedly learned that they had been subpoenaed not through process servers, who somehow missed their Saturday deliveries, but through a front-page story in the Sunday edition of the *Miami Herald*, which printed many of their workplace locations and home addresses beside their full legal names.

More chaos preceded Chairman Land's opening gavel in Miami. "The top guns of the segregation forces are converging on Florida in a stepped-up drive," trumpeted the *Miami Herald*. Integration oppo-nent John Kasper, considered a prophet of the white cause and a bomb inciter, sent his protégé Fred Hockett to Florida to recruit, threaten, foment disorder, and incite violence. Hockett was not a herald of the rural KKK but of a nouveau white urban movement—a "business-man's Klan"—called the White Citizens' Councils (WCC). "A little fire and some dynamite will show these niggers we mean business," Hockett preached to a backyard rally in Northwest Miami before marching the angry crowd to the home of an unsuspecting Black fam-ily, the LeGrees. Just before midnight that Saturday, Hockett crossed the boundary line onto the LeGree property and raised a kerosene-soaked cross.

According to Miami NAACP attorney Grattan Graves, who had a mole in Hockett's crew, Hockett's plan was to "shoot the place up" as the cross burned. Fortunately for the besieged family, police received the NAACP tip-off and arrested Hockett and his associates. In retali-ation for infiltrating and scuttling their house-burning mission, the WCC sent death threats to three NAACP leaders under subpoena to testify before FLIC that Monday: former Miami NAACP president Father Theodore Gibson, Grattan Graves, and Miami NAACP secre-tary Ruth Perry. Problematically for these frontline activists, their home and/or work addresses had already been announced to the would-be assassins via news outlets.

CHAPTER 5

First Strike

Father Theodore Gibson

February 25, 1957
(*Box 1, Box 3, Box 4, Florida Bar Association Papers*)

AT TEN A.M. sharp, Chairman Henry Land called for order in the East Circuit courtroom on the fourth floor of the Dade County courthouse. The courtroom setting, with committee members arrayed behind a judicial bench, lent the proceedings an inquisitorial air. This choice of location was deliberate, as FLIC wanted to make NAACP members feel as if they were charged with crimes. As the witnesses waited with a bailiff in an anteroom of the court, members of the Miami White Citizens' Council, who'd menaced the city over the weekend, filed into seats in the gallery's front rows.

When FLIC called Father Theodore Gibson, former president of the Miami NAACP, to the stand at 1:45 p.m., he carried himself with the gravity and dignity of a southern Black holy man. A civil rights leader, Christian preacher, and public litigant, Father Gibson served as the spearhead of Miami's desegregation movement. Pork Choppers like Charley Johns and Mark Hawes privately hoped they could make a public example of him. Father Gibson raised his right hand and swore an oath to God knowing that Senator Charley Johns sat poised to attack him with just one question: "Have you ever been or do you now belong to the Communist Party?"

Born in Miami in 1915, the same year that early voice for Black freedom Booker T. Washington died, Theodore Roosevelt Gibson was initially raised by his maternal grandparents in the Bahamas while his mother worked in Miami as a maid. Island life cultivated in him an early awareness of racial inequities; white Bahamians ran an apartheid system, though Black Bahamians outnumbered whites seven to one. "Racism was there," Gibson said. At age nine, Gibson returned to Miami to matriculate in Florida's dual-school system. He attended the segregated Booker T. Washington High School, where he gained the nickname "The Instigator" for his resistance to school policies.

Attending college in North Carolina and divinity school in Virginia, Theodore Gibson further bolstered his reputation for righteous agitation. Friends called the self-disciplined young man "God's angry child." Gibson received ordination in the Episcopal priesthood on March 3, 1944. He later affirmed that he entered the faith specifically to minister on racial matters and break down the "Berlin Wall" of neighborhood segregation. "I want to serve the Black people," he explained. Since 1945, Gibson had served as pastor of the Christ Episcopal Church in Coconut Grove, a then-developing neighborhood in south Miami, where he preached a practical theology of literacy, education, and hard-won class advancement to some eight hundred Black congregants.

Father Gibson, much like his hero Booker T. Washington, advocated for his fellow Black Americans to present themselves as upstanding and deserving of the freedoms they sought. A lifelong teetotaler, he opposed "juke joints next to our homes" and despised developers putting "whiskey dens under our noses." An exacting disciplinarian, he emphasized punctuality and cleanliness as moral philosophies. "His face is clean-cut and somber," noted the *Miami Herald*, commenting on his appearance with remarkable nonchalance. "And his dark skin contrasts vividly against the stark white circle of his cleric's collar."

This was Gibson's near-permanent look: pressed white collar on a dark shirt with a lapel pin on his blazer and a silver cross dangling from a simple chain.

A founding member of the Miami NAACP and a litigant on behalf of his son, Theodore Jr., in the eponymous *Gibson* case, Father Gibson was as iconic a "racial radical" as Miami could claim. Now on the witness stand of a Miami courtroom in front of white terrorists who'd promised him harm, the forty-one-year-old minister received no assurances of protection from Chief Attorney Mark Hawes. "How long have you been a member of the NAACP, Reverend?" Hawes asked. "As long as I could recall that I was classified as or grouped as a second-class citizen," answered Gibson sharply, "and that has been many years."

Sensing a formidable opponent, Hawes utilized several courtroom tactics designed to unsettle a witness. To break Gibson's rhythm and shake his confidence, Hawes frequently asked the court reporter to read and reread questions back from the hearing transcript. ("Now read the question, please." "Read the question.") Hawes mirrored and mocked Father Gibson's answers, while trying to trap the minister in inconsistencies.

GIBSON: I do not recall that sir.
HAWES: You don't recall that?
GIBSON: I do not recall.

Hawes instructed Gibson to read aloud from excerpts of an NAACP memorandum and a petition concerning the bringing of the *Gibson* lawsuit against Dade County. Gibson did not agree with Hawes's contention that the memo issued demands, contending that they were only "suggestions." At one point, Hawes nearly tricked Father Gibson into believing that he'd slipped up in his testimony and had himself called the memo a "directive." "You used that word 'directive,' I didn't use it. How were you using it?" asked Hawes. Perplexed, Father Gibson paused for a moment and then utilized the same power move as Hawes. Gibson asked the court reporter to reread Hawes's question from the record, "so that I might know where I got the word 'directive' from." Caught in his own trap, Hawes walked back his statement with a mea culpa: "Did I use the word? If I did, I apologize."

Such exchanges between lawyer and minister provoked Senator Charley Johns to jump into the fray with his own observations.

JOHNS: Mr. Chairman, this witness has been one of the most evasive witnesses that we have had come before this Committee. I want to insist that he either answer the question yes or no, or refuse to answer.

HAWES: May I proceed, Senator?

JOHNS: You may proceed.

Father Gibson tried to explain to Charley that he wanted to be "perfectly honest and frank," but also sought to understand "exactly what [he was] answering" when questions led or meandered. When finally asked by the committee why he'd filed suit against the state to take his son out of segregated schooling, Father Gibson opened his heart to the proceedings: "I say, with all the power of emphasis at my command, my boy will never, never get the necessary education that he ought to have as long as he is segregated as he is; there is something that happens to his personality, because at the very outset it stamps him as being inferior." Having sat through Father Gibson's oration, Charley Johns cut in.

JOHNS: Reverend —

GIBSON: Yes, sir.

JOHNS: Did you ever belong to the Communist Party?

GIBSON: No sir. Sir, no negro in the South, especially coming from Miami, would you ever find in the Communist Party.

JOHNS: Do you know whether any of the members of your Chapter belong to the Communist Party?

GIBSON: Sir . . . we have passed a law now that no member of the White Citizens' Council, no member of the Ku Klux Klan, no member of the Communist Party can be a member of the NAACP, and I was at the National Convention when such a law was passed. I helped pass it.

Maintaining his clerical poise, Gibson endured a quizzical and often sarcastic interrogation from Mark Hawes, with occasional snipes from Charley Johns, for the better part of an hour and a half. At the culmination of his testimony, Gibson identified NAACP secretary Ruth Perry as the keeper of the branch records for the Miami NAACP, and Chairman Land called recess.

Ruth Perry was a white Miami Beach librarian and a pro-integration personality on local radio. She joined the NAACP shortly before the 1951 assassination of Harry T. Moore. Subject to frequent bomb threats herself in the years that followed, Ruth Perry nevertheless assumed a growing profile. In 1956, she began writing the column Along Freedom's Road for the *Miami Times*, the city's major Black newspaper, and used her various platforms to blast FLIC—calling its probe of the NAACP a "foregone conclusion." Local members of the White Citizens' Council branded her as a race traitor.

Perry presented herself before FLIC conspicuously empty-handed. Although FLIC already possessed some of the Florida NAACP membership rolls through its alliance with Texas, Perry's subpoena had carried with it an additional order to bring all meeting minutes and membership lists for the Miami NAACP. This command posed a dilemma. As secretary of the organization, Perry had kept such records until just around the July 1956 special legislative session that created FLIC. Then, at an August 11 meeting of the Florida NAACP, chief counsel of the NAACP Legal Defense Fund, Thurgood Marshall, telephoned in and ordered the state's chapters to mail their records directly to his offices in New York.

Thurgood Marshall himself was a virulent anti-Communist, and he understood that white supremacists eagerly used any perceived Communist support of the NAACP as proof that the NAACP itself was a front for the Soviet Union. But he also knew that so-called anti-Communist panels like FLIC were not to be trusted or believed for their freedom-fighting rhetoric. By the time Governor LeRoy Collins allowed the FLIC bill to become law without his signature, all Ruth Perry's NAACP records had been passed beyond state lines, safely out of the reach of FLIC meddling.

Perry knew that she was about to provoke Mark Hawes by walking into her testimony sans documents. Settling in, she looked past the state attorney into the eyes of her would-be assassins from the WCC. What if one of them stood up with a gun or lit a stick of TNT? Would Charley

Johns protect her? Mark Hawes, sensing a visibly anxious person in the witness box, toyed with Perry. As he had done with Father Gibson, Hawes tried to get her to admit that it was national NAACP leadership who'd dragooned Father Gibson into filing the lawsuit and then rebuked her for disagreeing. Committee member Cliff Herrell cut in on one occasion and asked Perry to project her voice, a tactic known to fluster witnesses unaccustomed to public speaking.

Mark Hawes then lied on the record (an informally accepted deceptive interrogation tactic used by law enforcement) and told Ruth Perry that Father Gibson just testified under oath how the national NAACP had recommended the Dade County lawsuit to him before he filed his case. Perry, illegally held in a separate chamber during Father Gibson's testimony, couldn't have known that Gibson testified to the opposite. But Perry stood fast.

> HAWES: Did you know that he testified that the Miami Branch approved of the recommendation?
> PERRY: No, I didn't.
> HAWES: You think he is mistaken in that testimony?
> PERRY: I think he will have to speak for himself.

Turning to the same tension-ratcheting maneuver that had rattled Gibson, Hawes repeatedly asked Ruth Perry the same question by theatrically demanding for a court reporter to read and reread it back from the transcript: "Did the Miami Branch ever take any official action in regard to the Dade County federal lawsuit?" Perry, often cut off by Hawes and/or the court reporter mid-answer, attempted to respond six times: "I don't know. I don't understand what you are . . ."; "I thought the lawsuit was brought by individuals"; "I believe they agreed to pay the attorney . . ."; "I know that we—the Miami Branch—wanted an end to school segregation"; "I know we voted to give a certain proportion, a certain amount of our funds to pay the attorney . . ."; and, finally, "I think I answered that by my last statement."

Under pressure, Perry revealed under oath that she'd given up possession of her records nearly six months prior to the FLIC subpoena. When she did so, Hawes, in a move out of order for a state proceeding, turned his head and began to interrogate Perry and her NAACP attorney, Grattan Graves, in the courtroom simultaneously. With melo-dramatic flair, Hawes prompted Perry to engage in an awkward public pantomime with her attorney, who was seated in the chamber but not called to testify. Thus did the hearing devolve into full kangaroo status, with Hawes redefining the rules of decorum as he went.

> HAWES: Will you ask him to return those records to you?
> PERRY: You mean right this minute?
> HAWES: Yes.
> PERRY: Mr. Graves, will you return the records to me?
> GRAVES: Do you want me to answer the question? Or is she still on the stand?
> HAWES: Answer it.
> GRAVES: I don't have the records, sir.
> HAWES: To save time, are they in Dade County, Counsellor?
> GRAVES: All the records have been shipped out of state.

At various points in Perry's testimony, it became unclear if Hawes was grilling Graves in his seat or the witness on the stand. Facing the brunt of state ire, Perry and Graves became sacrificial lambs fated to explain how badly FLIC had been outmaneuvered by Thurgood Marshall, a legal genius. Finally, Hawes invited committee members to air additional questions, and Senator Charley Johns seized on his refrain.

"Mrs. Perry," Charley asked, "do you now or have you ever belonged to the Communist Party?" "No, sir," Perry answered. "That is all," Charley declared. As Perry stepped down, Hawes called on the NAACP lawyer to testify formally. Grattan Graves, under oath, revealed how Thurgood Marshall had demanded the records of all NAACP branches "from Palm Beach to Key West." Given that Ruth Perry had just publicly asked Graves to retrieve her records, Graves assured the committee that he would promptly wire the request to Marshall.

> HAWES: Do you have any idea whether or not he will honor your request to release those records and ship them back to Florida?
> GRAVES: In view of the commitments that I am making here, I hope so, but I have no control over him. I can only make a request. He made a demand.

HAWES: Do you have any strong personal feeling as to whether or not you will be able to get them back—just as a matter of personal information?

GRAVES: You know as well as I do, Counsellor. I don't know.

With Thurgood Marshall residing in New York and FLIC unable to hold Graves or Perry in contempt outside a full vote of the legislature during session, it became clear that FLIC's efforts to publicly unmask NAACP miscreants had been anticipated and thwarted. At nine thirty-six that evening, as promised to FLIC, Graves wired Thurgood Marshall a telegram:

THURGOOD MARSHALL FEBRUARY 25, 1957
NEED ALL MIAMI NAACP RECORDS MAILED TO YOU IMMEDIATELY FOR
FLORIDA INVESTIGATION COMMITTEE. REPLY BY RETURN WIRE.

To protect the Miami NAACP's interests, Marshall did not respond himself. After deliberating internally the next day, the NAACP drafted a statement it decided to never release, instead leaving its position toward FLIC a mystery. With power and procedure moving against them, the committee realized its deadlocked position. What could they hope to accomplish in Miami if the NAACP wouldn't cooperate? Witnesses were excused and the hearing recessed until 9:30 a.m. the next day.

Then a front-page headline from the morning's *Miami Herald* set off a veritable hurricane of terror: "Will Dynamite Set Off Racial War in Miami?" The *Herald* quoted a White Citizens' Council insider claiming that cross-burner Hockett and his henchmen had a hundred boxes of dynamite cached somewhere outside city limits. After a few days in lockup for the LeGree incident, Hockett was fresh on the streets and initiating a master plan. According to the article, Hockett promised that his mentor, "fiery" John Kasper, would be "sneaked" into Miami to help decide "the right place and the right time to let go with the big blast." Unavoidably, and unfortunately for the likes of Senator Charley Johns, these Tuesday bomb threats superseded FLIC's pursuit of integrationist "Pinks."

CHAPTER 6

Courthouse Stand

*Chief Attorney Mark Hawes leads a
FLIC meeting in Tallahassee*

February 1957 (*Box 3, Box 4*)

WHEN HEARINGS RECOMMENCED in the Dade County
courtroom on Wednesday, February 27, the judge's bench sat nearly
empty. Nearly half the FLIC membership had packed up and fled in
the night—suddenly wary of the consequences of their own proceedings. Surprisingly, Senator Charley Johns elected to stay on to stabilize
the situation and dismiss any notions of dangerous Caucasians with
TNT. Into the wee hours, white supremacists received hand-delivered
subpoenas to appear at the courthouse, and the remaining FLIC members expressed a readiness to defuse the *Miami Herald*'s sensational
reporting.

Fred Hockett, out on bail following his failed cross-burning, was
called to testify under markedly friendlier terms than Father Theodore
Gibson. In contrast to the circuitous modes of inquiry employed the
day before, Hawes peppered Hockett with straightforward yes-or-no

questions such as "Does your organization advocate the use of violence?" to which he allowed Hockett to answer without rejoinder, "It absolutely does not; it talks against violence." Under oath, Hockett cast himself as the victim of flagrant misreporting by the *Herald* and a libelous "misquote." He characterized his attempted cross-burning on the property of the LeGree family over the previous weekend as a political act carefully engineered to publicize "the deplorable situation" for whites in northwest Miami but "not meant to frighten anybody whatsoever."

On the record, Hawes permitted Hockett to venture a guess at the name of the NAACP mole in his operation who'd squealed to the police about the LeGrees, although exposing a potential informant publicly could endanger the man's life. Hockett nonetheless pronounced the suspected spy to be Harold Shaver, a man already under FLIC subpoena. Hockett had met Shaver only when he breezed into Miami, and the odds that he possessed a reliable biography of this new acquaintance were low. Nonetheless, after Hockett aired the accusation, Hawes gave him ample opportunity to impugn Shaver's future testimony by describing him as "a publicity hound" who once had "amnesia for seven or eight years" and was therefore "a little demented."

Curiously, Charley didn't ask Fred Hockett or other WCC members in good standing if they were members of the Communist Party during this phase of the hearings, though he'd treated the question as mandatory for NAACP affiliates.

Up to testify next, *Miami Herald* executive editor Allen Neuharth faced the full fury of FLIC. The Pork Choppers of Tallahassee felt that newspapermen should be nothing but civic boosters—as the *Columbia Journalism Review* put it ironically, to "make the community feel good about itself—because nobody else was." However, there also existed an odd "syndrome" of the "crusading country journalist" in the swamp of the "South's quest to know (or not know) itself," whose job title was sure to be "gone with the wind" when he asked questions in the wrong places.

Charley Johns and Hawes recognized that they had an undomesticated journalist on their hands who needed breaking.

Allen Neuharth sat alone on the witness stand as Mark Hawes

pressed him for names. "Who wrote that article?" Hawes asked point-blank. Neuharth felt the eyes of everyone in the chamber, including the international press, upon him. He knew that answering such a question could imperil lives. To protect *Herald* reporters who might be targeted for assassination if names were released, the "Dynamite" article had appeared with no byline. For the same reason, all quotes from sources were kept anonymous, lest the *Herald*'s NAACP contacts in white supremacist cells suddenly vanish and turn up in the mouths of alligators in the Everglades.

Taking a breath, Allen Neuharth, a longtime journalist and World War II veteran awarded the Bronze Star for battlefield heroism, attempted to make the sensitive situation clear to the FLIC attorney. "That article was the combined effort of several employees of the *Herald*," Neuharth stated. Hawes pounced on the vagueness. His courtroom style of strutting like a rooster while oozing southern politesse much resembled the Looney Tunes character Foghorn Leghorn. Southern juries tended to love this showmanship.

The night before, Neuharth spoke via telephone to the chief attorney on all these points, while offering the committee "the utmost cooperation." Neuharth had recommended to Hawes that, to identify the *Herald*'s confidential source, he simply request the available witness statements on the dynamite case from the Miami Police Department. The *Herald*'s source, Neuharth had confided, appeared by name in those materials. Thus did Neuharth provide the precise means for the state to acquire intel without drawing publicity to the whistleblower.

Ignoring this broad hint from Neuharth, Hawes leveraged his extralegal powers at the courthouse to browbeat the witness in front of others. Hawes demanded the name of the *Herald*'s confidential informant. Neuharth declined, as he'd assured Hawes he would over the phone, standing by the hard journalistic principle of source anonymity. As consolation, Neuharth offered to personally take Hawes "by the hand" and lead him "to the source or sources" by pointing out the exact police documentation he'd require.

Hawes took Neuharth through a series of circular questions, much like Perry and Gibson, each query subtly rephrased to make it appear that he wasn't asking for the same piece of information. Each attempt resulted in Neuharth's refusal to name names. Ultimately, Hawes felt provoked enough to shout, "Do you refuse to give us that information?" Neuharth responded, "For the reasons that I have already stated, yes." Remarkably, a random male speaker in the courthouse gallery interrupted Neuharth during his testimony, and Hawes allowed it. This unidentified man, likely a Miami WCC member in league with Fred Hockett, shouted at the editor, "Will you talk a little louder, please? We can't hear you." This interjection, which was entered into the official record, comprised a thinly veiled threat from a spectator—implying "watch what you say."

Turning theatrically to the Florida Legislative Investigation Committee members—including Senator Charley Johns—arrayed like inquisitors behind the courtroom bench, Mark Hawes appealed to his higher powers: "I ask, for the record, Mr. Chairman, that the witness be instructed to give us that information." FLIC chairman pro tem Cliff Herrell pointed at Allen Neuharth. "You will be instructed to answer the question," he ordered. On this impasse, with the white supremacists involved in the dynamite plot sitting in the front row of the gallery, Mark Hawes, a lawyer who was technically not acting in the capacity of a prosecutor, grilled a newsman under subpoena for more than an hour.

Not six months after Governor LeRoy Collins assured Floridians that a legislative investigation committee would not "abuse the broad powers granted them," the primary concern of FLIC was not a dynamite threat on a population center. Instead, it was a newspaperman who'd dared to suggest that white Floridians used tactics of terrorism. Resolute in refusing to name his source, Neuharth stepped down from the stand under threat of contempt from the Florida legislature.

Soon after on the stand, NAACP lawyer Grattan Graves also received a verbal thrashing for his practice of employing spies within the Miami WCC for the purposes of threat assessment. When Hawes demanded that Graves reveal to the courtroom the identity of his WCC spies, Graves stated, "I don't think it is proper for me to divulge it to the public. If you would like to discuss it with me for Committee purposes, then I will be glad to give it to you privately." But Hawes declined any such accommodation.

The next day, the NAACP spy within WCC, Hampton Earl Shaver, sat visibly shaking before FLIC. As it turns out, Mark Hawes hadn't required any of the previous theatrics with Neuharth and Graves to issue a subpoena to the right person. As the questioning began, Shaver asked for a lawyer, but Hawes blamed him for not making prior arrangements. He then used a rereading of the transcripts from the court reporter to spook and embarrass Shaver into proceeding without counsel.

> SHAVER: I can get George Clark Smith to represent me.
> HAWES: Have you talked to him about coming here?
> SHAVER: Not here, no.
> HAWES: Why haven't you?
> SHAVER: I didn't think it was necessary until you asked me about it.
> HAWES: Why do you suddenly think it is necessary?
> SHAVER: Well, he's known me for quite a while here in town.
> HAWES: Read the question, Mr. Lee.
> REPORTER: (Reading) "Why do you suddenly think it is necessary?"
> SHAVER: I really couldn't say on that part, sir.
> HAWES: What?
> SHAVER: I really couldn't say on that part. I have nothing to hide.
> HAWES: Are you able to answer questions pertaining to your own personal knowledge?
> SHAVER: That's right, sir.
> HAWES: You can do that without the advice of counsel?
> SHAVER: That's right.

Throughout this courtroom exchange, Hawes sidestepped Shaver's constitutional protection against self-incrimination by maneuvering him out of an explicit plea for a lawyer in a public setting, with an entire courtroom gallery overhearing the request.

Bullied into testifying by Hawes, Shaver described how talk among Miami White Citizens' Council members had escalated following Hockett's arrest and turned to the topic of dynamite. Hawes responded to Shaver's story with incredulity. Under pressure, as Shaver stared at the very WCC agents he'd informed upon in the courtroom gallery, his testimony unraveled. He admitted to being Neuharth's source, which Hawes already knew, and ended up accusing both white and Black groups in Miami of possessing guns and bombs. Charley Johns interjected to caution the NAACP informant against affirming knowledge of the dynamite cache's location.

> SHAVER: That is a story out in Colored Town and in a lot of these associations—approximately that many [100] boxes of dynamite. . . .
> JOHNS: Mr. Hawes.
> HAWES: Yes, sir.
> JOHNS: This witness doesn't have counsel here. I think you should tell him what the penalty is for perjury. Maybe he don't know.

Chairman pro tem Herrell adjourned the Miami hearings at 2:15 p.m. on February 28. He expressed gratitude to "members of the press and the TV stations who have covered the hearings" as well as "spectators who have taken time out of their busy endeavors." Although he was powerless to censure uncooperative witnesses, Herrell reproached "those witnesses who, for reasons known only to themselves or stated in the record, have declined to give full testimony" with "knowledge of the responsibility that they owed to this Committee."

FLIC hearings resumed on March 11, 1957, in Tallahassee, provoked in large part by the recent appearance in Florida of white firebrand John Kasper. Kasper had embarked on a statewide speaking tour through Pork Chopper terrain. He began by addressing a Ku Klux Klan rally of two hundred outside a gas station lit by a fiery cross in Chiefland. Accompanied by William "Bill" Hendrix, Grand Dragon of the Florida Knights of the KKK, Kasper called for a "new breed" of Floridians and warned the crowd that "the Negro can be handled on a segregated basis rather, but we are not so sure how the Jew can be handled."

Called to testify under oath in committee room 50 of the state capitol, Kasper received a dignified forum to air his pet conspiracy of Communists, Blacks, and Jews colluding to overthrow the U.S. government through integration. *The Palm Beach Post* described the man as "tall, slightly stoop shouldered, sharp featured, and handsome." Speaking with enchanting rhythm, Kasper mesmerized like-minded members of the Florida public with his piercing blue eyes and expressive hands. Moreover, he appreciated the niceties of testifying from a polished table in a committee room instead of from a witness box in a Miami court.

Occupying the chair of any ordinary petitioner of the state, Kasper ranted, "Civil rights is that broad term used by the Communists and the Left Wing to cover up the almost exclusively 'nigger rights . . .' [because] sometimes these niggers frame up a police officer, somebody does, and it's happened before, where they'd claim that—some police brutal slaying, or police brutality of some kind, when it never occurred at all." The man was a magician with crowds, and Hawes did not so much as chide Kasper for using anti-Black slurs in a state building:

> HAWES: During the proceedings here, your testimony here, I've noticed you've used the word "nigger" over and over again. Where did you learn that?
>
> KASPER: Oh, I definitely, I guess have used that more down South, but up there, they had another word, which we used quite freely among ourselves, which, in a way, I think is similar to a white man. . . . You might say, in a friendly manner down in the South, the Deep South, calling a nigger a "nigger," and reserving the "Negro" for the Northern nigger, but up north, we use the "spook" a lot.
>
> HAWES: "Spook"?

Unlike *Herald* editor Allen Neuharth, Kasper left his FLIC deposition free of the legal threat of contempt, though Kasper was the ringleader of a string of southern bombings and Neuharth had never bombed anything.

Arriving late to his appointed hearing time, Miami dynamite informant Hampton Earl Shaver presented himself to FLIC at the state capitol in an alarmingly disheveled state. As *Jet* magazine described, Shaver showed up "with two black eyes." Shaver "claimed he had been kidnapped by whites, and his life and that of his wife threatened if he testified." After being unmasked as an NAACP spy that February, Shaver had attempted to go off-grid in the Florida Everglades. But when FLIC subpoenaed him to Tallahassee, Shaver was forced to resurface. When his bus pulled into the Tallahassee Greyhound terminal on Monday morning, March 11, agents of the WCC stood waiting. They abducted him at gunpoint, bundled him into a car, drove him to a remote location, and roughed him up for a day.

Highly skeptical of Shaver's horrifying excuse for his lateness, Hawes probed the story for discrepancies.

> HAWES: What kind of a gun?
> SHAVER: It looked like a thirty-eight.
> HAWES: How big was it?
> SHAVER: Had about a six-inch barrel on it.
> HAWES: About a ten-inch gun overall?
> SHAVER: Yes sir.
> HAWES: Revolver?
> SHAVER: Yes sir.
> HAWES: Put it right on you?
> SHAVER: Yes sir . . .
> HAWES: What did they ask you about?
> SHAVER: Different associations, and all that; what I knew about them, and all.
> HAWES: What associations did they ask you about?
> SHAVER: Dade County Property Owners Association, NAACP, Civil Liberties Union . . .

Hawes had Fred Hockett stand in the Capitol room so that Shaver could identify him more easily, and at the conclusion of the testimony, Hawes released the man without state protection. More concerned that Shaver might become a flight risk, Hawes instructed the witness to provide his current phone number and mailing address before excusing him into a room in which sat the men he'd double-crossed. To members of the public, Shaver's treatment served as a tacit demonstration of how FLIC would handle race traitors. Members of the Florida public wrote Senator Charley Johns a fan letter for these tactics during the 1957 hearings: "Dear sir, please keep up the good work of your committee, as I feel many may be vindicated of charges and publicity as well as the uncovering of many culprits that all good Americans should know by name," wrote Ruby S. Johnson of Jacksonville.

Seemingly untouchable given the wide public approval for their methods, Senators Johns, Rawls, and Johnson introduced a bill in the 1957 session to renew FLIC for another two years and expand its powers to use the Florida court system to file contempt charges against witnesses. This beefed-up renewal bill passed in the Florida senate by a veto-proof vote of 36 to 1 on April 24. A companion bill passed the Florida House unanimously. Invigorated, the Florida house and senate passed a joint resolution that April supporting interposition and declaring, "The Legislature of Florida denies that the Supreme Court of the United States has the right which it asserted in the school cases decided by it on May 17, 1954." Governor Collins handwrote and attached the following bitter statement to the bottom of the interposition bill:

> This concurrent resolution of "Interposition" crosses the Governor's desk as a matter of routine. I have no authority to veto it. I take this means however to advise the student of government, who may examine this document in the archives of the state in the years to come that the Governor of Florida expressed open and vigorous opposition thereto. I feel that the U.S. Supreme Court has improperly usurped powers reserved to the states under the constitution. I have joined in protesting such and in seeking legal means of avoidance. But if this resolution declaring the decisions of the court to be "null and void" is to be taken seriously, it is anarchy and rebellion against the nation which must remain "indivisible under God" if it is to survive. Not only will I not condone "interposition" as so many have sought me to do, I decry it as an evil thing.

FLIC's first official report to the legislature, delivered on May 30, 1957, near the end of the session, warned that "the NAACP has formulated a plan calling for the full, complete and absolute integration of the races in this country in every phase of life by 1963," including interracial marriage. The report minimized the white supremacist un-

derworld throughout the state and devoted generous space to the issue
of Black organizations that "secretly removed" records. Lastly, regretfully according to the report, FLIC chastised the "willful, open and
continued defiance" of the testimony of *Miami Herald* editor Allen
Neuharth. Having "repeatedly declined the lawful instructions . . . to
answer relevant and lawful questions propounded to him without assigning any lawful excuse for his failure," FLIC recommended for the
newspaperman to be held in "contempt of the Legislature." After reading their report aloud to a bicameral session, FLIC duly filed the document.

In a news conference soon after, Governor LeRoy Collins called
FLIC's conduct "praiseworthy" and assessed that the committee "could
continue to serve a useful purpose." Not a single piece of legislation
recommended by FLIC would pass, and even the recommendation to
hold Allen Neuharth in contempt of the legislature went unheeded, its
brio merely symbolic. But with his attention monopolized by open legislative defiance on interposition, Collins again allowed the FLIC bill
to become law without his signature or a condemnatory statement.
The fully reconstituted FLIC received a budget increase, from $50,000
to $75,000, and greater leeway to act against "subversive organiza-
tions." No report on its investigations would be due to the legislature
until 1959, so the committee could effectively run silent for the next
two years.

Senator Rawls and Senator Johnson, two of three original cospon-
sors of FLIC, soon left the group, and Senator Charley Johns made
sure to stack their empty seats with loyalists. On July 8, 1957, former
acting governor Charley E. Johns officially took the reins as FLIC
chairman. Charley's months of haranguing FLIC witnesses with the
infamous question "Have you ever belonged to the Communist Party?"
paid off by spotlighting his leadership capabilities. "Charley used to
expound on the floor pretty good," agreed Cliff Herrell, "so that the
press would eat it up." As the sole representative authorized to speak
on FLIC investigations, known and clandestine, Chairman Charley
Johns held all the cards of a vaguely defined and open-ended state investigation in his hands.

Using the rules of Florida to his favor, Charley had rebuilt his reputation in less than two years from a political has-been into a force to be

feared. Noting Charley's promotion to chairman, the president of the Florida NAACP, Robert Saunders, wrote an emergency letter to the national NAACP in New York:

> Chairman of the Committee is Charley E. Johns, staunch segregationist and reported to be a former Ku Klux Klan member. Johns' stand on racial issues has been well pronounced since he has voted for and pushed legislation calling for everything from closing schools to interposition. We can expect every effort to be made to label the Association as Communistic and to even see some of our folk facing jail sentences.

CHAPTER 7

Quorum of One

A Typical Lane Scene, ot Key West, Florida 25

*Racialized depiction of poor kids
in Key West*

July 24, 1957
(*Florida Bar Association Papers, Box 3, Box 8*)

CHAIRMAN CHARLEY JOHNS commenced his reign by testing the loyalties of subordinates and settling scores. His committee unanimously formalized new "rules of procedure" that permitted FLIC to directly seek the "aid of the circuit court of the state" for contempt citations—bypassing the legislature as a check against FLIC's power to punish. At Charley Johns's second FLIC meeting on July 24, former FLIC chairman Henry Land resigned in frustration. Accepting Land's departure without delay, the committee seized on his exodus to boldly redefine its rules for quorum. From that day forward, "one or more members" present at a FLIC meeting met the legal bar for an official FLIC function—no more worries about absentee slips. One committee member could potentially transform any conversation or situation into an official proceeding, thereby cloaking said committee member with legal immunity.

Charley Johns managed to find a way for one man in a room, who was not a judge or a jury, to become a king at court—embodying and enforcing the laws of the state. Meanwhile, he released a statement about a former FLIC investigator named John Chesty, who'd resigned the prior year and squealed to the press that he couldn't work with "skunks" like Mark Hawes and Remus Strickland. Charley clarified to the public that Chesty had actually been fired in December 1956 for "excessive expense accounts," although these excesses were neither specified nor substantiated. Charley's rebuke, nearly six months after Chesty's departure, sent a warning to those who'd allege bias on the part of FLIC or impugn its lieutenants.

Charley then shifted his focus to the committee's sole contempt recommendation: *Miami Herald* editor Allen Neuharth. He appointed two FLIC allies to resolve the newsman's ethical and legal quagmire. Senator Bart Knight, a Pork Chopper from the Panhandle, issued a derisive report on the journalist:

> It is my opinion that the witness was most evasive, and discourteous to the Committee, and in his refusal to answer direct questions, under an assumed confidential relationship or privileged communication, amounted to contempt, since I am not familiar with any immunization afforded newspaper editors by our courts.

Knight's conclusion amounted to an apple-polishing performance that much pleased Chairman Charley Johns. Cliff Herrell, chairman pro tem at the Miami hearings, spoke next about Neuharth. In a classic "pay no attention to the man behind the curtain" speech, Herrell punted on the proposition of the committee using its new rules to post hoc punish Neuharth. Instead, Herrell argued that the contempt recommendation should remain within the purview of the full Florida legislature, which could act or not act as desired. Herrell's prescription won over fellow committee members, who didn't want to be responsible for blowback from a First Amendment fight. Allen Neuharth thus escaped the prospect of fighting a FLIC charge through the courts and also dodged any prospect of a legislative contempt threat, as the full legislature couldn't take up the matter until it met again in 1959, and memory in the Florida legislature was famously short-term.

Endowed with his "quorum of one," Chairman Charley Johns saw no need for his committee to meet again until early fall. For months, he effectively went dark as he consolidated authority over allied law enforcement and FLIC staff. Foreboding silence on the part of Charley, who did not post a committee calendar or make announcements for future hearings, led the *Orlando Sentinel* to speculate about the new Johns Committee. The name stuck. *The Miami News* also began to refer to FLIC as the Johns Committee, indelibly linking the fate of the committee to the personality and whims of the new chairman.

Concurrent with Chairman Charley Johns's co-optation of the committee, integration troubles came to the forefront in places like Pinellas County, a liberal bastion with the gall to send Republican representatives to the legislature. In January 1957, a Black senior at Gibbs High School named Thomas "Tommie" Lee Jennings Jr. kicked off a small scandal by asking St. Petersburg Junior College, the local white community college, for an application. The son of a trash hauler and a maid, the middle child of five, Jennings was raised in humble environs at 1344 Fargo Street in a residence that abutted the interstate.

With a curious mind and a varsity lineman's ability to proverbially take a hit, young Jennings became pegged from an early age for bigger things. Underserved in his segregated education, but hoping to develop business correspondence skills nonetheless, he took typewriting courses in high school. Jennings made his expectations of enrollment known to the St. Petersburg Junior College registrar in a misspelling-laden letter that, courageously, specified his home address:

> I am a senior at Gibbs High School and as I shall graduate in June, I would like to inter your school in September.
>> Will you kindly send me an application blank and any other information that I will need to enter
>>> Respectfully Your
>>> Tommie L. Jennings. Jr.

School district underlings forwarded Jenning's letter, as if radioactive, up the chain to Pinellas school superintendent Floyd T. Christian, and Christian tap-danced in his response to the high school senior. "There has been no established policy for the admittance of Gibbs High School students to the Junior College," Christian wrote. As if to provide cover to his student, Gibbs High School principal John W. Rembert asked the school district if money was available to create a "Negro junior college." Working with Rembert, Superintendent Christian informed Jennings that they'd need to "defer action" until Pinellas County could determine whether they'd create a brand-new Black junior college for "grades 13 and 14 at Gibbs High School" rather than integrate the white school. Heatedly, Jennings wrote back to the white school superintendent:

> You said that there had been no established Policy for the admittance of a Gibbs High School student; But may I remind you that on May 17, 1954 the Supreme Court made the decision that Segregated school violated the Constitution and as a legal instrument, is dead. As an American Citizen, I am granted the right to go to any Public College I wish to go to, regardless of the High School I went to.
> Very sincerely your
> Tommie L. Jennings. Jr.

Meanwhile, Superintendent Christian sought guidance from his boss, Florida superintendent of public instruction Thomas D. Bailey. Rather than offer Jennings enrollment, Pinellas County decided to establish the separate "Negro junior college" at greater cost. Some $151,000 was earmarked for graduates of "Gibbs Negro high school" wishing to pursue further studies, while the standard annual appropriation of $1.2 million would go to St. Petersburg Junior College. Tommie L. Jennings Jr., at the age of nineteen, was being rebuffed by a forty-two-year-old white administrator who did not honor his requests, who smiled while ignoring edicts of the U.S. Supreme Court. The lesson must have been bitter. All the while, Superintendent Christian had the temerity to claim that local Blacks were "well pleased" with their segregated facilities. "The academic achievement of our Negro youth exceeds that of Negroes in other parts of the state," Christian bragged. Although Tommie Jennings would receive a special class award at Gibbs's senior commencement that June, historical records seem to indicate that he forewent junior college to enlist in the U.S. Army as his ticket out of limitation and later became a banner member of his local church.

The new "Gibbs Junior College" needed to hire Black staff that fall to teach the incoming class of Black students. Among the first nine instructors recruited by the newly promoted Gibbs Junior College president John W. Rembert was a humanities professor and choir director with a pencil-thin mustache named William James Neal, a Black gay man who'd eventually become the bane of Charley Johns. Neal was an Orlando native who'd earned a master's degree from Columbia University and toured nationally as a solo pianist before venturing back to the South to teach music. Within weeks of Neal's arrival, Gibbs Junior College received its official listing in the national Directory of Higher Education, and the debonair music director led the William Neal Choir in its first public performance in the school chapel.

That September 1957, chief attorney Mark Hawes wrote the president of the Florida Bar Association to commence a clandestine campaign for the disbarment of NAACP lawyers under the direction of Chairman Charley Johns. Hawes's strategy was to eliminate the NAACP legal threat by taking its attorneys, such as Grattan Graves, out of commission. If Black attorneys lost their licenses to practice, Hawes foresaw that Black plaintiffs would be forced to represent themselves and thus would be doomed to failure in court. Moreover, if Black plaintiffs appealed their own cases, the adverse decisions that resulted would set legal precedents beneficial to the cause of segregation. In a letter to the Florida bar, Mark Hawes accused the NAACP of the following:

> In my judgement, the sworn testimony of these attorneys and their clients, together with certain documentary evidence in our Committee's files . . . discloses various violations of the ethics of the Bar. . . . I have this date received from Chairman Charley E.

Johns a letter expressing his hope that this matter will be followed up by the Bar in conformity with the entire Committee's recommendation in that respect.

In spite of Hawes's insistence to the contrary, of course, FLIC had not met since July 1957, and the committee hadn't voted to pursue these disciplinary actions. Chairman Charley Johns, as a "quorum of one," was pursuing a solo gambit, with Hawes working at his exclusive direction. The Florida bar, while sympathetic to Charley Johns, concluded that though NAACP attorneys acted in "interest to the colored race," they could not find "unethical conduct." A report by an outside attorney concurred that no NAACP attorneys were "guilty of the unauthorized practice of law." Due to the confidentiality of these deliberations and the quasi-private nature of the Florida Bar Association, none of these backroom skirmishes would be known or reported to the public for years.

Separate from Hawes's disbarment campaign, Chairman Charley Johns sent FLIC investigator Remus Strickland to Gainesville for two weeks to scrutinize "a matter." Details of Strickland's furtive trip were not revealed, although his confidential expense records were. In all likelihood, Chairman Charley Johns dispatched Strickland to follow up on a concern he'd expressed in a letter that January 1957 to University of Florida president J. Wayne Reitz. At the time, Charley noted an issue with "negro men janitors" in female dormitories at "all hours," with girls having "complained to their parents." Although President Reitz researched the matter and reported back to Charley how certain jobs in dormitories required "heavy-duty male workmen" and that "no adverse report" existed, it appears that specific mixed-race scenario stuck in Charley's craw. Perhaps it's no coincidence, as the political and the personal often conflated in Charley's mind, that daughter MarkleyAnn Johns had just reached high school age at this time.

Months later, Charley directed Strickland to reexamine the Gainesville situation without Reitz's knowledge or permission, although Strickland operated as a state agent on university property. Charley's paranoia at the notion of Black flirtation played on popular fears of innocent white female coeds being romantically hoodwinked into interracial courtship by oversexed Black laborers. As late as 1961, the

Johns Committee would deliberate in meetings on the nonissue of female UF students "approached for dates by colored male janitors working in female dormitories," which President Reitz felt compelled to repeatedly research for the committee and concluded to be a false claim.

Charley disclosed the Gainesville operation to the rest of FLIC several weeks after the fact. That October 2, 1957, Chairman Charley Johns reconvened the committee in Tallahassee to acknowledge R. J. Strickland's activities and formally hire him with the title chief investigator on a salary of $650 per month—raised to $700 in a separate meeting days later at Charley's private camp in Starke. Strickland's pay rate for "services rendered" in Gainesville was authorized ad hoc, and several more rubber-stamp votes authorized Charley's protocol breaches.

Chief Attorney Mark Hawes belatedly reported on the chairman's request to submit hearing transcripts to the Florida Bar Association for "study and recommendation on what appeared to be unethical conduct in the practice of law" by NAACP lawyers. Obviously, Hawes's letter and the transcripts had already circulated, and this request to proceed was stagecraft. Charley goaded fellow committee members, who were unaware that the game with the Florida bar was already afoot, to vote yes on the measure and provide cover for the chairman for further incursions.

CHAPTER 8

A Johns Committee

*Charley Johns with ice pick at the Starke Ice
Plant, 1953*

December 1957
(Clerk of the House Papers, Box 4)

DESPITE GROWING CRITICISM of Hawes and Strickland
for conducting shadow campaigns in parts unknown while receiving
state salaries, Chairman Charley Johns announced that FLIC would
not be meeting again until 1958. Frustrated, Pork Chopper loyalist
Bart Knight, previously a Charley Johns ally, expressed puzzlement
about committee activities and threatened to resign.

Smelling a scoop, an enterprising *Miami News* journalist named
Robert Delaney dug into the résumé and reimbursement requests of
chief investigator Remus Strickland. Strickland, it turned out, racked
up an eye-popping $700 in auto expenses (more than a down payment

on a luxury vehicle) between August and December 1957, and also spent $960 for "records and a transcript from a confidential source."

Solidifying his status as a thorn in Strickland's side, Delaney then published a piece on his track record of career errors, firings, and malfeasance. Prior to being a Tallahassee detective, Strickland had served as a Leon County sheriff's deputy. In 1953, Strickland was sacked by an incoming sheriff who took a look into his cases and removed him "for the good of the department." On the heels of that dismissal, Strickland began a stint with the state beverage department on "high recommendations" that ended in another abrupt departure. Delaney confirmed that Strickland's dismissal occurred because, as later stated by the state beverage director, "His investigations were not reliable." This coverage called into question how Charley Johns could entrust such a man with extrajudicial powers.

That December 11, Strickland wrote a confidential letter to Mark Hawes concerning NAACP subversion and enclosed "a list of 148 names of persons who have been associated with either the Communist Party or some organization listed as subversive." Strickland had acquired these names from a questionable historic source. Back in 1954, a state attorney for Dade County named George Brautigam had conducted a small-scale Communist hunt in Greater Miami following the William T. Simpson murder/homosexual scare that identified suspects based on rumor and unearthed a flyer titled "Communist Rules for Revolution," which turned out to be bogus. Brautigam, at the time, claimed to secure this intel through an anonymous but "known member of the Communist Party."

The name of Brautigam's mole was never revealed publicly, and most of Brautigam's crusade, according to the *Tallahassee Democrat*, entailed little more than the prosecutor "hauling a lot of alleged or former Communists in before the grand jury, asking them questions, then citing them for contempt when they refuse to answer." Compliant grand juries could be abused by prosecutors like Brautigam to issue subpoenas and compel sworn testimony without the mitigating approval of judges—thus functioning as courts unto themselves, or courts within courts. Evidently, before state attorney Brautigam died of a heart attack in 1958, either he or his Dade County successor Richard Gerstein leaked the files from the 1954 grand jury proceedings—supposedly sealed from review—to chief investigator Remus Strickland of the Johns Committee.

Strickland relayed the Brautigam files to Chief Attorney Hawes, who then made ample (and questionably legal, should access to sealed files become known) use of the information in public proceedings by identifying every person on the old list as a card-carrying Communist. Meanwhile, Chairman Charley Johns reassured a nervous Florida citizenry that he was "completely satisfied" with his investigators "running down information." In the new year, on January 7, 1958, Hawes and Strickland met privately with Chairman Charley Johns at the offices of the Charley E. Johns Insurance Agency in Starke, Florida. There they deposed Sylvia Crouch, ex-wife of the notorious Communist informant Paul Crouch. In Crouch's FLIC interrogation, Hawes put to use the lessons he'd gleaned from Brautigam's investigation.

> HAWES: Can you tell me whether or not it was an official aim of the Communist Party of the United States to divide the negro and white races and set them one against the other on the race issue?
>
> CROUCH: Yes sir, that was one of the ways the Party hoped to gain influence in the South. Of course, the Communist Party was not interested in bettering the conditions of either the southern white workers or the negroes but only in furthering the advancement of the Party, and they could do that by better playing one against the other and by creating incidents that the Communist Party could use as propaganda.

Surprisingly, in this interrogation, Hawes delved deeper into the sexual politics of Communism, no doubt guided by the fraudulent pamphlet in the Brautigam files titled "Communist Rules for Revolution," which stated that Communists embraced "corrupt" sexuality.

> HAWES: Is it a fair statement to say that the Communist Party's official position is to break down the family as a unit, so there won't be any possibility of close personal ties that

might conflict with an undivided loyalty towards
Communism?

CROUCH: Yes, that would be correct.

HAWES: Is that correct?

CROUCH: Yes, it is.

HAWES: Do they generally discourage, under this Manifesto,
permanent marriage relations between men and women?

CROUCH: Yes, they discourage that, although they changed
their tactics a little bit. . . .

HAWES: Can you tell us whether or not the Communist Party,
that seeks all this racial agitation as one of their primary
aims in the South—are they, truly and in fact, integrated?
Has that Party truly integrated itself, as a matter of fact, in
practice?

CROUCH: You mean as a whole?

HAWES: Yes.

CROUCH: No.

HAWES: Would you say that the integration that does exist
there is for the tactical purposes of furthering their appeal
to the minority members of the races?

CROUCH: Yes. I know, for instance, in the Party in certain
instances certain white girls would be instructed to have
close relations with negro boys.

With guidance from the Crouch deposition, Chairman Charley
Johns reopened meetings with the full FLIC membership later that
January. The committee voted to resume public hearings in Tallahassee and Miami. On February 7, 1958, the chairman issued what he
believed to be a Johns Committee declaration of war:

The Committee is possessed of information regarding Communists activities in several vital phases of life in Florida and other
states. . . . Our first hearing in Tallahassee is for the primary
purpose of developing the general aims, methods, and means of
operating adopted by the Communist Party.

Subsequent hearings will develop the facts as to efforts to
carry out these aims in Florida.

One of the aims of the Communist Party in Florida, as elsewhere in the South, is to agitate racial conflict and unrest.

FLIC hearings restarted with fanfare in the state capitol on February 10, with the testimony of a celebrity anti-Communist: Dr. Joseph
Brown "J.B." Matthews, who agreed to appear for an undisclosed
honorarium. Matthews was the former director of research and counsel of the House Un-American Activities Committee from 1938 to 1945
and a former aide to Wisconsin senator Joseph McCarthy. In the
popular imagination, Matthews represented a righteous convert to
Americanism willing to name his former Communist comrades. Well
credentialed, white, and sharply dressed in a navy-blue suit, Matthews
was touted by Chairman Charley as "the leading authority on Communism in this country."

Matthews coolly assured the committee that "the record will show
conclusively that the Communist apparatus has registered a degree
of success in penetrating the NAACP which is not paralleled in the
case of any other non-Communist organization." In his ensuing testimony, Matthews received carte blanche from FLIC to use the chamber
as a professorial stage. The witness bragged that his private anti-
Communist library, amassed during "the past 30 years," contained
some twelve rooms' worth of materials valued at approximately $1
million. Hawes permitted Matthews, under oath, to answer most of
the committee's softball questions with long digressions full of invec-
tive and conjecture.

Matthews submitted to the committee a list of forty-six people on
NAACP letterhead who, he insisted, were previously affiliated with
so-called Communist-sympathizing or Communist-front organizations.
Among the accused were celebrities such as former first lady Eleanor
Roosevelt and American lyricist, librettist, and theatrical producer
Oscar Hammerstein II. Inconveniently for Chairman Charley Johns,
none of the impugned were Florida residents or members of the Florida
NAACP. Hawes later claimed that Matthews's 46 suspects were cross-
checked against FLIC's files of 150 card-carrying Communists—
acquired from the Brautigam grand jury. As Hawes contended, names
contained in both Matthews's and Brautigam's lists could potentially
be compared against Florida NAACP membership roll (plus the Flor-

ida NAACP leadership list already in his possession through the state of Texas). Through this unscientific method of collation, using inaccurate and ill-gotten directories created by whisper campaigns, Hawes purported that FLIC could establish "how many of the known Communists in its files had penetrated the NAACP."

Miami News journalist Robert Delaney, covering the Matthews testimony, noted in his after-action report that FLIC's unabashed purpose in hosting such a professional informant was "to link the NAACP and the Communist party." Following Matthews's testimony, the Georgia Commission on Education published Matthews's Communist suspect list as an educational pamphlet. Misleadingly titled "Communism and the NAACP," the leaflet circulated widely throughout the United States, and as late as 1964, citizens requested the propaganda booklet as part of community educational efforts to set neighbors and/or progressive youth straight on the menace posed by civil rights. "My son-in-law and others are being deceived by Martin Luther King's writings, and I would greatly appreciate it if you would send me the pamphlet giving Dr. J. B. Matthews' sworn testimony on 'Communism and the NAACP,'" wrote Reverend Roy B. Smith of York, Pennsylvania, to FLIC.

The same day as the Matthews testimony, Chairman Charley announced his intention to extend the Communist hunt to the University of Florida in Gainesville. "There is a probability of Red influence among the faculty of any large institution," Charley stated, while contradictorily claiming to possess preliminary evidence on the school that "horrified" him. When contacted by the UF student newspaper *The Alligator* to explain the discrepancy, Charley backpedaled and expressed the hope that there wasn't "too much Communism in the University, just a sprinkling." Charley then made the blanket assurance that there would be "no witch-hunting."

Sensing an aggressive Johns Committee telegraphing its next play, the Florida NAACP sought relief through its national organization, and the NAACP Legal Defense Fund sent one of its best attorneys, Robert L. Carter, from New York City. Chairman Charley Johns began his February 26, 1958, hearings with a bang at 10:00 a.m. in the north courtroom, on the fourth floor of the Dade County courthouse. In a courtroom packed with flashing cameras, Charley issued broad opening remarks that made ample use of the hot-button word *Communist* to prime his audience.

Seeking to head off accusations of character assassination by the mere fact of being called as a witness before FLIC, the chairman instructed Hawes to read a statement to all men and women present under subpoena:

> There are some people who seem to think that because a witness has been subpoenaed before this Committee, that some inference or accusation that such a person is a Communist results. . . . It is not the intention of this Committee to make any such inference. . . .
>
> If you feel that any unfair inference has been made or assumed by anyone against you because you have been subpoenaed before this body, you may have the privilege of making a short and concise statement denying that you are now or ever have been a member of the Communist Party itself, or of any Communist front or Communist action group, if you so desire.

Hawes recommended that all witnesses be barred from listening to each other's testimony and compelled to remain "out of the courtroom" except when called to testify. Banging his gavel, Chairman Charley agreed. When a witness in the "courtroom," as Hawes repeatedly referred to the hearing space, objected on the grounds that "this is not a judicial proceeding," the chairman overruled him.

Defense attorneys instructed NAACP witnesses to decline any question that displayed a lack of "pertinence" to prevent any unwarranted fishing expeditions into their private lives. This instruction led to the first group of witnesses—including Reverend Ed Graham, vice president of the Miami NAACP; and Grattan Graves, the Miami NAACP attorney—refusing to answer questions on constitutional grounds and being held in contempt for their silence. As the hearing continued, committee members verbally lashed out at signs of noncompliance and performatively displayed their disgust.

By the time Hawes called NAACP secretary Ruth Perry to the stand, the Johns Committee seemed spring-loaded for retribution. Though FLIC had ordered Perry to bring with her all Florida NAACP records reclaimed from Thurgood Marshall, Perry once again arrived with nothing. Perry raised her hand and swore an oath to answer truthfully all questions posed as WCC members, again seated in the front row, sneered at her. Perry began her testimony by challenging the pertinency of a question from Hawes about her profession as a librarian. When Chairman Charley overruled her objections, Perry gave a prepared answer that she would repeat countless times in her hour and a half of testimony: "I respectfully refuse to answer on the grounds of the First and Fourteenth Amendments to the Constitution of the United States."

After blustering to test her resolve and trying to maneuver around her right to challenge his questions, Hawes at last gave Perry the opportunity to read from a written statement:

> I have been requested by the subpoena to bring all records and lists of membership pertaining to the National Association for the Advancement of Colored People. While I appear personally, and will answer all lawful and pertinent questions, I have brought no records or lists of memberships. I consider the Committee's demand for such records and memberships invalid and an invasion of my rights to due process of law and freedom of speech and association.

Mark Hawes compared Perry's principled silence that day against her more forthcoming 1957 testimony. "Give me her testimony," Hawes yelled to an underling. "It's in that black bag there!" Hawes asked why, if she and her attorney were acting in good faith, Perry agreed under oath the prior year that she would attempt to get "records back in this state." Perry objected to the pertinency of the question. When Chairman Charley overruled her objection, Perry again refused to answer. In a stage-managed moment, a frustrated Hawes told Ruth Perry to "come down" from the witness stand, but committee members seemed to belie that instruction, and Perry half stood—perhaps still a witness and perhaps not.

Representative Cliff Herrell, in a fit of rage, left the rostrum and paced the courtroom floor. He spoke a series of extemporaneous remarks that culminated in a personal attack, stating that Perry was "not fit to be a citizen of the State of Florida" and calling for her to be cited for contempt. Herrell's tirade incited pandemonium, his words meeting with equal parts cheers and jeers. Charley Johns demanded order in the chamber as if he were an appointed judge. The chairman then recognized committee member J. B. Hopkins, who was given the floor as Perry remained awkwardly half frozen in the box.

Speechifying like Herrell, Hopkins asked the chamber rhetorically, "When the people who are identified with these groups, who claim that they are noble, fine groups, and are not subversive, come in and constantly and continually refuse to cooperate, how can we draw but one conclusion?" The committee voted unanimously to hold the librarian and NAACP race traitor Ruth Perry in contempt. Perry's attorney asked for a pause so that his client might make a statement to rebut these insults. The committee attempted to deny her such a moment, but ultimately Perry was allowed to speak. "I would like to say that I have never been a member of the Communist Party," Perry said, choking back tears. Hawes then "excused" her, although technically she had already been dismissed approximately ten minutes earlier. Chairman Charley Johns called recess for lunch.

Father Theodore Gibson, up next on the witness docket, bristled with fury at the maltreatment of Perry. "They abused her," Gibson was heard saying. "They abused her." When the hearing resumed at two p.m., Chairman Charley Johns denied a request for Grattan Graves to register a legal objection to the Johns Committee's assault on Perry's "character and integrity." Striding then into the courtroom in full ministerial vestment, Father Gibson demanded to read from a prepared statement. Hawes asked the minister if he'd brought along "any of the books, papers and membership lists called for by that subpoena with you, Reverend," but the deep-voiced preacher ignored him and recited what amounted to a sermon:

> In view of the fact that Mr. Herrell . . . has stated openly that Mrs. Perry and all other witnesses prior to her appearance and those who might come subsequently, are—if they fail to answer questions propounded to her, them, or to any other witness by this Committee—unfit to be a citizen of this State, I think, Brethren, that this Committee by virtue of such a statement and

a position has disqualified itself to be a Committee who is investigating actions carried on by organizations in this State impartially.

Chairman Charley called the witness out of order. Father Gibson persisted, raising his voice:

I was born and reared in Dade County. I am an American citizen. I believe in the heritage of America. I believe in the principles of the Constitution of the United States. I would not permit this Committee or any other Committee to intimidate me nor to deny me my lawful Constitutional rights, and for such a reason, and none other, I want to state—let me state further, rather, that I have not been a Communist; I am not a Communist; I am not a Communist sympathizer; and for the previous reason or reasons I've given with regard to the statement made by Mr. Herrell, I refuse, as of now, to answer any questions, and I, therefore, consider myself no longer obligated to the Committee.

Gibson rose from the stand as the gallery erupted in spontaneous applause. Chairman Charley Johns banged his gavel and tried to save face, but the instinct to restore order was too late. Father Gibson stepped down and made for the center aisle with his head high and his gaze forward.

HAWES: Reverend, are you refusing to submit to the subpoena any further, and refusing to answer any question that might be propounded to you by this Committee?
GIBSON: That's my position, sir.
HAWES: And are you now leaving the hearing room?
GIBSON: I am, sir.

Before the committee could bring a motion to hold the minister in contempt, the man nicknamed "God's angry child" left the building. The legislators voted to hold him in contempt in absentia. Equally indignant, the next witness, NAACP treasurer Vernell Albury, took the stand.

Albury refused to cooperate or field any questions, instead reading directly from a statement: "In light of the other evidences of the 'star chamber' nature of these proceedings, I believe that this Committee had disqualified itself to sit as an objective fact-finding body." Albury stood and left, like Gibson. Her departure was so swift that she left her statement in the witness box. With the room in bedlam, FLIC adjourned its afternoon session. A total of fourteen FLIC witnesses would be held in contempt by that Friday, February 28. With no witnesses talking, rather than continue what Mark Hawes characterized as "pointless" proceedings, the chairman called the hearings to an early close.

Before disbanding, the Johns Committee agreed to show impartiality toward "both colored and white organizations," fomenting unrest by holding future hearings in Tallahassee to investigate the Florida Ku Klux Klan. When Charley reflected on FLIC's Miami excursion, especially Gibson's comportment, his broad misgivings in the near term—"the Communist Party and the NAACP are tied up together"— built to ire in the long haul: "Ridiculous! I feel this Committee should go back down there and call those witnesses before us to testify, and if they refuse, we should put them in jail and let them stay there."

Two weeks after Gibson's courthouse stand, several hundred KKK members of Manatee County paraded in mask and robe through the Black district of the Gulf Coast town of Bradenton. Waving flags and lighting fireworks, they rabble-roused in a cavalcade of about twenty cars led by county sheriff Roy Baden. Klansmen said they rode in protest of a "recent move by a Negro group which told the Manatee School Board it wanted a new school building in Bradenton or it would seek to integrate the junior and senior high schools." The NAACP petitioned Governor LeRoy Collins to investigate the incident. Chairman Charley offered no comment.

CHAPTER 9

White Knights

A cross burns at a Tallahassee KKK rally

April 1958 (*Box 1, Box 3, Box 4*)

A FLURRY OF fan mail met Chairman Charley Johns when he returned to the seat of Pork Chopper power. "I am happy to know that you are Chairman of the Committee on Communist Investigation," wrote Mrs. Kenneth Williams. James Weatherford—an ailing eighty-four-year-old retired farmhand living in Tampa—wrote to inform Charley of the suspicious activities of his neighbor and inquire whether he could be of service by acting as a FLIC spy. Remus Strickland responded to Weatherford via letter on April 7, 1958:

> *If your health permits, it would indeed be a great help to this Committee, and to me as Investigator, for you to study and observe the action that is being taken in house which you mentioned in your letter.*
>
> *My suggestion is if you could obtain any tag numbers of individuals and other information in regards to people who you see going in and out of said house, and submit it to me, it*

would eliminate my having to appear on the scene for that
investigation. . . .

    The act that you are committing is wholeheartedly looked
upon as true Americanism, therefore, it is something to be
proud of. With warmest personal regards, I remain,
    Yours truly,
    Remus Strickland
    Chief Investigator

Johns Committee hearings would not resume until after chief at-
torney Mark Hawes obtained a circuit court ruling to substantiate
FLIC's contempt citations. Dade County circuit court judge J. Fritz
Gordon speedily ruled in FLIC's favor, but in a setback, the Florida
Supreme Court granted an appeal to the NAACP on the question of
the broader constitutionality of FLIC. Within days of that appeal, a
cache of dynamite exploded in the school annex of Temple Beth El in
Miami, causing $30,000 in damage.

That April 16, 1958, the Florida Supreme Court issued a stay on all
FLIC operations and halted its NAACP investigations pending a final
judgment. Charley found himself suddenly defanged and unable to try
NAACP leaders in the court of public opinion. With near-eldritch timing, two more bombings struck in Jacksonville. On April 28, a bomb
blast left a crater in the entrance of the Jacksonville Jewish Center, and
a separate detonation struck a Black middle school named for James
Weldon Johnson. Anonymous callers to police, identifying themselves
alternately as the "Confederate Union" and the "Confederate Underground," claimed responsibility for the destruction, with one declaring, "Every segregationist in the South must go free; Jews will not be
allowed in Florida except at Miami Beach. . . . We are ready to kill
every Negro who votes." Governor Collins pledged the full force of the
state to track down "guilty hoodlums."

While NAACP leaders hurried to Jacksonville to rally locals against
racial violence, Chairman Charley Johns, perhaps forgetting the court
order freezing FLIC operations, sent his chief investigator, Remus
Strickland, to survey the damage. "I am for segregation, but these dynamitings have no place in Florida," explained Charley. "If our Committee can do anything to see that they are stopped, then we're going

to do it." Strickland devoted the majority of his efforts in Jacksonville to tailing the NAACP leaders who were engaged in the community triage operation.

The impasse on FLIC proceedings broke on June 18, 1958, when the Florida Supreme Court ruled unanimously for the state. Quoting almost verbatim from Mark Hawes's legal briefs, the Florida Supreme Court deemed FLIC to be fully within its constitutional bounds to subpoena witnesses and request NAACP membership records. Furthermore, the court ruled that the admissibility of questions stood at the sole discretion of the committee and its chairman. If Chairman Charley Johns ruled a question as in order, it instantly became so. "This is what we've been waiting for!" Charley proclaimed, delighted with the ruling. Days later, he announced that his committee would resume "the Klan phase of our investigation."

The Klan hearings in the state capitol began on June 25, 1958, with an eyebrow-raising sidebar: Johns Committee member Senator Bart Knight confessed to the chamber that he was a former Klan member. "Prior to 1936, more than twenty years ago, I was a member of the Ku Klux Klan," he attested. He asked Charley point-blank if this former affiliation might pose a conflict of interest: "Am I disqualified to sit in this hearing?" Chairman Charley Johns, in his now-unquestionable authority, answered casually, "I wouldn't think so."

KNIGHT: I don't want somebody to come out with a newspaper story, saying that I was investigating the Ku Klux, and I was a former member of it.
JOHNS: No, I don't think that would make any difference.
KNIGHT: If the Committee thinks I am not disqualified, I'll be glad to stay.

The Johns Committee called its first KKK witness: a sixty-eight-year-old private detective from Tampa named William Joshua "W. J." Griffin. Griffin, who'd until recently served as Grand Dragon of the Association of Florida Klans, took the stand with self-assurance. He, like most Florida Klansmen under subpoena, presented himself as a relatable citizen in sober business attire. By testifying from a shiny table of state, like John Kasper, he carried an unspoken factor of legitimization that favored his cause. As part of Griffin's subpoena, FLIC ordered him to bring Klan membership lists and records of operations. However, Griffin explained away the absence of these records casually.

> HAWES: You had kept records of your Klan operations. . . .
> GRIFFIN: We had a typed out list of the different officers, but we burned all that stuff.
> HAWES: When did you burn that, sir?
> GRIFFIN: That was in March of this year.
> HAWES: March 1958?
> GRIFFIN: That's right.

Undeniably, the timing of Griffin's destruction of the records reflected the Klansmen's anticipation of a subpoena following Chairman Charley's announcement at the Miami hearings in late February—a four-month window during which inconvenient KKK papers disappeared. Rather than disparage Griffin for tampering with potential evidence, as he had with NAACP secretary Ruth Perry, or move to hold the witness in contempt, Mark Hawes accepted the information at face value.

FLIC was presently prosecuting NAACP leaders for their failure to produce membership records that FLIC did not require to conduct its investigations and that Florida NAACP leaders did not possess. The NAACP, however, did not have the audacity to destroy those records in anticipation of a subpoena and casually admit to it under oath. For white Klansmen to go unpunished for destroying materials and for NAACP leaders to be charged for failing to produce them reflected the flouting of an extrajudicial process that professed to be color-blind.

In testimony, former Grand Dragon W. J. Griffin expounded at length about a 1955 "flogging" case that fell beyond the state statute of limitations—a fact that Mark Hawes and Chairman Charley Johns well understood going into the hearing room. By investigating an archival white crime, FLIC could gain the appearance of being tough on Klan violence without the dilemma of having to refer any findings to the state attorney general.

The term *flogging*, as widely used by Florida Klansmen and state officials, meant a nonfatal lynching. A southern euphemism, "flogging" was designed to make its racial violence sound run-of-the-mill and folksy, almost like an agricultural process. According to his testimony, Griffin learned during a 1955 visit to Live Oak of a violent "flogging" infraction. Suwannee County sheriff Hugh Lewis told Griffin about this crime when the incident was fresh.

Approximately half a dozen Live Oak Klansmen posing as sheriff's deputies kidnapped and tortured a local Black farmhand named Richard Cooks that June 1. Klansmen tied the thirty-five-year-old father of nine to a tree beside the Suwannee River and whipped him for hours while threatening to feed him to the alligators and do the same to his children. Two white ringleaders who impersonated deputy sheriffs during the abduction, local Klansmen Fred Sweat and Johnny Smith, later confessed their crimes to Sheriff Lewis. Yet after interviewing the victim, Sheriff Lewis declined to press charges against Sweat or Smith because Cooks, as he lay injured in bed, could not recall an exact enough description of his attackers to a standard that satisfied the lawman.

Family members who witnessed Cooks's kidnapping were not consulted by Sheriff Lewis as witnesses, and none of the whites present at the flogging could seem to remember who else was there. Determined not to capsize the lives of two local boys, Sheriff Lewis instead called upon Grand Dragon W. J. Griffin to internally discipline Sweat and Smith as errant Klansmen. Griffin continued at the hearing:

> He [the sheriff] says, "Well, I wish you'd give them a good scolding. Somebody around here needs talking to." He says, "We can't put up with stuff like this." I says, "I don't blame you, Sheriff." I says, "If you know anything about it, why don't you put them in jail?" He says, "Well, I know who done it, I know who did it." He says, "I discussed it with them," and he says, "They admitted it to me, the two of them."

When questioned by FLIC attorney Mark Hawes on the Cooks case, state attorney William Randall Slaughter, who'd called the 1955 grand jury that failed to indict Sweat and Smith, covered for Sheriff Lewis by repeatedly complaining about a lack of resources in his rural district. Slaughter blamed Cooks's own testimony for the county's failure to indict the two confessed assailants. The prosecutor, a state officer under oath, repeatedly referred to Cooks using racial euphemisms, reflecting his infantilization of Black citizens:

> He's a good old, humble darky. I've known him a long time. All his white neighbors up there gave him a good word, because we went and interviewed and talked to every one of them to try to find a motive.
>
> They gave him a good, high name. We could never establish a motive for this. While my opinion is only my opinion, sir, I have never yet figured out why anybody would want to go up and hurt this humble, old darky. He had never done—he wasn't bigoted. He wasn't a . . . Just a good darky, that's all he was, to tell you the truth about it.

State Attorney Slaughter theorized that a mouthy local Black man advocating for integrated schools must have been the true target of the white mob, but the mob accidentally "got the wrong house and the wrong negro." Slaughter's testimony drew to a close with the FLIC chairman praising him for prosecutorial tenacity. "You did everything in your power," comforted Charley.

When Sheriff Lewis took the stand, he caused a commotion by confessing that he was a former member of the Live Oak klavern of the KKK. Lewis stated that he quit the order in 1955, the same year he oversaw the Cooks case. As it would be relevant if a sheriff with Klan ties showed favoritism toward fellow Klansmen, it was crucial for Mark Hawes to pin down the timeline of Lewis's exit from the Klan and press him for any overlap. Yet once more, a vital fact within Hawes's grasp received only glancing attention.

> HAWES: Were you Sheriff in the months of May and June 1955?
> LEWIS: I were.
> HAWES: Are you now, or have you ever been, a member of the Ku Klux Klan?
> LEWIS: Yes sir.
> HAWES: Were you a member of the Suwannee Klavern of the Association of the Florida Klans in May and June 1955?

LEWIS: I was a member from along 1950, up until the early part
of 1955.
HAWES: Now, what do you mean by "the early part," Sheriff?
LEWIS: I'd say sometime during the first part of the year.
HAWES: How did you come to get out of the Klan in the first
part of the year 1955?

Thus did Hawes, with his "How did you come to get out of the Klan" question, let Sheriff Lewis off the hook by changing the subject without establishing whether Lewis was a member during the 1955 investigation. As Hawes probed for details about the Cooks incident, Sheriff Lewis was at first cooperative. The sheriff, however, stonewalled FLIC on any question pertaining to the suspects Sweat and Smith; their confessions to him; or the person(s) who first brought the attack to his attention. "I refuse to give you his name, on the account that it might cause him to be killed," stated Sheriff Lewis. After offering this rationale, the sheriff immediately contradicted that statement with "It's confidential information, and it might incriminate me."

Lewis's last statement, pertaining to a sheriff's capacity for self-incrimination, was revealing, since the Florida statute of limitations for the Richard Cooks attack—two years—had lapsed, but the federal statute of limitations—five years—had not. Federal charges could still be brought against a law enforcement official who'd conspired to deprive Cooks of his due process as an American citizen. Sheriff Lewis, advised by counsel on the federal risks, pleaded the Fifth Amendment more than a dozen times.

Meanwhile, Hawes permitted Lewis to casually call a Black citizen a "nigger" without addressing this observable prejudice. After Lewis stepped down, Fred Sweat and Johnny Smith were called to testify. Hawes assured both men that the Florida statute of limitations had passed—their crimes annulled by time. But still, sitting with legal representation, both men repeatedly refused to answer any significant question posed by FLIC "on the ground that it may be incriminating." When asked, "Have you ever been a member of the Ku Klux Klan?" Smith protested by mispronouncing the legal term that his attorney told him to speak.

SMITH: I refuse to answer, on the ground that it may
   inscriminate me.
HAWES: Would you talk a little louder, please, sir?
SMITH: I say, I refuse to answer, on the ground that it may
   inscriminate me.
COURT REPORTER: May what?
SMITH: Inscriminate.

Here paraded before the Florida public were the lowliest forms of uneducated whites—inept, lawbreaking, violent, and corrupt. Chairman Charley Johns, at first confident in the low-stakes nature of these hearings, now feared the possibility of federal charges arising accidentally as a consequence of their disastrous testimony. When former Klansman senator Bart Knight attempted to prevent a KKK witness from being held in contempt, saying, "He's already answered all questions with any pertinence," the witness shouted, "No, I haven't!" FLIC then made the unprecedented move to shut down proceedings so as to get the Klansmen an attorney, with committee members Hodges and Herrell agreeing to pay for the lawyer out of their own pockets.

The chairman attempted to shuffle witnesses off the stand quickly. For example, when Fred Sweat refused to answer a final question, Mark Hawes stated that he had no further questions, and Chairman Charley instructed quickly, "The witness may come down." Had other committee members not been paying attention that very second, a white witness who'd refused to answer questions would have been allowed to walk away scot-free. Committee members Hopkins and Herrell, however, were observant and interjected with "Just a moment" and "Wait just a moment. I think this man ought to be cited," respectively. Thus did a contempt vote proceed, despite Chairman Charley's attempt to evade it.

The abductor and flogger Fred Sweat was officially cited with contempt of FLIC. The testimony of Johnny Smith proceeded in the same pattern, with Chairman Charley and Hawes trying to excuse the defiant witness—"*Chairman:* The witness come down. *Hawes:* Wait out there, Mr. Smith"—before committee members protested and voted to cite him for contempt.

FLIC's contempt vote against Sheriff Lewis ensued even more bizarrely, with Senator Bart Knight, the former Klansman, insisting that FLIC go into executive session, or closed proceedings, to discuss the matter. To this date, no one knows what the Johns Committee discussed among themselves about Sheriff Lewis at this juncture. Returning to regular order after secret deliberation, FLIC advanced the contempt vote. Yet Senator Knight again interjected, this time quoting a federal lawbook. "I am a lawyer," thundered Knight, "and I reserve the right to interpret the law myself." FLIC split into camps for and against Lewis and ended up voting 4 to 2 (with Senator Randolph Hodges joining Senator Knight) to file contempt charges against the sheriff. It was the closest contempt vote that the committee ever conducted. Had just one more *nay* strayed to the Knight camp, Charley would have been forced to take a public stand on an issue he did not want to touch by casting the tiebreaker.

Within the disorder of that day, three curious moments surfaced that called into question whether Chairman Charley Johns himself had Klan affiliations. First, Joe Hand, former president of the KKK of Eustis, Florida, a small town about two hours south of Starke, refused to name fellow Klan members, citing his obligation of secrecy to the organization. When pressured on the matter by Hawes, Hand turned to Chairman Charley Johns and addressed him directly with a question that seemed to carry overtones beyond Charley's powers as leader of the Committee.

HAND: Mr. Chairman, do I have to give the names of those, or
    is it necessary to give the names?
JOHNS: Yes sir, it's necessary.
HAND: Necessary for me to give the names?
JOHNS: Yes sir.
HAND: All right, sir.

This dialogue between witness and chairman ignored the prosecuting attorney and unfolded with a tone of familiarity. Conceivably, Hand could have been asking for permission to break a Klan rule within the "necessary" context of a legal bind or emergency. Within Klan law, which operated with rigorous hierarchy, the only way to seek such an exception would be from a superior officer.

Moments of coded language and in-speak continued. Eldon "E. L." Edwards, Imperial Wizard of the U.S. Knights of the Ku Klux Klan, the man who'd personally rebuilt the national Klan from his home base of Atlanta in 1953, testified about leadership of the Starke klavern. But something went awry.

> HAWES: Do you have an organization in Starke, Florida?
> EDWARDS: Starke? I believe so. I'm not positive, but I believe we do.
> HAWES: Do you know the Cyclops [local leader] of it?
> EDWARDS: Not the gentleman there (Indicating the Chairman).
> HERRELL: Did he say it was the Senator?
> HAWES: He said it was not.
> HAWES: Mr. Edwards, do you have an organization in Miami?

Edwards, in this exchange, briefly stunned the chamber into silence. Chairman Charley made no verbal retort for his being pointed out and simultaneously dismissed as the head of his hometown klavern. As the seconds ticked by, the former acting governor didn't utter a word. Starke was not a well-known location. How could an Imperial Wizard from Georgia know about such a dusty place and also know for sure that the chairman hailed from it? What made Starke and Charley Johns so significant in the mind of an Imperial Wizard that he offhandedly connected them?

Furthermore, why would Edwards identify but also deny a person's association if not as a mind game? The Imperial Wizard's specific words said no concerning Charley, but his phraseology alluded to yes. When committee member Herrell asked for an explanation, it was Mark Hawes who gave the clipped response, followed up by a brand-new question. Undoubtedly in the record, Hawes stepped in to protect the chairman, but from what? At the end of his questioning of the Imperial Wizard, Hawes advocated for hurrying Edwards to the Tallahassee airport, explaining, "He has a plane commitment to get out of here."

Any sore feelings on the part of Charley came to a head when FLIC called former FBI Klan mole Dick Ashe as a witness. Now outed as a former Klan spy and running as a candidate for state legislature, Ashe described the klavern's regular meetings at a local gun club, which served as military-style preparation for future operations. He explained how it was vital for klaverns to operate as gun club fronts so that "they could buy guns and ammunition at a wholesale price, and also in large quantities." Arming themselves for an anticipated day of "forced integration," they stood prepared to kick off a race war. Then Ashe's testimony took a turn.

He stated that an Orlando Klansman named Edgar Brooklyn once bragged about how he'd participated in the 1951 bombing assassination of NAACP leader Harry T. Moore at Moore's home in Mims, Florida. According to FBI surveillance files, Brooklyn was a known accomplice to the bombing who possessed the floor plans to Moore's house. The murders of Moore and his wife represented the first major political slayings of NAACP leadership in midcentury America, although they wouldn't be the last. For the Johns Committee to accidentally unearth a substantiative lead loomed, for the chairman, as a startling prospect, a potential political anchor that would sink his Pork Chopper base.

As Ashe testified about attending a Klan rally in Charley's hometown, he rattled off the names of Starke Klan members as well as sympathetic neighbors and officials. Charley Johns, sitting by uncomfortably, interrupted Ashe to lash out at one of his own committee members.

JOHNS: Mr. Ashe, Representative Hopkins would like to know
    if you've ever seen the Chairman at any of those meetings.
ASHE: No sir, I never have.
HOPKINS: That was a joke, Charley, and you know it.

What's bizarre about this moment is the way that the chairman chose to confront committee member Hopkins about Klan insinuations instead of committee member Herrell, who'd previously asked the question about whether Imperial Wizard Edwards had identified Charley as a Klan leader. Charley appears to have deliberately gone after the wrong man with his rebuke. Hopkins, as point of fact, was an ally and a fellow Pork Chopper, and he used the chairman's first name when appealing for mercy, asking Charley to remember prior bonds and not to a hold a grudge over this small misunderstanding.

By acting forceful, the chairman made a bolder point. *Look at what I can do*, the chairman seemed to be saying to his committee. *I can make you grovel in a second.* With an adept maneuver, Charley wiped his name clean by pulling rank. But the object of his attack, non–Pork Chopper Cliff Herrell, watched as a bystander observant to the warning. Had Charley attacked Herrell directly, members of the press and the public would likely have perceived the incident as a rebuke for Herrell's prior comment.

Uncharacteristically exhausted after Ashe's testimony, Chairman Charley Johns ended the KKK hearings without a concluding speech. No future Klan arrests would be made by state authorities based on revelations uncovered by FLIC. Orlando Klansman Brooklyn would not be charged or questioned further for his alleged involvement in the 1951 assassination by dynamite of NAACP president Harry T. Moore. For a time, a tiny number of FLIC contempt charges against defiant Klansmen proceeded through the circuit courts, but eventually it appears those charges were dismissed or allowed to quietly fade out.

Over the next year, more court decisions erratically jerked the Johns Committee forward and backward on the NAACP issue, which left FLIC attorney Mark Hawes with a near-manic workload. The very life of Charley Johns's committee seemed to be on trial with each new ruling. In early July 1958, Miami circuit judge Ray Pearson ruled that thirteen NAACP witnesses under contempt charges from the Miami hearings should receive the opportunity to reappear before FLIC with the requested membership lists and records. But in late July, the Florida Supreme Court granted the NAACP an appeal, which froze Judge Pearson's order. Once again, the NAACP created a work stoppage.

Mark Hawes vented pent-up frustrations in oral arguments before the Florida Supreme Court on August 1, 1958. Accusing the NAACP of stall tactics reminiscent of Communists, Hawes charged, "They [the NAACP] have but one aim and that is to kill off the Committee." If the court didn't act swiftly, Hawes warned, FLIC would be unable to deliver its mandatory report to the legislature in 1959. Hawes argued that Florida's security concerns provided sufficient rationale to violate the NAACP's federally protected freedom of association. Miami NAACP leader Reverend Theodore Gibson, commenting on the FLIC attorney's tone, quipped that Hawes "sounds like a frustrated man."

The end game of FLIC's investigations, Hawes revealed in the brief he submitted, was the state of Florida's intention to petition federally for a constitutional amendment to enshrine the right of all state legislatures to investigate subversion. Contra to Hawes's far-reaching claims, the NAACP argued that its campaigns fell outside FLIC's authorization to investigate organizations promoting violence or violating state laws.

Six days before Christmas 1958, the Florida Supreme Court handed down a unanimous opinion affirming the constitutionality of FLIC and its right to hold witnesses in contempt. The committee possessed sufficient fact-finding powers to demand that the NAACP answer its questions and wielded such power with "moderation, restraint and caution."

Supplementarily, the court found committee member Cliff Herrell's personal tirade against NAACP secretary Ruth Perry—whom Herrell accused of being "not fit to be a citizen of the State"—to be without "bias or prejudice." It was the NAACP that stood in legal breach. The court declared Father Theodore Gibson's walkout from the Miami hearing to be "defiant" conduct and praised committee members for their "patience." The court ordered four NAACP witnesses—including Father Gibson—to give the requested membership information to state agents. Although the NAACP intended to appeal to the U.S. Supreme Court, the legal ice trapping Charley Johns and his committee was beginning to thin.

Then the fates changed course. Three days later, in a hearing for *Gibson v. Board of Public Instruction of Dade County*, federal judge Joseph J. Lieb handed the NAACP a history-making gift by nullifying Florida's constitutional mandate for segregation in education. Thus was the Article XII, Section 12 clause, "White and colored children shall not be taught in the same school, but impartial provision shall be made for both," rendered vestigial, void, patently in violation of the Fourteenth Amendment to the Constitution of the United States. A phrase that defined the political framework of the Pork Choppers, a phrase that meant so much to Charley Johns personally, was knocked out of the state's founding document, and it was gone because of a lawsuit brought by Father Theodore Gibson on behalf of his son.

Executing a stall tactic in the name of judicial restraint, Judge Lieb chose not to rule against Florida's pupil assignment law, though the law almost certainly violated standards set forth by *Brown*. "Lieb denied Gibson's petition for immediate integration of Dade County schools," read a dry article in the *Tallahassee Democrat*. "He said the Negro had not gone through all the steps provided by the pupil assignment law for those objecting to the placement of their children." The NAACP made clear its intention to challenge and nullify the pupil assignment law. For Father Gibson, the ruling came several months too late to deliver a much-prayed-for equal education for his now high-school-age son, who'd enrolled that fall as a freshman in the local segregated high school, Booker T. Washington—the alma mater of his father. The man's efforts could alter a constitution, but still couldn't get his kid into a white school. The struggle endured.

Even before these divergent rulings, Chairman Charley ordered his staff to expand the scope of their investigations to meet a faster pace of progress in subversion hunting. Charley instructed Chief Inspector Strickland to return to the University of Florida, the state's flagship campus, that summer 1958 to search for more Pinks and Reds like former UF professor John Reynolds. "We were concerned with the influence of the professors would have on the student body," recalled Strickland, "and I found it was really, really strong."

Within former professor Reynolds's coterie of community players at the Gainesville Little Theatre was a fifty-two-year-old bachelor named Claude L. Murphree—a UF music professor, world-famous organist, and nephew of former UF president A. A. Murphree. Strickland almost instantly suspected Murphree of foul play. "Card-carrying member of the Communist party," Strickland declared, with no clear evidence. "Had a certain following at UF that remained loyal to him, so the Committee couldn't catch him."

Problematically, as he was being surveilled by the Johns Committee on June 17, 1958, Murphree died under odd circumstances. Struck by his own 1955 Chrysler as it rolled down a hillside, the music professor was crushed under the car's wheels and killed almost instantly. It's unknown if committee agents witnessed the death firsthand, but a suspicious death did kick off their Gainesville undertaking. "Reported to Hawes," recalled Strickland. "I recommended we go into full swing, which we did." As Murphree was an unmarried globe-trotter with friends on multiple continents, Strickland staked out the man's funeral to see who showed. "The moment he was dead, and by his [Murphree's] popularity and presence no longer shielded, other homosexuals on the faculty—they started to be persecuted," confirmed a UF insider. With serendipitous timing, a new tip came in. "I had some knowledge of some individuals that were alleged to be gay," recalled Officer Tileston of the UF campus police department. "I had come onto it purely accidentally, not thinking about it, and I thought that my chief should know about the information. I told him about it, and a few weeks after that he called me into the office and introduced me to R. J. Strickland."

Although FLIC's operating statute technically did not authorize the right to investigate a nonviolent sexual subculture, the preamble to the law made use of the nebulous word *subversive* in the context of "certain activities of on the part of organizations and individuals," which Charley encouraged FLIC staff to read expansively, especially if it involved punishing an unpopular class of folk. Public sentiment tilted so far against homosexuality in the late 1950s that juries in Florida rarely presumed innocence for queer-related charges. "As a defense counsel, I can say that the entire area of sex deviation is so charged with emotion that a defendant, if the case ever gets to a jury, is usually lost," wrote Florida attorney Albert N. Fitts to the Johns Committee. "More innocent men have either lost their liberty or reputations by virtue of F.S. 800.04 [the crime against nature statute] than by any other statute in our history."

Southern men and women who felt the urge to engage in homosexual flings, once deemed permissible in their system of racial apartheid wherein any vice could be tolerated so long as it wasn't miscegenation, now became hunted and branded with labels tying them to activities they didn't want promulgated or named. Thus did the "deviate" few of Florida disguise themselves even further. They exiled the behavior from the rest of their lives. They tended to meet furtively in underworld settings, where they identified through aliases; many remained married with families, professed love for their spouses, and attended church each Sunday. Emblematically, a gay person from Dixie in 1953 wrote the editors of the Los Angeles–based "homophile" magazine *One* to lodge a complaint in their first issue: "Why in the hell are you idiots drawing a lot of attention to us by starting a magazine?" A gay Floridian from the Panhandle also wrote *One* to explain how the South "has nothing to offer but grief for the flamboyant, the flaunting homosexual," while the "quiet and self-respecting" gay did not attract the klieg lights of authorities.

The Johns Committee was an investigation in search of something new to investigate, and it undeniably found a prime target posing a danger to the American family through Tileston's tip-off lurking in the Gainesville Little Theatre company or party houses on the border of the major state university. Charley Johns, a devout Baptist who professed to being with only one woman his entire life, speculated that men who hid a sex secret surely conspired to hide more. Charley's chief lieutenants, Mark Hawes and Remus Strickland, were World War II veterans who once stood in draft lines and served in units where homosexuals were singled out as 4F—unfit for service—or were dishonorably discharged. Already seeing anti-gay sentiment as nothing but common sense, they grasped a political opening to enforce their beliefs.

If the committee's first pursuit (race) was a mandate, its second pursuit (sex) was an opportunity. "We first looked at University of Florida for Communists," Strickland said of his order of operations, "then we came back and did the homosexual purge."

On August 18, Charley subpoenaed "all records of personal misconduct on all faculty personnel, past and present; all records of Communists or Communist Front Affiliations of all personnel or faculty; all records of integration activities of all personal and/or faculty members" from UF president J. Wayne Reitz. And on October 1, 1958, Strickland purchased three thousand feet of tape with committee funds for a portable reel-to-reel recorder.

ACT II.

Liftoff

CHAPTER 10

Sons of Florida

*Art Copleston,
circa 1958*

January 20, 1959 (*Box 7, Copleston Papers*)

"HOW ARE YOU, Mr. Tileston?" asked Art Copleston, interrupting chief attorney Mark Hawes. It was 10:15 a.m. on January 20, 1959, and the University of Florida student had just been pulled from his accounting final exam by state highway patrolmen.

Copleston found himself in a seedy roadside motel on the edge of Gainesville, across the table from a state lawyer, chief investigator Remus Strickland, Florida senator Randolph Hodges from Cedar Key, and a few more uniformed men. Senator Hodges was a conservative Pork Chopper Democrat who, like Charley Johns, briefly attended the University of Florida before dropping out. Copleston could tell that saying hello to Tileston, a supposed undercover FLIC operative, embarrassed Hawes and Strickland in front of the senator. How secret could their operation be if a witness identified a mole on sight?

Chief attorney Hawes took a beat before continuing. "We've asked you to come out here because this committee is conducting, as quietly as we can with as little notoriety as we can, an investigation into the extent of homosexual activity here on this campus." Leaning into the word *investigation* when he spoke it, Hawes had made the term sound like "infestation," which is what Copleston heard. Copleston nodded. "Yes, I heard about it," he answered.

Copleston had spent all his life pretending to be normal, constructing a heterosexual persona, but none of that mattered now. Tileston had sniffed him out at the Burger House in the summer of 1958 just by looking at him. Hardly tripping over a syllable while reciting legalese, much as he had with Father Gibson in Miami, Hawes stipulated how the Johns Committee possessed the subpoena power to haul Copleston into questioning at a public hearing about sex crimes with the press in attendance. Or, Hawes qualified, everyone could just cooperate on the record, right here in this room. "Under those conditions," Hawes asked, "Art Copleston, are you willing to give us a voluntary statement of what you know or might know about this matter?" The lawyer paused. He leaned forward and smiled benignly, as if saying between the lines, "Just help us out a bit, and we can all go home."

Copleston could barely shake the feeling of being wrapped in a python's coils. Visions of every affair, all his lovers and gay friends, flooded his mind. Those faceless partners in the second-floor bathroom of the UF library, where he cruised during study breaks; the married chemical engineering professor, Dr. Thomas "Tim" Reed, with whom he made love in the faculty showers of the university recreation center; the closeted gay English professor, Dr. Stephen Fogle, with whom he'd listen to Metropolitan Opera radio broadcasts on Saturday afternoons; his buddy Bill Moore, part of his underground gay student cohort. Could these names be the ammunition he needed to get himself out of this chair? "I'll tell you, sir," Copleston answered, "before I make any recorded statement right now—I am willing to, but I tell you I am not homosexual."

Twenty-six-year-old Art Copleston stood and put his right hand in the air. A court reporter, ready with a Bible, duly swore him in.

Mark Hawes quickly lost the chumminess. At a breakneck pace, Hawes took Copleston through a series of contradictory instructions designed to instigate panic, to confuse Copleston and throw him off balance—a deceptive interrogation tactic called disorientation. Though this wasn't a criminal investigation, Hawes told Copleston, it was "a civil investigation, seeking information to inform the legislature as to the extent of this problem here." Copleston could be found criminally liable for any way that he might perjure himself in this deposition. "You know what—anything about the penalty for perjury in this state?" Hawes asked. "It's a penitentiary offense." If Copleston lied or evaded going forward, said Hawes, he could land himself in state prison on a perjury charge with the same mandatory sentence as a "crime against nature" for homosexual acts: twenty years.

Copleston's face flushed. The thought of being a cockroach in the spotlight terrified him. This lawyer had just said things that sounded like they made sense, but they really didn't at all. Afraid of looking stupid in front of a stranger, Art Copleston let stand a bewildering string of contradictions. Although Hawes, on the one hand, insisted that this wasn't a "criminal investigation," on the other he implied that he was watching out for instances of perjury and, if necessary, could advance charges. Never once did Hawes remind Copleston of the right to remain silent or ask if he'd like an attorney present, as such liberties did not exist in the kingdom of Charley Johns, much less in a nation without Miranda right protections. Nor did Hawes inform Copleston that Senator Hodges's presence in the room satisfied a Johns Committee requirement that "one or more members will constitute a quorum," which turned this spur-of-the-moment motel gathering into a state hearing, with legal implications.

HAWES: Art, do you know any member of the faculty at the University to be a homosexual?

COPLESTON: No, I do not.

HAWES: Do you know any student out here to be a homosexual?

COPLESTON: No, I do not.

HAWES: Now, you're talking about your personal knowledge?

COPLESTON: Yes.

HAWES: You never had any personal relationship, sexual relationship, with any of them?

COPLESTON: Definitely not. . . .

HAWES: And you've been in the Service. You know a little
something about homosexuals, don't you?

Art Copleston happened to be a military veteran attending college
on the G.I. Bill, which covered his per-semester student fees. Hawes
had just slyly reminded Copleston of that financial dependency. Copleston had enrolled as an undergraduate at UF in the fall of 1957, with
classes beginning on his twenty-fifth birthday. His mother, Margaret,
and stepfather, Pat, had proudly helped move him into his dormitory,
Thomas Hall.

ART COPLESTON WAS a son of New Florida. Born on September 16,
1932, in Charleston, South Carolina, his family moved to Tampa in
1937 with an influx of newcomers who felt that ineffable pull to the
land of sunshine. Copey, as his family called him, was a shy young boy.
His earliest memories were of his mother drunkenly calling for him
from in front of her bedroom vanity mirror, where she'd weep for
hours.

Copey's father, Arthur Sr., routinely drank himself into a stupor
while staring ahead with silent and furious intensity in his sitting-
room chair. Hired by Pan American World Airways as part of the national World War II mobilization, Arthur Sr. uprooted the family to a
one-bedroom apartment in Miami. "Playground of the young," wrote
famed Florida geographer Sigismond Diettrich, whom Copleston
would eventually meet, of Miami. The Magic City was where Copey's
dreams took root. In junior high school, he tried his hand at the sousa-
phone in band. By luck, the teacher sat him beside a gifted baritone
saxophone player, reputedly the son of a locally famous political family.
The boy's name was Donald Bouterse, but Copey called him Dee-Dee.

All of a sudden, Copey and Dee-Dee were in each other's lives every
day. As they planned after-school dates, Dee-Dee would instruct
Copey to sneak out at an appointed time from his family apartment,
where Copey slept on a pullout sofa. Copey would walk the five blocks
to catch a bus from Southwest 8th Street to Bayfront Park. The bus
swung by Dee-Dee's house, where Dee-Dee would hop aboard. Then
the boys would casually sit beside each other and lean across the divide

to give a playful nudge whenever another cute boy got on the bus. They would stand up and exit when they saw the glistening waters of Biscayne Bay appear between the downtown office buildings. Post–World War II, Bayfront Park was an internationally renowned gay cruising mecca, a sexually charged zone where the boys could literally count the condoms spilling from the mouth of the Miami River into the saltwater bay. Visions of almost nonstop man-sex, the boys knew, awaited in the bushes of their beloved park.

On weekends, Copey's oblivious father drove the boys south to Matheson Hammock Park, a lagoon recreation and swimming area. Arthur Sr. would typically go home to drink, so Copey and Dee-Dee spent whole Saturdays and Sundays unsupervised. Sometimes they wandered farther into mangrove thickets, where resourceful cruisers had assembled tree huts for anonymous hookups. On their wildest weekends, Copey and Dee-Dee mustered up the nerve to swim across a fifty-yard channel, reputedly filled with sharks, to a nearby island, where they peeled off their swimsuits and spent the day nude in the seclusion of the Australian pine trees.

Resting together, they charted out their futures. Ahead beckoned high school and four years of freedom at the vaunted University of Florida in Gainesville. Although they were not exclusive, they shared an erotic infatuation that continued through their years at Miami High School, where they hoped to graduate with the Class of 1950. Arthur Sr. had other plans.

At the beginning of Copey's senior year, Arthur Sr. announced that he was moving the family north to rural Fort Pierce, the ancestral home of former governor Dan McCarty and famous for little else. "I would be amazed if it had ever occurred to them that pulling me out of high school was destabilizing," Copleston recalled. "My father would have easily justified it because, after all, he was the only person who counted. He was the one having to bring home all the money." Copey rode his bike to Dee-Dee's house on 63rd Avenue to bid his special friend goodbye. They almost broke down several times as they spoke, but they couldn't reveal more, not with Dee-Dee's mother watching their parting.

As his parents sank deeper into drink in Fort Pierce, Copey struggled to make new friends as an incoming high school senior. After Copey's high school commencement, Arthur Sr. informed the boy that

Donald Bouterse, 1950

the family had no savings for his college education. Meanwhile, Dee-Dee graduated from Miami High School and enrolled in 1950 as an architecture student at the University of Florida, just as he'd daydreamed at the Matheson Hammock beach.

As a freshman in Gainesville, Dee-Dee met a male lover named Andres "Max" Fabregas. Both intellectually gifted, Dee-Dee and Max became celebrated as the "Golden Couple" among the Gainesville bohemian set, living a life that Art "Copey" Copleston could fantasize about but not realize. Dee-Dee graduated from the University of Florida in 1954, and he and Max eventually co-founded an architectural firm with offices in Paris, Miami, and São Paulo. Thrilled by their success, Copleston also felt inferior through natural comparisons. (Starchitect Donald Bouterse would go on to design such structures as Miami Beach City Hall and Miami International Airport Concourses B and D before perishing in 1985 during the AIDS crisis.)

Unwilling or unable to continue paying rent in inexpensive Fort Pierce, Arthur Sr. moved the Coplestons into the West Palm Beach home of his in-laws, Copey's maternal grandparents. In West Palm Beach, his parents' situation devolved further into days-long alcoholic benders. With his meals and lodging fully provided for, Arthur Sr. saw no need to work. To contribute financially, Copleston went to work as a ramp jockey for Eastern Airlines at the West Palm Beach airport.

Eventually, Copleston decided he needed to get the hell out of there. One day in January 1951, he stood up at dinner and announced his enlistment in the U.S. Air Force. Copleston foresaw that the G.I. Bill could provide a viable route to pay for his education at the University of Florida. Shipping off to basic training and then assigned to the Air Police squadron at Tyndall Air Force Base near Panama City for three years, Copleston did his time for Uncle Sam to qualify for a one-way ticket to college. The plan was "bachelor's degree or bust." There were no financial contingencies, and he knew there'd be no second chances if he was sent packing from Gainesville for a sex crime.

BEING A FULL seven years older than most of his UF classmates, Copleston didn't find his transition to campus life easy. Gainesville at the time existed as an Eden of white Protestants, with few Jewish students and fewer Catholics. The school had gone coeducational only in 1947. For most of the students, college represented a bastion of jocular rites of passage. Academic standards weren't high, and fraternity and sorority rush season made headlines in the student newspaper, the *Alligator*. During rush season, Art Copleston vowed never to pledge a fraternity because he couldn't risk being in a hazing situation where his sexuality might be exposed. All it would take was one misbegotten erection, and he'd become the target of spitballs or worse in the hallways and beatings in the showers until one day he'd have to bolt.

Student journalism in the *Alligator*, which Senator Charley Johns regularly read to gauge youth sentiment, largely parroted the agenda of the UF administration, which could judiciously exercise veto power over content. Stories that might tarnish the reputation of the institution would be killed, while cautionary tales about students carrying on too freely would make the pages of the paper. For example, administrators killed a 1955 student investigative piece into homosexual faculty, while allowing a 1958 story about a nineteen-year-old freshman girl who gave birth to a stillborn baby in her dorm room on a Friday night and left the remains in a box on the steps of the university auditorium.

Incidents concerning racial issues received more prominent ink. On the front page of the *Alligator* that fall of 1958 ran the headline "First Negro Student Enrolls at University." The *Alligator* requested that the university's inaugural Black student, a man named George H. Starke, publicly disclose his exam scores so as to justify his admission to the state's elite law school, but the paper simultaneously attempted to mollify student suspicions by describing Starke as "quiet, mild mannered." Meanwhile, as Starke was closely scrutinized, *Alligator* editors took no issue with white law graduates who blamed an "unduly difficult" test for their flunking the Florida bar that year and then re-took an easier exam.

Starke occupied a circumscribed space in Gainesville. He lived off campus with relatives and couldn't frequent the white-run restaurants or bars bordering the school. In his courses, he often stood out as the only student in suit and tie. He made sure to sit in the back of rooms so as not to bring undue attention to his presence and never volunteered an answer to a question unless called upon, until midway through his second semester. Starke received undercover protection from state troopers, who foiled a kidnapping plot by the KKK. (After three se-mesters, he would be forced to leave UF when he turned up five min-utes late to an exam and an opportunistic professor leveraged the technicality to fail him in the course. In frustration, he disenrolled.)

Because he didn't belong to a fraternity and wasn't a UF legacy stu-dent, with a family backing him, Art Copleston knew he had to estab-lish credentials on campus to avoid being bullied, so he took to lifting weights at the university recreation center. Copleston decided to major in business administration—not because he longed to be a company man but because he knew that he'd be the "only financial provider" in his lifetime, and he wanted to blend in. In a short time, Copleston had molded himself into a masculine ideal, admired by women and esteemed by his male peers, who assumed his muscles and personal magnetism made him a "field player." It was at the gym, ritualistically pumping iron, that Copleston spotted a strapping middle-aged Adonis across the weight room. The object of his infatuation turned out to be Dr. Thomas "Tim" Reed, an associate professor of chemical engineering.

One day, Professor Reed invited Copleston back for a chat in the faculty locker rooms, which they found empty. They stripped and soaped each other down in the faculty showers and mutually mastur-bated. Reed, as it turned out, had a wife and two daughters, whom Copleston soon met and befriended. Through that freshman year, Reed "mentored" Copleston on various outdoor excursions, including week-end jaunts to Daytona Beach and a canoeing trip to a remote section of Cedar Key. But no matter how high on himself a secret relationship with Tim Reed made him feel, Copleston knew to never share details about his clandestine beau, lest the rumors destroy them both.

Copleston found the Burger House off West University Avenue in late 1957 and continued to frequent the "guy bar" until the fateful day in June 1958 when Tileston eyeballed him. Suddenly all his friends started getting pulled out of their classrooms and dormitory rooms by the police. Copleston heard bloodcurdling rumors that after these incidents, these same friends spent extra time with therapists at the Florida Center for Clinical Services, the student health center steps away from President J. Wayne Reitz's office in the Administration Building, or at the newly opened psychiatry unit of the UF College of Medicine on the edge of campus.

In fact, several active and future informants for the Johns Committee prowled the Burger House that summer and fall. On October 1, 1958, a graduate student named David Meuser, who worked part-time as a Burger House bartender, broke in interrogation with Strickland at the university police station. Meuser was the son of a Lutheran minister in Miami. He was majoring in secondary education at UF with a specialization in social studies, and he'd recently married a fellow education major, who was now pregnant with their first child. Meuser

Dr. Thomas "Tim" Reed, Daytona Beach, 1957

had everything to lose if his young wife or his religious kin discovered his habit of accepting fellatio from other men.

In a soundproof basement room, formerly the broadcast studios of the college radio station, Meuser the part-time bartender confessed to participating in homosexual activity on a "passive basis" in the past. In this era, the depths of homosexual "sickness" were gauged in terms of "active" or "passive" homosexual activities. As the Johns Committee saw it, any man who merely received gratification from another man was a "passive," whereas any man who gave gratification to a member of the same sex irrevocably became an "active" participant. Those in law enforcement like Hawes and Strickland were of the opinion that active homosexuals tempted and "recruited" passives deeper into their aberrant lifestyle, and thus did homosexuality spread through society.

Johns Committee agents tapped into an eager team of UF physicians and social scientists to bolster their baseline assumptions about gayness with the latest theories and practices. These helpful clinicians included Dr. Justin E. Harlow Jr., head of the Psychology Clinic at the student health center; Dr. Winston Wallace Ehrmann, head of the Marriage and Family Clinic at the student health center; and Dr. Peter Regan, head of psychiatry at the UF College of Medicine. "A homosexual will get someone to be a homosexual," Ehrmann affirmed to Mark Hawes of FLIC. "Say, a person who's right on the borderline, or say, a person who's lonely and rejected, or something like that, and a homosexual is nice to them and inveigles them into homosexual activity, and then they get involved."

Experts like Ehrmann believed that once the homosexual impulse was fully triggered, it compounded into an affliction like alcoholism, with even the most reformed addict fighting to avoid sexual relapse one day, one minute at a time for the rest of their lives. Through their roles as counselors to students and faculty, the expert trio of Ehrmann, Harlow, and Regan also became linchpins in Strickland's intelligence network—taking confessions from ex-homosexual informants under the guise of therapy sessions and funneling new insights and suspects' names back to Strickland as action items.

Baseline assumptions of both the committee agents and their clinician cohorts about homosexuality were also drawn from prevailing sources, a fusion of nascent science and religious superstition revolutionizing popular culture. Three major texts were involved: the Revised Standard Version (RSV) of the Bible, Kinsey's *Sexual Behavior in the Human Male*, and the American Psychiatric Association's *Diagnostic and Statistical Manual of Mental Disorders* (DSM). Respectively, these reinforced the notions that homosexuality was a sin, a fearful social phenomenon, and a disease.

First, in 1946, the publication of the Revised Standard Version of the Bible marked the first modern English-language translation of the ancient Greek texts to include the German-derived word *homosexual*. The contextual placement was not positive: "Do not be deceived; neither the immoral, nor idolaters, nor adulterers, nor homosexuals, nor thieves, nor the greedy, nor drunkards, nor revilers, nor robbers will inherit the kingdom of God" (1 Corinthians 6:9). Thus was homosexual behavior made explicitly sinful. The first printing of this Bible, "said to be the biggest undertaking in book publishing history" as reported by *The New York Times*, totaled nearly 1 million.

Second, in 1948, the publication of Dr. Alfred Kinsey's sociological study *Sexual Behavior in the Human Male* provided objective evidence that homosexuality was a phenomenon practiced by males in every sector of American society. The "Kinsey Report," as it was nicknamed, constituted the first major empirical inquiry into the sex lives of white American males. Nearly half of all white male survey respondents described erotic behavior involving members of the same sex, and 37 percent said they had engaged in at least one homosexual act since adolescence.

The Kinsey Report portrayed homosexual activity as taking place "in every age group, in every social level, in every conceivable occupation, in cities and on farms, and in the most remote areas of the country." *Sexual Behavior in the Human Male*, published as a staid statistical tome, sold more than half a million copies and insulted broad swaths of the American public by informing them that the average white American male was, in some measure, part queer.

Conservative institutions expressed outrage, which contributed to a backlash against Dr. Kinsey, which led to congressional scrutiny of his funding at the University of Indiana. A counterattack on homosexuality ensued—ironically, using many of the findings from Kinsey's study, which became tools for authorities to size up potential threats. For example, Dr. Harlow, the head of the Psychology Clinic at the UF Center of Clinical Services, referenced Kinsey to Mark Hawes in his statement to the Johns Committee that "males in college, who were over the age of twenty, twenty-six percent of them admitted to some kind of homosexual contact, casual or chronic." Law enforcement and the military began campaigns to steer mostly heterosexual or slightly homosexual men on the Kinsey scale away from becoming repeat offenders.

Third, the 1952 publication of the American Psychiatric Association's *Diagnostic and Statistical Manual of Mental Disorders* codified homosexuality as a mental illness, specifically a sociopathic personality disturbance. Religious and political groups latched onto the pathogenic status of gayness to buttress their respective spiritual and ideological texts. For physicians and psychiatrists, homosexuality became a disease to treat aggressively, like cancer. Dr. Regan, head of psychiatry at the UF College of Medicine, signaled to Hawes that some diagnosed homosexuals required extreme treatments, including "electric shock treatment, Metrazol, the use of hormones, the use of restraint, and sedation of various sorts." Despite these measures, Regan concluded that "none of the physical treatment available offered any hope."

Regan, at the time of these interviews, was actively treating a closeted gay English professor named Dr. James Congleton for homosexual disorder, which Congleton admitted in a separate interview with Hawes. Yet when Hawes asked, "What are we to do with these people bearing in mind that the statutes of Florida make such conduct a criminal felony?" Regan answered bluntly.

> REGAN: When you get to out-and-out anti-social activity, I see no alternative to firing these people.
> HAWES: Sir?
> REGAN: I see no alternative to firing these people.
> HAWES: As a minimum step?
> REGAN: Yes, but I would emphasize this: That it would be of real importance to me to emphasize in this that there is more to the problem than the firing of these people.

CHAPTER 11

Tightening Web

Ernest Salley, left, plays a tape recording he made as an undercover investigator for the Florida Legislative Investigating Committee, 1961

October 1958 (*Box 6, Box 7, Copleston Papers*)

AMERICAN POLICE, MANY former armed services, imposed criminal penalties on as many as a million gay men and lesbians post–World War II through the end of the 1950s. All the while, federal agents actively purged practitioners of "sex perversion" from the State Department and among defense contractors in a "Lavender Scare" that resulted from President Eisenhower's executive order 10450 decreeing homosexuality to be grounds for termination. Gays were vulnerable and could be pressed into treason, or so went the logic of militarists from four-star generals to Remus Strickland. During the Eisenhower decade, 20 percent of the American workforce were federal contractors or employees, so classifying homosexuality as a violation of state loyalty or security oaths, especially when homosexuals already lived at risk of private arrest, had an all-embracing impact across society.

Given the cultural four-alarm fire surrounding homosexuality, it's understandable why David Meuser—an expectant father, aspiring social studies teacher, and part-time bartender at the Burger House who was desperate to finish out his final semester at UF—would qualify himself as "passive" to state interrogators. Hearing the "passive" plea and weighing Meuser's pregnant wife as proof of Meuser's reform, Strickland—an aggressive, broad-chested man—changed his approach with the bartender.

Now believing this "passive" Meuser to have rejoined the straight fold, Strickland made him a proposition: "Are you willing to work in conjunction with this Committee as a whole in trying to obtain the names and other data necessary in finding out who the students and faculty members are that are committing overt acts of homosexuality?" The Burger House bartender, faced with a choice between the destruction of his own reputation, not to mention the concurrent harm to his wife and unborn child, and the destruction of the lives of others, responded unequivocally, "Yes, sir, I would." By the end of questioning, Strickland and Meuser were joking and laughing together. "I am queer for women," Meuser said. "Let's put it that way."

In exchange for lists of confirmed and suspected homosexuals, Strickland agreed to make the "necessary arrangements" for Meuser to receive ongoing psychological and psychiatric care for any lingering "passive" issues through Dr. Harlow at the Florida Center of Clinical Services and Dr. Regan at the UF College of Medicine. "Students were offered the option of staying at the University of Florida as long as they underwent psychiatric treatment," Strickland insisted years later. "Many chose to leave," he then qualified, seemingly unaware that most of those who "chose to leave" were expelled for refusing compulsory treatments.

Like clockwork, on October 13, a marketing junior and army veteran named James William Graves confessed to homosexual contact in exchange for informing on Burger House customers, receiving "psychiatrist treatment," and getting to stay in school. And on November 4, a reformed ex-homosexual botany major named Joe Trice was told to spy on the Burger House crowd and submit any tips on the "homosexually inclined." Trice, a twenty-nine-year-old military vet who'd served with the Army Signal Corps during the Korean War, was attending UF on the G.I. Bill like Art Copleston. In 1957, he'd been forced to take a break from school after he was accused of sexually propositioning a Black male janitor. On the advice of a fellow U.S. Army veteran on the UF faculty named Lawrence Wathen, Trice struck a deal with a dean that allowed him to be reaccepted to UF under the provision that he seek mental health care from Dr. Justin E. Harlow. Harlow, in turn, informed Hawes and Strickland on the progress of Trice's sessions.

Last, an engineering junior named Don Steinbrecher, who lived just a short walk from the Burger House, confessed to homosexual activities and named Burger House owner Bill Woodbury in a sexually charged scenario. One or all of these informants—David Meuser, James William Graves, Joe Trice, and/or Don Steinbrecher—gave up the name Art Copleston in interrogation or a therapy session. Meuser and Steinbrecher also implicated a UF English professor named Stephen Fogle, with whom Art Copleston spent many Saturdays. "Runs around in Bermuda shorts," said Meuser. "The way he carries himself, he wears these French berets." Johns Committee investigators upgraded Fogle's risk factor in their files: "Known in and around Gainesville area to be homosexual."

Student witnesses like Meuser, Graves, Trice, and Steinbrecher received only a few seconds' grace time from Strickland to speak plainly or face a public hearing when confronted with exposure of their most embarrassing behaviors. Furthermore, many of these youngsters were of the southern cadre who viewed homosexuality as a playful activity, a personal indulgence distinct from "real" sex with women, and were traumatized when Strickland made their actions consequential and tied their play to their reputations. Additionally, each student caught in the net tended to have a personal pressure point that, if pressed, resulted in compliance. Strickland just needed to figure out where to push. "We were careful about students who held grudges," said Strickland in defense of his practices. One informant's letter addressed to Charley Johns and referred to Strickland read as follows:

Dear Sir,

As homosexuality is now being investigated at our University, I send and submit to you the following individuals who are known to be homosexual:

[name redacted by state], Sigma Alpha Epsilon
[name redacted by state], Tolbert Hall
[name redacted by state], Phi Kappa Alpha
[name redacted by state], Sigma Chi
[name redacted by state], Tolbert Hall

The rally point for these individuals seems to be Jacksonville bars (Howard's) on weekends.
    Cordially,
    One who wishes to remain
    Anonymous

That fall, unlike with the NAACP hearings, the Johns Committee kept mum on Strickland's activities and purposes in Gainesville. Charley Johns told a nosy reporter that to divulge such information would "ruin the investigation."

Strickland's expense vouchers confirmed that he spent ten days in August, seven in September, and twelve in October in the university town, where he stayed in various local hotels and spent $165 on bribes and rewards to secure the compliance of informants. As an additional development, given Meuser's and Trice's status as military veterans, Strickland reported back to the committee that he suspected the armed forces to be homosexual incubators and that they should specifically target students who were veterans. Being ex-military and financially vulnerable through the G.I. Bill, therefore, put a bull's-eye on Art Copleston.

Copleston's association with Stephen Fogle only made things worse. Fogle was hired in 1946 to teach the C-3 freshman English course, which was where he met the wiry former Air Force private in the fall of 1957. Copleston found himself bewitched by Fogle's lectures, wherein every deliberate word concerning poetry was accompanied by a unique facial expression and a toss of the head. "Poetry has proven to be one of the lasting delights of humankind," Fogle wrote in the introduction to a poetry anthology. "Sometimes what the poet does for us is to make us see freshly and exactly the different parts of our own past, things which we ourselves have done."

Copleston excelled in Fogle's classes and earned two A's. They struck up a friendship centered around a shared love of classical music and single-malt scotch. For a weight lifter who tirelessly sculpted his physique to portray himself as manly, Copleston perceived that Fogle's feyness could provide him with additional camouflage. When standing next to Fogle, a man whose sexuality basically oozed from his pores, Copleston believed, "No one would suspect me as the gay one."

Fogle enjoyed showing off his newly built cottage on Northwest 36th Road by inviting faculty and students back home for supper clubs and intellectual salons. "At Stephen's house, the party generally consisted of intellectual discussions," recalled the student informant Don Steinbrecher to the Johns Committee. "Art or music or Broadway plays or any of the number of fine arts that are taking place in the United States. . . . Drinks were served, and music was provided by Hi Fi."

Half-bald, bespectacled, and "pear-shaped," as Copleston put it, Fogle was hardly an object of sexual longing, but he did serve a crucial advisory role for male students who preferred other male students and wanted to enjoy their lives in college. A lymphoma survivor, Fogle bore a deep scar running down the right side of his throat. He knew he didn't have long to live and thus insisted upon being the star of each gathering, the epicenter of attention, while his disease remained in remission.

In university towns like Gainesville, it was homosexual code for men like Fogle to tip their hats to fellow bachelors by inviting them over on Saturday afternoons for the radio broadcast of the Metropolitan Opera. Throughout his freshman year, Art Copleston delighted in "Opera Saturdays." For Copleston, these live broadcasts functioned like homosexual church. Lying back on Fogle's sofa, Copleston reveled in the sonic river emanating from the Old Metropolitan Opera House at 1411 Broadway in Manhattan, which flowed through the airwaves before cascading into a Florida radio. At the conclusion of each broadcast, Fogle served snacks and drinks to an intimate group, generally composed of him, Art Copleston, and another gay undergrad named

Bill Moore. The three would converse for hours. "Those Saturdays with Steve," Copleston reminisced, "got me interested in opera for life."

As an intellectual specimen more mature than the typical undergrad, Art Copleston charmed his way into Fogle's inner circle. The professor trusted him enough to hire him as catering help for exclusive cocktail parties. Fogle hosted these invitation-only get-togethers for other homosexual members of the faculty, and discretion was paramount. Donning a bow tie and cummerbund and holding a silver tray, Copleston bore witness to a slew of university professors and deans, such as geography department head Sigismond Diettrich and English professor James Congleton, reveling as queens of the evening. After one particularly late event, Copleston decided to crash in Fogle's guest room. At some point, he became vaguely aware of the feeling of being touched and awoke to Professor Fogle fondling him. "NO!" Copleston shouted loudly and just once, and Fogle scrambled off.

It was Professor Fogle who tipped Copleston off to Gainesville's most active gay hot spot. Hiding in plain sight, it was located within an edifice of the law: the Alachua County courthouse. Soon afterward, Copleston walked the five blocks from his dorm to check out the courthouse himself, and the hookup scene there delivered beyond all rumors.

The Alachua County courthouse bustled with so much sex traffic that clerk of the circuit court George E. Evans kept a flashlight ready whenever he worked late so that he could catch men in the act. One night that August, Evans swore he saw UF assistant dean of arts and sciences Charles F. Byers "carrying on" in a hallway corner. Attorney Mark Hawes called the courthouse a "cesspool." For the closeted homosexuals of Gainesville, it was closer to paradise—a passion pit in a basement washroom accessed by an outside staircase, for easy entry and escape.

Scrawled upon the walls of that basement niche were sketches of penises and graffiti mosaics of male nudes in various coupling positions, which set the erotic stage for the anonymous many who stepped before one of the two standing urinals, located opposite the two doorless toilet stalls. Etched into the porcelain of one of the urinals was an unmistakable message: "Show It Hard!" Some held forth at the urinals by swinging their genitals until they found a taker. Others progressed into one of the two doorless stalls, where they found phone numbers of

Florida society men scrawled on virtually every surface and a generously sized hole, through which those in the opposite stall would wiggle their fingers and beckon. "Let me see it," some would say. Allegedly, that phrase was the calling card of UF geography department chairman Sigismond Diettrich.

Art Copleston found the spot too dingy and dangerous for his liking. He visited the courthouse only once. But passing truck drivers and local butchers and a Presbyterian minister from McIntosh named Paul Kapperman, as well as closeted professors and students, found satisfaction there dozens of times. Alachua County sheriff Joe Crevasse, who had known about the traffic for years and had already taken down the stall doors as a mitigation tactic, agreed to make the bathroom a staging ground for the Johns Committee: "Upon the recommendation of Mr. Strickland, we've kept it open a couple of hours longer in the evening." Strickland authorized Tileston and other agents to "importune," or make requests and demonstrations of homosexual intent so as to draw out unsuspecting gays. "Mr. Strickland had an individual who was then a trusty [informant] of his who did most of that," remembered Tileston. "He would go down and expose himself to people."

Through Professor Fogle and the crew of Burger House informants, Art Copleston got caught in the sights of the committee from multiple angles. Inexplicable events that gave him the creeps started to occur around him. At the beginning of the fall 1958 semester, the housing office denied Copleston his requested roommate—a friend—and instead assigned him a total stranger named Jim Steinbrenner. The two had never had classes together, and something about Steinbrenner made Copleston not trust him. Copleston began to worry about all of Fogle's indiscretions and double-entendre-laden phone messages (written down by random peers and tacked to a corkboard in the dorm hallway), lest the mother hen implicate her entire squadron of gay chicks.

Copleston could remember when he first got the knock from Officer Tileston on Thursday, October 16. It was on the door to his Biological Sciences classroom, which met late in the morning at Flint Hall. "We have information," Officer Tileston informed Copleston as with an odd grin he guided him into the hallway. "Come with me."

Copleston could read in the lawman's face that he relished what he was doing. For a lowly campus cop accustomed to punishing students for throwing gum wrappers on the sidewalk to be given such control over another human being created what military folk identified as a "power high."

Thrilled to be working with state police in a situation that might advance his career, Tileston nonetheless felt guilt and expressed misgivings to his mother. "My mother was an artist, and a lot of her personal friends I'm sure were of that persuasion," he later explained. "She said it was a witch hunt, it was just awful, and I shouldn't be involved in any way, shape, fashion, or form. She was adamant that I get out of it." Tileston loved his mother, but he'd chosen his profession and donned the uniform in an explicit rebuke of her, a gesture saying that he was his own person. "I, too, knew what my responsibilities to my chief and my department were and such as that," he reflected. "And I knew that there were statutes being violated."

The first time Copleston sat in campus lockup, he knew from his military experience to deny all accusations. Tileston had marched him down to a basement room with darkened windows in the university police station. The room had been staged like a noir movie set. A light bulb on a string dangled from a ceiling fixture that hung over a rectangular wooden table. There sat three chairs and a tape recorder. Just outside the light circle stood an imposing figure. The man was clean-shaven, if a bit jowly and overweight in a Sears suit, with dark hair comb-slicked in a style reminiscent of FBI agents. This was Remus Strickland, chief investigator of the most powerful legislator in the state.

Strickland cleared his throat, identified himself generically as a lawyer representing the governor of the state of Florida, and pressed a button on the tape recorder. They all sat. Rapid-fire, Strickland and Tileston traded questions, each time attempting to catch Copleston in a discrepancy: "I now ask you, are you a homosexual?" "Have you ever been involved in homosexual activity?" "At this time, I want to know have you ever been approached by anyone—any student or member of the faculty of the University of Florida—in a homosexual manner?" Copleston issued blanket denials and attempted to portray his presence in the interrogation room as a case of guilt by association.

Copleston thought Strickland and Tileston would force him to sign something or press harder and expel him from college at the culmination of this grilling. So Copleston couldn't believe it when his wild lies stuck. Strickland let him go, releasing him without apology or explanation. But Officer Tileston let him know that he was on call for the Johns Committee: "Whenever we want you."

After Copleston was released that first time, his mail began taking several days longer to reach him. When it did arrive, he noticed that some of the envelopes seemed to be wrinkled, as if they had been steamed open. Having written recently for several physique magazines (homosexual-oriented fare that proliferated when bodybuilding was a new offshoot of weight lifting), Copleston now feared the day those materials would be intercepted. He spent long sessions sitting on the john tearing letters and papers into pieces and flushing them down the toilet. Copleston destroyed nearly every record he could find of his affair with Professor Tim Reed, although he couldn't bring himself to rip up two risqué photographs of Reed flexing in a swimsuit on Daytona Beach. Those he hid. On long walks to class, Copleston repeatedly saw Officer Tileston with his roommate Jim Steinbrenner. Alternately, he noticed an array of thirtysomething men in cheap suits, some of whom carried cameras, milling around the dorms for no clear reason.

One evening that fall, Jim Steinbrenner undressed in front of Copleston and began to masturbate. Steinbrenner asked Copleston if he'd ever had sex with a man before. When Copleston refused the advance, Steinbrenner broke down crying and admitted that a police detective had put him up to it. "He told me he was working for the committee to help pay his UF tuition," Copleston recalled. "His family was all very poor." Disgusted, Copleston grabbed his books and headed for the library. When he returned a few hours later, he found Steinbrenner's side of the room completely emptied out. Copleston didn't see his former roommate for the rest of that year, and the UF housing office didn't fill the vacancy. To this day, it's unclear who Jim Steinbrenner really was. No student with that name graduated from the university. Years later, when examining a 1960 UF yearbook photo of Johns Committee informant Don Steinbrecher, Copleston exclaimed, "I think we have our man!" The names Steinbrecher and Steinbrenner were so similar as to be laughable. The slipperiest lies of all, Copleston concluded, are cloaked by a piece of the truth. "It's him. But we are talking almost eighty years ago."

Verging on paranoia, Copleston withdrew from society and adapted more or less to life as a loner—celibate, silent in the mess hall, all but invisible in class. Ironically, his grades were never better that fall term: four A's and a B, a 3.81 GPA. He disconnected from other "bachelors" from the Burger House and, believing the hallway pay phone in his dorm to be tapped, began making collect calls to Professor Tim Reed from a gas station. They both judged it too dangerous to even weight-lift at the same time. He lived in continual terror. "You never knew when one of the blue-uniformed, jackbooted guys was going to walk in and shout your name," Copleston recalled.

Gainesville's "guy" culture, so vibrant in the years of Copey's friend Don "Dee-Dee" Bouterse, retreated under duress. Copleston's visits to Professor Stephen Fogle's house for "Opera Saturdays" involved precautions verging on spy craft, with Fogle driving his car past a street corner at a specified time and Copleston hopping into the back seat and lying flat until Fogle pulled the vehicle into his carport. Copleston's exit from "Opera Saturdays" reversed the routine, with him being deposited on a different corner. Still, Copleston fretted these visits might end in a police raid.

One Saturday, as the professor, Art, and Bill Moore chatted in the living room, they heard a car pull into the driveway. Suddenly tense, Fogle signaled them to be silent as he went outside for a conversation beyond the carport door. Copleston heard another muffled male voice. For some reason, Fogle needed that person to believe that he was alone.

Sensing that Copleston was close to a nervous breakdown, Fogle suggested they indulge in a weekend getaway at Jacksonville Beach. Copleston went warily, and Fogle ended up endangering them both at a beach bar, where he picked up a random sailor and brought him back to the motel for a casual exchange of cash for sex. When Fogle refused to pay the man afterward, the sailor caused a ruckus. The police were called, and Copleston had to speed away in his car.

How could Steve be so flagrant? Copleston wondered as he put miles between himself and the embroilment. Every other gay professor feared the Johns Committee and mitigated risks. Ultimately feeling bad for abandoning a friend, Copleston called the Jacksonville motel from a pay phone. The desk clerk informed him that Fogle had already checked out and passed the message that he'd gone back to Gainesville. Somehow Fogle had talked his way out of impossible trouble. (For context, in 1962, UF senior assistant resident of psychiatry James Alton Hill would be fired for the same crime of picking up a Jacksonville sailor.)

Even with these close calls and lucky breaks, uniformed investigators visited Art Copleston repeatedly throughout the year. "I used to sit in my dorm room, by the window," he recalled, "looking down at the sidewalk between the buildings, always expecting to see Tileston come into view." But pulling him out of a final exam on January 20, 1959, was by far their most egregious act yet, signaling that neither the Johns Committee nor the university gave a goddamn about his academic performance.

AT THE MANOR Motel with chief attorney Mark Hawes of the Johns Committee, Copleston sensed his future riding on the next few seconds. Hawes drilled into Copleston's particulars and asked him why he frequented the Burger House. The lawyer prodded him as to why he remained a bachelor at age twenty-six, when so many of his generation had gotten hitched. There was no clock in the room, and Hawes turned a tape recorder on and off at will, eager to catch Copleston in a slipup. The lawyer sometimes leaned forward to whisper questions, but ordinarily maintained a theatrical volume as he slurped down cup after cup of coffee.

Throughout this span, Copleston was permitted neither food nor water nor the use of bathroom facilities. To keep his detainee off balance, Hawes sometimes pretended he couldn't hear Copleston and made him repeat the same statement for clarity. Hawes would then have a transcriber read back each version of his answer to examine for inconsistencies. In a climactic tirade, Hawes presented Copleston with the correct telephone number of his mother, Margaret, and said that he might just dial it to inform her "what a disgusting son she had." The threat nearly snapped Art Copleston in half.

Margaret was nearly two years sober in January 1959. Back when Copleston left his parents in West Palm Beach, his mother became so hopped up on amphetamine diet pills that she began having heart troubles and fainting. Copleston decided that his alcoholic father was "unsalvageable," but that he might save his mother, so he decided to get her out of the house. He announced to his parents that they were going to divorce, and when he told his mother the news, she was too stoned on pills to do anything but agree. After the divorce was finalized in 1956, Arthur Sr. became homeless, and Margaret speedily remarried an Alcoholics Anonymous sponsor named Pat, who was able to help her quit the pill habit.

Copleston loved his mother, but he was certain that his mother would be "driven right back into the bottle" if she ever got the call confirming that her only son was a "fairy." He could hear in his head the exact words she would speak: "How could you do this to me?" Worse, if Arthur Sr. found out that a child of his was gay, Copleston wondered if the man's silent fury might snap into a rampage. Would Arthur Sr. steal a car and drive while intoxicated, get arrested for public nudity, or harm himself and then blame his son to stir up pity? It was in that moment, just when he felt ready to snap, ready to snitch on Professor Fogle and Professor Tim Reed and the rest, that Art Copleston's military training clicked into place like muscle memory.

During his interrogation, Hawes couldn't have known certain facts about Copleston's tenure with the U.S. Air Force because the details remained classified, and his military record identified him only as a "Basic Airman" working for the Air Police squadron. But from 1952 to 1954, Staff Sergeant Arthur S. Copleston Jr. also served on covert missions at Tyndall Air Force Base near Panama City, Florida, for the Office of Special Investigations (OSI). The OSI was a specialized division within the Air Force tasked with, among other duties, identifying and purging homosexuals from the armed services. It became the military mantra that homosexuals, due to their illicit behaviors, made themselves susceptible to Communist blackmail—although no evidence of Communist/homosexual collusion ever surfaced, despite enormous efforts to identify "security risks." Soldiers like Art Copleston understood that they were policing morality, not really working to ensure national security.

Staff Sergeant Copleston was a self-described "paper shuffler" by day, tending to files on homosexual suspects at the base. At night, officers conscripted him for operations to shadow and expose sexual deviates. Copleston was the flirty decoy, the young and lean-muscled lure used to entice a mark. Staff Sergeant Art Copleston was the Officer Tileston of the Johns Committee in an earlier era, with both men deployed as lures because they were the right age and body type—early twenties and slim—as opposed to a man like Strickland, who was "heavy-set" and "slightly going to pot," in the words of a Johns Committee witness. If Copleston refused to participate in Air Force entrapment missions at Tyndall, he would have been labeled a suspect himself, and so he did the Air Police's and OSI's bidding for his term of service: three years, eleven months, and five days. It was dirty work, and Copleston knew it.

During his off-hours, Copleston freely picked up guys at roadside bars and fellated them in the front seat of his Plymouth convertible. That Plymouth, ironically, got commandeered by senior officers in need of temporary love nests to cheat on their wives amid a military culture that conspired to hide rampant male adultery. Because Copleston was part of the OSI team and a keeper of his superiors' secrets, his behavior didn't receive close scrutiny.

It was at Tyndall Air Force Base that Copleston mastered the art of moving between worlds, navigating the layers of the military and its sexual substrata. He had firsthand insight that most interrogations of homosexuals hinged on a confession. Because most homosexuals engaged in sexual encounters in clandestine spots, it was rare for authorities like the OSI to catch two or more queers in a flagrant act. Copleston knew for certain that if homosexual suspects in most interrogations had either stuck to their lies or kept their traps shut, they would have walked free.

Copleston exhaled and rebalanced himself before Mark Hawes. "They weren't going to crack me," Copleston recalled. "This you are not going to like," Copleston heard himself say to the state lawyer, "but I have to take this stand: I am not a homosexual myself." These words felt dissociated from the walls and ceiling and floor of this grimy interrogation room.

It's ironic that the U.S. military, through its efforts to purge homosexuals, trained another homosexual to resist interrogation. Hawes sighed, and the tension in the room dissipated. His lawyerly weapons, the threat of jail and parental exposure, failed to create the necessary crack. When Hawes released Copleston from detention, he walked the quarter mile back to Thomas Hall. He hoped that no one had tossed his room. He prayed that another set of officers from another agency wouldn't be waiting to recollect him. Heading up the front staircase to his dorm, it dawned on him that he had nothing to go back to. Had he failed Elementary Accounting?

Art Copleston called his accounting professor from the hallway pay phone. I've graded your test, the instructor informed him, and you failed. This public educator, who would point police toward a student during an exam, mentioned nothing about the hullabaloo during class. "He didn't even ask a question," Copleston remembered with amazement. The professor did, however, offer to make a onetime exception and permit Copleston to take a makeup test.

CHAPTER 12

Trusty Informants

An animal trainer feeds a dolphin at a Florida marine park

October 1958 (*Box 3, Box 6, Box 13*)

AFTER COLLECTING MINOR informants for months, the Johns Committee investigation switched its primary focus. Instead of undergraduate students, tenured professors, already in the committee's crosshairs through the informant frenzy, became prime targets. Still, Chairman Charley Johns stayed mum on the true purposes of his Gainesville task force. How could Hawes or Strickland ever reasonably explain to a wide-eyed public how a John Reynolds anti-Communist stakeout at UF led them to a sexual netherworld of men masturbating in the local courthouse bathroom, which merited the spotlight of the state?

Outside of judicial filings against the NAACP, Johns Committee members and staff had little else to fill their workdays but to read the weekly action reports of Strickland's Gainesville amusements. Time was not on the side of Charley Johns. With Florida's 1959 regular legislative session set to begin on April 7, Charley had to face that his beloved Johns Committee had spent four years and $125,000 without exposing a single Communist or jailing even one NAACP operative. His committee needed proverbial heads on spikes to remind the state about internal enemies and reinforce who could be trusted as their protector.

On Thursday, October 2, 1958, Strickland and Tileston staked out the residence of a University of Florida humanities professor named Clyde J. Miller in rural Cross Creek, Florida. Miller resided in a home gifted to the university by the estate of Pulitzer Prize–winning Florida "authoress" Marjorie Kinnan Rawlings after her death in 1953. It was considered a great honor for a man of letters like Professor Clyde Miller to occupy such hallowed literary ground. Over his three years residing at Cross Creek, Miller was known for holding the occasional faculty/student bash and providing tours to university VIPs.

After tailing students to Cross Creek, Strickland and Tileston hid in the brush with binoculars. Though they observed nothing in the realm of unsuitable behavior, they portrayed the presence of three students at a late-night gathering with the professor as cause for condemnation in their surveillance report. These students, who committed no offense other than driving to a professor's house, were now flagged to be interviewed. Several weeks later, on October 20, 1958, the University of Florida sent notice to Miller that he was to immediately vacate the property.

Days later, the *Alligator* began to speculate in the open about the cloak-and-dagger activities of the Johns Committee, noting Officer Tileston's practice of conspicuously pulling students out of classrooms. Even visitors in town for homecoming heard rumblings of a Communist hunt. "I heard, true or false, that your Committee has had an investigator checking on the funny activities of some of the professors," wrote a UF alumnus turned hotshot Miami attorney named Edward Clyde Vining to Charley Johns. Chairman Charley Johns maintained his poker face and did not respond to the intimations.

The Johns Committee achieved a small breakthrough on the afternoon of Tuesday, November 18, 1958, with the entrapment of UF music professor and glee club director John Faircloth Park in the courthouse bathroom. Seated in one of the restroom stalls for approximately one hour, Park was surveilled by several state spies and then captured. "Mr. Tileston went into the men's restroom and submitted himself for an approach to be made from Mr. Park and then returned outside waiting for him to come out," read the report. When Park exited the men's room facilities, expecting to find enchantment in a tryst, Tileston apprehended him and demanded that he come at once to the university police department.

Twenty-eight-year-old Park was the committee's first professor caught in the act. He'd taught at UF since 1956. Tall, young, and svelte, he arrived in Florida as a catch to fellow bachelors, and he'd made himself a regular at cruising grounds. At the police station, Park was shattered emotionally when Strickland entered the interrogation room and made clear his purpose: a state investigation into "homosexual relations." Park gave multiple conflicting explanations for his courthouse conduct and then pleaded. As it turned out, much like desperate students, a desperate professor made an ideal tipster. Although Park confessed to having lifelong desires for other men, he attested that he now had his personal situation under control.

He offered, as proof of his recovery, to assist the Johns Committee with insider knowledge before Strickland could even ask. "He cooperated fully," Tileston's report of the interrogation confirmed. Park quickly divulged his participation in oral sex with a tenured humanities professor named Lawrence Wathen. Gaining confidence as he spoke, Park described another scenario involving university speech professor John Edward Van Meter. Evidently, he and Van Meter met at a local newsstand and arranged for a sexual rendezvous in a nearby pine forest. Lastly, racking his brain, Park remembered and implicated Harold Elwood Carter, an elementary school art teacher working in Jacksonville who occasionally ventured to UF.

Noting the excitement with which Strickland and Tileston jotted down his testimony, Park believed himself to be a man who'd earned his way into state protection. "Park was not promised anything so far as immunity in regard to his job at the University of Florida," countered Tileston in the report. "He has apparently come to that conclusion, at this time, that nothing will come of this investigation, that he will not be discharged."

On December 12, Officer Tileston similarly ensnared John Faircloth Park's music department colleague Russell Danburg in a courthouse stall. Danburg represented a bigger catch for the committee, as

Danburg had taught at the University of Florida since 1948, and his orchestral compositions were performed nationwide. President J. Wayne Reitz dubbed him the university's "Victor Borge," comparing the professor to the virtuoso pianist and entertainer. Tileston demanded that Danburg proceed with him upstairs to the Alachua County sheriff's office, where Strickland pounced. Russell Danburg was married and had an eleven-year-old son, which made for easy leverage when Strickland pressed him for names.

Danburg appealed for mercy as a family man. He graphically recounted his struggles with same-sex cruising and his efforts to control the urge. He claimed that he had committed his first homosexual act in 1942, while serving in the music division of the U.S. Army Special Services during World War II. Danburg admitted to seeking out the courthouse for personal release since 1948, his first year of teaching at UF. Contradictorily, Danburg also went to great lengths to describe himself as a passive homosexual who reservedly accepted male gratifications. He declared that he'd experienced a moment of revelation through the humiliation of his being caught by Tileston and insinuated, like the student informant David Meuser, that his child was proof that he maintained sexual relations with his wife.

Danburg requested state immunity so that he could prove the totality of his rehabilitation. As a down payment of good faith, he rattled off the names of every so-called fellow traveler he'd ever recognized while out cruising. Danburg, in fact, was the tattletale who tipped off the committee to a second homosexual hub flourishing in the second-floor men's restroom of the university library, where three private stalls with courtesy doors provided ample concealment. "Professor Danburg states that he has observed Professor Congleton in the rest room on the 2nd floor library in close contact with another subject and that he has observed Congleton in such positions as there is no doubt, he is a homosexual," reported FLIC. Danburg recalled seeing Sigismond Dietrich in said bathroom giving a "foot wiggling signal" to invite homosexual contact and, on another occasion, "on his hands and knees" receiving fellatio. Lastly, Danburg named humanities professor Lawrence Wathen as "one of the worst homosexuals in that University," a man who "is always talking about sex while teaching mixed classes of boys and girls."

Slowly building a foundation of professor informers, FLIC experienced a windfall on December 5, 1958. It was on that Friday morning that Officer Tileston apprehended the tenured English professor Dr. James E. Congleton in the courthouse basement. A married fifty-seven-year-old educator from Kentucky who'd taught at the University of Florida since 1937, Congleton was an academic star with a lot on the line. He was a member of the Modern Language Association and the National Council of Teachers of English, and his textbook *Theories of Pastoral Poetry in England, 1684–1798* had been published in multiple languages.

Congleton had recently completed a year abroad lecturing in Turin, Italy, on a Fulbright fellowship. On the home front, Congleton and his wife had an adult daughter named Caroll, who'd recently married a famous "Gator" athlete named Bernie Parrish—an All-American college baseball player who'd signed with the Cincinnati Reds. Inconveniently, any sexual kerfuffle from Congleton would surely be amplified by virtue of his son-in-law's celebrity.

That fall semester, Congleton taught a lighter load. He had a Monday/Wednesday afternoon class called "Effective Writing" and a Tuesday/Thursday seminar. Fridays, he was freed up for extracurriculars. Observed in the act of masturbating at the courthouse that December 5, Congleton readily agreed "to be a receptive partner in a homosexual act with Officer Tileston." Tileston dropped the act and brought Congleton upstairs to the sheriff's office, where the professor expounded on his life story more or less unprompted.

Congleton claimed to first feel the thunderbolt of same-sex desire at the age of five in Kentucky, when he observed a group of boys swimming together. Decades later as a UF professor, he'd needed to use the restroom one day after shopping at the downtown Sears, Roebuck. "I saw the condition there," Congleton confessed, "and there was something that appealed to me." As if bewitched, Congleton returned repeatedly, often breezing down that half a flight of stairs on his way to and from lectures. "If I have knelt to pray about it once I have done it about a thousand times," he expressed. "I think I can repeat the prayer that I would say when I would kneel. Should I or not, Mr. Tileston?"

Congleton described how his never-ending hunger metastasized with middle age and became so unbearable that he sought medical relief. "When I was in Italy last year, I went to a famous doctor in Rome," Congleton shared of his Fulbright year. "He told me a lot and prescribed sex hormone capsules. At this time I could really tell a difference and conditions became more normal—completely normal in fact between me and my wife while I was in England. It is impossible to get those capsules in America, though you can get them in Italy by paying for them. They are all gone except a few, and I have been hoarding them for some emergency."

Periodically, the professor's eyes darted from Strickland to Tileston to the sheriff's deputies at their desks and back as if disassociating from reality. He began to hyperventilate and threatened self-harm, stating that "if he was brought out into the open in the homosexual investigation that he was going to commit suicide." Intuiting what his captors desired, he launched into allegations about and indictments of companions in his secret lifestyle. As the interrogation report noted, the professor "agreed to cooperate with this investigation in obtaining names and dates and other information that he could gather in regard to other homosexuals both students and faculty members at the University." Within minutes, Congleton provided a list of homosexual colleagues to the Johns Committee.

In a bout of anxiety typical of informants following their first confession, Congleton clearly feared his token cooperation wouldn't be enough to save his skin. So three days later, at 10:45 a.m. on December 8, Congleton called Tileston and asked him to stop by his office on the third floor of Anderson Hall. There, Congleton provided FLIC with an additional list of "other homosexuals" and tried to secure a formal "agreement of immunity." The Johns Committee noticed a special rapport between Tileston and Congleton—a unique dependency that can develop between cop and informant. It was exhilarating, almost intoxicating, for Tileston to have a former Fulbright scholar so firmly under his thumb.

Tileston repeatedly emphasized to Congleton that all facts would be turned over to proper authorities, but Congleton read some sympathy between the lines. Thus did Congleton continue to pass intel to the campus cop. As is to be expected, due to the moral compromise of informing, Congleton came to rely upon his confidential meetings with Tileston for support. Tileston's willingness to see Congleton again and again offered him misleading reassurance that his tormentors felt some stake in what was bound to happen to his future.

Through repeated contact, Congleton transcended his informer status and became a committee collaborator. That December 15, Congleton voluntarily went to the university police department again for yet another statement on the record. "I am going to try to close this now and maybe be like an ostrich," he said concerning his former homosexual contacts, "and go about my own work, which is perfectly normal, happy and successful." In session, Congleton hammered hardest on gays he knew personally, men he'd befriended or watched having sex or engaged sexually with on a passive basis. "It is really a relief to talk to someone who is aware and sympathetic and knows the problem," Congleton shared about the benefits of sharing with Tileston as well as psychiatrist/collaborator Dr. Peter Regan. "And I do want to try to overcome this and grow old gracefully and with honor and not lose everything I have because my estate is my profession." When he ran short of firsthand material, Congleton began implicating colleagues through gut feeling alone. Concerning Lawrence Wathen, Congleton attacked the man's chummy style with students. Concerning Sigismond Diettrich, Congleton condemned him through hearsay and association:

> TILESTON: Have you ever seen him at the courthouse or rest rooms in the library at any time?
> CONGLETON: Both.
> TILESTON: Would you say that he has patronized these two places on a great number of occasions?
> CONGLETON: Not a great number, no, but I would say an unnecessary number of times and out of the way to do it.
> TILESTON: In your opinion, would you say this man has homosexual tendencies?
> CONGLETON: Yes, I would say in my opinion he has.

With an active collaborator network in place, the stage was set for ritual slaughter. Congleton, Danburg, and Park had each turned informant with their lives and careers at risk. Each feared how a convicted sex criminal would be treated in prison. Much like the student informant David Meuser, Professor Congleton and Professor Danburg also had the reputations of their wives and children to consider. In the right circumstances, fear of shame being brought upon a loved one can make a person capable of anything. And once they crossed that line into betraying their colleagues, none of these men reexamined their initial choice to speak at all. Together, they betrayed the privacy of bachelors and married folk who for years had safeguarded a communal coexistence.

IN JANUARY 1959, chief attorney Mark Hawes and Chairman Charley Johns traveled to Gainesville with a "cleanup crew" to mop up the big wins. Perhaps, through surprise and pressure, Hawes and Charley Johns could make a few more witnesses sing.

Forces moved. A Florida state trooper knocked on the cottage door of humanities professor Lawrence Wathen on Monday morning, January 5. The trooper told the former Fulbright scholar that he was wanted immediately for questioning by Florida authorities. Standing more than six feet tall, speaking with the curious twang of a worldly aesthete disguising a Texas drawl, Wathen stood out as one of the more outsize personalities in Gainesville. Masculine yet libertine, cowboy-esque but with a penchant for berets, Wathen taught the comprehensive course "C-5: The Humanities" to all university sophomores, a course "designed to acquaint the student with the great literature, philosophy, art and music of Western Civilization." His classes had long wait lists, and he barely found time to learn the names of students before the next batch arrived each semester. Snooping around that fall and winter, Strickland and Tileston confidentially questioned a sampling of the athletes and fraternity members whom the eccentric professor tutored on his own time.

Despite his flamboyant "spaghetti supper club" style, Lawrence Wathen remained conservative in his politics, and he grounded his intellectual passions in military discipline. After devoting five years to the U.S. Army in World War II, Wathen enlisted in the Army Reserves. "I go to camp every summer," he liked to share. At fifty, he still served as an Army Reserve major, belying a level of fitness unique for a man who branded himself as an epicurean. "I have certainly been around," he often added suggestively.

Face-to-face with a state trooper, Major Lawrence Wathen felt inwardly unnerved, but nonetheless turned on his charisma. Almost every homosexual in Gainesville knew what Charley Johns and his committee were snooping around for, and Wathen was no tenderfoot. He had morning classes that couldn't be canceled, the professor explained regretfully, which bought him a few extra hours. Still blocking the doorway, the state trooper informed the professor that he could voluntarily meet at the Hotel Thomas at 2:30 p.m. or face a subpoena. The lawman marched off, and Wathen telephoned an attorney. He agreed to pay the man $300 for a consultation on the spot. The lawyer gave the professor one simple instruction: "Deny."

CHAPTER 13

Crossfire

An FSU football game

January 5, 1959
(Box 6, Box 7, James T. Sears Papers)

TRUE TO HIS military training, Lawrence Wathen arrived for his little appointment with the state at 2:30 p.m. on the dot. To throw the military man off his game, the committee made him sit and wait. The preceding witness, Russell Danburg, finished up his testimony around 1:00 p.m., and Hawes and Strickland must have decided to enjoy a long lunch. Danburg, without much prodding, had reimplicated Wathen in sordid conduct. Under oath, he decried Wathen as "an obnoxious person," a letch "pawing" at male students while dropping expletives like "Oh, shit!" and talking "about sex an awful lot."

For an hour and a half, Wathen alternately sat in a chair, tapped his foot, or paced in an anteroom as his inquisitors toyed with him. When the agents finally called his name, they invited him, psychologically fatigued, into a conference room and sat him in a hardbacked chair. Trying to regain his bearings, Wathen looked around. State troopers and sheriff's deputies, leaning and leering, guarded doors and windows. Then a man with a prosecutorial stride entered the space and waved for others to follow. Grave-faced, the retinue marched in one by one, arranged themselves behind the boardroom table, and sat in unison: Mark Hawes, Remus Strickland, Officer Tileston, a court reporter named Daniel Lee, and Senator Charley Johns himself, twirling a watch chain.

Instantly, Wathen recognized the jowly face of Senator Charley Johns from the newspapers. "Mr. Wathen," Hawes began, "I am Counsel for the Florida Legislative Investigation Committee. Senator Johns here is Chairman of the Committee. We are conducting an investigation." After compelling the professor to swear an oath and issuing threats of a public subpoena and/or perjury charges absent total cooperation, Hawes made the accusation: "We're investigating homosexual activities at the University of Florida, and we have been given evidence and sworn testimony that you have been participating in that sort of activity." Marshaling his energies, Wathen managed to pull off what no other person in the hot seat had done before. The professor not only denied the claim but also made an intellectual defense of sexual liberty.

Wathen's spontaneous oration, a lecture for the committee's sole benefit, lasted about thirty minutes:

> I've always been rather independent in what I do and say. I think that this is a free country, and I think that one of the things we ought to do is have more people just be themselves and stop all this business of aid and of conformity and this sort of planned paternalistic idea that affects so many people now, so that they are afraid of saying anything, afraid to be anything, afraid to do anything. . . .
>
> I have a lot of friends of all types and all kinds, and I am sure that all sorts of things are often said about me, as they are about other people. You can't expect anything else. I know five or six years ago when I was driving along University Avenue, going to classes, I picked up some student on University Avenue, and as we drove he said, "Do you know that man over there?" I said, "Yes, he teaches in the English Department." He said, "He is a queer." I said, "Do you know him?" He said, "No, but he is a queer." I said, "He looks like it." There you are.

I don't know the man too well. He is not a personal friend of mine. He has never been to my house, and I've never been to his. He married and has a couple of children, and as far as I know, he is a very responsible man and a reputable man, as far as I know. . . . You know, these people bandy about terms and say things all the time that they really don't know anything about. And they don't actually mean. I think, in many instances in these days, that if people don't like somebody, they call them a queer or a Red.

Unfazed by Wathen's outpouring, Mark Hawes continued on with the inquiry.

HAWES: I'm going to ask you whether or not you have ever had homosexual relations with a man named John Faircloth Park, an instructor in the Music Department at the University of Florida?

WATHEN: I know Mr. Park. I never had homosexual relations with Mr. Park. I met him, I think, when he first came here two or three or four years ago. And, as far as I can remember, he was in my house one time. I have seen him, but I don't think I have even gone to any social affairs where he was. I do know him.

HAWES: Did you, shortly after he came here in 1956, call him on the telephone and invite him over to your home?

WATHEN: Yes, I did. Yes.

HAWES: Did you on that occasion—and I should tell you here, Mr. Wathen, that we have sworn testimony in our record concerning it, concerning the matter that I am fixing to ask you about.

WATHEN: All right.

Catching his stride, Wathen told the story of how he'd counseled a UF student (and Johns Committee informant) Joe Trice. When Trice got expelled for sexually propositioning a Black janitor at his UF dormitory, Wathen took pity on him because Trice was a fellow Army man. Trice returned to his studies at UF on Wathen's recommendation that he press his case with the dean of men, Lester Hale. "Later he told me that he had gotten back in the University," Wathen revealed, "and that he was seeing a psychologist, I think, regularly."

Concerning Wathen, Joe Trice swore to his committee confessors, "With God as my witness, he has never approached me. Never." Changing tack, Mark Hawes attempted to stroke the scholar's ego. "Mr. Wathen, you have a good command of the English language," said Hawes. "I can tell as you sit here and talk." Flattering the man, Hawes commenced a second line of attack and steered the conversation toward the bawdy specifics of his entanglement with Professor John Faircloth Park.

> HAWES: You all had a homosexual relationship, with him
>   taking your penis in his mouth and you taking his. Is that
>   true or false?
> WATHEN: No, that is not true.
> HAWES: I should tell you that he also testified that that
>   occurred again approximately three to six weeks after the
>   first time.
> WATHEN: Well, I don't know why he would say that.
> HAWES: Do you know of any reason he had for saying a thing
>   like that if it were not true?

Wathen proceeded to almost think out loud, as if grasping for an explanation that would not impugn himself:

> I can't imagine why he would dislike or hate me that much. I
> really can't. I know that when he was in my house the one time
> that he was there, which was one afternoon, we talked about
> music and things, and I did not find him an interesting person,
> did not find him a person that I wanted to have a friendship
> with. . . . I suppose you might say that I dropped him like a hot
> cake.

Wathen's only admission to Hawes involved a rather innocent masturbation scenario when he was a Boy Scout in Texas at the age of thirteen. Concerning homosexual rumors involving his colleagues, he dismissed the wisdom of the grapevine. "As far as this casual stuff about this person or that person, I have no idea whether it is true and in many cases I don't give a damn," said the professor. By 4:58 p.m., having spent the better part of an hour dominating Hawes, Wathen received a conditional release.

Uncharacteristically, Chairman Charley stayed mum throughout Wathen's sermonizing. The professor, by Charley's lights, was an argumentative queer soon to be outed, fired, and shamed, and there was little point in debating such a man as a counterpart. "All right, Mr. Wathen, thank you very much," said Hawes in dismissal. Wathen left feeling triumphant, but without the slightest forewarning that he might be recalled for further cross-examination.

Unmistakably, the Johns Committee faced a dilemma with Wathen: The witness had explicitly contradicted the testimony of their pet informant John Faircloth Park. As Park's testimony likewise incriminated a second professor up for interrogation, UF speech instructor John Edward Van Meter, the committee resolved that they might need to employ more extreme measures with Lawrence Wathen until the man submitted. Later that evening, Mark Hawes sweated Van Meter in the hot seat.

HAWES: I'm going to ask if you know a man named John Faircloth Park?
VAN METER: I know of a faculty member by that name.
HAWES: Did you ever have occasion to meet him at a newsstand over by the Fire Station?
VAN METER: No.
HAWES: You never did?
VAN METER: No . . .
HAWES: Have you ever had homosexual contact with that man?
VAN METER: No.
HAWES: Are you sure of that?
VAN METER: Positive.

Before Van Meter could contradict John Faircloth Park any further, Hawes released him with the admonition, "I would appreciate it if you didn't say anything to anybody about this investigation or your being called here or what we discussed." When Van Meter asked if he was free to pose questions, Hawes answered, "Yes, sir, but I may or may not answer them." Van Meter raised his voice and began to inquire, "Why should you think I would know something about this? What source of information do you have?" But Hawes cut him short with a curt "Thank you." Now two key witnesses had each refuted the testimony of Park.

Only minutes later, FLIC collaborator Professor James Congleton walked into the conference room under the misapprehension that, because of his relationship with Tileston, he was a protected man. The former Fulbright scholar was in fact so loquacious that Hawes complained at one point, "It is getting a little late." Refusing to take a hint, Congleton persisted in his testimony and reiterated the name of virtually any known or suspected homosexual who'd crossed his path in his decades at the university. Congleton confessed to mutual masturbation and fellatio with assistant professor of the social sciences Herbert Doherty. He confessed to seeing Sigismond Diettrich on his knees fellating business education professor James Loyd on the cold tile floor between bathroom stalls in the university library.

He implicated Robert Gustus, chief pharmacist of the Student Health Center, in cruising the men's room of the student union. He confessed to repeatedly fellating and being fellated by the married coach of the University of Florida golf team, Andy Bracken, who he said eventually burst into his office and told him, "I can't do this!" And he accused English professor Stephen Fogle of being a notorious effeminate who sashayed about the Alachua County courthouse unabashedly: "If he is not homosexual, as somebody has said, he ought to pull in his sign."

Throughout the rundown of his Rolodex, despite his admission of fellating the golf coach, Congleton maintained his own status of sexual passivity. Congleton ended the session by begging for clemency. "If I were only thinking of myself, I would resign at the end of the semester," the professor asserted. "But I have my home here." Congleton leaned into his friendship with UF president J. Wayne Reitz—"His daughter and my daughter are in the same class, and they were little sweethearts of girls"—and the shock it would mean to "drag him through this, as busy a man as he is." The Johns Committee discharged

Congleton without promises when he finished his tirade at 10:01 p.m. "I know I will have a restless night," Congleton said ruefully as they parted.

Professor Stephen Fogle, labeled in Johns Committee files as a known "homosexual" and ID'd as gay by numerous witnesses, was not included in the procession of shamed scholars up for questioning at the Hotel Thomas. Instead, as Wathen shared years later to the historian James T. Sears using the alias "Arlen Davies" because of lingering fear, Fogle hired a $3,000 lawyer and gained an inside track on FLIC activities around town. The few witnesses like Fogle who retained lawyers or brought counsel into the room did tend to walk free. For students like Art Copleston and colleagues like Lawrence Wathen, who didn't have the finances to seek representation pre–*Gideon v. Wainwright* (the U.S. Supreme Court decision that created the institution of free public defenders), Fogle took on the role of a confidant and provided accurate advance notice to whoever was up next for questioning.

Fogle's warnings proved so prescient that Wathen began to regularly meet with the English professor for advice. Fearing that their vehicles were bugged, they'd drive separate cars to a woodland park and confide in each other while hiking. Taking similar precautionary measures, UF students Art Copleston and Bill Moore rode their bicycles out to farm fields adjoining Gainesville and strategized about their future in abandoned barns. On a hike one Tuesday, Wathen alerted Fogle that John Faircloth Park, a guest at several of Fogle's soirees, had turned informant and was now actively cooperating. Incensed at the betrayal of a former lover, Wathen took the unwise step to telephone Park at his home and demand that they meet.

Park expressed terror at the idea, but the towering U.S. Army Reserve major Lawrence Wathen turned up at his doorstep. We're going for a drive, Wathen told him. They rode around the North Florida countryside for hours, during which Park more than once broke down and confessed his predicament. "They put the screws on him," Wathen realized, mustering some pity. Park told Wathen that if he gave the committee names, they'd assured him that he would keep his job. "You can ruin my life," Wathen told him. "You can ruin my life."

Hawes's tactics evolved over time. When Gainesville witnesses asked for lawyers, Hawes started playing a game of pretending not to hear them or trying to embarrass them into declining their right to an attorney—a strategy he'd deployed to success in 1957 with the NAACP informant Hampton Earl Shaver, whose life became imperiled. In interrogation at the Hotel Thomas, Mark Hawes was able to trick a twenty-seven-year-old public school teacher named Earl Fender, from Merritt Island, a small Atlantic coast town, out of legal counsel by asking him to sweat out a few anxious minutes thinking it over in a windowless room. "They didn't know about calling an attorney and exercising their rights," said Tileston, blaming the witnesses for their predicaments. "They had their rights, but they didn't exercise [them]."

In the hot seat without representation, Earl Fender named assistant professor of the UF College of Education Leslie Murray as a former lover. Fender described being courted by Murray and accurately recalled Murray's physical features as well as his Gainesville address. Fender also sexually implicated the Jacksonville elementary school art teacher Harold Elwood Carter, corroborating one aspect of committee informant John Faircloth Park's otherwise unreliable tips. Professor Leslie Murray sat in questioning soon after Fender and repeatedly denied Fender's accusation. Deciding to face his accuser head-on, Murray arranged a midnight rendezvous with Earl Fender on a remote bridge in a backwater lake town called Palatka. There, Murray threatened Fender with "serious trouble" and made the man speak under duress at a pay phone to Murray's attorney, a Mr. Eastman, to whom Fender denied the homosexual relationship.

When confronted by Hawes about this flagrant act of witness tampering, Professor Leslie Murray attempted to delay questioning until his lawyer could arrive at the hearing: "You know, Mr. Hawes, I believe I had better wait for my lawyer Mr. Eastman because you are a very, very smart man." Hawes tried another ruse to prolong the proceedings.

MURRAY: Can't we postpone the hearing until he gets here?
HAWES: No, I'm going to ask you these questions. I'm not
    going to even compel you to answer them. You don't have to
    answer them. Do you understand that?
MURRAY: Yes. He told me he thought that you would honor a
    request for postponement.

HAWES: And I will. Yes, I will, but I'm going to ask you certain
questions about the activities last night and this morning,
which you can either answer or decline to answer. Do you
understand that?
MURRAY: Yes.

Murray continued to rebuff any attempts at questioning until the
state lawyer relented and agreed to reconvene. When Murray's attorney turned up, Mr. Eastman objected to thorny questions involving the
bridge confrontation with Fender as well as Leslie Murray's ongoing
divorce from his second wife, who'd threatened in a marital deposition
to make public how Murray "engaged in homosexual conduct." Murray nullified and quashed Fender's accusations to FLIC by having his
first wife, a nurse at Alachua General Hospital, testify to his heterosexual virility. Hawes seemed to have his doubts about the ex-wife's
ploy, but Chairman Charley Johns, present for the testimony, felt convinced. Charley couldn't imagine why a woman would lie for a man
she once loved, so Professor Leslie Murray kept his job, regardless of
the documented attempt to intimidate a FLIC witness. As in the Miami hearings with the White Citizens' Council, intimidation didn't
matter so much to Charley if it happened in service of helping the
"good guys" defend the way of life.

In due course, the Johns Committee referred Earl Fender to state
prosecutors on charges of perjury, although the preponderance of evidence pointed toward Fender's being truthful about his former relationship with Murray, and Fender's intel on the Jacksonville art teacher
proved accurate. Evidently, in FLIC's hall of mirrors, what mattered
more than catching a homosexual professor or teacher was showing
results to constituents. Fender had disrespected the committee by
wasting its time on Murray, or so Charley believed. Charley made sure
that Fender's "false affidavit" was made available to the Florida state
attorney "to determine whether or not said state Attorney would prosecute said witness."

On Wednesday, January 7, the committee pulled John Faircloth
Park out of a lecture and escorted him back to the Hotel Thomas. As
two of Park's three admitted sexual partners had failed to confess, the
committee needed answers. (The art teacher Harold Elwood Carter,

perhaps to pile pressure upon Park, had yet to be interrogated.) Using another "make 'em sweat" technique, Hawes accused Park of withholding information relevant to the investigation.

> HAWES: We are not going to let any witness come in here and give us what we know to be false testimony, or learn to be false testimony, and walk away from here with immunity. Do you understand that, sir?
>
> PARK: Yes, sir. Are you accusing me of giving false testimony?
>
> HAWES: I am saying that you did not tell us all you knew about this situation.

Park expressed genuine confusion about any information he'd left out of prior statements. Hawes gave Park a pad and a pencil and ordered the man to come back in five minutes with new names written down. But before he sent Park out of the room, Hawes tipped his hand toward his true reason for roughing him up that day.

> HAWES: By the way, while you are here, have you heard anything from anybody about your appearance here Monday?
>
> PARK: Anyone?
>
> HAWES: Yes.
>
> PARK: No.
>
> HAWES: Nobody has contacted you.
>
> PARK: No sir, just the man who called me here.

The state lawyer somehow knew about Park's little drive with Lawrence Wathen from another informant. Now Hawes saw the different game afoot: His rat was playing two sides. Fearing physical harm from a colleague, Park told a barefaced lie to a state official. As if in consolation, Park began tripping over his words to drum up new folks to inculpate.

> HAWES: Diettrich.
>
> PARK: Yes. He teaches geography or geology.
>
> HAWES: Have you had anything to do with him?

PARK: No, sir.

HAWES: Do you know anything about him?

PARK: No, sir.

HAWES: Have you heard anything about him?

PARK: No. I have met him and his wife at concerts. He is tall, a big man, dark hair, dark face. I think he does some extra music at the Catholic church. I always speak to him, but I don't know anything about him. . . .

HAWES: And you can't remember any people that have been connected with your choir that you have had homosexual relations with?

PARK: Having a rehearsal today, I remember seeing them, and there is no one in there.

HAWES: There never has been one in there?

PARK: In the Glee Club, no; no member of the Glee Club. . . .

HAWES: When you go in those restrooms out on the campus and pick up men for homosexual contact, Mr. Park, don't you realize that you are picking up students?

PARK: Not necessarily.

HAWES: Don't you realize that most of them are bound to be students?

PARK: Yes, it is a risk that I took and have regretted.

Bingo. An admission of *possible* student contact gave Hawes enough rope to cut the informant loose. By the end of this session, Park appeared to lose all nerve and sought to appease his former masters.

PARK: How about the outcome of all this investigation? Does this mean that I am going to get fired right off the bat? If I am, I should make plans.

HAWES: Mr. Park, none of us is in a position to tell you what the outcome of this thing is going to be yet.

PARK: What would you advise me to do? I haven't done anything.

HAWES: What do you mean, you haven't done anything?

PARK: I haven't met anyone since I talked to this man and Mr. Strickland.

HAWES: The only thing I can advise you to do is to go about
   your daily business in a normal fashion.

John Faircloth Park left the interrogation at 5:05 p.m. with his prospects diminished. Meanwhile, *Gainesville Sun* reporters noticed Chairman Charley's presence in town. They began nosing around the Hotel Thomas and noting down witnesses as they came and went. *The Gainesville Sun* attracted *The Miami News* in the way that one fly can draw many, and both news teams wondered if the committee had dredged up an honest-to-goodness Communist cell in North Florida. With journalists buzzing about, the committee felt compelled to uproot themselves from downtown to a new base of operations—to preserve the integrity of their investigation.

CHAPTER 14

Trapdoors

Alachua County courthouse, stakeout location of the Johns Committee

January 8, 1959
(*Box 7, University of Florida Archives, Diettrich Papers*)

BY THE TIME the Johns Committee recalled Lawrence Wathen for interrogation on Thursday, January 8, the committee had migrated to the Manor Motel, the edge-of-town motor court. Wathen, feeling that he'd stated his case persuasively the first time, expressed confusion at being under the microscope once again—and in shabbier environs. What more could they possibly want? Hawes informed Wathen that "we've had further sworn testimony." The scholar seethed, forming the mental weather that Hawes sought to create: a slow breakdown of the self in response to overstimulation and burnout. Wathen began by filibustering. He waxed philosophical to Hawes in a plea for common decency.

> WATHEN: I am puzzled, worried, concerned, and so forth, at the fact that I have been more or less, I mean, the focus of

something which seems to be, you almost think would be a plot or . . . I'm going to be the fall guy for something. I have heard all sorts of things around the University. Oh, the Burger House and this, that and the other and so forth. But . . . and you hear of various people, groups, cliques, of course, whom mostly I do not know. In most cases, their names mean nothing to me. You hear these things year after year, this, that and the other. And then here I, all of a sudden, seem to be the sort of focus of a hell of a lot of stuff.

HAWES: Mr. Wathen, let me tell you something: This Committee is not trying to make any fall guy out of you.

WATHEN: No sir, I didn't say you were. Mr. Hawes, I didn't say you were at all. But I mean, I can't understand. You know . . . I didn't imply that; I don't think you meant . . . I mean, that I actually said that. . . .

HAWES: Now, you said there seems to be a plot against you.

WATHEN: No, well, I mean . . .

HAWES: What did you mean by that?

The professor's powers of articulation, overworked since Monday of that week, failed, and he found himself at a rare loss for words. To Mark Hawes, Wathen represented wounded prey, a witness who kept calling his captor "sir" and repeating the same tired phrases. Since Wathen didn't want a public hearing, Hawes intuited that he could keep interviewing the man in secret rooms until his great mind caved. Perhaps if Hawes offered a little warmth, some expression of care, Wathen would momentarily soften and pen himself into a corner.

HAWES: You couldn't have had enough contact with him [Park] for him to dislike you extremely, could you? To the point of making a false accusation of this kind?

WATHEN: Well, the only thing . . . the only thing, Mr. Hawes, that I could think of was at the end of our testimony the other day, Monday, I believe. I thought that since I did know him, know who he was, and we talked. We have . . . our interests, only on musical subjects.

The professor stood directly above Hawes's trapdoor. "All right, just a minute, sir," Hawes said, pretending to close out the conversation. "Mr. Wathen, will you be good enough to wait here a few more minutes over here." The witness cooperated exactly as Hawes anticipated, moving to an anteroom. "All right, sir," Wathen answered, as if to a military superior. Having primed the humanities instructor for an ambush, Hawes made Wathen sit by and stew in his own juices.

At just the right moment, he called Wathen back into the room. There, waiting for the professor in the hot seat, sat his former lover, John Faircloth Park. Park did not speak a word when Wathen entered, though their eyes locked briefly. It was a setup that gave the state lawyer pride, a misdirection meant to invoke complete surrender. With Wathen seated to the side, Hawes forced the professor to endure every second of Park's lurid testimony against him. Upon the table, the Johns Committee tape recorder whirred. Park slowly and deliberately described to Hawes what transpired between them at Wathen's residence in 1956. Perhaps Park hoped that by spouting these truths, he would return into the committee's good graces.

PARK: We both committed oral contact upon each other.
HAWES: Did you take his penis into your mouth?
PARK: That's correct.
HAWES: Did he take yours in his?
PARK: That is correct.
HAWES: A full, complete homosexual act on the part of both of you?
PARK: That is correct, to my knowledge.
HAWES: Did you undress?
PARK: I am sure we did.
HAWES: All right, Mr. Park. Thank you. Do you want to ask him any questions, Mr. Wathen?

Hawes lifted his eyes and cocked his head cutely when he asked the professor the question. The words echoed in Wathen's brain. He wanted to scream. It was the worst sort of invasion: being backstabbed by a former intimate. Hawes set up Wathen perfectly to capitulate to rage and temporarily forget himself. But Wathen could see the tape turning in the recorder on the table. From the base of his throat, Wathen uttered three words to let pass this monster.

> HAWES: All right, Mr. Park. Thank you. Do you want to ask
>   him any questions, Mr. Wathen?
> WATHEN: No, I don't.

Sent home, Wathen telephoned his friend Professor Fogle for support. Fogle told Wathen that he still hadn't received notice of the place and time for his own interrogation. Indeed, despite the fact that many people described Fogle as the campus "queen," no committee records survive of his being called to testify. If we consider Fogle's flagrant sexual pass at his former student Art Copleston, his behavior in Jacksonville, his insider knowledge of committee activities, and his eagerness to dish with witnesses, it's reasonable to wonder whether Professor Stephen Fogle was a protected man. Theoretically, could one think of a better infiltrator into a secret network of gay academics than the chamberlain and party host, who knew virtually all the campus dirt?

For years, Art Copleston thought it was his classmate Bill Moore who pointed the finger at him and Fogle, but Moore's testimony revealed nothing of the sort.

> HAWES: Mr. Moore, do you know any faculty member in the
>   University of Florida campus out here who are homosexual?
> MOORE: No sir, I don't.
> HAWES: You never saw anything out of one that . . .
> MOORE: No sir.
> HAWES: Do you know any student who is?
> MOORE: No sir, I don't.
> HAWES: Have you ever seen any homosexual activity since
>   you've been on this campus up here?
> MOORE: No sir.
> HAWES: And never participated in any yourself?
> MOORE: No sir, I don't.

All Fogle's known circle of gay contacts—James Congleton, John Faircloth Park, Lawrence Wathen, Art Copleston, and Bill Moore—faced the inquisitors. But not the man in the silk-lined cape.

The same day that Wathen suffered a second session with the Johns Committee, *The Gainesville Sun* finally published an editorial about the investigation into "shocking irregularities in the conduct of a handful of faculty members and other personnel at the University of Florida." The *Sun* laid out the case for public firings: "Without a discharge to follow those whose guilt is established, they will easily find positions elsewhere in the academic life of the United States. We must be concerned with young people everywhere, as there are no arbitrary limits to the necessity for moral strength." Without naming what these "irregularities" concerned, the piece warned that some suspected professors might seek to quietly retreat through resignations. Alert to the *Sun*'s scoop, UF president J. Wayne Reitz attempted to head off future coverage by meeting with the editors and bringing along a known psychiatric expert, Dr. Peter Regan of the University Medical Center, to make a case on the dangers of publicizing political or sexual deviancy.

J. Wayne Reitz was under the gun financially. He had broad ambitions for the University of Florida, but most of his budget came from state funding. Nineteen fifty-nine was a legislative year, and Reitz was about to ask the Florida legislature for a record $48 million biennial appropriation—a $7 million increase—to grow his school from about 12,000 students to a planned 20,000 by 1970. To secure this sum, Reitz needed support from the Senate Appropriations Committee, on which sat none other than Senator Charley Johns. Reitz found himself in a pinch: Fail to cooperate with Chairman Charley Johns's investigations, and the senator would block his funding. Cooperate too freely, and the university would suffer such reputational damage that no senator of sound mind would back an expansion plan. Hence, when reporters asked Reitz about Strickland on campus, he felt compelled to give a noncommittal "Seen him passing," or risk seeming incompetent to his board, before also giving a "No comment," or risk defying Charley Johns.

In response to the *Sun* editorial on "irregularities," journalist Charles F. Hesser, a UF alumnus, published an investigative piece on the front page of *The Miami News* that dispensed with innuendo and leveled with the public. "Homosexual Probe Hits Florida U," read the

headline. All of Florida henceforth understood that the Johns Committee had switched from hunting Communists to hunting queers. Exactly why had Chairman Charley Johns changed his strategy? Nobody
on the FLIC staff seemed eager or authorized to address this question,
and for obvious and embarrassing reasons, the committee stonewalled
on any concession that basically one damned thing led to another
damned thing—a Gainesville Little Theatre to a Burger House to a
courthouse bathroom—in its sordid investigatory seduction. Regardless, given the bottom-basement status of his well-chosen marks,
Charley knew that few would leap to the defense of any perverted academic. "It was a popular thing," recalled FLIC member Cliff Herrell,
"and the public generally felt that maybe we could clean up the state."
Why he was investigating such people didn't matter to the public so
much as *that* he was investigating them.

Though campus gossip about the Johns Committee reverberated as
policemen pulled professors out of classes, the editors of the *Alligator*
delayed publishing all but op-eds on these incidents of high newswor-
thiness. Student journalists like *Alligator* columnist Dave Levy and Al
Quentel, a former staff reporter now at the UF law school, actively
assisted Strickland and Hawes by sharing intel and keeping coverage
minimal. Levy and Quentel offered testimony directly to Charley
Johns on Friday, January 9. Chairman Charley, who'd never served in
the military himself, bandied a theory to them about the military being a queer recruitment hub: "Like in the Army and Navy; we've found
out a lot of it started when they were in service."

Faculty fared no better. The UF chapter of the American Association of University Professors (AAUP), established to safeguard the intellectual freedoms of UF educators, offered scant guidance to its
constituents:

Dear Colleague,
   *A committee, commonly called the Johns Committee, au-
thorized by the legislature and with assurances of cooperation
from the Board of Control and the University Administration is
conducting an investigation. . . . We feel confident when we
speak for most of the faculty when we say we are deeply concerned with the welfare of the University and are, therefore,*

glad to cooperate in legally authorized, properly approved, and
properly conducted investigations which may aid in improving
conditions. . . .

As it happened, the president of the AAUP chapter at UF was none
other than sociologist Dr. Winston Wallace Ehrmann—a Johns Committee expert witness and therapist collaborator in the informant network at the Florida Center for Clinical Services, who understandably
did not reveal these conflicts of interest. As a point man in frequent
contact with both faculty and students, Ehrmann readily tipped off
FLIC about the ripest gay suspects. "Dr. Reitz gave his full assurance
that all innocent persons would be given full protection," he later
stated in his defense to *The Gainesville Sun.*

At a chapter meeting of the UF AAUP, Ehrmann allowed V. W.
Clark, a professor of law, to misadvise the faculty that if they refused
a Johns Committee "summons" or declined to answer questions, they
could be "taken to Circuit Court." The chapter voted by a ratio of two
to one to investigate Strickland's and Hawes's methods, but their efforts to head off FLIC were undermined at each turn by the chapter
president, who kept the findings buried. "We're keeping in close touch
with the situation," Ehrmann told his members cryptically. "Much of
what I've learned I've been able to share only with members of the
[AAUP] executive committee."

With the student press, the faculty union, and the Florida public
aligning in sympathy with Charley Johns, department heads and deans
understood they would be unsupported if and when they faced an onslaught. Because they were so-called high-value targets, FLIC had
been building cases against them for months. But Hawes first dispensed with proverbial low-hanging fruit on Friday, January 16. He
finally followed up on the tip from disgraced informants John Faircloth Park and Earl Fender about the Jacksonville elementary school
art teacher, Harold Elwood Carter. In interrogation, Hawes tricked
Carter out of seeking an attorney and then bludgeoned him verbally
when he refused to name other men involved in his indiscretions.

Sent out of the room by Hawes to ponder resisting at his "own
peril," Carter returned terror-stricken, having been denied the opportunity to consult with "any counsel whatsoever" during his time-out.

Carter asked for an extension so as to hire an attorney, but Hawes took the proceedings off the record to make direct threats. With the tape recorder back on minutes later, Carter made the mistake of describing Hawes's pressure tactics in a way that could be preserved: "I will make the testimony, but I make it under very strong emotional pressure—I don't know if you want this on the record." In response to Carter's disclosure, Hawes blew his stack.

HAWES: Mr. Carter, you don't have to testify; I've told you that. You can walk right out of this room and go about your business. There is nobody going to make you testify here, not a single soul. Now, you're either going to decide to testify, or you are going to decline to answer, and you're free to do as you wish.

CARTER: All right, I'll testify under emotional pressure, Mr. Hawes. But what I am doing, all I am doing, is telling the truth.

HAWES: What sort of emotional pressure are you talking about? You're not going to sit here and give me any testimony, Mr. Carter, prefacing, in the record, with a statement that you are being pressured, that you are being compelled to give any statement here.

CARTER: I realize that, Mr. Hawes. You don't have to raise your voice. Now, I want to testify.

Hawes had his fish on a hook. Carter named Professor Stephen Fogle as a former lover and Professor Park as a known homosexual associate—unfortunately entangling a gay professor the committee, for whatever reason, did not want to look at and, inconveniently, validating testimony from an otherwise disgraced informant. For his confessions, Harold Elwood Carter was not accorded mercy. The man was fired by the Florida Department of Education, and his teaching credentials were pulled.

Mark Hawes, having cut his teeth on Carter, walked out of the interrogation feeling sharpened and exhilarated. He was ready to bring down his biggest game yet.

CHAPTER 15

Queer Geography

Map of Florida, circa 1776

January 19, 1959 (*Diettrich Papers, OSI Files*)

UNIVERSITY OF FLORIDA department chairman Sigismond deRudesheim Diettrich received his call from the Johns Committee on a Monday evening in mid-January. That afternoon, the renowned authority on Florida geography had administered a final exam to his afternoon class and then returned home to 1418 Northwest 17th Terrace.

Drained from a long semester, Diettrich found a plush chair and fell into a dreamless slumber. His schedule hardly let up all year round. His wife, Iren, who taught piano lessons from their home, had constant health expenses stemming from a nervous condition aggravated by the Florida climate. Then there were the never-ending rounds of grading, due for students this semester by January 29, and his production responsibilities for the Gainesville Little Theatre renewed every season regardless of academic demands. After daily and nightly extracurriculars, Diettrich answered correspondence and crafted grant proposals at his home office until well after two or three in the morning. Every

Sunday, Diettrich rejuvenated his body and spirit as choir director for St. Patrick Catholic Church, where Iren played the organ.

A Hungarian Catholic immigrant, Diettrich had become a naturalized U.S. citizen in 1938 and reveled in the "mighty fine feeling" of being American and a Floridian. Compared to the hovels of his upbringing, he now lived in a palatial North Florida estate—three bedrooms, two bathrooms, fully electrified, built in 1955, all paid for out of his annual state salary of $9,300. For Diettrich, this single-family home represented the promise of an American century made manifest. He and Iren had raised a daughter, Rosemary, and seen her married off well to a good Catholic man.

An internationally celebrated man of letters, in 1953 Diettrich had been president of the Florida Academy of Sciences, and in 1955 he was chairman of the Resource-Use Committee of the National Council of Geography Teachers. He was listed in the compendium *Who's Who in America* and had written more than thirty books and journal articles. And deep within that geographer's brain, an eternal flame burned for his adopted home of Florida. Diettrich rejoiced in the world-class geography department he'd assembled in Gainesville and celebrated its landmark achievements. When Francis McCoy became the first UF student to graduate with an advanced degree in geography in 1951, Diettrich beamed with pride. Few thought more about Florida and its bounty, its climate, its factories and ecology, its tourism and urbanism, its farmlands and fisheries on an hour-to-hour basis than the UF geography department chairman.

At around 6:00 p.m., the Florida sun had already set, and the house sat in eerie darkness. Cutting through the stillness, the telephone rang. Roused from his nap, Diettrich supposed it might be a colleague or a student panicked about final examinations. Mentees in the graduate program did feel comfortable calling him at home and had lovingly nicknamed him "Dr. D." He picked up the receiver. Holding it to his ear, he must have looked cherubically tousled. He had a kind round face that many strangers took to be unformidable at first glance. He stood a mere five feet eight, with dark brown hair that, ordinarily slicked back, fell into his face when he hustled. Slightly round about the waist, he was wont to tuck his button-down shirts in his khaki pants and cinch everything high with a belt.

"Hello, this is Sig," Diettrich spoke into the receiver clearly and deliberately, his speech lightly accented. Diettrich, as did many of his generation, treated someone on the other end of a telephone line with a form of reverence. "It was somebody or other most politely inviting me to appear before Charley Johns' committee right away," recalled Diettrich. "I went." The drive from his house to the out-of-the-way Manor Motel, two miles north of town on U.S. 441, took less than fifteen minutes. As with Professor Lawrence Wathen, the Johns Committee made Diettrich sweat out an hour in an anteroom, during which he must have asked himself: How was this happening? Had he failed to prove himself to Uncle Sam?

When the United States had declared war on Germany and the Axis powers, Diettrich threw himself into the national mobilization effort. Without question, he chose his allegiance to his new nation over his loyalties to the old. He taught U.S. Army War Training classes to more than 750 G.I.s at the Second Army Corps School in Camp Blanding, Florida. Graduates of Diettrich's war geography courses reached high ranks in the armed forces. Taking note, then University of Florida president John Tigert promoted Sigismond Diettrich to the role of acting chairman of the geography department. Around that time, Diettrich received an encrypted offer from the Office of Strategic Services (the precursor to the CIA) to travel to Washington, D.C., as "a Consultant for a temporary position with the Europe-Africa Division."

Granted leave from university, Diettrich wired U.S. military command in Norfolk an emphatic message: "REPORTING FOR DUTY." Working for the OSS in the nation's capital, Diettrich swore an oath to defend the Constitution of the United States "against all enemies." Throughout the tense months of 1943 and 1944, he eagerly provided his consultancy for a meager stipend of $10 per day.

Indeed, Diettrich's "topographic intelligence" for the European theater coincided with the Allied invasions of Sicily and Italy as well as the amphibious assault in Normandy, France. The geographer's last advisory day, June 19, 1944, was D+12—when the northern, southern, and eastern Allied fronts executed a multipronged pinch of the Axis forces in Central Europe.

That June, Diettrich vacated his wartime lodgings and returned to Gainesville to take the reins as geography chairman of the University of Florida. No public notice or acknowledgment of Diettrich's unique services against the fascists would be included in VE-Day celebrations. His contributions to a grateful nation were, by necessity, thankless. Diettrich knew he could receive no formal recognition, lest he be assassinated by Eastern Bloc spies or his relations in Budapest be kidnapped and tortured for intelligence blackmail.

As Diettrich waited in the whites-only Manor Motel, he must have looked more like an academic than a patriot. No one from the Johns Committee knew they were staring at a war hero, much less the preeminent scholar of the state they claimed to be protecting. Vital projects still hung in the balance for this assiduous man. The U.S. State Department had recently awarded Sigismond Diettrich a one-year Fulbright fellowship to teach and research at Dacca University in East Pakistan. It was one of academia's highest honors, and Diettrich was scheduled to leave that May. Meanwhile, the University of Florida Press finally agreed to publish a geographic *Atlas of Florida*, with Diettrich as the primary author. What would happen now with his Fulbright? With his beloved *Atlas of Florida*?

Agents called him into the room. "Then," remembered Diettrich, "my ordeal began." In front of him sat Hawes, Strickland, and Tileston, plus a Florida state senator by the name of William O'Neil, whose presence satisfied FLIC rules for quorum. Hawes began by scaring the professor about potential "attendant publicity from the news reporters" if the delicate subject of their conversation was not handed "as quietly and discreetly as possible." He compelled Diettrich to swear an oath to answer all questions propounded.

From the outset, Mark Hawes wielded Congleton's and Danburg's damningly vivid testimony against Diettrich to great effectiveness. With reams of material from the informant network, Hawes barely needed a confession to doom this foreign-born man. "They were nice, polite, even sympathetic," Diettrich recalled of his subjugators. "But anyone reading the record would have the most horrible picture of me. I was trapped." As a boon to the committee, Diettrich, the penitent Catholic, quickly fell back on the Sacrament of Penance, or confession. In what could best be described as a psychological hitch, Diettrich confessed on the belief that a sorrowful admission of sin would precede the forgiveness of a pastoral authority.

HAWES: Mr. Diettrich, have you participated in any homosexual activity since you've been a member of the faculty out here?

DIETTRICH: Well, no, I wouldn't . . . I wouldn't say that.

HAWES: Now, Mr. Diettrich.

DIETTRICH: Oh.

HAWES: You know whether you have or not. Have you?

DIETTRICH: Well, how would you define it?

HAWES: You know what sex is, don't you?

DIETTRICH: Yes.

HAWES: Have you had any sexual activity between—with another man?

DIETTRICH: Well, mutual masturbation, yes.

Ten minutes into the interrogation, Diettrich sowed the seeds of his own destruction. Taken aback at the speed of the man's confession, Hawes backpedaled with a sympathetic sidebar. Diettrich was so compliant and remorseful that Hawes could hardly get out a sentence without the witness cutting in to register self-disgust.

HAWES: But over what period of time? How long have you been doing that, sir?

DIETTRICH: Well, I would say, oh, about ten years.

HAWES: Now, Mr. Diettrich?

DIETTRICH: Yes sir.

HAWES: I'm not asking you these questions in an attempt to embarrass you or . . .

DIETTRICH: No, I . . .

HAWES: . . . to pry into your affairs, as such. Do you understand that?

DIETTRICH: Yes sir.

HAWES: I'm asking you these questions for this Committee's information, and because it's our duty to . . .

DIETTRICH: Yes sir.

HAWES: . . . determine the extent of this thing out here. Now . . . and because, of course, we didn't pull your name out of a hat.

Hawes exploited the fully compliant witness and tried various angles to expand the scope of his confessions, so as to incriminate colleagues and corroborate past dalliances on university soil. Weeping, the professor held back nothing to his confessors but the identities of his former lovers. Even under threat of exposure to his wife, Diettrich did not name names. Melodramatically, Hawes slapped a stack of several thousand printed pages onto the table and claimed that within said stack was testimony describing every one of Diettrich's sex habits at the Alachua County courthouse.

Diettrich denied ever using the restroom for cruising, but claimed that a "loose bowel" condition sometimes made it medically necessary for him to use those facilities. Hawes upped the ante by having Diettrich review photographs of pornographic graffiti in the bathroom, as if implying that Diettrich's tolerance of such imagery constituted proof in itself.

HAWES: Doctor, that's a dirty, filthy, stinking place down there
    at that Court House, isn't it?
DIETTRICH: Yes, it is.
HAWES: It's filthy from a sanitary standpoint down there, isn't it?
DIETTRICH: It is.
HAWES: It smells very foul down there of urine.
DIETTRICH: Yes.
HAWES: And other odors, doesn't it?
DIETTRICH: Mostly urine.
HAWES: It's always dirty down there isn't it, filthy?
DIETTRICH: Well, most of the time it's not clean. . . .

Diettrich then related an excruciating story, which drew momentary silence from even Mark Hawes. Approximately ten years prior, in 1948, his wife Iren's health condition became life-threatening. At times, she was near paralysis, and physicians advised the couple to immediately cease sexual relations or risk debilitating harm to her body. In an era when a wife's denying a husband sexual satisfaction could constitute grounds for divorce, Diettrich agreed to abide by the doctor's orders to aid her recovery. He hoped the abstinence would save her life, and Iren's health did improve.

Eventually, one afternoon, he was sitting in a public bathroom at the university, and someone in the opposite stall started tapping his foot. "You go in, and you don't think about anything," Diettrich expounded to the Johns Committee. "And somebody starts to . . . sort of a tap, tap signal, and then you feel there is a sort of moving around you." Someone reached a hand beneath the stall partition and touched Diettrich in a way that he had not been touched in years. He felt alive. He climaxed. He instinctively wanted to return the gesture, but the anonymous partner stood and left before Diettrich could see his face.

It was during this difficult and lonely span in Gainesville, with Iren healing, that Diettrich turned to male-male encounters for regular release, as he felt that an affair with another woman would make him unfaithful to his wedding vows, and southern mores of the time did not categorize discreet horseplay among gentlemen as objectionable. In Diettrich's mind, what he did with other men was not sex. Diettrich emphasized to Hawes that these brief rendezvous, generally consisting of mutual masturbation scenarios, were utilitarian, and he therefore stoutly refused to reveal the identities of his sundry partners. Almost as soon as the act was over, he'd put it out of his mind and purge it from memory: "As long as you do it that way, it's sort of hidden and what-have-you, then you don't think much about it."

This provisional arrangement, nonetheless, aroused in Diettrich unspeakable Catholic guilt.

His wife and her health constituted the rawest of nerves. Even a friend broaching the subject could make him shake. As Hawes proceeded through his customary questions, he noticed the professor flinch at any probe into female relationships. Diettrich's confession of his wife's malaria gave Hawes an opening, and the state lawyer decided to pull on that thread.

Hawes expressed dissatisfaction with Diettrich's explanation of his and Iren's marital compromise. Diettrich countered that Iren was "the only woman I ever loved and cared to love." Going in for the kill, Hawes at last succeeded in breaking the witness.

DIETTRICH: Every now and then we try to recall the olden
    days, but I am sort of weak now.
HAWES: Sort of what?

DIETTRICH: Weak.

HAWES: What you do mean, "weak"?

DIETTRICH: Oh gentlemen, you know what it means to be impotent?

HAWES: Yes sir.

DIETTRICH: Well it's not . . . I'm not quite that bad, but I cannot complete the sexual act.

HAWES: You can't maintain an erection?

DIETTRICH: Yes sir.

HAWES: For sufficient time to complete?

DIETTRICH: Yes sir.

HAWES: The act? Is that what you're telling us?

DIETTRICH: Yes sir.

HAWES: Have you sought any medical attention for that?

DIETTRICH: I talked to a doctor once, but oh, I saw all sorts of specialists and what-have-you, and we just left it off. Now, since we are down here to the rock bottom of a man's inner life, that I have never mentioned to anybody. . . .

After about an hour and a half, Hawes was done playing with the department head, and the great geographer's psyche lay in shards. When the committee excused him, Diettrich asked his tormentors, "What shall I do now?" Someone told him to "act normally as ever." The geographer wandered back to his car and drove home, feeling the "scarlet letter" branded upon his soul. Something terrible was bound to happen, he was sure. Blurry days bled into each other.

As it turned out, UF president J. Wayne Reitz's assurances to the press about his intention to wait for an official report from FLIC to begin a crackdown were false. Around fifty UF professors and students had been hauled into closed hearings with the Johns Committee during those first three weeks of 1959, and actionable intel had already reached his office. Three university employees, including humanities professor Clyde Miller (evicted from the Rawlings house), were terminated by the Reitz administration on January 31. That same day, UF assistant dean of arts and sciences Charles F. Byers announced a sudden resignation for "health reasons" after being caught "carrying on" with another man by Alachua County clerk of the circuit court George

E. Evans. *The Gainesville Sun* ran a small but revealing piece about Byers's departure and printed that the man had been "a patient in the University Teaching Hospital for the past several days" to cue the public that something was off. Because he resigned, the former dean retired with full UF benefits. He passed away quietly, in relative obscurity, in 1981.

Reitz was only getting started. On Valentine's Day 1959, as reported in the *Alligator*, the Johns Committee held a closed meeting in executive session in Jacksonville. At last they delivered their typewritten report to the university president. The final document stood two feet high—purportedly, no fewer than 1,900 pages of depositions, surveillance sheets, personal records, and closed hearing testimony. Despite assurances from Hawes and Strickland about witness immunity and confidentiality, little to no information was denied President Reitz, who was almost immediately pressured by Charley Johns to validate the findings and "take such action as was deemed necessary." This report was "not for the purpose of damaging any institution or individual," Charley assured the press. Among the named names were many of Reitz's personal friends.

Sigismond Diettrich never knew when the hammer blow would strike. He frequently sat at home in darkness. He shuddered when the phone rang.

CHAPTER 16

Victim of Opportunity

*J. Wayne Reitz, left,
at an appropriations hearing, 1959*

February 1959 (*Diettrich Papers*)

WITH THE RELEASE of FLIC's report to Reitz, Chairman Charley Johns began pressing his case on the need to extend his committee for two more years during the next session. The Florida legislature would open for business on April 7, 1959. "There is still a lot of work be done," Charley said. "However, we have but one investigator," he cautioned. To voters, Charley painted a picture of the world that Markley had imprinted in his childhood mind, in which small forces of goodness held back an oncoming darkness.

On the racial front in Florida, the Dade County school board voted to integrate the first school in the state by admitting "four Negroes" at the elementary level for the 1959 school year. In response, Florida legislators held an impromptu summit at the grand opening of the Daytona Beach International Speedway, a 2.5-mile asphalt track for NASCAR perched at the edge of Pork Chopper country. In the stands at the speedway's inaugural race, legislators drafted a "manifesto" in which they pledged to shut down all public schools in Florida before submitting to integration. State senators, including Charley Johns, quickly registered their agreement, with senate president pro tem Dewey Johnson bemoaning the right of whites to receive "an education in keeping with our beliefs." Meanwhile, FLIC received bad news from Washington, D.C. The U.S. Supreme Court agreed to issue a stay on contempt proceedings against four members of the Miami NAACP, including Reverend Theodore Gibson, pending a final Supreme Court action on the NAACP's official appeal. "Not at all surprised," reacted Senator Charley Johns. "The NAACP controls the U.S. Supreme Court."

Back in Gainesville, tensions grew as the purge commenced in earnest. After months in the pocket of Hawes and Strickland, student journalists at the *Alligator* finally began publishing criticism of the disruptive effects of ongoing committee activities on their undergraduate education and college experience. "Watchdog Charley," as students nicknamed him, alarmed even the campus contingent of the Ku Klux Klan. On February 17, *The Miami Herald* reported that more than "500 students had been involved in the investigation." On February 20, the *Alligator* ran the front-page headline "15–16 Suspects Named in Report of Johns Group." The Florida Civil Liberties Union denounced the Johns Committee's investigation as causing "tremendous and permanent damage" by slandering professors and students. "No concern of mine," responded Charley, adding that he'd heard the group was trying to radicalize a campus contingent.

From the voluminous FLIC report, President J. Wayne Reitz drew up a list of names and proceeded down its pages more or less alphabetically. Tenure meant next to nothing to Reitz, when compared to his vision for the institution. Sigismond Diettrich knew just what would happen when his friend, his boss, reached the D's. Diettrich acquired a lethal dose of aspirin (the only pills he could get his hands on quickly) and threw himself into his last days of labor. "I don't think I ever gave better lectures in my life," Diettrich wrote. "The intensity of imminent disaster seemed to sharpen my wits. . . . Feverishly, I tried to finish everything."

Time was up that Monday, March 16, 1959. Early in the morning, dean of the College of Arts and Sciences, Ralph Page, phoned Diettrich at his office in Floyd Hall. Page had been waiting all weekend to make the move, but didn't want to startle the condemned man by calling him at home. "I knew what it was," wrote Diettrich. "His voice was as dead as my heart." President Reitz wanted to see them both in the Administration Building at 2:00 p.m.

Diettrich dialed his parish priest, Father Thomas Gross, and Gross came to Diettrich's office. They prayed together. Determined to maintain a productive morning, Diettrich went to a scheduled meeting with Linton Grinter, dean of the graduate school. They discussed expanding the geography department and extending Harvard cartographer Erwin Raisz's appointment as "distinguished research professor," so that Raisz could help Diettrich finish the *Atlas of Florida*. Even as a proverbial dead man walking, Diettrich continued to advocate on behalf of others. He asked the dean for $85 so that the department might purchase a better copy machine. On the spot, Grinter approved the funds. "It is always a pleasure to have you come by my office," declared Grinter, emotion overflowing as Diettrich left. What did he know? Diettrich wondered.

Diettrich went home for lunch. Iren, aware that something was terribly wrong, plied her husband with questions. Diettrich gave spare answers. As 2:00 p.m. approached, he returned to Floyd Hall and called Dean Page, who was already at Reitz's office. Diettrich joined Page in the president's waiting room at the Administration Building. The two were warmhearted colleagues. Even their wives were friends. "He was nice but preoccupied," Diettrich recalled. A few minutes of polite conversation passed, and then President Reitz breezed through.

J. Wayne Reitz wore shiny gold spectacles that glinted in the light. Clean-shaven, with the slightest dimple in his chin, he fit the role of a sprightly academic—a veritable fountain of youth fed on knowledge itself. Reitz gelled and parted his hair slightly to the side, with not a lock out of place. He flashed his white teeth. He greeted Diettrich and Page as comrades and guided them into

J. Wayne Reitz, circa 1955

his domain as a secretary shut the door. They sat in stuffed leather chairs. Reitz stood, leaning back on his desk. It was Reitz who broke the ice. "Sig, this is a most serious and to me most unpleasant task," he said, using Diettrich's nickname to soften the blow. "Yes, I know," Diettrich conceded, grieving for a visionary called to perform such a chore.

"Wayne was the nicest ever," Diettrich recalled. "I felt so sorry for him that he had to do this to a friend of his. I felt sorry for Page, who also liked me." Diettrich blamed himself: "How could I have betrayed them, who trusted me?" When the geographer received his opportunity to speak in response to the charges, his voice was drained of life. He didn't dispute a single fact. To the Johns Committee, Reitz would say that Diettrich was fired and list him as "terminated." In truth, in this administrative cloister, Reitz formally requested for his friend Sigismond Diettrich to resign the chairmanship of his department and retire with full benefits.

Diettrich complied without fuss. Through Reitz's insistence on a resignation, the president ensured that his friend would keep his state teacher's pension and be provided for as a member of emeritus faculty. The only snag, given his sudden and early retirement, was that Diettrich's pension could not become active until he reached the age of fifty-five on August 31, 1961. Until that date, he and Iren would have to fend for themselves financially. "By the way, Dr. Reitz assured me that my resignation will not affect in any way the Fulbright," Diettrich wrote to a confidant. Gently Dean Page put his arm around the geographer and told him that, though he was stunned and confused by these charges, he still loved him. "It was," Diettrich recalled, "a nice and reassuring goodbye."

Twenty minutes ticked by on the clock in J. Wayne Reitz's office. Twenty minutes to end a career.

Somehow Diettrich held it together during those painful moments until no one had anything left to say. When Diettrich realized that his two bosses were sitting in silence, waiting for him to leave, he rose and made himself scarce. Once out of eyeshot, he ran from the building, on the brink of psychosis. "The enormity of my weakness just dawned upon me!" Diettrich later wrote in a mad stream of consciousness to his best friend. "I was a traitor to everyone who loved me and respected me. I was proud all my life, self-assured and in a nice way but arrogant. I, though always upset afterwards, thought I could make my own little agreements and covenants even with the Lord! And get away with it." Outside, it had started to rain. He sprinted to Floyd Hall and found Father Gross in his office. To the priest, he raved. "I was out of my mind," Diettrich recalled. Just then a younger parish priest named Father Neil Sager, a geography student and chaplain of the university, returned from classes, and Diettrich confessed his sins to a pupil who'd venerated him. "I shall never, never forget his look," Diettrich wrote. Then a strange calm overcame him, and he resolved to execute his plan.

Diettrich ran to St. Patrick Catholic Church, kneeled before the altar, and began to argue with God: "Killing myself is a necessity and cannot be a sin." All debate settled, he returned to Floyd Hall and downed the eighty-five aspirin with a glass of water. As if by muscle memory, somehow, he wobbled over to classroom 205 in Floyd Hall and taught his 3:40 seminar, "Development of Geographic Thought." "I talked about the creed of geography," he wrote. "To them it may not have made too much sense, but it did to me." Once his lecture was complete, another emotional trapdoor gave way.

Diettrich ran upstairs to the department study hall on the third floor. Chasing a student out of the room, he demanded a cup of coffee with new imperiousness. Then the geographer climbed out a window onto the roof of Floyd Hall. Nearly everyone in the department knew how to access this clandestine roof deck. It was where graduate students went to smoke cannabis during study breaks.

It was still raining. He stared down at the concrete sidewalk. He looked across the wet lawn toward Peabody Hall and the rest of the campus. A few students were passing below, but nobody saw him perched at such a height, unmoving. With a cruel arithmetic, he weighed the merits of the perpetuation of his life against an instant death.

For decades, Sigismond Diettrich had truly loved something—the geography of a new American culture flourishing on a bountiful peninsula. At first only he had been aware of it. He'd studied and charted and nourished its dream. He'd written columns for Florida's major newspapers and been named to committees by the governor. Then that culture had noticed him, a little ant on the ground, and found him wanting.

He crouched to jump and started counting down in his head. Five, four, three, two . . . At the end of the countdown, he froze. Diettrich tried again. He counted from ten to zero. He tried once more. "I could not jump," he wrote. Diettrich could not even move. "Those were frightful minutes that seemed to hang on eternity," he wrote. Part of what prevented him from leaping, no doubt, was the realization that his death by suicide and the ensuing publicity would give fuel to the Johns Committee—proof, in the form of a literal body of evidence, that they were truly onto something. Then the aspirin in Diettrich's bloodstream kicked in and made him dizzy. He slipped backward, falling through the study hall window. Water dripping from his hair, Diettrich returned to his office downstairs complaining of a headache. His secretary gave him two more aspirin, which he swallowed straightaway.

Father Sager and the secretary sensed something frightening, almost maniacal in his manner, and they convinced Diettrich to cancel his evening lecture for his favorite class, aptly titled "The Geography of Florida." Somehow Diettrich managed to make it home. Iren served dinner. He made attempts at mealtime conversation. Finally Iren asked him what the hell was going on, and Diettrich answered, "I've lost my job."

She asked him why. The only woman he'd ever loved asked him why, and he told her the truth. "I am afraid if I had plunged a knife into her heart, I could not have hurt her worse," Diettrich wrote. "Oh that damn curse over my head that I can't but bring sorrow and disaster to all I love and who love me."

Diettrich sat at the table as Iren whimpered and did not touch her food. He prayed for the poison in his blood to work. He phoned Father Thomas Gross again, and the priest came to minister to Iren. As if detaching himself from the physical world, Diettrich drifted into drowsiness, his heartbeat faltering, his palms clammy. Around nine p.m., the priest left, and Iren retired to their daughter Rosemary's old bedroom. Diettrich collapsed alone in their marital bed. Coldness crept over him, and he felt strange relief. A million hammers pounded in his ears just as his legs grew numb. When the numbness reached his heart, he knew, the plan would be complete.

He wanted to cry out for help, but to whom? "I have lost all I had," he wrote, "all I lived for in my proud vanity." From miles away, it seemed, Diettrich heard the chiming of bells. He thought it might be angels from heaven. The noise grew louder, as if nearing. Soon the clamor was all he could hear. Diettrich awoke. His house phone was ringing. The geographer ran to answer it, as if by training. He picked up the receiver, but couldn't hear a word. Was the line down in the storm? He babbled something incoherent and called for Iren. Deafness engulfed him. He must have fainted. He lost an hour. Sometime later, in his living room, he stood before his parish priests once more. A hallucination, he concluded. Diettrich laughed maniacally and told them he'd "taken enough aspirin to kill a cow." He watched the priests call a doctor. He fainted again.

When he came to, Iren sat next to his chair as a doctor pumped a bitter syrup down his throat. Dizziness. Queasiness. Vomiting. At two a.m., he fell asleep. At ten a.m., Diettrich woke alone and remembered his final departmental duties. He'd promised his friend J. Wayne Reitz that he would draft a letter of resignation and lie about why. He had to transfer the chairmanship, his keys, and his office to a protégé named Professor William Pierson. Diettrich phoned his secretary and told her to call an all-staff meeting for ten the next morning, March 18, 1959. He canceled all his geography classes, pending the emergency conclave. Diettrich left instructions for a colleague to pick him up promptly at 9:45 a.m. that Wednesday and take him to Floyd Hall.

And then all these logistics became too much for his wounded brain. He crumpled into another crying spell and lost consciousness. Later he couldn't remember how he got off the phone with his secretary. Within that span of blankness, friends made plans to get him and Iren out of town as soon as possible—a tropical getaway, somewhere south. Wednesday morning came. Iren gave her husband a pep talk about not having a breakdown during his farewell speech. Diettrich packed up everything he kept at home that belonged to the university. And he found himself afraid of seeing the new acting chair of the department, Professor William Pierson. One time, Pierson had made a crack about homosexuals.

Head up, mustering what courage he still possessed, Sigismond Diettrich walked into Floyd Hall for the last time. And there they all stood in one room, his entire department "loving and sorrowful." Most were crying. Most knew about his attempt on his life. "And Bill," Diettrich wrote of his successor, "how could I have ever doubted his friendship and loyalty?" Still ashamed, Diettrich could not bring himself to look many colleagues in the eye. His secretary came into the room to take down his last dictation, and he poured from his brain all that he could marshal to help the department—plans, hopes, aspirations, technicalities, problems, nuances, budgets. He imparted a lifetime's worth of expertise in two hours.

Finally, he gave his office keys to Professor William Pierson. "The tragedy came to its curtain," Diettrich recalled. Diettrich wandered off alone, one last time, through the department he'd led since 1943. "It may not be much," Diettrich wrote, "and not too pretty to look at, but it was mine, it was the Department, my life, my love, my ambition."

A priest drove him home. They hopped immediately into the family car. With Iren at the wheel, the two of them left Gainesville. "While driving through the beautiful citrus belt I was gently crying," Diettrich recalled. "Will I ever see it again? Oh how I love Florida! How much I know about it! What a waste to throw me away like a squeezed-out orange." Throughout the week, Diettrich's former department continued to lie and obfuscate about his status. In a March 19 letter, Diettrich's ex-secretary wrote to a geography professor in North Carolina: "I regret to inform you that Dr. Diettrich is ill at present." That Sunday, *The Gainesville Sun* got the scoop and reported how the great geographer "quit." The speed of his departure and the lack of an explanation in the resignation letter said everything to local readers.

The Diettrichs returned home that March 22 to pick up the shards of their shattered lives. Humiliated from the "shock" of her husband's waywardness, Iren kept the house curtains closed. She rebuffed visitors and refused to answer the telephone. Dreading his next move, Diettrich went to Floyd Hall to pick up boxes of materials from his office. Next, Diettrich had to figure out what to do about his in-progress *Atlas of Florida*, still under contract with the University of Florida Press. Raisz, his coauthor and illustrator, had tried to secure special permission for Diettrich to work on the manuscript at the campus library. But on March 24, the UF academic council met and denied the proposal. "I am not welcome on campus," Diettrich wrote, "the campus I helped to build!"

Iren, who taught piano out of their home, feared her students would quit rather than be associated with her family's scandal. "All her pupils came back," Diettrich wrote a friend reassuringly, "and when they heard the news that she is not going to come with me to Pakistan, they were overjoyed." Upon the advice of President Reitz, Diettrich began a series of psychiatric sessions with Dr. Peter Regan of the UF Medical Center. "He is supposed to be a great expert," Diettrich wrote Erwin Raisz in Hungarian, perhaps on the odd chance that FLIC was eavesdropping on his mail. "Everyone has great confidence in him. I wish only I did! But I decided to go, if only because perhaps he might be able to 'cure' me, or at least give me a certificate that he cured me." Iren eventually forgave her husband for his indiscretions, and the two did not divorce.

As travel plans solidified for his Fulbright in East Pakistan, Diettrich charted a course to leave Gainesville on the last of May with intervening stops in Hawaii, the Philippines, Tokyo, Bangkok, Rangoon, Calcutta, and New Delhi for lectures at major universities. Diettrich's final destination and home for the 1959–1960 school year would be the budding Department of Geography at the University of Dacca—a department well-funded for regional studies. Tainted in Gainesville, Diettrich nevertheless remained one of the most sought-after geographers on the planet. The Johns Committee blacklist couldn't extend beyond the power and influence of Chairman Charley Johns and his acolytes, largely adherents to a fading southern way of life.

To maximize the benefit of his journeys, Diettrich convinced the American Geographical Society, along with the trade publisher Nelson Doubleday, to commission him to write a booklet on the geography of the Philippine Islands during a ten-day "field trip" on his way to Dacca. Meanwhile, Diettrich dropped in and out of melancholy, worrying Erwin Raisz. He frequently stared morosely into space—likely a side effect of overmedication by Dr. Peter Regan. If Diettrich could just keep on living until his fifty-fifth birthday, his university pension would kick in, and everyone he loved would be provided for.

Diettrich left Florida for East Pakistan on May 31, 1959. His ten-day tour of the Philippines was a smashing success, with the "hospitality and help of many" facilitating the rapid delivery of a sixty-three-page booklet to Nelson Doubleday in New York by 1960. Published as *The Philippine Islands* by Sigismond Diettrich, "Professor of Geography, University of Dacca," this text provided one of the first modern geographic surveys of the Philippine Islands. In Dacca, Diettrich's ambitious lectures and photographic fieldwork, including of the "Naked Mru" indigenous culture, won him an extension of his Fulbright into the 1960–61 school year.

Since his UF pension activated on August 31, 1961, his family now possessed the financial security that he was afraid he had denied them forever. Although the Fulbright Committee recognized Diettrich's worth, the University of Florida could not forgive the geographer his offenses. Once Diettrich was settled in East Pakistan, the University of Florida Press convinced Erwin Raisz to cut him out of the *Atlas of Florida* project, though Diettrich was the book's originator.

When the *Atlas* was published, Raisz received credit as the sole author, with "text by John R. Dunkle," a former protégé who once ferried Diettrich to and from psychiatric appointments at UF Hospital with Dr. Regan. Much of Diettrich's original writing received a light polish from Dunkle, who nonetheless received authorial credit from the press, and the acknowledgments section of the book downplayed the great geographer's contributions. In the foreword to the book, the Florida governor gushed, "The research which has made this book possible demonstrates significantly the service rendered to our state by the University of Florida."

The rave review of the *Atlas* in *The Miami Herald* conspicuously credited Diettrich as the "brain-father" of the project and described him as the "guiding genius" of the UF geography department, while characterizing Erwin Raisz as the book's "compiler." Although the full-color *Atlas of Florida* sold exceedingly well through several printings, neither Diettrich nor his family received a royalty check from the University of Florida Press for the work.

Despite infamy, Sigismond Diettrich was not a man to retire young. After his Fulbright ended, he searched for work and took a position in the U.S. territories as chairman of social sciences at the University of Puerto Rico in San Juan. In 1963, Delta Tau Kappa, an honor society science fraternity, named Dr. Sigismond Diettrich as its international chancellor, though the man was still not welcome to study at the UF library.

It's unknown when Diettrich retired and finally went home to Gainesville. He lived out his final years quietly and cherished time with his daughter, Rosemary, and his grandchildren. The Diettrichs established a local nonprofit called the Foundation for the Promotion of Music, which assisted young classical musicians with scholarships and sponsored concerts. When, in 1987, Diettrich was dying of cancer, he asked to be buried in his old academic regalia. The family saw to it that Sigismond deRudesheim Diettrich's papers and letters, detailing his persecution at the hands of state agents, were donated for the benefit of future researchers to the university department he once led—though at the time, Charley Johns and his admirers were still alive to silence stories and guard his reputation.

CHAPTER 17

Hands That Feed

*The Century Tower looming on
the University of Florida campus*

March 1959 (*Box 6, Box 7, Box 19*)

CONFUSINGLY, THE FATES of many FLIC informants who
compromised their principles tended to match the fates of countless
non-informers who did not. In spite of his substantial collaboration
with Officer Tileston, tenured English professor and former Fulbright
fellow James Congleton was terminated by President J. Wayne Reitz
on March 15, 1959. Evidently, the Johns Committee viewed Congleton's spying efforts as well as the medical intervention for his homosexuality through Dr. Regan as insufficient to spare him. Thus did
Congleton's twenty-two years of service to the state end in ignominy
and private disgrace. "He has been associated with the University since
1937," reported *The Gainesville Sun*. "It was reported that the resignation was due to ill health."

Similarly, on March 28, music professor, glee club instructor, and
committee collaborator John Faircloth Park was called in and fired de-

spite testimony impugning two professors, including Lawrence Wathen, and one art teacher. Fellow informer Harold Elwood Carter stood among the first K-12 teachers in Florida fired as a result of the Johns Committee relaying his testimony back to a local school district. Duval County Public Schools dismissed the art teacher for cause, and Carter's name appeared on an educational blacklist passed throughout the South. Earl Fender, the sixth-grade teacher at Merritt Island Elementary School, was not only fired and blacklisted but castigated before members of the Florida legislature in a session led by Charley Johns.

Contrarily, music professor and committee collaborator Russell Danburg received a pardon for his infractions. He kept his career, though he was witnessed in the act of masturbating at the courthouse by Tileston and his admitted encounters in the library and the student union bathrooms had likely occurred with undergraduate students. Evidently, testimony that led to the successful firing of Sigismond Diettrich proved helpful enough to save Danburg's neck. Additionally, Danburg's avowals that he was only passively homosexual "in a mild way" rang true with the committee, for some reason. Maybe Hawes and Strickland needed to believe that a talent like Danburg was capable of reform. More likely, some unnamed admirer of Danburg's compositions protected him from on high.

> HAWES: Do you think that a man with sufficient willpower can
>   unlearn that [homosexuality], like any bad habit?
> DANBURG: Most definitely. Since talking to Mr. Strickland and
>   Mr. Tileston I know, from a very definite personal
>   experience, that it can be done, because I say under Oath
>   that I have had no homosexual experience.

Notwithstanding the damage his testimony caused so many others, Russell Danburg continued teaching as a celebrated member of the UF faculty for decades. As part of the UF oral history program, he gave a retrospective interview about his life and career in which he made no mention of the Johns Committee. When he retired, the Russell L. Danburg Scholarship was established at UF to perpetually support one talented junior or senior studying piano or music theory. The scholarship still bears his name.

Several established informants and collaborators kept their jobs through more elaborate means. For example, twice-divorced assistant professor of the College of Education Leslie Murray, embroiled through liaisons with schoolteacher and accused perjurer Earl Fender, courted and then married a third wife in December 1960. They divorced several years later. Other UF professors were permitted to finish out teaching the 1959 spring term, but then were expected to take leaves of absence. That way, these informants could pretend they'd been fired to conceal their committee work and avoid the risk of collegial retribution. AAUP chapter president, student counselor, and Johns Committee spy Winston Wallace Ehrmann continued to serve as the local AAUP president until the firings, at which point he received a year's leave from the administration and moved to teach at Colorado State University.

Campus figures unaccountably shielded from troubles followed the same path as privileged informants. For example, Dr. Stephen Fogle took a leave of absence in the fall of 1959. Fogle then splurged on a trip to Key West to enjoy the sights. For a brief stint, Fogle taught composition at a community college in the Long Island town of Sayville, across the bay from Fire Island and its queer summer migrants. But the academic aesthete described the teaching gig as "beneath him" to Art Copleston and Bill Moore and complained endlessly of chill winters. "He led us to believe he'd been kicked out of Gainesville," Copleston explained.

Eventually, Stephen Fogle secured a visiting professor position at Bowling Green University in Ohio. In his hiring announcement, Bowling Green listed Fogle as "Professor of English at the University of Florida." Fogle eventually returned to Gainesville to reclaim his tenured post and his place on the gay social calendar. Innocuously, on May 7, 1965, the *Alligator* announced the retirement of several faculty members, including "Dr. Stephen Francis Fogle, Professor of English, 19 years." Not long after, in April 1967, Fogle died from cancer in an Alachua County hospital.

On March 19, President Reitz proclaimed the good news that he'd received his record appropriation from the legislature. Gleefully, Reitz held a freshman class forum and bragged of the $7 million "for new campus buildings" and dormitories. "In a democratic society," Reitz told the freshmen, "a university is the well-spring of progress." Both student enrollment and the university's physical footprint, he boasted, would nearly double by 1970.

Reitz's faculty massacre became national news by early April, when the Associated Press ran a piece headlined "Florida U. Dismisses 14 for Homosexuality." In that story, Reitz confirmed that at least fourteen employees had been dismissed for homosexual conduct, with action also taken against offending students and "suitable procedures" established to prevent future perversion. "President Reitz is to be commended for the action he has taken," chimed in *The Gainesville Sun*, characterizing the firings as a "morals cleanup." Charley Johns told the paper he was "well pleased" to see the situation "under control," with a large university taking steps to address an unfortunate matter that was "impossible to clean" up entirely, but necessary to keep "at a minimum."

So lurid was the material within FLIC's private 1,900-page report to Reitz that the UF president declined to make it available to anyone outside of his inner circle. From a public relations standpoint, Reitz sought to defend the honor of his institution against detractors. "I again want to emphasize that there is no reason to believe that the extent of the homosexual conduct at the University of Florida is unique and that other public institutions have any less of a problem," he averred. Though none of the accused would ever be brought up on criminal charges, the North Florida public applauded Reitz's actions and scorned the denigrated professors. "You might be interested in knowing that of the 14 staff members dismissed, 12 of them had been on the staff prior to my assuming the presidency," Reitz wrote in his own defense.

In angry letters to the *Alligator*, progressive UF students demanded explanations for the classroom chaos:

> *No information has been released as to proof of these alleged offenses nor how the (great and honorable) Charley E. Johns obtained this proof. The campus should be in mourning, yet we see no black flags. This is an issue that concerns all students and for that matter all citizens of Florida. Boldly stated, the issue is whether a legislative committee or Kangaroo court can run our institutions of higher learning or whether control of these institutions is better left to faculty and administration.*

Can we the citizens of Florida allow a politician to procure
political ammunition at the expense of our school system?
  Charles D. Edelstein
  Ross P. Beckerman

On April 9, 1959, authorities called UF student Arthur Sidney Copleston Jr. into the offices of dean of men Lester Hale in the Administration Building. Copleston was convinced that he was about to get "kicked out" out of school. Dean Hale asked Copleston to shut the door behind him—a classic power move. "I have some bad news," Hale said before either could sit down. Hale signaled for Copleston to take the chair in front of his desk. "I'm sorry," Copleston tried to say, but Hale spoke faster. "Your father died this morning," he said. After a brief pause to the let the news sink in, the dean continued. "He was panhandling in front of the Woolworth's department store in West Palm Beach and had a heart attack."

Copleston couldn't breathe. It was if all the air on earth got sucked into outer space. "Oh, thank God," he instinctively thought or maybe said. He couldn't be sure. It just slipped out. It was how he felt. Then, realizing his father was dead, Copleston winced in pain. Dean Hale crossed over from his desk and tried to comfort the student. He awkwardly put a hand on Copleston's shoulder, as men of the era weren't supposed to touch with affection and, if called for, never for too long. With a feeling of unreality, Copleston stood and nodded to Dean Hale and left the room. He couldn't see straight as he walked down the hallway. Those around him appeared as blurry shapes, and he tried to hide his face, wet with tears as it registered relief.

Copleston thought they really had him: Tileston, Strickland, and Charley Johns. He thought his life was over, but it was just that his dad had died.

Art Copleston was never sure when the Johns Committee would finally get around to killing his future, and he tried to mentally prepare for the next "sweat session." With a dedication verging on obsession, Officer Tileston developed a habit of hanging out in the hallways and stairwells of Thomas Hall near Copleston's dorm room. Especially after the reassignment of his former roommate, Copleston would periodically open the door to leave for class and find Officer Tileston standing right there, as if listening through the barrier into Copleston's last ten feet of private space.

Meanwhile, Senator Charley Johns wasted little time in the 1959 session. On April 10, he introduced a bill calling for another two-year extension of FLIC and solicited the senate for another $75,000. Charley let it be known that he expected no opposition. That same day, with reapportionment on the docket and Governor Collins pushing for an expansion of the number of senate seats, Charley called for an eighty-minute closed-door session of the legislature to critique the governor's efforts to "coerce" radical reform. This wouldn't be Charley's only use of off-the-record time. Three days later, on April 13, 1959, the Johns Committee met in Tallahassee to retroactively approve a practice, in use by Charley since March, that "files showing homosexual conduct on the part of all public employees" should be referred to "superiors with a request that such superiors report back to the Committee the action taken thereon within thirty (30) days." The measure, ensuring that FLIC would be better able to publicize its punishments, passed unanimously.

Four days later, a somewhat innocuous bill authorizing the Florida board of education to conduct investigations for "charges alleging misconduct of any public-school teacher" was introduced in the senate. Said bill, No. 237, passed unanimously with the support of Charley Johns, paving the way for an expanded round of FLIC inquiries. Then at 11:42 a.m. on April 29, the senate went into executive session for Chairman Charley Johns to deliver FLIC's written report and allow Hawes and Strickland to verbally convey the salacious details that couldn't be written down.

It was showtime. With the senate side of the capitol on lockdown and media barred from the chamber, Chairman Charley Johns waved pages with a clenched first and spoke impromptu. In FLIC's report on subversion in the state from 1957 to 1959, Charley and company made quick work of the NAACP. "Since February 1958, the Committee has been subjected to numerous sustained legal assaults designed to destroy the Committee or obstruct and frustrate the Committee's investigations until it expired," the report read. Charley listed the obstructive tactics: thirty circuit-level litigation actions, one case in district court of appeals, two combined appeals of the Supreme Court of Florida, one case in federal district court, and one case "now presently engaged in litigation in the United States Supreme Court."

Charley speedily moved on to the more salacious section of the report, titled "Homosexuality in Public Education." Skipping past the question of why the committee had looked into homosexuality in the first place, the report included generous use of the passive voice and made an appeal to legislators that though "it has been, and still is, the prime concern of the Committee that nothing be done to injure the good name of the University [of Florida]," the sexual misdeeds uncovered by happenstance necessitated that "some action be taken." What FLIC found involving "homosexual practices" at the University of Florida was "absolutely appalling," given the realities that "the greatest danger of a homosexual is his or her recruitment of other people" and that "a surprisingly large percentage of young people are subject to be influenced into homosexual practices."

FLIC presented a list of "salient facts" to corroborate its queer claims. As an example, Charley cited an investigation into "one public school teacher," who purportedly had "homosexual contact with 32 teenage students between the ages of 14 and 16.5 years." Cross-referencing this claim with the Johns Committee files, this allegation appears to be sourced from a February 6, 1959, deposition of a former Hillsborough County deputy sheriff named Bill Donaldson. Donaldson's testimony to FLIC concerned a former teacher at Riverview High School named Charles Howard Montague Jr. In January 1959, Montague had resigned his English teaching post following his arrest on charges of corrupting a minor. Montague was sentenced to a variable six months to twenty years for an "abominable and detestable crime against nature" against a juvenile.

The notion of a pedophile with a penchant for boys staking out a classroom to corrupt the scions of families "prominent in this state" stoked alarm in the senate chamber. The overriding fear of FLIC, and legislators more broadly, was not that adolescents were assaulted by an adult but that Montague may have created more "confirmed practicing homosexuals" through his heinous actions. Anticipating such shock, FLIC made assurances in its report that some of Montague's victims were "able to take one or several homosexual acts in stride and go on to live perfectly normal and natural lives."

As another "appalling" example of sex crime run amok, Chairman Charley told of a 1957 moral turpitude investigation that embroiled "approximately 27 teachers" in the Hillsborough County School District. Charley neglected to mention that this investigation had also been conducted by former deputy sheriff Bill Donaldson. In the report, FLIC grumbled that Tampa's 1957 inquiry had been cut short when investigators were bogusly "pulled off" the trail by superiors—resulting in an absence of evidence that constituted positive proof of guilt.

Most of the homosexual anecdotes paraded before the legislature in FLIC's 1959 report stemmed in fact from Donaldson's testimony—one interview of one disgruntled former deputy on one day in February. Upon analysis of the documentation, FLIC's "salient facts" appear to be little more than a single ex-lawman's calumnies—lifted without citation, remixed for greatest effect, and repackaged to the legislature as the committee's original work. Naturally, FLIC's insistence on confidentiality allowed them to freely co-opt information from other constituencies and take credit for any embellished or fictionalized findings.

Through an emphasis on secret intelligence gathering, Charley, Hawes, and Strickland made themselves look indispensable to the legislature. Having driven the senate chamber into an anti-homosexual panic, Charley posited FLIC as their savior: "It is not difficult for a qualified investigator who knows what to look for . . . to ferret out concrete proof on the vast majority of all practicing homosexuals." As a result of FLIC's exemplary detective work in Gainesville, Charley read aloud, "a total of fifteen instructional and staff personnel were dismissed with their records appropriately marked indicating the reason therefor." At the end of Charley's reading, the legislature sat stunned but admiring. Representatives jostled with one another to shake the hands of Johns, Hawes, and Strickland. At 1:05 p.m., the senate emerged from executive session and took roll call, with all thirty-eight senators present. Chairman Charley Johns submitted a copy of his report, and precisely one minute later, the senate adjourned for the day.

In late April 1959, just when humanities professor Lawrence Wathen started to believe that he might have escaped culpability, President Reitz hit the W's on his alphabetical list, and Wathen received a call from his immediate superior, Ralph Emerson Page, dean of the UF College of Arts and Sciences. As he had with Diettrich, Page met Wathen over at the offices of an unnamed university vice president. Their meeting began with a charged but productive discussion about the consequences of state intervention into private lives, involving Nazi Germany and its suffocation of expression. From there, the vice president pivoted to Wathen and said, "This is the whole big thing." He slapped down a large file with a blue cover. Within it were copies of all the condemnatory materials gathered by the committee on Wathen—accuser statements and surveillance accounts, plus Wathen's own depositions and denials. Reitz has reviewed these materials, the vice president said, and we are going to have to release you.

Wathen's position was terminated immediately for reason of "gross indecency." Though the committee never caught Wathen in a sexual act or secured his confession, they'd assembled a small trove of circumstantial paperwork, the quantity of which transformed chance insinuations into a reason for the administration to act.

Unsure what to do next, the former professor remained in Gainesville and hid in his house for the rest of the spring term. He told family members back in Dallas that he was taking the year off because of heart troubles. When the U.S. Army Reserves learned of Major Wathen's dismissal, they dishonorably discharged him, which cost him his monthly military pension. Unable to earn income, Wathen lost his home and lived for a year in his 1954 Plymouth. Destitute at the age of forty-nine, Wathen slept on the couches of acquaintances. He wandered. He mooched. He took out so-called loans from former students for simple car repairs.

Meanwhile, Wathen applied to teaching job after teaching job, even driving overnight to Alabama for one misbegotten interview. A prospective administrator flat-out told him that he couldn't "take a chance" on a Johns committee suspect. In 1961, a prestigious university seemed ready to hire him and showed Wathen his new desk. They phoned his former UF department chair, Robert Davidson, for a character reference, and when asked if he'd hire Wathen back to his former post, Davidson answered no. It took Lawrence Wathen until 1964 to find his way back into a lecture hall at a community college in Texas. Over time, Wathen's warmly received lectures rebuilt a student fandom, and he earned his way into a professorship at the University of Houston, where he taught humanities until his retirement.

Of the student moles tied to the Burger House (Don Steinbrecher, James William Graves, Joe Trice, and David Meuser), the results of their collaboration with the committee were mixed. Don Steinbrecher, now accused by Art Copleston of being the impostor roommate Jim Steinbrenner, graduated from University of Florida with a master's degree in engineering in 1960. James William Graves did not graduate from UF; it's unclear why. The military veteran Joseph "Joe" Morris Trice also did not graduate, though he'd agreed to an intensive bout of therapy from Dr. Justin E. Harlow Jr. of the Student Health Center in exchange for reenrollment; it appears, in fact, that Trice was expelled alongside his former mentor James Wathen in his final semester of school.

David Meuser, the newlywed and expectant father with a penchant for accepting fellatio from men, graduated from the University of Florida with a master's degree in secondary education. He took a job teaching social studies at a high school in West Melbourne, Florida, near Cape Canaveral. As proof of his full rehabilitation, the former "passive" bartender at the Burger House developed an "Americanism vs. Communism" course to inform local high school students of the "evils, dangers, and fallacies of the Communist movement," as reported in the Cocoa Beach *Evening Tribune*.

Impressed, Florida DOE superintendent and Johns Committee collaborator Thomas Bailey tapped the handsome, pompadoured young educator for a special committee to expand the "Americanism vs. Communism" class to all Florida schools. Soon Meuser was lecturing on anti-Communism at women's clubs and being courted to write a textbook. He and his wife, Patricia, had a second child, though something widened between them behind the scenes. On March 11, 1970, Patricia and David Meuser divorced, and she speedily rewed in what was hailed as the first interracial marriage in Florida's state capital.

Student sentiment in Gainesville turned in waves against Charley Johns and his noxious committee with the delivery of the 1959 FLIC report that characterized UF as a "homo" bastion. Undergraduates railed at the mid-semester loss of some of their most popular professors and reeled at the insult of Charley damaging the standing of their school. How was this fair to those paying fees and making the grade and earning degrees? Hadn't they silently assented every time they ignored some unlucky sod being escorted out of class? Hadn't they tolerated the childish and obvious presence of plainclothes agents at their libraries and hangouts, their football games and fraternity bashes? What would it take for someone to make these bastards leave their college years alone?

On April 30, students hung an effigy of Charley Johns from a tree in the most trafficked campus quad. Campus police cut down the stuffed statue by eleven a.m., but not before thousands passed and cheered the visage with the accompanying sign: "Charley Johns has condemned freedom here!! Shall we allow it to die? No!"

Dams burst in Gainesville on May 6, in near-perfect rhythm with the legislature's maneuvers to renew FLIC. In Tallahassee, Charley railroaded the Johns Committee extension bill through the Florida senate, securing passage by a 37 to 1 vote. Only Senator Frank Houghton of St. Petersburg, the lone Republican in the chamber, dared to say no. Charley's bill, with a $75,000 appropriation price tag attached, sped to the Florida house, where it was all but assured to pass despite Senator Tom Adams of the tax committee muttering that no one knew how the Johns Committee had exhausted its previous budget.

Around eight o'clock that evening, UF students gave into "the brunt of rising emotions" and mutinied when the power suddenly cut out of their dormitories, and rumors went wild from room to room that Charley Johns was shutting down their school. Vitriol unleashed toward one vague target: the man who'd invaded their minds and tried to cage what was theirs. Emerging outdoors, nearly a thousand students gathered before the "whites only" College Inn cafeteria on West University Avenue. Then someone shouted, "Panty raid!" and an uprising ensued.

The mob streamed toward the female dormitories, where it seethed in full release of the year's prudery. In response to shirtless men climbing trees and begging, "Panties, please!" female students flashed their nightgowns. Voices shouted, "We want panties!" as well as "We want Charley Johns!" In vain, dean of men Lester Hale attempted to drown out obscene cries by leading renditions of the UF fight song. Then male students pushed a nearby dumpster into the street and set it ablaze.

Heaving rocks and bricks, students bashed streetlamps and drove back a phalanx of university cops. One deputy campus policeman suffered an arm fracture. "A trail of blood led almost the entire length of the sidewalk," the *Alligator* reported. Dean Hale threatened suspensions and even expelled one track star. Covering the mob action, reporters attempted to categorize this act of rebellion as a "panty raid" to diminish its political import, but the event marked a spontaneous mass rejection of government intrusion into sexuality.

Standing near the Century Tower, a mid-campus clock building, Art Copleston watched the mob from a safe distance while pretending to feed Albert, the captive nine-foot-long alligator that the university kept as a mascot in a concrete pen. With police rhythmically pounding their nightsticks and the mob rallying and re-rallying, the bedlam from faraway looked and sounded like a prison-break scene in a movie. A curious part of him felt drawn to the action, while the more rational part of him knew that he couldn't risk joining a disruptive crowd. Besides, Copleston had loaded up on six classes that semester in a mad rush to graduate before administrators changed their minds about him.

Hardly seeing much of Professor Fogle or Bill Moore anymore, Copleston studied in his hermitage, stretched into Jim Steinbrenner's former section of the room, and fantasized about a future beyond the reach of Charley Johns. Somehow he got three A's that term. His only C was in "Elementary Accounting II." After getting pulled out of the final exam for introductory accounting by the Johns Committee, he never could rekindle a passion for the subject.

Copleston's case file clearly fell by the wayside, with bigger men in FLIC's crosshairs. He finished out the semester without any more classroom abductions or trips to a soundproof basement. For the upcoming fall, he was approved as a dorm counselor with a small associated stipend. His being awarded this position of authority over fellow students served as an indicator to Copleston that he might temporarily be out of the spotlight. He resumed his intensive weight-lifting regimen at the Florida Gym again, although he swore that Officer Tileston still tailed him to and from classes—chasing the dragon of a power high that he'd never quite feel again.

As Charley Johns turned his attentions to the burgeoning queer menace in Tampa, Tallahassee, and elsewhere, UF president J. Wayne

Reitz agreed to train his campus officers for moral "self-policing" with ongoing guidance from the committee; this would lead to the dismissal of at least six more faculty members and the departure of untold numbers of students, including future NOW activist and *Rubyfruit Jungle* author Rita Mae Brown, between the years of 1959 and 1965.

ACT III.

Orbit

CHAPTER 18

Open Season

*Hotel signage near the air
force base in Cocoa Beach*

June 1959 (*NAACP Files, DOE Files, Box 7*)

THROUGHOUT THE YEAR, federal missiles and rockets launched off Cape Canaveral in Florida at an accelerating clip. The coastal cape was first selected by the U.S. military as a launch site to take advantage of the Earth's rotation, since the planet's linear velocity is greatest toward the equator. Beyond scientific considerations, residents on the Cape and nearby Merritt Island were predominantly poor whites or poor Blacks and therefore more easily displaced via eminent domain. On February 6, the U.S. military achieved its first successful test firing of the Titan I intercontinental ballistic missile, which flew some three hundred miles off the coastline before plunging into the Atlantic.

With rocket propulsion science advancing on a weekly basis at Cape Canaveral, the comparatively antique and inefficient state of

Florida stood by at a distance—almost wholly cut off from NASA and learning of the latest developments through the press. A détente between state and federal powers took place: We won't interfere with your sweeping vision of the future, and you won't interfere with our daydream of "moonlight and magnolias" along de Sewanee River plantation. Besides, Democrats vying for a presidential slot—like Lyndon Johnson and John F. Kennedy—needed the southern Dixiecrats, including the Pork Choppers, aboard their wobbly coalition if they were going to seize the White House.

That June 1959, for the third time running, Democratic governor of Florida LeRoy Collins allowed a FLIC bill "to investigate certain organizations" to become law without his signature or signing statement. His silence gave the newly re-formed committee a veneer of carte blanche. On Monday, June 22, 1959, the U.S. Supreme Court officially denied a hearing to the Miami NAACP plaintiffs, including Father Theodore Gibson, who sought redress for the FLIC abuses of 1958. By a vote of 6 to 3, with Chief Justice Earl Warren dissenting, the high court decided, without stated rationale, to allow a December 1958 verdict of the Florida Supreme Court to stand against the NAACP. "I feel very good about the court ruling," gloated Charley Johns. "Hearings will be resumed." NAACP Legal Defense Fund attorney Robert L. Carter wrote the plaintiffs and identified a note of hope:

> I am not sure what the denial means. It could be based on the fact that conceivably the judgement is not final in view of the fact that we could go through another round in the courts by standing on our rights.

"I expect they will be breathing down our necks soon," Ruth Perry wrote back Carter. "I also imagine that you have noted that Cliff Herrell, my mortal enemy, is slated for the chairmanship. Well, as I see it from here, it all adds up to a regular witch hunt."

With Mark Hawes gearing up for more NAACP hearings that fall, chief investigator Remus Strickland recognized that he was freed up to pursue educators statewide. His experience with the way sixth-grade teacher Earl Fender, for example, had so quickly informed upon others assured him of more confessions leading to other teacher targets in his future. De-leashed, he tested the boundaries of his position and found them to be nonexistent.

By early summer, Strickland's extracurricular work had already led to several homosexual schoolteachers being outed and fired by the Florida Department of Education (DOE) as part of a planned 1959 purge. On June 15, four educators had their teaching certificates revoked for being "found guilty of committing acts of immoral nature." The DOE mailed the teachers identical form revocation letters, which included their names and certificate numbers:

> *Dear Sir:*
> *You are hereby notified that the certificates for the following persons have been revoked by the State Board of Education on June 16, 1959:*
>
> *Raymond Bruce Capella, Graduate Certificate 23656*
> *Lester Robinson McCartney, Graduate Certificate 74203*
> *Charles Howard Montague, Jr., Graduate Certificate 82868*
> *Jack Vernon Priest, Post Graduate Certificate 91864*
>
> *The above action is in accordance with the provisions of Sections 229.17(16), 231.28 and 230.33(21), Florida Statutes.*
> *Cordially Yours,*
> *Thomas D. Bailey, Secretary*
> *State Board of Education*

Two of the revocation notices, those sent to Capella and Priest, came back undelivered, suggesting that the men chose to flee rather than face an oncoming disgrace. The former Sarasota high school English teacher Charles Howard Montague Jr. already sat in prison, convicted of the aforementioned "crime against nature" involving a teenage boy, and it appeared that Capella had fled probation for a similar assault. Lester Robinson McCartney, a married father of three entrapped by Strickland at the Alachua County courthouse, wrote back that he "did not wish to appear before the Board and would not contest the revocation." McCartney's children would all have been younger than ten years old at the time.

Carelessly, the press treated McCartney's noncriminal indiscretions as equal to Montague's and Capella's convictions of pedophilia as well as Priest's conviction for "immoral" conduct. The educators' names appeared lumped together in Florida newspapers alongside a vague rationale for their dismissals. "Four Teachers Fired by State Cabinet on Morals Charge," read the *Pensacola News Journal*. "Cabinet Revokes Certificates of Four Teachers," wrote *The Tampa Tribune*. Although the Florida Department of Education attested to the press that all four teachers had been "found guilty" of something reprehensible, the DOE's own dismissal records for Lester Robinson McCartney clearly specify that he had only "admitted under oath to the Florida Legislative Investigation Committee of having participated in numerous homosexual contacts." McCartney was never charged, indicted, or convicted in court. The inaccuracy in the public malignment of McCartney made it crucial, from a risk management standpoint, for the defamed man to confirm that he would "not contest," lest the lawsuit commence. As with the UF professors whose names appeared in *The Gainesville Sun*, Florida authorities used publicity to convict the man in spirit.

That August, testing his ever-expanding clout, Remus Strickland issued a memorandum to all Florida school superintendents demanding the names of every teacher dismissed on morals charges in the past five years "to weed out known homosexuals who are now affiliated with the public school systems." Teachers who were confirmed subversives, Strickland well understood, could be pressed into giving up all their deviate friends in the profession, who otherwise remain incognito from school to school. "We are trying to set up some type of centralized file or system whereby School Superintendents throughout the State can be informed, upon request, in re: of any such person or persons whose name is contained in such a file," Strickland informed in the memorandum, which he drafted and distributed without a committee vote.

On June 24, 1959, Charley Johns reconvened the Johns Committee in house room 50 of the state capitol. The required rotation of the chairmanship between senators and house members meant that Char-

ley couldn't hold on to the position, so he called for his FLIC lieutenant, "big-city Pork Chopper" Cliff Herrell, to bravely lead the troops
into the next session. After being unanimously approved, Chairman
Herrell made it his first act to formally commend the great Charley
Johns for the "excellent manner in which he handled the chairmanship
of the previous Committee." This would be the only meeting of FLIC
until late 1960, when Chairman Herrell would be elevated to the Florida senate and compelled, in turn, to hand over his FLIC position to a
Florida house member.

From mid-1959 until that time, Herrell led in name only. The bulk
of FLIC's activities under his rule transpired in an intelligence vacuum—
unknown often even to him. FLIC staff, rather than committee members, took the initiative in a quiet coup. "My instructions came through
Hawes, and he informed on a daily basis to the Chairman," Strickland
blustered. "I reported to Hawes just about every day over the telephone." In truth, Hawes and Strickland planned their own missions,
maintaining their own calendars and notifying Chairman Herrell only
when they needed his statutory powers to clear their way. "As long as
this investigation is producing in the manner that it is at the present
time," Strickland wrote to Mark Hawes, "that maybe the best thing to
do would be to continue on as we are now without stepping in with
any member of the Committee."

As if gazing at a full map of possibilities, Strickland chose a new
investigatory turf for 1959 and 1960: the Florida Sun Coast, a gleam-
ing wonderland of New Florida, which differed markedly from old-
timey Gainesville. Tampa and St. Petersburg, twin cities on Tampa
Bay, were linked in prosperity and innovative spirit by a fourteen-mile-
long bridge system named the Sunshine Skyway. The trestle design of
the Skyway, opened in 1954, was a feat of modern engineering, and
Charley Johns presided over its dedication. Altogether, the Sun Coast
region boasted some 630,000 Floridians, with such a baby boom that
it educated no less than 115,000 school-age children. To meet statewide enrollment demand, most pronounced along the Sun Coast, state
superintendent Thomas Bailey of the Florida Department of Education oversaw a hiring spree that in 1957 alone brought in some 5,000
new educators.

But hidden in this metropole of the Sunshine Skyway was a "deviate" underground. Bars like the Knotty Pine served gay Tampans, while Jimmy White's Tavern catered to lesbians. Tampa detectives called their city Florida's new homosexual "headquarters," but most Sun Coasters tried to overlook unsavoriness, as it was certain to lower property values if it was publicized. Police supposedly kept a lid on bachelors, fans of the "ill-famed," "B-drinkers," and sexual eccentrics by harassing gay men and, it was rumored, sexually engaging with the odd lesbian to set her straight. "We never had it so good!" boasted a local real estate advertisement. "A neighborhood we are proud to live in, our own Citrus Trees and top it all CENTRALLY LOCATED!"

Post-Gainesville, school administrators and officials like DOE superintendent Thomas Bailey were suddenly concerned about the morality of whomever they'd thrown in front of classrooms in the mad dash to staff schools. Could it be, Bailey and Strickland worried, that a few perverts snuck in with the bunch? Encouraged by the results of his initial interrogation sessions of homosexual instructors, Strickland sensed a need to press the local school districts harder for answers. State law mandated that Florida schoolteachers "by precept and example" exemplify "patriotism and the practice of every Christian virtue." Charges against teachers could therefore entail any range of personal or professional conduct that violated social norms. In other words, an investigator like Strickland had wide leeway to hit his mark.

Though in its 1959 report to the legislature FLIC got an audible reaction from legislators by describing former deputy sheriff Bill Donaldson's foiled investigation involving twenty-seven homosexual teachers salted throughout Tampa's Hillsborough County, FLIC still had yet to properly vet the allegation. Months later, Strickland sought retrospective evidence to back up what his committee had already disclosed in writing to the entire state government. Strickland's excursion into Hillsborough County looking for the fabled twenty-seven teachers turned up few clues tying to the historic investigation, but Strickland did uncover tangential new leads through his aggressive tactics and menacing presence. "I consider myself determined," Strickland explained in his defense. "I don't play hanky-panky, and I'm not the most diplomatic person. . . . An attorney once called me uncouth." He knew any firings he could drum up personally would pad FLIC's tally of exposed "perverts" and add to his job security. Swinging his ax widely time and again, the executioner eventually struck a neck.

As about 73 percent of Florida's schoolteachers were women in the 1959 school year, Strickland soon found himself interrogating a bounty of female educators in Tampa for the first time. Former deputy Donaldson had warned FLIC, "The hardest that I found to break is the females; they go right to the bitter end before they finally give up," and Strickland revealed himself befuddled by several basic nuances of womanhood.

For example, in an interrogation of a divorced woman named Evelyn in Tampa on October 6, 1959, Strickland revealed himself as perplexed about how two female bodies might arrange themselves to facilitate sexual climax.

STRICKLAND: In making love to the female, what part do you play?

EVELYN: Strictly a woman myself.

STRICKLAND: You play the fem or the butch?

EVELYN: I told you, I guess the woman.

STRICKLAND: In other words, you play the fem. Have you ever played the butch part?

EVELYN: No, I don't think so.

STRICKLAND: Well, either you have, or you haven't.

EVELYN: Have you heard of any such thing in your life?

Yet through several eager-to-please informants who came forward such as Kathryn, a morally conscientious Florida State ex-coed, Strickland got an education about women. He became fixated on the notion of lesbian softball players, as if the primary function of a women's softball league wasn't sporting competition and socialization but lesbian incubation.

Hot on the trail of a lead, Strickland asked an East Bay High School gym teacher named Pat Wilson, a woman falsely accused of frequenting the Tampa lesbian bar Jimmy White's, for the names of members of her softball team as well as its playing roster. In a separate interrogation of Tarpon Springs High School physical education teacher

Margie DeGrow, Strickland asked for the names of DeGrow's softball team members, and DeGrow, reading Strickland's rather telegraphed intent, declined to take part in the "vicious circle" by naming them. Absent confessions, softball players DeGrow and Wilson kept their names and careers intact from those who would meddle.

Shadowing public school teachers and junior college instructors, rather than university professors, required Strickland to collaborate closely with State Superintendent Thomas Bailey and the Florida Department of Education, an entirely different department from the Florida Board of Control (BOC), which oversaw the state university system. The DOE's statutory process for firing a hypothetical kindergarten teacher and revoking a teaching certificate, as laid out by Senate Bill 237 (passed unanimously in 1959 with the support of Charley Johns), was cumbersome, involving more bureaucratic steps than the BOC dismissing the odd university professor for cause.

Under Senate Bill 237, there was a mandatory procedure. The DOE couldn't just send an investigator to look into a suspected teacher. Rather, a valid morals claim had to originate autonomously. When such a claim arose, the DOE could then empanel an investigating committee to research the allegation. If probable cause of misconduct could be established, a DOE hearing officer would then set a hearing date and notify the teacher of charges.

Rather than obey this newly enshrined law, Strickland violated it in the spirit of subversion hunting. He struck an off-the-record "gentleman's agreement" with DOE superintendent Thomas Bailey. Their handshake deal permitted Strickland to conduct preliminary "probable cause" work, claim or no claim against an educator. Within sixty days of the passage of SB-237, the head of the DOE himself invited an extrajudicial investigator to circumvent the law he'd lobbied into passage. Any Strickland-gathered materials "pertaining to the activities of teachers in the state" were to be "furnished to the state superintendent's office" so that Bailey could use them as evidence in DOE disciplinary proceedings and firings.

Strickland thus became a roving authority. All the powers of Florida—executive, legislative, judicial, and extrajudicial—coursed through his fingers, just as he steadily filed his per diem and car mileage reimbursements and cashed his $700-per-month paychecks. In response to Strickland's 1959 memorandum to all school superintendents for intelligence from the past five years "to weed out known homosexuals," many school districts initially reacted with caution and referred Strickland back to Superintendent Bailey, their highest authority. Bailey assuaged their concerns, and by that September, the DOE rank and file accepted their marching orders: Help the man or else.

CHAPTER 19

Predator/Prey

A mother escorts her two daughters to Orchard Villa Elementary School

1959 (*Box 7, Box 8*)

K-12 EDUCATORS—BLINDSIDED BY homosexual accusations, humiliated by the casual use of sexual terminology, and given no advanced warning of charges against them—stood little chance against Remus Strickland. Under duress, they inevitably tried to appease the hefty man they believed to be an irate state lawyer quoting confusing legalese. Time and again, the chief investigator secured his tape-recorded confession.

In St. Petersburg, Strickland bilked an admission of homosexual guilt out of Tyrone Junior High School librarian Bill Livingston, who was fired. On December 7, 1959, Strickland interrogated St. Petersburg Junior College social sciences professor Glenn McRae under oath at a remote location. After personally swearing in McRae and reminding the witness of the penalties of perjury, Strickland pressured the junior college professor into conceding his participation in homosexual contact. It was a textbook evisceration. First, Strickland used McRae's admission of serving in the federal Civilian Conservation Corps to imply that he may have met homosexuals in his travels.

> STRICKLAND: You say that while you were in the service you
>   did come in contact with these type of people on occasions,
>   didn't you, sir?
> McRAE: Yes, sir.

Next, Strickland asked McRae to testify to his whereabouts during the past few days and warned the witness about giving false testimony.

> STRICKLAND: I furthermore intend to go in this record that you
>   are under oath, sir.
> McRAE: Yes, sir.
> STRICKLAND: You have already violated that oath, sir.
> McRAE: In what way?
> STRICKLAND: On more than one occasion. Now I'm trying to
>   be as fair with you as I possibly can.
> McRAE: I'm trying to be as honest with you as I can, Mr.
>   Strickland.
> STRICKLAND: But I in turn expect the same thing with you. I'm
>   asking in good faith about these people because I know who
>   they are. If I didn't, I would have asked you. Well . . .

McRae started to protest, "I mean, to me this violates . . ." before Strickland cut him off. "You did not go to your mother's home as you stated yesterday afternoon," Strickland said flatly. McRae then began rattling off the names of homosexual friends in a panic, admitting to Strickland, "This naming of names, I can't think straight, and this isn't an act, either." Watching the witness squirm, Strickland sprang another trap while ignoring McRae's implied request for a lawyer.

STRICKLAND: Mr. McRae, have you yourself personally within the last year had any type of homosexual activity, sir?

McRAE: Yes, sir.

STRICKLAND: Where was that, sir?

McRAE: Here again I feel as though I am being backed up in a corner. I realize your statement, and I am trying to accept it in all faith, but I feel as though, is this not the point where I should have some advice?

STRICKLAND: Mr. McRae, this is a fact-finding Committee, not a prosecuting one.

McRAE: Well, what's going to happen?

Strickland gave the standard monologue, which he'd learned from Mark Hawes, to bewilder McRae into believing there would be no consequences to his confession, while feigning to inform him of his legal options. Oblivious to the illegality of Strickland's methods during his deposition, Glenn McRae did his best to accommodate the exasperated lawman pressing for answers. At one point, Strickland provoked McRae into revealing the investigator's habit of turning the deposition tape on and off—in essence, tampering with evidence. "When I expressed to you a while ago when the tape was off," McRae said, "I would have come to you if I knew of any instance where professional people were using their professional sources or occupations as a source of procurement." Rather than get heated at the prospect of having his tactics laid bare, Strickland barreled ahead cheerfully. Evidently, at this stage in the probe, Strickland understood himself to be above the rules.

Despite Strickland's vague assurances of protection from prosecution, he almost immediately reported to Chairman Herrell that the junior college professor "admitted his participation in homosexual activity and in turn named three other teachers." Glenn McRae was fired, and his teaching certificate was revoked.

Strickland often tried to unsettle witnesses into confessions by using profane language or making shocking statements. On October 14, 1960, when interrogating a married St. Petersburg High School social studies teacher and father of four named LeRoy Kaufman, Strickland employed this gambit.

STRICKLAND: Mr. Kaufman, have you ever made the statement
    to a student that you can recall whereas you stated that
    there was no lunch like the cream of the crotch?
KAUFMAN: That I have no knowledge of.
STRICKLAND: You don't remember making the statement?
KAUFMAN: Me?
STRICKLAND: Yes.
KAUFMAN: No. I don't remember making the statement. I
    might have, but I don't remember, I don't remember the
    statement. . . .

Later in the interrogation, Strickland tried to confuse Kaufman
into agreeing that he'd stated the phrase first.

STRICKLAND: You made the statement as I said before that
    you've made the statement that you've never eaten lunch
    until you've had the cream of a crotch. . . .
KAUFMAN: I never made the statement. That I'm positive of. I
    will say that under oath.

Kaufman denied inappropriate contact with students or any homosexual conduct. As a result, the father of four kept his job of three decades, his reputation, his family, and his teaching credentials.

Often, Strickland swooped down on educators already arrested for
gay offenses so as to interrogate them at his leisure. For example, Ellis
Vern Clack was a Merritt Island Elementary School principal charged
in July 1959 with "unlawfully and feloniously fondling a minor boy
aged 15." A Boy Scout leader and sponsor of a gun club for teenagers,
Clack had been one of several local leaders who'd co-created a summer
recreation program for Merritt Island boys. In anticipation of oncoming legal charges, Clack had announced his early retirement as school
principal and tried to skip town. According to one *Miami Herald* report, Clack planned to move back to Mississippi due to a heart ailment
and "live quietly" with his mother. Authorities caught Ellis Vern Clack
as he was packing his bags to get away.

As the last vulture to tear at the carrion, Remus Strickland descended upon Clack while the man awaited his court hearing—out on

bond that August 6, 1959. Strickland claimed to be particularly interested in the case because, as Merritt Island school principal, Clack had known Earl Fender, the Merritt Island teacher up on FLIC perjury charges for his relationship with UF professor Leslie Murray.

After Strickland placed Clack under oath, the witness revealed himself to be a serial pedophile with predilections for male children, a predator who hid among local homosexuals as social cover, but who did not share their same desires for consensual adult relations.

STRICKLAND: You then state your conduct has been only in the handling and playing with other organs of younger boys, is that correct, sir?

CLACK: Yes.

STRICKLAND: Have you ever done that with another adult person, sir?

CLACK: No, sir.

STRICKLAND: Can you tell me why this is attractive to you, sir?

CLACK: No, probably from their approaches.

STRICKLAND: What do you mean, "from their approaches"?

CLACK: The way they approach it themselves.

STRICKLAND: In what way, sir?

CLACK: In playing around.

Somehow, by wantonly violating the privacy of countless teachers, Strickland had unwittingly found himself face-to-face with a pedophile confessing on the record. Yet Strickland's devotion to recruitment theory, to preventing youth from being "influenced into homosexual practices," kept him from seeing pedophilia as anything other than a mechanism for homosexual recruitment, a means for homosexuals to propagate themselves rather than a separate disorder targeting children who were blameless for their abusers' violations.

After Strickland elicited Clack's admission, his main concern in the interrogation was the degree to which Clack's serial pedophilia may have converted Clark's adolescent and preadolescent victims into homosexuals.

STRICKLAND: Mr. Clack, did it ever occur to you that by handling these boys in such a manner that there was a great possibility that once these students became older that this might have a bearing on them, from a sexual standpoint, in their future life?

CLACK: No, sir, because if it was regular, yes, it might have.

STRICKLAND: Didn't you fully realize that this might destroy those boys, socially and otherwise, sir?

CLACK: No, sir, because if it had been a regular type of thing, it would have.

STRICKLAND: If a student tells me that he has been around you, with you, and participated with you in this type of thing for the last four or five years, is that true or false?

CLACK: I would say it would be false.

STRICKLAND: If this happened, don't you think there would be a danger of that boy becoming a confirmed homosexual?

CLACK: Sure.

STRICKLAND: In the near future?

CLACK: Regularly, yes.

STRICKLAND: Is there any student you know of, Mr. Clack, in your school, from having been around them, with them, and looking after them, you think now might be served by giving them some kind of treatment or having them consult a psychiatrist?

CLACK: No.

STRICKLAND: Do you think any of these boys have gone so far there might be a salvage for them, should we conduct a program at this time of having them submitted for the correct type of treatment that might be demanded?

CLACK: I don't know of anybody that is that far.

STRICKLAND: Do you know of any of them that have far enough gone that it would be beneficial to them to take them in?

CLACK: No, sir.

Ellis Vern Clack's declarations under oath resulted in no FLIC outreach to provide support and/or psychological counseling to the victims of Clack's serial abuse. In fact, Clack's victims appear to have been treated as sexually suspect—in essence, maligned and blamed as accessories to their abuser. Many Merritt Island parents did not wish to stigmatize their sons or to put them at further risk of becoming homosexual by inviting them to dwell upon the inappropriate contact.

Other than having his teaching credentials case referred to the DOE, which speedily revoked them, the former principal Ellis Vern Clack did not face a reckoning from FLIC for his string of crimes, and the story of his arrest for "fondling" disappeared from state newspapers by August 12, 1959. Puzzlingly, FLIC did not make moves to capitalize on Clark's confession of pedophilia to Strickland through the press, as it chose to do concerning the confession of homosexual acts by married high school teacher Lester Robinson McCartney, a nonpedophile who was not charged with a sex crime by law enforcement.

Ellis Vern Clack died as a free man in a veteran's hospital in Jackson, Mississippi, on September 11, 1965. His obituary in the Mississippi newspaper *The Clarion-Ledger* described him as "a former school teacher" who'd "made his home in Jackson for the past four years." A World War II veteran, Clark received burial with full military honors.

In the midst of Strickland's one-man war on the Florida Sun Coast, the Dade County School Board made good on its promise to "voluntarily" integrate the first public grade school under Florida's pupil assignment law "or the federal courts will stuff it down our throats." That September 8, the first calendar day of the 1959 schoolyear, four Black pupils—Jan Errol Glover, nine; Irene Amanda Glover, seven; Sherry Marie Joseph, six; and Gary Chandler Range, six—arrived outside Miami's Orchard Villa Elementary School.

Unlike the violent desegregation scenes happening in front of Clinton High School in 1956 Tennessee or Central High School in 1957 Arkansas, Jan and Irene Glover simply said goodbye to their mother and walked without police escort alongside white peers into the building. Florida governor LeRoy Collins offered few words for the historic moment: "I can't see anything which would warrant any comment from me." State superintendent Thomas Bailey hedged his reaction by noting that local school boards were legally authorized to integrate or not integrate as desired. "This school board is operating under the provisions of the state pupil assignment law," said Bailey, "and from apparent reports I have received is apparently doing so in a peaceful atmosphere."

As Jan and Irene Glover strode into Orchard Villa Elementary, NAACP Miami president Father Theodore Gibson stood across the street with tears in his eyes, but declined to comment, wary of causing racial incitement. "I would not want to make any statement that might interfere with progress in the schools," Gibson explained. Although Florida White Citizens' Council leader Fred Hockett arrived at Orchard Villa ready to stir up a ruckus, the school principal denied him access to the opening-day press conference. Slack-jawed, Hockett was forced to stand back and observe the integration from a safe distance.

Five years post-*Brown*, an equal education had arrived in time for four Black youngsters—but not for one single more of the state's estimated 187,742 "Negro" schoolchildren. Days later in mid-Florida, eleven Black students were formally denied admittance to the new all-white Dixie M. Hollins High School in Pinellas County. Per usual, defenders of the "way" changed the ground rules and invented new means to prevail.

CHAPTER 20

King of Florida

A postcard advertising Florida
wildlife

October 1959 (*Box 2, Box 3, Box 7, Box 8*)

STRICKLAND PLUGGED AWAY in his teacher investigations throughout the state from early 1959 throughout 1960. With his secret inquisitions unchallenged, he expanded his probe at will from Hillsborough and Pinellas Counties to Bradford, Brevard, Citrus, Collier, Columbia, Dade, Duval, Gilcrest, Hardee, Highlands, Lake, Manatee, Orange, Palm Beach, and Sarasota. Strickland offhandedly wrote to Chairman Herrell: "Leaving the office this morning to make a final sweep of the State in an attempt to gather all information and data possible in re: of the 141 teachers whom we have names." Operating with legal free rein, he went wherever the new leads, racial or sexual, took him.

The pace of his findings and the scope of his task soon overwhelmed the stout detective, and he began to campaign FLIC superiors for more staffers. A sympathetic Charley Johns took up the issue with the governor's office. "Personally, and confidentially, we have asked the Cabinet for some help," Charley wrote Senator W. Turner Davis. "They will give Strick two or three men who are presently employed." Ultimately, Strickland commanded a staff of twelve, including seven field officers.

Nightmare stories circulated from all corners of the Panhandle and peninsula. On a trip to Miami that October 1959, Strickland ordered the Florida highway patrol to detain one Frank S. Wright, a political insider who'd helped run Pork Chopper Fuller Warren's gubernatorial campaign. The highway patrol arrested Warren and held him without charges for two days. On February 3, 1960, Remus Strickland instructed a Naples police officer to handcuff a fifth-grade schoolteacher named John B. Rooney Jr., in front of his elementary school. They hauled off the teacher and youth basketball coach, his arms full of team jerseys, for a so-called sweat session. The Strickland/Rooney encounter transpired with Kafkaesque degrees of menace, as later avowed by Rooney in an affidavit:

> [Police] forced the affiant [Rooney] to submit to being hand-cuffed and put into the police car and was taken to police headquarters in the City of Naples where the affiant was ushered into a room and the door was locked behind him.
>
> Affiant later learned and saw a tape recorder in operation concealed and disguised. Affiant was introduced to a man who stated that his name was R. J. Strickland of Gainesville, Florida and who said he was a lawyer and exhibited a card to show that he was an investigator for the State Board of Education. . . .

Strickland recorded only about 40 minutes of his 3.5-hour deposition with the fifth-grade teacher, during which Rooney did not confess despite several attempts to humiliate him into compliance by implying that he liked to dress in drag. Unluckily for Strickland, this elementary school teacher he manhandled turned out to be politically well connected—brother-in-law to Florida senator G. W. "Dick" Williams of Hardee County. A defense attorney and longtime friend of the Rooney family sent an irate letter to the DOE on June 22, 1960. "This young man's father [John B. Rooney Sr.] was Superintendent of Public Instruction for many years," wrote the lawyer. "They are a pioneer family."

The defense attorney poked holes in Strickland's interrogation.

"The procedure for the exercise of power of investigation and disqual-
ification of teachers has been completely ignored, with no chance to be
heard, with an arrest as a common criminal for no reason on earth,"
he noted. Stumbling over himself in response, Florida DOE superintendent Thomas Bailey wrote back sorrowfully, but declined to take
responsibility: "Mr. R. J. Strickland is not employed by the State Board
of Education. . . . As State Superintendent of Public Instruction, I have
neither authority nor responsibility for Mr. Strickland's investigative
procedures."

When Strickland caught wind of the lawyer's letter and read the
victim's statement, he wrote an angry rejoinder. In the subtext of
Rooney's affidavit was the accusation that the chief investigator was
practicing law without a license—a jailable offense, if noticed. Undoubtedly, Strickland cut corners by pretending to be a state attorney
when it suited him and swearing witnesses under oath for testimony
through the random happenstance of his being a public notary in his
free time—but not a court official.

Before anyone could realize they had him dead to rights, he attacked. Threatening perjury charges against Rooney, Strickland promised to make the allegations public. "I am sure that Mr. Hawes will
advise you that Mr. Rooney is entitled to a public hearing before this
Committee," Strickland blustered. The chief investigator played the
public hearing card, knowing full well that Florida elites would do virtually anything to avoid an incident that would embroil a state senator
who voted with the Pork Choppers. On a mission that day, Strickland
typed out a second letter suggesting a public hearing—this one to
FLIC chairman Cliff Herrell.

Hurt and frightened by the language that the defense lawyer had
used, Strickland sought vindication through Johns Committee ave-
nues. Strickland's overreaction did scare Rooney back to the bargain-
ing table, pressuring the man to cut a deal so that Strickland would
work his levers to quash the committee's nuclear option of publicity.
Rather than acknowledge his unlawful arrest and false imprisonment,
this wrongfully accused Florida insider with powerful relatives decided to deal. The Florida DOE did not terminate or sully the name of
fifth-grade teacher John B. Rooney Jr., and Strickland agreed to forget
the whole thing and investigate others.

March 1960 brought a new wave of sit-ins and protests across Florida. In Tampa, thirty-six high school members of the local NAACP youth council staged a demonstration at white lunch counters. On March 12, a consortium of about sixty integrationist leaders from assorted groups, including the Southern Conference Educational Fund (SCEF) and the NAACP, met at the Unitarian Church in Orlando to set up a communications hub to conduct a coordinated civil rights campaign in Florida and to "watch the legislature."

Strickland recruited three white Floridians to infiltrate the meeting and sent them in undercover. Posing as integrationists, these citizen snoops—Mrs. Fannie Collins, the wife of an Orlando dentist; Ernest Salley, a state road commission employee; and Mary Mueller, a former secretary of the Florida Legislative Investigation Committee—acted as Strickland's eyes and ears. Each informant received a wholly unauthorized memorandum "TO WHOM IT MAY CONCERN" from Strickland deputizing them as a state spy. For this work, they each received $25 in compensation out of FLIC's revolving fund.

At the SCEF summit in Orlando, Strickland's little birdies came in contact with mainstream civil rights group like the NAACP, along with members of the civil rights fringe, such as a committee to "secure justice" for atomic spies Julius and Ethel Rosenberg. FLIC's agents signed up to receive the SCEF mailing list at their home addresses and thereby gained access to the SCEF membership rolls for Florida, which they dutifully passed on to their spymasters. Tantalizingly for Hawes and Strickland, SCEF members on that list staffed the leadership ranks of the Florida NAACP.

The Orlando dentist's wife Fannie Collins attended a workshop and was able to confirm to Strickland that the SCEF summit was led by none other than Carl Braden. Braden was an NAACP member previously cited by the House Un-American Activities Committee as a "card-carrying" Communist. Hawes and Strickland did a bit more digging and discovered that the SCEF had been characterized as "closely allied with the Communist Party" by one HUAC representative named Donald L. Jackson in 1958. In the press, FLIC made hay out of Carl Braden's Communist affiliations and announced a plan to subpoena him in Tallahassee for a new round of FLIC hearings. Mark Hawes hoped that ensnaring Braden on perjury charges could lead to subpoenaing Braden's colleagues in the movement. Hawes particularly salivated on the notion of getting Dr. Martin Luther King Jr. under oath.

In response to the racial unrest, Governor LeRoy Collins took to the airwaves at 5:30 p.m. on March 20, 1960. Addressing his state at large, the governor pivoted from his moderate stance on segregation toward something unexpected. "I believe very deeply that I represent every man, woman, and child in this state as their governor, whether that person is black or white," Collins began as preamble. Indeed, in his final, lame-duck year as chief executive, Collins found his voice for integration. "I believe that the face of Florida—the image of Florida—is not in its pine trees or in its palm trees or even in its orange trees, but in the people of this state; I believe that large star on our map of the United States that represents Florida stands for the people of Florida," he continued.

Over the course of his thirty-minute broadcast, Collins emerged as the first southern governor to speak on the moral need to end segregation. Collins linked Florida's racial dilemma to broader stakes of America in the Cold War and rebuked the established position of Pork Choppers that racial issues would get solved by quashing Black activism:

> Friends, we must find answers. There is absolutely nothing that can aid the Communists more at this time in establishing supremacy over the United States—and that is their ambition—than racial strife in this country.
>
> Now friends, that's not a Christian point of view. That's not a democratic point of view. That's a realistic point of view. We can never stop Americans from struggling to be free. We can never stop Americans from hoping and praying that someday in some way, this ideal that is embedded in our Declaration of Independence is one of these truths that are inevitable: that all men are created equal, that, that somehow will be a reality and not just an illusory distant goal.

The top story in *The Miami Herald* the next day read "Let Negroes Eat in Stores Where They Trade—Collins." In letters to the editor, white Florida voters accused Collins of "adding fuel to the fire" and making their state a laughingstock. Theodore Gibson declared Collins "one of the greatest statesmen Florida has ever known." Senator Charley Johns boiled with anger at the words of his former opponent. This never would have happened had he kept the mansion, he exclaimed to allies. How can segregationists expect to stay in power when they lose the southern trump card of segregation?

That May 1960, for the first time in recent memory, Charley Johns faced a contested primary for his Union County and Bradford County senate seat. "Word is out that Charley, now a bank president, has been too busy with private business affairs to keep up the 'grass roots' contact with many old friends," reported *The Miami Herald*. Campaigning feverishly, Charley held lengthy rallies that featured the loud horn-blowing of supporters, and voters swept Charley Johns back into office by a three-to-one margin in the first primary vote.

Other veteran Pork Choppers faced the same sort of primary challenges from the next generation of white Floridians. Almost unthinkably, the Pork Choppers lost a stalwart voice: three-term senator Newman Brackin, a former senate president from the Panhandle. Though the Pork Choppers still mustered a legislative majority, these small defeats sent a ripple through the tribal ranks. If Brackin could go down swinging, who might be next?

National Democratic Party leaders rewarded outgoing Florida governor LeRoy Collins for his newfound racial stances by naming him chairman of the 1960 Democratic National Convention. Party pundits considered him a possible nominee for Senator John F. Kennedy's vice presidential ticket as part of the Democratic southern strategy, although the Kennedys eventually went with Senate Majority Leader Lyndon B. Johnson of Texas.

Collins's successor to the Florida governorship, former state house speaker Farris Bryant, squeaked into the Democratic nomination in a nail-biter by running on Collins's former platform of states' rights and stay the course. Warnings from opposing candidate Doyle E. Carlton Jr. that Bryant would "turn back the clock" went ignored, and Bryant vowed to avoid the subject of race as governor-elect: "The less said about segregation, the better. To talk about it merely incites the people." (Florida governors Collins and Bryant, respectively, would accept future positions in the Johnson administration as point persons to southern governors during implementation of the Civil Rights Act.)

As Remus Strickland inserted himself into the affairs of school after school, his dogged pursuit of alleged homosexuals verged on megalomania. He interceded in the hiring processes of Florida junior colleges. In June 1960, for example, Strickland sent a letter to Florida senator-elect Dempsey J. Barron about a candidate for the presidential position at Panama City Junior College in Barron's hometown. The candidate in question, Dr. Marion Jennings Rice, was a reputable professor at the University of Georgia. But Rice had previously worked overseas for the U.S. Department of State, and Strickland had the instinct to write the feds for his background file. When the inquiry, according to Strickland, "could not be answered due to their rules and regulations concerning the giving out of confidential information," Strickland telephoned a personal contact at the State Department to glean what needed to be known. As Strickland relayed:

> Since I had been so helpful to them in handing various matters of interest to that Department, they wanted to inform me that Mr. Rice had been asked to resign from his duties with the Department of State in 1957 due to the facts that had been uncovered involving his conduct and participation in moral conduct charges.

Strickland conveyed this unfounded rumor from a possibly nonexistent source back to the Florida DOE, and Rice was not hired. Afterward, the Panama City Junior College hiring committee wrote Charley Johns to thank FLIC for its assistance: "In the last several weeks I have had the opportunity to work with Mr. R. J. Strickland, a member of your Committee, in working on some unpleasant problems in our county. I, now, better understand the problem that your Committee is faced with [and], therefore, hope that we can be of some help to you."

Reaching full force as a stand-alone investigator and state punisher, Strickland developed a habit of bypassing the DOE's disciplinary processes entirely to jump straight into sentencing. In an illegal stratagem that he tape-recorded for posterity, Strickland would demand that cer-

tain teachers in the hot seat surrender their certificate directly to him
to save everyone the time and aggravation. For example, on October
11, 1960, Strickland visited a former Monroe Junior High School music teacher from Tampa named Paul Stephen Houk, who sat in Pinellas
County jail. Houk, a World War II veteran turned educator, was arrested on August 18, 1960, for "contributing to the delinquency of a
minor" and convicted shortly thereafter. Rather than permit the Florida DOE to initiate a revocation process against Houk, Strickland
took that process upon himself.

> STRICKLAND: Mr. Houk, previously explaining to you the
>   nature of the charges against you and the position that will
>   be taken by the State Board of Education, as far as
>   revocation of your certificate is concerned, do you
>   understand that?
> HOUK: Yes, sir. I believe so.
> STRICKLAND: You understand that under the conditions as they
>   exist today and under subsection 16, section 229.08 Florida
>   Statutes, that your certificate will be revoked?
> HOUK: Yes, sir.
> STRICKLAND: Do you wish to have revocation served upon you
>   by the State Department of Education, or do you prefer to
>   voluntarily submit your certificate or surrender your
>   certificate to the State Department?
> HOUK: I voluntarily surrender my certificate to the State
>   Department.

When a teacher Strickland interrogated at a Florida highway patrol
station in Tampa resigned immediately after the encounter, which dis-
satisfied Stickland, the chief investigator chased the man through the
mail with scare tactics to ensure that he never taught again:

> I am therefore asking that you submit your Certificate #28851 to
> the State Department of Education for revocation, along with a
> letter surrendering same . . . [or] submit to a polygraph test to
> such questions that I might choose to propound you.

Few FLIC members made the effort to learn of Strickland's exploits, except to manage the rare bout of negative press or political blowback. Men like Chairman Herrell appreciated Strickland's results and frequently passed on their compliments. As he had done during the Gainesville campaign, Strickland demurred when asked by the press about his agenda at Sun Coast schools. "I can't tell you my purpose," he told the *Tampa Bay Times*. He then falsely implied that Black activists were his target: "Due to the recent Negro sit-downs, everyone around the state is tense." Racial unrest functioned as convenient cover.

The one and only official to whom Strickland stood accountable from 1959 to 1961, FLIC chairman Cliff Herrell, was largely preoccupied with a state senate campaign, and his leadership style, when compared with that of Charley Johns, was remarkably at arm's length. Why mess with what worked? "As an investigator, he got out of hand," Herrell later conceded without taking responsibility for his failure to take Strickland to task. "He got overzealous," Herrell qualified, balancing criticism with admiration for the man's pluck. A white go-getter cop could hardly be a threat to the law of the South.

CHAPTER 21

Radical Steps

A postcard of the Sunshine Skyway

October 1960 (*NAACP Papers, Box 8*)

CHIEF INVESTIGATOR REMUS Strickland's forays into Tampa's and St. Petersburg's segregated school systems inevitably placed him in isolated rooms with Black educators accused of sexual offenses, which brought to light an awkward intersection of prejudices among both white and Black elites.

Broadly speaking, the civil rights movement strove for racial equality through an end to segregation while batting down constant accusations of un-Americanism and treason lobbed by white supremacists. The movement largely eschewed tangential topics that risked distracting it from its primary goal. Major figures like NAACP executive director Roy Wilkins viewed Black homosexuals as a liability to the cause, and the NAACP maintained no official stance on homosexuality other than it being an illegal act worthy of arrest or military discharge. When James Farmer, executive director of the Congress of Racial Equality, better known as CORE, issued a call in 1961 for Freedom Riders to test illegal segregation in interstate bus travel, he made sure to character-test the candidates for their very public roles. "We recruited a small group of 13 persons, carefully selected and screened,"

Farmer affirmed, choosing his words conscientiously, "because we wanted to be sure that our adversaries could not dig up derogatory information on any individual and use that to smear the movement." Black gay men who were civil rights leaders, such as author James Baldwin or Southern Christian Leadership Conference (SCLC) strategist Bayard Rustin, were expected to keep their private lives private so as not to enrage Black church folk or the white populace.

Bayard Rustin was a former high school football player. A Pennsylvania Quaker, he applied for a World War II draft deferment as a religious conscientious objector, for which he served a federal prison term. In 1942 he co-formed the Congress of Racial Equality with James Farmer to protest segregation in the U.S. Armed Forces and the Deep South. Farmer had a famously "strained" working relationship with Rustin, which led to Rustin eventually leaving the organization. After a speech in Pasadena, California, in 1953, then-forty-year-old Bayard Rustin was arrested for a "morals charge" involving the performance of oral sex upon two twenty-three-year-old white men in the back seat of a parked car. Rustin served a sixty-day sentence in California prison without incident, but the arrest left a stain on his reputation and was trotted out by opponents of integration. "J. Edgar Hoover would periodically send notes to people where Bayard was supposed to appear," recalled Walter Naegle, Rustin's former lover and the executor of his estate. "Occasionally, he would enclose Bayard's arrest record."

Rustin's fellow Southern Christian Leadership Conference leaders, including Reverend Dr. Martin Luther King Jr., knew not to acknowledge Rustin's sexual preferences in a public forum. Instead, the SCLC adhered to the strategy of tolerating Rustin in good times and expelling him when heated accusations rose to a point of crisis. After the controversies died down, the movement inevitably welcomed Rustin back—agreeing once more to keep the man's open secret until it was time yet again to feign shock and temporarily banish him. During the Montgomery bus boycott of 1954, for example, Black civil rights leaders warned that Rustin, only recently freed from California prison, could "set back the whole cause."

If a man like Dr. King would not put himself on the line for his on-the-ground planner Bayard Rustin, called the "Socrates of the Civil

Rights Movement," the NAACP and its executive director, Roy Wilkins, would certainly not do so for a few Black Florida teachers.

At times in Strickland's interrogations of Black educators, it became unclear if FLIC's chief investigator was on the lookout for racial infractions, homosexual infractions, or some combination thereof. Strickland addressed the great many importuning white men dragged out of courthouse bathrooms as "mister" or "sir," but elected to called Black schoolteachers by either their first name or their last name without the appropriate honorific, even when the correct honorific was "Dr."

On October 13, 1960, Strickland interrogated a Black former Fulbright scholar named Thomas Franklin Pinson, chair of the English Department at segregated Gibbs Junior College, in the offices of Pinson's boss, assistant superintendent for Pinellas County schools Dr. Albert Craig. In addition to Albert Craig, an undercover officer for St. Petersburg police named Don McQuaig stood by during questioning to serve as an intimidating face. Pinson was a married Black man with three children ranging in age from five years to seven months.

With a master's degree from Atlanta University, Pinson was hired to teach French and English to undergrads in 1957 after Pinellas County decided to expand segregated Gibbs High School for grades 13 and 14 rather than integrate St. Petersburg Junior College. That October day, Pinson gave two interviews under oath to Strickland. The interrogation was interrupted at a key moment to allow statements against the witness by two white St. Petersburg policemen, whom Strickland didn't want to keep waiting.

In his first sitting, Thomas Pinson described himself as a "restless" person who suffered from insomnia and had a habit of taking late-night drives around St. Petersburg. He denied partaking in homosexual acts and even described a past scenario where he reported his roommate at Morehouse College to administrators for making an illicit advance. On two separate occasions since 1957, police had arrested and charged the former Fulbright scholar for making white women uncomfortable with his driving.

> STRICKLAND: You were accused of following a white lady, were you not?

PINSON: That's right.

STRICKLAND: In fact, you were picked up by the police, were you not?

PINSON: That's right. I don't think it was really a question of following the lady. It seems that she was putting out trash at the time I decided to turn around. And I turned around in her driveway, and she got the idea that I was trying to get her attention. And then of course . . .

STRICKLAND: Have you made any passes by that house in the car?

PINSON: Obviously, evidently, rather, I had, but I wasn't aware of the fact that I was passing the same house. That is, I didn't do it consciously.

STRICKLAND: What charge was placed against you by the officers at that time? Do you recall?

PINSON: I do. Night prowling.

For this crime, to which Thomas Pinson pleaded guilty to avoid racial blowback, a local court fined Pinson $25. When Gibbs Junior College administrators learned of the offense, they suspended Pinson from work for ten days.

Strickland upped the ante by accusing Pinson of participating in homosexual "cruising" scenarios during his late-night drives. Pinson denied these allegations by explaining how he limited his driving after his "night prowling" indiscretion. Gibbs Junior College officials had sent him a letter forewarning him that he would be terminated for cause if he was "ever guilty of such indiscretion again."

Ordering the former Fulbright scholar to stand aside in silence as two white police officers from St. Petersburg testified against him, Strickland encouraged the lawmen to describe in detail what they'd allegedly caught the man doing at Bayfront Park, a notorious waterfront cruising zone. According to the officers, Pinson parked his car at a secluded location with a man named Theo Edmondson. Though they never explicitly witnessed Pinson and Edmondson in a sexual act, the cops described the suspicious whereabouts and time of day as proof enough.

Having sat through Pinson's denials and the contradictory testimony of two white officers, assistant superintendent Albert Craig interceded in the questioning. "Should Pinson decide to change his original statements in the deposition, is he still in the position of having perjured himself?" Craig asked Strickland. The assistant superintendent for Pinellas County then paused the proceeding to confer with Pinson off the record. It is unknown what Craig threatened or promised to this married father of three during their sidebar. Yet immediately after this chat of unknown length, Pinson returned resolute, as summed up by Strickland in the deposition recording, to "answer truthfully and correctly such questions as he has formerly, falsely testified to."

What Pinson admitted to was in actuality a receptive bisexual act of accepting a blow job from another male while also enjoying the company of a wife and several girlfriends, but as a member of the Black middle class, he didn't possess the requisite language to characterize himself as "passive" and therefore reformable. Though he'd offered such exemptions to UF informants Professor Russell Danburg and David Meuser for the same behavior, Strickland declined to help Pinson out of this jam. After Pinson was strong-armed into the confession by his white boss, that same white boss recommended to the DOE that the Black English Department chair be fired. Thereafter, the state of Florida revoked Pinson's teaching certificate and placed him on a teacher blacklist sent by FLIC to administrators of neighboring states.

Unquestionably, having ensnared yet another former Fulbright scholar, Strickland was riding high. But while pushing his powers to their zenith, he interrogated a group of schoolteachers with the gumption to counterattack. The same day that he spoke to Thomas Pinson, Strickland deposed a Black music professor from Gibbs Junior College named William James Neal in the office of Pinellas County superintendent Floyd T. Christian.

Neal was a tall, svelte concert pianist with a pencil-thin mustache. Born in 1927 in New Smyrna, Florida, a town on the Atlantic coast with a sizable Black population, he was called Willie as a child. By 1940, his family had moved to the flourishing city of Orlando, where young Willie entered the segregated school system and began taking piano lessons. As the oldest of four siblings, Willie was burdened by the expectations of his working-class father, a hotel bellhop who raised him to work like a horse and expect little as reward.

Playful Willie Neal transformed into formidable William James Neal when he sat down at those piano keys. The pride of his mother Sadie, he graduated high in his segregated high school class and enrolled at Fisk University in Nashville to study music on a scholarship. So formidable were his talents that when he was an eighteen-year-old college freshman, he was among a rare coterie of Black males in America who qualified for a World War II draft deferment.

After graduating, William James Neal was speedily recruited to lead the music department at Gibbs High School. Moving up in the world, he next served as choir director for segregated Bethune-Cookman College in Daytona Beach before pausing his life as "Chorus Master" to enter the Korean War. After twenty-four months of active duty, Private First Class William James Neal received an honorable discharge on October 23, 1952, and he spent five more years in the U.S. Army Reserve service as a "Clerk Typist."

Back in civilian life, Neal relocated to New York City to pursue a master of arts in music at Columbia University. He toured North America as a solo pianist, a virtuoso act performing with orchestras and classical ensembles in such places as Ontario, Cleveland, Philadelphia, and Washington, D.C. Neal ventured back south in 1957 to accept a professorship teaching music and humanities with the inaugural staff of the new Gibbs Junior College.

Thriving in his role as a member of Florida's Black intellectual elite, he produced the "William J. Neal" choir's weekly AM radio hour while touring the state and holding campus recitals of rigorous works by Debussy and Khachaturian. Happy to contribute as a Gibbs faculty member, Neal worked as a summer school instructor for "grades seven through 12" from June to August 1958. All the while, Neal was slowly hacking away at his PhD studies with Columbia University. Little but segregation and compulsory military service had slowed his trajectory until Remus Strickland beckoned him into the office of a school superior that October 13, 1960.

Strickland tape-recorded just thirty minutes of his marathon session with William James Neal in Superintendent Floyd T. Christian's office, but the upshot would shake the state. "You're an educated Nigra," Strickland remarked to Neal at the outset.

Similar to Strickland's interview with Neals's doomed Gibbs Junior College colleague Thomas Pinson, the interrogation was supervised by both a police officer and Assistant Superintendent Albert Craig. Exercising public notary powers separate from his powers as a FLIC investigator, Strickland placed Neal under oath and touched on the man's military service and family background. He then pointedly asked, "Have you ever participated in any homosexual activity?" To which Neal answered faintly, "Not here."

For the accused, to be confronted and insulted by a "belligerent, condescending" detective constituted an "invasion of privacy" that his brain could hardly fathom. Strickland followed up the allegation with his usual sequence of verbal switchbacks.

> STRICKLAND: If this Committee holds a file, evidence to the contrary of your statement, is that true or false?
> NEAL: Would you repeat yourself slowly, please?
> STRICKLAND: I said if this Committee holds in its files evidence contrary to the statement that you have just made, is that true or false?
> NEAL: It should be false.
> STRICKLAND: I know. Is it, or isn't it?
> NEAL: It is.

To test the witness's endurance, Strickland asked Neal about his willingness to start over and redo the entire testimony under polygraph. It was at this point, conspicuously without mention in the deposition transcript, that Neal asked to pause the proceedings. "He told me he had proof I was a homosexual," recalled Neal. "He told me I would never teach within the continental limits of the United States."

As defense lawyers would later state in Neal's case to the Florida courts, "Petitioner saw after three hours of questioning that he was going to be constantly harangued until he told the police investigators what they wanted to hear; so he made up a story and ended the session." William James Neal invented a novel means of escape: If he could confess to something impossible, he would fool Strickland and Craig into releasing him.

STRICKLAND: William, I have given you the opportunity of a private conference with Dr. Craig, have I not?

NEAL: That's right.

STRICKLAND: After having discussed this situation with him privately, is there any part of this testimony up until this time that you want to make a statement change?

NEAL: Do you have reference to one specific part?

STRICKLAND: Pardon?

NEAL: Do you have reference to one specific part?

STRICKLAND: Is there part of it that you want to change?

NEAL: Well, perhaps I'd like to give a further statement for clarity.

STRICKLAND: William, I believe a few moments ago, you stated that although it wasn't in the State of Florida, that you had had an act on a couple of occasions with person or persons in Rochester, New York, did you not?

NEAL: New York City.

The hitch here, which Strickland and Craig didn't realize, was that despite anything William James Neal said, he wasn't in New York City during that window of time. Neal was in fact teaching summer classes at Gibbs Junior College, as could be validated by a July 1958 report in the *Tampa Bay Times*.

Neal knew he could offer proof—his class syllabus, graded papers, a news report—that he was teaching at Gibbs in the summer of 1958 to call attention to the smoke-filled, closed-door attempt at entrapment. Under duress, he gave verifiably false testimony so he would be permitted to leave the room. For his confirmation of homosexual activities, William James Neal was summarily suspended from Gibbs Junior College pending a DOE revocation hearing.

Just as he wrapped up with Pinson and Neal, Strickland wrangled several more confessions from female instructors at neighboring white schools. However, several of the women fought back when they caught wind of the illegality of Strickland's methods. Strickland, in his inquest into local lesbianism, became fascinated with the idea of female roommates—a relatively common living arrangement among unmarried women in Florida and elsewhere. Mary Frances Bradshaw, a teacher at Pinellas County's Mirror Lake Junior High School, happened to live with her colleagues Anne Louise Poston and Ina Jane Riggs. Enter Remus Strickland.

In an interrogation room for two hours that October 19, during which he periodically flipped the tape recorder on and off, Strickland pressured Mary Frances Bradshaw to reveal the nature of her relationship with her roommates.

> STRICKLAND: I asked the question if you had become involved in any type of homosexual activity with another person of the same sex.
> BRADSHAW: I believe you said if I had the opportunity.
> STRICKLAND: Well, have you?
> BRADSHAW: Have I had the opportunity?
> STRICKLAND: Have you been involved?
> BRADSHAW: It's all according to what you call being involved.
> STRICKLAND: To any degree, realizing of course, that there are various degrees.
> BRADSHAW: Realizing that there are various degrees, yes.
> STRICKLAND: Would you please state as to what degree?
> BRADSHAW: I have to think. I have been close to one person.

A conspicuous pause also occurred in Bradshaw's FLIC transcript. With the deposition tape turned off at will, Bradshaw sensed that evidence against her would be misrepresentative unless she found a way of getting the surreptitious practice into the record. Thus did Bradshaw take the unprecedented step of leaning over the table, grabbing the microphone from Strickland, and making a direct address: "I have asked Mr. Strickland to discontinue the tape because, since the same questions will be asked at the hearing, I feel that it is not necessary for me to go through this procedure twice." Bradshaw's explanatory statement called attention to the curated nature of the so-called evidence mustered against her.

Only fourteen pages of Bradshaw transcript, occupying what Strickland estimated as "approximately 40 minutes" worth of tape, emerged from the two-hour interview. The rest of Strickland's time with Bradshaw would forever be missing from the record. Nevertheless, having made a half admission on tape to "various degrees" of same-sex conduct, Mary Frances Bradshaw was suspended from work, pending a DOE hearing, by Superintendent Christian.

In parallel with the Bradshaw and Neal interrogations, Strickland deposed Mary Frances Bradshaw's roommate, Mirror Lake Junior High physical education teacher Anne Louise Poston. Only a fraction of Poston's three hours of deposition would be recorded. As a misdirection tactic, Strickland pulled Poston out of her classroom under the false pretenses of receiving a job promotion. When she walked into her administrator's office, FLIC investigators caught her off balance by asking her to give a statement concerning the prevention of child molestation. Once they got her under oath, they revealed their true purposes and began to interrogate her about homosexual conduct.

Confused but wanting to be helpful, Poston confessed to wild times as an undergrad at the University of Florida. Strickland got Poston to agree that she'd possibly been in the room with "some degree" of homosexual activity. He then tried to get Poston to lower her defenses through a leading question: "You had begun to try to fight this thing and to get it away from you, which you had been successful in doing through your religion?" To which Poston responded, "That is true."

Off tape, Strickland introduced the word *caressing* as a characterization of intimate female-female relations into the deposition. Turning the tape recorder back on, Strickland steered Poston into speaking the word *caressing* on the record. Discombobulated, Poston confessed to faint, fuzzy homosexual horseplay with or perhaps just feelings about her roommate and colleague Mary Frances Bradshaw.

> STRICKLAND: Miss Poston, in your acts with Miss Bradshaw, whom you referred to on this record, would she play the part of the aggressor?
> POSTON: Yes.
> STRICKLAND: In other words, she was known as the butch, is that true?
> POSTON: Yes.
> STRICKLAND: Was there on any occasion any oral copulation made by Miss Bradshaw?
> POSTON: At one time that I could remember, there was.

STRICKLAND: Could there have been more than once?
POSTON: Possibly but if so only one more time.

Poston, as with Neal, would later forswear this testimony in its entirety. Testifying before a DOE hearing officer named George Georgieff in defense of her roommate and colleague Mary Frances Bradshaw, Poston denied engaging in homosexual activities and explained the process whereby Strickland had frightened her into making misleading or counterfactual allusions.

GEORGIEFF: Are you able to state if at any time during your
    acquaintance with Miss Bradshaw, from the beginning until
    October 19 of 1960, did you ever caress any part of her
    body?
POSTON: No sir, I have not caressed her body.
GEORGIEFF: Or any portion of it?
POSTON: No sir, I have not.
GEORGIEFF: You are certain of that?
POSTON: Yes.
GEORGIEFF: Have you ever made any statement to the effect
    that you did?
POSTON: Yes sir. Mr. Strickland put the word "caress" in my
    mouth, and I under such duress. It was his word, not mine.

The DOE hearing officer asked Poston to clarify how Strickland went about menacing her, and Poston answered at length, occasionally pointing to the printed transcript of her FLIC deposition for emphasis. Poston cast such doubt upon Strickland's deposition, in fact, that the DOE would decline to submit the FLIC transcript as evidence during Poston's revocation hearing.

POSTON: Mr. Georgieff, when I was in there with Mr.
    Strickland, there were quite a few threats, etc., that went on
    that I can't tell you about. I can't even remember what I
    said, and some of this in here [gesturing to FLIC transcript]
    I did not say. I cannot remember to this day.
GEORGIEFF: What kind of threats?

POSTON: The penitentiary.

GEORGIEFF: Are you saying that that man threatened you with the penitentiary, with penal servitude of some kind?

POSTON: Yes, but what I am trying to say is I was in complete duress. Those are my words. They didn't come from anybody.

GEORGIEFF: I understand, and I am asking you to elaborate, if you will. . . .

POSTON: Why was I under duress? By being called out of my classroom. I did not know why. I really thought it was for a promotion. Mr. Strickland didn't think that was very funny, but I was told that when I walked in. I had no idea that anything that would be said would be held against me, because I wasn't planning on saying anything against myself, because I haven't done anything like that.

Strickland deposed Poston, Bradshaw, and Neal within hours of each other that October 1960. Afterward, the district suspended them all without pay on an indefinite basis, though their disciplinary proceedings were ongoing. Strickland's harsh interrogation tactics against them, particularly, generated rumors among educators throughout the region, and Pinellas County administrators fielded questions from panicked members of staff, who feared they would lose their livelihoods through one deposition with that man.

Speculation whirled about what would ultimately happen to the teachers up on the DOE block. Pinellas County superintendent Floyd T. Christian wrote the Florida DOE and implored them to make haste. "These teachers have, of course, all employed attorneys and recently have gone to the Classroom Teachers Association to ask the NEA to bring an investigating committee because they feel their rights have been denied," Superintendent Christian complained. "Far too much time has been lost from the date of the suspensions, October 20, until the time of the hearings, which makes it very difficult to keep down the rumors and also affects the peace of mind of other teachers who are fearful of this Legislative Investigation Committee." Christian urged the DOE to do what need be done and dispose of the educators "once and for all."

CHAPTER 22

Backlash

The bombed home of Harry T. Moore

November 1959
(*Clerk of the House Papers, FBI Papers, Mississippi Papers, Box 9*)

WHILE CHIEF INVESTIGATOR Remus Strickland had his way with the teaching profession of Florida, chief attorney Mark Hawes, on the orders of Charley Johns, continued his smear campaign against the Florida NAACP. Developments came to a head for Hawes and Strickland at the same time.

On November 4, 1959, Gibson, Graham, and other Florida NAACP members were again subpoenaed to the state capital and ordered to bring membership lists, accounting books, and other records. "We are going to continue the hearings that were interrupted in Miami due to court suits," Chairman Herrell told the press. Flanked by attorneys, Father Theodore Gibson appeared congenial but brought no papers, as he did not possess them, and the issue reverted to the court system again. Somehow over the years of legal jockeying through various appellate layers of the Florida judicial system, most of the NAACP plaintiffs subject to FLIC contempt citations had been winnowed down to two big fish: Father Gibson and Reverend Edward Graham. These men were the primary architects of school and bus integration in Miami, and Hawes fantasized about the public relations boon of photographing either of them hitched to a chain gang on the Florida roadside.

FLIC and Florida courts traded Gibson and Graham back and forth like chess pawns until August 30, 1960, when a Tallahassee judge finally found the Black men guilty of criminal contempt. "When the time comes that a member of the NAACP or any other voluntary association can disobey a committee of the legislature of Florida and a mandate of the state judiciary, democracy will crumble and freedom will be destroyed," the judge ruled after eight months of vacillation. He sentenced the plaintiffs each to six months in prison and a $1,200 fine. Before Mark Hawes could exhale, the NAACP appealed the ruling to the Florida Supreme Court, which kept Gibson and Graham out of prison stripes.

At year's end, the Florida high court unanimously upheld Gibson's contempt conviction. But growing weary of FLIC shenanigans, the court performed an about-face on Graham and ruled unanimously that the minister's refusal to answer FLIC questions was an aspect of his "right to assemble and to speak freely."

Father Gibson, the de-segregator of the Dade County public school system, now stood alone as the NAACP test case and whipping boy for the Pork Chopper segregationists. Almost overnight, Gibson's lawyers appealed to the U.S. Supreme Court in Washington, D.C. The matter sat on the docket weightily. With the threat of jail time looming for "God's angry child," the spring 1961 plea convinced the court justices, at last, to hear the case *Gibson v. Florida Legislative Investigation Committee.*

Just prior to Florida's 1961 legislative session, a menacing case in argument before the U.S. Supreme Court called *Baker v. Carr* threatened the southern political order by questioning whether federal court action could be taken to force state reapportionment. To make matters more tenuous for Pork Choppers, FLIC—for the first time—faced an adversary to its re-extension: the American Civil Liberties Union. "They have been trying to produce subversives," noted ACLU attorney Tobias Simon, aligned with the NAACP. "And they haven't found one Communist. The Committee has spent $150,000 during the past four years. Nobody knows who got this money."

Rallying with a power play in the face of critique, the Pork Choppers of the Florida senate unanimously passed a bill in April 1961 to mandate the respectful treatment of the Confederate battle flag. "Ridiculous," decried the NAACP. "The Florida legislature retrogresses into history." Ignoring issues being raised by Yankee progressives, the legislature instead devoted floor time to debating the illegality of mutilating, defacing, or casting contempt upon the beloved stars and bars.

In another statement of Pork Chopper solidarity, three days after the U.S. Supreme Court agreed to hear the *Gibson* case, the Florida senate extended FLIC yet another two years by unanimous vote of 38 to 0. The bill expanded FLIC's authorities and, for the first time, unambiguously authorized its investigation into sexual perversion.

Through Charley's goading, the 1961 statute legally connected FLIC's pursuit of "organizations and individuals advocating violence" with the "infiltration of agencies supported by state funds by practicing homosexuals." The threefold conspiracies of Communism, integration, and homosexuality were thus interwoven as fact in the lawbooks. FLIC received an additional $75,000 to finance their ongoing work, and on May 24, 1961, the new Florida governor, Farris Bryant, signed the bill into law. The stroke of his pen marked the first time a Florida governor lent Charley's "special interim bicameral committee" the support of the executive branch.

The next day, FLIC delivered its mandatory report to the legislature on subversion between the years 1959 and 1961. As FLIC was already a fully funded entity, the reading of this report served little more than to stoke the legislature for a planned operational expansion. The Johns Committee opened by noting the peril of the *Gibson* case sitting on the U.S. Supreme Court docket. FLIC touted its use of state snoops to infiltrate a March 12, 1960, meeting of the SCEF in Orlando and then published the full names and home addresses of approximately 120 Florida citizens allegedly on an SCEF mailing list. Although such an action could expose private citizens charged with no crime to vigilante justice, FLIC blamed any consequential danger on the accused.

> The Committee makes no accusation that every member of SCEP or every person associated with the SCEF is a Communist. . . . The Committee does say that every such person is either knowingly

or unknowingly lending aid to the subversive threat of the Communist Party in Florida. There seems to be little excuse for any reasonably well-informed citizen of Florida to continue association with this organization, unless said association is knowingly intended.

Battling Florida's much-touted homosexual problem, FLIC proudly included a numerical tally of the firings from Hawes's and Strickland's crusades in its report:

> Since July 1, 1959, a total of 39 public school teachers' teaching certificates have been revoked, most of them at the investigation of and on evidence supplied by the Committee. Fourteen revocation cases are presently pending before the State Board of Education. The Committee is in possession of sworn testimony concerning homosexual conduct in excess of 75 additional public school teachers.

The committee announced, among a new set of "salient facts," the uncovering of a homosexual "call ring" in an unnamed Florida city, which operated through an alleged "mailing list of over 8,000 men all over the world." (The number 8,000, repeated for effect, seemed a favored FLIC marker for "numerous.") Purportedly, each person on the homosexual mailing list received pornographic photographs of "properly trained" Florida boys "between the ages of 13 and 17." To substantiate the mailing list, FLIC also claimed to possess "in excess of 8,000 pieces of pornographic paraphernalia." Hawes and Strickland maintained that though they wished to share more about specific cases against perverts and pedophiles, the "premature disclosure of details of said investigation at this time would destroy entirely its effectiveness."

Perplexingly, the names and home locations of the 120 SCEF members printed in the 1961 report were safe to advertise, but not even one homosexual suspect could be identified without jeopardizing FLIC security.

Justifiably shocked from the bombshells contained in the 1961 report, *One* magazine fact-checked FLIC's claims for its homophile readership and found them to be bogus. "We have for years been hearing about supposed homosexual 'rings' and 'clubs' that serve their membership playboy style. I defy anyone to show me one," a reporter for *One* said. Taking FLIC's claims at face value, Florida governor Farris Bryant relayed the 1961 report to FBI director J. Edgar Hoover. The report received the highest-level urgency of the Bureau: "Immediate and preferred attention." Hoover sent a memorandum to four FBI field offices—Atlanta, Jacksonville, Miami, and Tampa—and ordered them to commence parallel investigations to bring to light the vile crimes discovered by FLIC.

Remus Strickland, at first blush, appeared to be flattered by this FBI interest. The man did have a high opinion of himself. Within days, however, Strickland began playing cat and mouse with federal agents seeking to depose him. The FBI reported the chief investigator as "having questionable associates, displaying an apparent disregard for the truth." Strickland set a meeting with the FBI at the state capitol to go through his pornography cache but then didn't show up or leave "any obscene matter in his office for review."

Baffled, the FBI agents tracked him down halfway across the state. When reached by phone, Strickland insisted without apology that he had to leave on a case. Furthermore, he explained that he'd transferred his pornography samples for the benefit of "a display" for Florida legislators, but couldn't share the display location. "It appears obvious that Strickland does not intend to cooperate," the FBI Jacksonville field office noted in a confidential communiqué. "He is a devious individual and cannot be trusted."

When the FBI rescheduled with Strickland to review the pornography cache, the man backtracked and began to speculate that Dade County state attorney Richard Gerstein might now have some of the evidence, while the remainder might be with Hillsborough County state attorney Paul Johnson in Tampa. When contacted by the Tampa field office, Paul Johnson told the FBI that "he is acquainted with Remus Strickland but does not recall Strickland or the Florida Legislative Investigation Committee ever turning any pornographic material over to him." When asked why Strickland might have referred the feds to him, Johnson expressed perplexity, given that his one and only meeting with Strickland had occurred in 1956.

FBI Jacksonville agents now cautioned fellow operatives about the accuracy of anything in FLIC's report. For example, heated assertions about the SCEF being a Communist front were speedily debunked by agents adept at exposing Soviet spies. A majority of Strickland's work produced on the civil rights movement, the feds confirmed, had been directly lifted in an uncredited manner from the investigations of two other state entities: "Strickland has done nothing more than obtain materials or information from those two sources."

One by one, FLIC's "salient facts" about a homosexual conspiracy went up in smoke when exposed to fact-based analysis. Concerning the so-called urban call ring of male teenage prostitutes being trafficked by a homosexual cabal, the FBI Miami field office contacted Dade County detective sergeant James Barker, who'd spent the prior five years leading the Juvenile Crime Division of the Department of Public Safety. Barker informed the FBI that Strickland must be mistaken about any gay training school existing in the area: "There is no such school in Dade County to his knowledge."

Concerning the 8,000-member homosexual mailing list, the FBI determined this list to be a "known asset," a historical document circulated widely among state and local law enforcement agencies following the federal raid of a Washington, D.C., muscle magazine company called the Guild Press in 1960. "The fact that this is a mailing list does not, of itself, establish that all the names listed are practicing homosexuals and is an interpretation placed thereon by the Florida Legislative Investigation Committee," critiqued FBI director J. Edgar Hoover.

Through elementary casework, FBI agents debunked the entirety of the 1961 FLIC report by that November. It was amateur hour in Florida, they determined. The bureau's entire involvement with Remus Strickland was deemed to be an utter waste of resources. The FBI rebuked FLIC in its final summary. They repeated a line that the Tampa prosecutor had shared in confidence: "The Committee might have tried to sensationalize their activities in order to justify their existence." Unfortunately, these FBI assessments did not circulate beyond the Bureau. For reasons unspecified, likely to avoid state interference with rocket and missile testing on the Atlantic coastline, federal authorities did not notify the Florida public that they'd been bamboozled by Charley Johns.

With an almost comic level of gall, while he dodged corruption charges from an FBI inquiry, Strickland actively colluded against federal power in meetings with agents of other southern states. Southern officials first met confidentially in Atlanta, Georgia, in June 1961 for the purpose of establishing closer ties between state agencies "to familiarize those present with past and current activities of Communistic, Socialistic, Subversive and Agitative individuals and groups." In attendance were law enforcement representatives of every state in the Deep South, plus North Carolina and Oklahoma. Florida's emissary that June 5 and June 6 was none other than Remus Strickland. The agents nicknamed their clandestine group of agents the Southern States Investigator's Association, and Remus Strickland volunteered Florida as host site for the next meeting in November.

After the Atlanta summit, a Mississippi Sovereignty Commission investigator wrote to Strickland to compliment "the excellent work you and your investigators are doing for your Committee." Days later, on June 28, 1961, Remus Strickland wrote Mississippi investigator Andy Hopkins a letter promising the delivery of vital FLIC intelligence:

> Dear Andy,
>   . . . Enclosed is a list of the teachers in the State of Florida whose certificates have been revoked to teach in this state, most of which was due to practice of homosexuality. These people were not prosecuted, due to the fact that this agency is a fact-finding body rather than a prosecuting Committee; therefore no criminal record has been established in re of individuals named herein.
>   Trusting that I can be of assistance to you in your endeavors, I remain with warm personal regards,
>   Sincerely yours,
>   R.J. Strickland

Soon after, FLIC's full teacher blacklist sailed through the mail to Jackson, Mississippi, and out of Florida hands forever.

The committee assembled that September 22, 1961, for the first time in nearly a year. At that meeting, Senator Charley Johns was unanimously reapproved as chairman. As his first act, Chairman Charley Johns reaffirmed past behavior and offered pardon for any spirited infractions. He commended chief counsel Mark Hawes and chief investigator Strickland for their "outstanding job" and "their untiring efforts," and the committee voted to retain them at their current salaries. The committee voted to send yet another letter to UF president J. Wayne Reitz about Black male janitors employed in white female dorms.

As new business, Mark Hawes agreed that FLIC should continue its investigation into "homosexual practices in the public school system," but, in a territorial backstep, affirmed that the committee would "comply with the State Department of Education's request to be furnished a list of the names of all teachers about whom the Committee had information or statements on file." Finally, Strickland convinced the renewed Johns Committee, as a gesture of alliance, to send its thanks to Georgia Bureau of Investigation lieutenant H. A. Poole for "furthering the Committee's investigations" and for organizing cooperative summits to protect the southern way of life.

Meanwhile, Strickland's micromanagement of President Reitz's "self-policing" effort in Gainesville continued unabated. On October 7, 1961, University of Florida foreign student advisor Dr. Ivan J. Putman Jr. was entrapped and arrested in Washington, D.C., while in town for an academic conference. According to police, Putman solicited sex in a public urinal from an undercover officer. Humiliated by the ordeal, Putman fled back to Gainesville, but his failure to appear in court to answer to the charges was, in the eyes of the court, an implied "admission of guilt."

Several weeks later, UF president J. Wayne Reitz learned of the incident and called Putman into his office. Putman admitted to being intrigued by homosexuality from an intellectual standpoint. "[I] got an erection from the stimulus," Putman testified. "I have always been interested in talking to them to find out how they get this way and what sort of people they are." Following a tack similar to the one he had used with Diettrich, President Reitz resolved not to outright fire the forty-nine-year-old married father of three, who'd served UF for a decade. But he made clear that Putman needed to find work elsewhere by that summer.

Remus Strickland discovered this arrangement and interrogated Putman. Pretending to be mutually "curious" about the subject of homosexuality, Strickland homed in on the timing of Reitz's disciplinary review, perhaps hoping that Putman would embroil the university president.

> STRICKLAND: Just a few weeks ago, then, that you were requested in his office? And this subject matter was brought up?
>
> PUTMAN: Yes.
>
> STRICKLAND: What determination did Reitz make on this report that he had?
>
> PUTMAN: I don't think it's proper for me to indicate this. This is something that he should—
>
> STRICKLAND: Did you discuss it with him?
>
> PUTMAN: Yes.
>
> STRICKLAND: Well, what did he tell you about it?
>
> PUTMAN: I think this is information he should give you. I'm sorry.

Strickland became furious when he learned that Putman had been permitted to land a new job as dean of students at the New York State University College, Fredonia, with a good word from his UF colleagues. He wrote Chairman Charley Johns in a huff to protest Reitz's underhanded leniency and implied he needed to look into the matter. It's unknown how Charley responded.

That spring, a staff editorial of the *Alligator* bid Ivan J. Putman adieu by naming him Alligator Man of the Year: "We recognize Dr. Putman's contributions not only to the UF and to the state but feel that through his dealings with thousands of foreign students, Dr. Putman has helped to create a good image of both the UF and the United States." U.S. Senator George Smathers of Florida also hailed Putman's "outstanding daily contribution to the UF." Despite this impressive showing of support, yet another UF asset left the school under the full force of Charley's boot.

CHAPTER 23

Trench Warfare

*The Greyhound bus station, stakeout location of
the Johns Committee*

January 1961 (*Box 2, Box 9*)

WHEN NEWS OF Charley's resumption of power hit the
newspapers, members of the public acclaimed his return. "We have
had many requests from county school authorities throughout the
state to help them with the problem of homosexuals who have infiltrated into instructional staffs," Charley said that mid-November
1961, more than two years into Strickland's foray into Florida school
districts. Demand for their services had never been higher.

Chairman Charley reassured the media that FLIC would continue
the noble work. Apprised of Charley's reascension, the Florida NAACP
wrote a letter of warning to its members: "We can expect an attack at
any time." In a spirit of celebration, Strickland hosted ten states of
the Southern States Investigator's Association at the Di Lido Hotel on
Miami Beach that November 1961. *The New York Times* expressed
skepticism in an editorial after uncovering the secret organization's
existence:

> It is a little difficult to believe that the South is threatened today
> by subversion, Communist or any other kind. It is likely that the

new organization's backers may have in mind as targets the movements to end racial discrimination.

As the summit on subversion continued apace, Charley sought pre-approval from Florida State University (FSU) president Gordon W. Blackwell to begin an anti-homosexual operation around Tallahassee and on his campus. "I assure you that we have been giving much thought and careful attention to this problem and that we will be happy to co-operate with your committee in every way," President Blackwell wrote back on November 16, 1961. That same day, Blackwell granted associate dean of students Harry P. Day, a married man with two children rumored by several FSU students to be bisexual, two years' leave to serve at an American studies seminar in Salzburg, Austria. Given the timing and the reality that Day would not return until the 1961 iteration of FLIC had disbanded, it appears that Blackwell was providing preemptive cover for a much-valued asset in the leadership pipeline.

Fresh from the summit, Strickland received authorization from Chairman Charley Johns in early December to stake out one of Tallahassee's well-known homosexual tearooms: the men's restroom of the Greyhound bus terminal. Strickland hoped to use the bus terminal as an entrée into the netherworld of FSU, similar to how the 1958 Alachua County courthouse stakeout kicked off the University of Florida purge. This entrapment campaign would utilize both FSU student recruits and a handsome thirtysomething policeman aptly named Sergeant Peacock as Greyhound station marks, in much the same way that Officer John Tileston had once lured Gainesville queers from the county courthouse.

Sergeant Burl Peacock, head of Tallahassee's two-man liquor and gambling squad, leapt at the opportunity to expand his vice beat. In what became a monthlong sting, Strickland and Peacock rounded up more than forty men for sexual solicitation and hauled them before Judge John Rudd in city court. Among those caught in Peacock's nets were three FSU professors, three state employees, a high school football coach, an Army private, and a U.S. Air Force sergeant stationed at Tyndall Air Force Base.

Each man was interrogated and then charged with "lewd and lascivious acts." Each arrestee then bore the indignity of having their name appear in the *Tallahassee Democrat*. For example, Strickland entrapped an FSU social welfare instructor named Lucian C. Reed, who was fired by FSU president Gordon Blackwell ahead of his trial date, as reported by *The Tampa Tribune*. Once in court, however, Reed contested the charges and received a directed verdict of acquittal from Judge Rudd. Even though Reed was legally vindicated, he still didn't get his job back.

Nearly apoplectic at the filth so close to his Tallahassee doorstep, Governor Farris Bryant held a press conference to announce a state-wide program to identify homosexuals under the collective authority of the Florida Legislative Investigation Committee, the Florida Children's Commission, and other assorted morals agencies. "We are going to have to come out in the open and let people know the dangers," Governor Bryant expounded, "and how to prevent it, repress it and provide rehabilitation." Reporting for the *Orlando Sentinel*, journalist Robert Delaney noted that while Governor Bryant made no direct criticism of the Johns Committee's methods, the governor did admit that the state had "not yet developed proper procedure for dealing with this problem." FLIC agents like Strickland took the comment as a personal insult.

Days after President Blackwell granted Dean Harry P. Day leave and announced his departure to Salzburg, Sergeant Peacock entrapped Carl Wilson Stewart Jr., a sophomore theater kid at FSU. Stewart confirmed the major homosexual hot spots around town to Strickland and Peacock.

> STRICKLAND: After having come to Florida, has all of your
>   contact been in and around Tallahassee?
> STEWART: Yes.
> STRICKLAND: Where have your contacts been made here?
> STEWART: At the Greyhound Bus Station and at the Cypress
>   Lounge. You mean contacts, what do you mean by contacts?
> STRICKLAND: For homosexual acts, to go out someplace and
>   have acts.

With Stewart proving so helpful, Strickland and Peacock inquired about racially integrated homosexual parties around town. Stewart said there were none to his knowledge. Stewart also confessed to hearing "rumors to the effect that [Dean Day] was a homosexual and that a friend of mine had seen him at a 'gay' party in Atlanta, Georgia." For his misconduct, Carl Wilson Stewart Jr. would be booted out of FSU. Strickland delayed action on any of Stewart's tips, and by the time he tried to interview Dean Harry P. Day, the married father of two had with exemplary timing departed for Austria.

On December 11, 1961, Strickland ensnared an FSU senior named Leslie Powell, a social studies major who worked as an associate editor and a news columnist at the student newspaper *The Florida Flambeau*. Facing an adept inquisitor in Strickland, twenty-six-year-old Powell doomed himself from the outset when he agreed to speak without a lawyer.

> STRICKLAND: Leslie, was this subject whom we have spoken of, what part of the act did you take in the situation?
>
> POWELL: That has been a mutual thing.
>
> STRICKLAND: All right. Now, what type, what about this fellow whom you were caught with last night?
>
> POWELL: That was also mutual.
>
> STRICKLAND: Last night?
>
> POWELL: Last night, it would have been, only I.
>
> STRICKLAND: You were the aggressor last night?
>
> POWELL: I was last night.

Powell admitted to having his first homosexual encounter while serving in the U.S. Air Force during the Korean War. Attending FSU on the G.I. Bill, a financial pressure point that intrigued Strickland, Powell had moved to Tallahassee in 1959 and found himself tempted by the Greyhound station. "The first year I was here, I just behaved myself," recalled Powell. "The second year it was a little more frequent; last year, well." Strickland asked about sexual activities of FSU creative writing teacher James T. Cox, but Powell did not implicate his married mentor.

Although Powell was not charged at the city courthouse, he did not graduate with his FSU class that spring 1962 or in subsequent semesters. It seems, however, that President Blackwell and Strickland may have dangled the possibility of his attending commencement for lever-age. Given Powell's compromised position with the committee and his influence as a student editor, it's clear why *The Florida Flambeau* failed to devote any coverage to the faculty firings and student expulsions that resulted from Strickland's investigations.

Leslie Powell's final column in *The Florida Flambeau* that September 12, 1962, was an ode to his fallen mentor James "Jim" Cox, who'd perished earlier that week by self-inflicted gunshot wound at the age of forty-one. Deputy sheriffs claimed they found no suicide note from Cox, and it's unknown if the death of the married father of two was related to the ongoing Johns Committee investigation. "He was instrumental in the revival of student interest in writing," eulogized Leslie Powell. "Dr. Jim was ours . . . he belonged to the students . . . we belonged to him." Posthumously, James T. Cox received an O. Henry Award for a story called "That Gold Crane" about an alcoholic father with secrets living in Tallahassee, Florida.

President Blackwell struck a collaboration agreement between FSU security officers and the Johns Committee. Campus police subsequently relayed to Strickland background details about Leslie Powell's former mentors as well as a supplementary list of forty-two names of suspected homosexuals, including thirty-three students, seven graduate student lecturers, and two faculty members. The first faculty member on the hit list was a hard-to-fire visiting lecturer and research associate from the University of London named Dr. Oliver Heavens. The other was Professor Lucian C. Reed, whom Blackwell had already sacked.

Much like Reitz, Blackwell played a double game of pacifying Strickland while shielding key staff from termination, and far fewer faculty would depart FSU than UF during the purges. "Florida State was a relatively new university, and we didn't find the problems there that we found in University of Florida," FLIC member Cliff Herrell later confirmed. FSU also did not boast a team of physician informants and campus counselors eager to test their theories by performing FLIC's scut work.

Meanwhile, the Pinellas County teacher revocation processes wound through various arbitration and court hearings. The Black professor William James Neal retained the services of William F. Daniel, a white

Tallahassee defense attorney and a UF law school graduate. The NAACP took no legal interest in William James Neal's case, despite Neal's being a Black Floridian targeted by the same committee harassing their plaintiff Father Theodore Gibson, who was receiving the NAACP's finest legal representation.

Neither Neal's name nor his case appears in a single file or letter or memorandum in the NAACP's archival files on the Johns Committee. Thus the Florida music professor was on his own from October 13, 1960, when Strickland interrogated him, to January 13, 1961, when the Florida DOE notified him of a scheduled hearing to review and possibly revoke his teaching license. The notice, written by Florida assistant attorney general George Georgieff, ran afoul of Florida's teacher revocation law by neglecting to inform Neal of the charges against him.

When Neal turned up with a lawyer for a closed hearing in the boardroom of the Pinellas County School District that January 25, 1961, the man's private nightmare was not yet a matter of public record. At the hearing, Georgieff served as both prosecutor and jury over Neal, whose defense team brought forward four witnesses to speak to the professor's stature and character. Gibbs Junior College president Dr. John Rembert, who'd earned a PhD from Columbia University, testified that Neal had an "exemplary record" as a tenured instructor for Gibbs and that he knew of "no evidence of any misconduct." Other defense witnesses corroborated Rembert.

Remus Strickland, the DOE's star witness, was forced under oath to admit that he did not work for the Florida DOE, that he'd placed Neal's home under surveillance, that he found "no evidence of wrongdoing," and that he had no personal knowledge of Neal's participating in a homosexual act.

Then William James Neal got his chance to tell his side of things. He scorched Strickland's methods, repudiated his FLIC deposition, and described the "third degree" conditions under which Strickland, in a "three-hour duress-filled interrogation session," bilked a false confession out of him. Neal attested that he made up a story on the spot about a blow job in New York City because the investigator was "agitating for an answer" and he otherwise would have been detained indefinitely. The ruse, once unpacked, emasculated Strickland before his comrades at the DOE. Neal's attorney offered proof that Neal was in fact teaching at Gibbs Junior College in the summer semester of 1958.

It wasn't until April 4, 1961, that William James Neal found out through newspaper headlines that the state cabinet of the Florida executive branch met without notifying him to render a final judgment on his case. Alarmed by Neal's absence during the rushed proceeding, Florida House Representative Tom Whitaker of Tampa warned against "methods employed by R. J. Strickland." Imperially, the state cabinet revoked Neal's teaching license alongside the licenses of four female educators from Pinellas County, including those of Mary Frances Bradshaw and Anne Louise Poston.

Unlike the hushed firings that resulted from most of Strickland's previous investigations, the state cabinet's action was treated by FLIC as a much-prayed-for victory and a public relations coup. Each of the teachers had their name and the stated reason for termination—"moral turpitude"—broadcast across television and radio stations and emblazoned on the front pages of Florida newspapers. Perhaps, Strickland figured, if FLIC went as big with this as it did in 1959 with Lester Robinson McCartney, the scapegoats would be too ashamed to retaliate.

"Five Teachers Lose Licenses," read the *Tallahassee Democrat*, which reported the dismissals as due to homosexual charges. "State Fires 5 Teachers," wrote the *Miami Herald*. The *Pensacola News Journal* went with the more hair-raising "Sex Charge: Teachers Ousted." Given the national phobia about homosexuality, the chances of any of these plaintiffs finding future work while applying for a teaching position with their birth name were close to zero. Tellingly, in news reports, state legislators acknowledged Strickland's unconventional inclusion in the proceedings. But members of the Bryant cabinet defended the investigator and blamed the insufficiency of state law for Strickland being in violation of statutes. Governor Farris Bryant said the pertinent question was not whether Strickland had violated procedure but whether the accused individuals were "fit to teach." To provide back-end protection to FLIC and the DOE, the 1961 legislature had amended and corrected this legalese that May to retroactively permit Strickland's involvement in DOE firings.

The broadcasting of William James Neal's homosexual disgrace banished this honorably discharged veteran from the fold of the churchgoing Black elite of Florida. His life, as he knew it, was done. "I went to a friend's house and slept for three days," Neal later recalled to the *Tampa Bay Times*. "I was like a block of ice; I don't know when I fell asleep, and I don't know when I woke up. The blow was so devastating that a lesser person, I suppose, would have committed suicide." Perhaps he just couldn't stand to be ruined by a buffoon who degraded him with the label "educated Nigra." It was in this condition that Neal resolved to do what no other victim of the Johns Committee dared before: He sued.

Neal directed his attorney to appeal to the Florida Supreme Court. Soon afterward, Neal packed his bags and crossed state lines to avoid retribution. Neal's lawyers filed their complaint on June 2, 1961, and the Florida Supreme Court set the initial hearing to determine jurisdiction. Neal's race was not made explicit in his team's legal documents nor in the state's rebuttals, and Neal was not expected to appear or take the stand. At a pretrial hearing, Neal's attorney William F. Daniel, a credible white man, told the full story of a how an exemplary music professor and military veteran was "yanked out of his class" and subjected to an illicit grilling by an unsanctioned state agent. Arguing for the state, assistant attorney general George Georgieff, vexed to be in court on the subject of his own DOE revocation ruling, falsely asserted that Neal denied experiencing duress during Strickland's interview process.

Perhaps for the first time, Remus Strickland's methods would fall under the scrutiny of a panel of judges. But the prosecution stood firmly by his side. During a break from arguing the case, Georgieff accepted Strickland's invitation to speak at the clandestine Miami summit of southern lawmen colluding against the U.S. government. By year's end, two of the besmirched white teachers from Pinellas County, Mary Frances Bradshaw and Anne Louise Poston, had joined Neal's lawsuit, but William James Neal maintained his status as the named plaintiff. With sympathetic women now part of the case, the fact that Neal was Black receded further into the background. *The Tampa Tribune* did not include Neal's race as a detail in its ongoing coverage. To preserve what privacy was left for him, Neal stayed out of state and let his lawyers do the speaking in the landmark case to come, *Neal v. Bryant*.

CHAPTER 24

Friends of the Court

Supreme Court of the State of Florida

December 1961
(*Bonnie Stark Papers, NAACP Papers, U.S. Supreme Court Records*)

THE FLORIDA SUPREME Court met in Tallahassee on December 13, 1961, nearly eight months from William James Neal's termination, to consider the constitutionality and legality of his firing. The word *negro* appeared nowhere, neither in the legal documents nor in the oral arguments. Neal's lawyers argued that all Pinellas County teachers in the lawsuit should have their jobs and certifications restored due to investigative infractions on the part of FLIC chief investigator Remus Strickland, who had operated outside the law as a non-DOE employee. The defense attorneys propounded:

> The question posed by this case then is the necessity for due process of law and protection of basic individual rights against

forced self-incrimination; and even further, the necessity for in-dependent proof of the occurrence of facts to support a license revocation on a vague charge of immoral behavior. Otherwise, police can extract an admission out of a citizen by whatever method they choose. . . .

For the state, assistant attorney general Georgieff and Mark Hawes mockingly restated Neal's assertions, rather than taking efforts to re-but them: "The Petitioner would have the Court believe that there was an essential departure from the requirements of law. . . ." Defending his actions to the press, Remus Strickland described his well-honed ways and means. As Strickland maintained, "Whenever I questioned a teacher, he knew what it was about."

The Florida Supreme Court, in all likelihood reticent to rule against a white-run committee that had flouted state standards, proceeded to sit like hens on *Neal v. Bryant* for months on end, buying Charley and Strickland more time to ply their craft freely. Anticipating an adverse decision, Florida governor Farris Bryant, still reeling from the 1961 FLIC report, leapt on the homosexual issue himself. By executive order on December 27, Bryant directed the Florida Children's Commission to study the statewide problem of homosexuality and funded it with approximately $17,000 from his executive budget. To serve on Bryant's new Advisory Committee on Homosexuality, the governor named Senator Charley Johns; Hillsborough County school superintendent J. Crockett Farnell, who'd collaborated with Strickland in the Tampa purges; Remus Strickland; and chairman of psychiatry at the UF College of Medicine Dr. Peter Regan, who'd assisted with the Gainesville investigation against his UF colleagues. At a January 22, 1962, commission meeting in Tallahassee, Regan advised the state that morals education and warnings about venereal diseases were "not going to stop the homosexual," but that elevated awareness on the part of mothers, fathers, and teachers could help them "take legitimate measures" with at-risk children.

Sensing new power in the governor's coalition and getting nervous about the *Neal* case, Strickland issued a memorandum to his FLIC staffers on March 8, 1962, telling them what to do in the event of future lawsuits:

No employee of said Committee can be compelled to testify about his or her work or work pertaining to the Committee and its functions. . . . If subpoenaed by Grand Jury or State's Attorney, by lawful subpoena, appear as directed but respectfully decline answering questions propounded by claiming legislative immunity, unless authorized by Chairman. . . .

Meanwhile, Florida's political fault lines yielded an earthquake. State elections in May 1962 shook the Pork Chopper base to its core. Five-term Pork Chopper stalwart and former senate president W. Turner Davis of Madison was unseated by an upstart Democrat. "Davis—who created the Pork Chop Gang in 1953 and 1955 with Sen. Charley E. Johns—was the cohesive force which kept the gang intact," reported the *Tampa Bay Times*. Confederate flag enthusiast and Pork Chopper senator Wayne Ripley also lost to a newcomer. "The myth that 'Governors come and Governors go, but the Pork Chop Gang goes on forever' is at least badly cracked," continued *The Tampa Tribune*. Luckily for Charley Johns, his seat was safe until 1964. Though the Pork Choppers, through historical riggings, clung to a bare majority of twenty-one out of thirty-eight senators in the upper chamber, the voters had roundly rebuked Old Florida rule.

All the while, Charley's steady stream of fan letters kept pouring in from an adoring public. "I want you to know that I highly approve of the work your Committee is doing and firmly believe that most of the those that are critical are ignorant of what you've accomplished," wrote Louise Hill of Miami. Interestingly, the FLIC fan mail almost always came addressed to Charley Johns, even when someone else was temporarily chairman.

From the Florida Supreme Court building, a legal grenade flew high and dropped directly at the feet of Remus Strickland. On October 19, 1962, after more than ten months of overscrupulous review from the justices on the controversial matter, a conservative Florida high court delivered a nevertheless landmark *Neal v. Bryant* decision. In a dazzling riposte to all things Johns Committee, the Court ruled five to two in favor of the maligned educators.

Only two stalwart North Florida justices, William Glenn Terrell and Bonnie Kaslo Roberts, stayed the course with Charley Johns, while the majority affirmed that the Florida DOE "had not complied with the statutory procedure" and called the revocations "improper." As the firings that resulted from the revocation inquiries were also deemed inappropriate, the teachers' positions within the Pinellas County School District could, if so requested by Neal or others, be restored.

The court held back little in its repudiation of the investigatory practices of Strickland:

> In lieu of following the statute, the State Board relied upon a so-called investigation by an investigator (Strickland) for the State Legislative Investigations Committee. This man had not been appointed by the State Board. . . .
>
> When the Legislative Committee investigator conducted the interviews, he had no power whatsoever to do so under the controlling statute which was Chapter 59-207, Laws of 1959. This statute created the Legislative Committee entirely for the purpose of investigating subversive activities. We have held that the power of this Committee to investigate is limited and circumscribed by the creating statute. *Gibson v. Florida Legislative Investigating Committee*, Fla., 108 So.2d 729.
>
> When the Committee investigator set himself up to delve into the homosexual problem, there was no semblance of authority for so doing. . . . Actually, the Committee had no such power to investigate these people at that time. The statements which they allegedly made were obviously extracted from them under a threat of publicity.

The court also noted that a post hoc maneuver by the 1961 legislature to legitimize Strickland's actions by loosening up the revocation law was immaterial to the *Neal v. Bryant* case, since Strickland's deeds transpired under prior law. The Florida DOE was forced to return the rescinded teaching credentials back to Neal and the other plaintiffs.

In a panic, the Pinellas County school district strategized on what do if these teachers contacted them to resume employment. "I thought you ought to be posted on the action that we are planning to take here in Pinellas County in reference to the three teachers," wrote

Superintendent Floyd Christian to the DOE. "The Board has decided that they would not take any action until they were contacted either by the individual teachers or by their attorneys and that their course of action, of course, would be largely determined by their request. If they ask for a full reinstatement and back salary, I intend to put up a fight." Christian proposed sizable payoffs to keep the teachers away.

Neal v. Bryant dealt an instant deathblow to Strickland's ability to wage his war against homosexuals. The broad language of the *Neal v. Bryant* ruling affected not just the three Pinellas County teachers but also FLIC's constitutional capacity to investigate homosexuals under the blanket of "subversive." The committee's legal authority to hunt homosexuals pre-1961—in Gainesville, Tampa, and elsewhere—lay in shambles.

Stung by this reversal of fortune, Chairman Charley sought a rehearing. In a wild petition for a redo with the Florida Supreme Court, state attorneys Georgieff and Hawes argued that FLIC must be authorized to pursue homosexuals because such teachers were "turncoats" susceptible to blackmail by "the Marxist cult," though they declined to accuse Neal, Bradshaw, and Poston of Communist actions, as the state would then be compelled to produce evidence, and it possessed none. Nonplussed, the Florida Supreme Court denied the state a final rehearing on February 27, 1963.

Following his victory over the Johns Committee, William James Neal remained a veritable ghost as the named plaintiff. In all likelihood, Neal feared what would happen to the people he loved if he came back to Florida and showed his face—and his race—to the press. Indeed, media powers deemed it a bridge too far, dangerous even, to disseminate news that a Black teacher accused of homosexuality had defeated a segregated state on its own turf.

Not even legal redemption could restore Neal to his prior standing among the southern Black elite, who were so closely tied to church culture. Thus did William James Neal of *Neal v. Bryant* choose to live in exile. He found work teaching music in a suburban Maryland school system and remained there, in service to students, until his retirement in 1987.

In 1993, at the age of sixty-seven, Neal found the courage to tell a portion of his story when a reporter from the *Tampa Bay Times* came calling. "As you grow older," he reflected, "those scars from the past become stripes of success." When William James Neal died on February 17, 2008, he did not receive a substantial obituary in any major newspaper. A private mass of Christian burial was held in Washington, D.C., and his remains were interred at a cemetery in Maryland. The epitaph on his gravestone reads: "Beloved Friend."

Taking steps to dilute Neal's Blackness, Florida newspapers in 1962 simply listed William James Neal alongside his fellow plaintiffs, as if all enjoyed equal status under the law of the South. "The action stemmed from challenges by Miss Mary Frances Bradshaw and Miss Anne Louise Poston of Pinellas County secondary schools, and William James Neal, a teacher at Gibbs junior college in Pinellas County," *The Tampa Tribune* wrote. Only Floridians from Pinellas County would discern from the casual mention that Gibbs was a segregated junior college, and Neal was thus likely a Black citizen. Additionally, Florida newspapers failed to mention the fact that his fellow white plaintiffs joined the lawsuit only after Neal initiated it.

Few, if any, professors or teachers fired prior to 1961 were motivated to seek redress under the new ruling. Likewise, the Florida NAACP didn't know or didn't wish to acknowledge that a Black plaintiff had emerged triumphant over the same Johns Committee that continued to hound Father Theodore Gibson.

Reeling from the legal defeat in Tallahassee, Mark Hawes and the Johns Committee turned to face an even bigger case looming on the U.S. Supreme Court docket.

On December 5, 1961, in Washington, D.C., the full bench of justices heard opening arguments for *Gibson v. Florida Legislative Investigation Committee*. Mark Hawes, instead of the Florida attorney general, represented the state. It was the epitome of conceit for Charley Johns to assess that FLIC's best chance of winning stood with its chief attorney, rather than with the Florida attorney general. Meanwhile, former *Brown* attorney Robert L. Carter represented plaintiff Theodore Gibson.

Carter was a Black American born in segregated Florida in 1917, but his family fled to the North with the Great Migration and resettled in New Jersey. Carter graduated high in his class at the Columbia University Law School in 1941 and wrote an influential thesis on the

freedom of association in the First Amendment. He fought in the U.S.
Army Air Corps during World War II before being tapped to work
with the star attorney of the NAACP Legal Defense Fund, Thurgood
Marshall, with whom Carter would argue the case *Brown v. Board of
Education.*

In contrast, Mark Hawes attended the University of Florida College of Law and graduated without high distinction. He passed the
Florida bar in 1950 and served with his mentor Florida attorney general Richard Ervin for one and a half years before entering private law
practice and then applying to work for FLIC. By 1961, Robert L.
Carter had appeared before the Supreme Court more than ten times,
while Mark Hawes would be making his solo debut before the highest-
ranking judicial body in the country.

The mismatch of appellate experience in a courtroom where whites
did not receive Tallahassee-style deference unfolded brutally for Hawes.
Addressing the U.S. Supreme Court first, Robert L. Carter pointed to
the complete absence of facts connecting Father Gibson or the Miami
NAACP with anti-American subversion. The state had no security interest, Carter argued, for FLIC's demand that Gibson violate his freedom of association. The ensuing contempt citation, Carter continued,
must therefore be nullified because it was predicated on the violation
of an inalienable right.

Chief Justice Earl Warren gave Mark Hawes equal time to refute
Carter's points. Hawes, playing the country lawyer, wasted his opening seconds by complaining of a cold and then trailing off with an in-
decipherable mumble.

> HAWES: If your honors please. I hope you will indulge my
> rough voice. I am just overcoming a severe sinus attack. I'll
> try to stand in form of the facts with one opinion. If my
> opinion is too much, please indicate, and I'll try to [end of
> sentence].

Finding his self-assurance after these flubs, Hawes contended that
it was imperative for the court to uphold Gibson's conviction regardless of whether the initial charge was just or legitimate. Hawes devoted
the remainder of his time to insisting that if the court ruled for FLIC,

Gibson somehow wouldn't end up in prison. Hawes assured the justices that if Gibson finally came up with the required lists, he would personally try to get Gibson's sentence set aside or reduced, as if Pork Chopper rules applied everywhere.

> JUSTICE POTTER STEWART: What if this Court should decide that you were right, that you were entitled to have him bring with him the membership list so that he could refer to them in answering questions about specific individuals, would he be given a local penitentiary or would he have to serve six months in jail?
>
> HAWES: I will say this to Your Honor. I don't know of course what position my Committee would take. If it takes the same position it has always taken, we have permitted several witnesses to purge themselves. We are civilized people down there in the legislature of Florida, Your Honor. And I know that for myself, I have no desire to see Reverend Gibson in jail at all.

Chief Justice Earl Warren invited Carter to retort, and Carter executed an impassioned soliloquy that incorporated Hawes's language into his own comprehensive point.

> CARTER: I think that the statement that Mr. Hawes made really succinctly places the problem before the Court. Mr. Hawes says that the Committee doesn't want to stop every time they ask whether a person is a member of the party and the person decides to stand on his constitutional rights. But it seems to us, if the Court please, that is a particular issue here. The fact that the constitutional guarantees remain mean that the Committee cannot violate the constitutional guarantees and cannot freely violate constitutional guarantees.

The justices then quizzed Carter on possible precedents to the *Gibson* case, and the day ended with the chief justice calling for recess without asking Hawes to speak again—signaling that the Florida attorney had not impressed the court. As the court's calendar was packed with civil rights cases, oral re-arguments of the *Gibson* case would not be heard until October 1962.

In that long span of time between argument and re-argument, as Mark Hawes pressed FLIC's case to the highest court, Remus Strickland attended yet another southern conference to plot against federal power.

Between June 10 and 12, southern investigators gathered in the resort town of Hot Springs, Arkansas, for a confab hosted by Arkansas assistant attorney general Garland Lyell. Attendees formally voted to ban press from their meetings, and the Georgia Bureau of Investigation lectured on "handling demonstrators" using high-powered hoses. Lieutenant Howard Chandler of the Arkansas state police answered questions about CORE, the NAACP, and "other groups of agitators."

Remus Strickland took the floor to give a keynote lecture on homosexuality's playing "a big part in our present racial problems and in the promotion of Communism." An Illinois businessman demonstrated the latest compact listening devices "for the purpose of recording speeches or secret information." At final adjournment, the group agreed to meet again in one year in Montgomery, Alabama—a sly nod toward Dr. Martin Luther King Jr.'s 1954 Montgomery bus boycott, as if signaling to King himself that the guardians of old ways were taking back their precious land.

ACT IV.

Reentry

CHAPTER 25

A Closer Squeeze

Art Copleston on graduation day
with his mother and stepfather

January 1961
(*U.S. Supreme Court Records, NAACP Papers*)

ART COPLESTON SPENT two quiet years in Gainesville finishing up his degree in industrial management while serving as a dorm counselor at Thomas Hall. In his senior year, he got recruited at a campus career fair to work for the Armstrong Cork Company, a vinyl manufacturer based in Pennsylvania. Despite all the efforts of Officer Tileston and Remus Strickland, Copleston stood poised to achieve his dream of a bachelor's degree and a white-collar job as an entrée into financial freedom.

Feeling brave during his last days at UF, Copleston invited a male "fling" from the Burger House back to his private dorm room in Thomas Hall under the auspices of studying maps, over which he'd charted his route out of state. As they sampled a bottle of scotch, one thing led to another behind closed doors in a symbolic rebuke to Tileston, who'd given up the stalking. "When I came to Gainesville, I originally had thought about staying and going for a master's degree," Copleston reflected. "But after what happened, I just had to get out of here as rapidly as I could, but I think I was shortchanged." Art Copleston graduated from the University of Florida on January 28, 1961, with honors and a 3.8 GPA. His mother drove up to attend his commencement. Then Copleston packed his life into a Plymouth Valiant. He resolved to abandon the land of sunshine, barring a family emergency or a medical event. A child of New Florida, he ran away forever.

Copleston received his first work placement in Braintree, a New England industrial town ten miles south of Boston. Rather than live in a suburb, he rented a studio downtown on Commonwealth Avenue, so he could explore the nightlife of the city. Butch in appearance, polite in demeanor, and inured to police corruption, Copleston made up for lost time in Boston's code-heavy underworld for gentlemen bachelors. Copleston made himself a regular at the Napoleon Club, a private "gentlemen's" haunt on an obscure side street accessed by knocking on a wooden door with a peephole guarded by an elegant woman named Marie, who was usually dressed in a ballgown. It was a piano bar for those in the know, where local acts were occasionally joined by luminaries like Liberace or Ms. Judy Garland herself. "It's rumored JFK frequented it when he was at Harvard," *Boston* magazine noted. Copleston also took a liking to a smoke-filled gay dive called Sporters, located in the Beacon Hill neighborhood. It was at Sporters, wearing his tightest pair of jeans, that Copleston connected romantically with a new boyfriend named Dr. William Edward "Bill" Huckabee, a Boston University School of Medicine professor and cardiovascular disease researcher.

A late-in-life divorcé, Huckabee owned a small mansion on a prime piece of real estate off Boston Common. Copleston found Dr. Bill's lifestyle to be enchanting. "The sun and the stars set over Bill's head," he recalled. The couple established a standing date night on Fridays at a men's-only restaurant called Locke-Ober. Then Copleston's bosses at Armstrong Cork recognized his talent, and he was promoted and transferred back to the corporate home base in Pennsylvania, which split up him and Dr. Bill. (Dr. William Huckabee would die "apparently of a heart attack" in 1986 at the age of fifty-nine, as stated in his *Boston Globe* obituary, during the height of the AIDS crisis.)

After settling into life in Lancaster, Copleston playfully "enlisted" a new nineteen-year-old lover named Hank from the local army base. But Copleston's mother, Margaret, based in Florida, soon sent him a letter informing him that she could no longer live independently. At fifty-eight, she threatened to hop into her Cadillac in her pajamas and drive straight to Lancaster. "It was like a guillotine," Copleston recalled, "just waiting for her to walk in that door."

When Margaret arrived in Pennsylvania to move in with thirty-eight-year-old Copleston, she relapsed into alcoholism almost immediately and remained clueless that her son's live-in "roommate" Hank was actually his boyfriend. Eventually Hank tired of tiptoeing around the subject. It was a Friday, Copleston remembered. Hank spent the afternoon with Margaret, and when Copey arrived home from work around 6:30 p.m., Hank was waiting at the front door with a drink in his hand. "I think you're gonna need this," he said.

Copleston found Margaret slouched in a living room chair. She looked up at her only son, her eyes full of betrayal. Margaret slurred the words that Copleston had predicted in his nightmares and always feared. "How could you do this to me?" she asked.

AFTER SUBMITTING FOR reimbursement the usual mileage and per diem travel receipts from his interrogation trips around the state, Remus Strickland returned to Tallahassee in mid-1962 to learn that the Johns Committee was broke. Chairman Charley Johns had been hiding their insolvency since late December. Indeed, between all of Strickland's traveling and hosting duties, the Florida State University investigation, the *Neal v. Bryant* case, an ongoing investigation at the University of South Florida, and the *Gibson v. Florida Legislative Investigation Committee* case, FLIC had exhausted its two-year, $75,000 appropriation from the legislature in six months' time.

FLIC payroll records revealed that the committee had increased its staff from three to seven since 1961, largely to provide deputies for Strickland such as a former policeman named Norman Sikes. With the Florida legislature out of session for another eight months, Chairman Charley Johns had to go hat in hand to the state cabinet for a replenishment. Astonishingly, without undo protest, the state cabinet granted

$67,150, defined as an "auxiliary appropriation," for the purposes of reinforcing investigations, paying staff, and arguing the *Gibson* case before the U.S. Supreme Court.

Paid in the nick of time to get back to Washington, D.C., Chief Attorney Mark Hawes sat in the oval courtroom of the U.S. Supreme Court on October 10, 1962, for re-argument of the NAACP's challenge. Once again, Robert L. Carter confidently dominated time with the justices. Carter unpacked in full why even the implication that the NAACP harbored Communists was counterfactual, given Gibson and Remus Strickland's own testimony.

> CARTER: There is no evidence in this record, independent evidence in this record, that anybody named as a Communist or alleged to be a communist was a member of the NAACP at any time.
>
> JUSTICE ARTHUR J. GOLDBERG: Mr. Carter, there was some action that the NAACP itself adopted—
>
> CARTER: Yes sir. The evidence on this point Mr. Justice Goldberg was that in 1950, the NAACP had adopted an anti-communist resolution baring persons from the organization. All of the resolutions on that fact up to 1959 was submitted to the committee and because at the last argument here, counsel for the committee seemed to me to have given the Court an erroneous conclusion as to what was in the resolutions passed since 1950. We have those resolutions prejudiced so that the Court could itself see exactly the resolutions which had been adopted by the national organization beginning with 1950 through 1962. . . . The Committee itself had no knowledge of any Communist infiltration.

Chief Justice Earl Warren called recess for the day without giving Hawes a moment to speak, and Robert L. Carter controlled the play clock for much of the next morning. When Mark Hawes received his chance for rebuttal, his Foghorn Leghorn style worked against him. Talking over justices and laughing at his own jokes, the man came across as a blowhard.

JUSTICE WILLIAM O. DOUGLAS: I thought—

HAWES: Because if we don't—

DOUGLAS: I thought the question is whether or not there
is any evidence that the organization that you're
investigating was engaged in—engaging in communist
activities.

HAWES: That is the question that has evolved here orally,
if Your Honor pleases. I agree with that. I disagree
violently that that is the question legally before the Court.
[Attempt to Laughter] Now, here's the situation.

Hawes fumbled on the fundamental constitutional question of the
case when the justices asked him to clarify how potential membership
in a subversive organization might be relevant or irrelevant to state
interests. Instead of addressing the question directly, he played martyr
and framed his answer around the supposed unfairness of the accusations leveled against FLIC.

HAWES: It has been said that this committee that I represent is
here to simply trying to smear the NAACP.

DOUGLAS: I didn't suggest that.

HAWES: It has been said, now by counsel. Now, if Your Honors
please, it's a fact.

By Hawes's own assessment, Communist Party membership ceased
to be a relevant societal threat after a lapsed period of ten years. But
the NAACP still posed a clear and present danger to states like Florida, Hawes contended, even if governors and legislatures happened to
be operating in violation of the *Brown* edicts. Chief Justice Earl Warren ended the re-argument with a foreboding "I think not," which
took on a resonance beyond the questions at hand.

As days blended into weeks of waiting for the *Gibson* ruling, Chairman Charley Johns expressed confidence. "I think the people are behind us," he told the *Tampa Bay Times*. "The Committee is doing
good work, and the job isn't finished yet."

Meanwhile, feeling an itch for power and with few else to harass
following the judicial constraints imposed by *Neal v. Bryant*, Strickland

put a new operation in motion to entrap Florida news reporter Robert W. Delaney.

For almost the entire lifetime of the committee, Delaney had covered FLIC as his news beat—first for the *Tampa Bay Times* and then for *The Miami News* and now for the *Orlando Sentinel*. Adding salt to Strickland's wounded pride, Delaney broke the story of how Strickland's 1953 firing as a county deputy was deemed "in the best interest of the sheriff's office." And in late 1962, Delaney had agreed to be a featured speaker for a Florida State student group called the Liberal Forum. There he warned students about the under-the-radar Johns Committee assault occurring at FSU—calling it a witch hunt so insidious that it was "reaching the point that people dare not raise their voices in criticism because if they do they will be smeared." Delaney's blowing the whistle on an ongoing investigation registered as a last straw for the watchmen of the state.

Strickland had payback in mind that February 1963 when he pressured Janice Wilkes, a "pudgy black-haired bartender from Pensacola" with a rap sheet for lesbianism, to lure the journalist into a situation that would lead to an arrest.

A forty-five-year-old married man with a past of his own, Robert Delaney was now a teetotaler in alcoholic recovery who sat on the Governor's Advisory Council for the Rehabilitation of Alcoholics. Out of nowhere, Delaney got the feeling that he was being followed to AA meetings and while he was out reporting. For a time, he wondered if he was losing his mind. Colleagues with whom he shared his suspicions called him paranoid, but state forces were closing the net around him.

Strickland instructed Janice Wilkes, a paid mole, to manipulate the highly social aspects of AA recovery in order to enter Delaney's life as "Jan Lee," a penitent drunk. Delaney initially met Jan Lee on February 8, 1963, at a Tallahassee club called the Driftwood. "She told me she had a big liquor problem and asked me if I could come by her motel and help her out," Delaney recalled in his defense to the *Orlando Sentinel*. He realized too late that Lee brought up her boozing apropos of nothing, which might have tipped him off that something was fishy.

Delaney drove Lee around town that Saturday, February 9, offering her counsel. As an AA sponsor, Delaney spoke of the grace of sobriety and the twelve steps of the program. Around midnight on February 10, he returned to Lee's motel room because he believed her to be a suicide risk. "The rest of it was my fault," admitted Delaney. Lee opened the door wearing a robe open at the waist, her dishevelment suggesting that she was inebriated and unaware of her appearance. He went in.

Almost as suddenly as she clicked the lights out without warning, Jan Lee shouted a signal to a gang of state and local officers waiting in an adjoining motel room. On cue, she shoved the journalist's head down into her bosom. Flashbulbs went off in time for a police photographer to capture that defining moment, though the image of the compromising pose came out blurry and couldn't be used as evidence.

Tallahassee police sergeant Burl Peacock barreled into the room and shouted gleefully at Delaney, "I caught you!" Lawmen laughed and slapped their knees. "It took us a long time," Peacock told Delaney, "but we did." Later at the police station, who should waltz over but Remus Strickland with the biggest shit-eating grin he could muster.

In a surprise move to the trustee Janice Wilkes/Jan Lee, who was earning $400 per month for the sting operation, Strickland arrested Delaney and her together on the morals charge of "abominable and detestable crime against nature—adultery." To the press, Strickland denied a plot against their fellow reporter. But an uninhibited and euphoric Sergeant Peacock let slip how Strickland had helped the Tallahassee Police Department set the trap in a "50-50" operation.

Strickland soon reversed himself in the media and copped to booking the adjoining motel room used to help ensnare Delaney. To give himself an alibi, Strickland swore up and down to the media that Delaney got himself stupidly caught in a random trap intended for a run-of-the-mill Johns Committee target: "a lesbian." When police released Delaney, the city referred his case to a state attorney, who announced that he would prosecute even though the details of the case pointed toward the accused being framed.

Jan Lee, who filed a false statement to police with her alias name, disappeared and forfeited bond. When asked flatly by *The Miami News* if Lee was a paid stooge of the Johns Committee, Strickland threatened legal action against "lies" but neither confirmed nor denied the allegation. When reached for questioning on the Delaney incident, Chairman Charley acted surprised and then said the quiet part loudly. "I've heard statements that Strickland set out to trap Delaney because

Delaney was critical of the Committee," Charley said. "I asked him if he'd done that, and he told me he hadn't."

Although the Delaney operation might appear clownish, its fallout irreparably damaged the journalist. In court, Robert Delaney refused to admit guilt to a lesser charge as part of a plea offer. After going through the rigmarole of a first criminal trial, resulting in a hung jury, Delaney sat in a Tallahassee courthouse again on "attempted crime against nature" charges. This second time around, a jury of his peers convicted him of conspiring to cheat on his wife without his actually doing so.

At sentencing, Delaney received five years' probation, and the *Orlando Sentinel* fired him on the spot. Delaney transplanted his family to Miami to try to turn the page, but his wife could not forgive him for the humiliation. When the Delaneys divorced in 1968, Remus Strickland enjoyed a belly laugh over his former critic.

Despite Strickland's gloating, the Delaney affair broke out as a full-fledged media scandal, a pointed example of the Johns Committee's overreaches into the realm of private conduct. It stood out conspicuously that in all of FLIC's years of operation, the first and only court conviction tied to their investigations was of a journalist covering their news beat.

Then, at one p.m. on March 25, 1963, the worst came to pass for Charley Johns. NAACP attorney Robert L. Carter found out first via telegram from the Supreme Court Clerk:

JUDGEMENT GIBSON AGAINST FLORIDA LEGISLATIVE INVESTIGATION COMMITTEE REVERSED TODAY AND CASE REMANDED

After an ultramarathon pursuit of the NAACP, the U.S. Supreme Court ruled by a margin of 5 to 4 in favor of the plaintiff Father Theodore Gibson, with Chief Justice Earl Warren acting as the swing vote. Despite Mark Hawes's poor showing before the justices, the case had indeed been that close.

With the *Gibson v. Florida Legislative Investigation Committee* decision, the U.S. Supreme Court overturned the Florida Supreme Court's ruling that the Johns Committee had demonstrated a "compelling interest" to violate the constitutional rights and guarantees of

NAACP officials. Hewing their decision to the FLIC statute, the court let loose a legal broadside that no doubt stung Mark Hawes and Chairman Charley Johns. "We hold simply," wrote Justice Arthur Goldberg, "that groups which themselves are neither engaged in subversive or other illegal or improper activities, nor demonstrated to have any substantial connection with such, are to be protected in their rights of free and private association."

Declining to rule on the question of FLIC's right to exist or investigate per se, Supreme Court Justice Goldberg, author of the majority opinion, nonetheless reasserted the First and Fourteenth Amendment rights of anyone labeled as subversive: "To impose a lesser standard than we here do would be inconsistent with the maintenance of those essential conditions basic to the preservation of our democracy." The majority also defended the right of Father Theodore Gibson and the NAACP to refuse to produce records and/or answer impertinent questions.

By the power of the U.S. Supreme Court, Father Theodore Gibson's contempt conviction in the State of Florida was nullified and cast aside.

"I thank my God and rejoice!" Father Gibson proclaimed in a statement that graced the front page of the *Miami Herald*. "The NAACP, as I have said time and time again, is not Communistic," he continued. "The NAACP is simply a good American organization." Mark Hawes, when asked for comment, told reporters disingenuously that he hadn't read the opinion. "But," Hawes added sourly, "it seems to me the majority of the court has held that before you can make an investigation of a group which is, on the face of it, legitimate, you must be able to prove that there has been a substantial amount of subversion. . . . Of course, if you could prove that, there would be no need for the investigation."

Once again, the State of Florida lost a live-or-die case in court to a Black citizen. And this time around, since the ruling came out of Washington, D.C., the Florida press couldn't credibly underplay the racial overtones of the ruling. The Associated Press newswire reported internationally how the decision put "a brake on fishing expeditions by legislative committees that lack a legitimate excuse for asking questions." The front-page headline in *The New York Times* read: "Supreme Court Tightens States' Red Inquiry Rules."

Through the *Gibson* ruling, the Johns Committee was soundly defeated in its battle of attrition against integrationists. From 1957 through 1963, the NAACP had resisted Charley Johns, stalled committee hearings, and delayed contempt proceedings. The Johns Committee, meanwhile, killed time and delayed access to fundamental freedoms that, said the U.S. Supreme Court, should have been freely available to begin with. The stated goal of the Johns Committee, the restriction of NAACP operations and lawsuits in Florida, had failed through its inability to jail the prime mover of desegregation in Miami. At an appropriations price tag of nearly $350,000 and counting, all the committee could claim that it had achieved against the NAACP during those years of pestering was bad press for Black witnesses and postponing the inevitable reversal of the "way of life" in Dixieland.

CHAPTER 26

Lonely Hunters

A newscaster at Daytona
International Speedway

March 1963 (*Clerk of the House Papers, Bonnie Stark Papers, Box 2*)

AS OF MARCH 1963, there was no great enemy left for FLIC to haul out and question with one iota of legal authority. *Neal v. Bryant* blunted the homosexual operation, and *Gibson* knocked the teeth out of their Black investigation. Two of their three targets were out of bounds, and FLIC investigators had yet to demonstrate any track record of or skill at finding Communists. Thus, with little rationale to justify FLIC's extension in the 1963 session, Charley's enemies began to speak up. "The Johns Committee should be abolished," Senator John E. Mathews of Jacksonville came right out and said. House Speaker Mallory Horne of Tallahassee questioned the "value" of another two years of Hawes and Strickland.

Representative Fred Karl of Daytona Beach noted that the committee's activities at USF and elsewhere had "all the characteristics of *witch hunts*." The term *witch hunt*, evoking the worst abuses of McCarthyism, was perceived by Florida politicos as so toxic a phrase, so capable of turning public sentiment against campaigns, that Representative

George Stallings, a FLIC member, could not let it stand. "If Karl had bothered to read the entire report of the committee's investigation," Stalling responded pugnaciously, "I cannot understand how he can call such activity 'witch hunting.'" His words were too little, too late.

Witch-hunting was increasingly used in reference to Charley and company. "The witch-hunting Johns Committee appears unable to become organized," asserted *The Miami News*. FLIC carried the dark mark not just in the press but in common gossip. A concerned citizen named Mary Ann Moorhouse of St. Petersburg wrote FLIC to warn of the turning tides of public sentiment:

> We were out looking for a boat at one of the local marinas and got into a conversation with the manager, which somehow turned to the subject of the Johns Committee. This man referred to it as a 'witch-hunting' outfit, etc., etc.

Newspapers like the *Tampa Times* avoided the term while offering a stunning critique: "The Committee has been acting as a roving grand jury without sanction of law." Given the publicity around the *Gibson* ruling, members of the Florida public questioned why an anti-Communist organization like FLIC had spent more than half a decade chasing down non-Communist foes.

Charley Johns, working with the slimmest Pork Chopper majority in the twentieth century, nonetheless expressed certainty that a bill to extend his beloved committee would pass, regardless of outlier opinions. On April 18, 1963, as part of a push for extension that welcomed the press into the chamber, Charley and Mark Hawes presented FLIC's biennial report to a joint session of the legislature. Governor Bryant and the press observed the presentation from the balcony, nullifying past "executive session" overtures in favor of spectacle.

Charley took the podium to make his introductory comments from the heart. "The work of this Committee has got to go on," he avowed. "It's larger than any of us." Brimming with emotion in the fight for his political life, Charley held back little in reserve. He believed in the committee so much, he assured the legislature, that he would step down as chairman for the next term so that it could continue. All but freshman legislators, however, understood that the FLIC chairmanship alternated between house and senate members and therefore couldn't be held by Charley for the next term. These were a salesman's tricks.

Touting FLIC's statistical wins, Charley asserted that FLIC's investigations had led to the firing of seventy-one public school teachers as well as thirty-nine deans and professors at state universities, with sixty-three other cases still pending. Mark Hawes then took the podium to deliver a hodgepodge of commentary on the Johns Committee's major investigations into Florida State University as well as secondary investigations into other public educational institutions, such as Florida A&M University in Tallahassee and the University of South Florida (USF) in Tampa.

Puzzling the press, Mark Hawes didn't dwell much on the topic of homosexuality, but instead pivoted to address another elephant in the room: the Strickland/Delaney affair. Speaking passionately in Remus Strickland's defense, Hawes assured the legislature that he'd personally investigated the matter. Delaney's arrest did not "constitute entrapment," Hawes declared, seeing that "police and Strickland told me under oath they were not after the newsman." The chief attorney conceded that the journalist Robert Delaney's co-arrestee Janice Wilkes, aka "Jan Lee," had operated with a false name as a paid agent of the state.

Hawes also confirmed that, despite Strickland's denials, the Tallahassee police force did seek out the chief investigator's expertise to stage-manage Delaney's arrest and the bugging of the motel. Hawes concluded magnanimously, on the good word of his colleague, that *Orlando Sentinel* reporter Robert Delaney was merely a bad guy who "got caught" doing something dirty.

Noting skeptical faces in the chamber, Chairman Charley Johns jumped into the fray with a tangential defense of Strickland. Charley made public a confidential anecdote about Strickland's disrupting a homosexual plot that year, a planned kidnapping of the eleven-year-old son of Tallahassee judge John Rudd, a city magistrate who'd adjudicated the bus boycott car poolers and the men arrested through Strickland's FSU/Greyhound sting. "If Strickland never does anything," Charley Johns concluded, with tears streaming from his eyes, "he's earned every dime this Committee has paid him."

The identities of the homosexual men in Charley's anecdote were never revealed, although Judge John Rudd did confirm that Strickland had told him about the plot. Given Strickland's reputation for cutting corners, some members of the legislature wondered whether this alleged kidnapping scheme may have been fabricated for the purposes of making the investigator appear a savior.

Charley's wild story ended FLIC's ninety-minute presentation to the legislature. Immediately afterward, more legislators voiced opposition to Charley and the Johns Committee. Senator Tom Whitaker said the report demonstrated "there is absolutely no justification for the Committee's continued existence." Representative Tom Sessums of Hillsborough called the report "one-sided," with a "great deal of rank hearsay." Given the poor showing, Sessums felt it necessary for the legislature to "set up a committee to investigate the Committee" and conduct an audit of all previous FLIC activities.

On May 6, 1963, despite frenzied opposition from senate Lamb Choppers, a Pork Chopper–dominated committee voted to advance an extension bill for another two years of FLIC, with an augmented budget of $155,000. That figure was more than twice the appropriation of 1961, a raise factoring in how the Johns Committee had to dip back into state coffers halfway through the previous term. In an almost-party-line North Florida/South Florida split, the upper chamber approved a new Johns Committee by thirty yeas to fourteen nays.

Those fourteen nays marked the largest margin of disapproval for FLIC in its seven years of existence. "Whenever you try to preserve America for Americans, this is the type of obstruction you run into," Charley later said, thumbing his nose at his detractors.

Governor Farris Bryant again felt obliged to put pen to page and sign the legislation into law—a symbolic victory for Charley, the senatorial lion. From the muck of the prior two years, Charley seemed to emerge as feisty as ever. But in reality, 1963 marked a narrow escape. Hawes and Strickland, celebrating at sine die, had no inkling they might be pawns in a broader bargain.

With FLIC's stock dropping fast, Chairman Charley Johns cut a backroom deal to maintain his grip. In exchange for two more years of investigatory capacity, he offered opponents the heads of his chief lieutenants Mark Hawes and Remus Strickland. "Numerous members, including some members of the Pork Choppers, felt that Strickland and Hawes had created a secret police agency and had gone far afield from the proper purpose of an interim investigating committee," recalled Florida senator Ed Price. "Some of the strong members of the Pork Choppers conditioned their vote for the appropriation for another two years for Senator Johns' Committee on his agreement to get rid of Strickland and Hawes."

Despite Strickland's and Hawes's steadfast devotion to Charley and their belief that following his orders would be a springboard to higher office, Charley axed them to politically save himself. But when he pulled Strickland and Hawes aside to explain the deal, he couldn't admit what he had done to their faces. "He [Charley] didn't know about it until the night before," Strickland insisted years later, still fooled. "He called us into his hotel room in Jacksonville, and said, 'Boy, look out. They are going to bust us.'" Charley's clever use of *us* in that key moment preserved his friendships with two men who'd risked their reputations on his behalf. By fudging the petty details, he kept their loyalty and their silence in place.

At 10:00 a.m. on August 8, 1963, the reconstituted Florida Legislative Investigation Committee met in room 602 of the Robert Meyer Hotel in Jacksonville. As promised, Charley relinquished the chairmanship, and the job went to a Pork Chopper representative from Tallahassee named Richard Mitchell. As Chairman Mitchell's first act, he called FLIC into executive session as Hawes and Strickland stepped into a hallway.

The committee embarked on a riotous debate, during which no notes were taken. Hawes and Strickland listened to raised voices through the doorway as Charley Johns attempted to back out of the pledge he'd made. When the room went quiet, Chairman Mitchell invited Hawes and Strickland back inside. Officiously, Mitchell informed the twosome that the committee no longer required their services. They could resign or be fired, effective immediately.

Resolutely, Strickland and Hawes attempted to beg and bargain to keep their positions for the better part of an hour. Their jobs, including the dirty work they'd performed in service of Charley Johns, were supposed to punch their ticket to "the good life" among party elites. The committee meeting notes read:

> The Committee received the resignation of its Chief Counsel Mark R. Hawes and its Chief Investigator R. J. Strickland together with his staff. Mr. Hawes' resignation was accepted effective October 6, 1963. Mr. Strickland's resignation was accepted effective sixty days from this date, and the Committee ordered that each employee be paid for annual leave due him.

Grim-faced, Hawes and Strickland emerged into the hotel hallway. "What went on in there?" a reporter asked. "A meeting," Hawes answered at a clip. They couldn't fathom how their allegiances had led them astray. "Two Quit Johns Group" read the headline to the *Orlando Sentinel* story, by none other than Robert W. Delaney. After they recovered their emotional bearings, Hawes told reporters that he planned to return full time to his private law practice. Strickland revealed no immediate plans. He was out on his ass, as the saying goes, virtually unemployable now that Hawes had corroborated every base detail of the Delaney scandal.

For his part, Charley expressed no contrition for his handling of the controversial pair, whom he'd mentored only to toss away. "My heart and conscience are clear about my actions," said Charley. "No apologies to make to anyone." As Strickland still held on to the chief investigator title for the next sixty days, he seized upon the chance to prevent any replacement from taking a closer look into his unique ways of working. In the FLIC offices, Strickland oversaw the destruction of all of his suspect photographs as well as the photo negatives and documents detailing his statewide network of collaborators, informants, and acolytes. Thus did the chief investigator exercise his last bit of leeway to close the circle tight and clear away the record of his activities in a row of smoldering wastebins. You can do anything you want in the name of the law in Florida, he confirmed, if your second act as a lawman is saving yourself from the consequences of the first.

After Strickland departed, a perplexed administrative assistant for FLIC wrote the newly unemployed man at his Tallahassee residence on

October 9, 1963, to ask about the location of key FLIC records and the return of state equipment:

> *Dear Strick,*
>
> *You mentioned to me about pornographic files which were, you thought, in the Secretary of State's vault. I would appreciate it if you could give me any more information concerning this, as they know nothing about it in the Secretary of State's Office.*

There is no record that Strickland answered this memo. He resolved to get lost and stay there, and Charley Johns saw to it that the others let him be.

The former chief investigator fell on hard times. As late as October 1964, Charley Johns expressed puzzlement how "one of the best investigators in the state" had been "unable to secure employment." The ongoing trial of *Orlando Sentinel* journalist Robert Delaney complicated Strickland's efforts to present himself legitimately as a prospect to other law enforcement entities.

Separate from the Delaney affair, in October 1965, Strickland was charged with grand larceny alongside a former female informant for the Johns Committee for allegedly stealing $4,200 worth of whiskey from a restaurant in Cross Creek, Florida, owned by the brother of Mark Hawes. When Hawes intervened, the prosecution of the man who was once the state's most feared policeman did not proceed.

CHAPTER 27

Shock Technique

Crowd greeting President John F. Kennedy
in Miami, Florida

April 1963
(Clerk of the House Papers, Bonnie Stark Papers, Box 2)

CIVIL UNREST ERUPTED in April 1963 in Birmingham, Alabama, as the Southern Christian Leadership Conference intensified
its campaign for integration. Since 1945, the southern city had experienced more than forty unsolved bombings of Black and Jewish sites
by white supremacist groups—so many that the city earned the nickname "Bombingham" and one neighborhood was called "Dynamite
Hill." To help advise on the Birmingham push, Reverend Dr. Martin
Luther King Jr. called upon his exiled counselor Bayard Rustin, who'd
co-conceived the SCLC with King back in 1957 but been sidelined
in 1960 when Democratic congressman Adam Clayton Powell Jr.

had threatened to falsely implicate King and Rustin in a homosexual affair.

Rustin, the movement's great logistics and public relations point person, arrived just in time. On Good Friday, April 12, 1963, King was arrested by Birmingham authorities, led by commissioner of public safety Eugene "Bull" Connor for violating an anti-protest injunction. While in solitary confinement, King penned the beginnings of his famous "Letter from Birmingham Jail" in the margins of the local newspaper, which Rustin recognized as noteworthy and helped get out to the world.

On May 2, several thousand Black students led a nonviolent march downtown, and images circulated internationally of Connor's white lawmen repelling the Black youngsters with dogs and fire hoses. Entering the fray in response, President John F. Kennedy called on Congress to pass a civil rights act to end Black oppression on American soil. The civil rights bill would struggle through Congress and meet with one of the longest filibusters in Senate history, filling more than 63,000 pages of the Congressional Record with exposition from southern senators intent on stalling for time.

All the while, Rustin engaged his social action network for a massive March on Washington for Jobs and Freedom to protest economic equality. Roy Wilkins, executive director of the NAACP, expressed reservations about the optics of Rustin's participation. "I don't want you leading that march on Washington," Wilkins said to Rustin. "I'll have to defend draft dodging. I'll have to defend promiscuity." The March leaders met with President Kennedy at the White House, and less than two weeks later, King handed the logistical reins back to Rustin, which gave the libertine Black idealist eight weeks to plan an estimated 100,000-person march to the Lincoln Memorial.

In St. Augustine, Florida, separate but equal still reigned. The Florida advisory committee to the U.S. Civil Rights Commission called St. Augustine a "segregated superbomb aimed at the heart of Florida's economic prosperity." The city's upcoming four-hundredth-anniversary celebration in 1965 was to be a celebratory extravaganza organized and funded by President Kennedy's Quadricentennial Commission. On July 18, 1963, a Black sit-in at the local Woolworth's ended in the imprisonment of sixteen Black protesters, among them seven Black juveniles. A judge sentenced four of these youth to reform school and transferred them into state custody as juvenile prisoners.

On August 13, 1963, South Carolina senator Strom Thurmond took to the Senate floor in the U.S. Capitol with opposition files on Bayard Rustin, acquired via a strategic info drop by FBI director J. Edgar Hoover. Thurmond mocked how "Mr. March-on-Washington" could be portrayed as "smelling like a rose and looking like a gilded lily" when he was in fact a former Communist guilty of "sex perversion." Ignoring Thurmond's character attacks, Rustin conflated his morality arrests with his more than twenty-two career arrests at civil rights demonstrations. As the fate of the march rested on Rustin's oblique denials, sympathetic media outlets played a party to the misdirection.

The New York Times focused largely on Thurmond's Communist accusations in its coverage of the affair, noting how a youthful Rustin had joined the Young Communist League in 1941 but quit when he realized "the organization was not interested in social justice." Concerning the charges against Rustin for homosexual behavior, the *Times* allowed Rustin a circuitous answer: "An individual involved in a character charge cannot deal with it himself. . . . This must be done by my peers who as you know are the Christian ministers of the Negro communities and the civil rights leaders." These were hardly the words of a man coming out of the closet to his nation. Rather, Rustin gave *Times* readers the mistaken impression that he'd fought and resolved a personal issue through Christian teachings. The march proceeded. From Miami, Father Theodore Gibson encouraged his flock to travel to Washington, D.C., with him.

Although Rustin devoted countless days and sleepless nights to the March at its headquarters, he was not included in the main order of speakers to address the more than 200,000-person crowd from the podium on August 28. While King said, "I still have a dream," he stood in the background. Organizers prevented Black gay author James Baldwin from addressing the crowd for fear of what he was liable to say. Likewise, victorious Black southerners like William James Neal were not invited to share their unique experiences at white hands. Although his presence went overlooked at a global happening that featured the likes of Rosa Parks and Bob Dylan, Father Theodore Gibson stood stoically at the front of his Miami contingent before the Lincoln Memorial shouting, "Freedom now!"

In September, Klansmen staged a rally on the outskirts of St. Augustine. In robes, they abducted local NAACP leader Dr. Robert Hayling, a Black dentist whose practice helped Blacks avoid local animal hospitals for oral care, and beat him bloody with chains in a ritual ceremony. Nearly four hundred locals attended the rally where Hayling received this flogging, but *The St. Augustine Record* reported the event the next day as a "meeting." Afterward, Sheriff L. O. Davis turned up on cue to find Hayling and three other activists "lying on the ground"; he charged Hayling for allegedly assaulting two Klansmen at a prior rally. On October 25, 1963, four armed whites drove a car down a street in the "Negro section" while discharging firearms and expressed outrage when their car received return fire. Local white resident William David Kinard, age twenty-four, died in the vehicle.

In desperation to quell the bloodshed, the local NAACP turned to King and the SCLC, and the Black dentist Robert Hayling resigned his local NAACP position hoping that "less militant" leaders would take his place. Weeks later, an unidentified assailant in an unidentified car fired four loads of buckshot into Hayling's home, killing his dog.

On November 15, President John F. Kennedy flew in Air Force One for a restful weekend in Palm Beach, Florida. Sporting a suntan, the president decided to take a day trip in a chopper to tour the Cape Canaveral space center. No less than a billion federal dollars had gone into that 87,000-acre, state-of-the-art spaceport. The influx of capital had transformed the sleepy working-class Black region into the mostly white Space Coast. At launch Complex 37, Kennedy stood awestruck before the gargantuan Saturn I rocket, the largest of its era. "Wonderful," the president said of the day. "Wonderful."

The following Monday, President Kennedy campaigned for reelection throughout Tampa. "Suncoast Smiles on Kennedy," read the front page of the *St. Petersburg Times*. Teenage girls screamed "with glee and turned away in embarrassment, and then one breathed, as if she'd just seen Elvis Presley." Newspapers noted how, in northern style, Kennedy shook the hands of "Negroes" as well as whites. By that Friday afternoon, this handsome man with idealistic notions in his head, who'd courted Black voters in Florida, would be dead in Dallas.

Gears of a new and improved FLIC began turning apace. A man named John Evans, former special assistant to Governor Farris Bryant, was named the new FLIC staff director. Evans's new role primarily involved public relations, at which he was adroit. Introducing Evans and his staff to the public in the week after President Kennedy's assassination, Chairman Mitchell attempted to align FLIC's new mission with the national outcry against subversive actors like accused gunman Lee Harvey Oswald. "We must find sound ways to combat those forces that warped minds and hatreds, and, unchecked, can lead to violence and tragedy," said Mitchell in a press conference.

Unlike his FLIC predecessor Charley Johns, who waited every two years to give a report to the legislature, Richard Mitchell began the practice of delivering regular status updates to the senate, signaling that the days of "Johns Committee" secrecy were over. The committee planned to meet before Christmas to get a jump start on its two-year operations, but they closed the books on 1963 having accomplished little more than firing a few loose cannons.

Trying to make a splash in the New Year by fulfilling a long-promised proposal from several anti-homosexual groups, Evans proposed the creation and publication of a FLIC report on the dangers of homosexuality. Given that Governor Bryant's Advisory Committee on Homosexuality had concluded in 1962 that a so-called shock technique might be needed for public education on the issue, Evans's proposal received a warm response throughout the capitol.

So on January 2, 1964, FLIC held a special executive session meeting at the Algiers Hotel on Miami Beach to codify the printing of a homosexuality report as part of their new direction. Former chairman Charley Johns, the only legislator who'd been part of every iteration of FLIC since 1956, was absent at a key moment once again. New committee staff delivered an internal report and recommendations on the problem of homosexuality in Florida:

> To pursue the approach and maintain the pace set by the Legislative Investigation Committee during the 1961–63 biennium, we could expend 10 years of effort and still only uncover some 20 percent of the estimated 60,000 practicing homosexuals in Florida today. Clearly, we must foster increased activity on the

part of others. . . . We recommend that the results of our inquiries, and the summation of the information developed by our predecessors, be embodied into a report suitable for presentation to the Committee at its first public meeting and for publication.

FLIC set a public hearing for January 29 in senate room 31 of the capitol to hammer out what should go into the public record via the report. The committee convened at 10:00 a.m. with all hands on deck, including Senator Charley Johns. Together they reviewed a draft "Report on Homosexuality" and moved to publish the proposed text, with distribution limited to "members of the Legislature, law enforcement officials, educators, members of the press, and to such groups as parent-teacher associations, city police departments and others properly concerned." Senator Charley Johns seconded the motion, and the plan was approved unanimously.

FLIC's long-anticipated homosexuality report—a fifty-two-page 9-by-6-inch booklet, entitled "Homosexuality and Citizenship in Florida: A Report of the Florida Legislative Investigation Committee"— had its public premiere when it turned up in senatorial mailboxes on March 11. It was the culmination of more than six years of anti-gay research, and Evans intended it to serve as a foundation for FLIC to tout their conclusions and expertise to the nation.

The initial print run was limited to 2,000 copies at a total cost of $720, with the first 300 copies distributed to state leadership. Its arrival on the Florida landscape ushered in nothing less than a political Waterloo.

Readers who were able to get past the surrealistic purple artwork on the front cover opened the booklet to come upon a black-and-white photograph of two white gay men naked to the waist, with visible pubic hair, engaging in an open-mouth embrace. In an era when Lucille Ball's portrayal of pregnancy and divorce on television or Clark Gable saying *damn* in *Gone with the Wind* stoked controversy, the image of two men lip to lip was one that many Floridians had never witnessed and could not unsee.

"Given the background and the opportunity, we innocently provided what we thought was a nice, non-specific abstract cover," offered

Evans, who evaded comment on the internal imagery. Next in the booklet came a strong warning to "every parent and every individual concerned with the moral climate of the state." But before readers actually got to the report, they were confronted with another shocking photo, this one of a blond teenage boy in a G-string flexing his sinewed abdominals, his torso tied with white bondage rope to what appeared to be a garden trellis.

The FLIC report that followed the images, if readers made it that far, channeled Dr. Kinsey's research in *Sexual Behavior in the Human Male* by stating assertively that "the best and current estimate of active homosexuals in Florida is 60,000 individuals." Unwittingly half quoting and conflating the Revised Standard Version of the Bible with the American Psychiatric Association's *DSM-I* handbook, the pamphlet advised the public that "the origins of homosexuality are obscure, as is the question of whether it is sin or sickness." The booklet warned of rampant corruption of at-risk youth into homosexual practices in a subsection entitled "Why Be Concerned?":

> The plain fact of the matter is that a great many homosexuals have an insatiable appetite for sexual activities and find special gratification in the recruitment to their ranks of youth.
>
> There is a tendency to lump together the homosexuals who seek out youth and the child molesters. To most people the child molester seems to pose the greatest threat to society. The child molester attacks but seldom kills or physically cripples his victim. The outlook for the victim of molestation is generally good for recovery from the mental and physical shocks involved and for the enjoyment of a normal life.
>
> The homosexual, on the other hand, prefers to reach out for the child at the time of normal sexual awakening and to conduct a psychological preliminary to the physical contact. The homosexual's goal and part of his satisfaction is to "bring over" the young person, to hook him for homosexuality.
>
> Whether it be with youth or with older individuals, homosexuality is unique among the sexual assaults considered by our laws in that the person affected by the practicing homosexual is

first a victim, then an accomplice, and finally himself a perpetrator of homosexual acts.

The final section of the pamphlet was devoted to a ten-page "Glossary of Homosexual and Deviate Acts," a veritable how-to on the homosexual lifestyle. The glossary defined such terms for public edification as *dyke*, "a female homosexual"; *trade*, "people who like to be passive partners in sexual relations with homosexuals; one-sided affairs"; *chicken*, "an extremely young-looking homosexual or a homosexual under 21 years"; and *anilingus*, "sexual pleasure obtained through the use of the mouth on the anus." On the very last page of the report appeared something more than a public advisory: an advertisement.

Additional copies of this report are available at single copy cost of twenty-five cents, including mailing. Special prices on purchases of 100 or more copies. Write Report, P.O. Box 1044, Tallahassee, for copies or information.

The purple back cover bore the official seal of the State of Florida, reflecting its status as a government document created and paid for with tax dollars. If the verbiage of FLIC's report purported to be educational, the images were irrefutably offensive by standards of the day, and the invitation for readers to send payment made its production a commercial endeavor.

At 12:00 p.m. on March 18, within hours of receiving the report in the mail, Richard E. Gerstein, state attorney for Dade County, wired Staff Director Evans a directive:

Complaints from public officials and citizens indicate that the recent pamphlet published by Florida Legislative Investigation Committee contains obscene and pornographic material. While you may feel the distribution of this pamphlet is necessary for legislative or governmental purposes, offering it indiscriminately to anyone who will pay 25 cents is unnecessary and may well constitute a violation of Florida Statute 874.011 governing obscenity. I direct you to immediately cease distribution.

John Evans, clicking into public relations mode, tried to fudge with Gerstein by relaying him the minutes to FLIC's January 29, 1964, meeting and highlighting the language about limited circulation. By misdirecting through another document, Evans gambled that Gerstein was reacting to rumor and not yet in possession of the homosexuality report. Unfortunately for Evans, Gerstein already had the document. Describing the booklet back to FLIC, Gerstein wrote matter-of-factly: "The note at the end of the pamphlet did not reflect the decision made at your January 29th meeting in which the distribution was to be limited."

That same day, Florida representative Murray Dubbin called the report "nauseating" and said, "I'm certainly glad that it wasn't mailed to my home." Representative Robert Mann of Tampa "strongly objected" to the material. Florida senator Whitaker found himself "flabbergasted." Representative Maxine Baker said the report validated her 1963 vote against the Johns Committee. Gubernatorial candidate Fred Karl called the state pamphlet "nothing but obscenity." Senate president Wilson Carraway, a Tallahassee Pork Chopper, reportedly threw the report in the trash when he saw the first picture.

On the citizen front, Mrs. Thelma Wells, president of the Women's Service Club of Clearwater, Florida, wired FLIC chairman Mitchell that her group was "definitely opposed to the publication." Staff Director Evans, attempting to assuage the likes of Wells, called the report a "jumping off point for a serious and meaningful consideration" among Florida citizens. "It is important to show this up for the sordid business it is," Evans wrote. On March 19, the following day, Florida attorney general James W. Keynes released a carefully worded statement:

> The pictorial exhibitions were clearly repulsive and shocking, and if any of the reports have been disseminated to the public, they should be promptly withdrawn. The committee, in making an effort to educate appropriate legal agencies as to this problem in Florida, included material that was not constructive.

That afternoon, Governor Farris Bryant held a press conference to address the divisive document. Bryant, loath to criticize his former aide Evans, said that the committee had "good motives" to educate about "bad practices." The governor feigned ignorance when asked to defend particulars by asserting that he had not yet seen the report himself. On March 20, the Hillsborough County Children's Committee wired Governor Bryant to criticize the report's "availability to the public, which includes children and adolescents."

Governor Bryant responded to an onslaught of letters from concerned citizens with cut-and-paste answers, lightly tailored for each complainant: "The publication to which you refer was issued by a legislative committee over which, of course, I have no control." "I agree with you one thousand percent." "I have been assured by the Chairman of the Legislative Committee that its report on homosexuality is being given a very limited circulation and that distribution of it has been stopped."

Staff Director Evans stressed to the *Miami Herald* that those "who bothered to find out what was in the report" would find it to be valuable. Rallying to the report's defense, Pork Chopper and FLIC member Leo Jones backed Evans by explaining that the point of the document was to "alert" the state. Senator C. W. "Bill" Young, another FLIC member, equivocated that the content was "not pleasant" but necessary. With this comment, Young appeared to give himself political distance should the heat intensify. That same day, the *Miami Herald* published a front-page story in which Dade County solicitor Joel Davies claimed to personally see nothing wrong with the so-called purple pamphlet published by FLIC, although he noted that it "caused considerable furor."

The nickname Purple Pamphlet stuck like superglue. It was suddenly impossible for Floridians to remember the report's official title. Overnight, FLIC's steady stream of fan mail started yielding hate mail, letter for letter. An anonymous "Good Citizen" wrote to Chairman Mitchell:

> I personally hope that you and every member of your infamous legislative investigation committee, and your staff henchman, John Evans, get just what you deserve—to rot in hell. How does it feel to be on the other side of the fence . . . to be getting a royal fucking instead of giving one? P.S. Your present ill-fame only serves to prove that you and your crowd have the dirtiest minds in the whole state.

Following the instructions on the last page of the Purple Pamphlet, hundreds of requests for the booklet flooded FLIC's official post office box along with quarters to pay the advertised price tag. Florida Representative Richard Pettigrew sent the committee four dollars in change for sixteen copies. Evans, barefacedly denying the content of the report's back cover to an elected official, told Pettigrew that booklet was "not for sale" and furnished him the copies gratis to "be handled with the care due them." Trying to get a handle on distribution concerns, Chairman Mitchell attempted to force individuals to sign a certified document to receive a copy of the pamphlet for "use in conformance with the policy of the Committee."

Requesters of the report who opposed FLIC politically were conveniently deemed unfit to receive the document by Evans, who then blamed the "strictly limited" print run. Flatterers and friends, however, readily received the report, even after copies of the initial printing were supposedly exhausted. Evans went to the trouble and expense of making pre-Xerox-technology copies of the pamphlet and mailing them to perceived allies.

Robert Delaney, the former *Orlando Sentinel* reporter entrapped by Strickland and now working as a *Time* magazine correspondent, requested a copy for his publication. Evans, clearly unaware of Delaney's history with FLIC, mailed the pamphlet to Paul Welsh, *Time*'s Chicago bureau chief.

With supply and distribution pinched on the FLIC side but reader demand growing, a private publisher stepped in to fill the void. In Washington, D.C., a mail-order distributor of homosexual print fare and muscle magazines called the Guild Book Service formatted and re-published for sale an exact facsimile of the Purple Pamphlet, cover page and all. There was no need to embellish or create new content to make the booklet fit their erotic list. Adding it to their pornographic catalogue, the Guild Book Service offered to ship the Purple Pamphlet anywhere in the continental United States for the price of $2. Since the report had been printed with state money and therefore could not be copyrighted, there was little the state of Florida could do to stop the reproduction.

The Purple Pamphlet stayed on the gay market in this way, campily displayed on coffee tables from Florida to San Francisco, for several decades. In 1967, for example, *Miami Herald* reporters noted that the Purple Pamphlet still sold well on the national "smut market" for queer readers. "A Potomac News Co. order blank sent from Washington to dealers lists the 'Florida Report on Homosexuality' among the books available," reported the *Herald*, "along with such other publications as 'The Hell of Loneliness,' 'Carnal Matters,' and 'Of Hot Nights and Damp Beds.'"

CHAPTER 28

Purple Panic

An advertisement for a Purple Pamphlet
reprint by a gay book service

April 1964 (*Clerk of the House Papers, Box 1, Box 2*)

THE NATIONAL PRESS, smelling the blood in the gulf waters, descended upon the story. "The war to protect the people of Florida from the dangerous homosexuals who are alleged to lurk in the state's universities has taken a rather odd turn," reported *The New Republic*. "Such is the book's fame that an envelope addressed only 'Sex, Tallahassee' reached the proper destination." Harold "Hal" Call, president of the Mattachine Society in San Francisco, penned an open letter to the "Johns Committee" about the Purple Pamphlet in an issue of the *Mattachine Review*:

> I would like to join with other responsible Americans in expressing my shock and concern at the report on homosexual-

ity recently issued by the Florida Legislative Investigation Committee. No wonder that I was unable to obtain a copy of the report from the office of the staff director or that the committee seems now—despite its original intent to do precisely the opposite—to be doing everything in its power to prevent further circulation and discussion of its notorious masterpiece. Rarely do legislative bodies come up with material that is so irresponsible, inaccurate, inflammatory or obviously biased.

Bringing the Purple Pamphlet scandal to the American mainstream, *Life* magazine hopped on the bandwagon and included FLIC as an example of "irresponsible" state behavior in its feature story "Homosexuality in America."

Attempting to win back core supporters, Staff Director Evans gave a keynote address on April 15, 1964, to the Annual Convention of the Florida Federation of Women's Clubs in Jacksonville. Evans, parroting the common "you may have heard / but I say to you" format of southern preachers, won over the crowd of conservative religious women:

You may have heard that the report was lewd, pornographic, indecent, obscene and a number of other terms designed to conjure up visions of a really vile publication. The fact is while, to the eyes of some beholders the factual reporting and presentation of an inherently ugly and repugnant reality may be all of those things, not one competent authority has so classified it. . . .

In the files of our predecessors of the Legislative Investigation Committee created by the 1961 Legislature, there were allegations of homosexuality and references to 123 individuals then, and presumably now, teaching in Florida schools. These allegations need to be refuted or affirmed.

Chairman Mitchell was so delighted by Evans's performance that he had the speech transcribed that same day and mailed to every member of the Legislature with an attached note.

> *Gentlemen of the Legislature:*
>
> *Because there has been so much misconception about the preparation, distribution and reception of this Committee's recent report and of its overall activities, I believe you would find of interest the enclosed talk. . . .*
>
> > *Cordially,*
> > *Dick*
> > *Chairman*

Mitchell's instinct to distribute this transcript created complications, as Evans never intended for his cited figure of 123 pending homosexual teacher cases to serve as anything other than a crowd-pleaser for Jacksonville mothers. Attempting to rally his own troops, Mitchell sent a separate note about Evans's speech to fellow committee members.

> *Gentlemen of the Committee . . .*
>
> *At the conclusion of John's speech, he received a tremendous ovation. Mrs. Mark W. Emmel, President of the FFWC, then said, "I think you can tell from the response you have received that the women of Florida are solidly behind you and the Committee." Another two-minute ovation followed.*

Invariably, legislators shared the transcription with members of the media, who then quoted the estimate. For FLIC opponents, this relatively large number of teacher suspects sounded suspicious. After all, *Neal v. Bryant* had shut down the FLIC teacher interrogations. This approximation of 123 could only have come from one archival FLIC memo labeled "10-45," which itemized Remus Strickland's running tallies of fired educators as of July 1, 1961—approximately two years prior to Evans's arrival. "10-45" listed 19 pending cases against college professors and 105 pending cases against schoolteachers on the docket that year, totaling 124. In his desperation to repair FLIC's standing, Evans either miscalculated these figures or rounded down, because after all, 123 had a better ring to it.

Rather than admit to sloppiness, Evans tried to jibe his way out of the jam. In letters and comments to media outlets, he split hairs and claimed he had not said what he said publicly in a speech witnessed by more than two hundred people. "I did not say that 123 teachers have been identified in the public school teacher system," Evans wrote to the *Evening Independent* in St. Petersburg on April 27. "I did say that in the files of the Committee at the time of reorganization, there were allegations and references to 123 individuals who were then teaching." Meanwhile, FLIC member Leo Jones signaled to the committee that he would be ramping down his contributions and possibly resign because "other commitments would prevent his participation."

From Miami, an essentially one-man gay political movement called the Atheneum Society, led by a gay taxi driver named Richard Inman, responded to the Purple Pamphlet with a furious letter-writing campaign. Inman claimed that the pamphlet's estimate of 60,000 homosexual Floridians was inaccurate. "A figure closer to 200,000 would probably be closer to the number that actually exists," Inman insisted. Inman penned several letters to Dade County's representative Richard Pettigrew in Tallahassee, and Pettigrew's office responded encouragingly. This was the state recognizing an openly gay citizen in the body politic. "As of now, it seems that the Johns Committee will definitely be abolished," reported Inman to gay colleagues.

Inman networked with national gay leaders of the Mattachine Society in Washington, D.C., and San Francisco to reform his organization as Florida Mattachine. A gay political consciousness was surfacing in Florida at last, with an organizing trajectory in search of social equality that historian Craig Loftin would call a civil rights impulse. "Prejudices of the era, whether in the form of job discrimination, police harassment or family ostracism, sparked anger, outrage, and ultimately, a civil rights impulse among gays and lesbians," Loftin wrote in *Masked Voices: Gay Men and Lesbians in Cold War America*. "The 1950s Black civil rights movement also influenced the civil rights impulse of many gay and lesbian Americans, but this influence should not be overstated either. . . . Early gay activists drew their models and inspiration from a broad range of social movements."

Almost concurrently on the racial front, Dr. Martin Luther King Jr. came to Orlando and rallied a crowd of 2,000 at Tinker Field. Segregation, King told mid-Florida, was on its deathbed amid the "wind of change." The only question, King said, was "how expensive its funeral is going to be." Nearly a hundred miles away, St. Augustine had transformed into the epicenter of the national civil rights fight. The freeing of the "St. Augustine Four" juvenile protesters of the NAACP from state custody, by special order of the Bryant cabinet, led to more local sit-ins and demonstrations as well as controversial Black actions involving armed self-defense. In response, white nationalists organized a militia of more than 1,400 to "keep our kids white for the next 100 generations."

Promising a "long, hot summer," where a racial reckoning would come to the fore, King paid the city a visit on May 18, 1964, to assess conditions on the ground. Once there, he declared St. Augustine "a small Birmingham" and vowed to raise a "Nonviolent Army." A King-organized march downtown initiated a new strategy of "flooding the jails" to foil police. He descried St. Augustine as "the most lawless city I've ever visited." He enjoined President Lyndon Johnson to monitor developments and, if necessary, enter the fray with military force.

Events seemed to bounce like a Ping-Pong ball between the nation's capital and the nation's oldest city. On June 10, the U.S. Senate broke its seventy-five-day filibuster of the Civil Rights Act. The next morning, King and SCLC leadership were arrested at St. Augustine's Monson Motor Lodge when they attempted to be served at the motel's whites-only restaurant. Fearing that King would be lynched while in state custody, Governor Farris Bryant invoked emergency powers and ordered a 150-man special task force to occupy the city. From the St. Augustine lockup, King penned a "Letter from the St. Augustine Jail" to civil rights ally Rabbi Israel Dresner in New Jersey. "I am dictating this letter from the St. Augustine City Jail," King wrote. "Perhaps if this letter could be read to your brethren next week, it might be considered a 'call.'" King's letter motivated a host of rabbis and lay Jewish leaders to board southbound buses.

Change was afoot even among Black moderates. In his weekly "Sermon of the Week" in *The Miami News*, Father Theodore Gibson addressed the troubles in St. Augustine and praised all northern activists traveling to join the demonstrations. "Do not be a spectator; be a participant," Gibson beseeched. "When the call comes, whom shall we send, and who will go for us? How will you answer?"

On June 12, the Ku Klux Klan held a rally at the Old Slave Market in St. Augustine to mock the Black protesters. "The Kluxers were walking in pairs of two, with one policeman per pair and one dog for every five pairs," reported *The Florida Alligator.* "The Klansmen bore Confederate flags and two signs which said wistfully, 'Kill the Civil Rights Bill.'" Jubilant Klansmen then paraded with police escort through St. Augustine's "Negro Section," after which the local sheriff L. O. Davis proclaimed to race traitors, "If you marched with the niggers, the Klansmen would pull you out of the line and kill you."

In an unauthorized FLIC operation snuck under the nose of Chairman Mitchell, Senator Charley Johns hired private agents to embed with the St. Augustine Klansmen and act as go-betweens for the White Knights and police forces. "Lynch location (be careful of this, his wife wrote it down for me as I promised some pictures is __[redacted by state]__)," noted one FLIC associate, posing as a photojournalist, in a field report. Several who attended Klan rallies were spotted but offered protection after being vetted and confirmed as Charley's men.

The city walked on what the *Miami Herald* called "the cliff's edge of a crisis." That June 18, either fifteen or sixteen rabbis, depending on the source, who'd heeded Dr. King's call were arrested for forming an interracial prayer circle in the parking lot of the Monson Motor Lodge. Two more of the group were arrested for joining a sit-in with three Black activists at the nearby Chimes Restaurant. It would constitute the largest mass arrest of rabbis in American history. Later that day, a local grand jury ordered King and the SCLC to depart St. Augustine for one month to restore "racial harmony." King called the grand jury's request "immoral."

The next day, the U.S. Senate passed the Civil Rights Act by a vote of 73 to 27. On July 1, Governor Farris Bryant announced the formation of a biracial committee for interracial negotiations in St. Augustine. King declared it a victory. "The purpose of our direct action was to create a crisis . . . so that they would talk to us," he said. "Now they have agreed." The SCLC announced a two-week suspension of protests, and as a further gesture of goodwill, King left the city.

From Miami, Father Theodore Gibson abided by the suspension but warned that the area could end up like Birmingham "if we are not careful." Pork Choppers threw up their hands when Governor

Bryant's biracial committee was not staffed in the days that followed and declared the enterprise a "hoax" for King and Johnson.

The day after King departed St. Augustine, July 2, 1964, the U.S. House of Representatives passed the Civil Rights Act. The Johnson administration planned for the president to sign the historic bill on July 4, but the man just couldn't wait. At 6:45 p.m. on July 2, President Lyndon Johnson entered the East Room of the White House with Dr. King and Rosa Parks in attendance. "My fellow citizens, we have come now to a time of testing," the president told the nation. "We must not fail. Let us close the springs of racial poison."

A few months later, in October 1964, Reverend Dr. Martin Luther King Jr. received word that he'd won the Nobel Peace Prize. In a bitter rebuke, St. Augustine police chief Virgil Stuart called King's prize win "one of the biggest jokes of the year." An exuberant Lyndon Johnson, campaigning for reelection at an Atlanta hotel, proclaimed, "The New South is here," highlighting the economic and social successes of his administration. Unwisely, Johnson, the man who'd signed the Civil Rights Act, bastardized an iconic anti-Reconstructionist phrase, coined by whites to symbolize a resurgent Dixie absent Black leadership, for his own purposes, as if signaling to proponents of Jim Crow that he was taking back their words, too. Few Pork Chopper Dixiecrats, who worshipped "Old Folks at Home," would be able to forgive Johnson or the Democratic coalition.

Back on the homosexual front, FLIC Staff Director Evans's citation of 123 pending homosexual teacher cases in Florida continued to plague him. On June 1, the *Tampa Bay Times* ran the story, "Teacher 'Morals' Case List Said to Be Nonexistent." J. T. Kelley, certifications director for the DOE, was quoted as saying, "I don't know what Evans is talking about. I don't know what he means by 123 names." The next day, Florida DOE superintendent Thomas Bailey requested all the "remaining lead sheets held by the Committee." Readily transferring those files, Evans abandoned FLIC's pursuit of homosexuals.

In midsummer 1964, Chairman Richard Mitchell became diagnosed with cancer right when he was needed at the helm. With the chairman medically incapacitated, his duties transferred to FLIC member Senator Robert Williams, although Williams did not particularly want the responsibility. Evans, much like Strickland before him, was left to his own devices while Mitchell was ill, and he largely ignored the commotion in St. Augustine in deference to Governor Bryant, his former mentor. Sensing an opening, members within FLIC—prodded by Senator Charley Johns and Representative Bill Young—began to meet independently about St. Augustine, creating a committee within the committee.

On the morning of September 3, Chairman Mitchell, having emerged from a successful surgery, reconvened FLIC. Senator Williams voiced concerns "with activities of the Committee during the illness of the Chairman." At 11:55 a.m., the committee went into executive session to debate St. Augustine, and Evans left the room. Confidentially, the committee reviewed an unauthorized report on the city's race riots prepared by an unnamed investigator hired without permission by Senator Charley Johns. Forty minutes later, FLIC emerged from the secret session, and Evans was invited back in.

Chairman Mitchell "advised the staff that it was the will of the Committee that work on all projects other than St. Augustine be terminated." He announced his intention to hold hearings on St. Augustine in mid-October 1964 and planned to issue "an appearance subpoena for Dr. Martin Luther King, Jr." Goaded by Charley Johns, FLIC resumed its pattern of after-the-fact justification for unapproved actions by doubling down on Charley's unsanctioned investigations into King and the SCLC when Mitchell was out of commission. At this key point in the meeting, Chairman Mitchell keeled over in agony and recessed, explaining how "he doubted it would be possible for him to return for the afternoon."

Minutes later, for reasons unexplained, the committee reconvened without its chairman and agreed to a media blackout during the "maximum work effort on the St. Augustine Situation." FLIC members Stallings and Williams ordered Evans to "ride herd on this project and go to work," looking especially hard into Governor Bryant's biracial committee. Staff Director Evans expressed unmanageable conflict at being called to investigate the doings of Governor Bryant's biracial committee. In a countermove on Tuesday, September 8, Evans, along with his entire staff, resigned in protest from the Florida Legislative Investigation Committee. The outgoing staff director penned a 2,000-word resignation letter to Chairman Mitchell:

Dear Dick:

Last December First, I assumed, at your request, the duties of Staff Director. . . . At the time your new staff took office, the Committee had no discernable investigative program. . . . The files of the Committee were in disarray with indices either far outdated, incomplete or nonexistent. Liaison with local, state and federal law enforcement and investigative agencies was nil, and there was a considerable hesitancy on the part of most of those agencies to deal with the Committee, due to the extensive unfavorable press it had received. . . .

Because of my pride in our progress and pleasure at the associations that have been part of each day's work, it is with real regret that I now tender my resignation as Staff Director of the Committee. The policies adopted and procedures followed during the period of your illness and absence from the Committee leadership are at sufficient variance with my own concepts and convictions that continued association with the Committee would be untenable to me.

Mitchell accepted Evans's resignation with "great regret." After giving his notice, the former staff director broke the media blackout to share with the *Miami Herald* that his departure had to do with "not so much what we were told to investigate as how." Evans contended that his dilemma was not with the committee's order but with Senator Charley Johns taking advantage of Mitchell's infirmity to run surreptitious operations. In turn, FLIC member George Stallings broke the media blackout to attack Evans and the governor. "When a staff is supposed to be working for a Committee, it should do what it's told," Stallings told the *Herald*.

Unable to resist jumping into the fray, Senator Charley Johns called Evans's claims overblown. Days later, Evans received confirmation through third parties that Charley Johns did in fact hire an investigator to seek "inside dope" in St. Augustine and learned the man's surname: Norris. Despite Charley's gaslighting to the contrary, the menace of which Evans spoke wasn't illusory. As *The Tampa Tribune* reported, "Staff members learned the committee was holding a series of 'secret' meetings, with the staff absent; it was also reported that some committee members initiated investigations of their own."

In a bind over his St. Augustine subterfuge and exposed to fellow Pork Choppers as powerless to run his old committee either as alpha or omega, through intimidation or charm, Senator Charley Johns announced his sudden resignation from FLIC alongside acting chairman Robert Williams on September 30, 1964. Senate president Wilson Carraway confirmed that neither of their two committee seats would be filled, and so the exodus left FLIC with a bare quorum of five.

As if dousing the bridge in kerosene behind him, Charley told reporters that FLIC should "close the office, lock up the records and save the taxpayers of Florida the remainder of the $155,000 appropriation." These were earthshaking words from a man who'd devoted nearly a quarter of his legislative career to the FLIC experiment.

Still sitting on the committee, Representative George Stallings retorted, "I disagree that there isn't much that could be accomplished, and I have no intention of resigning." Charley hit back at FLIC's failures and took credit for its achievements by exclaiming, "The only thing the Committee has accomplished during this interim is to get out two reports taken from prior records." Infighting between Charley and Stallings devolved into a series of stories and counterstories in various Florida newspapers. "Charley Johns is not afraid of investigating St. Augustine or anything else," Charley crowed. "Our able chairman, as you know, is disabled." The little boy shivering in the flour-sack underwear was provoked.

ACT V.

Crash Landing

CHAPTER 29

Death Stroke

Florida senators on the senate floor during a 1965 session

October 1964 (*Bonnie Stark Papers*)

WITH FIVE LEGISLATORS and no remaining staff, Chairman Mitchell emerged from a second set of surgeries in the fall of 1964. He announced his intention to pick up the pieces of FLIC and conclude the St. Augustine investigation. Perhaps unsurprisingly, the final FLIC report, entitled "Racial and Civil Disorders in St. Augustine," was published in a slow-motion rollout between February and May 1965 to little public notice. Unimpressed, newly elected Pork Chopper governor Hayden Burns declared that the Florida Legislative Investigation Committee now served no purpose. "The sooner it is eliminated, the better off the state will be," remarked Governor Burns.

When the 1965 legislative session opened on April 6, 1965, Chairman Mitchell did not sponsor an extension bill. The legislature took its cue to drop the curtain with minimal fuss, and so the Johns Committee died with a whimper on June 1, 1965, when its final enabling statute expired.

In its nine years of life, the Florida Legislative Investigation Committee exhausted nearly half a million taxpayer dollars ($497,150) on sub-rosa and open operations that had failed to unearth one Communist or jail a single NAACP activist. On balance, all FLIC officials were able to pull off in their time was prosecute one journalist; collude to fire several hundred suspected homosexual professors, teachers, and state employees; and expel an unknown number of students deemed sexually deviate. State newspapers mostly did not deem FLIC's demise to be worthy of coverage, and so no articles reported the procedural mischief undertaken by former FLIC members to cover their retreats as they headed for the capitol exits.

Florida senate staff lawyers declared all FLIC records, transcripts, tapes, and reports to have transpired under "executive session" rules and sealed them from review in perpetuity using an obscure provision of Article III of the 1885 constitution. It's difficult to parse how that particular provision, applying to the use of executive session in the Florida senate when the "doors of each House" were otherwise to be "kept open" by decree during session, might apply to a bicameral committee that operated and met mostly out of session. But Florida senate lawyers deemed the provision to be directly applicable. Much like Strickland's archival purges in 1963, troves of FLIC documents and photo negatives were tossed into flaming wastebaskets. The remainder was boxed up by legislative staff and transferred to an undisclosed location under the Florida Department of Law Enforcement. It's unknown, in the final days of FLIC, who precisely packed away the nine years of records, who decided what would be saved or what would perish, or even who turned out the lights.

Entering the 1965 session, Senator Charley Johns read the shifting polities and tried to secure greater pension payments for outgoing senators (like, possibly, himself), who were still paid a measly salary of $100 a month for their work. "He proposed, therefore, writing into law a myth that their pension would be figured on a schedule which would pretend their annual salary all along had been $7,500," reported *The Tampa Tribune*. "Oh, how those in the 'Pork Chop' crowd look out for themselves!" Just as a Florida judge had once legally changed Markley Johns's age so he could practice law, Charley tried and failed, by a ratio of two to one, to retroactively alter the record of his salary so as to boost future pension payments.

Charley Johns's tenure as a lion of the senate died when true reapportionment was thrust upon Florida from the outside. On June 22, 1964, the U.S. Supreme Court case *Swann v. Adams* kicked back a prior district court decision that had allowed a Pork Chopper reapportionment to stand on the grounds that Florida's traditional method of representation "should not be completely overturned." Now with federal court cases hanging overhead like guillotine blades, the legislature acted, and the resultingly dramatic reapportionment of 1965 obliterated Charley's beloved 15th senatorial district of Bradford and Union Counties.

The 1965 plan replaced the old 15th District with a brand-new 5th District, stretching across twenty-four North Florida counties, including portions of Alachua (home to the former Johns Committee turf of Gainesville). Imagine two to twenty-four counties in one leap. His vote had been disenfranchising to that proportional degree. As if unable to help himself, Charley did try to tamper with his new boundaries, but the Florida senate slapped down the measure.

To stay in the Florida senate through the 1967 session, Charley now had to win the same number of votes as any other member elected to the upper chamber. Charlie was unnerved by these developments, and his health declined. His gallbladder condition, dormant since 1953, returned. That December, at the age of sixty, Charley Johns entered a Jacksonville hospital to undergo surgery to remove his gallbladder. After the operation, his condition stabilized, and the Johns family told reporters that his outlook was "good." But for the first time in his legislative career, and the third in his political career, Charley Johns would face a truly democratic election. He fared about as well as he'd fared in past efforts when he didn't have his finger on the scale.

"We can't quite see how the experience and background of Charley Johns could give him much advantage in the newly reapportioned Senate," assessed the *Tallahassee Democrat*, which endorsed his Democratic opponent Hal Davis. Davis, a graduate of the University of Florida College of Law with the Class of 1958, could recall the worst of the Johns Committee's abuses. Attesting to his resiliency, Charley won the May 1966 primary over Davis, but he failed to secure a majority share. Lacking the stamina for a long campaign, Charley lost the runoff against Davis by a tally of 52,604 votes to 52,886. It was a squeaker, a 282-vote margin that took days to confirm.

"Charley Johns Beaten," reported the *Pensacola News Journal*, which went on to state inaccurately that Charley had served in the Florida senate "except for a 15-month term as acting governor" continuously since 1936. Charley's failed 1940 campaign for the U.S. Congress, resulting in a four-year absence from the legislature during World War II, was omitted from most newspaper accounts of his storied career. Although Charley claimed that he "heard there were some discrepancies" in the vote, "especially in Alachua County," he accepted the results.

"'Pork Choppers' Fall by Wayside," read another *Pensacola News Journal* headline. Indeed, the rural Pork Choppers held on to just seven seats in the senate, losing their factional majority in a swing that enfranchised Florida Republicans, who expanded their presence in the chamber from two to twenty. In an even more shocking outcome that November, Republican Claude R. Kirk Jr. was elected governor of Florida following months of Democratic Pork Chopper/Lamb Chopper infighting. The unthinkable had transpired: the election of the first Republican governor of Florida since 1877—the end of Reconstruction. The Pork Chopper dynasty, the system of one-party rule as Florida knew it, had suddenly died out, which sowed further uncertainty.

Charley closed up his offices in the capitol and packed his car for Starke. "I'm going to leave the headaches to him," Charley said of his successor Hal Davis. He exited at the right moment for a man loath to embrace the New South.

In 1967, a newly representative Florida legislature, with twenty Republicans and twenty-eight Democrats, met in session. They passed the Government in the Sunshine Law, or simply the "Sunshine Law," which banned closed meetings of all public bodies at state, county, and local levels. Senator J. Emory Cross of Gainesville, a man who understood the damage that secret meetings could bring, had introduced and sponsored the legislation for four consecutive sessions—since 1961—but never got it out of committee until Pork Chopper domination ended. "Executive session," a polite term used by the likes of Charley Johns to bar citizens from any watchdog capacity, was rendered illegal, and violators became subject to up to six months' imprisonment and a fine of $500.

When the U.S. Supreme Court revisited *Swann v. Adams* that same year, it officially struck down Florida's 1965 reapportionment plan as unconstitutional on the basis that it still failed to meet a "one man, one vote" standard. During an ensuing special session in June and July of 1968, the Florida legislature jettisoned Florida's 1885 constitution for its failure to fairly apportion districts and/or provide remedy for voting malapportionment through the political process. In its place, legislators enshrined what became known as the state's 1968 constitution. It was a new governing document that offered a clean slate, set population as the standard for voting districts, and wrote Florida's eighty-three-year experiment in apartheid out of the lawbooks.

When racial conflict didn't up and disappear with the state's new framework, Father Theodore Gibson stood at the ready. In the New Florida, where government agents could no longer de jure endorse white supremacy, men of true ability like Father Gibson received the chances they'd always deserved to lead communities. In 1968, Gibson mediated a standoff between the University of Miami president Henry King Stanford and fourteen Black students staging a sit-in demonstration in his administration office. After the student protesters were forcibly removed and arrested, Gibson visited them at the police station and joined with the nonviolent demonstrators in defending their right to protest.

When King was assassinated in Memphis, Gibson pastored to a city in grief. "That man has not died in vain," he counseled. "This tragedy ought to make all of us in Dade County, black and white, examine ourselves." On April 20, 1970, Father Gibson, a man once threatened with prison and hounded by state agents to the steps of the U.S. Supreme Court, led an opening prayer for the Florida legislature. His now-raspy voice echoed throughout the sunny chamber of the Florida house as he prayed for each of its members:

> As they engage in the government of this state, grant to them integrity of purpose and unfailing devotion to the cause of righteousness. May all their legislation be such as will promote all of our welfare, to the succor of the poor, the relief of the oppressed,

the putting down of all social evils, and the redress of all social wrongs.

On April 18, 1972, when former NAACP leader and *Gibson v. Florida Legislative Investigation Committee* plaintiff Edward Graham resigned from the Miami city commission to take another post, city leaders nominated Father Theodore Gibson to take his place, though he'd never considered holding political office.

Allies coalesced around the preacher, and fifty-six-year-old Gibson was approved on a unanimous ballot as the new city commissioner. "Politics is not my way of life," Gibson confessed. "I have no preconceived notions. I am open to whatever is before us." Gibson's style of quiet persuasion earned him a reputation as a political peacemaker. In 1973, Gibson became the vice-mayor of Miami, and in November of that year, he successfully ran for a new four-year term on the Miami commission.

In November 1980, Miami's Dixie Park was renamed the Theodore R. Gibson Park. One month later, a biopsy test revealed that Father Gibson had prostate cancer, which required aggressive surgery. He announced soon afterward that after nine and a half years of service, he would not be seeking reelection.

One year later, at age sixty-seven, Father Theodore R. Gibson took his final breath. A caravan of shiny cars created a traffic jam in Coconut Grove as hundreds filed by his casket at Christ Episcopal Church. Gibson's obituary appeared, among other notable places, in *The New York Times*. "In 1959, he was sentenced to a six-month term for contempt for refusing to turn over a membership list of Miami NAACP members to a state legislative committee investigating 'subversives,'" wrote the paper of record. "The decision was later overturned by the Supreme Court." Beneath the shade of an old tree in the City of Miami Cemetery, he was laid to rest.

Congressman Dante Fascell, a Democrat representing metro Jacksonville, honored Gibson with a eulogy in the Congressional Record: "He was beloved by south Floridians—black and white alike. He was their conscience."

No longer officially a public official, Charley Johns nonetheless continued to hold court from his cluttered desk in the offices of the

Charley E. Johns Insurance Agency in Starke, Florida. He also ran the local bank down the street. The nameplate on his desk read "Charley E. Johns, Governor." It didn't matter to locals that he'd never held that particular title. No one would dare give Charley Johns a hard time in his hometown, where he doled out reward and punishment from a deeply cushioned leather chair. He was governor in their hearts.

Evenings, he'd sit on his porch and regale listeners with stories of past battles. "The Johns Committee—that's how it's known, you know," he joked in 1972, "and I reckon when I die, it'll be headlined, 'Charley Johns of the Johns Committee Has Died.'"

Looking back, Charley blamed the homosexual investigations of his famous Johns Committee for embroiling his legacy: "We went investigating the homosexuals down at the University of Florida. They did not like that. It got me into a lot of trouble. We got rid of seventeen of them at the University of Florida and did not scratch the surface." He wished, in retrospect, that he'd remained "naïve" to all matters regarding so-called homosexualism.

However, casting his actions in a gallant light, he described any such sacrifice as worthwhile. "I tell you, I don't get no love out of hurting people," Charley insisted. "But that situation in Gainesville, my Lord a'mercy, I never saw anything like it in my life. If we saved one boy from being made homosexual, it was justified." As it turned out, Charley's ideological bequest to the state not only lingered but thrived. He'd planted his ideological seeds deep. Still, when the first FLIC scholar came calling for an interview, he rebuffed her request.

CHAPTER 30

Days of Future, Passed

Floyd T. Christian after federal sentencing

1977 (*Bonnie Stark Papers, National Stonewall Archives*)

IN THE LATE sixties, Mark Hawes reemerged from private practice to run for Tampa's state senate seat. Despite his infamous resignation from FLIC, Hawes never gave up his aspirations for higher office. During his campaign, Hawes expressed qualified regret for his involvement with the Johns Committee. "From my experience as counsel for that body, I learned that educational institutions should not be investigated," he said. He avoided outright repudiation of FLIC's goals and operations because aspects of his anti-homosexual and anti-Black crusades polled well with white voters. When Hawes received a furious thumping at the ballot box, he blamed the loss on local Democrats and began a new political courtship that culminated in his "big switch" to the Republican Party—part of the drift of Southern Democrats who rebranded themselves following the Civil Rights

Act. At some point, Hawes also considered a run for Hillsborough County solicitor, which didn't pan out for him either.

Hawes ran for office again in 1972, this time as an appellate judge for the Florida Second District Court of Appeals—a politically unaffiliated post. Conspicuously, Hawes omitted his nearly seven years of participation with the Johns Committee and his one Supreme Court appellate experience in campaign advertisements. He lost his bid for the judgeship, fulfilling a lifelong pattern of un-electability. In the late 1970s, Hawes suffered a debilitating stroke that claimed his ability to speak. The swaggering lawyer who once laughed to himself while jousting with the NAACP in the U.S. Supreme Court now struggled to string together a single sentence. After Hawes was robbed of his gift of gab, the Hawes family fell from grace financially, and he and his wife had to downscale from their Tampa residence to a trailer park in Zephyrhills, Florida. The Hawes family kept scrapbooks of the various phases of their patriarch's life, which they periodically reviewed with him to preserve his memories.

Many of Hawes's FLIC allies didn't do much better. Hillsborough county superintendent Floyd T. Christian received a promotion to Florida DOE superintendent before he became the first Florida cabinet member to wear prison stripes. In 1975, he went to jail for income tax evasion after failing to report $29,000 in bribes on his income taxes as well as awarding $1.5 million in no-bid contracts to friends. The former school official, who denied an equal education to many such as Tommie Jennings, served 135 days in a federal prison.

Mark Hawes died on April 24, 1985, at the young age of sixty. But before he perished, he agreed to meet at his home in rural Zephyrhills with the first Johns Committee scholar, a woman named Bonnie Stark, who reviewed his personal archive as he nodded with oxygen tubes in his nostrils.

BORN IN 1954, the year of the *Brown* decision, Bonnie Sue Stark was a child of the New South. Her family moved from Brooklyn to Miami, where she thrived as a young girl in the generation after Art Copleston's. A public school kid active in extracurriculars, Bonnie graduated from

Miami Norland Senior High School with the Class of 1972. After receiving her associate's degree from Miami-Dade Community College, she moved to Tampa to attend the University of South Florida, where she graduated with dual bachelor's degrees in American history and American literature.

A tireless student of her adoptive state, much like Sigismond Dietrich, she watched the culture of the New Florida evolve and sometimes return to its old ways, which inspired her to enroll in grad school for further studies. While pursuing her master's degree in American history, Bonnie Stark took a graduate seminar at USF on McCarthyism taught by a civil rights history professor named Dr. Steven F. Lawson. "I was sitting in class with Dr. Lawson," recalled Stark. "And he told us about the Johns Committee, and it hit—like a lightning bolt."

A contingent of the university maintained an institutional memory of Charley Johns's attempts to repeat the Gainesville purges on their turf. "There were colleagues at USF who were here during those times," validated Lawson. "I became aware that it went from race, it went on to Communism in the schools, and then of course the gay and lesbian angle." Stark found the story of this opportunistic committee fascinating, and Lawson encouraged her to make FLIC the focus of her master's thesis. "She was a prodigious researcher," Lawson recalled. "She would go anywhere she needed to go to uncover new materials. She knew that you should have historical objectivity, and she tried to maintain that, but she also felt deeply, deeply moved and pained by what this committee had done."

Another Floridian found her purpose in a different way while tracing the bread-crumb trail of Charley Johns. On January 1977, the Dade County Commission, with jurisdiction over Miami, proposed an ordinance to outlaw discrimination on the basis of sexual orientation in employment, housing, and public services. This legislation, heralded as a boon for homosexuals in Dade County, birthed an unexpected backlash from conservative Christians. Anita Bryant, a singer and spokesperson for Florida orange juice, became encouraged by her minister at Miami's Northwest Baptist Church to use her celebrity status to take a stand.

Bryant got a real taste for politics when she spoke against the ordinance in a community forum:

I've been a resident of Florida for 16 years. . . . I come here today with no prejudice in my heart, with no hate, no anger, or judgment of my fellow man. But what I do is come with a very deep burden on my heart for my county, for my community, especially because of this issue. And for my children . . .

I believe that I represent many people, and we urge you, the Dade County Commission, to be responsible to a vast majority of your constituents to not discriminate and to vote no.

Bryant's heartfelt words met with long applause. But over Bryant's objections, the anti-discrimination ordinance passed the Dade County Commission by vote of five to three. "This is just the beginning of our fight," vowed the singer.

Bryant felt public sentiment at her side, even if the 1950s moralism and pseudoscience behind her arguments had withered under expert critique. Several recent edits to the Revised Standard Version of the Bible and the American Psychiatric Association's *Diagnostic and Statistical Manual of Mental Disorders* handbook had modified their language on homosexuality. A quiet revision to the RSV Bible in 1971 changed 1 Corinthian's 6:9 infamous condemnatory word from *homosexuals* to *sexual perverts*. Likewise in 1973, a change was made to the second edition of the *DSM*, in recognition of the fact that its prior codification of homosexuality as a mental disease created stigmatization and became "misused by some people outside of our profession." By amending the disease definition to "Sexual Orientation Disturbance," the American Psychiatric Association hoped they would "be removing one of the justifications for the denial of civil rights to individuals."

Following her initial political loss, Bryant pivoted and launched a one-woman Save Our Children campaign out of her thirty-three-room mansion on Biscayne Bay. With the passage of the Dade County ordinance, Bryant feared that local homosexuals were "trying to recruit our children" at places like Northwest Christian Academy, the private school her four kids attended.

As Bryant was a Florida resident and had been a Baptist congregant during the Purple Pamphlet scandal, she'd internalized many of the Johns Committee's warnings about homosexual dangers to youth.

FLIC's old message, however, took on fresh resonance when she channeled its verbiage through the delivery system of a former Miss Oklahoma turned picture-perfect mother figure. Almost immediately, Bryant built a small army of followers in fellow Florida moms who aspired to be "like Anita."

Her anti-homosexual arguments parroted those of Charley Johns almost verbatim—homosexuality was an affront to God and America as well as a public nuisance and a threat to youth—but she never once quoted or mentioned the name of the former FLIC chairman. Records of the Johns Committee had been sealed for more than a decade. Few in the state could quite put their finger on what Charley's cabal may have done to the NAACP; how they tried to stop the Civil Rights Act by abetting a race war in St. Augustine; how they conspired against the U.S. government; and how they turned to homosexuality only when miscegenation ceased to be the primary sexual boogeyman. In April 1972, the Florida Department of Law Enforcement transferred the FLIC records for safekeeping to the Florida State Archives under the following agreement: "Records shall be preserved permanently or until such time as the destruction may be authorized by the Division of Archives, History and Records Management."

With evidence of Charley's savagery primed for annihilation at the check of a box, individuals like Anita Bryant unknowingly kept his ideology alive. With her painstakingly crafted hairdos and appeals to the wholesomeness of the traditional family, Bryant embodied the voice and style of a rebounding conservative segment of Americana. "As a mother, I know that homosexuals cannot biologically reproduce children; therefore, they must recruit," Bryant assured *The Palm Beach Post*.

Within weeks of organizing, Save Our Children submitted a petition with a record 64,304 signatures to put the Dade County ordinance up for a voter referendum in June 1977. Riding the Bryant anti-homosexual wave, legislators in Tallahassee sponsored two anti-homosexual bills to prohibit gay couples from marrying or adopting children to form households, and both passed resoundingly. "The problem is homosexuals are surfacing to such an extent that they're beginning to aggravate ordinary folks," said Senator Curtis Peterson of Lakeland, echoing the talking points of Save Our Children. "They are trying to flaunt it."

The Save Our Children campaign mobilized the largest voter turnout for a special election in Dade County history. By a stunning ratio of 69 percent to 31 percent on June 7, 1977, voters successfully revoked the ordinance for nondiscrimination.

Save Our Children's triumph represented not just a defeat for homosexual rights in Florida but also a revelatory win for conservative Christian forces nationwide. "We won 2 to 1, which is proof that the country sees homosexuals as child molesters and religious heretics," asserted a Save Our Children spokesperson. Elated, Anita Bryant danced a jig before news cameras at the celebratory rally. She told *The New York Times*, "With God's continued help, we will prevail in our fight to repeal similar laws throughout the nation." Similar legislative campaigns were brewing in California, Kansas, Minnesota, Oregon, Texas, and Washington.

The day after Dade County voters struck down the ordinance, the Florida governor signed the anti-homosexual adoption bill and the anti-same-sex marriage bill into law. Anita Bryant was riding high. Yet for the first time in her carefully managed singing and advertising career, she found herself embroiled in controversy. A key segment of Bryant's audience abhorred unpleasantness, so she experienced a drop in popularity and a barrage of negative publicity. Ordinarily performing up to a hundred concerts per year, she performed less than five in 1977 due to cancellations. A contract to host a daytime television sewing show evaporated. The unthinkable came to pass when the Florida Citrus Commission allowed her spokesperson contract to expire in 1980.

Meanwhile, graduate student Bonnie Stark stepped into untested legal waters searching for documentation of the state's past. Determined to make use of the Florida Sunshine Laws to reopen FLIC records, she wrote the Florida State Archives on May 27, 1980, to request access to the files. "I was very naïve when I started," she admitted. Attorney D. Stephen Kahn, staff lawyer of the Florida senate, responded to Stark on June 26, 1980, using the letterhead of the office of the senate president:

Dear Ms. Stark,

Your letter of May 27 to the Florida State Archives has been referred to me.

The investigative activities of the Florida Legislative Investigation Committee, commonly known as the Johns Committee, were conducted in "executive session" and were closed under a provision of Article III of the 1885 Constitution, then in effect.

That means the transcripts and materials were confidential when made and continue to be so. . . .

Sincerely yours,

D. Stephen Kahn

Hitting brick walls wherever she turned, Stark improvised novel ways to complete her thesis without access to the FLIC files. By collating and compiling archival newspaper and court records, Stark began reconstructing a fragmented picture of what Charley Johns and his committee perpetrated. She spent hours each day rummaging through case folders and painstakingly reviewing microfiche under lights. In the early 1980s, Bonnie Stark moved from Tampa to Tallahassee to facilitate her research. She requested an interview from one Charley E. Johns, who declined to speak to her via letter on February 19, 1982. Charley maintained that he was old and no longer possessed a recollection of the people he may or may not have hurt through his work.

To be fair, Charley truly was in poor health. In his late seventies, he became, according the *New-Press*, "confined to his home because of a series of strokes." At his eightieth-birthday reception, he stayed parked in a chair while well-wishers, some of whom he could not remember, filed past—an alarming sign for a man who once possessed near-perfect recall. When the local newspaper asked him to pose for a snapshot, Charley stared like death into the lens. It was as if time had closed a loop and rendered him as helpless as the boy in the flour-sack underwear. "He died a horrible, horrible death," agreed his former colleague Cliff Herrell.

In April 1984, Bonnie Stark met and interviewed former chief investigator Remus Strickland in his office at the Florida Department of Natural Resources (DNR) in the state capital. By exhibiting the professional style of a paralegal, Stark had long ago perfected the art of inviting the underestimation of males, in order to get them to drop their guards. Around 1970, Strickland told her, he'd found his way back into state employment, and he got hired by DNR on the recommendation of former FLIC officials. There, for more than a decade, he'd toiled in relative obscurity as a state investigator for waterfront projects. But his bureaucratic niche came under fire on May 6, 1980.

That Tuesday, U.S. attorneys unsealed a twenty-page indictment of Strickland. They charged him with four counts of perjury for his false testimony about personal ties to a kickback scheme with a construction firm in Panama City. The FBI had Strickland on tape acknowledging that he expected to receive 25 percent of a $6,000 overpayment of federal hurricane recovery loan funds in exchange for inside dirt about DNR approvals and future construction jobs. Unaware of the audio evidence, Strickland denied these points under oath to a federal grand jury. It was the ultimate irony that a former investigator who used the threat of perjury to wring out countless tape-recorded confessions ended up charged with that very crime.

Strickland was arrested, perp-walked out of the Florida DNR, and suspended from his $17,415-per-year state position. In court, Strickland maintained that he'd plum "forgotten" his conversations with the Panama City firm during his grand jury testimony. He testified that he'd always intended to quit his DNR job should other lucrative opportunities arise. The fact that FBI surveillance shut down the venture was, according to Strickland's lawyers, immaterial.

Jurors deliberated late into Thursday evening, July 3, but the presiding judge refused to release the jury pool when they asked if they could go home to sleep and reconvene the next morning. So at 2:15 a.m. on the Fourth of July 1980, the jury delivered its verdict: not guilty on all counts. Strickland emerged in the clear, once again, by the skin of his teeth.

Thus was Remus Strickland still employed by the state when Bonnie Stark approached him in 1984. Somehow, through her unassuming style and talents as an interviewer, Stark got Strickland to speak candidly. He spoke on the record and at length. "It [the committee] deserves a role in the history of the state as an eye-opener," Strickland contended. "It was the beginning of an era of public awareness to some of the things that were put away in the closet for too many years." It was the only interview he ever gave about his history with FLIC.

Although Strickland expressed bitterness about accusations involving his misuse of authority, he stood resolute on the importance of his work for "heart of gold" Charley Johns. "I was very pleased with the service I did for the people," he told Bonnie Stark, "especially children, inasmuch as I was a part of exposing a serious problem in the school system." When Remus James "Strick" Strickland died at the age of seventy on November 1, 1992, he received only a small death notice in the *Tallahassee Democrat*, which did not mention his Johns Committee work. Despite a lifetime of clambering toward the limelight while pushing down others he viewed as unworthy or in his way, the man did not receive a public memorial. Few but Bonnie Stark observed his passing, and even she did not put flowers on his grave.

Bonnie Stark submitted her master's thesis, "McCarthyism in Florida: Charley Johns and the Florida Legislative Investigation Committee" in April 1985. Her USF thesis committee, led by Professor Steven Lawson, enthusiastically accepted the work and awarded her the degree.

CHAPTER 31

Truth Will Out

Copleston's first photograph of Dennis Fillmore, captioned "The day we met"

1971 (*Art Copleston Papers, Beutke Papers, Bonnie Stark Papers*)

FOR MUCH OF his life, Art Copleston had a hard time thinking about his mother without feeling enraged. After he was outed to her in such a painful manner, he regarded her as an inherently unhappy person. Somehow they cohabitated in misery for another two years before he reached a breaking point. In 1971, Copleston quit his job in Pennsylvania, packed up his mom in the car, and drove across the country to Merced, California. There he shoved her off on her gay, alcoholic brother. Feeling freed of a tremendous burden, Copleston drove to San Francisco ready to start fresh.

In Merced, after a brief stay at the Belmont Psychiatric Hospital, Margaret Copleston managed to get sober and regain her mental health. She spent the last twenty-three years of her life without a single drop of alcohol. Yet, as she was what Copleston called "generationally incapable" of admitting fault, Margaret never found the grace to apologize for the manner in which she'd lived, parented, punished, levied expectations, and otherwise traumatized her only child.

Art Copleston found love in the Bay Area. He never could forget the day they met: June 2, 1972. On a weekend camping trip in the Sierra foothills with a group of gay friends, Copleston climbed down a cliff to explore the shoreline of the Yuba River. When Copleston glanced back up toward the summit, there he stood in khaki shorts and a striped T-shirt: Dennis "Denny" Fillmore. They gazed at each other in mutual fascination. The attraction was strong and immediate. When they got to talking, they discovered they both were ex-military. They both were only children. They both had self-centered mothers, and as a result, both were masters at controlling their emotions.

Copleston and Denny would spend the next thirty years together, investing in real estate and attending black-tie openings of the San Francisco Opera, which Denny also adored. The couple hosted lavish dinners and Super Bowl watch parties in their gated home on 1270 Panorama Drive overlooking the Berkeley Hills. Still, trauma plagued Art Copleston. "You never enjoy anything," Denny told him one day, pinpointing Copleston's "memory attacks" as reason to seek out professional counseling.

He tried to get better. "I am a tarnished, less-than-normal person," Copleston explained. "I didn't ever feel that way until I met Mr. Tileston that night at the Burger House. And I have felt that way ever since."

Copleston bore the scars of the Johns Committee, not just psychologically but bodily. "It became clear that while [Denny] really, really preferred anal sex, I didn't want anything to do with anal sex," Copleston said. Though he didn't like delving into why, Copleston couldn't bring himself to engage in anal intercourse with a lover, even in his wildest Boston days. He couldn't attempt the physical act without feeling sick to his stomach. The couple sought out a sex therapist, who spent countless hours in sessions with them working to repair the psychological wound.

At one point, Denny and the sex therapist arranged a weekend in Honolulu to create the ideal conditions. From the floor of their rented condo, Copleston broke down and told Denny, "Honey, I can't do this." Art Copleston never thought to tell a shrink about what happened to him back in Gainesville, and when he tried to broach the subject with Denny, Denny couldn't see how it related. After all, besides the Purple Pamphlet, little documentation about the Johns Committee existed, and Denny was a logic-driven man.

Thus an unspoken arrangement developed. Denny "went off on his own" privately and sought outside partners, while he and Copleston maintained a loving domestic bubble. For Copleston, it was a painful but necessary accommodation so that they could stay a couple.

In 1986, Denny came home to 1270 Panorama Drive and announced loudly, "I'm HIV positive!" before storming to their bedroom and slamming the door. When Denny emerged, Copleston poured two glasses of wine, and they rationally discussed what to do next. Copleston got tested and confirmed that he was HIV negative. The couple were determined to not let their HIV status dominate their lives, and they went on long vacations to Australia, Europe, Key West, and elsewhere around the world.

Dennis "Denny" Fillmore lived for another sixteen years. When he passed in 2002, Copleston had his remains interred in a mausoleum for two at Forest Lawn Cemetery in Cathedral City, California. The epitaph on his gravestone reads:

We Met in Mountain Majesty, in Love Three Score Ago
In Desert Splendor We Rest Together, Now and Evermore

Copleston's last name is already etched into the marble cairn, along with his birth date. When his death date finally appears in stone, Copleston will reside in the berth beside the love of his life, where they'll rest together. Even now, at the age of ninety-two, Art Copleston finds it hard to admit, as it renders him so powerless, that the Johns Committee did such damage to him that it not only permanently altered his relationship to his own body but possibly played a supporting role in the suffering and death of his great love, Dennis Fillmore.

When Denny died, Art Copleston lost his emotional connection to the gay world. He retreated indoors. The identifying word *queer*, as it returned to the fore in a reclaimed "queer studies" context by the mid-2000s, lingered as such a painful slur in his mind, so visceral a reminder of the day Tileston "tarnished" him, that he could not stand to hear it. Copleston often asks younger gay folk not to speak the word so freely in his presence—people who say they understand, but in truth fault him for lack of enlightenment. (I must admit, I was one of them.)

"Had the demeaning and belittling experiences as a target of Johns Committee permanently warped my sense of self?" Copleston asked himself in a self-published memoir. "Was I projecting onto all gay people all of the negative stereotypes of gays that had been promoted by Strickland and Tileston? To this day, I have not been able to successfully answer these important questions."

Then in 1999, a communications major at the University of Florida researching the Johns Committee named Allyson Beutke sent an email to Art Copleston requesting an interview, and Copleston readily agreed to speak on-camera for a class documentary assignment. He flew down to Gainesville to relive his memories in the places where they occurred. In a jolt to Copleston, Officer John "Bill" Tileston, recently retired from a career in law enforcement and still living in mid-Florida, also resurfaced to participate in Beutke's project.

In the final cut of Beutke's documentary, titled *Behind Closed Doors: The Dark Legacy of the Johns Committee*, she intermingled portions of Tileston's interview with Copleston's recollections. Tileston admitted to using harsh apprehension techniques to terrorize UF students: "They were asked to come to the university police department, and they were asked in such a way that they really didn't have much of a choice."

But ultimately, Tileston could not fully repudiate what he'd done as an arm of the law for Charley Johns. "I can't say that I ever regret anything that I've done professionally," he said. "I've worked very hard for thirty-two years in my profession. There was some things I would have liked to have changed, but I was not in any position to change those things." For Art Copleston, anything short of an unqualified apology in person from Tileston felt "flimsy and self-serving," and Copleston viewed the editorial decision to air Tileston's commentary side by side with his own as unfortunate.

Tileston continued to participate in several other Johns Committee documentaries, articles, and educational panels throughout his golden years. Beutke guessed that these were efforts aimed to advertise his freelance private detective business. "He was looking for redemption,"

Copleston concluded. "But he certainly wasn't begging for mercy or begging for understanding and appreciation and love. He expected all of that. Because he's a cop." When Officer John Tileston passed away in 2014, he represented the only former agent of FLIC who regularly made himself available to describe what he'd done.

Unable to remember or account for his actions in his final breaths, Charles Eugene "Charley" Johns closed his eyes and died at Alachua County Hospital in Gainesville on January 23, 1990. As a former acting governor of a populous state, he received a loud public send-off. "Charley Johns: End of an Era," rang out the headline in the *Orlando Sentinel*. "Mr. [LeRoy] Collins was the first of the new style of governors, and Mr. Johns was the last of the old," read the obituary. "Long offstage, long has the curtain on his era been closed." Florida governor Bob Martinez ordered state flags to be flown at half-staff. "He was always very personable and amiable," remembered LeRoy Collins, his former rival.

A pitched battle ensued to determine the man's legacy. "In 1961, he was presented a plaque for meritorious service by members of the Legislature as the Senator most effective in committee," reported the *Bradford County Telegraph* of Starke. "Although he was a sometimes controversial figure—as all politicians must be—Johns was noted, especially during his term as Acting Governor, for being a friend to the elderly and unemployed," stated the *Telegraph*. The *Miami Herald* was cutting: "Floridians undoubtedly felt mixed emotions following the death this week of former Gov. Charley Johns. Their human sympathies were tempered by unpleasant memories of the harm that he inflicted upon lives and careers."

The Johns family held the funeral at the First Baptist Church in Starke, with a Masonic burial following at the Crosby Lake Cemetery. More than three hundred state leaders, friends, and relatives attended the service. "Charley Johns cared about his constituents," preached the pastor of the First Baptist Church. "He was many things to many people," qualified another pastor, "but to those who knew him, he was just Charley."

Charley's death did bring to the forefront fresh debate about the notorious, yet mysterious and oft overlooked Johns Committee. "Should death wipe the slate clean?" asked a *Herald* columnist. "What

I remember from those days is . . . the Johns Committee's 'destructive witch hunts.'" Former political allies stepped forward to defend Charley Johns and his eponymous committee's work. "Some reporter asked me if I thought anybody's civil rights had been violated," recalled Cliff Herrell. "I said well, if they were, it wasn't a question thirty years ago. They were wrong and doing wrong, or at least accused of doing wrong, and the public supported the inquiry." Renewed coverage of FLIC inspired additional calls to unseal the records, which were stored in the Florida State Archives until the Office of the Secretary of the Florida Senate requested them back, likely for extra protection.

Senate staff attorney Stephen Kahn, on behalf of the senate president Gwen Margolis, repeatedly denied requests to release the records, and Margolis ultimately decreed that the files would not become available until December 31, 2028. As it happened, anyone involved in the Johns Committee affair would be dead and buried by 2028 and therefore unable to seek recourse. Bonnie Stark petitioned Stephen Kahn again to open the records on June 26, 1992. Not only did Kahn deny her request again, but he enclosed a copy of his original denial letter, sent to her twelve years prior to the day: June 26, 1980.

Then in November 1992, voters tipped the scales in Bonnie Stark's favor. Florida citizens overwhelmingly approved a constitutional amendment to "grant public access to records and meetings of the executive, judicial, and legislative branches of state government, and other governmental entities; to allow the Legislature to enact exemptions and rules." The full weight of the 1968 Florida constitution now mandated access to Johns Committee records unless otherwise specifically exempted by vote of the legislature by June 30, 1993.

The FLIC records dilemma, thus, got kicked back to the legislature with the game clock ticking. State senators like Betty Holzendorf of Jacksonville mused about destroying the inconvenient files rather than having to pass onerous exemptions on a tight timeline. "Any we're in doubt of, we can always throw away," said Senator Holzendorf. "It doesn't work that way, Senator," countered an advocate for open records.

During the 1993 session, the legislature drafted and passed an overreaching bill to exempt from public review all current and historic work papers, drafts, and supporting documentation from their branch of government. On May 14, 1993, Florida governor Lawton Chiles sent the bill back to the legislature with a strong veto message. In response, the legislature was forced to enter special session to prevent whole caches of documents from becoming public domain with their sensitive information intact.

Senate lawyer Stephen Kahn worked overtime to draft a more modest bill that limited exemptions to notable cases. He defined one such exemption as 2(e): "Portions of records of former legislative investigating committees whose records are sealed or confidential as of June 30, 1993, which may reveal the identity of any person to whom reference is made in such records."

In a panic on May 25, 1993, Bonnie Stark wrote to Senator Toni Jennings, chairman of the senate committee on rules and calendar. "This language could be interpreted to exempt even records that identify noncontroversial names such as legislators who served on this committee, staff members," Stark warned. The next day, the Senate Committee had Stark in the chamber to testify. She stood in the capitol as a lone advocate for amending a law that stood to censor all of FLIC's operational papers.

Patiently, Bonnie Stark waited to be recognized by the committee chairman, and then she spoke:

> I believe that when the Florida voters voted on the constitutional amendment on November 3, 1992, to ensure public access to records of the legislature, that in doing so, they did not intend for exemptions that would circumvent the intent of that constitutional amendment. . . . As a student of Florida history and a Florida citizen, it is important that once the records of committees like the Johns Committee are opened, that every effort is made to ensure that their historical integrity remains intact and that the complete history of these types of committees can be told in Florida history books. I thank you all for your attention. . . .

As Stark addressed the committee, she looked up several times and noticed how only one senator—Fred Dudley—returned eye contact and seemed to be paying attention. All other senators had their heads turned to whisper to aides. In a question-and-answer session that followed, Senator Dudley asked Bonnie Stark, "So in other words, you would have us limit it [exemption 2e] so that, for example, if a legislator made a statement or had taken a position, that portion of the record would not be deleted?" Stark, playing the underestimation game once again, sensed an opportunity to preserve half of every FLIC transcript by keeping the names of state officials and staff untouched. She responded: "Exactly, senator." To counter Stark's points, senate attorney Stephen Kahn took the microphone:

> When the Johns Committee met, the records that are in the public domain of the Johns Committee show a policy between Senator Johns and others that said enough for me to conclude that the witnesses and the targets were both given an assurance, to the extent that that committee could do, that information developed would be kept confidential.

Couching his testimony with the legal qualifier "enough for me to conclude," the senate lawyer who'd denied Stark access for thirteen years played loose linguistically with an inconvenient truth: Victim confidentiality was hardly the modus operandi of FLIC, a state body whose primary weapon was public shame. Impressed by Stark's testimony, Senator Dudley proposed a revised clause for the FLIC exemption, which he drafted while Kahn was speaking. It passed the committee by a vote of nine to one.

The senate rules committee then clarified, through Kahn, that Dudley's revised exemption to allow public access to redacted records would supersede Senate President Margolis's planned full and uncensored release of the FLIC files in 2028. These material exclusions wouldn't precede a full release in the twenty-first century; they would occur instead of a full release. Any names redacted or made confidential through the exemption process in 1993 would be redacted, said committee lawyers, "forever."

When Senate Bill 20-B reached the chamber, thirty-one legislators voted yea and six opposed. Despite the clear legislative bias that was demonstrated against open access, Bonnie Stark's testimony spared half of every FLIC hearing and interrogation transcript from being redacted in full. Her clever maneuver left open the possibility of future

FLIC researchers using official titles, dates, identifying details, and excision mistakes to recover the mutilated record in later years.

On June 13, 1993, Florida governor Lawton Chiles allowed Senate Bill 20-B to become law without his signature—joining the passive assent of governors past. It was a final abandonment of responsibility in favor of the reduction of liability. To argue that erasing the names of citizens on the original documents protected FLIC victims from further harm was to overlook the reality that every name on a piece of paper constituted potential evidence, should any FLIC victim have sought an official apology or tried to make a case for reparations. Because the names of the victims would be deleted, the state could continue to credibly deny responsibility for those they'd hurt.

CHAPTER 32

The Great Erasure

*Redacted transcript of FLIC agents hired
by Johns who attended 1964 Klan meeting*

July 1993 (*Bonnie Stark Papers*)

THE REDACTION PROCEDURE commenced almost imme-
diately in the basement of the senate office building. Senate secretary
Joe Brown hired a team of three undergraduate students from Florida
State University to cull through an estimated 30,000 pages of FLIC documents, stacked in twenty-one boxes. As instructed, the students used
dark markers to ink over the names of committee targets, witnesses,
and informants as well as revealing details that could point toward an
easy identification. The students made line-by-line deletions directly
upon the historic materials so as to make the erasures permanent.

As amateur censors racing to complete their mission during the
month of June, the students were both imperfect and overeager in their
textual modifications. Attempting to be exhaustive, they unlawfully deleted the names of key FLIC witnesses who were known to the public

record in 1993, such as plaintiff Virgil D. Hawkins, *Miami Herald* editor Allen Neuharth, and NAACP leader Father Theodore Gibson. The student censors also blacked out the names of key individuals interrogated behind closed doors for alleged infractions but who then became publicized in the media pre-1993, such as William James Neal of *Neal v. Bryant*, convicted child predator Charles Howard Montague Jr., and former University of Florida geography chairman Sigismond Diettrich. "They were just kids," Bonnie Stark remembered, shaking her head.

In the rush to redact longer transcripts, the student censors often accidentally left exposed first or last names of private individuals interrogated in private settings—identities, by law, meant for exemption. Or they left portions of first and last letters of names visible with their marker dashes. Or they left portions of letters with descenders, such as *g* and *p*, and letters with ascenders, such as *t* and *h*, observable. Or they struck out a name so precisely as to leave exposed the exact number of letters in the name. "You could track and trace down a lot of them," admitted senate secretary Joe Brown, "if somebody really wanted to."

Lastly, the student censors unlawfully and permanently deleted the names of countless public officials who were not exempt, such as the school superintendent of Lake County; the sheriff of Suwannee County; the chairman of the state board of control; and the acting director of the Florida Children's Commission, just for starters. In addition, Joe Brown confirmed to the *Miami Herald* that all photographs of homosexual activity amassed by FLIC were "incinerated" in 1963—Strickland's last year as chief investigator.

Bonnie Stark was there at eight a.m. on July 1, 1993, when the state of Florida opened the doors to room A of the senate office building. Like cicadas, reporters and academics descended upon the harvest.

For easier access, senate secretary Brown made two copies of the twenty-one FLIC boxes and then broke the chain of custody by divvying up the juiciest materials into three large piles: homosexual activity, Communist activity, miscellaneous activity. Nearly every major paper in Florida and most publications in the continental United States, from *The Philadelphia Inquirer* to the *San Francisco Examiner*, covered the story of the document release. "Florida Examines Era of Suspicion," announced *The New York Times*. Most reports were one-offs, written by journalists on tight deadlines eager to fly back home.

As Bonnie Stark recalls, the crowd in room A dwindled by the week's end, and within three weeks, the investigative journalists doing long-form pieces had departed. Soon Stark found herself more or less alone with the FLIC files, and room A became akin to her private library. Joe Brown determined that it was time to transfer the 30,000-plus papers back to the Florida State Archives. Taking mercy on Bonnie Stark, keeping in mind that he'd made two copies of all materials (marked version A and version B), aides to Brown exercised their discretion to give Bonnie Stark the full second set of FLIC records: twenty-one boxes, which she packed up in her car and hauled back to her house.

With an unprecedented records cache on her hands, Stark received a contract from the University of Florida Press to expand her Johns Committee thesis into a book. But just then, her legal career with a Tallahassee litigation firm took off. "I always put my professional work first," Stark explained. Time blurred, and she struggled to carve out the necessary headspace to finish even a chapter. However, she was not bashful with telling others about her possession of the secret second set of the Johns Committee records. "My friends knew I had the boxes," Stark insisted, and she participated in several FLIC history panels where she publicly attested to their existence. It seems, however, that academics in the growing Johns Committee subfield of queer southern history overlooked her. Even Stark's mentor and master's thesis advisor Stephen Lawson was taken aback when he learned of Stark's private archive in September 2024. Likewise, agents of the state moved on with their daily affairs and forgot all about Bonnie Stark.

In 1994, Republican Florida gubernatorial candidate Jeb Bush stated that Florida gays and lesbians should not receive "additional" legal protections from discrimination, resurrecting Anita Bryant's bygone argument about gays wanting extra privileges in the guise of so-called basic guarantees. Bush reiterated that landlords and employers should have the right to turn gays and lesbians away. "I don't think we need to hurt people," said Bush. "But I'm totally opposed to the expansion of additional legal rights for people based on their sexual preference."

Governor Jeb Bush, elected in 1998, rigorously defended Florida's Anita Bryant–era gay adoption law as his state became a kingmaker, politically and culturally, in the new century. During the 2000 presidential election, Governor Bush recused himself from the hotly contested Florida vote recount, which ultimately sent his brother, Texas governor George W. Bush, to the White House on a winning margin of 537 votes from the Sunshine State. It was the closest presidential contest of all time.

Charley's seeds of distrust and discord, his longing to return to a past where "de old folks stay," had burrowed deep into the state's unconscious—often provoking "Johns-ian" revivals that didn't even know they cribbed the man's style. In 2008, voters amended the state constitution to explicitly deny same-sex couples the right to marriage:

Inasmuch as marriage is the legal union of only one man and one woman as husband and wife, no other legal union that is treated as marriage or the substantial equivalent thereof shall be valid or recognized.

A complete lack of digital access to the FLIC records and constraints to view the redacted records in paper form had the net result of obscuring Charley Johns's durable stamp on state politics. For example, in the summer 2005 issue of the University of Florida alumni magazine *UF Today*, Charley Johns was highlighted among eighty-one distinguished "Gators You Should Know," though he never graduated from the school.

Meanwhile, advocates for garden-variety Florida sentimentality fought to have old things remembered in fond ways, which helped keep former UF president J. Wayne Reitz's name on the UF student union in Gainesville as well as Charley's name on the Johns Building, a state office structure at 725 South Bronough Street in Tallahassee that got demolished in the late 2000s.

It wasn't until 2008 that the official song of the State of Florida, the minstrel tune "Old Folks at Home," was revised to remove slavery references. "Still longing for de old plantation" changed to "Still longing for my childhood station." And "Oh, darkies, how my heart grows weary" transformed to "O dear ones, how my heart grows weary." Florida's Anita Bryant–era anti-gay adoption ban, passed in 1977, endured until 2010, when it was struck down by a Florida judge, though it remained vestigial on the books, unenforceable but lingering as part of state law, until 2015. Some Floridians still have a hard time letting that one go.

CHAPTER 33

Arc of History

State of Florida Archives building

Present times

IN 2018, FLORIDA representative Evan Jenne, a South Florida Democrat from Broward County, decided it was past due for the
State of Florida to acknowledge and apologize for the abuses of the
Johns Committee. His father, a Florida senator in the late 1970s,
"pointed it out to me at a young age," recalled Jenne, "saying this was
an instance where the government of the State of Florida specifically
targeted individuals because of who they were and tried to destroy
their lives at every turn."

Jenne reached out to another scholar on the Johns Committee, Dr.
Stacy Braukman (author of the prizewinning 2012 monograph on the
Johns Committee, *Communists and Perverts Under the Palms*), to
compose the language of his resolution. Braukman delivered the draft
to Jenne in December 2018. Her 700-word resolution was a master-
work of concision that provided an unambiguous repudiation and tally
of the committee's abuses:

A concurrent resolution acknowledging the injustices perpetrated against the targets of the Florida Legislative Investigation

Committee between 1956 and 1965, and offering a formal and heartfelt apology to those whose lives, well-being, and livelihoods were damaged or destroyed by the activities and public pronouncements of those who served on the committee.

Measure in hand, Representative Jenne submitted the FLIC apology resolution to the civil justice subcommittee of the Florida house for consideration on February 18, 2019. His ally Senator Lauren Book submitted the same resolution to a Florida senate committee the next day.

"I couldn't get an answer on anything," recalled Jenne. "Finally, two friends from the other side of the aisle came to me . . . and they just said, 'They're not going to do it. They're not going to do it. They do not want to talk about this stuff.'" Stalled in committee, the apology resolution did not proceed to a floor vote. Undiscouraged, the legislators cosponsored the same apology resolution in 2020, and it died in committee again. The legislators tried in 2021 to the same results.

Just as Republican governor Ron DeSantis voiced his support for the Florida Parental Rights in Education Act in 2022, commonly called the Don't Say Gay bill, to prohibit LGBT+ instruction in classrooms from kindergarten to grade three, Representative Jenne submitted his FLIC apology resolution a fourth time, and Republican colleagues wiped the floor with it on March 14, 2022. Fourteen days later, Governor DeSantis signed the Don't Say Gay bill. Weeks after that, DeSantis signed the Individual Freedom Act, nicknamed the Stop WOKE Act, to prohibit any K–12 instruction that would induce students to "feel guilt, anguish, or other forms of psychological distress because of actions, in which the individual played no part, committed in the past by other members of the same race."

In a classic case of everything old is new again, Charley Johns's breed of Pork Chopper politics, which embraced nostalgia by disremembering past traumas, apologized for nothing, and bent the law for personal spoils, resurfaced with a vengeance. DeSantis supporters in the legislature often claimed to target queers and "woke" Black scholars in defense of children and moral sanctity.

Representative Evan Jenne was term-limited out of office in 2022 and rendered unable to lead the FLIC apology effort. Nonetheless,

Representative Jenne's and Stacy Braukman's resolution language endured archivally in the state record, readily available to legislators, who could no longer fully plead ignorance.

The FLIC apology resolution was last proposed in 2023 and 2024, where it languished just as anti-trans bathroom bills and gender-affirming-care bans advanced to chamber votes. Meanwhile, Governor Ron DeSantis's Department of Education rejected a proposed AP African American studies course for high school students, calling it "indoctrination masquerading as education."

I EMAILED BONNIE Stark at her Tallahassee law firm on August 18, 2021. The totality of the FLIC records, I had been led to believe by other Florida historians, were held in redacted paper form in one place in the world: the Soviet-like edifice of the State Archives complex of the capital city. I'd already spent several months traveling there to peruse and photograph each document, kept under lock and key by an archival staff that permitted me to handle only one folder at a time and allowed me to view that folder's contents only while sitting in one specific seat that directly faced their desks.

I reached out to Stark hoping to find an ally in the trenches. I'd read and loved her thesis "McCarthyism in Florida," which she had generously offered to the Florida Heritage website in May 2000 for digitization and free availability online. Almost as soon as I finished the last page, I knew I had to ask her what happened to the transcript of her now-priceless interview with Remus Strickland back in 1984. As it turns out, she held on to it. She had the instinct to hold on to everything, even when she couldn't rationally explain why.

Bonnie Stark had been hard at work, I would soon discover. Hacking away at the Johns Committee in her own time, Bonnie Stark catalogued her twenty-one boxes and ferried them through several moves, sometimes keeping her nest egg safe at her paralegal office. Still periodically digging through the State Archives on Saturdays, Stark stumbled by chance upon a possible decryption key to a series of censored FLIC documents—a single list that could be used to recover names censored from the interrogation transcripts of Gainesville professors during the 1958 and 1959 University of Florida purges.

This black-and-white list of fired UF scholars, titled "University of Florida Resignations," sat for decades in the 1959 section of the Governor LeRoy Collins papers until Bonnie Stark reached into the haystack and pulled forth a needle. Eventually, as she would share with me, she came to understand why the misdeeds of the Johns Committee so "deeply, deeply moved and pained her," in the words of her mentor. Because she was a child born the year of the *Brown* decision, it was preternaturally her life's mission to ensure that the committee's violations of the U.S. Constitution be widely known.

I experienced a separate research coup in the digital archives of the Mississippi Sovereignty Commission. Because of Remus Strickland's hubris back in 1961, at the height of his Johns Committee powers, a full list of the names of fired Florida teachers had been mailed across state lines to a Mississippi agent named Andy Hopkins. That list, perfectly preserved from the day it arrived on Hopkins's desk on June 30, 1961, traded hands until it sat in a vault of the Mississippi Department of Archives and History. Then in March 1998, following a multi-decade ACLU lawsuit, those records went public in their entirety.

In 2002, the Mississippi Sovereignty Commission collection was digitized and made freely available online, which is where I found Strickland's pristine letter.

On Tuesday, August 24, 2021, the Florida State Archives formally denied me access to the only unredacted box of FLIC materials that I'd located in their collections. They told me that the box's contents, filed by the Florida Clerk of the House, weren't important. (It contained the sole surviving copies of the FLIC meeting minutes, the very same minutes that senate lawyer Stephen Kahn had reviewed in 1993.) The archivists explained to me that they'd need to initiate a review process with the state general counsel, which could take months, and the result might be that they would have to, according to strictures of the 1993 law, redact those materials in a present-day effort—so that neither I nor any future researcher could view them in original form.

I tried not to raise my voice. I implored them, in such a case, not to perform their redactions upon the originals, not to deface any more history. I composed an email for the State Archives team to relay to the general counsel, whose name I still don't know, arguing that the 1993 FLIC statute did not call for post hoc redactions to materials available to the public since the 1980s. The archival team assured me that they would include my thoughts in a "request package" to "legal," but I have no way of verifying if this was done.

Objectively, Florida had checked my king. Its knot of evasiveness appeared too convoluted to unwind with patience. I'd tried to help a historic cause, and instead I hurt it by failing to notice that my efforts were being watched. I'd exhausted my book advance spending weeks as a gay guy at an archive near the Florida Panhandle, and I had only made a bad situation worse by drawing the state's attention to the last piece of the past they'd neglected to harm.

My naïveté seemed boundless. I was about to email my editor to tell her that I couldn't fulfill the terms of our publishing contract. But before I pulled that lever, I hopped onto a video chat with the first Johns Committee scholar. "I've lugged these around forever," Bonnie Stark told me, pointing to the boxes teetering in her small legal office. She'd held on to the second set all this time. "Right now, they're in my office at work. I know," she said, laughing. "And I want to give them to you."

Cloud Reading

Present day

THE BOX CAME back to me. It came back whole and intact. They didn't disappear or deface its contents. The only explanation I can venture is that the woman to whom I sent the email believed in what I was doing and stuck her neck out to help. There are friends of Dorothy in any system.

Once I cross-referenced the disappearing/reappearing box with the Bonnie Stark collection and the "University of Florida Resignations" list and the Mississippi Sovereignty Commission decoding sheet, it was as if a portal to a past opened, and I stepped through it. The winding route I once took to fathom how Tallahassee politics become national politics resolved itself as more or less a straight line through Charley Johns. Standing in the middle of a palace of information, I finally understood how it would be possible to decensor more than 75 percent of the FLIC papers for the first time in history. I would be able to take the shards of all those tantrums and lies and conspiracies and reassemble a mosaic of the truth, because that is what Americans do best besides scaring the ever-living shit out of one another: putting America back together again.

It was the ultimate blessing and fait accompli that the psychological hang-ups of a few white tyrants in Florida and Mississippi, and their instincts to save their trophies, kept the story of the Johns Committee in a condition where it could be retrieved. Perhaps the greatest liberty in any country is the freedom to know one's country, and I felt truly free. I stepped outside in New Orleans to let my mind dance across the rising thunderheads of the southern sky, and a bracing new knowledge rolled toward me on waves.

ACKNOWLEDGMENTS

NO BOOK HAPPENS by accident, and no book happens alone. Recovering and writing queer history reminds me of the Goethe phrase "Be bold, and mighty forces will come to your aid." These are the forces that came to mine. *American Scare* happened because a coalescence of events and allies brought the story into my life. Every person in that chain deserves a share of credit.

First, a tremendously talented queer history scholar and Floridian named Dr. Julio Capó Jr. curated an important 2019 exhibit at the HistoryMiami Museum titled "Queer Miami: A History of LGBTQ Communities." By happenstance, my writing and journalistic mentor Samuel G. Freedman visited that exhibit in March 2019 and told me that I absolutely had to make the trip.

I was broke at the time, but I scrounged up enough for a cheap morning flight on July 16, 2019, and my life changed. The "Queer Miami" exhibition featured a section of video interviews about a little-known anti-queer cabal in the 1950s called the Johns Committee, and a FLIC scholar named Stacy Braukman, who I did not yet know, made the following statement: "Today, I'm not sure how many people know about the Johns Committee at all." Why not? I wondered. Braukman was baiting me. I asked myself a follow-up question, "What's with Florida?," which sent my brain whirring. I was baited and hooked.

My agent, Peter Steinberg, believed in my queer Florida book proposal enough to pitch it to publishers on the open market, and my future editors at Dutton, Grace Layer, Stephen Morrow, and Hannah Feeney, believed in the dream enough to fund it and offered safe harbor on Mardi Gras Day 2020.

After the COVID lockdown delayed my ability research the Florida Legislative Investigation Committee collection at the State of Florida Archives for more than a year, I turned up in Tallahassee on May 17, 2021, to find the documents heavily redacted and virtually unusable, except for perhaps by an ethnographer who didn't need to note names and locations. Several hopeless months in the archive stacks led to my desperately reaching out to the first Johns Committee scholar, a Tallahassee paralegal named Bonnie Stark, in August 2021, and the rest is now part of the historical record. Stark's generous gift of the secret second set of the FLIC files for use in *American Scare* began an odyssey of decensorship. Stark gave my book life and momentum, and I will be forever thankful to her.

Along the way, I developed a rich reporter/source relationship with Art Copleston, among the last living Johns Committee survivors. We were able to build a level of trust that transcended the parameters of this book, and I consider him a friend. Not only did we interview dozens of times about his recollections over the phone, but I was able to fly out to Palm Springs, California, to visit his and Denny's home and enjoyed several fine meals and conversations with that brave nonagenarian gay man, who lives in true style.

I must tip my hat to the archivists at the George A. Smathers Libraries and Special Collections at the University of Florida and especially Sarah Coates, who so graciously scanned PDFs of whole collections for me free of charge when in-person visits were impossible during the COVID epidemic, as well as the Samuel Proctor Oral History Program at the University of Florida, which had the foresight to interview vital historic figures like Charley Johns and digitize the transcriptions. I've gone back and forth with whether to express gratitude to the staff of the State of Archives of Florida, and I've decided, without jeopardizing their employment by naming them individually, that

I want to thank those archivists who used the rules and norms at their disposal to help this book in the face of colleagues who facilitated the problem. It takes bravery to gamble job security in a situation where virtually no state employee feels safe.

I also owe debts of gratitude to the staff of the Rubenstein Rare Book & Manuscript Library at Duke University, who facilitated my research into the papers of the retired queer historian James T. Sears, who wrote about the Johns Committee using pseudonyms in his 1997 book *Lonely Hunters*; fortunately for *American Scare*, Sears used so many pseudonyms that he had to write down and save a key to decipher them all. Likewise, my deepest thanks to Emery Grant and the staff at the National Stonewall Archives in Fort Lauderdale, who helped me round out my research into Anita Bryant with original transcripts. Additionally, the team behind the Mississippi State Sovereignty Commission digital archive deserve an award for their tireless preservation of unredacted documents and their mission to make them freely available to the public—a step Florida has never taken.

Writing anything substantive on the queer American past means treading into the terrain of colossal minds on whose coattails one rides in service of an ever-advancing historical inquiry. Members of a small club of fellow obsessives, we speed each other forward. I must therefore recognize Dr. Stephen Lawson, author of the first peer-reviewed essay on the Johns Committee, "The Florida Legislative Investigation Committee and the Constitutional Readjustment of Race Relations, 1956–1963," in addition to the aforementioned Bonnie Stark and James T. Sears. Karen L. Grave's 2009 *And They Were Wonderful Teachers* remains the definitive work on the Johns Committee's violations of academic freedoms, while Stacy Braukman's *Communists and Perverts Under the Palms* remains the definitive FLIC monograph. Lastly, the historian Judith Poucher's biographical personification of major FLIC figures in her esteemed 2014 work *State of Defiance* lit a lamp in the lighthouse for me and demonstrated adeptly that it was possible to not only educate but also emotionally move readers with the Johns Committee story. The journalist and documentarian Allyson Beutke DeVito has rightly installed herself as a dean and statesperson of FLIC history not only through her 2000 film *Behind Closed Doors* but also through the generous guidance and encouragement she's provided to successive generations of FLIC scholars as they've started their journeys. I must also tout Dan Bertwell's published research in *The Florida Historical Quarterly* and Emma Pettit's journalism in *The Chronicle of Higher Education*. Bravo! And I can't forget René Merino, Joshua Goodman, or Claudia Adrien for the deep insight they showed me regarding Florida history.

Several arts and literary organizations stepped up to support *American Scare* in its nearly six-year gestation, and I'd like to acknowledge them here: the Robert B. Silvers Foundation, the Studios of Key West, the Watermill Center, the Logan Nonfiction Program, the Bread Loaf Writers' Conference, and the Sewanee Writers' Conference. In 2022, the Columbia Journalism School and the Nieman Foundation for Journalism at Harvard University named *American Scare* a finalist for the J. Anthony Lukas Work-in-Progress Award, which was an astounding honor. Additionally, about 80 percent of the way through my book-writing funnel, the Department of History at Tulane University recruited me into their PhD program with ample funding and provided ongoing guidance on the book's development through independent study seminars led by my advisor, Randy Sparks. In this same vein, I must also thank my Tulane history professors Blake Gilpin, Karissa Haugeberg, Kris Lane, and Justin Wolfe for their advice and counsel, in addition to the entire support structure at the Tulane Mellon Fellowship program, including Carol Bebelle, Lucas Diaz, and Ryan McBride. My ultra-supportive PhD cohort also merits a shout-out here: Jason Bedolla Acevedo, Jordette Cummings, and Sara Small. Thank you for believing all my book talk wasn't just a fantasy.

It's so important to me to recognize my family for their tireless encouragement, even when the writing process ran long, and also my friend Kelly Anderson, who put me up at reduced rent in Tallahassee during my major archival spelunking into the Johns Committee records. My in-laws Ron and Deb Leitner stepped in at the pivotal moment to steady the ship, and they know what I mean. My dad reminded me when I deserved a Bob Wiley–style vacation. My goddaughter Riley and my nieces Josie and Penny kept me honest about what really mattered when the tasks of writing became oh so very important in my mind, and my elder terrier and best friend and spirit animal Chompers, who sadly did not make it with me to the end of this particular book journey, helped and continues to help me find hope and solace in dark places.

But most of all, I'd like to praise my husband and life partner, the artist Ryan Leitner, for the grace he's shown me on a daily basis during the painstaking process of bringing this book into being. He sacrificed one quarter of our living space so that I could live and work among the Bonnie Stark Papers, and he put up with me on days when I was cursing with a magnifying glass over transcripts while trying to piece together names and details of a thoroughly maimed past. He's ridden the roller-coaster ride of my career, such as it is, while holding my hand and assuring me that the gamble of following my dreams is all going to turn out okay. I cannot do any of this without him.

NOTES

PREFACE

xiii **New World Eden:** "Life In Tallahassee, Florida in the 1950s—Black, White and Red All Over," Flashbak, September 17, 2020, https://flashbak.com /life-in-tallahassee-florida-in-the-1950s-black-white-and-red-all-over-432539.

xiv **"in my office at work":** Bonnie Stark, interview by Robert Fieseler, August 22, 2021.

xiv **as many as five hundred:** John B. McDermott, "Probers Suspect Many Students of Secret Activities," *Miami Herald*, February 17, 1959, 2; "Florida Legislative Investigation Committee," circa 1961, #10-45, Bonnie Stark Papers.

xv **"use it to pick on anyone":** Lauren Book, interview by Robert Fieseler, March 9, 2023.

xv **Bonnie Stark's legal office:** Bonnie Stark, text message to Robert Fieseler, September 4, 2021.

xv **shocked her mentor:** Stephen Lawson, interview with Robert Fieseler, September 5, 2024.

xv **"I remember thinking":** Bonnie Stark, email to Robert Fieseler, December 16, 2024.

INTRODUCTION I. RACE

1 **"any and all enemies":** "Persona Attending Meeting Southern States Investigator's . . . ," November 1961, Box 2, FLIC Papers; Remus Strickland, SCR ID # 3-6A-2-22-1-1-1, November 1961, Mississippi Sovereignty

Commission Online (hereafter called Mississippi Papers), https://da.mdah
.ms.gov/sovcom/; SCR ID # 3-6A-2-21-1-1-1, circa 1961, Mississippi
Sovereignty Commission Online.

1   for "massive resistance" in Dixieland: Associated Press, "Byrd Calls on South
to Challenge Court," *New York Times*, February 26, 1956.

2   Florida, with just five desegregated school districts: "School Desegregation in
the Southern and Border States, November 1961 Statistics," Southern
Education Reporting Service, November 1961, accessed through South
Carolina Digital Library, https://cdm16821.contentdm.oclc.org/digital
/collection/p16821coll22/id/1706/rec/2; "Segregation-Desegregation Status,"
Southern School News, December 1, 1961, 1, https://gahistoricnewspapers
.galileo.usg.edu/lccn/sn59049440/1961-12-01/ed-1/seq-1/.

2   close down public pools: Ana Goñi-Lessan, "TLH 200: Tallahassee Closed
the Pools to Keep Civil Rights Activists Quiet. It Didn't Work," *Tallahassee
Democrat*, accessed November 20, 2024, https://www.tallahassee.com/story
/news/local/bicentennial/2024/02/16/in-1960s-tallahassee-closed-swimming
-pools-to-thwart-civil-rights/71738582007/.

2   white man without calling him "mister": Vivien M. L. Miller, *Hard Labor
and Hard Time: Florida's "Sunshine Prison" and Chain Gangs*, New
Perspectives on the History of the South (University Press of Florida,
2012), 200.

2   called "darky" by prosecutors: Testimony of State Attorney William Randall
Slaughter, June 26, 1958, Box 4, Florida Legislative Investigation Committee
Papers (hereafter called FLIC Papers), State Archives of Florida; "Old Folks
at Home," audio, Library of Congress, 1914, https://www.loc.gov/item
/jukebox-186869/.

2   Between 1924 and 1941: Miller, *Hard Labor*, 145.

3   "outside forces are now attacking": Tom Scarborough, SCR ID # 3-6A-2-20-
1-1-1, November 13–15, 1961, Mississippi Papers.

3   "The Magic City, the Tropical Playland": Sigismond Diettrich, "Greater
Miami," Folder 15, 1, Sigismond deRudesheim Diettrich Papers (hereafter
called Diettrich Papers), University of Florida Archives.

4   "encouraged white southerners to": Charles Reagan Wilson, *The Southern
Way of Life: Meanings of Culture and Civilization in the American South*
(University of North Carolina Press, 2022), 5.

4   "Not strong, not open": Remus Strickland, transcript of interview with
Bonnie Stark, April 1984, Bonnie Stark Papers.

4   house representative Richard O. Mitchell: Carillon Hotel, letter to R. J.
Strickland, November 9, 1961, Document #12-340, Box 2, FLIC Papers.

4   called the meeting to order: Scarborough, SCR ID # 3-6A-2-20-1-1-1,
Mississippi Papers.

4   "Cuban problem": Scarborough, SCR ID # 3-6A-2-20-1-1-1, Mississippi
Papers.

4   part of the notorious "Red" plan: J. B. Matthews, *Communism and the
NAACP*, vol. 2 (Georgia Commission on Education, 1958), Florida
Investigation Committee, July 1957–March 1958, NAACP Papers, Library of
Congress.

5   "with us on agitative groups": Tom Scarborough, SCR ID # 3-6A-2-20-2-1-1, November 13–15, 1961, Mississippi Papers.

5   "one state to another confidential": Tom Scarborough, SCR ID # 3-6A-2-20-2-1-1, November 13–15, 1961, Mississippi Papers.

5   "running loose today": Tom Scarborough, SCR ID # 3-6A-2-20-2-1-1, November 13–15, 1961, Mississippi Papers.

5   "made bond or were imprisoned": Tom Scarborough, SCR ID # 3-6A-2-20-3-1-1, November 13–15, 1961, Mississippi Papers.

5   T. B. Birdsong, who led: Associated Press, "Communist Led, Says Birdsong," *Memphis Press-Scimitar*, June 30, 1961, 5.

5   "Communists, should they take over": Tom Scarborough, SCR ID # 3-6A-2-20-4-1-1, November 13–15, 1961, Mississippi Papers.

6   "for them to get armed": Tom Scarborough, SCR ID # 3-6A-2-20-4-1-1, November 13–15, 1961, Mississippi Papers.

6   This homosexual "purge": Strickland, interview with Stark.

6   "teach in Florida for life": Tom Scarborough, SCR ID # 3-6A-2-20-4-1-1, Mississippi Papers.

7   "our form of government": SCR ID # 3-6A-2-21-1-1-1, circa 1961, Mississippi Papers.

7   a popular southern spa town: Tom Scarborough, SCR ID # 3-6A-2-20-4-1-1, November 13–15, 1961, Mississippi Papers.

7   Café Le Can Can in a nearby tower: Carillon Hotel, letter to R. J. Strickland, November 9, 1961.

7   The Louisiana Bureau of Criminal Identification: Major Billy Booth, letter to R. J. Strickland, December 27, 1961, #11-1744, Box 2, FLIC Papers.

7   an educational blacklist: R. J. Strickland to Andy Hopkins, SCR ID # 3-6A-2-12-1-1-1, June 30, 1961, Mississippi Papers.

8   "expose and let the public itself destroy": R. J. Strickland, SCR ID # 13-0-3-4-4-1-1, June 3, 1961, Mississippi Papers.

8   gushed President H. A. Poole: H. A. Poole, letter to R. J. Strickland, November 17, 1961, Box 2, FLIC Papers.

8   Strickland's boss, "Mr. R. J.": H. A. Poole, letter to Charley Johns, November 17, 1961, Box 2, FLIC Papers.

8   "Security Bureau Formed in South": Claude Sitton, "Security Bureau Formed in South," *New York Times*, November 22, 1961, 1.

8   H. A. Poole petitioned: H. A. Poole, letter to R. J. Strickland, December 5, 1961, Box 2, FLIC Papers.

8   "tinker's damn about": R. J. Strickland, letter to H. A. Poole, December 7, 1961, Box 2, FLIC Papers.

8   Southern States Investigator's Association: SCR ID # 3-6A-2-21-1-1-1, circa 1961, Mississippi Papers.

8   "first line of defense": Tom Scarborough, SCR ID # 3-6A-2-20-4-1-1, November 13–15, Mississippi Papers.

8   Dixie, lest she vanish: A. L. Hopkins, SCR ID # 3-16A-2-113-1-1-1, June 10–12, 1962, Mississippi Papers.

Introduction II. Sex

9 **was taking his final exam:** Art Copleston, FLIC interrogation transcript, January 20, 1958 [misdated year], #4-16, Box 7, FLIC Papers; "The University Record of the University of Florida, 1958–1959," publication of the University of Florida Registrar, 1958, 4–5, University of Florida Archives.

9 **seats of Matherly Hall:** "The University Record of the University of Florida, Schedule of Courses First Semester, 1958–1959," publication of the University of Florida Registrar, 1958, 25, University of Florida Archives.

9 **James F. Moore:** "The University Record of the University of Florida, 1958–1959," publication of the University of Florida Registrar, 1958, 43, University of Florida Archives.

9 **the twenty-six-year-old college sophomore:** Art Copleston, video interview with Allyson Beutke, 1999, DVD 3, Allyson Beutke Personal Papers (hereafter called Beutke Papers).

10 **Why wasn't a public educator:** Art Copleston, video interview with Allyson Beutke.

10 **Tan and trim with a crew cut:** Art Copleston photograph, circa 1958, Art Copleston Personal Papers (hereafter called Art Copleston Papers).

10 **"benefit of shock," noted Officer John Tileston:** John Tileston, interview in the documentary *The Committee*, 2017, produced by Burnett Honors College, University of Central Florida.

10 **"The physical factors of Florida's":** Sigismond Diettrich, "An Outline of the Role of the Geographic Factor in Florida's History," Folder 17, 1, Diettrich Papers, University of Florida Archives.

11 **More than twelve thousand strapping youths:** "Enrollment Hits Record; 9,266 Men, 3,038 Coeds," *Florida Alligator*, October 3, 1958, 1, https://ufdc.ufl.edu/UF00028291/01841/images.

11 **policy of interposition:** "Interposition Resolution in Response to *Brown v. Board of Education*, 1957," Florida House of Representatives, May 2, 1952, Series S222, State Archives of Florida.

11 **rebuked as "unlawful":** Ron Chernow, *Alexander Hamilton* (Penguin, 2005), 599.

11 **have no "moral obligation":** Jack Detweiler, "U. of F. Professors Say They Have No 'Obligation' to Advocate Integration," *Tampa Tribune*, February 18, 1958, 6.

11 **UF law school dean rejected interposition:** Karen L. Graves, *And They Were Wonderful Teachers: Florida's Purge of Gay and Lesbian Teachers* (University of Illinois Press, 2009), 71.

11 **J. B. Matthews, an American ex-Communist:** John L. Boyles, "Red Gains in NAACP Charged," *Miami Herald*, February 11, 1958, 1.

12 **University of Florida for only two months:** Ben Field, "The Charley E. Johns Story," *Orlando Sentinel Magazine*, May 1, 1954, 39; Charles Johns, oral history interview with Ray Washington, 1979, Samuel Proctor Oral History Program, University of Florida Archives.

12 **professor named John H. Reynolds:** "Confidential Report of Informant— Gainesville Area," June 1–8, 1958, #8-28, FLIC Papers.

12 "I refuse to answer": Herbert D. Cameron and Sam Mase, "Professors Say They're Obligated to Answer Congress Questions," *Tampa Tribune*, July 7, 1953, 1, 6.

12 for "Pink" integration: Cameron and Mase, "Professors Say They're Obligated to Answer Congress Questions."

12 free use of his campus police officer: "Minutes, Florida Legislative Investigation Committee," September 27, 1958, 2, Clerk of the House Papers, State of Florida Archives; John Tileston, transcript of interview with Allyson Beutke, April 12, 1999, Beutke Papers; John Stanton Tileston Sr., *Legacy*, accessed December 2024, https://www.legacy.com/obituaries/name/john-tileston-obituary?pid=171827969.

12 "queers and the Communists on campus": Tileston, interview in the documentary *The Committee*.

13 in loco parentis: Graves, *And They Were Wonderful Teachers*, 16.

13 kill segregation: "NAACP Mapping Plans to Kill Segregation," *Panama City News-Herald*, May 23, 1953, 12; James Schnur, "Closet Crusaders: The Johns Committee and Homophobia, 1956–1965," in *Carryin' On in the Lesbian and Gay South*, ed. John Howard (New York University Press, 1997), 133.

13 "advocated racial integration": Charley Johns, press conference clip in the documentary *The Committee*.

13 "Strick," as Charley lovingly: Charley Johns, letter to R. J. Strickland, January 19, 1963, Box 2, FLIC Papers; "City Attempts to Establish Car Pool Angle," *Tallahassee Democrat*, October 18, 1956, 1.

13 Strickland's tactics: Glenda Alice Rabby, *The Pain and the Promise: The Struggle for Civil Rights in Tallahassee, Florida* (University of Georgia Press, 1999), 30–31.

13 as one of the worst "Pinks": Confidential Report, #8-28, FLIC Papers; David Lane, FLIC suspect sheet, #13-419, Box 13, FLIC Papers; Ernest Ford, FLIC suspect sheet, #13-420, Box 13, FLIC Papers.

13 all faculty records: Subpoena, President University of Florida, August 18, 1958, #13-98 and #13-99, Box 1, FLIC Papers.

14 Reitz's driveway: Charley Johns, letter to J. Wayne Reitz, November 9, 1956, Box 40, Reitz Papers, University of Florida Archives.

14 knew it as the Johns Committee: Robert W. Delaney, "Johns Committee Mum," *Miami News*, December 15, 1957, 25.

14 of $75,000 for a "State FBI": Jim Hardee, "Part-Time Attorney Paid More Than Ervin Assistants," *Orlando Sentinel*, December 3, 1957, 3; Judith Poucher, *State of Defiance: Challenging the Johns Committee's Assault on Civil Liberties* (University Press of Florida, 2014), 11.

14 itself "hamstrung" by the NAACP: Graves, *And They Were Wonderful Teachers*, 68; Stacy Braukman, "'Nothing Else Matters but Sex': Cold War Narratives of Deviance and the Search for Lesbian Teachers in Florida, 1959–1963," *Feminist Studies* 27, no. 3 (2001): 557.

14 immune from liability: George E. Owen, letter to Henry Land, October 4, 1956, #11-1664, Box 3, FLIC Papers.

14 Gainesville Little Theatre: "Little Theatre to Offer 'Dark of the Moon,'"

Gainesville Daily Sun, May 11, 1958, 4; "Full House Greets New Show of Little Theatre," *Gainesville Daily Sun*, January 31, 1950, 5.

14 **Arthur "Hoyle" Wyman, owner:** Arthur Wyman, interrogation by Mark Hawes, January 9, 1959, Box 7, FLIC Papers; "Dress Rehearsal Set Tonight for Little Theatre Play," *Gainesville Daily Sun*, December 13, 1956, 17.

15 **roommate Lonnie Rhoden:** Lonnie Rhoden, 1950 U.S. Census.

15 **called the Burger House:** Wyman, interrogation by Hawes, January 9, 1959, 998, Box 7, FLIC Papers.

15 **open after dark, and the prospect proved:** Joe Crevasse, Transcript of Testimony, January 22, 1959, 1507, Box 7, FLIC Papers.

15 **above said bathroom:** "Minutes, Florida Legislative," September 27, 1958, Clerk of the House Papers.

15 **"not send down any word":** "Minutes, Florida Legislative," September 27, 1958, Clerk of the House Papers.

15 **"advocating violence or a course of conduct":** "Exhibit A: Statement to be made by Chairman at opening of public hearing in Miami on February 26, 1958," February 1958, Clerk of the House Papers.

15 **"abominable and detestable crime against nature":** George Painter, "Florida," Sodomy Laws, 1991, Gay & Lesbian Archives of the Pacific Northwest, https://www.glapn.org/sodomylaws/sensibilities/florida.htm.

15 **infractions involving "moral turpitude":** Bonnie Stark, "McCarthyism in Florida: Charley Johns and the Florida Legislative Investigation Committee July, 1956 to July, 1965" (master's thesis, University of South Florida, 1985), 97, https://palmm.digital.flvc.org/islandora/object/usf%3A49370#page/title/mode/1up.

16 **uncovered a "considerable homosexual operation":** "Progress Report of Chief Investigator R. J. Strickland . . . ," October 16, 1958, #3-159, Box 1, FLIC Papers.

16 **establish a causal link:** Graves, *And They Were Wonderful Teachers*, 95–97.

16 **"mutual discretion":** John Howard, *Men Like That: A Southern Queer History* (University of Chicago Press, 1999), 46.

16 **"Prejudice will fade away":** Letter to the Editor, *One* 1, no. 1 (January 1953): 22, https://archive.org/details/one-magazine/.

16 **toward the Manor Motel:** Manor Motel, postcard by Dexter Press, 1964, University of Florida Archives, https://original-ufdc.uflib.ufl.edu/MH00001199/00001/citation.

16 **past summer at the Burger House:** Art Copleston, *Demons and Deliverance* (published by author, 2014), Kindle, 152.

16 **was a "3.2 bar":** Art Copleston, interviews with Robert Fieseler, October 28, 2019, May 3, 2020.

16 **"bohemian" establishment:** Art Copleston, Transcript of Testimony, January 20, 1959, 1304, #4-16, Box 7, FLIC Papers.

16 **it was a "fairyland":** James Wathen, interrogation by Mark Hawes, January 8, 1959, 81, #2-77, Box 7, FLIC Papers.

17 **"of strange investigation":** Copleston, interview, May 3, 2020.

17 **during repeated interrogations at:** Art Copleston, interrogation by Remus Strickland, October 16, 1958, #1-142, Box 8, FLIC Papers.

17   **a military veteran:** Art Copleston, interview with Robert Fieseler, April 26, 2020.

17   **It was about 10:15 a.m.:** Copleston, interrogation by Hawes, January 20, 1959, #4-16, Box 7, FLIC Papers.

17   **"Mark Hawes":** Copleston, interrogation by Hawes, January 20, 1959, #4-16, Box 7, FLIC Papers.

17   **"barrel-chested, gravel-voiced":** Ronald Hutchinson, "Three Dominate Trial," *Tampa Bay Times*, March 1, 1970, 16.

18   **"How are you, Senator?":** Copleston, interrogation by Hawes, January 20, 1959, #4-16, Box 7, FLIC Papers.

18   **"How are you, Mr.":** Copleston, interrogation by Hawes, January 20, 1959, #4-16, Box 7, FLIC Papers.

CHAPTER 1. CALL ME CHARLEY

21   **admire his portrait in his last hours:** "Tallahassee Prepares for Inauguration," *Tampa Tribune*, January 1, 1955, 2; "'Johns' Photo Ruffles Darby," *Tallahassee Democrat*, January 2, 1955, 7; "MarkleyAnn Johns Unveiling Her Father's Portrait," Florida Memory, circa 1953, https://www.floridamemory.com/items/show/45287.

21   **hobby was working:** Allen Morris, "Meet Your Lawmakers," *Pensacola News Journal*, April 4, 1945, 4.

21   **"All Florida Needs" before:** "Let's Keep Charley Johns Our Governor," political ad, *Southern Jewish Weekly*, April 30, 1954, 6.

22   **"Pork Chopper" faction:** Dom Bonafede, "'Plum' Pressure by Johns Revealed," *Miami Herald*, April 19, 1959, 7.

22   **in the Grove Mansion, the ancestral:** Theo Sommerkamp, "Debate over Site Stalls Building of New Mansion," *Tallahassee Democrat*, January 4, 1955, 37.

22   **turned over the keys:** "Johns Turns Over Executive Mansion," *Miami News*, December 31, 1954, 12.

22   **Johnses' family possessions:** "Tallahassee Prepares," *Tampa Tribune*, January 1, 1955; "Johns, Fighting Cold, Has Busy Final Day in Office," *Tampa Tribune*, January 4, 1955, 4.

22   **Tuesday morning, January 4:** Jim Powell, "Tallahassean Will Become State's 33rd in Office; Johns Returns to Senate," *Tampa Tribune*, January 4, 1955, 1, 4.

22   **twirled his chain watch:** "From Railroad Conductor to Governor's Mansion, Charley Johns Carved Out Self-Made Career," *Bradford County Telegraph*, January 25, 1990, 4, https://newspapers.uflib.ufl.edu/UF00027795/01848/zoom/3.

22   **exhibited signs of disrepair:** "The Mansion Is Florida's 'Old House,'" *Tampa Times*, January 3, 1955, 5; Ann Liberman, *Governors' Mansions of the South* (University of Missouri Press, 2008), 30–36.

22   **Florida constitution of 1885:** James Anthony Schnur, "LeRoy Collins and Legislative Interposition: A Portrait of Emerging Moderation in Gubernatorial Politics" (master's paper, University of South Florida, 1989), 2,

https://digitalcommons.usf.edu/cgi/viewcontent.cgi?article=4038&context
=fac_publications.

22 pioneered a model for Black disenfranchisement: Edward C. Williamson, "The Constitutional Convention of 1885," *Florida Historical Quarterly* 41, no. 2 (October 1962): 116–26.

23 housed fifteen of Florida's: Liberman, *Governors' Mansions of the South*, 32.

23 it the "State Shack": "New Governor Reveals Plan to Newsmen," *Orlando Sentinel*, January 8, 1953, 13.

23 nickname itself: "Grammar School Notes," *Mendocino Coast Beacon*, October 21, 1933, 5.

23 school-age daughter, MarkleyAnn: Barbara Frye, "Florida's New First Lady Is 'Homebody,'" *Miami Herald*, October 16, 1953, 2; Haines Colbert, "Charley Johns Feels He's Doing Good Job," *Miami News*, November 13, 1951, 1.

23 met in session: "Session Ended amid 11th Hour Uproar, Time-Honored Ceremony," *Tampa Tribune*, June 6, 1953, 4; Charlton W. Tebeau, *A History of Florida* (University of Miami Press, 1971), 253; Seth Weitz, "Bourbon, Pork Chops, and Red Peppers: Political Immorality in Florida, 1945–1968," PhD dissertation, Florida State University, 2007, https://repository.lib.fsu.edu /islandora/object/fsu:175753.

23 rented a small room: Charles Johns, oral history interview by Ray Washington, 1979, 4, Samuel Proctor Oral History Program, University of Florida Archives.

23 *two-jobbing*: "Two-Jobbers Again?," *Tampa Tribune*, June 30, 1937, 4.

23 "I worked so hard": "Senate Sets Race Probe," *Miami Herald*, April 15, 1939, 2.

24 Baptist deacon: "Chatter," *Bradenton Herald*, February 7, 1854, 12.

24 strictures of the 1885 constitution: Seth Weitz, "Defending the Old South: The Myth of the Lost Cause and Political Immorality in Florida, 1865–1968," *The Historian* 71, no. 1 (2009): 79–92; Berkeley Miller and William Canak, "From 'Porkchoppers' to 'Lambchoppers': The Passage of Florida's Public Employee Relations Act," *ILR Review* 44, no. 2 (1991): 349–66, https://doi .org/10.2307/2524814.

24 was routinely filled: Robert Buccellato, *Finding Dan McCarty* (published by author, 2016), Location 517.

24 prevented the printing of legislative: James Nathan Miller, "How Florida Threw Out the Pork Chop Gang," *National Civic Review* 60, no. 7 (July 1971): 366–80.

24 "Enact in haste, repent at leisure": Kenneth Ballinger, "Affairs of State," *Orlando Sentinel*, October 15, 1937, 4.

24 "pet bill night": Jack Thale, "It's Not Official, But—," *Tampa Bay Times*, May 28, 1941, 8.

24 Six feet tall: Charley Eugene Johns, WWII Draft Card, Ancestry.com.

24 "You can't resist liking him": John Perry, "Charley Johns, the Controversial Candidate," *Tampa Bay Times*, March 6, 1954, 1.

25 "I was for making the University": "Co-Education to Be Big Issue," *Tallahassee Democrat*, March 28, 1945, 3.

25   "Out of all the members of the senate": Cliff Herrell, interview with Bonnie
     Stark, circa 1993, Bonnie Stark Papers.

25   exploded from 400,000 to about 3.5 million: Charlton W. Tebeau, *A History
     of Florida* (University of Miami Press, 1971) 292; Erwin Raisz and associates,
     Atlas of Florida (University of Florida Press, 1964), 1.

25   most like a winter vacation: "Florida, California Top Winter Favorites,"
     Herald and News, January 19, 1949, 6.

25   a third of the world's citrus: Raisz and associates, *Atlas*, 23.

25   Florida manufacturing surpassed: Raisz and associates, *Atlas*, 30.

26   no reapportionment occurred for four decades: "Business, Market and
     Financial News," *Orlando Sentinel*, May 26, 1925, 9.

26   "gentleman's agreement": "Re-apportion Bill Passed by Senate," *Tampa
     Times*, April 30, 1925, 1.

26   This steamrollering: "Re-apportion Bill Passed by Senate," *Tampa
     Times*, 1.

26   bill sail through the Florida house: "Reapportionment Bill Passes House
     Without Amendment of Senate," *Smith's Weekly*, May 29, 1925, 11.

26   malapportionment: William Havard and Loren Beth, *The Politics of
     Mis-Representation: Rural-Urban Conflict in the Florida Legislature*
     (Louisiana State University Press, 1962), 1; "Reapportionment by
     Legislatures," *Bradenton Herald*, January 21, 1941, 4.

26   held more citizens than the entire state: Havard and Beth, *The Politics of*, 2.

26   500,000 Dade County residents: Miller, "How Florida Threw Out the
     Pork Chop Gang," 366; "Grab of Power Defies Voters," *Tampa Tribune*,
     December 20, 1953, 27.

26   nicknamed the Pork Choppers: Miller, "How Florida Threw Out the Pork
     Chop Gang," 366; "Grab of Power Defies Voters," 27.

26   "took a blood oath": Ed Price, transcript of interview with Bonnie Stark,
     September 20, 1984, Bonnie Stark Papers; Kevin N. Klein, "Guarding the
     Baggage: Florida's Pork Chop Gang and Its Defense of the Old South," PhD
     dissertation, Florida State University, 1995, 5–7, ProQuest (304215209).

27   Johns–led loyalty ceremony: Martin, "Pork Chop Gang Fills Void Left by
     Ball," *Tampa Bay Times*, February 17, 1964, 1; "The Aucilla River Hideaway
     of Florida's 'Pork Chop Gang,'" Florida Memory, July 7, 2014, https://www
     .floridamemory.com/items/show/295187; Weitz, "Bourbon, Pork Chops, and
     Red Peppers," 3.

27   less than 15 percent: Miller, "How Florida Threw Out the Pork Chop
     Gang," 366.

27   1947 to 1965: Judith Poucher, *State of Defiance: Challenging the Johns
     Committee's Assault on Civil Liberties* (University Press of Florida,
     2014), 4.

CHAPTER 2. THE FLOUR-SACK BOY

28   founding ancestral lines: Judith Poucher, *State of Defiance: Challenging the
     Johns Committee's Assault on Civil Liberties* (University Press of Florida,
     2014), 1.

28   grandfather: Ben Field, "The Charley E. Johns Story," *Orlando Sentinel Magazine,* May 1, 1954; Journal of the House of Representatives, April 5, 1887, 6, University of Florida Archives, https://ufdc.ufl.edu/UF00027834/00001/images/5.

28   **Nassau County chief deputy sheriff:** John Perry, "Charley Johns, the Controversial Candidate," *Tampa Bay Times,* March 6, 1954, 1.

28   **spare cloth from flour sacks:** "Johns Didn't Like Governor Stint," *Miami Herald,* December 19, 1977, 110.

28   **hide behind the bushes:** "Johns Didn't Like Governor Stint."

29   **Charley's many retellings:** "Johns Didn't Like Governor Stint"; Ray Washington, "The Porkchopper Governor," May 27, 1979, A5; "'Porkchopper' Charley Johns: Didn't Like Job," *Playground Daily News,* December 19, 1977, 15.

29   **Charley liked to stop and listen:** Washington, "The Porkchopper Governor," A5.

29   **faction of the Ku Klux Klan:** Dick Ashe, testimony to FLIC, June 27, 1958, 1086, FLIC Papers.

29   **graduated with high honors:** Poucher, *State of Defiance,* 2.

29   **"He was not but 19":** Charles Johns, oral history interview with Ray Washington, 1979, 14, Samuel Proctor Oral History Program, University of Florida Archives.

29   **state senate in 1928:** Field, "The Charley E. Johns Story."

29   **at only thirty-five:** Poucher, *State of Defiance,* 2.

29   **Markley Johns perished:** "Upper House Action Surprise," *Tallahassee Democrat,* April 10, 1951, 1.

29   **"I just loved Markley":** "Johns Self-Styled Old Cracker Boy from Bradford," *Panama City News-Herald,* May 23, 1954, 12.

29   **as a baseball and basketball player:** Allen Morris, "Meet Your Lawmakers," *Pensacola News Journal,* April 4, 1945, 4.

30   **his sweetheart, Thelma:** Charles Johns, oral history, 1979, 14, Samuel Proctor Oral History.

30   **the first state to mandate segregated:** Pauli Murray, *States' Laws on Race and Color* (Women's Division of Christian Service, 1951), 85.

30   **"He had a memory":** Jerome Johns, transcript of interview with Bonnie Stark, April 4, 1996, 10.

30   *Miami Herald* **trumpeted the election:** Kenneth Ballinger, "Mann Urges Racing Fund for Pensions," *Miami Herald,* March 19, 1935, 13.

30   **in a unanimous Florida house:** "'S'wannee River' Voted Official Florida Melody," *Miami News,* May 22, 1935, 1.

30   **voters elevated Charley:** "Charley Johns Beaten After 32 Years," *Pensacola News Journal,* May 29, 1966, 48.

30   **"Remember What Charley":** Campaign ad for Charley Johns, *Cocoa Tribune,* May 21, 1954, evening edition, 10.

30   **tires of his Model T coupe:** Charles Johns, oral history, 1979, 16, Samuel Proctor Oral History; "Road Built for Johns' Brother," *Tampa Tribune,* January 31, 1953, 1.

31   widows of Confederate veterans: "Johns Asks Hike in Confederate Widows' Pensions," *Tampa Tribune*, May 5, 1961, 24.

31   Charley E. Johns Insurance: "Put Up the Sign Charley," *Tampa Tribune*, September 4, 1954, 4.

31   "It was a big job," agreed: Charles Johns, oral history, 1979, 11, Samuel Proctor Oral History.

31   earn a conductor post: Charles Johns, oral history, 1979, 16, Samuel Proctor Oral History.

31   the *Orange Blossom Special*: Charles Johns, oral history, 1979, 17, Samuel Proctor Oral History; Ben Brotemarkle, "Iconic Train Inspired Iconic Song," *Florida Today*, June 9, 2015, 9A.

31   "invested with all the powers": Murray, *States' Laws*, 85.

31   he ran for a U.S. congressional seat: "Elect State Senator Charley E. Johns to Congress," *Southern Jewish Weekly*, March 22, 1940, 7.

31   neglected to requalify: "Adams, Hentz Candidates for State Senator," *Panama City News-Herald*, March 25, 1940, 6.

31   Lex Green also hailed: "Lex Green Qualifies," *Bradenton Herald*, January 12, 1940, 10.

31   he was out of the race: "Green Is Leading in Congress Race," *Tallahassee Democract*, May 8, 1940, 1.

31   he would excise this campaign: Charles Johns, oral history, 1979, 8, Samuel Proctor Oral History; "Present and Past Members of the Florida Legislative Investigation Committee," circa 1963, #10-47, Bonnie Stark Papers.

32   he received his draft card: Charley Eugene Johns, WWII Draft Card, Ancestry.com.

32   named MarkleyAnn: Field, "The Charley E. Johns Story."

32   "I promise when you elect": "Johns Announces Candidacy for State Senate," *Bradford County Telegraph*, January 14, 1944, 1.

32   "which permit the membership": "More Than Third of 38-Member '45 Senate Will Be Newcomers," *Tallahassee Democrat*, February 2, 1944, 1.

32   as president pro tem: Poucher, *State of Defiance*, 4.

32   by voting to hang his brother's portrait: "Senate to Get Portrait of Johns," *Tallahassee Democrat*, May 18, 1951, 8.

32   by being unanimously elected: "Johns Says State Welfare Workers Fighting Him," *Tampa Times*, May 1, 1954, 3.

32   jockeying in a small skirmish: Allen Morris, "Cracker Politics," *Tallahassee Democrat*, April 29, 1951, 6; "Upper House," *Tallahassee Democrat*, April 10, 1951.

33   "He is no more for": "Governor Gets Watch as Gift," *Orlando Sentinel*, November 10, 1951, 11.

33   Charley Johns collapsed in Starke: Perry, "Charley Johns, the Controversial."

33   "was going to let Markley": Perry, "Charley Johns, the Controversial."

33   up the family car: Robert Buccellato, *Finding Dan McCarty* (published by author, 2016), Location 891, Kindle.

33   "I am in the people's corner": Buccellato, *Finding Dan*.

33   series of open houses: Buccellato, *Finding Dan*.

33 **cardiac arrest:** "McCarty Has Heart Attack," *Tampa Tribune*, February 27, 1953, 1; "Gov. Dan McCarty's Condition Not Critical, Says Physician," *Palm Beach Post*, February 28, 1953, 1; John Hopkins, "McCarty Heart Attack Points Up Necessity for Aide to Executive," *Fort Lauderdale News*, March 11, 1953, 13.

34 **downgraded to a gallbladder issue:** "Johns in Good Physical Shape Doctors Say," *Panama City News-Herald*, November 8, 1953, 3.

34 **"I would feel in my":** Hampton Dunn, "Dan's Example Is Inspiration for Youth," *Tampa Times*, October 3, 1953, 6.

34 **reported on March 2, 1953:** "Lieutenant Governor Plan Gets Approval," *Orlando Evening Star*, March 2, 1953, 11.

34 **"A sentimental quest will have a storybook":** "Long Ambition of Legislator Becomes Real," *Fort Lauderdale News*, March 16, 1953, 30.

34 **"achieving a goal that has":** "Johns Takes Oath as Senate Chief," *Bradford County Telegraph*, April 10, 1953, 1.

34 **held an "informal reception":** "Sen. Johns Entertains Guests at Informal Reception," *Tallahassee Democrat*, April 8, 1953, 6.

Chapter 3. Acting Governor

35 **from a bedroom of the Executive:** Robert Buccellato, *Finding Dan McCarty* (published by author, 2016), Location 891, Kindle.

35 **LeRoy Collins opposed:** Judith Poucher, *State of Defiance: Challenging the Johns Committee's Assault on Civil Liberties* (University Press of Florida, 2014), 5; Bonnie Stark, "McCarthyism in Florida: Charley Johns and the Florida Legislative Investigation Committee July, 1956 to July, 1965" (master's thesis, University of South Florida, 1985), https://palmm.digital .flvc.org/islandora/object/usf%3A49370#page/title/mode/1up, 6; "Senate Fails to Override Racing Veto," *Orlando Sentinel*, June 4, 1953, 1.

35 **questioned the renewal:** "Charley Johns, in Line as Governor, Broke with McCarty on Gulfstream," *Miami News*, September 23, 1953, 1; "M'Carty Says Webb Is Out; Hits Johns' State Business," *Tampa Tribune*, January 13, 1953, 1.

36 **"joint legislative committee to":** Journal of the Senate, Regular Session, 1953, 770, State of Florida Archives.

36 **would be authorized:** Journal of the Senate, Regular Session, 1953, 770, State of Florida Archives; "Senators in Row over Crime Probers," *Orlando Sentinel*, May 23, 1953, 3.

36 **"God-fearing":** "Senators in Row."

36 **"grovel around in the rocks":** Jim Powell, "Johns' Investigation Bill Stirs Hot Senate Debate, Passes Test," *Tampa Tribune*, May 23, 1953, 1, 8.

36 **"apostles of the":** Jim Powell, "Senate Vote Kills Inquiry Bill," *Tampa Tribune*, May 27, 1953, 1.

36 **"I don't want to see innocent":** "Senate Defeats Bill to Set Up Probe Group," *Miami Herald*, May 27, 1953, 1.

36 **one of two potential bills:** "Three Florida Ex-Governors Back Succession Law Change," *Tampa Tribune*, December 30, 1953, 10.

36   passed the two succession bills: "Lieutenant Governor Constitutional
Provision Wins House Approval," *Tampa Tribune*, May 13, 1953, 9; "Two
McCarty Bills Hacked to Death," *Tallahassee Democrat*, May 31, 1953, 1.

37   He rejected both options: "Three Florida Ex-Governors."

37   two senate committees: "Summer Date for Jai-Alai, Dogs Fading," *Miami
Herald*, June 1, 1953, 15.

37   sine die closing: "Session Ended Amid 11th," *Tampa Tribune*, June 6,
1954, 4.

37   second heart attack: Charles F. Hesser, "Gov. Dan McCarty Is Dead; Johns
to Take Oath Today," *Miami News*, September 29, 1953, 1.

37   in the capitol rotunda: John McDermott, "Johns Sworn In as Acting Governor;
McCarty Funeral Today at Ft. Pierce," *Miami Herald*, September 30, 1953, 4.

38   stood in the senate chamber: Holmes Alexander, "Senator Johns Is Sworn In
to Perform Governor Duties in Quiet Capitol Ceremony," *Tampa Tribune*,
September 30, 1953, 1.

38   son, Jerome Johns: Alexander, "Senator Johns Is Sworn In"; "President of the
Senate Disclaims Any Fixed Policy at This Time," *Palm Beach Post*,
September 30, 1953, 1.

38   As he waited for: Bill Baggs, ". . . Up in Room 401," *Miami News*, November
15, 1953, 23; "Duval Hotel No 'Mansion Pro-Tem,'" *Orlando Sentinel*,
October 11, 1953, 6.

38   "Johns frequently uses the third person": "Charley Johns Feels He's Doing
Good Job," *Miami News*, November 13, 1953, 1.

38   "Charley Johns is for": Baggs, ". . . Up in Room 401."

38   "Why it got so in Tallahassee": Baggs, ". . . Up in Room 401."

38   "acting governor" as his proper: "Supreme Court Rules on Signing Pay Roll,"
Tampa Bay Times, September 30, 1953, 2; "Grab of Power," *Tampa Tribune*,
December 20, 1953.

38   Johns family took possession: Barbara Frye, "Johns Family Quietly Moves
Into Governor's Mansion," *Tampa Tribune*, October 16, 1953, 1.

38   Battleship Florida punch bowl: "The Battleship Florida Silver Service," state
pamphlet, circa 1953, Box 11, Dan McCarty Papers, State Archives of
Florida.

38   demanded the resignations: Poucher, *State of Defiance*, 6; "The Empty
Chair," *Tampa Tribune*, December 16, 1954, 22.

38   "If I don't have men in there": Clyde Shaffer, "Johns Says 'Little Cabinet'
Should Resign, Thus Giving Acting Governor a Free Hand," *Tampa Tribune*,
October 11, 1953, 1.

39   fired them on charges: Poucher, *State of Defiance*, 6; Jim Powell, "Johns Must
Give Cause in Ousters," *Tampa Tribune*, October 20, 1953, 1; Jim Powell,
"Road Board, Hotel Commissioner Are Suspended; They Call Charges
'Trumped Up, Smears, Asinine,'" *Tampa Tribune*, December 12, 1953, 1;
"Johns May Tell Plans This Week," *Tampa Tribune*, January 3, 1954, 6.

39   "look over": Jim Powell, "Reitz Still Sought for School Job," *Tampa Tribune*,
September 24, 1954, 1.

39   "The acting governor told me the engineers": "Simpson Says Acting
Governor Sought Favors," *Tampa Times*, December 13, 1954, 8.

39   Johns was eligible to run: "Uncle Charley Gets the Nod," *Tampa Tribune*, February 21, 1954, 27; "Gov. Johns 'Very Happy' About Ruling," *Tampa Bay Times*, February 17, 1954, 1.

39   "Let's KEEP Charley": "Let's Keep Charley Johns," political ad, *Orlando Evening Star*, May 24, 1954, 14.

39   1956 gubernatorial election: Sumner Rand, "Odham Leaves 6-Year Term Question Open," *Orlando Sentinel*, March 16, 1954, 13.

39   on roadbuilding: "Smarter Than He Thinks," *Tampa Tribune*, April 7, 1954, 12.

39   Black participation in state primaries: "'White Primary' Measure Is Placed Before Legislature," *Pensacola News Journal*, April 11, 1947, 1; "State Legislators Oppose Florida White Primary Act," *Bradenton Herald*, March 9, 1947, 5.

39   Johns had voted against a 1951 bill: "'A Very Dangerous Bill,'" *Tampa Tribune*, May 11, 1954, 8.

39   no fewer than 315 Black citizens: "Lynching in America: Confronting the Legacy of Racial Terror, County Data Supplement," Equal Justice Initiative, February 2020, 3–4, https://eji.org/wp-content/uploads/2020/02/02-07-20 -lynching-in-america-county-supplement.pdf.

40   even in private schools: Pauli Murray, *States' Laws on Race and Color* (Women's Division of Christian Service, 1951), 14, 78; Joseph A. Tomberlin, "Florida and the School Desegregation Issue, 1954–1959: A Summary View," *Journal of Negro Education* 43, no. 4 (Autumn 1954): 457–67; Irvin D. S. Winsboro and Abel A. Bartley, "Race, Education, and Regionalism: The Long and Troubling History of School Desegregation in the Sunshine State," *Florida Historical Quarterly* 92, no. 4 (2014): 714–45.

40   "Mixed Schools and Mixed Blood": Herbert Ravenel Sass, "Mixed Schools and Mixed Blood," pamphlet reprint from *The Atlantic*, November 1956, Clerk of the House Papers, State of Florida Archives.

40   "'keeping the breed pure'": Sass, "Mixed Schools and Mixed Blood."

40   adultery or fornication: Murray, *States' Laws*, 18, 30, 83–84.

40   town of Ocoee, Florida: Charlton W. Tebeau, *A History of Florida* (University of Miami Press, 1971), 366.

40   village of Rosewood: Tebeau, *A History of Florida*, 366; David R. Colburn, "Rosewood and America in the Early Twentieth Century," *Florida Historical Quarterly* 76, no. 2 (1997): 175–92.

40   to challenge a white sheriff: Harry T. Moore, "Florida NAACP Sponsors Groveland Defense Sun.," *Miami Times*, October 20, 1951, 5; Gilbert King, *Devil in the Grove: Thurgood Marshall, the Groveland Boys, and the Dawn of a New America* (Harper, 2012), 83, 103; Don Rider, "Executive Secretary of NAACP Visits Fatal Explosion Scene, Moore's Widow," *Orlando Sentinel*, December 29, 1951, 9.

40   Moore's front porch: James C. Clark, "New Evidence Surfaces in Death of Florida Civil Rights Activist," *Times-Tribune*, October 20, 1991, 2; "SAC, Miami (44-270)," March 10, 1952, 4, FBI Records, obtained via FOIA request.

40   explosion left Moore: "Mother of Slain Negro Tells of Fatal Explosion," *Orlando Sentinel*, December 27, 1951, 13; Stephen Trumbull, "Bomb Explosion Kills Florida Negro Leader," *Miami Herald*, December 27, 1951, 1.

40   long ambulance ride: "Mother of Slain Negro Tells of Fatal Explosion."

40   more or less by evisceration: "Bomb Kills Mims NAACP Leader," *Orlando Evening Star*, December 26, 1951, 1.

40   dynamite left on the steps: "Fizzle Averts Miami Blast," *Orlando Sentinel*, November 2, 1951, 1; "From Persecution Arises Anarchy," *Tampa Bay Times*, December 26, 1951, 6.

40   the first Black man to apply to the University of Florida: Poucher, *State of Defiance*, 11–15.

41   "Black Monday": Susan Plauché, "Brown, the Civil Rights Act of 1964, and the NAACP's Impact on Avoyelles Parish Public Schools: 1954–1988," *Louisiana History: The Journal of the Louisiana Historical Association* 54, no. 2 (2013): 172–99; Joseph A. Tomberlin, "Florida Whites and the *Brown* Decision of 1954," *Florida Historical Quarterly* 51, no. 1 (July 1972): 22–25, https://www.jstor.org/stable/30150269.

41   being at a "brief loss": Stephen Trumbell, "Collins Raps Foe: Johns Woods Aged," *Miami Herald*, May 18, 1954, 1.

41   stump speeches: "No More Talk on Debates, Johns Says," *Miami News*, May 17, 1954, 18.

41   "Are you going to permit Negroes": "Johns Says He May Call Legislature," *Miami Herald*, May 18, 1954, 1.

41   "We should call": "Florida Leaders Appeal for Calm Race Issue Study," *Dothan Eagle*, May 18, 1954, 5.

41   won the first round: "Johns and Collins in Runoff," *Tampa Bay Times*, May 5, 1954, 1.

41   debate that May 13: Stacy Braukman, *Communists and Perverts Under the Palms: The Johns Committee in Florida, 1956–1965* (University Press of Florida, 2012), 19.

42   taken out an ad: Poucher, *State of Defiance*, 8.

42   "Earthshaking": Cliff Herrell, interview with Bonnie Stark, August 3, 1993.

42   "That's not Charley Johns": "Debate Between Governor Charley Johns and Future Governor LeRoy Collins (1954)," Florida Memory, video on YouTube, https://www.youtube.com/watch?v=89EHbs4UlN0.

42   attempted to talk over: Braukman, *Communists and Perverts Under the Palms*, 20.

42   "to run on his own": Harold Park, "Final Drive for Dade Vote Set by Johns," *Key West Citizen*, May 12, 1954.

42   Senator LeRoy Collins trounced: "Collins Easy Winner," *Miami Herald*, May 26, 1954, 1.

42   plans to hold hearings: "Collins May Set December Hearings on Johns Ousters," *Tampa Tribune*, November 7, 1954, 1; "17 Ousted by Johns Get Hearing This Week," *Tampa Tribune*, December 12, 1954, 1.

42   "Spoilsman Johns": "Put Up the Sign," *Tampa Tribune*, September 4, 1954.

42   the Southern Governors' Conference: "Johns Said Now Seriously Considering Calling Special Session on Segregation Issue," *Tampa Tribune*, December 2, 1954, 9.

42   **"our most serious problem"**: "Johns to Push Agency to Fight Crime in State," *News-Press*, December 19, 1954, 1.

43   **"create a state FBI"**: "Johns Proposes State 'FBI' to Curb Criminal Elements," *Orlando Sentinel*, December 19, 1954, 14.

43   **Simpson was murdered in Miami**: Milt Sosin and Sanford Schnier, "EAL Man Is Slain on 'Lovers Lane,'" *Miami News*, August 3, 1954, 1; James T. Sears, *Lonely Hunters: An Oral History of Lesbian and Gay Southern Life, 1948–1968* (Westview Press, 1997), 12; Fred Fejes, "Murder, Perversion, and Moral Panic: The 1954 Media Campaign Against Miami's Homosexuals and the Discourse of Civic Betterment," *Journal of the History of Sexuality* 9, no. 3 (July 2000): 305–47, https://www.jstor.org/stable/3704569.

43   **Charles Lawrence**: "Killing Brings to Light Miami Colony of Perverts," *Fort Worth Star-Telegram*, August 10, 1954, 4; "2 Brazen Youths Re-Enact Murder of Airline Steward in North Miami," *Miami Herald*, August 9, 1954, 21.

43   **Lewis Richard Killen**: "2 Brazen Youths."

43   **he bled out**: James Polchin, *Indecent Advances: A Hidden History of True Crime and Prejudice Before Stonewall* (Counterpoint, 2019), 177–84.

43   **"unnatural sex act"**: J. L. (Dixie) Smith, "Defense to Ask Dismissal," *Miami Herald*, November 6, 1954, 23; Richard Rundell, "Pair Faces 20 Years Maximum," *Miami Herald*, November 8, 1954, 23.

43   **"shall suffer death"**: George Painter, "Florida," Sodomy Laws, 1991, Gay & Lesbian Archives of the Pacific Northwest, https://www.glapn.org/sodomylaws/sensibilities/florida.htm.

43   **a "Grade 1" felon**: Vivien M. L. Miller, *Hard Labor and Hard Time: Florida's "Sunshine Prison" and Chain Gangs*, New Perspectives on the History of the South (Gainesville: University Press of Florida, 2012), 2, 264.

43   **an "in-kind contribution"**: Miller, *Hard Labor*, 46.

43   **"teenage Miami boys"**: Richard Rundell, "Two Youths Convicted in Slaying," *Miami Herald*, November 8, 1954, 1.

44   **"Pervert Colony Uncovered . . ."**: Milt Sosin, "Pervert Colony Uncovered in Simpson Slaying Probe," *Miami News*, August 9, 1954, 1.

44   **"a colony of some 500 male homosexuals"**: Sosin, "Pervert Colony Uncovered . . ."; "Civilization of Past Plagued by Deviates," *Miami News*, August 16, 1954, 5.

44   **than 8,000 homosexuals**: "Warning Seen for Miami in Pervert Colony," *Miami News*, August 15, 1954, 5.

44   **"Powder Puff Lane"**: "Enforcement Teamwork Must Break Up Crime," *Miami Herald*, July 9, 1954, 6; "Soft Police Policy Towards Perverts Results Only in Evil," *Miami Herald*, September 2, 1954, 6.

44   **his city manager an ultimatum**: Jack W. Roberts, "Mayor Threatened After Ultimatum," *Miami News*, August 27, 1954, 1.

44   **"males who act mighty like girls"**: Stephen J. Flynn, "Beach Police Round Up 35 in Pervert Crackdown," *Miami Herald*, August 13, 1954, 43; "Raiders Seize 19 in Pervert Roundup," *Miami News*, August 14, 1954, 1.

44   **"to cooperate with you"**: "Johns Names Aide to Fight Perverts," *Miami News*, September 7, 1954, 4.

44   **cost of $4,000 to taxpayers**: "Johns Has Busy Day on Eve of Departure,"

Orlando Sentinel, January 4, 1955, 13; "Johns Calls Road Building Major Achievement of Term," *Tallahassee Democrat*, January 4, 1955, 1.

44 **acknowledging a debt:** John Kilgore, "Johns SRB Also Ends Service," *Miami Herald*, January 4, 1955, 12.

44 **reinstate the wrongly fired McCarty:** "Formalities Over, Collins on Job; Reinstates Ousted McCarty Men," *Bradenton Herald*, January 5, 1955, 1; "Appointees of Johns Bow Out," *Miami Herald*, January 4, 1955, 12.

44 **Johns met governor-elect LeRoy Collins:** "Justice Terrell Gives Oath to New Governor," *Tampa Times*, January 4, 1955, 4.

44 **"as smooth a transition as possible":** "LeRoy Collins to Be Sworn In for Balance of McCarty Term as Governor at Noon Today," *Tampa Tribune*, January 4, 1955, 4.

44 **"political friends and foes":** "Johns Calls for Harmony," *Tampa Tribune*, January 5, 1955, 1.

45 **"Roy, I've left a little":** "Sidelights on Collins Inauguration," *Tampa Tribune*, January 5, 1955, 2.

45 **"Old Folks at Home":** "Official Inauguration Program," *Miami Herald*, January 2, 1955, 91.

45 **worthy reception hall:** Ann Liberman, *Governors' Mansions of the South* (University of Missouri Press, 2008), 32; "Governor Winner Can Build Mansion," *Miami Herald*, April 26, 1954, 30.

45 **on the present site:** "Collins Wants New Mansion on Site of Present," *Bradenton Herald*, January 18, 1955, 11; Liberman, *Governors' Mansions*, 33–34.

45 **for time capsules in:** "1907 'Cornerstone' Missing at Mansion," *Miami Herald*, August 2, 1955, 12.

CHAPTER 4. OATHS OF OFFICE

46 **proposed committee:** "Anti-Subversive Bill Sponsored by Johns," *Miami Herald*, May 11, 1955, 12; Bonnie Stark, "McCarthyism in Florida: Charley Johns and the Florida Legislative Investigation Committee July, 1956 to July, 1965" (master's thesis, University of South Florida, 1985), 97, https://palmm .digital.flvc.org/islandora/object/usf%3A49370#page/title/mode/1up, 9; Journal of the Senate, Regular Session, April 1955, 2.

46 **"red hunting":** "Red-Hunting Bill Offered by Sen. Johns," *Tampa Bay Times*, May 11, 1955, 17.

46 **Both measures failed:** Stark, "McCarthyism in Florida," 8–9; "Senators Ask FBI Advice on 'Red' Bill," *Tampa Tribune*, May 17, 1955, 8.

46 **"the first man in Florida's":** "Collins Is Winner in First Primary," *Tampa Tribune*, May 9, 1956, 1.

47 **Wilhelmina Jakes and Carrie Patterson:** Don Meikeljohn, "A&M Gets Bus Cases," *Tallahassee Democrat*, May 30, 1956, 1; Glenda Alice Rabby, *The Pain and the Promise: The Struggle for Civil Rights in Tallahassee, Florida* (University of Georgia Press, 1999), 9–13; "Field Reports on Desegregation in the South: Tallahassee, Florida," Anti-Defamation League of B'nai B'rith, February 1958, https://www.bjpa.org/content/upload/bjpa/fiel/FIELD %20REPORTS%20ON%20DESEGREGATION%20IN%20THE %20SOUTH%20TALLAHASSEE%20FL.pdf.

47   **cross was set aflame:** "Negro Coeds Scared by Cross Burning," *Orlando Evening Star*, May 28, 1956, 1.

47   **Inter-Civic Council:** Rabby, *The Pain and the Promise*, 5, 14–15.

47   **volunteer carpool system:** "Negro Community Joins Tallahassee Student Boycott," *News-Press*, May 30, 1956, 1.

47   **hemorrhaged money:** "Company Feels Pinch of Tallahassee Bus Boycott," *Miami Times*, June 2, 1956, 1; Rabby, *The Pain and the Promise*, 20, 49; "Capital Boycott Continues," *Orlando Sentinel*, June 21, 1956, 15.

47   **two redlined Black areas:** Rabby, *The Pain and the Promise*, 23.

47   **Remus J. Strickland:** Rabby, *The Pain and the Promise*, 30–31; "Car-Pool Roundup," *Tallahassee Democrat*, August 27, 1956, 1; "11th 'For Hire' Arrest Is Made," *Tallahassee Democrat*, August 29, 1956, 1.

47   **no knowledge of payments:** "City Attempts to Establish Car Pool Angle," *Tallahassee Democrat*, October 18, 1956, 1.

47   **special city prosecutor:** "Hawes Is Made Chief Attorney," *Tallahassee Democrat*, October 19, 1956, 1.

48   **"Divine Guidance to":** Rabby, *The Pain and the Promise*, 44.

48   **Inter-Civic Council raised:** Rabby, *The Pain and the Promise*, 45.

48   **"The war is not":** Rabby, *The Pain and the Promise*, 45.

48   **a contingent of six Black parents:** Carita Swanson Vonk, *Theodore R. Gibson: Priest, Prophet, and Politician* (Little River Press, 1997), 6, 66.

48   **on behalf of their children:** Juanita Greene, "6 Students' Fathers Also Sue," *Miami Herald*, June 13, 1956, 1.

48   **"made application to":** Vonk, *Theodore R. Gibson*, 66.

48   **"As Next Friend":** Vonk, *Theodore R. Gibson*, appendix copy of *Gibson v. Board of Public Instruction of Dade County*.

48   **called a special session:** "Mix Bills May Delay Session," *Orlando Sentinel*, July 29, 1956, 5; Judith Poucher, *State of Defiance: Challenging the Johns Committee's Assault on Civil Liberties* (University Press of Florida, 2014), 18; Senate Bill No. 11-XX, or the Pupil Assignment Act, Florida State University Archives, https://universityintransition.omeka.net/exhibits/show/a-university -in-transition/the-fabisinski-committee/the-pupil-assignment-law.

48   **"available facilities":** Senate Bill No. 11-XX, or the Pupil Assignment Act.

49   **usurpation of state sovereignty:** Journal of the Senate, Special Session, July 23, 1956, 6.

49   **an "interposition" resolution:** "David, Bryant Squabble over Resolution on Interposition," *Bradenton Herald*, August 1, 1956, 1; Stark, "McCarthyism in Florida," 12.

49   **alarm with allies:** "Klan Denounces Collins, Papers," *Orlando Sentinel*, September 2, 1956, 4.

49   **"advocating violence or a":** Journal of the Senate, Special Session, July 25, 1956, 27.

49   **"no other group the bill would fit":** Tom Raker, "Fund Voted to Probe NAACP," *Tampa Tribune*, July 26, 1956, 1.

49   **a resounding 28 to 7:** Journal of the Senate, Special Session, July 25, 1956, 27.

49   **six state senators:** Journal of the Senate, Special Session, July 26, 1956, 29.

49   **passed by a two-thirds margin:** Journal of the House of Representatives, July
      31, 1956, 137, University of Florida Archives, https://ufdc.ufl.edu/collections
      /fhrp/results?q=1956.

49   **succeeded in deadlocking:** Stark, "McCarthyism in Florida," 15.

50   **sine die:** "David, Bryant Squabble."

50   **took the unprecedented:** "Governor Ends Legislature in History-Making
      Move," *Tallahassee Democrat*, August 2, 1956, 1.

50   **"low blow":** "Collins Dissolves Special Session in Surprise Move," *Tampa
      Tribune*, August 2, 1956, 6.

50   **law without his signature:** Poucher, *State of Defiance*, 20.

50   **"I regard the matter as one":** "Group Set Up to Investigate NAACP, KKK,"
      Pensacola News Journal, August 22, 1956, 1.

50   **The first meeting:** FLIC Meeting Minutes for September 11, 1956, Clerk of
      the House Papers, State of Florida Archives.

50   **didn't show:** FLIC Meeting Minutes for September 11, 1956, Clerk of the
      House Papers, State of Florida Archives.

50   **"I have a Director meeting":** Charley Johns proxy vote slip, Clerk of the
      House Papers, State of Florida Archives.

50   **Proxy voting:** James Nathan Miller, "How Florida Threw Out the Pork Chop
      Gang," *National Civic Review* 60, no. 7 (July 1971): 367–68.

50   **"A terrible system":** Cliff Herrell, interview with Bonnie Stark, August 3,
      1993, Bonnie Stark Papers.

51   **"Where are the other six":** Cliff Herrell, interview with Bonnie Stark, August
      3, 1993.

51   **"secure all information":** FLIC Meeting Minutes for September 11, 1956.

51   **"big city Pork Chopper":** "Will Your Voice Be Heard?" *Tampa Times*, June
      5, 1965, 8.

51   **"He doesn't believe in fighting":** Rick Tuttle, "Big City Pork-Chopper?
      Herrell Just Smiles," *Miami Herald*, November 28, 1962, 7.

51   **"We will have to hear":** FLIC Meeting Minutes for September 11, 1956.

51   **"like the Un-American Activities":** FLIC Meeting Minutes for September 11,
      1956.

51   **on October 10, 1956:** FLIC Meeting Minutes for October 10, 1956, Clerk of
      the House Papers.

51   **"immune from what they do or say":** Richard W. Ervin, letter to Henry Land,
      October 4, 1956, Box 3, FLIC Papers.

51   **"neither an accusing (grand jury)":** FLIC Meeting Minutes for October 10,
      1956.

52   **"lead to big headlines":** FLIC Meeting Minutes for October 10, 1956.

52   **Remus Strickland and special city prosecutor Mark Hawes:** FLIC Meeting
      Minutes for October 18, 1956, Clerk of the House Papers; FLIC Meeting
      Minutes for November 13, 1956, Clerk of the House Papers.

52   **"an opportunity to serve":** Mark Hawes, letter to Henry Land, September 19,
      1956, 2, Clerk of the House Papers.

52   **a part-time salary of $11,000:** "Johns Backs $11,000 Pay for Legislatures'
      Racial Study Group Attorney," *Tampa Tribune*, December 4, 1957, 36;

"Probe's Part-Time Attorney Is Paid More Than Most of Ervin's Aides,"
Miami News, December 3, 1957, 6.

52 **entirely absent:** FLIC Meeting Minutes for November 13, 1957, Clerk of the
House Papers; FLIC Meeting Minutes for December 11, 1956, Clerk of the
House Papers.

52 **"or feared some":** "NAACP Investigation Group Says It's Met No Objection,"
Tampa Morning Tribune, November 16, 1956, 26.

52 **"general situation":** "Progress Reported to State," *Miami Herald*, November
14, 1956, 3.

52 **confidential memorandum:** R. J. Strickland memorandum, "Confidential,
To: All Chiefs of Police," circa 1956, Box 3, FLIC Papers.

53 **obtained a court order:** "U.S., State Laws Cited in Move to Lift NAACP
Ban," *Alabama Tribune*, July 6, 1956, 3.

53 **created a nine-member investigation:** "McFaddin Named Chairman of Group
Probing NAACP Here," *Times and Democrat*, July 19, 1956, 1.

53 **miniature HUACs and FBIs:** Dan Bertwell, "'A Veritable Refuge for
Practicing Homosexuals': The Johns Committee and the University of South
Florida," *Florida Historical Quarterly* 83, no. 4 (2005): 412; Poucher, *State
of Defiance*, 163; Stark, "McCarthyism in Florida," 18–19.

53 **December 24, 1956:** Rabby, *The Pain and the Promise*, 48.

53 *Browder v. Gayle*: Ken Hare, "'They Walked to Freedom,'" *Montgomery
Advertiser*, December 26, 2010, 4.

53 **act of mass revolt:** "Bus Mix Gets New Support," *Orlando Sentinel*,
December 31, 1956, 1.

53 **"preserve peaceful relations":** "Bus Franchise," *Tallahassee Democrat*,
December 27, 1956, 2.

53 **Bethel Baptist Church:** "Many Arrested, Birmingham Negroes Sit Up Front
in Buses," *Winston-Salem Journal*, December 27, 1956, 6.

53 **two integrated buses:** "Shots Pepper Two Montgomery Buses," *Shreveport
Journal*, December 27, 1956, 1, 2A; "Discord, Violence Mar Bus Riding in 4
Cities," *Montgomery Advertiser*, December 27, 1956, 1.

53 **ruled in favor:** Rabby, *The Pain and the Promise*, 51.

53 **"I have no hesitation":** Henry Cavendish, "Negroes Seek Ruling on Bus Seats
Feb. 4," *Miami News*, January 22, 1957, 17.

54 **Tallahassee repealed:** Rabby, *The Pain and the Promise*, 51.

54 **FLIC set their first open:** FLIC Meeting Minutes for January 17, 1957, Clerk
of the House Papers.

54 **subpoena more than twenty:** "NAACP Probers to Meet Monday at
Tallahassee," *Tampa Tribune*, February 3, 1957, 8; "State Opens Probe,"
Pensacola News Journal, February 5, 1957, 5.

54 **state capitol room 50:** Transcript of Testimony, February 4, 1957,
Volume 1, M81-17, Box 1, Florida Bar Association Records, State Archives
of Florida.

54 **Hawes had served:** George Anderson, "Veteran Iwo Marine Urges Bond
Buying," *Tallahassee Democrat*, May 17, 1945, 1; "Mark Hawes in State
Senate Race," *Tampa Tribune*, February 2, 1966, 19.

54 **"barratry":** Poucher, *State of Defiance*, 21.

54   **"Daytona Beach Negro who has waged":** Barbara Frye, "NAACP Probe to Dig Deeper into Help to Negro Student," *Miami News*, February 5, 1957, 27.

54   **Senator Charley Johns joined:** Transcript of Testimony, February 4, 1957, Volume 1, M81-17, Box 1, Florida Bar Association Records, State Archives of Florida.

54   **memory lapses:** Poucher, *State of Defiance*, 30; "Legislators Begin Probe of Bus Integration Drive," *Tampa Bay Times*, February 6, 1957, 1; "Negro Leader Charges Committee Is Trying to Outlaw State NAACP," *Tampa Bay Times*, February 5, 1957, 18.

54   **who couldn't recall how:** Transcript of Testimony, February 7, 1957, Box 4, FLIC Papers, State of Florida Archives.

54   **"obviously nettled by repeated":** "NAACP Succumbed to Hysteria Ex-President for State Claims," *Pensacola News Journal*, February 6, 1957, 9.

54   **"sheer luck":** Bob Delaney, "Chairman Says 'Luck' Aided Probe Committee," *Tampa Bay Times*, February 6, 1957, 1.

55   **"If the copies are authentic":** Delaney, "Chairman Says 'Luck' Aided Probe Committee."

55   **lawyers Hawes and Hill:** Transcript of Testimony, February 7, 1957.

55   **"Isn't this witness an attorney?":** Transcript of Testimony, February 7, 1957.

55   **"member of the Communist Party?":** Transcript of Testimony, February 7, 1957.

56   **"I never had been and":** Transcript of Testimony, February 7, 1957.

56   **"almost had to go home":** "Senator Loses Shoes at Probe," *Tallahassee Democrat*, February 6, 1957, 1.

56   **"I can find no provision of law which":** Richard W. Ervin, letter to Mark Hawes, February 8, 1957, 2, Box 3, FLIC Papers.

56   **the 1957 session wouldn't begin:** Journal of the Senate, Regular Session, April 2, 1957.

56   **no reason:** "NAACP Behind Mix Lawsuits, Rodriguez Says," *Tallahassee Democrat*, February 19, 1957, 1.

56   **Monday, February 25, 1957:** FLIC Meeting Minutes for February 5, 1957, Clerk of the House Papers.

56   **"any NAACP members in the Miami area":** "NAACP Probe Here Monday," *Miami Herald*, February 21, 1957, 5.

56   **servers delivered twenty-five court orders:** George Gilbody, "'Nothing to Hide'—Attorney," *Miami Herald*, February 24, 1957, Section B.

56   **attorney general of Texas:** FLIC Meeting Minutes for October 18, 1956, Clerk of the House Papers, State of Florida Archives.

57   **"bringing suits to integrate the schools":** "Committee Plans Dad Mix Probe," *Orlando Sentinel*, February 23, 1957, 3.

57   **workplace locations and home addresses:** Gilbody, "'Nothing to Hide'—Attorney."

57   **"The top guns of the":** Bert Collier, "Segregationist Big Guns Sounding Off in Florida," *Miami Herald*, February 24, 1957, 26.

57   **John Kasper, considered a prophet of the white:** Alec Marsh, *John Kasper and Ezra Pound: Saving the Republic* (Bloomsbury Academic, 2015), Location 107, 3478, Kindle.

57 "businessman's Klan": John Howard, *Men Like That: A Southern Queer History* (University of Chicago Press, 1999), 39.

57 "A little fire and some dynamite": "Will Dynamite Set Off Racial War in Miami?," *Miami Herald*, February 26, 1957, 1, 5.

57 kerosene-soaked cross: "Will Dynamite Set Off Racial War in Miami?"; James Buchanan, "Negro Householder Receives Bomb Threat," *Miami Herald*, February 26, 1957, 2; "Probe Planned of White Group Klan in State," *Pensacola News Journal*, February 27, 1957, 8.

57 "shoot the place up": Grattan Graves, testimony to FLIC, February 28, 1957, 1555, Florida Bar Association Papers, State Archives of Florida.

57 death threats: Poucher, *State of Defiance*, 49–50; "Daring Plot Against Miami Negroes," *Jet*, March 28, 1957, 12–14.

57 their home and/or work addresses: "Miami Probe of NAACP Opens Today," *Miami Herald*, February 25, 1957, 2.

CHAPTER 5. FIRST STRIKE

58 East Circuit courtroom: Transcript of Testimony, February 27, 1957, Florida Bar Association Papers, State Archives of Florida.

58 choice of location was deliberate: Mark Hawes, Confidential Memo to Dade County Circuit Court, February 13, 1957, Box 3, FLIC Papers.

58 waited with a bailiff: Transcript of Testimony, February 26, 1957, Florida Bar Association Papers, State Archives of Florida.

58 Miami White Citizens' Council: Judith Poucher, *State of Defiance: Challenging the Johns Committee's Assault on Civil Liberties* (University Press of Florida, 2014), 41.

58 the stand at 1:45 p.m.: Transcript of Testimony, February 25, 1957, 1096, Florida Bar Association Papers, State Archives of Florida.

59 Born in Miami in 1915: Carita Swanson Vonk, *Theodore R. Gibson: Priest, Prophet, and Politician* (Little River Press, 1997), 15.

59 "Racism was": Vonk, *Theodore R. Gibson*, 15.

59 "The Instigator": Vonk, *Theodore R. Gibson*, 16.

59 "God's angry child": Congressional Record, Proceedings and Debates of the 89th Congress, First Session, July 8, 1965.

59 "Berlin Wall": Jack Robert, "Coconut's 'Berlin Wall,'" *Miami News*, December 29, 1969, 5.

59 "I want to serve the Black people": Gibson, *Miami News*, September 21, 1982, 7.

59 some eight hundred Black congregants: Vonk, *Theodore R. Gibson*, 29.

59 "juke joints next to our homes": Larry Birger, "Negroes Attack Rezoning of Heights," *Miami News*, January 23, 1955, 8.

59 "His face is clean-cut and somber": "Negro Pastor Sees Hope in King's Death," *Miami Herald*, April 9, 1968, 50.

60 "How long have you been a member of the NAACP": Theodore Gibson, Transcript of Testimony, February 25, 1957.

60 "a second-class citizen": Theodore Gibson, Transcript of Testimony.

60 "Now read the question, please": Theodore Gibson, Transcript of Testimony.

60 "suggestions": Theodore Gibson, Transcript of Testimony.

60   mea culpa: Theodore Gibson, Transcript of Testimony.

61   "most evasive witnesses": Theodore Gibson, Transcript of Testimony.

61   "Did you ever belong to the Communist Party?": Theodore Gibson, Transcript of Testimony.

62   Miami Beach librarian: Bella Kelly, "Witnesses 'Surprised' by Call to Red Quiz," Miami News, February 8, 1958, 1; Poucher, State of Defiance, 43–44.

62   Along Freedom's Road: Ruth Perry, "Along Freedom's Road," Miami Times, August 24, 1957, 5.

62   "foregone conclusion": Ruth Perry, "Along Freedom's Road," Miami Times, February 23, 1957, 6.

62   bring all meeting minutes and membership lists: Stacy Braukman, Communists and Perverts Under the Palms: The Johns Committee in Florida, 1956–1965 (University Press of Florida, 2012), 49–50.

62   at an August 11: Ruth Perry, Transcript of Testimony, February 25, 1957; Francisco A. Rodriguez, letter to Constance Motley, August 6, 1956, NAACP Papers, Library of Congress.

62   beyond state lines: Ruth Perry, Transcript of Testimony, February 25, 1957.

63   Committee member Cliff Herrell: Ruth Perry, Transcript of Testimony.

63   "Did you know that he testified": Ruth Perry, Transcript of Testimony.

63   "Did the Miami Branch": Ruth Perry, Transcript of Testimony.

63   "I think I answered": Ruth Perry, Transcript of Testimony.

64   Graves, in the courtroom simultaneously: Ruth Perry, Transcript of Testimony.

64   Hawes was grilling Graves: Ruth Perry, Transcript of Testimony; Poucher, State of Defiance, 52.

64   "Mrs. Perry": Ruth Perry, Transcript of Testimony.

64   "from Palm Beach to Key West": "Miami Citizens Council Is Facing State Inquiry," Tallahassee Democrat, February 26, 1957, 9.

64   "Do you have any idea": Grattan Graves, Transcript of Testimony, February 25, 1957.

65   Graves wired Thurgood Marshall: Grattan Graves, Telegram to Thurgood Marshall, February 26, 1957, NAACP Papers, Library of Congress.

65   drafted a statement: NAACP Revised Draft Statement on Graves, February 26, 1957, NAACP Papers, Library of Congress.

65   Witnesses were excused: Transcript of Testimony, February 25, 1957.

65   "Will Dynamite Set": "Will Dynamite Set Off Racial War in Miami?" Miami Herald, February 26, 1957.

65   a hundred boxes of dynamite: "Will Dynamite Set Off Racial War in Miami?"

65   "fiery" John Kasper: "Will Dynamite Set Off Racial War in Miami?"

CHAPTER 6. COURTHOUSE STAND

66   Nearly half the FLIC membership: Transcript of Testimony, February 27, 1957, 1364, Florida Bar Association Papers, State of Florida Archives.

66   hand-delivered subpoenas: "4 Newsmen Subpoenaed in Hearings," Panama City News-Herald, February 28, 1957, 3.

67   "Does your organization advocate the use of violence?": Fred Hockett, Transcript of Testimony, February 27, 1957, 1371, Florida Bar Association

Papers, State of Florida Archives; "We Fight 'Legally'—Hockett," *Miami Herald*, February 28, 1957, 2.

67   **"misquote"**: Fred Hockett, Transcript of Testimony, February 27, 1957, 1374, Florida Bar Association Papers, State of Florida Archives.

67   **"not meant to frighten"**: Fred Hockett, Transcript of Testimony, February 27, 1957, 1375, Florida Bar Association Papers, State of Florida Archives.

67   **pronounced the suspected spy to be Harold Shaver**: Fred Hockett, Transcript of Testimony, February 27, 1957, 1446, Florida Bar Association Papers, State of Florida Archives.

67   **"a publicity hound"**: Fred Hockett, Transcript of Testimony, February 27, 1957, 1378, Florida Bar Association Papers, State of Florida Archives.

67   **to "make the community feel"**: Meredith Raimondo, "Dateline Atlanta: Place and the Social Construction of AIDS," in *Carryin' On in the Lesbian and Gay South*, ed. John Howard (New York University Press, 1997), 344–45.

67   **"crusading country journalist"**: Raimondo, "Dateline Atlanta."

68   **"Who wrote that article?"**: Allen Neuharth, Transcript of Testimony, February 27, 1957, 1383, Florida Bar Association Papers, State of Florida Archives.

68   **sources were kept anonymous**: Allen Neuharth, Transcript of Testimony, February 27, 1957, 1387, Florida Bar Association Papers, State of Florida Archives.

68   **World War II veteran**: "Legacy Allen 'Al' Neuharth," South Dakota Hall of Fame, https://www.sdexcellence.org/Allen_Neuharth_1980.

68   **"the combined effort of several"**: Allen Neuharth, Transcript of Testimony, February 27, 1957, 1383, Florida Bar Association Papers, State of Florida Archives.

68   **"the utmost cooperation"**: Allen Neuharth, Transcript of Testimony, February 27, 1957, 1400, Florida Bar Association Papers, State of Florida Archives.

68   **Miami Police Department**: Allen Neuharth, Transcript of Testimony, February 27, 1957, 1391, Florida Bar Association Papers, State of Florida Archives.

68   **"by the hand"**: Allen Neuharth, Transcript of Testimony, February 27, 1957, 1400, Florida Bar Association Papers, State of Florida Archives.

69   **"Do you refuse to give us that"**: Allen Neuharth, Transcript of Testimony, February 27, 1957, 1387, Florida Bar Association Papers, State of Florida Archives.

69   **"Will you talk a little louder, please?"**: Allen Neuharth, Transcript of Testimony, February 27, 1957, 1395, Florida Bar Association Papers, State of Florida Archives.

69   **"I ask, for the record, Mr. Chairman, that the witness"**: Allen Neuharth, Transcript of Testimony, February 27, 1957, 1387–88, Florida Bar Association Papers, State of Florida Archives.

69   **"abuse the broad powers"**: "Group Set Up," *Pensacola News Journal*, August 22, 1956.

69   **"I don't think it is proper for me to divulge it"**: Grattan Graves, Transcript of Testimony, February 27, 1957, 1436, Florida Bar Association Papers, State of Florida Archives.

69   Hampton Earl Shaver: Hampton Earl Shaver, Transcript of Testimony, February 28, 1957, 1462, Florida Bar Association Papers, State of Florida Archives.

70   "I can get George Clark Smith to represent me": Hampton Earl Shaver, Transcript of Testimony, February 28, 1957, 1463, Florida Bar Association Papers, State of Florida Archives.

71   "That is a story out in Colored Town": Hampton Earl Shaver, Transcript of Testimony, February 28, 1957, 1480, Florida Bar Association Papers, State of Florida Archives.

71   "members of the press and the TV": Cliff Herrell, Transcript of Testimony, February 28, 1957, 1607–9, Florida Bar Association Papers, State of Florida Archives.

71   "those witnesses who": Cliff Herrell, Transcript of Testimony.

71   March 11, 1957: Transcript of Testimony, March 11, 1957, Florida Bar Association Papers, State of Florida Archives; Alec Marsh, *John Kasper and Ezra Pound: Saving the Republic* (Bloomsbury Academic, 2015), Location 3904, Kindle.

71   He began by addressing: Marsh, *John Kasper and Ezra Pound*, Location 3905, Kindle.

71   "the Negro can be handled": Marsh, *John Kasper and Ezra Pound*, Location 3906, Kindle.

71   committee room 50: Transcript of Testimony, March 11, 1957, Florida Bar Association Papers.

72   "tall, slightly stoop shouldered, sharp featured": Don Meiklejohn, "Kasper Declares It's All States' Rights; in South, Segregate, in North, Integrate," *Palm Beach Post*, March 14, 1957, 28.

72   "Civil rights is that broad term used by the Communists": John Kasper, Transcript of Testimony, March 11, 1957, 1713–14, Florida Bar Association Papers.

72   "During the proceedings here": John Kasper, Transcript of Testimony, March 11, 1957, 1823, Florida Bar Association Papers.

72   alarmingly disheveled state: "Daring Plot Against Miami Negroes," *Jet*, March 28, 1957, 14.

72   "with two black eyes": "Daring Plot Against Miami Negroes."

73   abducted him at gunpoint: Hampton Earl Shaver, Transcript of Testimony, March 12, 1957, 1957–1962, 1823, Florida Bar Association Papers.

73   "What kind of a gun?": Hampton Earl Shaver, Transcript of Testimony, March 12, 1957, 1962–63, Florida Bar Association Papers.

73   had Fred Hockett stand: Hampton Earl Shaver, Transcript of Testimony, March 12, 1957, 1971, Florida Bar Association Papers.

73   current phone number: Hampton Earl Shaver, Transcript of Testimony, March 12, 1957, 2035, Florida Bar Association Papers.

73   "Dear sir, please keep up the good work of your committee": Ruby S. Johnson, letter to Charley Johns, April 18, 1957, 11-1119, Box 3, FLIC Papers.

74   1957 session to renew FLIC: Florida Journal of the Senate, April 24, 1957, 266.

74   **passed the Florida House unanimously:** Florida Journal of the House of
      Representatives, May 1, 1957, 625.
74   **"The Legislature of Florida denies":** House Concurrent Resolution No. 174,
      April 5, 1957, 71.
74   **"This concurrent resolution of 'Interposition'":** "Interposition
      Resolution by the Florida Legislature in Response to *Brown v. Board of
      Education*, 1957, with Handwritten Note by Florida Governor LeRoy
      Collins," Library of Congress, https://www.loc.gov/resource/gdcwdl.wdl
      _14196/.
74   **"the NAACP has formulated":** Report of the Florida Legislative Investigation
      Committee, 1957, 3, Clerk of the House Papers.
75   **"secretly removed":** Report of the Florida Legislative Investigation
      Committee, 1957, 3, Clerk of the House Papers.
75   **"willful, open and":** Report of the Florida Legislative Investigation
      Committee, 1957, 3, Clerk of the House Papers.
75   **conduct "praiseworthy":** "Interposition 'Lie' Says Gov. Collins," *Tallahassee
      Democrat*, April 21, 1957, 2; "Collins Terms Mix Curb Defiant 'Lie,'"
      Orlando Sentinel, April 21, 1957, 3.
75   **Not a single piece:** Bonnie Stark, "McCarthyism in Florida: Charley Johns
      and the Florida Legislative Investigation Committee July, 1956 to July, 1965"
      (master's thesis, University of South Florida, 1985), 97, https://palmm.digital
      .flvc.org/islandora/object/usf%3A49370#page/title/mode/1up, 28–30.
75   **without his signature:** Stacy Braukman, *Communists and Perverts Under the
      Palms: The Johns Committee in Florida, 1956–1965* (University Press of
      Florida, 2012), 51.
75   **"subversive":** Chapter 57-125, Senate Bill No. 347, Clerk of the House
      Papers.
75   **legislature until 1959:** Chapter 57-125, Senate Bill No. 347, Clerk of the
      House Papers.
75   **soon left the group:** FLIC Meeting Minutes for July 8, 1957, Clerk of the
      House Papers.
75   **"Charley used to expound":** Cliff Herrell, interview with Bonnie Stark, circa
      1993, Bonnie Stark Papers.
76   **"Chairman of the Committee is Charley E. Johns":** Robert Saunders, letter to
      Gloster Current, July 9, 1957, NAACP Papers, Library of Congress.

CHAPTER 7. QUORUM OF ONE

77   **"rules of procedure":** FLIC Meeting Minutes for July 8, 1957, Clerk of the
      House Papers.
77   **"one or more members":** FLIC Meeting Minutes for July 24, 1957, Clerk of
      the House Papers.
78   **released a statement:** Charley Johns, "Statement to Press Concerning
      Termination of John Cye Chesty," July 8, 1957, Clerk of the House Papers;
      "City Detective Called to Testify in Hoffa Trial," *Tallahassee Democrat*, July
      1, 1957, 11.

78   "excessive expense accounts": Johns, "Statement to Press."

78   two FLIC allies: FLIC Meeting Minutes for July 8, 1957, 5, Clerk of the
      House Papers.

78   "witness was most evasive": FLIC Meeting Minutes for July 24, 1957, 8,
      Clerk of the House Papers.

78   spoke next about Neuharth: FLIC Meeting Minutes for July 24, 1957, 8,
      Clerk of the House Papers.

79   again in 1959: Florida Journal of the Senate, Regular Session, April 16,
      1957.

79   until early fall: FLIC Meeting Minutes for October 2, 1957, Clerk of the
      House Papers.

79   Johns Committee: "'Last Resort' School Bill Considered," *Orlando Sentinel*,
      August 27, 1957, 3; Robert W. Delaney, "Johns Committee Mum," *Miami
      News*, December 15, 1957, 25.

79   Pinellas County: Frank E. Kennedy, "Early Canal Report Expected,"
      Orlando Sentinel, February 3, 1957, 10; "Absentee to Decide Two Races,"
      Orlando Sentinel, November 8, 1956, 3.

79   a Black senior: "Commencement Season Officially Opens Today," *Tampa
      Bay Times*, May 26, 1957, 14; Florida State Population Census, 1945,
      Ancestry.com; 1950 U.S. Census, Ancestry.com.

79   1344 Fargo Street: "About People You Know," *Tampa Bay Times*, July 11,
      1955, 12; Tommie Jennings, St. Petersburg City Directory, 1956, 438,
      Ancestry.com, https://www.ancestry.com/search/collections/2469/records
      /666039388.

79   varsity lineman's: Cal Adams, "Gibbs Meets Strong Quincy Squad Tonight,"
      Tampa Bay Times, November 16, 1956, 16.

79   he took typewriting courses: "Gibbs Students Get Practical Business
      Courses," *St. Petersburg Times*, October 31, 1956, 37.

79   "I am a senior at Gibbs High School": Thomas "Tommie" Jennings,
      letter to Registrar of St. Petersburg Junior College, January 18, 1957, Box 3,
      FLIC Papers.

80   "There has been no established policy": Floyd T. Christian, letter to Thomas
      Jennings, February 12, 1957, Box 3, FLIC Papers.

80   "Negro junior college": "County School Board Names Rembert as JC
      President," *St. Petersburg Times*, June 15, 1957, 15; Harry Dyer, "Gibbs
      Principal Asks for New Junior College," *Tampa Bay Times*, January 14,
      1957, 25.

80   "defer action": Christian, letter to Jennings, February 12, 1957.

80   "there had been no established Policy": Thomas Jennings, letter to Floyd T.
      Christian, February 15, 1957, Box 3, FLIC Papers.

80   Thomas D. Bailey: Thomas Bailey, letter to Floyd T. Christian, January 30,
      1957, Box 3, S1128, Board of Education Papers, State Archives of Florida;
      Thomas Bailey, letter to Floyd T. Christian, March 4, 1957, Box 3, S1128,
      Board of Education Papers, State Archives of Florida.

80    $151,000: Lowell Brandle, "Junior College Facilities Seen at Gibbs High,"
      Tampa Bay Times, March 23, 1957, 18.

80 "well pleased": Ralph Sumner, "Pinellas Superintenent Says Negroes 'Well Pleased' with Segregated School Facilities," *Tampa Tribune*, August 31, 1956, 8.

81 would receive a special class award: "Gibbs, Community Honor Top Grads During Awards Day Rites," *Tampa Bay Times*, June 5, 1957, 39.

81 became a banner member: "Tommy Jennings Takes Banner for His Church," *Tampa Bay Times*, March 2, 1962, 22; "Tommie Lee Jennings Obituary," Tribute Archive, accessed December 3, 2024, https://www.tributearchive .com/obituaries/22120887/tommy-lee-jennings/st-petersburg/florida/smith -funeral-home-cremation-services.

81 first nine instructors: "9 Instructors Are Listed for Gibbs Junior College," *Tampa Bay Times*, August 18, 1957, 22.

81 an Orlando native: "Personal Notes," *Tampa Bay Times*, June 25, 1950, 16; William J. Neal, 1950 U.S. Census, Ancestry.com; William James Neal, WWII Draft Card, Ancestry.com; "Talented Trio to Appear Here," *Tampa Bay Times*, March 19, 1958, 19; William James Neal, interrogation by Remus Strickland, October 13, 1960, # 1-95, Box 8, FLIC Papers, 2.

81 received its official listing: Bertha Dancil, "Choir to Make First Public Appearance," *Tampa Bay Times*, October 14, 1957, 12.

81 That September: Hawes, letter to Harrison, September 26, 1957, 1–2, Florida Bar Association Papers.

81 "In my judgement": Hawes, letter to Harrison, September 26, 1957, 1–2.

82 insistence to the contrary: Hawes, letter to Harrison, September 26, 1957, 1; FLIC Meeting Minutes for July 24, 1957, Clerk of the House Papers.

82 "interest to the colored race": "Investigation of Evidence Before the Florida Legislative Investigation Committee Relating to the Professional Conduct of Alex Akerman and Horace E. Hill," Grievance Committee, June 24, 1960, 2–3, Florida Bar Association Papers.

82 "guilty of the unauthorized practice": Jack A. Abbott, "Report of Unauthorized Practice of Law Committee of the Florida Bar, in re: Special Legislative Investigation Concerning the NAACP," May 15, 1959, 2, Florida Bar Association Papers.

82 "a matter": FLIC Meeting Minutes for October 2, 1957, Clerk of the House Papers.

82 confidential expense records: Mark Hawes, "Confidential Addition to Minutes of Sunday, October 27, 1957, not to be placed in our public files," Clerk of the House Papers.

82 "negro men janitors": Charley Johns, letter to J. Wayne Reitz, January 8, 1957, Box 40, Reitz Papers, University of Florida Archives.

82 "heavy-duty male workmen": J. Wayne Reitz, letter to Charley Johns, January 15, 1957, Box 40, Reitz Papers, University of Florida Archives.

82 daughter MarkleyAnn Johns: MarkleyAnn Johns, Bradford High School Yearbook, 1959, 52.

83 "dates by colored male janitors": FLIC Meeting Minutes for September 22, 1961, 6–7, Clerk of the House Papers.

83   disclosed the Gainesville: FLIC Meeting Minutes for October 2, 1957, Clerk
       of the House Papers.
83    $650 per month: FLIC Meeting Minutes for October 2, 1957, Clerk of the
       House Papers; FLIC Meeting Minutes for October 25, 1957, Clerk of the
       House Papers.
83   "services rendered": FLIC Meeting Minutes for October 2, 1957, 2, Clerk of
       the House Papers.
83   "study and recommendation": FLIC Meeting Minutes for January 17, 1958,
       4–5, Clerk of the House Papers.
83   to vote yes: FLIC Meeting Minutes for January 17, 1958, 4–5, Clerk of the
       House Papers.

CHAPTER 8. A JOHNS COMMITTEE

84   not be meeting again until 1958: Frank Trippett, "Johns Silent About
       Next Probe Target," *Tampa Bay Times*, November 6, 1957, 6; "Lawyer
       for Race Probers Mopping Up on Salaries," *Miami News*, December 3,
       1957, 6.
84   threatened to resign: John L. Boyles, "Senator Irked at Committee," *Miami
       Herald*, January 4, 1958, 2.
84   dug into the résumé and reimbursement requests: Robert Delaney, "Prober
       Spends $1,000 for Secret Records," *Miami News*, December 4, 1957, 8C.
84    $700 in auto expenses: Delaney, "Prober Spends $1,000 for Secret Records."
85   record of career errors, firings: Robert Delaney, "Comptroller Reports
       Expenses of Charley Johns' Aide," *Miami News*, December 4, 1957, 7C.
85   "for the good of the department": Delaney, "Comptroller Reports Expenses
       of Charley Johns' Aide."
85   "high recommendations": Robert Delaney, "Johns Committee Meets,
       Reorganizes," *Orlando Sentinel*, August 9, 1963, 1, 4.
85   "His investigations were not reliable": Haines Colbert, "Johns Committee
       Strays," *Orlando Sentinel*, March 30, 1963, 11A.
85   That December 11: Remus Strickland, letter to Mark Hawes, December 11,
       1957, 1, Clerk of the House Papers.
85   a small-scale Communist hunt: Damon Runyon Jr., "Reds Flee Miami to
       Escape Probe," *Miami News*, November 27, 1954, 1.
85   following the William T. Simpson: Milt Sosin, "Pervert Colony Uncovered,"
       Miami News, August 9, 1954; Donald Janson, "Communist 'Rules' for
       Revolt Viewed as Durable Fraud," *New York Times*, July 10, 1970, 1, 26.
85   "known member of the Communist": Janson, "Communist 'Rules' for
       Revolt," 26.
85   "hauling a lot of alleged or former Communists": "Are Red-Baiters
       Immune?" *Tallahassee Democrat*, October 19, 1954, 6.
85   died of a heart attack in 1958: "Eulogies Pour In for Brautigam, 52," *Miami
       News*, August 18, 1958, 1; "Jury Woes Follow Same Pattern," *Miami Herald*,
       October 18, 1957, 1.
86   "running down information": "Johns Defends Probe Attorney, Says
       Investigators Gathering Data," *Tampa Bay Times*, December 4, 1957, 10.

86   deposed Sylvia Crouch: John Boyles, "Mrs. Paul Crouch's Deposition Names
     Past, Present Miamians; Hearing to Shift Here on Feb. 26," *Miami Herald*,
     February 12, 1958, 2.
86   "Can you tell me whether": Sylvia Crouch, Transcript of Testimony, January
     7, 1958, 18–19, Box 6, FLIC Papers.
86   Communists embraced "corrupt" sexuality: "Communist Rules for
     Revolution," May 1919, Wisconsin Historical Society Papers, https://content
     .wisconsinhistory.org/digital/collection/p15932coll8/id/60855/.
86   "Is it a fair statement to say": Sylvia Crouch, Transcript of Testimony,
     January 7, 1958, 66–67, Box 6, FLIC Papers.
87   The committee voted to resume: FLIC Meeting Minutes for January 17, 1958,
     3, Clerk of the House Papers.
87   "The Committee is possessed": "Statement by Senator Charley E. Johns,
     Chairman," February 7, 1958, Clerk of the House Papers.
88   a celebrity anti-Communist: Robert Delaney, "State Red Quiz Hears
     Matthews," *Miami News*, February 10, 1958, 2; "Former Expert for Sen.
     McCarthy Called 'Too Left' by Socialists," *Tampa Bay Times*, February 11,
     1958, 10; Bonnie Stark, "McCarthyism in Florida: Charley Johns and the
     Florida Legislative Investigation Committee July, 1956 to July, 1965"
     (master's thesis, University of South Florida, 1985), 97, https://palmm.digital
     .flvc.org/islandora/object/usf%3A49370#page/title/mode/1up, 33.
88   dressed in a navy-blue suit: "Former Expert for Sen.," *Tampa Bay
     Times*.
88   "the record will show conclusively": Stark, "McCarthyism in
     Florida," 34.
88   "the past 30 years": Delaney, "State Red Quiz Hears Matthews," *Miami
     News*.
88   forty-six people on NAACP letterhead: "Ex-McCarthy Aide Testifies
     NAACP Red Infiltration Target 30 Years," *Tampa Bay Times*, February 11,
     1958, 10A.
88   first lady Eleanor Roosevelt: "Ex-McCarthy Aide Testifies NAACP Red
     Infiltration Target 30 Years," *Tampa Bay Times*.
89   "how many of the known Communists": *Gibson v. Florida Legislative
     Investigation Committee*, Brief of FLIC, 20, Bonnie Stark Papers.
89   "to link the NAACP and the Communist party": Robert Delaney, "Red
     Influence in NAACP Cited," *Miami News*, February 10, 1958, 2A.
89   Georgia Commission on Education: "Communism and the NAACP,"
     pamphlet by Georgia Commission on Education, circa 1958, NAACP
     Papers.
89   menace posed by civil rights: "Communism and the NAACP."
89   "My son-in-law and others are": Roy B. Smith, letter to FLIC, May 22, 1964,
     Box 2, FLIC Papers.
89   "There is a probability of Red": "Johns Plans Ouster of 'Red' Professors,"
     Florida Alligator, February 11, 1958, 1; Fred M. Frohock, "Acheson Speaks at
     UF; Students Air Views, Too," *Miami Herald*, February 23, 1958, 16E.
89   "too much Communism": "Johns Plans Ouster," *Florida Alligator*.

89   Robert L. Carter: Bella Kelly, "NAACP Attempts to Kill Federal Probe
      Subpoenas," *Miami News*, February 23, 1958, 10.

89   February 26, 1958, hearings: Transcript of Testimony, February 26, 1958,
      Box 4, FLIC Papers; John B. McDermott, "New Disclosures Foreseen of
      Commie 'Use' of NAACP," *Miami Herald*, February 26, 1958, 2A.

90   "There are some people who seem": Mark Hawes, Transcript of Testimony,
      February 26, 1958, Box 4, FLIC Papers.

90   "out of the courtroom": Hawes, Transcript of Testimony, February 26,
      1958.

90   "this is not a judicial proceeding": Transcript of Testimony, February 26,
      1958.

90   first group of witnesses: John B. McDermott, "Three Cited for Contempt at
      State NAACP Probe," *Miami Herald*, February 27, 1958, 1, 2A.

90   bring with her all Florida NAACP: Ruth Perry, Transcript of Testimony,
      February 27, 1958, Box 4, FLIC Papers; Judith Poucher, *State of Defiance:
      Challenging the Johns Committee's Assault on Civil Liberties* (University
      Press of Florida, 2014), 57; "Witnesses Refuse to Answer Queries of Racial
      Probers," *Palm Beach Post*, February 28, 1958, 20.

91   swore an oath: Ruth Perry, Transcript of Testimony, February 27, 1958;
      Poucher, *State of Defiance*, 57.

91   "I respectfully refuse to answer": Ruth Perry, Transcript of Testimony,
      February 27, 1958.

91   "I have been requested by the subpoena": Ruth Perry, Transcript of
      Testimony, February 27, 1958.

91   "Give me her testimony": Ruth Perry, Transcript of Testimony, February
      27, 1958.

91   "come down": Ruth Perry, Transcript of Testimony, February 27,
      1958.

92   "not fit to be a citizen of the State of Florida": Cliff Herrell, Transcript of
      Testimony, February 27, 1958.

92   "When the people who are identified": J. B. Hopkins, Cliff Herrell,
      Transcript of Testimony, February 27, 1958.

92   "I would like to say that": Ruth Perry, Transcript of Testimony, February
      27, 1958.

92   "They abused her": Jack Mann, "Gibson Breaks Witch Hunt by Charley
      Johns," *Miami Herald*, December 5, 1958, 1.

92   "character and integrity": Grattan Graves, Transcript of Testimony,
      February 27, 1958.

92   "any of the books, papers and membership lists": Mark Hawes, Transcript of
      Testimony, February 27, 1958.

92   "In view of the fact that Mr. Herrell": Theodore Gibson, Transcript of
      Testimony, February 27, 1958.

93   "I was born and reared in Dade County": Theodore Gibson, Transcript of
      Testimony, February 27, 1958.

93   erupted in spontaneous applause: "Four Witnesses Refuse to Talk at NAACP
      Probe," *Panama News-Journal*, February 28, 1958, 9A.

93   **"Reverend, are you refusing to submit"**: Theodore Gibson, Transcript of Testimony, February 27, 1958.

94   **"of the 'star chamber' nature"**: Vernell Albury, Transcript of Testimony, February 27, 1958; Statement of Vernell Albury, February 27, 1958, Clerk of the House Papers.

94   **FLIC adjourned its afternoon**: Transcript of Testimony, February 27, 1958.

94   **fourteen FLIC witnesses**: John B. McDermott, "10 More Cited in Red Hunt," *Miami Herald*, February 28, 1958, late edition, 1.

94   **"pointless"**: "Johns Group Stymied in Miami NAACP Probe," *Tampa Bay Times*, March 1, 1958, 8A; Mark Hawes, Transcript of Testimony, February 28, 1958, Box 4, FLIC Papers.

94   **"both colored and white"**: Transcript of Testimony, February 28, 1958.

94   **"put them in jail"**: John Boyles, "Court Upholds Red Probe of NAACP Here," *Miami Herald*, June 19, 1958, 2A; Charley Johns, press clip in the documentary *Behind Closed Doors*, 2000, produced by Allyson Beutke; "Strozier, State Probers 'Chat,'" *Tallahassee Democrat*, June 25, 1959, 2.

94   **several hundred KKK members**: "An Odd Way to Keep the Peace," *Bradenton Herald*, March 13, 1958, 4.

94   **The NAACP petitioned**: "NAACP Cites Klan Parade, Asks Probe," *Tampa Tribune*, March 11, 1958, 19.

CHAPTER 9. WHITE KNIGHTS

95   **"I am happy to"**: Mrs. Kenneth Williams, letter to Charley Johns, May 8, 1958, Box 3, FLIC Papers.

95   **James Weatherford**: James Weatherford, 1940 U.S Census, Ancestry.com; James Weatherford, 1950 U.S. Census, Ancestry.com.

95   **"If your health permits"**: Remus Strickland, letter to J. Weatherford, April 7, 1958, Box 3, FLIC Papers.

96   **obtained a circuit court ruling**: "Johns Group Stymied," *Tampa Bay Times*, March 1, 1958.

96   **judge J. Fritz Gordon**: "NAACP Takes Protest to Supreme Court," *Tallahassee Democrat*, March 8, 1958, Section 2.

96   **cache of dynamite**: Bob Swift, "Dynamite Bomb Blasts School at Synagogue," *Miami Herald*, March 17, 1958, 1.

96   **issued a stay**: Bonnie Stark, "McCarthyism in Florida: Charley Johns and the Florida Legislative Investigation Committee July, 1956 to July, 1965" (master's thesis, University of South Florida, 1985), 97, https://palmm.digital .flvc.org/islandora/object/usf%3A49370#page/title/mode/1up, 44.

96   **struck in Jacksonville**: "'Terror' Blasts Rock Jacksonville," *Tampa Bay Times*, April 29, 1958, 1; "To Act on Bombings," *New York Times*, May 1, 1958, 30, https://timesmachine.nytimes.com/timesmachine/1958/05/01 /issue.html; "Jacksonville Jewish Center Bombed; Community Meets Today on Action," Jewish Telegraphic Agency, April 29, 1958, 1, https://www.jta .org/archive/jacksonville-jewish-center-bombed-community-meets-today-on -action.

96   **Black middle school**: "'Terror' Blasts Rock Jacksonville."

96   "Confederate Union": "'Hate' Blasts Rip Jax," *Miami Herald*, April 29, 1958, Palm Beach ed., 1.
96   "Every segregationist in the South": "Threats to Jews by 'Underground' Follow Explosions," *Miami Herald*, April 29, 1958, 1; "Jacksonville Synagogue, Negro School Blasted," *Orlando Sentinel*, April 29, 1958, 1.
96   "guilty hoodlums": "Jacksonville Synagogue."
96   sent his chief investigator: "Jacksonville Synagogue."
96   "If our Committee can do anything": "Johns, Collins Pledge to Probe Jax Dynamitings," *Pensacola News Journal*, April 29, 1958, 3B.
97   Strickland devoted: FLIC Meeting Minutes for June 6, 1958, Clerk of the House Papers; Cliff Herrell, interview with Bonnie Stark, circa 1993, Bonnie Stark Papers.
97   Florida Supreme Court ruled unanimously: Stark, "McCarthyism in Florida," 45; Boyles, "Court Upholds Red Probe," *Miami Herald*, June 19, 1958; Robert Delaney and Jack W. Roberts, "Court Says NAACP Must Bare Records," *Miami News*, June 18, 1958, 1.
97   admissibility of questions: "Court Says Johns Group Can Question NAACP," *Tampa Tribune*, June 19, 1958, 4B.
97   "This is what we've": Delaney and Roberts, "Court Says NAACP."
97   "the Klan phase of our investigation: Charles F. Hesser, "Legislators Will Meet Thursday," *Miami News*, June 22, 1958, 1.
97   eyebrow-raising sidebar: Transcript of Testimony, June 25, 1958, # 5-56, Box 4, FLIC Papers; Don Meiklejohn, "Sen. Bart Knight Said Former Member of KKK," *Jackson County Floridan*, June 26, 1958, 1.
97   "Prior to 1936, more than": Bart Knight, Transcript of Testimony, June 25, 1958.
97   "I wouldn't think so": Charley Johns, Transcript of Testimony, June 25, 1958.
97   "I don't want somebody to come": Bart Knight, Transcript of Testimony, June 25, 1958.
97   private detective: Jim Hardee, "Mount Dora Klux Meeting Disorderly, Ex Chief Says," *Orlando Sentinel*, June 26, 1958, 1B; W. J. Griffin, Transcript of Testimony, June 25, 1958.
97   sober business attire: John Laboyles, "Klan Tied to Making of Bombs," June 26, 1958, 1.
98   Griffin explained away: "Tampan Tells Probes of Klan Disbanding," *Tampa Times*, June 25, 1958, 5.
98   "You had kept records of your Klan operations": W. J. Griffin, Transcript of Testimony, June 25, 1958.
98   announcement at the Miami hearings: John B. McDermott, "States' Rights Chief Denies Race Baiting," *Miami Herald*, May 4, 1958, 5A.
98   accepted the information: Mark Hawes, Transcript of Testimony, June 25, 1958.
98   "flogging" case: Martin Waldron, "Johns Says Klan Faces Probe 'Top to Bottom," *Tampa Tribune*, June 24, 1958, 1.
98   The term *flogging*: Lisa Cardyn, "Sexualized Racism/Gendered Violence: Outraging the Body Politic in the Reconstruction South," *Michigan Law Review* 100, no. 4 (2002): 675–867, https://doi.org/10.2307/1290425.

99   during a 1955 visit: W. J. Griffin, Transcript of Testimony, June 25, 1958.

99   sheriff Hugh Lewis: Griffin, Transcript of Testimony, June 25, 1958.

99   June 1: "Collins Given Story of Negro's Flogging," *Miami Herald*, June 25, 1955, 2; "Live Oak Negro Bares Flogging," *Orlando Evening Star*, June 21, 1955, 1.

99   father of nine: Herbert D. Cameron, "Collins Asks Suwanee Official to Explain Flogging," *Tampa Tribune*, June 22, 1955, 1; "Live Oak Negro," *Orlando Evening Star*, June 21, 1955, 1.

99   Fred Sweat: W. J. Griffin, Transcript of Testimony, June 25, 1958; "Flogging Details Refused," *Tallahassee Democrat*, June 26, 1958, 1.

99   to a standard that satisfied: Hugh Lewis, Transcript of Testimony, June 26, 1958.

99   instead called upon Grand Dragon W. J. Griffin: W. J. Griffin, Transcript of Testimony, June 25, 1958.

99   "'Well, I wish you'd give'": W. J. Griffin, Transcript of Testimony, June 25, 1958.

99   who'd called the 1955 grand jury: "Grand Jury Called in Flogging," *Tampa Tribune*, June 26, 1955, 1; William Slaughter, Transcript of Testimony, June 25, 1958.

100   "He's a good old, humble darky": William Slaughter, Transcript of Testimony, June 25, 1958.

100   "got the wrong house and the wrong negro": William Slaughter, Transcript of Testimony, June 25, 1958.

100   "You did everything in your power": William Slaughter, Transcript of Testimony, June 25, 1958.

100   confessing that he was a former: Hugh Lewis, Transcript of Testimony, June 26, 1958; "Sheriff Defies Probers Here," *Tallahassee Democrat*, June 25, 1958, 6.

100   "Were you Sheriff in the months of May and June 1955?": Hugh Lewis, Transcript of Testimony, June 26, 1958.

101   "I refuse to give you his name": Hugh Lewis, Transcript of Testimony, June 26, 1958; "Governor, Do Your Duty!," *Tampa Tribune*, June 28, 1958, 8.

101   five years: "Concept Citations Are Sought for Two Live Oak Ku Klux Klansmen," *Fort Pierce Tribune*, June 26, 1958, 1; Hugh Lewis, Transcript of Testimony, June 26, 1958.

101   pleaded the Fifth Amendment: Hugh Lewis, Transcript of Testimony, June 26, 1958.

101   "nigger": Hugh Lewis, Transcript of Testimony, June 26, 1958.

101   "on the ground that it may be incriminating": Fred Sweat, Transcript of Testimony, June 26, 1958.

102   "may inscriminate me": Johnny Smith, Transcript of Testimony, June 26, 1958.

102   "He's already answered all": M. B. Sherrill, Transcript of Testimony, June 25, 1958; "Klan Probers Vote to Cite Silent Sheriff for Contempt," *Tampa Tribune*, June 27, 1958, 13.

102   out of their own pockets: M. B. Sherrill, Transcript of Testimony, June 25, 1958.

102   "The witness may come down": Fred Sweat, Transcript of Testimony, June 26, 1958.

102   "Just a moment": Fred Sweat, Transcript of Testimony, June 26, 1958.

102   "The witness come down": Johnny Smith, Transcript of Testimony, June 26, 1958.

103   FLIC go into executive session: Hugh Lewis, Transcript of Testimony, June 26, 1958.

103   "I am a lawyer," thundered: Hugh Lewis, Transcript of Testimony, June 26, 1958.

103   Joe Hand, former president of the KKK: Joe Hand, Transcript of Testimony, June 25, 1958; "Tampan Airs Klan's Dirty Linen at State Probe," *Tampa Tribune*, June 26, 1958, 7A.

103   "Mr. Chairman, do I have to give the names": Joe Hand, Transcript of Testimony, June 25, 1958.

103   "necessary": Joe Hand, Transcript of Testimony, June 25, 1958.

104   Eldon "E. L." Edwards: Eldon Edwards, Transcript of Testimony, June 26, 1958; "Klan Probers Vote to Cite Silent Sheriff for Contempt," *Tampa Tribune*.

104   "Do you have an organization": Edwards, Transcript of Testimony, June 26, 1958.

104   committee member Herrell: Edwards, Transcript of Testimony, June 26, 1958.

104   "He has a plane commitment to get out of here": Edwards, Transcript of Testimony, June 26, 1958.

104   Dick Ashe: Dick Ashe, Transcript of Testimony, June 27, 1958; "Ashe Says KKK Is Storing Arms," *Tallahassee Democrat*, June 28, 1958, 1.

105   "they could buy guns": Dick Ashe, Transcript of Testimony, June 27, 1958.

105   "forced integration": Ashe, Transcript of Testimony, June 27, 1958.

105   named Edgar Brooklyn: "Ashe Says KKK," *Tallahassee Democrat*; Harry T. Moore Assassination folder, FBI Records.

105   possessed the floor plans: "Investigation Regarding Suspect Earl J. Brooklyn," # 44-270, 3, FBI Records.

105   murders of Moore: Jim Hardee, "Klans in State Storing Arms, Dynamite: Ashe," *Orlando Sentinel*, June 28, 1958, 1.

105   attending a Klan rally in: Ashe, Transcript of Testimony, June 27, 1958.

105   "Mr. Ashe, Representative Hopkins": Ashe, Transcript of Testimony, June 27, 1958.

105   committee member Herrell: Edwards, Transcript of Testimony, June 26, 1958.

105   he used the chairman's first name: Ashe, Transcript of Testimony, June 27, 1958.

106   Johns ended the KKK hearings: Transcript of Testimony, June 27, 1958.

106   eventually it appears those charges: "Sheriff Questions Legislative Power," *Tampa Tribune*, October 14, 1958, 25; "Asks Dismissal," *Tampa Bay Times*, October 16, 1958, 9; "Liberal Florida Favors State Rights," *Tallahassee Democrat*, December 28, 1958, 2.

106   Miami circuit judge Ray Pearson: Stark, "McCarthyism in Florida," 51.

106   "have but one aim and that": "Court Maneuvers of NAACP Hamstring Legislative Probers; Hearings Delayed," *Tampa Tribune*, August 2, 1958, 16; Stark, "McCarthyism in Florida," 52.

107   "sounds like a frustrated": "Court Maneuvers of NAACP Hamstring Legislative Probers," *Tampa Tribune*; Stark, "McCarthyism in Florida," 52; Bella Kelly, "Tactics Hit by Probers," *Miami News*, August 1, 1958, Evening ed., 1.

107   constitutional amendment: *Gibson et al. v. Florida*, "Brief of Appellee," 15, Box 14, FLIC Papers.

107   NAACP argued: *Gibson et al. v. Florida*, "Brief of Appellants," 15, Box 14, FLIC Papers; Stark, "McCarthyism in Florida," 55–56.

107   unanimous opinion affirming: *Gibson et al. v. Florida*, "Opinion Filed December 19, 1958," 33, Box 14, FLIC Papers.

107   "moderation, restraint": *Gibson et al. v. Florida*, "Opinion Filed December 19, 1958," 12, Box 14, FLIC Papers.

107   "bias or prejudice": *Gibson et al. v. Florida*, "Opinion Filed December 19, 1958," 21, Box 14, FLIC Papers.

107   "defiant": *Gibson et al. v. Florida*, "Opinion Filed December 19, 1958," 21–22, Box 14, FLIC Papers.

107   appeal to the U.S. Supreme Court: Stark, "McCarthyism in Florida," 63.

107   Joseph J. Lieb: "Says U.S. Ruling Is 'Heartening,'" *Miami Herald*, December 24, 1958, 3; *Gibson v. Board of Public Instruction, Dade Country, Fla.*, accessed December 1, 2024, via Leagle.com, https://www.leagle.com/decision/19591035272f2d7631798.

107   "White and colored children shall": Florida Constitution of 1885, Florida Constitution Revision Commission, https://library.law.fsu.edu/Digital-Collections/CRC/CRC-1998/conhist/1885con.html.

108   "Lieb denied Gibson's petition for immediate": "Miami Judge Rules on Segregation," *Tallahassee Democrat*, December 23, 1958, 2.

108   challenge and nullify: "Says U.S. Ruling," *Miami Herald*, December 24, 1958.

108   now high-school-age son: Carita Swanson Vonk, *Theodore R. Gibson: Priest, Prophet, and Politician* (Little River Press, 1997), 18.

108   Chief Inspector Strickland: FLIC Meeting Minutes for September 27, 1958, Clerk of the House Papers; "Confidential Report of Informant—Gainesville Area," June 1–June 8, 1958, #8-28, FLIC Papers.

108   "We were concerned with": Remus Strickland, transcript of interview with Bonnie Stark, April 1984, Bonnie Stark Papers.

108   Claude L. Murphree: Remus Strickland, transcript of interview with Bonnie Stark, April 1984; "Capacity House Greets Little Theatre Play," *Gainesville Sun*, n.d., Diettrich Papers; "'The Curious Savage,' to Be Given as Curtain-Raiser at GHS Nov. 17," *Gainesville Sun*, November 6, 1955, 21; "Claude Murphree Killed," *Gainesville Sun*, June 18, 1958, 1.

108   "Card-carrying member": Remus Strickland, transcript of interview with Bonnie Stark, April 1984.

108   Murphree died under odd circumstances: "Claude Murphree Killed," *Gainesville Sun*.

108   music professor was crushed: "Florida U. Organist Dies in Accident," *Tampa Tribune*, June 18, 1958, 2.

109   "Reported to Hawes": Remus Strickland, transcript of interview with Bonnie Stark, April 1984.

109   "The moment he was dead": Didier Graeffe, transcript of interview with Bonnie Stark, December 1983, Bonnie Stark Papers.

109   "I had some knowledge": John Tileston, transcript of interview with Allyson Beutke, April 12, 1999, Beutke Papers.

109   *subversive*: Chapter 57-125, Senate Bill No. 347.

109   rarely presumed innocence: George Painter, "Florida," Sodomy Laws, 1991, Gay & Lesbian Archives of the Pacific Northwest, https://www.glapn.org/sodomylaws/sensibilities/florida.htm.

109   "As a defense counsel, I can say that the entire": Albert Fitts, letter to John Evans, March 19, 1964, Box 2, FLIC Papers.

109   system of racial apartheid: James T. Sears, *Growing Up Gay in the South: Race, Gender and Journeys of the Spirit* (Routledge, 1991), 13; Mab Segrest, "Drag You Off to Milledgeville," in *Queer South Rising: Voices of a Contested Place*, ed. Reta Ugena Whitlock (Information Age, 2013), 173.

110   lodge a complaint: Letter to the Editor, *One* 1, no. 1 (January 1953): 22.

110   "has nothing to offer but": Jerry T. Watkins, *Queering the Redneck Riviera: Sexuality and the Rise of Florida Tourism* (University Press of Florida, 2018), 1.

110   a devout Baptist: "Johns Promises Churchmen to Fight Gamblers," *Bradenton Herald*, November 12, 1953, 8A.

110   4F—unfit for service: Allan Bérubé, *Coming Out Under Fire: The History of Gay Men and Women in World War II*, 20th ann. ed. (University of North Carolina Press, 2010), 4.

110   "We first looked at University of Florida for Communists": Remus Strickland, transcript of interview with Bonnie Stark, April 1984.

110   "records of personal misconduct on all faculty": Subpoena, President, University of Florida, August 18, 1958.

110   Strickland purchased three thousand feet: Martin Waldron, "Race Probe Investigator in Gainesville for 29 Days," *Tampa Tribune*, October 28, 1958, 1, Clerk of the House Papers.

CHAPTER 10. SONS OF FLORIDA

113   "How are you": Copleston, interrogation by Hawes, January 20, 1959.

113   accounting final exam: Christiana Lilly, "The Johns Committee: State Sanctioned Homophobia," *SFGN* (*South Florida Gay News*), March 6, 2019, 18–21.

113   a state lawyer: Copleston, interrogation by Hawes, January 20, 1959.

113   briefly attended the University of Florida: "W. Randolph Hodges, 1914–2005," *Cedar Key News*, 2005, https://www.cedarkeynews.com/Archives/OLDSITE/Obituaries/2736-15.html.

113   "We've asked you": Copleston, interrogation by Hawes, January 20, 1959.

114 "infestation": Art Copleston, interview with Robert Fieseler, October 28, 2019.

114 "Yes, I heard": Copleston, interrogation by Hawes, January 20, 1959.

114 pretending to be normal: Art Copleston, interview with Robert Fieseler, October 28, 2019.

114 "Under those conditions": Copleston, interrogation by Hawes, January 20, 1959.

114 Thomas "Tim" Reed: Art Copleston, interview with Robert Fieseler, May 3, 2020.

114 "I'll tell you, sir": Copleston, interrogation by Hawes, January 20, 1959.

115 "a civil investigation, seeking information": Copleston, interrogation by Hawes, January 20, 1959.

115 "You know what": Copleston, interrogation by Hawes, January 20, 1959.

115 "crime against nature": George Painter, "Florida," Sodomy Laws, 1991, Gay & Lesbian Archives of the Pacific Northwest, https://www.glapn.org/sodomylaws/sensibilities/florida.htm.

115 cockroach in the spotlight: Art Copleston, interview with Robert Fieseler, May 3, 2020.

115 "criminal investigation": Copleston, interrogation by Hawes, January 20, 1959.

115 Miranda right protections: "Miranda v. Arizona," New York Times, October 2, 1966, 62.

115 "constitute a quorum": FLIC Meeting Minutes for July 24, 1957.

115 "Art, do you know any": Copleston, interrogation by Hawes, January 20, 1959.

116 the G.I. Bill: Art Copleston, interview with Robert Fieseler, April 26, 2020; "Legislature to Vote on Fees," Florida Alligator, March 20, 1959, 3.

116 his twenty-fifth birthday: Art Copleston, interview with Robert Fieseler, May 3, 2020.

116 Thomas Hall: Art Copleston, interrogation by Remus Strickland, October 16, 1958, Box 8, FLIC Papers.

116 September 16, 1932: Art Copleston, Demons and Deliverance (published by author, 2014), Kindle, 47.

116 Copey: Art Copleston, interview with Robert Fieseler, July 10, 2021.

116 drank himself into a stupor: Art Copleston, interview with Robert Fieseler, July 10, 2021.

116 "Playground of the young": Sigismond Diettrich, "An Outline of the Role of the Geographic Factor in Florida's History," n.d., Sigismond Diettrich Papers.

116 gifted baritone saxophone player: Art Copleston, interview with Robert Fieseler, July 10, 2021. Subsequent biographical details are also drawn from this interview.

117 "I would be amazed": Art Copleston, interview with Robert Fieseler, July 10, 2021.

118 family had no savings: Art Copleston, interview with Robert Fieseler, October 28, 2019.

118 architecture student: Art Copleston, interview with Robert Fieseler, July 10, 2021; Peter Aronson, "Death Won't Affect Pines City Hall Work," Fort Lauderdale News, July 28, 1985, 5SW.

118 **Andres "Max" Fabregas:** Barbara Capitman, "Donald Bouterse: A Great Artist Is Gone," Letter to the Editor, *Miami Herald*, August 5, 1985, 12.

118 **"Golden Couple":** Capitman, "Donald Bouterse: A Great Artist Is Gone."

118 **architectural firm:** Capitman, "Donald Bouterse: A Great Artist Is Gone"; Beth Dunlop, "Miami Architects Gain Acclaim for Style Tempered by Tropics," *Miami Herald*, March 15, 1981, L.

118 **Miami Beach City Hall:** Aronson, "Death Won't Affect."

118 **paying rent in inexpensive:** Art Copleston, interview with Robert Fieseler, July 10, 2021.

118 **meals and lodging:** Art Copleston, interview with Robert Fieseler, July 10, 2021.

118 **ramp jockey:** Art Copleston, interview with Robert Fieseler, April 26, 2020.

118 **announced his enlistment:** Art Copleston, interview with Robert Fieseler, July 10, 2021.

118 **Air Police squadron at Tyndall Air Force Base:** Art Copleston, Honorable Discharge, U.S. Air Force, Art Copleston Personal Papers; Copleston, *Demons and Deliverance*, 119–121.

119 **"bachelor's degree or bust":** Art Copleston, interview with Robert Fieseler, November 11, 2019.

119 **full seven years older:** Art Copleston, interview with Robert Fieseler, October 28, 2019.

119 **Eden of white Protestants:** James T. Sears, *Lonely Hunters: An Oral History of Lesbian and Gay Southern Life, 1948–1968* (Westview Press, 1997), 48.

119 **coeducational:** Jack Anderson, "State Colleges Enroll 40,000," *Miami Herald*, November 19, 1950, 15K.

119 **standards weren't high:** Sears, *Lonely Hunters*, 53; Jackie O'Quin, "Greeks Spotlight Rush," *Florida Alligator*, February 19, 1960, 2.

119 **vowed never to:** Copleston, interview with Fieseler, October 28, 2019.

119 **Johns regularly read:** Charley Johns, "Charley Johns Feels Slights in Recent Issues of *Alligator*," *Summer Gator*, June 19, 1959, 2.

119 **killed a 1955 student investigative:** Al Quentel, Transcript of Testimony, January 9, 1959, Box 7, FLIC Papers; "Inquest Clears UF Coed of Blame in Baby's Death," *Florida Alligator*, December 12, 1958, 1.

119 **"First Negro Student":** "First Negro Student Enrolls at University," *Florida Alligator*, September 19, 1958, 1.

119 **"quiet, mild-mannered":** "First Negro Student Enrolls at University."

119 **"unduly difficult":** "Students Can Retake Bar Exam," *Miami Herald*, July 12, 1958, 3B.

120 **lived off campus with:** Katheryn Russell-Brown, "Desegregation at UF, 60 Years Later," *Gainesville Sun*, September 17, 2018, https://www.gainesville.com/story/opinion/columns/more-voices/2018/09/15/katheryn-russell-brown-desegregation-at-uf-60-years-later/10283161007/.

120 **only student in suit and tie:** Emanuel Griffin, "The First Black Student at the University of Florida," Medium, January 15, 2018, https://medium.com/@emanuelgrif/the-first-black-student-at-the-university-of-florida-bd2c09ab012c.

120   **his second semester:** Griffin, "The First Black Student at the University of Florida."

120   **who foiled a kidnapping plot:** "UF Marks 60 Years of Desegregation," *UF News Archive*, November 2018, https://archive.news.ufl.edu/articles/2018/11/uf-marks-60-years-of-desegregation.html.

120   **After three semesters:** Griffin, "The First Black Student at the University of Florida."

120   **lifting weights:** Art Copleston, interview with Robert Fieseler, October 28, 2019.

120   **"only financial provider":** Art Copleston, interview with Robert Fieseler, October 28, 2019.

120   **Thomas "Tim" Reed:** Art Copleston, interview with Robert Fieseler, April 26, 2020; "Professor T. M. Reed, University of Florida," *Chemical Engineering Education*, Spring 1976, 59.

120   **faculty showers:** Art Copleston, interview with Robert Fieseler, April 26, 2020.

120   **Cedar Key:** Art Copleston, interview with Robert Fieseler, May 3, 2020.

121   **"guy bar":** Art Copleston, interview with Robert Fieseler, October 28, 2019.

121   **Florida Center for Clinical Services:** University Record of the University of Florida, 1958–1958, 107–8, University of Florida Archives; "UF Teaching Hospital Opened; First Patient Taken Yesterday," *Florida Alligator*, October 21, 1958, 1, 3.

121   **October 1, 1958:** David Meuser, interrogation by Remus Strickland, October 1, 1958, Box 6, FLIC Papers; Seminole 1958 yearbook, University of Florida, 383; Ann Bixler, "Caps and Gowns Are in Style," *Miami News*, January 26, 1958, 10D.

121   **Lutheran minister:** "Dr. Edwin Meuser Dies; Lutheran Mission Head," *Evening Star*, November 14, 1949, 14A.

121   **fellow education major:** "Tomlin-Meuser," *Miami Herald*, May 18, 1958, 7E.

121   **his young wife:** Meuser, interrogation by Strickland, October 1, 1958; "Meuser-Mathews," *Gainesville Sun*, July 10, 1979, 9A; Kris Meuser, Gainesville High School Yearbook, 1974, 245.

121   **college radio station:** Meuser, interrogation by Strickland, October 1, 1958; Linus Mitchell, "'The Voice of Florida' Comes to You from Campus Station," *Florida Alligator*, November 10, 1944, 1; Sarah Coates, email to Robert Fieseler, October 25, 2021.

121   **"passive":** Meuser, interrogation by Strickland, October 1, 1958.

121   **"recruited":** Audie Shuler, Transcript of Testimony, January 8, 1959, Box 7, 757, FLIC Papers.

122   **Dr. Justin E. Harlow:** "1,200 Get Psychological Aid," *Florida Alligator*, November 21, 1958, 5.

122   **"A homosexual will get":** Winston Wallace Ehrmann, Transcript of Testimony, January 19, 1959, Box 7, 1119; "1,200 Get," *Florida Alligator*.

122   word *homosexual*: Edward D. Andrews, "'HOMOSEXUAL' 1946: Was
There a Mistranslation That Shifted Culture?" *Christian Publishing House
Blog*, April 28, 2021, https://christianpublishinghouse.co/2021/04/28
/homosexual-1946-was-there-a-mistranslation-that-shifted-culture/; JD
Glass, "How a Bible Error Changed History and Turned Gays into Pariahs,"
Advocate, December 17, 2022, https://www.advocate.com/religion
/2022/12/17/how-bible-error-changed-history-and-turned-gays-pariahs.

123   "the biggest undertaking": "Million Copies of Bible," *New York Times*, July
25, 1951, 19.

123   *Sexual Behavior in the Human Male*: "Concerning Man's Basic Drive," *New
York Times*, January 4, 1948, 61.

123   "Kinsey Report": Justin E. Harlow, Transcript of Testimony, January 22,
1959, Box 7, 1519, FLIC Papers; Eric Cervini, *The Deviant's War: The
Homosexual vs. the United States of America* (Farrar, Straus and Giroux,
2020), 19; "Medicine: 5940 Women," *Time*, August 24, 1953, 53.

123   nearly half of all white male survey: Cervini, *The Deviant's War*, 18; Alfred
Kinsey, Wardell Pomeroy, and Clyde E. Martin, *Sexual Behavior in the
Human Male* (W. B. Saunders, 1948), 625–51.

123   "in every age group": Kinsey et al., *Sexual Behavior*, 634.

123   half a million: Regina Markell Morantz, "The Scientist as Sex Crusader:
Alfred C. Kinsey and American Culture," *American Quarterly* 29, no. 5
(1977): 563–89, 569.

123   led to congressional scrutiny of his funding: Roger Stuart, "Quizzer Kinsey
to Be Quizzed on Finances," *Evansville Press*, January 7, 1954, 15.

123   many of the findings from Kinsey's study: "Two Doctors Publish Book
Opposing Kinsey," *Kokomo Tribune*, January 5, 1954, 2; "Personality,
December 15, 1952," *Time*, December 15, 1952, https://time.com/archive
/6885203/personality-dec-15-1952/.

123   "males in college": Harlow, Transcript of Testimony, January 22, 1959,
1518.

123   sociopathic personality disturbance: *Diagnostic and Statistical Manual of
Mental Disorders* (American Psychiatric Association, 1952).

123   Religious and political groups: "Homosexuality and Sexual Orientation
Disturbance: Proposed Change in DSM-II, 6th Printing, page 44
POSITION STATEMENT (RETIRED)," American Psychiatric
Association, 1973.

124   "electric shock treatment": Regan, Transcript of Testimony, January 22,
1959, Box 7, FLIC Papers.

124   "none of the physical": Regan, Transcript of Testimony, January 22,
1959.

124   in a separate interview: James Congleton, Transcript of Testimony, January
5, 1959, Bonnie Stark Papers.

124   "What are we to do": Regan, Transcript of Testimony, January 22,
1959.

124   "When you get to out-and-out": Regan, Transcript of Testimony, January 22,
1959.

CHAPTER 11. TIGHTENING WEB

125 **as many as a million:** William N. Eskridge Jr., *Gaylaw: Challenging the Apartheid of the Closet* (Harvard University Press, 1999), 60.

125 **"Lavender Scare":** David K. Johnson, *The Lavender Scare: The Cold War Persecution of Gays and Lesbians in the Federal Government* (University of Chicago Press, 2004).

125 **Gays were vulnerable:** Johnson, *The Lavender Scare*, 5–7; Remus Strickland, transcript of interview with Bonnie Stark, April 1984.

125 **20 percent of the American workforce:** Margot Canaday, *Queer Career: Sexuality and Work in Modern America* (Princeton University Press, 2023), 38.

126 **"passive":** Meuser, interrogation by Strickland, October 1, 1958.

126 **"Are you willing to work":** Meuser, interrogation by Strickland, October 1, 1958.

126 **"I am queer for women":** Meuser, interrogation by Strickland, October 1, 1958.

126 **"necessary arrangements":** Meuser, interrogation by Strickland, October 1, 1958.

126 **"Students were offered":** Strickland, transcript of interview with Stark, April 1984.

126 **James William Graves:** James William Graves, interrogation by Remus Strickland, October 13, 1958, 2-62, Bonnie Stark Papers; James William Graves, Transcript of Testimony, January 8, 1959, Box 7, FLIC Papers; "James William Graves," U.S. Veterans' Gravesites, Ancestry.com, https://www.ancestry.com/search/collections/8750/records/4414314; Harold Elwood Carter, Transcript of Testimony, January 19, 1959, Box 7, FLIC Papers.

126 **Joe Trice:** Joe Trice, interrogation by Remus Strickland, November 4, 1958, 2-57, Bonnie Stark Papers; Lawrence Wathen, Transcript of Testimony, January 5, 1959, 4-43, Bonnie Stark Papers.

127 **twenty-nine-year-old military vet:** Trice, interrogation by Strickland, November 4, 1958; Ann Hollingsworth, "Small Talk," *Hollywood Sun-Tattler*, December 28, 1953, 6.

127 **a fellow U.S. Army veteran:** Trice, interrogation by Strickland, November 4, 1958; Wathen, Transcript of Testimony, January 5, 1959.

127 **Don Steinbrecher:** Don Steinbrecher, interrogation by John Tileston, October 30, 1958, 6-63, Bonnie Stark Papers; James William Graves, Transcript of Testimony, January 8, 1959.

127 **Meuser and Steinbrecher:** Meuser, interrogation by Strickland, October 1, 1958; Steinbrecher, interrogation by Tileston, October 30, 1958.

127 **"Bermuda shorts":** Meuser, interrogation by Strickland, October 1, 1958.

127 **"area to be homosexual":** Stephen Fogle, FLIC suspect sheet, #13-421, Box 13, FLIC Papers.

127 **"We were careful about":** Strickland, transcript of interview with Stark, April 1984.

128 "As homosexuality is now": Anonymous, letter to Charley Johns, circa 1958, 11-839, Bonnie Stark Papers.

128 "ruin the investigation": Jack Detwiler, "Reactions at Gainesville Hint Johns' Investigator Inquiring About Faculty," *Tampa Tribune*, October 29, 1958, 15A.

128 $165 on bribes: "Prober Haunts Gainesville," *Orlando Sentinel*, October 28, 1958, 5A.

128 hired in 1946: "The University Record of the University of Florida, 1958–1959," 24, 299; Arthur Sidney Copleston Jr., Unofficial Academic Transcript, University of Florida Registrar, Art Copleston Papers.

129 "Sometimes what the poet does": Stephen Francis Fogle, *Brief Anthology of Poetry* (American Book Company, 1951), xii.

129 earned two A's: Arthur Sidney Copleston Jr., Unofficial Academic Transcript.

129 classical music: Art Copleston, interview with Robert Fieseler, October 28, 2019.

129 "No one would suspect": Copleston, interview with Fieseler, October 28, 2019.

129 Northwest 36th Road: Gainesville City Directory, 1958, 98, Ancestry.com, https://www.ancestry.com/search/collections/2469/records/662204912?tid=&pid=&queryId=27d14c3f-4fe3-4f7d-aad3-636e2a54782c&_phsrc=Pmf984&_phstart=successSource.

129 "At Stephen's house": Steinbrecher, interrogation by Tileston, October 30, 1958.

129 "pear-shaped": Art Copleston, interview with Robert Fieseler, October 28, 2019.

129 lymphoma survivor: Art Copleston, interview with Robert Fieseler, November 11, 2019.

129 being the star: Art Copleston, interview with Robert Fieseler, July 10, 2021.

129 it was homosexual code: Art Copleston, interview with Robert Fieseler, November 11, 2019.

129 Fogle served snacks: Art Copleston, interview with Robert Fieseler, November 11, 2019.

130 "Those Saturdays": Art Copleston, interview with Robert Fieseler, November 11, 2019.

130 hire him as catering: Art Copleston, interview with Robert Fieseler, July 10, 2021.

130 Sigismond Diettrich: Art Copleston, interview with Robert Fieseler, July 10, 2021.

130 "NO!": Art Copleston, interview with Robert Fieseler, July 10, 2021; Art Copleston, email to Robert Fieseler, September 5, 2022.

130 Professor Fogle who tipped: Art Copleston, interview with Robert Fieseler, July 10, 2021; Art Copleston, email to Robert Fieseler, September 5, 2022.

130 George E. Evans: George E. Evans, Statement to Remus Strickland, August 12, 1958, 2-72, Bonnie Stark Papers.

130 Byers "carrying on": George E. Evans, Statement to Remus Strickland,

August 12, 1958, 2-72, Bonnie Stark Papers; Charles Byers, FLIC suspect sheet, #13-423, Box 13, FLIC Papers.

130 "cesspool": Mark Hawes, Transcript of Testimony, January 22, 1959, 1571, Box 7, FLIC Papers.

130 "Show It Hard!": Powell, Transcript of Testimony, January 18, 1959, 2-76, 1102, Box 7, FLIC Papers; Joe Crevasse, Transcript of Testimony, January 22, 1959, 1507–8, Box 7, FLIC Papers.

131 "Let me see it": Sigismond Diettrich, Transcript of Testimony, January 19, 1959, 2-76, Box 7, FLIC Papers.

131 spot too dingy: Art Copleston, interview with Robert Fieseler, July 10, 2021.

131 found satisfaction there: "Statement of Facts," circa 1958, 4-95, Box 1, FLIC Papers; Paul Kapperman, Transcript of Testimony, January 6, 1959, 4-44, Box 7, FLIC Papers; Powell, Transcript of Testimony, January 16, 1959; Sigismond Diettrich, Transcript of Testimony, January 19, 1959; Lester Robinson McCartney, Transcript of Testimony, January 16, 1959, 2-76, Box 7, FLIC Papers; Transcript of Testimony, January 7, 1959, 665-87, Box 7, FLIC Papers.

131 "recommendation of Mr. Strickland": Joe Crevasse, Transcript of Testimony, January 22, 1959.

131 "Mr. Strickland had an individual": John Tileston, transcript of interview with Allyson Beutke, April 12, 1999.

131 office denied Copleston: Art Copleston, interview with Robert Fieseler, November 11, 2019.

131 Thursday, October 16: Art Copleston, interrogation by Strickland, October 16, 1958.

131 "We have information": Art Copleston, interview with Robert Fieseler, April 26, 2020.

132 "power high": Art Copleston, email to Robert Fieseler, January 29, 2023.

132 "My mother was an artist": John Tileston, transcript of interview with Allyson Beutke, April 12, 1999.

132 "responsibilities to my chief": John Tileston, transcript of interview with Allyson Beutke, April 12, 1999.

132 military experience: Art Copleston, interview with Robert Fieseler, October 28, 2019.

132 staged like a noir movie set: Art Copleston, interview with Robert Fieseler, October 28, 2019.

132 jowly and overweight: Art Copleston, interview with Robert Fieseler, October 28, 2019; Transcript of Testimony, January 7, 1959, 666, Box 7, FLIC Papers.

132 as a lawyer: Art Copleston, interview with Robert Fieseler, October 28, 2019.

132 "I now ask you, are you": Copleston, interrogation by Strickland, October 16, 1958.

133 "Whenever we want you": Art Copleston, interview with Robert Fieseler, October 28, 2019.

133 his mail: Art Copleston, interview with Robert Fieseler, November 11, 2019.

133   **physique magazines:** Art Copleston, interview with Robert Fieseler, April 26, 2020.

133   **tearing letters and papers:** Art Copleston, *Demons and Deliverance* (published by author, 2014), Kindle, 153.

133   **repeatedly saw:** Art Copleston, outtake footage of *Behind Closed Doors*, 2000, produced by Allyson Beutke.

133   **began to masturbate:** Art Copleston, interview with Robert Fieseler, November 11, 2019.

133   **"He told me he was working":** Art Copleston, interview with Robert Fieseler, October 28, 2019.

133   **completely emptied out:** Art Copleston, interview with Robert Fieseler, November 11, 2019.

133   **1960 UF yearbook photo:** Seminole 1960 yearbook, University of Florida, 385.

134   **"It's him. But":** Art Copleston, email to Robert Fieseler, May 19, 2024.

134   **withdrew from society:** Art Copleston, interview with Robert Fieseler, October 28, 2019; Art Copleston, interview with Robert Fieseler, April 26, 2020.

134   **grades were never better:** Arthur Sidney Copleston Jr., Unofficial Academic Transcript.

134   **gas station:** Copleston, *Demons and Deliverance*, 157.

134   **"You never knew":** Art Copleston, interview with Robert Fieseler, October 28, 2019.

134   **Don "Dee-Dee" Bouterse:** Art Copleston, interview with Robert Fieseler, June 10, 2021.

134   **verging on spy craft:** Copleston, *Demons and Deliverance*, 158.

134   **heard a car pull:** Art Copleston, interview with Robert Fieseler, June 3, 2021.

134   **weekend getaway at Jacksonville:** Copleston, *Demons and Deliverance*, 159; Art Copleston, interview with Robert Fieseler, July 11, 2021.

134   **random sailor:** Copleston, *Demons and Deliverance*, 159; Art Copleston, interview with Robert Fieseler, July 11, 2021.

134   **speed away in his car:** Art Copleston, interview with Robert Fieseler, July 11, 2021.

134   **called the Jacksonville motel:** Art Copleston, interview with Robert Fieseler, July 11, 2021.

135   **James Alton Hill:** Charley Johns, letter to Norman Sikes, May 15, 1962, Bonnie Stark Papers; "The University Record of the University of Florida, 1962–1963," 32; "The University Record of the University of Florida, 1963–1964," 34.

135   **"I used to sit in my dorm room":** Copleston, *Demons and Deliverance*, 160; Art Copleston, interview with Robert Fieseler, October 28, 2019.

135   **January 20, 1959:** Art Copleston, Transcript of Testimony, January 20, 1959.

135   **his future riding:** Art Copleston, interview with Robert Fieseler, October 28, 2019.

135   **was no clock:** Art Copleston, interview with Robert Fieseler, October 28, 2019.

135   **neither food nor water:** Art Copleston, interview with Robert Fieseler, October 28, 2019.

135   **pretended he couldn't hear:** Art Copleston, Transcript of Testimony, January 20, 1959.

135   **"what a disgusting son":** Art Copleston, interview with Robert Fieseler, October 28, 2019.

135   **two years sober:** Art Copleston, interview with Robert Fieseler, July 12, 2021.

136   **amphetamine diet pills:** Art Copleston, interview with Robert Fieseler, July 10, 2021.

136   **"unsalvageable":** Art Copleston, interview with Robert Fieseler, July 10, 2021.

136   **stoned on pills:** Art Copleston, interview with Robert Fieseler, July 10, 2021.

136   **divorce was finalized in 1956:** Art Copleston, interview with Robert Fieseler, July 10, 2021.

136   **"driven right back into":** Art Copleston, interview with Robert Fieseler, October 28, 2019.

136   **military training:** Art Copleston, interview with Robert Fieseler, June 14, 2021.

136   **"Basic Airman":** Art Copleston, Honorable Discharge Papers, U.S. Air Force, Art Copleston Personal Papers.

136   **1952 to 1954:** Copleston, Honorable Discharge Papers; Copleston, *Demons and Deliverance*, 126; Copleston, interrogation by Strickland, October 16, 1958.

136   **"security risks":** Art Copleston, interview with Robert Fieseler, May 3, 2020.

136   **"paper shuffler":** Art Copleston, interview with Robert Fieseler, October 28, 2019.

137   **"heavy-set":** Transcript of Testimony, January 7, 1959, 666, Box 7, FLIC Papers.

137   **labeled a suspect himself:** Art Copleston, interview with Robert Fieseler, October 28, 2019.

137   **his Plymouth convertible:** Art Copleston, interview with Robert Fieseler, November 11, 2019.

137   **commandeered by senior officers:** Art Copleston, interview with Robert Fieseler, May 3, 2020.

137   **moving between worlds:** Copleston, *Demons and Deliverance*.

137   **kept their traps shut:** Copleston, *Demons and Deliverance*; Art Copleston, interview with Robert Fieseler, July 11, 2021.

137   **"They weren't going":** Art Copleston, interview with Robert Fieseler, May 3, 2020.

137   **"but I have to take":** Copleston, interrogation by Strickland, October 16, 1958.

138   **no one had tossed his room:** Copleston, *Demons and Deliverance*; Art Copleston, interview with Robert Fieseler, October 28, 2019.

138   **called his accounting professor:** Copleston, *Demons and Deliverance*; Art Copleston, interview with Robert Fieseler, November 11, 2019.

138   **"He didn't even ask":** Art Copleston, interview with Robert Fieseler, October 28, 2019; Arthur Sidney Copleston Jr., Unofficial Academic Transcript.

CHAPTER 12. TRUSTY INFORMANTS

139   **not on the side:** Judith Poucher, *State of Defiance: Challenging the Johns Committee's Assault on Civil Liberties* (University Press of Florida, 2014), 74; Stacy Braukman, *Communists and Perverts Under the Palms: The Johns Committee in Florida, 1956–1965* (University Press of Florida, 2012), 69; Bonnie Stark, "McCarthyism in Florida: Charley Johns and the Florida Legislative Investigation Committee July, 1956 to July, 1965" (master's thesis, University of South Florida, 1985), 97, https://palmm.digital.flvc.org /islandora/object/usf%3A49370#page/title/mode/1up, 91–93.

139   **set to begin on April 7:** Florida Journal of the Senate, Regular Session, April 7, 1959.

140   **October 2, 1958:** "Statement of Facts," FLIC report, October 2, 1958, 4-69, James T. Sears Papers, Duke University Archives; "The University Record of the University of Florida, 1958–1959," 42; "History, Marjorie Kinnan Rawlings Historic State Park," Florida State Parks, https://www .floridastateparks.org/parks-and-trails/marjorie-kinnan-rawlings-historic -state-park/history; Clyde J. Miller, Gainesville City Directory, 1958.

140   **"authoress":** G. B. Knowles Jr., "University of Florida," *Bradenton Herald*, March 23, 1941, 10; Ruth Smith, "Central Florida Women," *Orlando Sentinel*, January 19, 1954, 10; "Marjorie Kinnan Rawlings House and Farmyard," Atlas Obscura, accessed November 27, 2024, http://www .atlasobscura.com/places/marjorie-kinnan-rawlings-house-and-farmyard.

140   **three years residing:** Clyde Moore, Transcript of Testimony, January 5, 1959, 4-43, Box 6, FLIC Papers.

140   **tailing students to Cross Creek:** "Statement of Facts," FLIC report, October 2, 1958.

140   **October 20, 1958:** Clyde Moore, Transcript of Testimony, January 5, 1959.

140   **cloak-and-dagger activities:** "Investigating Group Checking on Faculty," *Florida Alligator*, October 31, 1958, 1; "Campus Cloak and Dagger," *Florida Alligator*, November 7, 1958, 4.

140   **"I heard, true or false":** Edward Clyde Vining, letter to Charley Johns, November 5, 1958, Box 3, FLIC Papers; Miami City Directory, 1958, 250; "Edward Clyde Vining, Jr.," Findagrave.com, https://www.findagrave.com /memorial/122002286/edward_clyde-vining.

140   **November 18, 1958:** "Statement of Facts," November 18, 1958, 4-67, James T. Sears Papers; John Faircloth Park, Transcript of Testimony, January 8, 1959, 2-77, Box 7, FLIC Papers; James T. Sears, "Johns Testimony Index," December 12, 1996, 7, James T. Sears Papers.

140   **"Mr. Tileston went into the":** "Statement of Facts," November 18, 1958, 4-67, James T. Sears Papers.

141   **UF since 1956:** John Faircloth Park, Transcript of Testimony, January 8, 1959.

141   **At the police station:** "Statement of Facts," November 18, 1958.

141   Park confessed: "Statement of Facts," November 18, 1958.

141   to assist the Johns Committee: "Statement of Facts," November 18, 1958.

141   in oral sex: "Statement of Facts," November 18, 1958; Lawrence Wathen, Transcript of Testimony, January 5, 1959.

141   John Edward Van Meter: "Statement of Facts," November 18, 1958; John Van Meter, Transcript of Testimony, January 5, 1959, Bonnie Stark Papers.

141   elementary school art teacher: "Statement of Facts," November 18, 1958; Harold Elwood Carter, Transcript of Testimony, January 19, 1959, Box 7, FLIC Papers.

141   "Park was not promised": "Statement of Facts," November 18, 1958; Harold Elwood Carter, Transcript of Testimony, January 19, 1959, Box 7, FLIC Papers.

141   December 12: "Statement of Facts," December 12, 1958, Box 1, FLIC Papers; Russell Danburg, FLIC suspect sheet, #13-410, Box 13, FLIC Papers.

142   since 1948: Russell Danburg, FLIC suspect sheet, #13-410, Box 13, FLIC Papers; "Business Growth Cited by Yates," *Orlando Sentinel*, January 19, 1958, 53.

142   "Victor Borge": Helen Wells, "It's the Gremlins That Push the Car Up Spook Hill!," *Miami Herald*, April 2, 1957, 22.

142   Danburg was married: Russell Danburg, FLIC suspect sheet, #13-410.

142   claimed that he had committed: "Statement of Facts," December 12, 1958.

142   release since 1948: Russell Danburg, Transcript of Testimony, January 5, 1959, Box 7, FLIC Papers; "The University Record of the University of Florida, 1958–1959," 20.

142   moment of revelation: "Statement of Facts," December 12, 1958.

142   restroom of the university library: "Statement of Facts," December 12, 1958.

142   "observed Professor Congleton": "Statement of Facts," December 12, 1958.

142   "foot wiggling signal": "Statement of Facts," December 12, 1958; Sigismond Diettrich, Transcript of Testimony, January 19, 1959.

142   "one of the worst homosexuals": "Statement of Facts," December 12, 1958; Lawrence Wathen, Transcript of Testimony, January 5, 1959.

143   December 5, 1958: "Statement of Facts," December 5, 1958, 3-160, Box 1, FLIC Papers; James Congleton, Transcript of Testimony, January 16, 1959.

143   University of Florida since 1937: "The University Record of the University of Florida, 1958–1959," 18; "Congleton of UF to Preside at Language Meet," *Gainesville Sun*, December 21, 1956, 3.

143   *Theories of Pastoral*: J. E. Congleton, *Theories of Pastoral Poetry in England, 1684–1798* (University of Florida Press, 1952), http://archive.org/details /theoriesofpastor0000jeco; James Congleton, FLIC suspect sheet, #13-409, Bonnie Stark Papers.

143   Turin, Italy: Ruth Weimer, "Congletons Plan Trip, Others Talk of Vacations," *Gainesville Sun*, September 22, 1957, 3.

143   daughter named Caroll: "Engagement of Miss Congleton and B. P. Parrish Is Revealed," *Gainesville Sun*, September 7, 1958, 17; "Congleton-Parrish

Wedding Held in Gainesville Episcopal Church," *Gainesville Sun*, October 5, 1958, 16; James Congleton, Transcript of Testimony, January 16, 1959.

143   **taught a lighter load:** "The University Record of the University of Florida, Schedule of Courses First Semester 1958–1959," 74–76.

143   **act of masturbating:** "Statement of Facts," December 5, 1958.

143   **age of five in Kentucky:** James Congleton, Transcript of Testimony, January 16, 1959.

143   **"I saw the condition":** James Congleton, Transcript of Testimony, January 16, 1959.

143   **"If I have knelt":** James Congleton, Transcript of Testimony, January 16, 1959.

144   **"When I was in Italy":** James Congleton, Transcript of Testimony, January 16, 1959.

144   **"if he was brought":** "Statement of Facts," December 5, 1958.

144   **"agreed to cooperate":** "Statement of Facts," December 5, 1958.

144   **So three days later:** "Statement of Facts," December 5, 1958.

144   **"other homosexuals":** "Statement of Facts," December 5, 1958.

144   **a special rapport:** "Statement of Facts," December 5, 1958.

144   **facts would be turned over:** "Statement of Facts," December 5, 1958.

145   **December 15:** James Congleton, deposition to Tileston, December 15, 1958, 3-153, Box 6, FLIC Papers.

145   **"I am going to try":** James Congleton, deposition to Tileston, December 15, 1958, 3-153, Box 6, FLIC Papers.

145   **"It is really a relief":** James Congleton, deposition to Tileston, December 15, 1958, 3-153, Box 6, FLIC Papers.

145   **"Have you ever seen him":** James Congleton, deposition to Tileston, December 15, 1958, 3-153, Box 6, FLIC Papers.

146   **knocked on the cottage door:** James T. Sears, *Lonely Hunters: An Oral History of Lesbian and Gay Southern Life, 1948–1968* (Westview Press, 1997), 66; Lawrence Wathen, Transcript of Testimony, January 5, 1959; Sears, "Johns Testimony Index," December 29, 1996, 1.

146   **six feet tall:** Lawrence Wathen, World War II Draft Card, Ancestry.com; Lawrence Wathen, Transcript of Testimony, January 5, 1959.

146   **course "C-5":** Lawrence Wathen, Transcript of Testimony, January 5, 1959; "The University Record of the University of Florida, 1958–1959," 301.

146   **long wait lists:** Lawrence Wathen, Transcript of Testimony, January 5, 1959; "The University Record of the University of Florida, 1958–1959," 301.

146   **sampling of the athletes:** Edwin Johns, interrogation by Remus Strickland, September 6, 1958, 3-44, Bonnie Stark Papers; Sears, *Lonely Hunters*, 54.

146   **"spaghetti supper club":** Johns, interrogation by Strickland, September 6, 1958; Sears, *Lonely Hunters*, 54.

146   **"I go to camp every summer":** Johns, interrogation by Strickland, September 6, 1958; Sears, *Lonely Hunters*, 53.

147   **Hotel Thomas at 2:30 p.m.:** Sears, *Lonely Hunters*, 66.

147   **"Deny":** Sears, *Lonely Hunters*, 66.

CHAPTER 13. CROSSFIRE

148   the preceding witness: Russell Danburg, Transcript of Testimony, January 5, 1959; Lawrence Wathen, Transcript of Testimony, January 5, 1959.

148   "an obnoxious person": Russell Danburg, Transcript of Testimony, January 5, 1959.

148   into a conference room: James T. Sears, *Lonely Hunters: An Oral History of Lesbian and Gay Southern Life, 1948–1968* (Westview Press, 1997), 67.

148   state troopers: Sears, *Lonely Hunters*, 67.

149   behind the boardroom table: Transcript of Testimony, January 5, 1959.

149   "Mr. Wathen": Lawrence Wathen, Transcript of Testimony, January 5, 1959.

149   "We're investigating homosexual": Lawrence Wathen, Transcript of Testimony, January 5, 1959.

149   "I've always been rather": Lawrence Wathen, Transcript of Testimony, January 5, 1959.

150   "I'm going to ask": Lawrence Wathen, Transcript of Testimony, January 5, 1959.

150   Trice got expelled: Lawrence Wathen, Transcript of Testimony, January 5, 1959; Trice, interrogation by Strickland, November 4, 1958.

151   "Later he told me that": Lawrence Wathen, Transcript of Testimony, January 5, 1959; Trice, interrogation by Strickland, November 4, 1958.

151   "With God as my witness": Joe Trice, Transcript of Testimony, January 6, 1959, 4-44, Box 7, FLIC Papers.

151   "Mr. Wathen, you": Lawrence Wathen, Transcript of Testimony, January 5, 1959.

151   "You all had a homosexual": Lawrence Wathen, Transcript of Testimony, January 5, 1959.

151   "I can't imagine why": Lawrence Wathen, Transcript of Testimony, January 5, 1959.

152   "As far as this casual": Lawrence Wathen, Transcript of Testimony, January 5, 1959.

152   "All right, Mr. Wathen": Lawrence Wathen, Transcript of Testimony, January 5, 1959.

152   John Faircloth Park: "Statement of Facts," November 18, 1958.

152   incriminated a second professor: "Statement of Facts," November 18, 1958.

152   "I'm going to ask if you": John Van Meter, Transcript of Testimony, January 5, 1959.

152   "I would appreciate": John Van Meter, Transcript of Testimony, January 5, 1959.

153   "Why should you think": John Van Meter, Transcript of Testimony, January 5, 1959.

153   Congleton walked into: James Congleton, Transcript of Testimony, January 16, 1959.

153   "It is getting a": James Congleton, Transcript of Testimony, January 16, 1959.

153   Congleton confessed: James Congleton, Transcript of Testimony, January 16, 1959.

153   implicated Robert Gustus: James Congleton, Transcript of Testimony, January 16, 1959.

153   golf team, Andy Bracken: James Congleton, Transcript of Testimony, January 16, 1959.

153   "If he is not homosexual": James Congleton, Transcript of Testimony, January 16, 1959.

153   "If I were only thinking": James Congleton, Transcript of Testimony, January 16, 1959.

154   "I know I will have a restless": James Congleton, Transcript of Testimony, January 16, 1959.

154   "homosexual": Stephen Fogle, FLIC suspect sheet, #13-421.

154   Fogle hired a $3,000 lawyer: Sears, Lonely Hunters, 74–75.

154   who retained lawyers: Robert Gustus, Transcript of Testimony, January 6, 1959, Bonnie Stark Papers.

154   accurate advance notice: Sears, Lonely Hunters, 75.

154   regularly meet: Sears, Lonely Hunters, 75.

154   rode their bicycles: Art Copleston, interview with Robert Fieseler, October 28, 2019; Art Copleston, interview with Robert Fieseler, November 11, 2019.

154   John Faircloth Park: Sears, Lonely Hunters, 63.

154   to telephone Park: Sears, Lonely Hunters, 63.

154   turned up at his: Sears, Lonely Hunters, 63.

154   for hours: Sears, Lonely Hunters, 63.

154   "They put the screws": Sears, Lonely Hunters, 63.

154   "You can ruin my life": Sears, Lonely Hunters, 63.

155   Earl Fender: Earl Fender, Transcript of Testimony, January 7, 1959, 503–64, #4-8, Box 7, FLIC Papers.

155   "They didn't know about": John Tileston, interview with Allyson Beutke, April 12, 1999.

155   without representation, Earl: Earl Fender, Transcript of Testimony, January 7, 1959.

155   Harold Elwood Carter: Earl Fender, Transcript of Testimony, January 7, 1959; Harold Elwood Carter, Transcript of Testimony, January 19, 1959.

155   Murray sat in questioning: Leslie Murray, Transcript of Testimony, January 7, 1959, 564–80, #4-8, Box 7, FLIC Papers.

155   midnight rendezvous: Earl Fender, Transcript of Testimony, January 8, 1959, #2-77, Box 7, FLIC Papers.

155   "serious trouble": Earl Fender, Transcript of Testimony, January 8, 1959, #2-77, Box 7, FLIC Papers.

155   "You know, Mr. Hawes, I believe": Leslie Murray, Transcript of Testimony, January 8, 1959, 2-77, Box 7, FLIC Papers.

155   "Can't we postpone the": Leslie Murray, Transcript of Testimony, January 8, 1959, 2-77, Box 7, FLIC Papers.

156   "engaged in homosexual": Leslie Murray, Transcript of Testimony, January 8, 1959, 2-77, Box 7, FLIC Papers.

156   Alachua General Hospital: Murray's ex-wife, Transcript of Testimony, January 19, 1959, 2-76, Box 7, FLIC Papers.

156   **White Citizens' Council:** Allen Neuharth, Transcript of Testimony, February 27, 1957.

156   **referred Earl Fender:** FLIC Meeting Minutes for April 13, 1959, 1, Clerk of the House Papers.

156   **"false affidavit":** FLIC Meeting Minutes for April 13, 1959, 1, Clerk of the House Papers.

156   **Park out of a lecture:** John Faircloth Park, Transcript of Testimony, January 7, 1959.

156   **Harold Elwood Carter:** Harold Elwood Carter, Transcript of Testimony, January 19, 1959.

157   **"We are not going to":** John Faircloth Park, Transcript of Testimony, January 7, 1959.

157   **"By the way, while you":** John Faircloth Park, Transcript of Testimony, January 7, 1959.

157   **Park's little drive:** Sears, *Lonely Hunters*, 63, 75.

157   **"Diettrich":** John Faircloth Park, Transcript of Testimony, January 7, 1959.

158   **"How about the outcome":** John Faircloth Park, Transcript of Testimony, January 7, 1959.

159   **at 5:05 p.m. with:** John Faircloth Park, Transcript of Testimony, January 7, 1959.

159   **began nosing around:** "Legislative Probe Chairman Huddles Here with Top Aides," *Gainesville Sun*, January 6, 1959, 1; "Johns Remains Quiet on Probe at University," *Gainesville Sun*, January 12, 1959, 1; "Time for Action," *Gainesville Sun*, February 1, 1959, 6.

159   ***The Miami News:*** Charles F. Hesser, "Let's Get Story in Open of Probe at U. of Florida," *Miami News*, January 12, 1959, 1.

159   **compelled to uproot:** Transcript of Testimony, January 7, 1959; Transcript of Testimony, January 8, 1959; Jack Detweiler, "Johns Mum After 5-Day Florida U. Staff Probe," *Tampa Tribune*, January 10, 1959, 10.

CHAPTER 14. TRAPDOORS

160   **recalled Lawrence Wathen:** Lawrence Wathen, Transcript of Testimony, January 9, 1959, 809–33, 2-77, Box 7, FLIC Papers.

160   **"we've had further":** Lawrence Wathen, Transcript of Testimony, January 9, 1959, 809–33, 2-77, Box 7, FLIC Papers.

160   **the scholar seethed:** James T. Sears, *Lonely Hunters: An Oral History of Lesbian and Gay Southern Life, 1948–1968* (Westview Press, 1997), 73–74.

160   **"I am puzzled, worried":** Lawrence Wathen, Transcript of Testimony, January 9, 1959, 836–70.

161   **"You couldn't have had":** Lawrence Wathen, Transcript of Testimony, January 9, 1959, 836–70.

162   **"All right, just a minute":** Lawrence Wathen, Transcript of Testimony, January 9, 1959, 836–70.

162   **Park did not speak a:** Lawrence Wathen, Transcript of Testimony, January 9, 1959, 836–70.

162   **endure every second:** Lawrence Wathen, Transcript of Testimony for January 9, 1959, 836–70.

162   "We both committed": John Faircloth Park, Transcript of Testimony, January 8, 1959.

163   "All right, Mr. Park": John Faircloth Park, Transcript of Testimony, January 8, 1959.

163   of the place and time for: Sears, *Lonely Hunters*, 81–82.

163   "Mr. Moore, do you know any": Bill Moore, Transcript of Testimony, January 22, 1959, 1469–77, #2-75, Box 7, FLIC Papers.

164   "shocking irregularities": "Dealing with Irregularities," *Gainesville Sun*, January 9, 1959, 4.

164   "Without a discharge": "Dealing with Irregularities," *Gainesville Sun*.

164   to head off future: "Evidence Needed Before Taking Action, Says Reitz," *Gainesville Sun*, January 13, 1959, 1; Bonnie Stark, "McCarthyism in Florida: Charley Johns and the Florida Legislative Investigation Committee July, 1956 to July, 1965" (master's thesis, University of South Florida, 1985), 97, https://palmm.digital.flvc.org/islandora/object/usf%3A49370#page/title/mode/1up, 107.

164   under the gun financially: Charles Hesser, "Homosexual Cleanup at UF Pledged," *Miami News*, January 13, 1959, 2A.

164   20,000 by 1970: "$48 Million UF Budget Approved," *Gainesville Sun*, January 30, 1959, 1; "Time for Action," *Gainesville Sun*, March 24, 1959, 4; "Reitz Predicts 20,000 Students at UF in 1970," *Florida Alligator*, March 25, 1959, 1.

164   Senate Appropriations Committee: Journal of the Senate, April 7, 1959, 7.

164   "irregularities": Charles F. Hesser, "Let's Get Story in Open of Probe at U. of Florida," *Miami News*, January 12, 1959.

164   "Homosexual Probe Hits Florida U": Hesser, "Let's Get Story in Open."

165   "It was a popular thing": Cliff Herrell, interview with Bonnie Stark, August 3, 1993.

165   Dave Levy and Al Quentel: Al Quentel, Transcript of Testimony, January 9, 1959.

165   "Like in the Army and Navy": Al Quentel, Transcript of Testimony, January 9, 1959.

165   "Dear Colleague": Franklin A. Doty, letter, "The American Association of University Professors, University of Florida Chapter, Gainesville, Florida," January 20, 1959, Johns Committee vertical file, University of Florida Archives.

166   Winston Wallace Ehrmann: Charles Hesser, "UF Told to Move on Vice," *Miami News*, February 16, 1959, 6A; Charles Hesser, "Public Hearing on U-F Morals?" *Miami* News, January 22, 1959, D1; Jack Detweiler, "Professors to Probe Sen. Johns' Investigation," *Tampa Tribune*, January 29, 1959, 4.

166   "that all innocent persons": Bob Mirandon, "Profs to Probe UF Investigation," January 28, 1959, *Gainesville Sun*, 1, 2.

166   Committee "summons": Mirandon, "Profs to Probe UF Investigation."

166   voted by a ratio of two to one: Mirandon, "Profs to Probe UF Investigation."

166 **"We're keeping in close touch":** "AAUP Group Still Studying Johns' Probe," *Gainesville Sun*, February 25, 1959, 8; "Probe of Johns' Investigation to Get Under Way," *Gainesville Sun*, January 29, 1959, 1.

166 **on Friday, January 16:** Harold Elwood Carter, Transcript of Testimony, January 19, 1959.

166 **tricked Carter out of:** Harold Elwood Carter, Transcript of Testimony, January 19, 1959.

166 **his "own peril":** Harold Elwood Carter, Transcript of Testimony, January 19, 1959.

167 **off the record:** Harold Elwood Carter, Transcript of Testimony, January 19, 1959.

167 **"I will make the testimony":** Harold Elwood Carter, Transcript of Testimony, January 19, 1959.

167 **"Mr. Carter, you":** Harold Elwood Carter, Transcript of Testimony, January 19, 1959.

167 **Fogle as a former:** Harold Elwood Carter, Transcript of Testimony, January 19, 1959.

167 **man was fired:** Andy Hopkins, SCR ID # 3-6A-2-12-1-1-1, June 30, 1961, Mississippi Papers.

CHAPTER 15. QUEER GEOGRAPHY

168 **Monday evening in mid-January:** Sigismond Diettrich, Transcript of Testimony, January 19, 1959; Sigismond Diettrich, letter to Raymond Crist, May 24, 1959, Diettrich Papers.

168 **administered a final exam:** "The University Record of the University of Florida, 1958–1959," 4; "The University Record of the University of Florida, Schedule of Courses First Semester, 1958–1959," 84; Sigismond Diettrich, letter to David Baker, April 21, 1959, Diettrich Papers.

168 **fell into a dreamless slumber:** Sigismond Diettrich, letter to Raymond Crist, May 24, 1959.

168 **taught piano lessons:** Sigismond Diettrich, letter to Father Joe Curtin, April 8, 1959; Judith Poucher, *State of Defiance: Challenging the Johns Committee's Assault on Civil Liberties* (University Press of Florida, 2014), 84; Sigismond Diettrich, letter to Wallace Atwood, March 15, 1939, Folder 1, Diettrich Papers.

168 **by January 29:** "The University Record of the University of Florida, 1958–1959," 4; "Director Announced for Little Theatre Play," *Gainesville Sun*, February 3, 1957, 4.

169 **St. Patrick Catholic Church:** "St. Patrick's Plans Services for Holy Week," *Gainesville Sun*, March 18, 1951, 8; Poucher, *State of Defiance*, 66.

169 **naturalized U.S. citizen in 1938:** "Stanley, Diettrich Made Naturalized Citizens of U.S.," *Gainesville Sun*, December 14, 1938, 5.

169 **built in 1955:** "1418 NW 17th Ter, Gainesville, FL 32605," Realtor.com, accessed November 28, 2024, https://www.realtor.com/realestateandhomes -detail/1418-NW-17th-Ter_Gainesville_FL_32605_M61244-55738; Sigismond Diettrich, Transcript of Testimony, January 19, 1959.

169   daughter, Rosemary: "Miss Rosemary Diettrich Becomes Bride of Charles E. Leedham Jr.," *Gainesville Sun*, 27, September 29, 1957.

169   in 1953 Diettrich had been president: Sigismond Diettrich, Curriculum Vitae, circa 1940, Diettrich Vertical File; "Florida Science Teachers to Take Part in Meeting," *Gainesville Sun*, December 3, 1953, 7; "Diettrich New President of Science Group," *Gainesville Sun*, December 6, 1953, Diettrich Vertical File; "Press Release," February 24, 1955, University of Florida News Bureau, Diettrich Vertical File.

169   Francis McCoy became: "Madagascar Is Next Stop for Globe-Trotting McCoy," *Tampa Bay Times*, August 25, 1951, 17.

169   Florida sun had: "Orlando 1959 Past Weather (Florida, United States)," Weather Spark, accessed November 28, 2024, https://weatherspark.com/h/y /17721/1959/Historical-Weather-during-1959-in-Orlando-Florida-United -States.

169   telephone rang: Sigismond Diettrich, letter to Raymond Crist, May 24, 1959.

169   colleague or a student: Sigismond Diettrich, letter to Raymond Crist, May 24, 1959.

169   "Dr. D.": M.J.W., letter to Sigismond Diettrich, March 13, 1959, Folder 4, Diettrich Papers.

169   five feet eight: Sigismond Diettrich, World War II Draft Card, Ancestry.com, https://www.ancestry.com/search/collections/2238/records/12332780?tid =&pid=&queryId=c21feb91-b02d-481d-b104-4cb631047984&_phsrc =Pmf1003&_phstart=successSource.

169   Slightly round: "Madagascar Is Next," *Tampa Bay Times*, August 25, 1951, 17; "Visitors to Silver Springs," *Orlando Sentinel*, June 14, 1956, 10.

170   "Hello, this is Sig": Sigismond Diettrich, letter to Raymond Crist, May 24, 1959; Sigismond Diettrich, Transcript of Testimony, January 19, 1959; "Red Cross," *Gainesville Sun*, November 25, 1956, 3.

170   "It was somebody": Sigismond Diettrich, letter to Raymond Crist, May 24, 1959.

170   Manor Motel: "Manor Motel," University of Florida Archives, accessed November 28, 2024, https://original-ufdc.uflib.ufl.edu/MH00001199/00001 /citation.

170   sweat out an hour in: Sigismond Diettrich, letter to Raymond Crist, May 24, 1959.

170   Diettrich threw himself: Sigismond Diettrich, Office of Strategic Services (OSS) Records, obtained via FOIA request; Sigismond Diettrich, letter to Wallace Atwood, October 5, 1942, Folder 1, Diettrich Papers.

170   Second Army Corps School: Albert B. Crowther, letter to Sigismond Diettrich, May 14, 1942, Diettrich Vertical File, Diettrich Papers; Sigismond Diettrich, letter to Wallace Atwood, March 22, 1943, Folder 1, Diettrich Papers.

170   reached high ranks: Sigismond Diettrich, letter to Wallace Atwood, July 23, 1943, Folder 1, Diettrich Papers.

170   Tigert promoted Sigismond: "Diettrich to Head Board in Washington," *Gainesville Sun*, March 26, 1944, 2.

170   travel to Washington, D.C.: "Diettrich to Head Board in Washington," *Gainesville Sun*.

170 **"REPORTING FOR DUTY":** Sigismond Diettrich, telegram to Norfolk, August 27, 1953, OSS Records.

170 **provided his consultancy:** Sigismond Diettrich, "Oath of Office, Affidavit," August 30, 1943, OSS Records.

170 **"topographic intelligence":** Sigismond Diettrich, "*Work Completed," June 22, 1944, OSS Records.

170 **last advisory day:** "Receipt for OSS Credentials," June 19, 1944, OSS Records.

170 **geography chairman:** Sigismond Diettrich, Curriculum Vitae, circa 1940, Diettrich Vertical File.

171 **relations in Budapest:** "Red Cross," *Gainesville Sun.*

171 *Atlas of Florida*: Sigismond Diettrich, letter May 19, 1959, Folder 4, Diettrich Records.

171 **"Then":** Sigismond Diettrich, letter to Raymond Crist, May 24, 1959.

171 **"attendant publicity from":** Sigismond Diettrich, Transcript of Testimony, January 19, 1959.

171 **"They were nice":** Sigismond Diettrich, letter to Raymond Crist, May 24, 1959.

172 **"Mr. Diettrich, have you participated":** Sigismond Diettrich, Transcript of Testimony, January 19, 1959.

172 **"But over what period":** Sigismond Diettrich, Transcript of Testimony, January 19, 1959.

173 **stack of several thousand:** Sigismond Diettrich, Transcript of Testimony, January 19, 1959.

173 **"loose bowel":** Sigismond Diettrich, Transcript of Testimony for January 19, 1959.

173 **"Doctor, that's a dirty":** Sigismond Diettrich, Transcript of Testimony, January 19, 1959.

173 **became life-threatening:** Sigismond Diettrich, Transcript of Testimony, January 19, 1959; Poucher, *State of Defiance*, 66–68.

173 **sexual relations:** Sigismond Diettrich, Transcript of Testimony, January 19, 1959.

174 **"You go in, and":** Sigismond Diettrich, Transcript of Testimony, January 19, 1959.

174 **wanted to return:** Sigismond Diettrich, Transcript of Testimony, January 19, 1959.

174 **for regular release:** Sigismond Diettrich, Transcript of Testimony, January 19, 1959.

174 **"As long as you":** Sigismond Diettrich, Transcript of Testimony, January 19, 1959; Poucher, *State of Defiance*, 68.

174 **unspeakable Catholic guilt:** Sigismond Diettrich, letter to Bob and Muriel, April 27, 1957, Folder 4, Diettrich Papers.

174 **"the only woman I":** Sigismond Diettrich, Transcript of Testimony, January 19, 1959.

174 **"Every now and then":** Sigismond Diettrich, Transcript of Testimony, January 19, 1959.

175   "act normally as ever": Sigismond Diettrich, Transcript of Testimony, January 19, 1959; Sigismond Diettrich, letter to Raymond Crist, May 24, 1959; Sigismond Diettrich, letter to Bob and Muriel, April 27, 1957.

175   "scarlet letter": Sigismond Diettrich, letter to Raymond Crist, May 24, 1959.

175   fifty UF professors and students: Charles Hesser, "Homosexual Cleanup," *Miami News*, January 13, 1959; Charles Hesser, "Let's Get Story," *Miami News*, January 12, 1959; "Florida University Morals Probed," *News-Press*, January 13, 1959, 1.

175   humanities professor Clyde Miller: "University of Florida Resignations," April 17, 1959, 6, Box 117, LeRoy Collins Papers, State of Florida Archives; Clyde Miller, Transcript of Testimony, January 5, 1959, Bonnie Stark Papers.

175   "health reasons": "Arts, Sciences Assistant Dean Byers Resigns," *Gainesville Sun*, February 1, 1959, 1; Charles Byers, FLIC suspect sheet, #13-423.

176   "a patient": "Arts, Sciences," *Gainesville Sun*, February 1, 1959.

176   passed away: "Charles Francis Byers" probate filing, *Gainesville Sun*, March 26, 1982, 20; "C Francis Byers," Findagrave.com, https://www .findagrave.com/memorial/72950235/c-francis-byers.

176   as reported in the *Alligator*: "Johns' Group Gives Findings to University," *Florida Alligator*, February 17, 1959, 1; FLIC Meeting Minutes for February 14, 1959, Clerk of the House Papers.

176   no fewer than 1,900 pages: FLIC Meeting Minutes for February 14, 1959, Clerk of the House Papers; "Johns Report Names 15–16 Florida U. Faculty Men," *Tampa Tribune*, February 18, 1959, 1.

176   "take such action": FLIC Meeting Minutes for February 14, 1959, Clerk of the House Papers.

176   "not for the purpose": "Mysterious University Quiz Shifted," *Pensacola News Journal*, February 17, 1959, 2.

176   hammer blow would: Sigismond Diettrich, letter to Raymond Crist, May 24, 1959.

Chapter 16. Victim of Opportunity

177   April 7, 1959: Journal of the Senate, April 7, 1959.

177   "There is still": Charles Hesser, "UF Told to Act in Morals Probe," *Miami News*, February 16, 1959, 1.

177   "four Negroes": John Boyles, "Race-School Laws Largely the Same," *Miami Herald*, June 6, 1959, 3-A.

177   impromptu summit: "Manifesto Hit," *Miami Herald*, April 8, 1959, 15.

177   "manifesto": Glenda Alice Rabby, *The Pain and the Promise: The Struggle for Civil Rights in Tallahassee, Florida* (University of Georgia Press, 1999), 220.

178   "an education in keeping": "'Manifesto' Pledges Integration Fight," *Fort Lauderdale News*, February 25, 1959, 5.

178   issue a stay: "U.S. Court Delays Probe of NAACP," *Miami Herald*, February 25, 1959, 8A.

178   **"Not at all surprised"**: "U.S. Court Delays Probe of NAACP."

178   **"Watchdog Charley"**: "Campus K.K.K.," letter to the editor, *Florida Alligator,* April 3, 1959, 4.

178   **"500 students had"**: John B. McDermott, "Probers Suspect Many Students of Secret Activities," *Miami Herald,* February 17, 1959.

178   **"15–16 Suspects"**: Bob Gilmour, "15–16 Suspects Named in Report of Johns Group," *Florida Alligator,* February 20, 1959, 1.

178   **"tremendous and permanent"**: "Civil Liberties Union Attacks Probe at AF," *Tallahassee Democrat,* February 11, 1959, 1.

178   **"No concern of mine"**: "Civil Liberties Union Attacks Probe at AF."

178   **more or less alphabetically**: Didier Graeffe, transcript of interview with Bonnie Stark, December 1983; Judith Poucher, *State of Defiance: Challenging the Johns Committee's Assault on Civil Liberties* (University Press of Florida, 2014), 87.

178   **Tenure meant next**: James T. Sears, *Lonely Hunters: An Oral History of Lesbian and Gay Southern Life, 1948–1968* (Westview Press, 1997), 81.

178   **lethal dose of aspirin**: Sigismond Diettrich, letter to Raymond Crist, May 24, 1959.

178   **"I don't think I ever"**: Sigismond Diettrich, letter to Raymond Crist, May 24, 1959.

178   **March 16, 1959**: Sigismond Diettrich, letter to Raymond Crist, May 24, 1959.

178   **Ralph Page**: Sigismond Diettrich, letter to Raymond Crist, May 24, 1959.

179   **"I knew what it was"**: Sigismond Diettrich, letter to Raymond Crist, May 24, 1959.

179   **Father Thomas Gross**: Sigismond Diettrich, letter to Raymond Crist, May 24, 1959; "49 Dads, Sons Here Talk by Father Gross," *Gainesville Sun,* March 9, 1959, 3.

179   **"distinguished research professor"**: Sigismond Diettrich, letter to Raymond Crist, May 24, 1959.

179   **"It is always a pleasure"**: Sigismond Diettrich, letter to Raymond Crist, May 24, 1959.

179   **Diettrich gave spare answers**: Sigismond Diettrich, letter to Raymond Crist, May 24, 1959.

179   **"He was nice but"**: Sigismond Diettrich, letter to Raymond Crist, May 24, 1959.

180   **"Sig, this is a most serious"**: Sigismond Diettrich, letter to Raymond Crist, May 24, 1959.

180   **"Wayne was the nicest ever"**: Sigismond Diettrich, letter to Raymond Crist, May 24, 1959.

180   **"terminated"**: "University of Florida Resignations," April 17, 1959, 6.

180   **Diettrich to resign**: Sigismond Diettrich, letter to Raymond Crist, May 24, 1959.

180   **pension could not**: Sigismond Diettrich, letter to Raymond Crist, May 24, 1959.

180   **"Dr. Reitz assured"**: Sigismond Diettrich, letter to Raymond Crist, May 24, 1959.

180   "reassuring goodbye": Sigismond Diettrich, letter to Raymond Crist, May 24, 1959.

180   "The enormity of my": Sigismond Diettrich, letter to Raymond Crist, May 24, 1959.

181   Father Neil Sager: Sigismond Diettrich, letter to Raymond Crist, May 24, 1959; "Priest Leaves G'ville," *Gainesville Sun*, January 13, 1960, 5.

181   "shall never, never": Sigismond Diettrich, letter to Raymond Crist, May 24, 1959.

181   "Killing myself": Sigismond Diettrich, letter to Raymond Crist, May 24, 1959.

181   "I talked about": Sigismond Diettrich, letter to Raymond Crist, May 24, 1959.

181   onto the roof: Sigismond Diettrich, letter to Raymond Crist, May 24, 1959.

181   cruel arithmetic: Sigismond Diettrich, letter to Raymond Crist, May 24, 1959.

182   "could not jump": Sigismond Diettrich, letter to Raymond Crist, May 24, 1959.

182   two more aspirin: Sigismond Diettrich, letter to Raymond Crist, May 24, 1959.

182   titled "The Geography of Florida": Sigismond Diettrich, letter to Raymond Crist, May 24, 1959; "The University Record of the University of Florida, Schedule of Courses Second Semester 1958–1959," 82.

182   "I've lost my job": Sigismond Diettrich, letter to Raymond Crist, May 24, 1959.

182   "I am afraid if I had": Sigismond Diettrich, letter to Raymond Crist, May 24, 1959.

182   A million hammers: Sigismond Diettrich, letter to Raymond Crist, May 24, 1959.

183   "have lost all I had": Sigismond Diettrich, letter to Raymond Crist, May 24, 1959.

183   "taken enough aspirin": Sigismond Diettrich, letter to Raymond Crist, May 24, 1959.

183   J. Wayne Reitz: Sigismond Diettrich, letter to Raymond Crist, May 24, 1959.

183   emergency conclave: Sigismond Diettrich, letter to Raymond Crist, May 24, 1959.

183   having a breakdown: Sigismond Diettrich, letter to Raymond Crist, May 24, 1959.

184   "loving and sorrowful": Sigismond Diettrich, letter to Raymond Crist, May 24, 1959.

184   his last dictation: Sigismond Diettrich, letter to Raymond Crist, May 24, 1959.

184   "The tragedy came to": Sigismond Diettrich, letter to Raymond Crist, May 24, 1959.

184   "While driving through": Sigismond Diettrich, letter to Raymond Crist, May 24, 1959.

184   "I regret to inform you that Dr. Diettrich": Sigismond Diettrich, letter to Raymond Crist, May 24, 1959.

184   "quit": "Diettrich Quits as Head of UF Geography Dept.," *Gainesville Sun*, March 22, 1959, 7.

184   that March 22: Sigismond Diettrich, letter to Raymond Crist, May 24, 1959.

184   "shock": Sigismond Diettrich, letter to Joe Curtain, April 8, 1959, Folder 4, Diettrich Papers.

184   went to Floyd Hall: Sigismond Diettrich, letter to Raymond Crist, May 24, 1959.

184   *Atlas of Florida*: Sigismond Dietrrich, letter to "Dear Ones," May 19, 1959, Folder 4, Diettrich Papers.

184   Raisz: Sigismond Diettrich, letter to Raymond Crist, May 24, 1959; Sigismond Diettrich, letter to Erwin Raisz, May 17, 1959, Folder 4, Diettrich Papers.

184   "I am not welcome on campus": Sigismond Diettrich, letter to Raymond Crist, May 24, 1959.

185   "All her pupils came back": Sigismond Diettrich, letter to Joe Curtain, April 8, 1959.

185   "He is supposed": Sigismond Diettrich, letter to Erwin Raisz, April 6, 1959, Folder 4, Diettrich Papers.

185   the last of May: Sigismond Diettrich, letter to Ray and Hilda, April 27, 1959, Folder 4, Diettrich Papers.

185   University of Dacca: "Dacca," *News from Geographic Centers* 11, no. 4 (1959): 22–25.

185   "field trip": Sigismond Diettrich, letter to Thomas, April 25, 1959, Folder 4, Diettrich Papers; Sigismond Diettrich, letter to Ray and Hilda, April 27, 1959.

186   "hospitality and help": Sigismond Diettrich, *The Philippine Islands* (Doubleday, 1961), 62.

186   "Naked Mru": William van Schendel, "A Politics of Nudity: Photographs of the 'Naked Mru' of Bangladesh," *Modern Asian Studies* 36, no. 2 (May 2002): 341–74; Poucher, *State of Defiance*, 87.

186   cut him out of the: Poucher, *State of Defiance*, 90; Erwin Raisz, *Atlas of Florida* (University of Florida Press, 1964).

186   "text by John R. Dunkle": Raisz, *Atlas of Florida*, front cover; Sigismond Diettrich, letter to Erwin Raisz, April 6, 1959.

186   "The research which has": Raisz, *Atlas of Florida*, 2.

186   "brain-father": Bert Collier, "All About Florida—in Just One Book," *Miami Herald*, May 5, 1964, 6AW.

186   royalty check: Poucher, *State of Defiance*, 90.

186   chairman of social sciences: "UB Honors Society Has Members in 10 Nations," *Bridgeport Post*, July 21, 1963, 17.

187   international chancellor: "UB Honors Society Has Members in 10 Nations."

187   Foundation for the Promotion of Music: "Sigismond deRudesheim Diettrich," *Gainesville Sun*, May 21, 1987, 12; "Past Presidents," Foundation for the Promotion of Music, https://www.thefpm.org/board-of-directors.

187   in 1987, Diettrich was dying: "Sigismond deRudesheim Diettrich," *Gainesville Sun*, May 21, 1987; Emma Pettit, "'Private Little Hell': A Florida

Committee Once Hunted for Gay People on Campuses. Sixty Years Later, the Effects Linger," *Chronicle of Higher Education*, November 28, 2022, https://www.chronicle.com/article/private-little-hell.

187 **Diettrich's papers and letters:** Sigismond deRudesheim Diettrich Papers, Special & Area Studies Collections, University of Florida Archives, accessed November 28, 2024, https://findingaids.uflib.ufl.edu/repositories/2/resources/1226.

CHAPTER 17. HANDS THAT FEED

188 **Congleton was terminated:** "University of Florida Resignations," April 17, 1959, 6.

188 **medical intervention:** James Congleton, Transcript of Testimony, January 5, 1959, Bonnie Stark Papers.

188 **"He has been associated":** "J. E. Congleton Resigns from UF," *Gainesville Sun*, March 18, 1959, 1.

188 **Park was called in and fired:** "University of Florida Resignations," April 17, 1959, 6.

189 **Carter stood among the first:** Andy Hopkins, SCR ID # 3-6A-2-12-1-1-1, June 30, 1961, Mississippi Papers; Harold Elwood Carter, Transcript of Testimony, January 19, 1959, Box 7, FLIC Papers.

189 **Earl Fender:** Earl Fender, Transcript of Testimony, January 7, 1959, #4-8, Box 7, FLIC Papers; "Champs in Spelling," *Orlando Sentinel*, March 28, 1958, 1B; FLIC Meeting Minutes for April 13, 1959, Clerk of the House Papers; Journal of the Senate, April 29, 1959, 280.

189 **Danburg received a pardon:** Russell Danburg, FLIC suspect sheet, #13-410, Bonnie Stark Papers.

189 **witnessed in the act:** "Statement of Facts," December 12, 1958; Russell Danburg, Transcript of Testimony, January 5, 1959, Box 7, FLIC Papers.

189 **"in a mild way":** Russell Danburg, Transcript of Testimony, January 5, 1959.

189 **"Do you think that a man":** Russell Danburg, Transcript of Testimony, January 5, 1959.

189 **Danburg continued teaching:** "The University Record of the University of Florida, 1961–1962," 18; "Craig to Sing This Weekend," *Florida Alligator*, April 7, 1965, 5; "Tale of Scrooge Reading Tonight," *Florida Alligator*, December 5, 1969, 18; "3 UF Faculty Members Are Retiring," *Gainesville Sun*, July 8, 1981, 10A; "Tape Recording 120," University of Florida Archives, accessed November 29, 2024, https://web.uflib.ufl.edu/spec/sound/ufaudio120.htm.

189 **retrospective interview:** Russell Danburg, oral history interview with Marian Ludlow, 1983, Samuel Proctor Oral History Program, University of Florida Archives.

189 **Russell L. Danburg Scholarship:** "Online Giving," University of Florida College of the Arts | University of Florida, accessed November 29, 2024, https://arts.ufl.edu/giving/online/list/.

190   **married a third wife:** Marriage Indexes, Florida Department of Health, 1960, Volume 1933, Certificate 37250, accessed via Ancestry.com; James T. Sears, *Lonely Hunters: An Oral History of Lesbian and Gay Southern Life, 1948–1968* (Westview Press, 1997), 81.

190   **received a year's leave:** Eleanor Crom, "To Attend Convention; Heils to Be Feted; Everet Yon III Arrives," *Gainesville Sun*, July 10, 1960, 18; "The University Record of the University of Florida, 1961–1962," 21.

190   **Fogle took a leave:** Sears, *Lonely Hunters*, 81; Art Copleston, interview with Robert Fieseler, November 11, 2019; "The University Record of the University of Florida, 1960–1961," 24.

190   **trip to Key West:** Stephen Fogle, "Arriving and Departing Passenger and Crew Lists for Key West, Florida, August 24, 1959," accessed via Ancestry .com, https://www.ancestry.com/search/collections/8842/records/4755402?tid =&pid=&queryId=7788c110-3164-4f5a-a8b8-892f23867b54&_phsrc =Pmf1023&_phstart=successSource.

190   **town of Sayville:** Art Copleston, interview with Robert Fieseler, November 11, 2019.

190   **as "beneath him":** Art Copleston, interview with Robert Fieseler, July 11, 2012.

190   **visiting professor:** "44 New Staff Members Join University Faculty," *Daily Sentinel-Tribune*, September 14, 1962, A1.

190   **May 7, 1965, the *Alligator*:** "18 of Faculty to Retire," *Florida Alligator*, May 7, 1965, 10.

190   **April 1967, Fogle died:** "Stephen Francis Fogle," Florida Death Index, 1967, accessed via Ancestry.com, https://www.ancestry.com/search/collections /7338/records/1170073?tid=&pid=&queryId=a9989893-50ad-41f8-a5ec -91416544a9aa&_phsrc=Pmf1025&_phstart=successSource.

190   **On March 19, President Reitz:** "Reitz Predicts 20,000 Students at UF in 1980," *Florida Alligator*, March 25, 1959, 1.

190   **"In a democratic society":** "Reitz Predicts 20,000 Students at UF in 1980."

191   **"Florida U. Dismisses 14":** "Florida U. Dismisses 14 for Homosexuality," Associated Press, April 4, 1959, James T. Sears Papers.

191   **"suitable procedures":** "Florida U. Dismisses 14 for Homosexuality."

191   **"President Reitz is to be":** "Suitable Procedures," *Gainesville Sun*, April 9, 1959, 4.

191   **"morals cleanup":** "14 Leave UF in Morals Cleanup, Reitz Reveals," *Gainesville Sun*, April 3, 1949, 1.

191   **"well pleased":** "14 Leave UF in Morals Cleanup, Reitz Reveals": "14 Fired After Probe of Florida U. Morals," *News-Press*, April 4, 1949, 1; "Homosexual Case Cleanup Pleases Senator Johns," *Tampa Tribune*, March 24, 1959, 6.

191   **1,900-page report:** FLIC Meeting Minutes for February 14, 1959, Clerk of the House Papers.

191   **"I again want to emphasize":** "14 Leave UF in Morals Cleanup, Reitz Reveals."

191   **"You might be interested in knowing":** J. Wayne Reitz, letter to Harrison Friese, May 26, 1959, Box 26, Reitz Papers, University of Florida Archives.

191   **"No information has been":** "Readers Want More Information About Investigation Firings," *Florida Alligator*, April 17, 1959, 4.

192   April 9, 1959: Art Copleston, interview with Robert Fieseler, July 10, 2021; Art Copleston interview with Robert Fieseler, October 28, 2019; "The University Record of the University of Florida, 1958–1959," 8.

192   "kicked out": Art Copleston, interview with Robert Fieseler, July 10, 2021.

192   "I have some bad news": Art Copleston, interview with Robert Fieseler, July 10, 2021.

192   "Your father died": Art Copleston, interview with Robert Fieseler, July 10, 2021.

192   "thank God," he instinctively: Art Copleston, interview with Robert Fieseler, October 28, 2019.

192   couldn't see straight: Art Copleston, interview with Robert Fieseler, October 28, 2019.

192   his dad had died: Art Copleston, interview with Robert Fieseler, October 28, 2019.

192   next "sweat session": Art Copleston, interview with Robert Fieseler, October 28, 2019.

192   a habit of hanging out: Art Copleston, interview with Robert Fieseler, October 28, 2019.

193   standing right there: Art Copleston, interview with Robert Fieseler, October 28, 2019; Art Copleston, *Demons and Deliverance* (published by author, 2014), Kindle.

193   April 10, he introduced: Journal of the Senate, April 10 1959, 28; "Senate Committee Votes $75,000 to Extend Life of Johns Investigating Group," *Tampa Tribune*, April 30, 1959, 1; "Racial Probes Victim of House Economy Ax," *Tampa Tribune*, May 15, 1959, 17A; Bonnie Stark, "McCarthyism in Florida: Charley Johns and the Florida Legislative Investigation Committee July, 1956 to July, 1965" (master's thesis, University of South Florida, 1985), 97, https://palmm.digital.flvc.org/islandora/object/usf%3A49370#page/title/mode/1up,111.

193   reapportionment on the: "Mix, Revision Bills Stir Legislative Pot," *Orlando Evening Star*, April 11, 1959, 2.

193   on April 13, 1959: FLIC Meeting Minutes for April 13, 1959, Clerk of the House Papers.

193   "files showing homosexual conduct": FLIC Meeting Minutes for April 13, 1959, Clerk of the House Papers.

193   passed unanimously: FLIC Meeting Minutes for April 13, 1959, Clerk of the House Papers.

193   "charges alleging misconduct": Journal of the Senate, April 17, 1959, 78.

193   Said bill, No. 237: Journal of the Senate, May 5, 1959. 373.

193   11:42 a.m. on April 29: Journal of the Senate, April 29, 1959, 280.

193   FLIC's written report: "Probers 'Appalled' by School Morals," *Miami Herald*, April 30, 1959, 14.

193   on lockdown and media barred: "Probers 'Appalled' by School Morals"; "Homosexual Activities Widespread," *Orlando Sentinel*, April 30, 1959, 17.

193   "Since February 1958, the Committee": "Report of the Florida Legislative Investigation Committee to the 1959 Session of the Legislature," 1959, #10-54–#10-55, Bonnie Stark Papers.

194   **"engaged in litigation":** "Report of the Florida Legislative Investigation Committee to the 1959 Session of the Legislature," 1959.

194   **"Homosexuality in Public Education":** "Report of the Florida Legislative Investigation Committee to the 1959 Session of the Legislature," 1959.

194   **"it has been, and still is, the prime":** "Report of the Florida Legislative Investigation Committee to the 1959 Session of the Legislature," 1959.

194   **"homosexual practices":** "Report of the Florida Legislative Investigation Committee to the 1959 Session of the Legislature," 1959.

194   **"salient facts":** "Report of the Florida Legislative Investigation Committee to the 1959 Session of the Legislature," 1959.

194   **"one public school teacher":** "Report of the Florida Legislative Investigation Committee to the 1959 Session of the Legislature," 1959.

194   **February 6, 1959:** Bill Donaldson, Transcript of Testimony, February 6, 1959, #4-12, Box 7, FLIC Papers.

194   **Charles Howard Montague:** "Sarasota Raid Breaks Sex Ring; Teacher Charged," *Tampa Tribune*, January 24, 1959, 1; "Morals Case Bonds Set," *Tampa Bay Times*, January 24, 1959, 8B.

194   **Montague had resigned:** "Sarasota Raid Breaks Sex Ring; Teacher Charged"; "Morals Case Bonds Set"; Andy Hopkins, SCR ID # 3-6A-2-12-1-1-1, June 30, 1961, Mississippi Papers.

194   **"abominable and detestable":** "Former Sarasota Teacher Gets 6 Months to 20 Years," *Tampa Tribune*, April 22, 1959, 3; George Painter, "Florida," Sodomy Laws, 1991, Gay & Lesbian Archives of the Pacific Northwest, https://www.glapn.org/sodomylaws/sensibilities/florida.htm.

194   **"prominent in this state":** "Report of the Florida Legislative Investigation Committee to the 1959 Session of the Legislature," 1959.

194   **"confirmed practicing homosexuals":** "Report of the Florida Legislative Investigation Committee to the 1959 Session of the Legislature," 1959.

195   **"homosexual acts in stride":** "Report of the Florida Legislative Investigation Committee to the 1959 Session of the Legislature," 1959.

195   **"appalling" example:** "Report of the Florida Legislative Investigation Committee to the 1959 Session of the Legislature," 1959; "Probers 'Appalled' by School Morals."

195   **conducted by former deputy:** Bill Donaldson, Transcript of Testimony, February 6, 1959.

195   **"pulled off":** "Report of the Florida Legislative Investigation Committee to the 1959 Session of the Legislature," 1959.

195   **"salient facts":** "Report of the Florida Legislative Investigation Committee to the 1959 Session of the Legislature," 1959; Bill Donaldson, Transcript of Testimony, February 6, 1959.

195   **"for a qualified investigator":** "Report of the Florida Legislative Investigation Committee to the 1959 Session of the Legislature," 1959.

195   **"a total of fifteen instructional":** "Report of the Florida Legislative Investigation Committee to the 1959 Session of the Legislature," 1959.

195   **At 1:05 p.m.:** Journal of the Senate, April 29, 1959, 280.

195   **alphabetical list:** Didier Graeffe, transcript of interview with Bonnie

Stark, December 1983; Sears, *Lonely Hunters*, 82; "The University Record of the University of Florida, 1958–1959," 8; "University of Florida Resignations," April 17, 1959, 6; Lawrence Wathen, Transcript of Testimony, January 5, 1959, Bonnie Stark Papers; Sigismond Diettrich, letter to Joe Curtain, April 8, 1959.

196   state intervention into private: Sears, *Lonely Hunters*, 82.
196   "This is the whole big thing": Sears, *Lonely Hunters*, 82.
196   copies of all: Sears, *Lonely Hunters*, 82.
196   "gross indecency": Sears, *Lonely Hunters*, 82.
196   hid in his house: Sears, *Lonely Hunters*, 82.
196   Army Reserves learned: Sears, *Lonely Hunters*, 83.
196   his 1954 Plymouth: Sears, *Lonely Hunters*, 83.
196   so-called loans: Sears, *Lonely Hunters*, 83.
196   "take a chance": Sears, *Lonely Hunters*, 83.
196   former UF department chair: Sears, *Lonely Hunters*, 83.
196   community college: Sears, *Lonely Hunters*, 83.
197   University of Houston: "Lawrence James Wathen," *Houston Chronicle*, June 15, 2003, https://www.legacy.com/us/obituaries/houstonchronicle/name/lawrence-wathen-obituary?id=28149122.
197   Don Steinbrecher: Seminole 1960 yearbook, University of Florida, 385.
197   James William Graves: Seminole 1959 yearbook, University of Florida; Seminole 1960 yearbook, University of Florida.
197   Trice also did not graduate: Seminole 1959 yearbook, University of Florida; Seminole 1960 yearbook, University of Florida, 359; Trice, interrogation by Strickland, November 4, 1958.
197   David Meuser: Seminole 1959 yearbook, University of Florida, 280; "Melbourne Teacher Named to State Group," *Cocoa Tribune*, October 5, 1961, evening edition, 1, 4.
197   social studies at a high school: "Melbourne Teacher Named to State Group."
197   "Americanism vs. Communism": "Melbourne Teacher Named to State Group"; Dan Brown, "Brevard to Lead State on Anti-Red Study," *Miami Herald*, October 12, 1961, Section B.
197   handsome, pompadoured: Jackie Reid, "Lecture Planned on Reds," *Orlando Evening Star*, February 2, 1962, 5.
197   at women's clubs: Reid, "Lecture Planned on Reds"; Brown, "Brevard to Lead State on Anti-Red Study."
197   second child: "Melbourne Teacher Named to State Group."
197   March 11, 1970: Florida Divorce Index, 1970, accessed via Ancestry.com, https://www.ancestry.com/search/collections/8837/records/1739004?tid=&pid=&queryId=ea8e4709-60fe-47ad-86e2-d517b381b3e7&_phsrc=Pmf1029&_phstart=successSource; "Sierra Leone Tradition," *Tallahassee Democrat*, August 2, 1970, 2C.
197   turned in waves: Fred Frohock, "Johns' Statement Irks UF Students," *Miami Herald*, May 10, 1959, 14E.
197   a "homo" bastion: "Readers Want More Information About Investigation

Firings," 4; "Reader Hits Johns' Professor Probe," *Florida Alligator*, April 27, 1959, 4; "Johns 'Appalled' by Homosexuality in States' Schools," *Florida Alligator*, May 1, 1959, 1.

198   **students hung an effigy:** "Unknown Students Hang Johns in Plaza Effigy," *Florida Alligator*, May 1, 1959, 1.

198   **"Charley Johns has":** "Johns Hung in Effigy on Florida U. Campus," *Tampa Tribune*, May 1, 1959, 7B.

198   **on May 6:** Jim McGuirk, "1,000 Students Riot in Raid on Coed Dorms," *Florida Alligator*, May, 1959, 1.

198   **37 to 1 vote:** Journal of the Senate, May 6, 1959, 398.

198   **dared to say no:** Journal of the Senate, May 6, 1959, 398.

198   **Tom Adams of the tax:** "Senate Votes to Close $32 Million Tax Loophole," *Tampa Tribune*, June 3, 1959, 9.

198   **"the brunt of rising emotions":** McGuirk, "1,000 Students Riot in Raid on Coed Dorms."

198   **"whites only":** David Finnerty, "Gator Dives of the Decades," University of Florida Advancement, accessed November 29, 2024, https://www.uff.ufl.edu/gatornation/gator-dives-of-the-decades/.

198   **"Panty raid!":** McGuirk, "1,000 Students Riot in Raid on Coed Dorms."

198   **"Panties, please!":** McGuirk, "1,000 Students Riot in Raid on Coed Dorms."

198   **"We want panties!":** McGuirk, "1,000 Students Riot in Raid on Coed Dorms."

199   **"A trail of blood":** McGuirk, "1,000 Students Riot in Raid on Coed Dorms."

199   **Covering the mob action:** "'Trial Unfair,' Says Expelled Panty Raider," *Tampa Bay Times*, May 11, 1959, 6; "Discipline Sought Against Five More U. Rioters," *Tampa Tribune*, May 15, 1959, 17.

199   **Art Copleston:** Art Copleston, interview with Robert Fieseler, February 1, 2025; Sarah Henry, "Mascot for Cruelty," *Atrium Magazine*, October 19, 2024, https://atriummag.org/mascot-for-cruelty/.

199   **bedlam from faraway:** Art Copleston, interview with Robert Fieseler, June 14, 2021.

199   **loaded up on six classes:** Arthur Sidney Copleston Jr., Unofficial Academic Transcript, Office of the University Registrar, University of Florida.

199   **got three A's:** Arthur Sidney Copleston Jr., Unofficial Academic Transcript.

199   **dorm counselor:** Art Copleston, interview with Robert Fieseler, November 11, 2019.

199   **Tileston still tailed him to:** Art Copleston, interview with Robert Fieseler, November 11, 2019; Art Copleston, email to Robert Fieseler, January 19, 2023.

200   **"self-policing":** Jim McGuirk, "UF Sanctioned Agents Uncover Homosexuals," *Florida Alligator*, February 19, 1960, 1; Stacy Braukman, *Communists and Perverts Under the Palms: The Johns Committee in Florida, 1956–1965* (University Press of Florida, 2012), 93.

200   **six more faculty members:** Karen L. Graves, *And They Were Wonderful Teachers: Florida's Purge of Gay and Lesbian Teachers* (University of Illinois Press, 2009), 6.

200   **Rita Mae Brown:** Rita Mae Brown, *Rita Will: Memoir of a Literary Rabble-Rouser* (Bantam Books, 1997), 181–85; Rita Mae Brown, *Rubyfruit Jungle* (Daughters, 1973).

CHAPTER 18. OPEN SEASON

203   **was first selected:** Panel 15, "Why Did NASA Choose Florida?" *The Moon, Stars, and Sunshine State* exhibit, 2019, Florida Historic Capitol Museum, courtesy of Tiffany Baker; Erwin Raisz, *Atlas of Florida* (University of Florida Press, 1964), 5.

203   **eminent domain:** "Video: Documentary Details Early Merritt Island History, NASA Development of Space Center," *Space Coast Daily*, July 14, 2016, https://spacecoastdaily.com/2016/07/video-documentary-details-early-merritt-island-history-nasa-development-of-space-center/.

203   **On February 6:** "Mighty U.S. Titan Missile Makes It Aloft on 3rd Try," *Tampa Tribune*, February 8, 1959, 1; Tony Long, "Feb. 6, 1959: Titan Launches; Cold War Heats Up," *Wired*, February 6, 2009, https://www.wired.com/2009/02/feb-6-1959-titan-launches-cold-war-heats-up-2/.

204   **of "moonlight and magnolias":** Kate Masur, "The South and the Nation 1840–1860," in *A New History of the American South*, ed. W. Fitzhugh Brundage (University of North Carolina Press, 2023), 231; "'S'wanee River' Voted Official Florida Melody," *Miami News*, May 22, 1935, 1.

204   **That June 1959:** Stacy Braukman, *Communists and Perverts Under the Palms: The Johns Committee in Florida, 1956–1965* (University Press of Florida, 2012), 103.

204   **June 22, 1959:** Bonnie Stark, "McCarthyism in Florida: Charley Johns and the Florida Legislative Investigation Committee July, 1956 to July, 1965" (master's thesis, University of South Florida, 1985), 97, https://palmm.digital.flvc.org/islandora/object/usf%3A49370#page/title/mode/1up, 65.

204   **By a vote of 6 to 3:** "Florida NAACP Denied Hearing," *Palm Beach Post*, June 23, 1959, 1; "U.S. Supreme Court Upholds NAACP Probe," *Orlando Sentinel*, June 23, 1959, 5.

204   **"I feel very good about":** "Supreme Court Tells NAACP It Must Testify," *Miami Herald*, June 25, 1959, 1.

204   **"I am not sure what":** Robert Carter, letter to plaintiffs, June 25, 1959, Florida NAACP Records 1959–1961, NAACP Papers, Library of Congress.

204   **"I expect they will be":** Ruth Perry, letter to Robert Carter, June 23, 1959, Florida NAACP Records 1959–1961, NAACP Papers, Library of Congress.

204   **teacher Earl Fender:** Earl Fender, Transcript of Testimony, January 7, 1959, #4-8, Box 7, FLIC Papers.

205   **"found guilty of committing":** Thomas Bailey, letter to Dear Sir, June 22, 1959, Box 13, DOE Papers, State Archives of Florida.

205   **"You are hereby notified"**: Thomas Bailey, letter to Dear Sir, June 22, 1959.

205   **came back undelivered**: J. T. Kelley, memo re: Raymond Bruce Capella to Thomas Bailey, June 15, 1959, Box 13, DOE Papers, State Archives of Florida; J. T. Kelley, memo re: Jack Vernon Priest to Thomas Bailey, June 15, 1959, Box 13, DOE Papers, State Archives of Florida.

205   **Montague Jr. already sat in prison**: J. T. Kelley, memo re: Charles Howard Montague Jr. to Thomas Bailey, June 15, 1959, Box 13, DOE Papers, State Archives of Florida; J. T. Kelley, memo re: Raymond Bruce Capella to Thomas Bailey, June 15, 1959.

205   **Lester Robinson McCartney**: J. T. Kelley, memo re: Lester Robinson McCartney to Thomas Bailey, June 15, 1959, Box 13, DOE Papers, State Archives of Florida; Lester Robinson McCartney, Transcript of Testimony, January 16, 1959, Box 7, FLIC Papers; Andy Hopkins, SCR ID # 3-6A-2-12-1-1-1, June 30, 1961, Mississippi Papers.

205   **"did not wish to appear"**: J. T. Kelley, memo re: Lester Robinson McCartney to Thomas Bailey, June 15, 1959.

206   **"Four Teachers Fired"**: "4 Teachers Fired by State Cabinet on Morals Charge," *Pensacola News Journal*, June 17, 1959, 5.

206   **"Cabinet Revokes Certificates"**: "Cabinet Revokes Certificates of Four Teachers," *Tampa Tribune*, June 17, 1959, 1.

206   **"found guilty"**: Thomas Bailey, letter to Dear Sir, June 22, 1959; J. T. Kelley, memo re: Lester Robinson McCartney to Thomas Bailey, June 15, 1959.

206   **"admitted under oath"**: J. T. Kelley, memo re: Lester Robinson McCartney to Thomas Bailey, June 15, 1959.

206   **"to weed out known homosexuals"**: Remus Strickland, memo to "All Superintendents of Public Instruction," August 1959, Box 3, FLIC Papers.

206   **"We are trying to set up"**: Remus Strickland, memo to "All Superintendents of Public Instruction," August 1959.

206   **June 24, 1959**: FLIC Meeting Minutes for June 24, 1959, Clerk of the House Papers.

207   **"big-city Pork Chopper"**: "Big City Pork-Chopper? Herrell Just Smiles," *Miami Herald*, November 28, 1962.

207   **"excellent manner in which"**: FLIC Meeting Minutes for June 24, 1959, Clerk of the House Papers.

207   **until late 1960**: FLIC Meeting Minutes for November 5, 1960, Clerk of the House Papers.

207   **"came through Hawes"**: Remus Strickland, transcript of interview with Bonnie Stark, April 1984, Bonnie Stark Papers.

207   **"this investigation is producing"**: Remus Strickland, letter to Cliff Herrell, December 15, 1959, #11-1674, Box 3, FLIC Papers.

207   **fourteen-mile-long bridge system**: "Tampa Bay Crossing Spans 14 Miles of Tidewater," *Popular Mechanics*, August 1954, 72–73.

207   **opened in 1954**: Wilton Martin, "$22 Million Sunshine Skyway Spans Beautiful Tampa Bay," *Tampa Times*, August 31, 1954, 17; "Van Fleet Sees No Atom War," *Tampa Tribune*, September 5, 1954, 8.

207   **some 630,000 Floridians**: Raisz, *Atlas of Florida*, 49.

207   **5,000 new educators:** "Teacher Shortage Problem Solved—Bailey," *Pensacola News Journal*, September 5, 1958, 18.

208   **Knotty Pine:** Judith Poucher, *State of Defiance: Challenging the Johns Committee's Assault on Civil Liberties* (University Press of Florida, 2014), 98.

208   **"headquarters":** Poucher, *State of Defiance*, 98; Chuck Hendrick, "13 Nabbed in Crackdown on Morals Offenders Here," *Tampa Tribune*, July 13, 1957, 2.

208   **"ill-famed":** Neal Brogdon, "Agents Say Closing of Bar Unwarranted," *Tampa Times*, August 16, 1960, 3; Poucher, *State of Defiance*, 100–101; Bob Turner, "Entertainers' Chief Promises Mayor Aid in B-Girl Control," *Tampa Times*, January 9, 1958, 3.

208   **"We never had it so":** "WE NEVER HAD IT SO GOOD!," *Tampa Bay Times*, November 4, 1959, 4C.

208   **"by precept and example":** Karen L. Graves, *And They Were Wonderful Teachers: Florida's Purge of Gay and Lesbian Teachers* (University of Illinois Press, 2009), 126; Thomas Bailey, "Proposed Teaching Guides on 'America's Moral and Spiritual Heritage,'" *Florida School Bulletin*, December 1955, 2.

208   **foiled investigation:** Bill Donaldson, Transcript of Testimony, February 6, 1959, #4-12, Box 7, FLIC Papers.

208   **"I consider myself determined":** Remus Strickland, transcript of interview with Bonnie Stark, April 1984.

209   **73 percent of Florida's:** Graves, *And They Were Wonderful Teachers*, 156.

209   **"The hardest that I found":** Bill Donaldson, Transcript of Testimony, February 6, 1959.

209   **October 6, 1959:** Evelyn, interrogation by Remus Strickland, October 6, 1959, #3-29, Box 7, FLIC Papers.

209   **"In making love":** Evelyn, interrogation by Strickland, October 6, 1959.

209   **Kathryn, a morally conscientious:** Braukman, *Communists and Perverts*, 109–11; Kathryn, interrogation by Remus Strickland, May 9, 1960, Box 8, FLIC Papers.

209   **Pat Wilson:** Pat Wilson, interrogation by Remus Strickland, September 4, 1960, #3-139, Box 8, FLIC Papers; Moroccan 1952 yearbook, University of Tampa; East Bay High School 1960 yearbook, 97.

210   **Margie DeGrow:** Margie DeGrow, interrogation by Remus Strickland, October 18, 1960, #1-16, Box 8, FLIC Papers; Sandra Young, "Tarpon High to Serve 'Sugar and Spice' Dec. 12," *Tampa Bay Times*, October 17, 1956, 21; Sandra Young, "Tarpon Springs High Sets Plans for Season," *Tampa Bay Times*, September 9, 1956, 5; Seminole yearbook 1953, University of Florida, 283.

210   **Florida Department of Education:** Graves, *And They Were Wonderful Teachers*, 83–85.

210   **statutory process:** Stark, "McCarthyism in Florida," 97.

210   **Senate Bill 237:** Graves, *And They Were Wonderful Teachers* , 83–85; "Brief of Petitioner," *Anne Louise Poston v. State Board of Education*, 2–7, Bonnie Stark Papers.

210   **probable cause:** "Brief of Petitioner," *Anne Louise Poston v. State Board of Education*, 3.

210 "gentleman's agreement": Stark, "McCarthyism in Florida," 114.

210 "pertaining to the activities": Stark, "McCarthyism in Florida," 114; "Brief of Petitioner," *Anne Louise Poston v. State Board of Education*, 12.

210 $700-per-month: FLIC Meeting Minutes for October 25, 1957, Clerk of the House Papers.

211 "to weed out": Remus Strickland, memo to "All Superintendents of Public Instruction," August 1959, Box 3, FLIC Papers.

211 accepted their marching orders: Braukman, *Communists and Perverts*, 131.

CHAPTER 19. PREDATOR/PREY

212 state lawyer: Art Copleston, interview with Robert Fieseler, October 28, 2019; John Rooney, affidavit re: Remus Strickland, June 13, 1960, Box 8, FLIC Papers.

212 Bill Livingston: Bill Livingston, interrogation by Remus Strickland, December 8, 1959, #2-153, Box 7, FLIC Papers; Peggy Lee and John Greene, "Tyrone JHS Band Drilling for Armistice Day Fete," *Tampa Bay Times*, October 30, 1955, 13C.

212 Glenn McRae: Glenn McRae, interrogation by Remus Strickland, December 7, 1959, #4-33, Box 7, FLIC Papers; Andy Hopkins, SCR ID # 3-6A-2-12-1-1-1, June 30, 1961, Mississippi Papers; St. Petersburg Junior College 1959 yearbook, 24, accessed via Ancestry.com.

213 swearing in McRae: McRae, interrogation by Strickland, December 7, 1959.

213 "You say that while": McRae, interrogation by Strickland, December 7, 1959.

213 "I furthermore intend": McRae, interrogation by Strickland, December 7, 1959.

213 "I mean, to me this violates": McRae, interrogation by Strickland, December 7, 1959.

213 "This naming of names": McRae, interrogation by Strickland, December 7, 1959.

214 "Mr. McRae, have you": McRae, interrogation by Strickland, December 7, 1959.

214 "When I expressed to you": McRae, interrogation by Strickland, December 7, 1959.

214 "admitted his participation": Remus Strickland, letter to Cliff Herrell, December 15, 1959, August 1959 Box 3, FLIC Papers; Andy Hopkins, SCR ID # 3-6A-2-12-1-1-1, June 30, 1961, Mississippi Papers.

214 LeRoy Kaufman: LeRoy Kaufman, interrogation by Remus Strickland, October 14, 1960, #2-165, Box 8, FLIC Papers; LeRoy Kaufman, "They Jeered Him and Fought Him, but His Genius Made Them Quake," *Tampa Bay Times*, March 4, 1961, 15A; LeRoy Kaufman, 1950 U.S. Census, Ancestry.com; LeRoy Louis Kaufman, World War II Draft Card, Ancestry.com; St. Petersburg High School 1955 yearbook, 11, 125.

215 "Mr. Kaufman, have you": Kaufman, interrogation by Strickland, October 14, 1960.

215 **"You made the statement"**: Kaufman, interrogation by Strickland, October 14, 1960.

215 **father of four kept his job**: St. Petersburg High School 1961 yearbook, 14; Andy Hopkins, SCR ID # 3-6A-2-12-1-1-1, June 30, 1961, Mississippi Papers.

215 **Ellis Vern Clack**: Andy Hopkins, SCR ID # 3-6A-2-12-1-1-1, June 30, 1961, Mississippi Papers; "School Head Selected for Florida Book," *Orlando Sentinel*, August 29, 1957, 24; "School Principal Ousted, Arrested on Fondling Charge," *Tampa Tribune*, August 11, 1959, 3.

215 **Boy Scout leader**: Edith E. Voss, "Indian War Cry Will Be Added to Rocket Roar," *Miami Herald*, August 4, 1959, 2B.

215 **tried to skip town**: Voss, "Indian War Cry Will Be Added to Rocket Roar."

215 **"live quietly"**: Voss, "Indian War Cry Will Be Added to Rocket Roar."

215 **caught Ellis Vern Clack**: "Former Principal Arrested," *Orlando Evening Star*, August 10, 1959, 24; "Ex-Principal Arrested in Brevard," *Miami Herald*, August 11, 1959, Section B.

216 **August 6, 1959**: Ellis Vern Clack, interrogation by Remus Strickland, August 9, 1959, #2-21, Box 7, FLIC Papers; Karl Hunziker, "Two Morals Cases Due on Docket," *Orlando Sentinel*, August 12, 1959, evening edition, 1.

216 **Earl Fender**: Clack, interrogation by Strickland, August 9, 1959; "Island Kiwanians Will Man Service Station Wednesday," *Cocoa Tribune*, March 31, 1958, evening edition, 5; FLIC Meeting Minutes for April 13, 1959, Clerk of the House Papers.

216 **"You then state your conduct"**: Clack, interrogation by Strickland, August 9, 1959.

216 **being "influenced into homosexual practices"**: "Report of the Florida Legislative Investigation Committee to the 1959 Session of the Legislature," 1959.

217 **"Mr. Clack, did it ever occur"**: Clack, interrogation by Strickland, August 9, 1959.

218 **teaching credentials case referred**: Andy Hopkins, SCR ID # 3-6A-2-12-1-1-1, June 30, 1961, Mississippi Papers; Hunziker, "Two Morals Cases Due on Docket."

218 **Lester Robinson McCartney**: "4 Teachers Fired by State Cabinet on Morals Charge," *Pensacola News Journal*, June 17, 1959, 5.

218 **Clack died as a free man**: "Ellis Vern Clack," *Clarion-Ledger*, September 12, 1965, 11A.

218 **"a former school teacher"**: "Ellis Vern Clack," *Clarion-Ledger*.

218 **burial with full military**: "Ellis Vern Clack," Findagrave.com, https://www.findagrave.com/memorial/125517510/ellis-vern-clack.

218 **"voluntarily" integrate**: "Civil Rights Planks Hike Integration Activities," *Miami Herald*, August 14, 1960, 18-B; Henrik J. Berns, "Dade Board Makes Historic Decision," *Miami News*, February 22, 1959, 18.

218 **That September 8**: "Orchard Villa Expects White, Negro Pupils," *Tampa Bay Times*, September 5, 1959, 12A; Gene Plowden, "Miami School

Integrated," *Tallahassee Democrat*, September 8, 1959, 1, 5; "12 New
White Pupils Enter Orchard Villa," *Tampa Bay Times*, September 10, 1959,
16A.

218   Jan and Irene Glover: "Mother Escorts Her Two Daughters to Orchard Villa
School," Florida Memory, September 8, 1959, https://www.floridamemory
.com/items/show/4534; John N. Popham, "9 Negroes Attend School in
Clinton," *New York Times*, September 5, 1956, 1, 12; George Barrett,
"Clinton Blocks Rally by Kasper," *New York Times*, September 10,
1956, 16; "Troops in Little Rock," *New York Times*, September 25,
1957, 28.

218   "I can't see anything": "Collins Has No Comment," *Tallahassee Democrat*,
September 8, 1959, 1.

218   "This school board is operating": "'Peaceful Atmosphere,'" *Tallahassee
Democrat*, September 8, 1959, 6.

219   "not want to make": "Miami School Integrated," *Tallahassee Democrat*,
September 8, 1959.

219   Hockett arrived at Orchard: Gene Plowden, "Miami School Integrated,"
Tallahassee Democrat, September 8, 1959, 1.

219   Hockett was forced to stand: "4 Negroes, 8 Whites Integrate Dade School,"
Tampa Tribune, September 9, 1959, 9.

219   187,742 "Negro" schoolchildren: "School Desegregation in the Southern and
Border States, May 1959 Statistics," Southern Education Reporting Service,
May 1959, 10, accessed through South Carolina Digital Library, https://
cdm16821.contentdm.oclc.org/digital/collection/p16821coll22/id/1360
/rec/1.

219   eleven Black students were formally denied: John Gardner, "11 Negroes
Denied Transfer to New Dixie Hollins High," *Tampa Bay Times*, September
10, 1959, B1.

CHAPTER 20. KING OF FLORIDA

220   expanded his probe: Assorted interrogations by Remus Strickland reviewed
and collated by Robert Fieseler, 1959–1962, Boxes 2, 3, 7, 8, 9, FLIC Papers;
assorted interrogations by Remus Strickland reviewed and collated by Robert
Fieseler, 1960–1963, Bonnie Stark Papers.

220   "Leaving the office": Karen L. Graves, *And They Were Wonderful Teachers:
Florida's Purge of Gay and Lesbian Teachers* (University of Illinois Press,
2009), 39; Remus Strickland, letter to Cliff Herrell, September 12, 1960, Box
3, FLIC Papers.

220   "Personally, and confidentially": Charley Johns, letter to W. Turner Davis,
December 8, 1961, Box 2, FLIC Papers.

221   a staff of twelve: Remus Strickland, transcript of interview with Bonnie
Stark, April 1984, Bonnie Stark Papers.

221   Frank S. Wright: Frank S. Wright, interrogation by Remus Strickland,
October 28–29, 1959, #8-45, Box 1, FLIC Papers; "Frank Wright Back on
State Payroll," *Bradenton Herald*, December 30, 1952, 1; "Education Talks
Off," *Tampa Bay Times*, November 30, 1960, 13.

221   **for two days:** Wright, interrogation by Strickland, October 28–29, 1959.
221   **February 3, 1960:** John B. Rooney, affidavit re: Remus Strickland, June 13, 1960, Box 8, FLIC Papers; John B. Rooney, interrogation by Remus Strickland, February 3, 1960, #1-118, Box 7, FLIC Papers.
221   **in front of his elementary school:** Rooney, affidavit re: Strickland, June 13, 1960; Rooney, interrogation by Strickland, February 3, 1960.
221   **"to submit to being handcuffed":** Rooney, affidavit re: Strickland, June 13, 1960; Rooney, interrogation by Strickland, February 3, 1960.
221   **his 3.5-hour deposition:** Rooney, affidavit re: Strickland, June 13, 1960; Rooney, interrogation by Strickland, February 3, 1960.
221   **brother-in-law to Florida senator:** Graves, *And They Were Wonderful Teachers*, 38; Wilbur Whitehurst, letter to Thomas Bailey, June 22, 1960, Box 3, Florida DOE Papers, State Archives of Florida; "3 New State Senators Elected; 4 in House Reelected, 4 Defeated," *Tampa Tribune*, May 26, 1960, B1.
221   **"This young man's father":** Whitehurst, letter to Bailey, June 22, 1960.
222   **"The procedure for the":** Whitehurst, letter to Bailey, June 22, 1960.
222   **"Mr. R. J. Strickland is not":** Thomas Bailey, letter to Wilbur Whitehurst, June 29, 1960, Box 13, FLIC Papers.
222   **Threatening perjury charges:** Remus Strickland, letter to Whitehurst, July 5, 1960, #11-1692 Box 3, Florida DOE Papers, State Archives of Florida.
222   **"I am sure that Mr. Hawes":** Strickland, letter to Whitehurst, July 5, 1960.
222   **a second letter:** Remus Strickland, letter to Cliff Herrell, July 5, 1960, #11-563, Box 3, Florida DOE Papers, State Archives of Florida.
222   **did not terminate:** Andy Hopkins, SCR ID # 3-6A-2-12-1-1-1, June 30, 1961, Mississippi Papers.
223   **thirty-six high school members:** "Sitdowns Hit 3 Florida Cities," *Miami Herald*, March 6, 1960, 2A; Howard A. Stewart and Duane Bradford, "Negroes Sit Down in 9 Places Here; One Fight; 2 Jailed," *Tampa Tribune*, March 2, 1960, 1.
223   **On March 12:** "Two NAACP Leaders Again Refuse to Answer Probers," *Tampa Tribune*, July 28, 1960, 4B; Lane Carter, "CORE Reported Behind Race Row," *Birmingham News*, March 29, 1961, 1; "Report of the Florida Legislative Investigation Committee to the 1961 Session of the Legislature," 1961, 10–13, #10-58, Bonnie Stark Papers; Martin Waldron, "Racial Agitation in Florida Partially 'Red-Inspired,' Says Legislative Committee," *Tampa Tribune*, February 10, 1961, 1, 3.
223   **three white Floridians:** "Revolving Fund for Florida Legislative Investigation Committee—1959–61," Clerk of the House Papers.
223   **citizen snoops:** "Racist Accused of Using Negro as Tool of Reds," *News-Press*, February 10, 1961, 1; Waldron, "Racial Agitation in Florida Partially 'Red-Inspired,' Says Legislative Committee," 1.
223   **"TO WHOM IT MAY":** Remus Strickland, form letter to "To Whom It May Concern," January 19, 1962, Box 2, FLIC Papers.
223   **$25 in compensation:** "Revolving Fund for Florida Legislative Investigation Committee—1959–61."

223   **"secure justice":** "Report of the Florida Legislative Investigation Committee to the 1961 Session of the Legislature," 1961.

223   **mailing list:** Waldron, "Racial Agitation in Florida Partially 'Red-Inspired,' Says Legislative Committee," 3.

223   **Fannie Collins:** Waldron, "Racial Agitation in Florida Partially 'Red-Inspired,' Says Legislative Committee," 1, 3.

223   **"card-carrying":** Bonnie Stark, "McCarthyism in Florida: Charley Johns and the Florida Legislative Investigation Committee July, 1956 to July, 1965" (master's thesis, University of South Florida, 1985), 97, https://palmm.digital .flvc.org/islandora/object/usf%3A49370#page/title/mode/1up, 77–78.

223   **"closely allied":** "Solon Charges Commies Duped Negro Leaders," *Alabama Tribune*, August 1, 1958, 8.

223   **plan to subpoena:** FLIC Meeting Minutes for November 5, 1960, Clerk of the House Papers; Stark, "McCarthyism in Florida," 70; "Integrationist Called for Quiz by NAACP Probers," *Tampa Tribune*, January 27, 1961, 10C.

224   **March 20, 1960:** LeRoy Collins, "Transcript of Statewide TV-Radio Talk to the People of Florida on Race Relations," March 20, 1960, University of North Florida Archives, https://digitalcommons.unf.edu/cgi/viewcontent.cgi ?article=1033&context=eartha_materials; Stacy Braukman, *Communists and Perverts Under the Palms: The Johns Committee in Florida, 1956–1965* (University Press of Florida, 2012), 117–18; Glenda Alice Rabby, *The Pain and the Promise: The Struggle for Civil Rights in Tallahassee, Florida* (University of Georgia Press, 1999), 107–8; "Counters Barring Negroes 'Unfair,' Collins Declares," *Tampa Tribune*, March 21, 1960, 1.

224   **"I believe very deeply":** Collins, "Transcript of Statewide TV-Radio Talk to the People of Florida on Race Relations."

224   **"I believe that the face":** Collins, "Transcript of Statewide TV-Radio Talk to the People of Florida on Race Relations."

224   **the first southern governor:** Martin Dyckman, "LeRoy Collins, Trent Lott: A Study in Contrasts," *St. Petersburg Times*, December 22, 2002, accessed via WaybackMachine, https://web.archive.org/web /20030218063543/https://www.sptimes.com/2002/12/22/Columns /LeRoy_Collins__Trent_.shtml.

224   **"Friends, we must find answers":** Collins, "Transcript of Statewide TV-Radio Talk to the People of Florida on Race Relations."

224   **"Let Negroes Eat":** John L. Boyles, "Let Negroes Eat in Stores Where They Trade—Collins," *Miami Herald*, March 21, 1960, 1.

225   **state a laughingstock:** "Collins Target in Florida," *New York Times*, March 27, 1960, 74.

225   **"one of the greatest statesmen":** Erwin Potts, "Collins Cheered—and Jeered," *Miami Herald*, March 21, 1960, 1.

225   **"Word is out that Charley":** John L. Boyles, "He's Running for an Office He Would Abolish," *Miami Herald*, March 28, 1960, 10F; "Voters Flock to Rallies," *Bradford County Telegraph*, April 7, 1960, 1.

225   **lengthy rallies:** "Senator Shocked by Accusations," *Bradford County Telegraph*, April 14, 1960, 1; "Johns, Patten, Kelly, Thomas, Score Heavy Vote to Win," *Bradford County Telegraph*, May 5, 1960, 1.

225   **Newman Brackin:** "Pork Choppers Keep Hold," *Orlando Sentinel*, May 5, 1960, evening edition, 1B; "Sikes, Bracken Rage at Russell Slight," *Pensacola News Journal*, May 18, 1952, 4.

225   **chairman of the 1960 Democratic:** "Collins Named Chairman of Convention," *Orlando Sentinel*, May 25, 1960, 1.

225   **possible nominee:** "Collins Named Chairman of Convention."

225   **Farris Bryant, squeaked:** "Victorious Bryant Pledges No New Taxes for Florida," *Tampa Times*, May 25, 1960, 1.

225   **"turn back the clock":** Charles Van Devaner, "Gov. Collins' Support Welcomed by Carlton," *Tampa Bay Times*, May 21, 1960, 1; "Florida Can Go Forward with Bryant," *News-Press*, May 26, 1960, 4.

226   **future positions:** "New Rights Agency Aims at Fairness," *Vancouver Sun*, July 4, 1964, 15; Lee Brandy, "Johnson Entertains Governors," *The State*, September 14, 1967, 3B.

226   **In June 1960:** Remus Strickland, "Memorandum, Subject: Marion Jennings Rice," July 6, 1960, #11-911, Box 1, FLIC Papers; "Hatcher Ousted; Barron Is Named," *Tallahassee Democrat*, May 26, 1960, 2.

226   **Marion Jennings Rice:** "Marion Rice," *Athens Banner-Herald*, March 17, 2015, https://www.legacy.com/us/obituaries/onlineathens/name/marion-rice-obituary?id=44276238.

226   **"could not be answered":** Strickland, "Memorandum, Subject: Marion Jennings Rice," July 6, 1960.

226   **"Since I had been so helpful":** Strickland, "Memorandum, Subject: Marion Jennings Rice," July 6, 1960.

226   **"In the last several":** Earl Cochran, letter to Charley Johns, December 1, 1961, #11-1447, Box 2, FLIC Papers.

227   **October 11, 1960:** Paul Stephen Houk, interrogation by Remus Strickland, October 11, 1960, #3-24, Box 8, FLIC Papers; "JP Court," *Tampa Bay Times*, September 24, 1960, 2B; Andy Hopkins, SCR ID # 3-6A-2-12-1-1-1, June 30, 1961, Mississippi Papers.

227   **"contributing to the":** "JP Court."

227   **"Mr. Houk, previously":** Houk, interrogation by Strickland, October 11, 1960.

227   **"I am therefore asking that you submit":** Remus Strickland, letter to [Unknown], October 10, 1960, #11-116, Bonnie Stark Papers.

228   **"I can't tell you my purpose":** Jack Alexander, "State Prober Checks School Homosexuality," *Tampa Bay Times*, March 18, 1960, 12.

228   **"Due to the recent":** Alexander, "State Prober Checks School Homosexuality."

228   **state senate campaign:** "Central Florida to Gain in Congressional Seats," *Orlando Sentinel*, June 19, 1960, 7.

228   **"As an investigator, he got out of hand"**: Cliff Herrell, interview with Bonnie Stark, August 3, 1993, Bonnie Stark Papers.

228   **"He got overzealous"**: Cliff Herrell, interview with Bonnie Stark, August 3, 1993.

CHAPTER 21. RADICAL STEPS

229   **Roy Wilkins viewed Black homosexuals**: Walter Naegle, interview with Robert Fieseler, March 14, 2023.

229   **"We recruited a small group"**: James Farmer, transcribed interview for PBS documentary *Eyes on the Prize*, American Archive of Public Broadcasting (GBH and the Library of Congress), November 1, 1985, http:// americanarchive.org/catalog/cpb-aacip-151-4b2x34nb4p.

230   **Black gay men**: John D'Emilio, "Remembering Bayard Rustin," *OAH Magazine of History* 20, no. 2 (March 1, 2006): 12–14, https://doi.org /10.1093/maghis/20.2.12; Eric Pace, "Bayard Rustin Is Dead at 75," *New York Times*, August 25, 1987, B8.

230   **former high school football**: "Rights March Chief Has Police Record," *Miami Herald*, August 15, 1963, 77.

230   **Quaker**: David Hardiman, *Gandhi in His Time and Ours: The Global Legacy of His Ideas* (Columbia University Press, 2003), 256; Junius Griffin, "He'll Lead March on Capital," *Miami News*, August 8, 1963, 9A; "How a Negro Wins Justice," *Des Moines Register*, November 4, 1942, 11.

230   **protest segregation**: D'Emilio, "Remembering Bayard Rustin"; Hardiman, *Gandhi in His Time and Ours*, 256; "Three-Day Conference Hits Discrimination," *Michigan Chronicle*, February 19, 1944, 3.

230   **famously "strained"**: John D'Emilio, *Lost Prophet* (Free Press, 2003), 62.

230   **a "morals charge"**: "Morals Charge Jails Booster of World Peace," *Chicago Tribune*, January 22, 1953, 2.

230   **served a sixty-day sentence**: "Lecturer Jailed on Morals Charge," *Arizona Daily Sun*, January 30, 1953, 2.

230   **"J. Edgar Hoover would periodically"**: Walter Naegle, interview with Robert Fieseler, March 14, 2023.

230   **knew not to acknowledge**: Walter Naegle, interview with Robert Fieseler, March 14, 2023.

230   **expelling him**: D'Emilio, "Remembering Bayard Rustin"; Taylor Branch, *Parting the Waters: America in the King Years, 1954–63* (Touchstone, 1988), 265.

230   **"set back the whole cause"**: Eric Cervini, *The Deviant's War: The Homosexual vs. the United States of America* (Farrar, Straus and Giroux, 2020), 157.

230   **"Socrates of the Civil"**: Jervis Anderson, *Bayard Rustin: Troubles I've Seen* (HarperCollins, 1997), 17–18.

231   **"mister" or "sir"**: David Meuser, interrogation by Remus Strickland, October 1, 1958, Box 6, FLIC Papers; Earl Fender, interrogation by Remus Strickland, December 5, 1958, #3-150, Box 6, FLIC Papers.

231   first name or their last name: Thomas Franklin Pinson, interrogation by Remus Strickland, October 13, 1960, #1-79, Box 8, FLIC Papers; William James Neal, interrogation by Remus Strickland, October 13, 1960, #1-95, Box 8, FLIC Papers.

231   October 13, 1960: Pinson, interrogation by Strickland, October 13, 1960.

231   Thomas Franklin Pinson: "Gibbs JC Getting Set for Opening," *Tampa Bay Times*, August 24, 1958, 19.

231   "restless": Pinson, interrogation by Strickland, October 13, 1960.

231   former Fulbright scholar: "Gibbs JC Getting Set for Opening."

231   "You were accused of": Pinson, interrogation by Strickland, October 13, 1960.

232   "cruising": Pinson, interrogation by Strickland, October 13, 1960.

232   two white police officers: Detective White, deposition with Remus Strickland, October 13, 1960, #1-78, Box 8, FLIC Papers.

232   Theo Edmondson: White, deposition with Strickland, October 13, 1960.

233   "Should Pinson decide to": Pinson, interrogation by Strickland, October 13, 1960.

233   "answer truthfully": Pinson, interrogation by Strickland, October 13, 1960.

233   "passive": Pinson, interrogation by Strickland, October 13, 1960.

233   revoked Pinson's teaching certificate: Andy Hopkins, SCR ID # 3-6A-2-12-1-1-1, June 30, 1961, Mississippi Papers.

233   William James Neal: Neal, interrogation by Strickland, October 13, 1960.

233   tall, svelte concert pianist: William James Neal, World War II Draft Card, Ancestry.com; "Talented Trio to Appear Here," *Tampa Bay Times*, March 19, 1958; "9 Instructors Are Listed for Gibbs Junior College," *Tampa Bay Times*, August 18, 1957, 22.

233   called Willie: Willie James Neal, 1930 U.S. Census; Willie James Neal, 1940 U.S. Census.

233   As the oldest of four siblings: Willie James Neal, 1930 U.S. Census; Willie James Neal, 1940 U.S. Census; William James Neal, 1950 U.S. Census.

234   to lead the music department: "Capacity Crowd at Negro Festival Donates $862.86," *Tampa Bay Times*, March 2, 1950, 1.

234   Bethune-Cookman College: "Local Students Play in College Pageant," *Tampa Bay Times*, December 13, 1953, 10C.

234   twenty-four months of active duty: Neal, interrogation by Strickland, October 13, 1960; William James Neal, "Report of Separation from the Armed Forces of the United States," October 1952, U.S. Army Records, acquired via FOIA request.

234   relocated to New York: "9 Instructors Are Listed for Gibbs Junior College"; Mamie Doyle Davis, "Pinellas Teachers Are Members of East's Better Degree Brigade," *Tampa Bay Times*, August 5, 1955, 27; "Personal Notes," *Tampa Bay Times*, June 21, 1950, 34.

234   toured North America: "Talented Trio to Appear Here."

234 weekly AM radio hour: "Gibbs Junior College Choir Making 2-Day, 3-City Tour," *Tampa Bay Times*, April 12, 1959, 195; "Station WTMP 1150 on Your Dial Proudly Presents the Gibbs Junior College Choir, Every Sunday at 3 p.m.," *Tampa Bay Times*, April 12, 1959, 195.

234 "grades seven through 12": "Registration Opens at Gibbs," *Tampa Bay Times*, July 15, 1958, 12.

234 tape-recorded just thirty minutes: Neal, interrogation by Strickland, October 13, 1960; "Brief of Petitioner," *Neal vs. Bryant*, 1961, 7–8, Bonnie Stark Papers.

234 "You're an educated Nigra": Neal, interrogation by Strickland, October 13, 1960.

235 "Have you ever participated": Neal, interrogation by Strickland, October 13, 1960.

235 "belligerent, condescending": David Barstow, "St. Petersburg Teacher Found Himself Target," *Tampa Bay Times*, July 2, 1993, 6A.

235 "If this Committee holds": Neal, interrogation by Strickland, October 13, 1960.

235 asked to pause: Neal, interrogation by Strickland, October 13, 1960.

235 "He told me he had proof": Barstow, "St. Petersburg Teacher Found Himself Target."

235 "Petitioner saw after three hours": "Brief of Petitioner," *Neal v. Bryant*, 1961, 7–8.

236 "William, I have given you": Neal, interrogation by Strickland, October 13, 1960.

236 teaching summer classes: "Registration Opens at Gibbs," *Tampa Bay Times*, July 15, 1958, 12.

236 smoke-filled, closed-door: "Brief of Petitioner," *Neal v. Bryant*, 1961, 7–8.

236 Neal was summarily suspended: Floyd T. Christian, letter to J. T. Kelly, March 21, 1963, Box 13, Florida DOE Papers, State Archives of Florida.

236 Mary Frances Bradshaw: Mary Francis Bradshaw, interrogation by Remus Strickland, October 19, 1960, #1-136, Bonnie Stark Papers; Anne Louise Poston, interrogation by Remus Strickland, October 18, 1960, #2-116, Box 8, FLIC Papers.

237 for two hours: "Brief of Petitioner," *Mary Francis Bradshaw v. Florida Board of Education*, 1961, 16–17, 23–27, Bonnie Stark Papers; "Hearing Held Before Hearings Officer . . . on January 24, 1961, beginning at the hour of 5:25 p.m.," *Mary Francis Bradshaw v. Florida Board of Education*, 1961, Bonnie Stark Papers.

237 "I asked the question": Bradshaw, interrogation by Strickland, October 19, 1960.

237 deposition tape turned off: "Brief of Petitioner," *Mary Francis Bradshaw v. Florida Board of Education*, 1961.

237 "I have asked Mr. Strickland": Bradshaw, interrogation by Strickland, October 19, 1960.

237 "approximately 40 minutes": "Hearing Held Before Hearings Officer . . . on January 24, 1961, beginning at the hour of 5:25 p.m.," *Mary Francis Bradshaw v. Florida Board of Education*, 1961.

238   "various degrees": Bradshaw, interrogation by Strickland, October 19, 1960; Floyd T. Christian, letter to J. T. Kelly, March 21, 1963.

238   Anne Louise Poston: Poston, interrogation by Strickland, October 18, 1960.

238   three hours of deposition: "Brief of Petitioner," *Anne Louise Poston v. Florida Board of Education*, 1961, 18–20, 23–30, Bonnie Stark Papers.

238   receiving a job promotion: "Brief of Petitioner," *Anne Louise Poston v. Florida Board of Education*, 1961, 18–20, 23–30.

238   of child molestation: "Brief of Petitioner," *Anne Louise Poston v. Florida Board of Education*, 1961, 18–20, 23–30.

238   about homosexual conduct: Poston, interrogation by Strickland, October 18, 1960.

238   "You had begun to try": Poston, interrogation by Strickland, October 18, 1960.

238   *caressing*: Poston, interrogation by Strickland, October 18, 1960; "Brief of Petitioner," *Anne Louise Poston v. Florida Board of Education*, 1961; Elinor Newman, interrogation by Remus Strickland, October 5, 1960, Bonnie Stark Papers.

238   "Miss Poston, in your acts": Poston, interrogation by Strickland, October 18, 1960.

239   Poston denied engaging: "Brief of Petitioner," *Anne Louise Poston v. Florida Board of Education*, 1961.

239   "Are you able to state": "Brief of Petitioner," *Anne Louise Poston v. Florida Board of Education*, 1961.

239   decline to submit the FLIC transcript: "Brief of Petitioner," *Anne Louise Poston v. Florida Board of Education*, 1961.

239   "I was in there with Mr. Strickland": "Brief of Petitioner," *Anne Louise Poston v. Florida Board of Education*, 1961.

240   the district suspended them: Floyd T. Christian, letter to J. T. Kelly, March 21, 1963.

240   "These teachers have, of course": Floyd T. Christian, letter to J. T. Kelly, December 6, 1960, Box 13, Florida DOE Papers, State Archives of Florida.

CHAPTER 22. BACKLASH

241   "We are going to continue the hearings": "NAACP Officials to Testify Today," *Miami Herald*, November 4, 1959, 23.

241   Somehow over the: Bonnie Stark, "McCarthyism in Florida: Charley Johns and the Florida Legislative Investigation Committee July, 1956 to July, 1965" (master's thesis, University of South Florida, 1985), 97, https://palmm.digital.flvc.org/islandora/object/usf%3A49370#page/title/mode/1up, 73–75.

242   August 30, 1960: "Two Miami NEEACP Leaders Given 6 Month Jail Terms," *Miami Herald*, August 31, 1960, Section C1; Stacy Braukman, *Communists and Perverts Under the Palms: The Johns Committee in Florida, 1956–1965* (University Press of Florida, 2012), 108.

242   "When the time comes that": "Two Miami NEEACP Leaders Given 6 Month Jail Terms."

242 **the NAACP appealed:** Stark, "McCarthyism in Florida," 74; Robert L. Carter, memorandum to Roy Wilkins, August 31, 1960, Gibson Case in Florida file, NAACP Papers, Library of Congress.

242 **unanimously upheld Gibson's:** Stark, "McCarthyism in Florida," 74; "High Court Backs Jailing of Gibson; Graham Goes Free," *Miami News*, December 20, 1960, 8A.

242 **"right to assemble and to speak freely":** "NAACP Jail Term Tossed Out," *Miami Herald*, December 21, 1960, 9.

242 **appealed to the U.S. Supreme Court:** Stark, "McCarthyism in Florida," 75–76.

242 **"God's angry child":** Congressional Record: Proceedings and Debates of the 89th Congress, First Session, July 8, 1965; "Father Gibson Wins Stay of Florida Jail Sentence Pending High Court Appeal," News from NAACP press release, January 19, 1961, Gibson Case in Florida file, NAACP Papers, Library of Congress; "High Court to Hear Case of Miami NAACP President," News from NAACP press release, May 13, 1961, Gibson Case in Florida file, NAACP Papers, Library of Congress.

242 **1961 legislative session:** Journal of the Florida Senate, April 4, 1961; "Supreme Court's Actions," *New York Times*, November 22, 1960, 29; "Supreme Court's Actions," *New York Times*, May 2, 1961, 28.

242 **"They have been trying":** Charles Hesser, "Quit Hunting Red Herrings, Liberties Group Asks," *Miami News*, February 15, 1961, C1; "Civil Liberties Union Would End Legislative Probe Committee," *Tampa Tribune*, February 16, 1961, 9.

243 **unanimously passed a bill:** "Confederate Flag Dignity Bill Okayed by Group," *Tampa Tribune*, April 27, 1961, 18; Journal of the Senate, April 25, 1961, 540.

243 **"Ridiculous":** "NAACP Hits Legislation for Flag of Confederacy," *Tampa Tribune*, May 13, 1961, 18.

243 **Florida senate extended FLIC:** Journal of the Senate, May 11, 1961, 1123; "Top Court to Hear Case of NAACP-Contempt," *Salt Lake Tribune*, May 9, 1961, 2.

243 **"organizations and individuals advocating violence":** Journal of the Senate, May 11, 1961, 1123.

243 **an additional $75,000:** Jack Nease, "Legislative Group Calls Florida Schools 'Refuge for Homosexuals,'" *Tampa Tribune*, May 26, 1961, 2B; Journal of the Senate, May 11, 1961, 1123; Journal of the Senate, June 2, 1961, 2250.

243 **the first time a Florida:** "$100-a-Night 'Call Boy' Racket Bared in Miami," *Orlando Sentinel*, May 26, 1961, 1B.

243 **mandatory report:** Nease, "Legislative Group Calls Florida Schools 'Refuge for Homosexuals'"; "'Call Boy' Ring, Baby-Sale Racket Uncovered in State," *Miami Herald*, May 26, 1961, 14C.

243 **noting the peril of the *Gibson*:** "Report of the Florida Legislative Investigation Committee to the 1961 Session of the Legislature," 1961.

243 **120 Florida citizens:** "Report of the Florida Legislative Investigation Committee to the 1961 Session of the Legislature," 1961.

243   "The Committee makes": "Report of the Florida Legislative Investigation
       Committee to the 1961 Session of the Legislature," 1961.

244   "Since July 1, 1959, a": "Report of the Florida Legislative Investigation
       Committee to the 1961 Session of the Legislature," 1961.

244   "salient facts": "Report of the Florida Legislative Investigation Committee to
       the 1961 Session of the Legislature," 1961.

244   "properly trained": "Report of the Florida Legislative Investigation
       Committee to the 1961 Session of the Legislature," 1961.

245   "We have for years been hearing": "Tallahassee," *One* 9, no. 7 (July 1961):
       18–19; Karen L. Graves, *And They Were Wonderful Teachers: Florida's
       Purge of Gay and Lesbian Teachers* (University of Illinois Press, 2009),
       166n179.

245   Bryant relayed the 1961 report: J. Edgar Hoover, memorandum to Florida
       offices, August 28, 1961, FBI Records, accessed via FOIA request; SAC
       Jacksonville to J. Edgar Hoover, September 7, 1961, FBI Records.

245   "Immediate and preferred": SAC Miami, airmail to J. Edgar Hoover,
       September 15, 1961, FBI Records.

245   appeared to be flattered: SAC Jacksonville, airmail to J. Edgar Hoover,
       September 1, 1961, FBI Records.

245   as "having questionable associates": SAC Jacksonville, airmail to Hoover,
       September 1, 1961.

245   "any obscene matter": SAC Jacksonville, airmail to Hoover, September 9,
       1961, FBI Records.

245   When reached by phone: SAC Jacksonville, airmail to Hoover, September 9,
       1961.

245   "a display": SAC Jacksonville, airmail to Hoover, September 1, 1961; SAC
       Jacksonville, airmail to Hoover, September 9, 1961.

245   "he is acquainted with": SAC Tampa, airmail to SAC Jacksonville, September
       16, 1961, FBI Records.

246   speedily debunked by agents: F. J. Baumgardner, memorandum to W. C.
       Sullivan, August 24, 1961, FBI Records.

246   "Strickland has done nothing": SAC Jacksonville, airmail to J. Edgar Hoover,
       September 13, 1961, FBI Records.

246   "salient facts" about a homosexual: "Report of the Florida Legislative
       Investigation Committee to the 1961 Session of the Legislature," 1961.

246   "There is no such": SAC Miami, airmail to J. Edgar Hoover, September 22,
       1961, FBI Records.

246   "known asset": J. Edgar Hoover, airmail to SAC Newark, October 9, 1961,
       FBI Records.

246   "The fact that": Hoover, airmail to SAC Newark, October 9, 1961.

246   The FBI rebuked FLIC: W. B. Welte, memorandum to Mr. Rosen, November
       2, 1961, FBI Records.

246   "The Committee might": SAC Tampa, airmail to SAC Jacksonville,
       September 15, 1961; SAC Miami, memorandum, October 31, 1961, FBI
       Records.

247   Atlanta, Georgia, in June 1961: H. A. Poole, SCR ID # 1-8-0-16-1-1-1,
       Mississippi Papers.

247 state in the Deep South: H. A. Poole, SCR ID # 3-6A-2-22-1-1-1, Mississippi Papers.

247 "excellent work": Andy Hopkins, letter to Remus Strickland, June 21, 1961, Box 3, FLIC Papers.

247 "Enclosed is a list of the teachers": Remus Stickland, letter to Andy Hopkins, June 28, 1961, #11-2, Box 3, FLIC Papers.

247 full teacher blacklist: Andy Hopkins, SCR ID # 3-6A-2-12-1-1-1, June 30, 1961, Mississippi Papers.

247 September 22, 1961: FLIC Meeting Minutes for September 22, 1961, Clerk of the House Papers.

248 "outstanding": FLIC Meeting Minutes for September 22, 1961.

248 "homosexual practices in the": FLIC Meeting Minutes for September 22, 1961.

248 "self-policing": Jim McGuirk, "UF Sanctioned Agents Uncover Homosexuals," Florida Alligator, February 19, 1960.

248 On October 7, 1961: Ivan Putman, interrogation by Remus Strickland, March 13, 1962, Box 9, FLIC Papers.

248 implied "admission": Putman, interrogation by Strickland, March 13, 1962; Remus Strickland, letter to Charley Johns, March 21, 1962, #11-1685, Box 2, FLIC Papers.

248 "got an erection": Putman, interrogation by Strickland, March 13, 1962; Remus Strickland, letter to Charley Johns, March 21, 1962.

249 "curious": Putman, interrogation by Strickland, March 13, 1962; Strickland, letter to Johns, March 21, 1962.

249 "Just a few weeks ago": Putman, interrogation by Strickland, March 13, 1962; Strickland, letter to Johns, March 21, 1962.

249 dean of students: Strickland, letter to Johns, March 21, 1962; "Forum Award Is Presented to W. Ellicott Girl," Buffalo News, February 25, 1963, 3.

249 Reitz's underhanded leniency: Strickland, letter to Johns, March 21, 1962.

249 Alligator Man of the Year: Tom Gibson, "Dr. Ivan Putman 'Man of the Year,'" Florida Alligator, May 22, 1962, 1.

249 "outstanding daily": Gibson, "Dr. Ivan Putman 'Man of the Year.'"

Chapter 23. Trench Warfare

250 "We have had many": "Homosexuals in Schools Prime Targets of Probers," Orlando Sentinel, November 15, 1961, 1B.

250 "We can expect an": Robert Saunders, letter to Florida NAACP, September 20, 1961, Florida NAACP Records 1959–1961, NAACP Papers, Library of Congress.

250 hosted ten states: "Persona Attending Meeting Southern States Investigator's . . . ," November 1961, Box 2, FLIC Papers.

250 "It is a little difficult": "'Subversion' in the South," New York Times, November 27, 1961, 28.

251 "I assure you that": Gordon Blackwell, letter to Charley Johns, November 16, 1961, #11-1530, Box 2, FLIC Papers.

251 Harry P. Day: "Control Board Delays Answer on Pay Raises," *Tallahassee Democrat*, November 17, 1961, 2; Carl Wilson Stewart, interrogation by Remus Strickland, January 10, 1962, #3-78, Box 9, FLIC Papers.

251 leadership pipeline: Ann Waldron, "Decline in Student Morals Seen at FSU," *Tampa Bay Times*, October 21, 1965, 59; "Use of Students to Help Nab Sex Deviates Blasted," *Tucson Citizen*, December 29, 1965, 21.

251 Greyhound bus terminal: "Tallahassee Fines 19 Men on Charges of Perversion," *Tampa Tribune*, January 5, 1962, 4.

251 Sergeant Peacock: Homer Frazier, interrogation by Burl Peacock and Remus Strickland, December 12, 1960, #13-45, Box 8, FLIC Papers; "Students Hired to Nab Deviates," *Miami Herald*, December 29, 1965, late edition, 1.

251 Tallahassee's two-man liquor: "Burl Peacock Promoted to Police Sergeant," *Tallahassee Democrat*, June 24, 1960, 9.

251 rounded up more than forty men: "Tallahassee Fines 19 Men on Charges of Perversion"; "Action Taken on 3 Accused of Lewd Acts," *Tallahassee Democrat*, January 7, 1962, 6; Charley Johns, letter to Ben Griffin, December 28, 1961, #10-62, Bonnie Stark Papers.

251 having their name appear: "36 Sentenced for Lewd Acts," *Tallahassee Democrat*, January 4, 1962, 13.

252 Lucian C. Reed: "3 Convicted in Roundup," *Pensacola News*, January 4, 1962, 1; "3 Accused Men Fired by State," *Tampa Tribune*, January 6, 1962, 6B.

252 directed verdict of acquittal: "3 Accused Men Fired by State."

252 announce a statewide program: "Many Obstacles Face Enforcers," *Pensacola News Journal*, January 6, 1962, 1; "Bryant Mapping Anti-Lewd Plan," *Tallahassee Democrat*, January 5, 1962, 3; "Governor Launches Drive on Deviates," *Pensacola News Journal*, January 5, 1962, 1; Martin Waldron, "Homosexuality Faces Strong State Action," *Tampa Bay Times*, March 6, 1962, 14.

252 "We are going to": "Many Obstacles Face Enforcers," 2.

252 Reporting for the *Orlando Sentinel*: Robert Delaney, "Bryant Pushes Task of Locating Perverts," *Orlando Sentinel*, January 18, 1962, 11D.

252 Carl Wilson Stewart Jr.: Stewart, interrogation by Strickland, January 10, 1962.

252 "After having come to Florida": Stewart, interrogation by Strickland, January 10, 1962.

253 "rumors to the effect that": Stewart, interrogation by Strickland, January 10, 1962.

253 booted out of FSU: TallyHo 1963 yearbook, Florida State University; TallyHo 1964 yearbook, Florida State University; TallyHo 1965 yearbook, Florida State University.

253 departed for Austria: "Dr. Harry Day Leaving FSU for Two Years," *Tallahassee Democrat*, November 22, 1961, 14.

253 December 11, 1961: Leslie Powell, interrogation by Remus Strickland, December 11, 1961, #1-26, Box 8, FLIC Papers; TallyHo 1961 yearbook, Florida State University, 137; Leslie Powell, "La Dolce Vita," *Florida Flambeau*, 2.

253   "Leslie, was this subject": Powell, interrogation by Strickland, December 11, 1961.

253   "The first year I was here": Powell, interrogation by Strickland, December 11, 1961.

253   he did not graduate: TallyHo 1962 yearbook, Florida State University; TallyHo 1963 yearbook, Florida State University.

254   September 12, 1962: Leslie Powell, "All You Can Ask," *Florida Flambeau*, September 12, 1962, 2; Georgiana Fry Batemen, "'You Know, It's Strange,'" *Florida Flambeau*, September 12, 1962, 2–3; "Memorial Services Set for Tomorrow," *Florida Flambeau*, September 12, 1962, 1; "FSU Teacher Is Found Dead of Gun Shot," *Tallahassee Democrat*, September 11, 1962, 1.

254   no suicide note: "FSU Teacher Is Found Dead of Gun Shot."

254   "He was instrumental": Powell, "All You Can Ask."

254   received an O. Henry: "Dr. Cox Story Is Chosen for O'Henry Award," *Tallahassee Democrat*, April 3, 1963, 4.

254   struck a collaboration: Gordon Blackwell, letter to Charley Johns, March 22, 1963, Box 2, FLIC Papers.

254   supplementary list of forty-two names: Blackwell, letter to Johns, March 22, 1963; Remus Strickland, letter to William Tanner, March 28, 1963, Box 3, FLIC Papers.

254   University of London: Blackwell, letter to Johns, March 22, 1963; "Laser Techniques to Be Viewed at Physics Colloquim," *Tallahassee Democrat*, April 9, 1963, 3.

254   Lucian C. Reed: Blackwell, letter to Johns, March 22, 1963; "3 Accused Men Fired by State."

254   "Florida State was a relatively": Cliff Herrell, interview with Bonnie Stark, August 3, 1993, Bonnie Stark Papers.

254   William F. Daniel: "Teacher Seeks Permit Return," *Tallahassee Democrat*, June 19, 1961, 2; "New Law Firm Formed in City," *Tallahassee Democrat*, May 25, 1958, 10.

255   in a single file or letter: Florida Legislative Investigation Committee files, NAACP Records, Library of Congress.

255   January 13, 1961: "Brief of Petitioner," *Neal v. Bryant*, 1961, 4–7, Bonnie Stark Papers.

255   neglecting to inform Neal: "Petition for Extraordinary Relief," *Neal v. Bryant*, June 2, 1961, Bonnie Stark Papers.

255   January 25, 1961: "Petition for Extraordinary Relief," *Neal v. Bryant*, June 2, 1961; Karen L. Graves, *And They Were Wonderful Teachers: Florida's Purge of Gay and Lesbian Teachers* (University of Illinois Press, 2009), 111–12.

255   forward four witnesses: "Petition for Extraordinary Relief," *Neal v. Bryant*, June 2, 1961; Graves, *And They Were Wonderful Teachers*, 8.

255   "exemplary record": "Petition for Extraordinary Relief," *Neal v. Bryant*, June 2, 1961; Judith Poucher, *State of Defiance: Challenging the Johns Committee's Assault on Civil Liberties* (University Press of Florida, 2014), 134.

255   was forced under oath to admit: "Petition for Extraordinary Relief," *Neal v.*

Bryant, June 2, 1961; "Brief of Petitioner," *Anne Louise Poston v. Florida Board of Education*, 1961, Bonnie Stark Papers.

255 **"third degree"**: "Petition for Extraordinary Relief," *Neal v. Bryant*, June 2, 1961; Graves, *And They Were Wonderful Teachers*, 101.

255 **"agitating for an answer"**: "Petition for Extraordinary Relief," *Neal v. Bryant*, June 2, 1961; Graves, *And They Were Wonderful Teachers*, 8.

256 **April 4, 1961**: "Petition for Extraordinary Relief," *Neal v. Bryant*, June 2, 1961; Bonnie Stark, "McCarthyism in Florida: Charley Johns and the Florida Legislative Investigation Committee July, 1956 to July, 1965" (master's thesis, University of South Florida, 1985), 112, https://palmm. digital.flvc.org/islandora/ object/usf%3A49370#page/title/mode/1up; "Brief of Petitioner," *Anne Louise Poston v. Florida Board of Education*, 1961; "Five Teachers Lose Licenses," *Tallahassee Democrat*, April 4, 1961, 3.

256 **"methods employed**: "Five Teachers Lose Licenses."

256 **four female educators**: "Five Teachers Lose Licenses"; Floyd Christian, letter to J. T. Kelly, March 21, 1963, Box 13, Florida DOE Papers, State Archives of Florida.

256 **"moral turpitude"**: "Five Teachers Lose Licenses."

256 **"Five Teachers"**: "Five Teachers Lose Licenses."

256 **"State Fires"**: "State Fires 5 Teachers," *Miami Herald*, April 5, 1961, 2B.

256 **"Sex Charge: Teachers"**: "Sex Charge: Teachers Ousted," *Pensacola News Journal*, April 4, 1961, 1.

256 **state legislators acknowledged**: "Sex Charge: Teachers Ousted," 2.

256 **blamed the insufficiency**: "Sex Charge: Teachers Ousted," 2.

256 **"fit to teach"**: "Five Teachers Lose Licenses."

256 **corrected this legalese**: Journal of the Senate, May 22, 1961, 1985; Journal of the Senate, May 25, 1961, 1596.

256 **honorably discharged veteran**: William James Neal, "Report of Separation from the Armed Forces of the United States," October 1952, U.S. Army Records, acquired via FOIA request.

257 **"I went to a friend's house"**: David Barstow, "St. Petersburg Teacher Found Himself Target," *Tampa Bay Times*, July 2, 1993.

257 **label "educated Nigra"**: William James Neal, interrogation by Remus Strickland, October 13, 1960, #1-95, Box 8, FLIC Papers.

257 **crossed state lines**: Barstow, "St. Petersburg Teacher Found Himself Target."

257 **June 2, 1961**: "Brief of Petitioner," *Neal v. Bryant*, 1961, Bonnie Stark Papers.

257 **"yanked out of his"**: "Teacher Seeks Permit Return," *Tallahassee Democrat*, June 19, 1961, 2.

257 **Neal denied experiencing duress**: "Teacher Seeks Permit Return."

257 **clandestine Miami summit**: Tom Scarborough, SCR ID # 3-6A-2-20-1-1-1, November 13–15, 1961, 1, Mississippi Papers.

257 **joined Neal's lawsuit**: *Neal v. Bryant* decision, October 19, 1962, 530, Bonnie Stark Papers.

257 **not include Neal's race**: "Court Asked to Reverse Ruling Against 3 Teachers," *Tampa Tribune*, December 14, 1961, 3.

CHAPTER 24. FRIENDS OF THE COURT

258 "The question posed": "Brief of Petitioner," *Neal v. Bryant*, 1961, Bonnie Stark Papers.

259 "The Petitioner would": "Brief of Respondent," *Neal v. Bryant*, 1961, Bonnie Stark Papers.

259 "Whenever I questioned": Remus Strickland, transcript of interview with Bonnie Stark, April 1984, Bonnie Stark Papers.

259 for months on end: *Neal v. Bryant* decision, October 19, 1962, Bonnie Stark Papers.

259 December 27: Robert Delaney, "Bryant Pushes Task of Location Perverts," *Orlando Sentinel*, January 18, 1962, 39; "Children's Board Gets Study Fund," *Tampa Tribune*, March 22, 1962, Box 57, Bryant Papers, State Archives of Florida; "Children's Board to Ask Funds to Fight Lewd Books," *Tampa Tribune*, March 19, 1962, Box 57, Bryant Papers, State Archives of Florida.

259 Dr. Peter Regan: Martin Waldron, "Homosexuality Faces Strong State Action," *Tampa Bay Times*, March 6, 1962.

259 January 22, 1962: "Problems on Homosexuality," Advisory Committee on Problems of Homosexuality in Florida, Meeting Minutes for January 22, 1962, Box 57, Bryant Papers.

260 "No employee of said": Remus Strickland, memorandum to FLIC staff, March 8, 1962, #11-125, Box 1, FLIC Papers.

260 Five-term Pork Chopper: Bonnie Stark, "McCarthyism in Florida: Charley Johns and the Florida Legislative Investigation Committee July, 1956 to July, 1965" (master's thesis, University of South Florida, 1985), 97, https://palmm .digital.flvc.org/islandora/object/usf%3A49370#page/title/mode/1up, 196.

260 "Davis—who created the Pork Chop": Martin Waldron, "Pork Chop Gang Cooked?" *Tampa Bay Times*, May 10, 1962, 13A.

260 senator Wayne Ripley: Stark, "McCarthyism in Florida," 196; Vernon Bradford, "'Pork Chop Gang' Loses Leader, 3 Stalwart Members," *Tampa Tribune*, May 10, 1962, 21; "Senate Votes to Build New Job Offices in Eight Cities," *Tampa Tribune*, April 26, 1961, 11.

260 "The myth that": "Handwriting Grows Larger," *Tampa Tribune*, May 11, 1962, 14A.

260 bare majority of twenty-one: "Handwriting Grows Larger."

260 "I want you to know": Louise Hill, letter to Charley Johns, November 11, 1962, #11-791, Box 2, FLIC Papers.

260 October 19, 1962: *Neal v. Bryant* decision, October 19, 1962.

260 five to two in favor: *Neal v. Bryant* decision, October 19, 1962; "Teacher Firings Illegal," *Miami Herald*, October 20, 1962, 2B.

260 Terrell and Bonnie Kaslo Roberts: *Neal v. Bryant* decision, October 19, 1962; "Teacher Firings Illegal"; Vernon Bradford, "Court Upsets Revocation of 3 Teachers' Permits, Says Legislative Probers Limited," *Tampa Tribune*, October 20, 1962, 4; "Former Justices," Florida Supreme Court, September 24, 2024, https://supremecourt.flcourts.gov/Justices/Former-Justices.

261   "In lieu of following": *Neal v. Bryant* decision, October 19, 1962.

261   was forced to return: "3 Teachers Are Returned Credentials," *Fort Lauderdale News*, March 19, 1963, 13.

261   "I thought you ought": Floyd Christian, letter to J. T. Kelly, March 21, 1963, Box 13, DOE Papers, State Archives of Florida; Stacy Braukman, *Communists and Perverts Under the Palms: The Johns Committee in Florida, 1956–1965* (University Press of Florida, 2012), 228n5.

262   "subversive": Journal of the House of Representatives, May 25, 1961, 2434; SB 64, 1959, Clerk of the House Papers.

262   sought a rehearing: *Neal v. Bryant* decision, October 19, 1962.

262   susceptible to blackmail: "Petition for Rehearing," *Neal v. Bryant*, 1963, Bonnie Stark Papers.

262   denied the state: *Neal v. Bryant* decision, October 19, 1962.

262   *Neal v. Bryant*: David Barstow, "St. Petersburg Teacher Found Himself Target," *Tampa Bay Times*, July 2, 1993.

263   "As you grow older": Barstow, "St. Petersburg Teacher Found Himself Target."

263   died on February 17, 2008: "William James Neal," *Washington Post*, February 20, 2008, https://www.legacy.com/us/obituaries/washingtonpost /name/william-neal-obituary?id=5610683; "William James Neal," Findagrave, https://www.findagrave.com/memorial/238908803/william -james-neal.

263   "The action stemmed from challenges": Bradford, "Court Upsets Revocation of 3 Teachers' Permits, Says Legislative Probers Limited," 2B.

263   December 5, 1961: *Gibson v. Florida Legislative Investigation Committee*, U.S. Supreme Court Records, accessed via Oyez, https://www.oyez.org/cases /1961/6.

263   segregated Florida in 1917: "Celebrating the Life of the Late Robert L. Carter," NAACP, January 1, 2012, https://naacp.org/resources/celebrating -life-late-robert-l-carter.

263   Law School in 1941: Roy Reed, "Robert L. Carter, an Architect of School Desegregation, Dies at 94," *New York Times*, January 3, 2012, https://www .nytimes.com/2012/01/04/nyregion/robert-l-carter-judge-and-desegregation -strategist-dies-at-94.html.

264   University of Florida College of Law: "Mark Hawes," *Tampa Bay Times*, September 10, 1972, 14-I; "Ex-Hillsborough Prosecutor Dies," *Tampa Tribune*, April 25, 1985, 11B.

264   one and a half years: "Mark Hawes"; "Ex-Hillsborough Prosecutor Dies."

264   more than ten times: Robert L. Carter, "Cases Argued," Oyez, https://www .oyez.org/advocates/robert_l_carter.

264   complete absence of facts: "Oral Argument—December 05, 1961," *Gibson v. Florida Legislative Investigation Committee*, Oyez, https://www.oyez.org /cases/1961/6.

264   be nullified because: *Gibson v. Florida Legislative Investigation Committee*.

264   wasted his opening: *Gibson v. Florida Legislative Investigation Committee*.

264   "If your honors please": *Gibson v. Florida Legislative Investigation Committee*.

265 "What if this Court should decide": *Gibson v. Florida Legislative Investigation Committee.*

265 "I think that the statement": *Gibson v. Florida Legislative Investigation Committee.*

265 The justices then quizzed: *Gibson v. Florida Legislative Investigation Committee.*

266 attended yet another: A. L. Hopkins, SCR ID # 3-16A-2-113-1-1-1, June 10–12, 1962, Mississippi Papers.

266 June 10 and 12: Hopkins, SCR ID # 3-16A-2-113-1-1-1, June 10–12, 1962.

266 Strickland took the floor: Hopkins, SCR ID # 3-16A-2-113-1-1-1, June 10–12, 1962.

CHAPTER 25. A CLOSER SQUEEZE

269 two quiet years: Art Copleston, interview with Robert Fieseler, November 11, 2019; Art Copleston, *Demons and Deliverance* (published by author, 2014), Kindle, 160–61.

269 Feeling brave during his: Copleston, *Demons and Deliverance*, 161; Art Copleston, interview with Robert Fieseler, July 11, 2021.

269 "When I came to Gainesville": Art Copleston, interview with Robert Fieseler, July 11, 2021.

270 with honors and a 3.8 GPA: Arthur Sidney Copleston Jr., Unofficial Academic Transcript, University of Florida Registrar, Art Copleston Papers.

270 His mother drove: Art Copleston, interviews with Robert Fieseler, November 11, 2019, and July 11, 2021.

270 Copleston received his first: Copleston, *Demons and Deliverance*, 163; Art Copleston, interview with Robert Fieseler, July 10, 2021.

270 the Napoleon Club: Art Copleston, interview with Robert Fieseler, July 10, 2021; "Former Gay Boston," Ron's Log, October 2004, https://ronslog .typepad.com/ronslog/2004/10/former_gay_bost.html.

270 "It's rumored JFK": "The Napoleon Club," *Boston Magazine* (blog), January 1, 1974, https://www.bostonmagazine.com/best-of-boston-archive/1974 /the-napoleon-club/; Keith Orr, "Clubland," *Boston Phoenix*, July 1998, https://bostonphoenix.com/archive/1in10/98/07/CLUBLAND.html.

270 William Edward "Bill" Huckabee: "Dr. William E. Huckabee, 59, Cardiovascular Disease Researcher," *Boston Globe*, July 14, 1986, 43.

270 owned a small mansion: "List of Boston Residents," 1966, Ancestry .com,https://www.ancestry.com/search/collections/62752/records/7323730 ?tid=&pid=&queryId=684d657c-eed8-4baa-b7fa-e17b9ef84d3e&_phsrc =Pmf1077&_phstart=successSource.

270 "The sun and the stars": Art Copleston, interview with Robert Fieseler, July 10, 2021.

270 Dr. William Huckabee: "Dr. William E. Huckabee, 59, Cardiovascular Disease Researcher."

271 nineteen-year-old lover named Hank: Art Copleston, interview with Robert Fieseler, July 11, 2021.

271   **"It was like a guillotine":** Art Copleston, interview with Robert Fieseler, July 11, 2021.

271   **When Margaret:** Art Copleston, interview with Robert Fieseler, July 11, 2021.

271   **"How could you do this to me?":** Art Copleston, interview with Robert Fieseler, July 10, 2021.

271   **Johns Committee was broke:** "Legislative Probe Body Gets $67,150 to Carry on Work," *Florida Times-Union*, August 29, 1962, 26.

271   **since late December:** Charley Johns, letter to Farris Bryant, December 28, 1961, #10-61, Bonnie Stark Papers.

271   **FLIC payroll records:** Vernon Bradford, "Cabinet Gives Johns Group $67,150 to Continue Probes," *Tampa Tribune*, August 29, 1962, 14A.

272   **"auxiliary appropriation":** Bradford, "Cabinet Gives Johns Group $67,150 to Continue Probes."

272   **October 10, 1962:** "Oral Reargument—October 10, 1962," *Gibson v. Florida Legislative Investigation Committee*, Oyez, https://www.oyez.org /cases/1961/6.

272   **"There is no evidence":** "Oral Reargument—October 10, 1962," *Gibson v. Florida Legislative Investigation Committee*.

272   **controlled the play clock:** "Oral Reargument—October 11, 1962," *Gibson v. Florida Legislative Investigation Committee*.

273   **"I thought":** "Oral Reargument—October 11, 1962," *Gibson v. Florida Legislative Investigation Committee*.

273   **"It has been said":** "Oral Reargument—October 11, 1962," *Gibson v. Florida Legislative Investigation Committee*.

273   **But the NAACP still:** "Oral Reargument—October 11, 1962," *Gibson v. Florida Legislative Investigation Committee*.

273   **"I think the people are behind us":** Rick Tuttle, "Johns Committee Is Facing Trouble," *Tampa Bay Times*, March 20, 1963, 9.

274   **Delaney had covered:** Robert Delaney, "Chairman Says 'Luck' Aided Probe Committee," *Tampa Bay Times*, February 6, 1957, 1; Robert Delaney, "State Red Quiz Hears Matthews," *Miami News*, February 10, 1958, 2; Robert Delaney, "Committee Approves Johns Group," *Orlando Sentinel*, May 24, 1963, 6.

274   **"in the best interest":** Robert Delaney, "Prober Spends $1,000 for Secret Records," *Miami News*, December 4, 1957, 18.

274   **called the Liberal Forum:** Haines Colbert, "Johns Committee Strays," *Orlando Sentinel*, March 30, 1963, 11.

274   **"reaching the point that":** Colbert, "Johns Committee Strays."

274   **"pudgy black-haired":** Bob Sherill, "Jury Convicts Newsman," *Orlando Sentinel*, January 7, 1965, 6A; Judith Poucher, *State of Defiance: Challenging the Johns Committee's Assault on Civil Liberties* (University Press of Florida, 2014), 133–34.

274   **forty-five-year-old married:** Haines Colbert, "Newsman Caught in Trap," *Orlando Sentinel*, March 28, 1963, 25; "Named to Council," *Tampa Tribune*, December 20, 1960, 30.

274   **got the feeling:** Haines Colbert, "Was Wrong Man Trapped?" *Orlando Sentinel*, March 29, 1963, 17A.

274   "Jan Lee": Colbert, "Was Wrong Man Trapped?"

274   "She told me she": Colbert, "Was Wrong Man Trapped?"

274   Saturday, February 9: Colbert, "Was Wrong Man Trapped?"; Colbert, "Newsman Caught in Trap."

275   Almost as suddenly as: Colbert, "Newsman Caught in Trap."

275   "I caught you!": Colbert, "Was Wrong Man Trapped?"

275   waltz over but Remus Strickland: Colbert, "Newsman Caught in Trap."

275   $400 per month: Robert Sherrill, "Women Ex-Con Helped Police Nab Newsman," *Miami Herald*, January 7, 1965, 17; "Delaney Trial Starts with Charge Denial," *Orlando Sentinel*, January 21, 1964, 4.

275   "a lesbian": Colbert, "Was Wrong Man Trapped?"

275   "I've heard statements that Strickland": Colbert, "Newsman Caught in Trap."

276   refused to admit guilt: "Delaney Trial Starts with Charge Denial."

276   "attempted crime against nature": Sherill, "Jury Convicts Newsman."

276   five years' probation: "Probation Term Against Delaney Upheld by Court," *Tallahassee Democrat*, September 29, 1966, 8; Donna O'Neal, "Sentinel Reporter Was Only Person Charged with Crime," *Orlando Sentinel*, June 27, 1993, A12.

276   family to Miami: "Reporter's Life Shattered by '60s Panel," *Contax*, August 11, 1993, 6, James T. Sears Papers.

276   March 25, 1963: John Davis, telegram to Robert Carter, March 25, 1963, NAACP Papers, Library of Congress.

276   a margin of 5 to 4: Anthony Lewis, "Supreme Court Tightens States' Red Inquiry Rules," *New York Times*, March 26, 1963, 1; James Marlow, "Marlow Comments on Ruling on Theodore Gibson Case," *Daily Mail*, March 26, 1963, 3.

276   *Gibson v. Florida*: *Gibson v. Florida Legislative Investigation Committee*, 372 U.S. 539 (1963), March 25, 1963, accessed via Justia, https://supreme.justia.com/cases/federal/us/372/539/#tab-opinion-1944202.

277   "We hold simply": *Gibson v. Florida Legislative Investigation Committee*, 372 U.S. 539 (1963), March 25, 1963.

277   "To impose a lesser": *Gibson v. Florida Legislative Investigation Committee*, 372 U.S. 539 (1963), March 25, 1963.

277   "I thank my God and": "Miami's Chief Cleared," *Miami Herald*, March 26, 1963, 1; Bonnie Stark, "McCarthyism in Florida: Charley Johns and the Florida Legislative Investigation Committee July, 1956 to July, 1965" (master's thesis, University of South Florida, 1985), 97, https://palmm.digital.flvc.org/islandora/object/usf%3A49370#page/title/mode/1up, 85.

277   "But," Hawes added: "Supreme Court Dismisses Contempt Charge Against Miami Negro NAACP Leader Gibson," *Pensacola News Journal*, March 26, 1963, 3.

277   "a brake on fishing expeditions": James Marlow, "Using Reds as Prying Excuse Unfair," *Harlan Daily Enterprise*, March 27, 1963, 4.

277   "Supreme Court Tightens": Lewis, "Supreme Court Tightens States' Red Inquiry Rules."

Chapter 26. Lonely Hunters

279   "should be abolished": Barbara Frye, "Johns Committee Activities Face Tight Controls," *Tampa Tribune*, March 25, 1963, 19.

279   "value": Frye, "Johns Committee Activities Face Tight Controls."

279   "all the characteristics": "Johns Group 'Witch Hunt' Slam Denied," *Tallahasse Democrat*, March 22, 1963, 13.

280   "I cannot understand": "Johns Group 'Witch Hunt' Slam Denied."

280   "The witch-hunting": "Johns Committee Should Quit," *Miami News*, July 31, 1963, 6; "Witch Hunt Charge of Probers Rapped," *Tampa Times*, March 22, 1963, 1.

280   "We were out looking": Mary Ann Moorhouse, letter to FLIC, September 9, 1963, Clerk of the House Papers.

280   "roving grand jury": "Johns Committee Exceeds Authority," *Tampa Times*, April 20, 1963, 8.

280   April 18, 1963: Douglas Starr, "Johns Probe Report Due at Session," *Tallahassee Democrat*, April 18, 1963, 13.

280   "executive session": Journal of the Senate, April 18, 1963, 206.

280   "The work of this": Martin Waldron, "Johns Committee Unleashes Final Fire," *Tampa Bay Times*, April 19, 1963, 1.

281   led to the firing: "Florida Legislature Investigation Committee," 1961, #10-45, Bonnie Stark Papers; Tom O'Connor, "Sen. Johns Raps USF, Dr. Allen," *Tampa Tribune*, April 19, 1963, 1A, 5B.

281   the Strickland/Delaney affair: O'Connor, "Sen. Johns Raps USF, Dr. Allen," 5B.

281   not "constitute entrapment": "Johns Defends Probers," *Orlando Sentinel*, April 19, 1963, 10; Martin Waldron, "Johns Committee Unleashes Final Fire," *Tampa Bay Times*, April 19, 1963, 13A.

281   who "got caught": Waldron, "Johns Committee Unleashes Final Fire."

281   kidnapping of the eleven-year-old: Waldron, "Johns Committee Unleashes Final Fire"; O'Connor, "Sen. Johns Raps USF, Dr. Allen," 5B.

282   John Rudd did confirm: "Kidnap Plot Said Thwarted in City," *Tallahassee Democrat*, April 19, 1963.

282   ninety-minute presentation: O'Connor, "Sen. Johns Raps USF, Dr. Allen," 1A.

282   demonstrated "there is absolutely": Bob Turner, "Delegation Raps Johns Probers," *Tampa Times*, April 19, 1963, 1.

282   "set up a committee to": Turner, "Delegation Raps Johns Probers."

282   On May 6, 1963: "Johns' Group Hearing Seat for Today," *Palm Beach Post*, May 6, 1963, 15; Bonnie Stark, "McCarthyism in Florida: Charley Johns and the Florida Legislative Investigation Committee July, 1956 to July, 1965" (master's thesis, University of South Florida, 1985), 97, https://palmm .digital.flvc.org/islandora/object/usf%3A49370#page/title/mode/1up, 201–2.

282   thirty yeas to fourteen nays: Journal of the Senate, May 9, 1963, 716.

282   "Whenever you try to": Vernon Bradford, "Bill to Label Books by Subversives Is Killed," *Tampa Tribune*, May 23, 1963, 13A.

282 **sign the legislation:** "Johns Committee Gets Final Okay," *Orlando Evening Star*, May 30, 1963, 1.

282 **in a broader bargain:** Martin Waldron, "Charley Johns Again Heads Probe Group," *Tampa Bay Times*, June 20, 1963, 1.

282 **backroom deal:** Stark, "McCarthyism in Florida," 212.

283 **"Numerous members":** Ed Price, transcript of interview with Bonnie Stark, September 20, 1984, Bonnie Stark Papers.

283 **"He [Charley] didn't know":** Remus Strickland, transcript of interview with Bonnie Stark, April 1984, Bonnie Stark Papers.

283 **on August 8, 1963:** FLIC Meeting Minutes for August 8, 1963, Clerk of the House Papers.

284 **"The Committee received":** FLIC Meeting Minutes for August 8, 1963, Clerk of the House Papers.

284 **"What went on in there?":** Robert Delaney, "Two Quit Johns Group," *Orlando Sentinel*, August 9, 1963, 1, 4A.

284 **"Two Quit Johns Group":** Delaney, "Two Quit Johns Group."

284 **private law practice:** "Legislative Probers Quit Posts," *Miami Herald*, August 9, 1963, 2.

284 **"My heart and conscience":** Stark, "McCarthyism in Florida," 213.

284 **destruction of all of his suspect photographs:** Davis McGriff, letter to Remus Strickland, October 9, 1963, #11-1646, Box 2, FLIC Papers; Michael Browning, Karen Branch, and Jack Wheat, "How Gays Were Once Hunted in Florida," *Miami Herald*, July 3, 1993, 12A.

285 **"Dear Strick":** Davis McGriff, letter to Remus Strickland, October 9, 1963.

285 **fell on hard times:** Remus Strickland, transcript of interview with Bonnie Stark, April 1984.

285 **"one of the best investigators in the state":** "Probe Favored by Sen. Johns," *Tampa Bay Times*, October 6, 1964, 2B.

285 **ongoing trial:** "Delaney Trial Starts with Charge Denial," *Orlando Sentinel*, January 21, 1964.

285 **charged with grand larceny:** Harold Rummel, "Two Former Investigators Are Charged," *Tampa Bay Times*, October 5, 1965, 3.

CHAPTER 27. SHOCK TECHNIQUE

286 **erupted in April 1963:** Jack Stillman, "Integration Question Affects Everyone in Troubled Birmingham," *Pensacola News Journal*, April 15, 1963, 7A; Foster Hailey, "Dr. King Arrested at Birmingham," *New York Times*, April 13, 1963, 1; Taylor Branch, *Pillar of Fire: America in the King Years, 1963–1965* (Simon & Schuster, 1998), xviii–xix.

286 **more than forty unsolved bombings:** "Birmingham's 'Dynamite Hill' Negroes Are Used to Bombs, Violence," *Fort Lauderdale News*, September 26, 1972, 13A; "St. Petersburg Mourns Bomb Victims Today," *Tampa Bay Times*, September 18, 1963, 8D; "Counterblast: How the Atlanta Temple Bombing Strengthened the Civil Rights Cause," *Southern Spaces*, June 22, 2009, https://southernspaces.org/2009/counterblast-how-atlanta-temple-bombing-strengthened-civil-rights-cause/; Branch, *Pillar of Fire*, 138.

286   **advise on the Birmingham push:** Jervis Anderson, *Bayard Rustin: Troubles I've Seen* (University of California Press, 1998), 243–44.

286   **his exiled counselor Bayard:** "Former King Aide Hits Silent Liberal," *Courier-News*, June 26, 1963, 7.

286   **co-conceived the SCLC:** Anderson, *Bayard Rustin*, 198.

286   **been sidelined in 1960:** Walter Naegle, interview with Robert Fieseler, March 14, 2023; "Powell, Adam Clayton, Jr.," Martin Luther King Jr. Research and Education Institute, accessed December 2, 2024, https://kinginstitute .stanford.edu/powell-adam-clayton-jr.; Martin Luther King, letter to Adam Clayton Powell, June 24, 1960, https://kinginstitute.stanford.edu/king -papers/documents/adam-clayton-powell-jr-1#fn3.

287   **April 12, 1963, King was arrested:** "Contempt March Leader on Trial," *Fort Lauderdale News*, April 22, 1963, 4B.

287   **"Letter from Birmingham Jail":** Branch, *Pillar of Fire*, 47–48; Walter Naegle, interview with Robert Fieseler, March 14, 2023.

287   **May 2, several thousand:** Foster Hailey, "500 Are Arrested in Negro Protest at Birmingham," *New York Times*, May 3, 1963, 1; "Thousands of Negroes March in Birmingham," *Orlando Sentinel*, May 3, 1963, 3.

287   **pass a civil rights act:** John F. Kennedy, "Televised Address to the Nation on Civil Rights," June 11, 1963, JFK Library, accessed December 2, 2024, https://www.jfklibrary.org/learn/about-jfk/historic-speeches/televised -address-to-the-nation-on-civil-rights.

287   **one of the longest filibusters:** Branch, *Pillar of Fire*, 336.

287   **March on Washington:** Jules Witcover, "Rights March Planner Hopes for New Social Order," *St. Louis Globe-Democrat*, July 29, 1963, 9A.

287   **"I don't want":** Gary Younge, "Bayard Rustin: The Gay Black Pacifist at the Heart of the March on Washington," World News, *The Guardian*, August 23, 2013, https://www.theguardian.com/world/2013/aug/23/bayard -rustin-march-on-washington.

287   **leaders met with President Kennedy:** Marjorie Hunter, "Negroes Inform Kennedy of Plan for New Protests," *New York Times*, June 23, 1963, 1; James Farmer, *Lay Bare the Heart: An Autobiography of the Civil Rights Movement* (Texas Christian University Press, 1998), 215; "Kennedy Pushes Civil Rights Drive," *Vancouver Sun*, June 17, 1963, 8.

287   **reins back to Rustin:** M. S. Handler, "City Groups Plan March on Capital," *New York Times*, July 26, 1963, 12; Taylor Branch, *Parting the Waters: America in the King Years, 1954–63* (Touchstone, 1989), 850–72.

287   **"segregated superbomb":** "St. Augustine 'a Segregated Super-Bomb,'" *Tampa Bay Times*, August 17, 1963, 3.

287   **four-hundredth-anniversary celebration:** "Racial and Civil Disorders in St. Augustine," FLIC, February 1965, 1–2, Box 57, Bryant Papers; "Johnson Heads Dignitaries for St. Augustine Event," *Tampa Tribune*, March 6, 1963, 8B.

287   **a Black sit-in:** "11 Negroes Arrested in Two Sit-ins Here," *The Shreveport Times*, July 20, 1963, 2; "Civil Rights Timeline," *St. Augustine Record*, May 18, 2014, https://web.archive.org/web/20180802215214/http://www .staugustine.com/content/stub-428.

288   **sentenced four of these youth:** Snow James, "Four Youths Shot, Jailed in Oldest 'American' Town," *New Pittsburgh Courier*, July 13, 1963, 1; Stacy M. Brown, "Celebrating Black History: The St. Augustine Four Is a Vital Part of Black History," Black Press USA, February 7, 2021, https://blackpressusa.com/celebrating-black-history-the-st-augustine-four-is-a-vital-part-of-black-history/.

288   **August 13, 1963:** "March Head a Pervert—Thurmond," *Tampa Tribune*, August 14, 1963, 8; M. S. Handler, "Negro Rally Aide Rebuts Senator," *New York Times*, August 16, 1963, 10; Eric Cervini, *The Deviant's War: The Homosexual vs. the United States of America* (Farrar, Straus and Giroux, 2020), 156; John D'Emilio, *Lost Prophet: The Life and Times of Bayard Rustin* (Free Press, 2003), 348; Congressional Record—Senate, August 13, 1963, https://www.govinfo.gov/content/pkg/GPO-CRECB-1963-pt11/pdf/GPO-CRECB-1963-pt11-7-2.pdf.

288   **Thurmond mocked:** "March Head a Pervert—Thurmond"; "Thurmond Spells Out Evidence Promoter of March Once Red," *The Item*, August 14, 1963, 1; Cervini, *The Deviant's War*, 156.

288   **twenty-two career arrests:** "Negro Rally Aide Rebuts Senator."

288   **outlets played a party:** "Rights March Chief Has Police Record," *Miami Herald*, August 15, 1963, 2A.

288   **"not interested in social justice":** "Negro Rally Aide Rebuts Senator."

288   **"An individual involved":** "Negro Rally Aide Rebuts Senator."

288   **From Miami, Father Theodore:** Lee Winfrey, "Miamians Encourage Marchers," *Miami Herald*, August 15, 1963, 8.

288   **devoted countless days:** "Rights March Chief Has Police Record"; E. W. Kenworthy, "200,000 March for Civil Rights in Orderly Washington Rally," *New York Times*, August 29, 1963, 1.

288   **in the background:** "Official Program for the March on Washington for Jobs and Freedom," August 28, 1963, accessed via National Archives, https://www.archives.gov/milestone-documents/official-program-for-the-march-on-washington.

288   **prevented Black gay author:** Neely Tucker, "Protests That Changed America: The March on Washington," Library of Congress Blogs, June 10, 2020, https://blogs.loc.gov/loc/2020/06/protests-that-changed-america-the-march-on-washington/.

289   **"Freedom now!":** "Rev. Theodore R. Gibson, President of Local NAACP . . . ," *Miami News*, August 31, 1963, 8; Lee Winfrey, "They Plan to Talk About Jobs for 'Troubled' Young People," *Miami Herald*, September 1, 1963, 20; Carita Swanson Vonk, *Theodore R. Gibson: Priest, Prophet, and Politician* (Little River Press, 1997), 79.

289   **September, Klansmen:** "Racial and Civil Disorders in St. Augustine," FLIC, February 1965, 3; Juanita Greene, "'Utter Hate Hurts Most,' Negro Klan Victim Says," *Miami Herald*, September 21, 1963, 1D; "Suit Filed by NAACP," *Miami Herald*, September 27, 1963, 40.

289   **"meeting":** "Racial and Civil Disorders in St. Augustine," FLIC, February 1965, 3.

289   **"lying on the ground":** Greene, "'Utter Hate Hurts Most,' Negro Klan

Victim Says"; "Negro Convicted in Klan Assault," *Miami Herald*, October 17, 1963, 1.

289   **October 25, 1963:** "Racial and Civil Disorders in St. Augustine," FLIC, February 1965, 4; "Shrimper Killed in Negro Quarter," *Pensacola News Journal*, October 26, 1963, 2.

289   **local NAACP turned to King:** "Racial and Civil Disorders in St. Augustine," FLIC, February 1965, 4, 9, Appendix 5; "Negro Aides Quit in St. Augustine," *Miami Herald*, December 20, 1963, 30.

289   **four loads of buckshot:** "Racial and Civil Disorders in St. Augustine," FLIC, February 1965, 5.

289   **November 15, President John:** "Kennedy Relaxes at Palm Beach," *Fort Lauderdale News*, November 16, 1963, 10; "Kennedy Goes to Sea for Polaris Launch," *Tampa Tribune*, November 17, 1963, 1.

289   **Cape Canaveral:** "Kennedy Visits Cape Canaveral," *Lima Citizen*, November 16, 1963, 1.

289   **a billion federal dollars:** "Kennedy Goes to Sea for Polaris Launch."

289   **transformed the sleepy:** Charlie Wadsworth, "Hush Puppies," *Orlando Sentinel*, November 16, 1963, 20.

289   **"Wonderful":** Wadsworth, "Hush Puppies."

289   **campaigned for reelection:** "Pres. Kennedy's Schedule," *Tampa Tribune*, November 17, 1963, 10.

289   **"Suncoast Smiles on":** "Suncoast Smiles on Kennedy," *St. Petersburg Times*, November 19, 1963, 1.

289   **"with glee and turned":** Tom O'Connor, "President Says Nation 'On the Move,'" *Tampa Tribune*, November 19, 1963, 1, 6.

289   **hands of "Negroes":** O'Connor, "President Says Nation 'On the Move.'"

290   **named John Evans:** "Rice Named Aide for Probe Body," *Tallahassee Democrat*, November 28, 1963, 17; FLIC Meeting Minutes for November 10, 1963, Clerk of the House Papers; John Evans, letter CC: Remus Strickland, March 15, 1963, Box 2, FLIC Papers; "Biographical Sketch, John Evans," circa 1963, Clerk of the House Papers; Bonnie Stark, "McCarthyism in Florida: Charley Johns and the Florida Legislative Investigation Committee July, 1956 to July, 1965" (master's thesis, University of South Florida, 1985), 97, https://palmm.digital.flvc.org/islandora/object/usf%3A49370#page/title/mode/1up, 214.

290   **"warped minds and hatreds":** Stacy Braukman, *Communists and Perverts Under the Palms: The Johns Committee in Florida, 1956–1965* (University Press of Florida, 2012), 167; "Ex-FBI Agent Hired by State Probing Group," *Tampa Bay Times*, November 28, 1963, 5B.

290   **delivering regular status:** Stark, "McCarthyism in Florida," 215.

290   **closed the books on 1963:** FLIC Meeting Minutes for January 2, 1964, Clerk of the House Papers.

290   **Evans proposed the creation:** FLIC Meeting Minutes for January 2, 1964; "Staff Report and Recommendation," FLIC, January 2, 1964, Clerk of the House Papers.

290   **shock technique:** "Memorandum," Advisory Committee on Homosexuality, June 4, 1962, 3, Box 57, Bryant Papers.

290 absent at a key moment: FLIC Meeting Minutes for January 2, 1964.

290 "To pursue the approach": "Staff Report and Recommendation," FLIC, January 2, 1964.

291 hearing for January 29: FLIC Meeting Minutes for January 29, 1964, Clerk of the House Papers.

291 "Report on Homosexuality": FLIC Meeting Minutes for January 29, 1964.

291 mailboxes on March 11: "Homosexuality and Citizenship in Florida: A Report of the Florida Legislative Investigation Committee, January 1964," FLIC, January 1964, Bonnie Stark Papers; John Evans, letter to Lester Kafer, March 2, 1964, Box 2, FLIC Papers; Richard Mitchell, letter to F. Wilson Carraway, March 11, 1964, Box 82, Bryant Papers; James Buchanan and Robert Sherrill, "Booklet on Homosexuality Shocks State Legislators," *Miami Herald*, March 18, 1964, 1.

291 limited to 2,000 copies: John Evans, letter to Ralph Guyette, July 2, 1964, Box 2, FLIC Papers; Buchanan and Sherrill, "Booklet on Homosexuality Shocks State Legislators," 1.

291 Readers who were: John Evans, letter to Ralph Guyette, July 2, 1964; Buchanan and Sherrill, "Booklet on Homosexuality Shocks State Legislators."

291 "Given the background": John Evans, letter to Bonnie Stark, September 27, 1984, Bonnie Stark Papers.

292 "every parent and every": "Homosexuality and Citizenship in Florida."

292 a blond teenage boy: "Homosexuality and Citizenship in Florida."

292 "the best and current estimate": "Homosexuality and Citizenship in Florida"; Alfred Kinsey, Wardell Pomeroy, and Clyde E. Martin, *Sexual Behavior in the Human Male* (W. B. Saunders, 1948); Justin E. Harlow, Transcript of Testimony, January 22, 1959, Box 7, 1518, FLIC Papers.

292 conflating the Revised Standard Version: "Homosexuality and Citizenship in Florida"; 1 Corinthians 6:9, RSV translation; *Diagnostic and Statistical Manual of Mental Disorders* (American Psychiatric Association, 1952).

292 "Why Be Concerned?": "Homosexuality and Citizenship in Florida."

293 "Glossary of Homosexual": "Homosexuality and Citizenship in Florida."

293 "Additional copies": "Homosexuality and Citizenship in Florida."

293 "Complaints from public": Richard Gerstein, telegram to John Evans, March 18, 1964, Box 2, FLIC Papers.

294 tried to fudge: Richard Mitchell, letter to Richard Gerstein, March 23, 1964, Box 2, FLIC Papers.

294 "The note at the end": Richard Gerstein, letter to Richard Mitchell, March 26, 1964, Box 2, FLIC Papers.

294 "nauseating": James Buchanen and Robert Sherrill, "Pervert Booklet Published," *Miami Herald*, March 18, 1964, 1B.

294 "strongly objected": "Report Raises Objections," *Tampa Times*, March 18, 1964, 1.

294 "flabbergasted": "Report Raises Objections."

294 Maxine Baker: "Solons Criticize Deviate Report," *Tallahassee Democrat*, March 18, 1964, 11.

294   **"nothing but obscenity"**: "Homosexuality Report Stirs 'Obscenity' Furor," *Fort Lauderdale News*, March 19, 1964, 4B.

294   **Wilson Carraway**: "Report on Homosexuality Denounced by Legislators," *News-Press*, March 19, 1964, 12.

294   **"definitely opposed"**: Thelma Wells, telegram to Richard Mitchell, March 18, 1964, Box 2, FLIC Papers.

294   **"jumping off point"**: "Solons Criticize Deviate Report."

294   **"The pictorial exhibitions"**: James W. Kynes, "For Immediate Release," March 19, 1964, Box 82, Bryant Papers.

294   **Bryant held a press**: "Bryant, Kynes Oppose Public Deviate Report," *Tallahassee Democrat*, March 20, 1964, 1.

294   **"good motives"**: "Bryant, Kynes Oppose Public Deviate Report."

295   **"availability to the public"**: J. E. Neblett, telegram to Farris Bryant, March 20, 1964, Box 82, Bryant Papers.

295   **"The publication to which"**: Farris Bryant, form response letter, circa March 1964, Box 82, Bryant Papers.

295   **"I have been assured"**: Farris Bryant, form response letter, circa March 1964.

295   **"who bothered to"**: Stark, "McCarthyism in Florida," 221.

295   **"alert"**: Barbara Frye, "Homosexuality Report Shocks Kynes, He Says," *Pensacola News Journal*, March 20, 1964, 6A.

295   **"not pleasant" but**: Stark, "McCarthyism in Florida," 220.

295   **purple pamphlet**: Tom Smith, "County Solicitor Defends Pamphlet on Homosexuals," *Miami Herald*, March 20, 1964, 1B.

295   **"I personally hope that you"**: Good Citizen, letter to Richard Mitchell, March 20, 1964, Box 2, FLIC Papers.

296   **Richard Pettigrew**: John Evans, letter to Richard Pettigrew, April 3, 1964, Box 2, FLIC Papers.

296   **"not for sale"**: Evans, letter to Pettigrew, April 3, 1964.

296   **"use in conformance"**: "By motion of the Legislative . . . ," circa 1964, Box 2, FLIC Papers.

296   **deemed unfit to receive**: Lawrence Rembeau, letter to John Evans, June 12, 1964, Box 2, FLIC Papers; John Evans, letter to Brent Wallis, March 25, 1964, Box 2, FLIC Papers; John Evans, letter to Dick Smith, March 25, 1964, Box 2, FLIC Papers.

296   **Flatterers and friends**: John Evans, letter to Elizabeth Egan, April 28, 1964, Box 2, FLIC Papers; John Evans, letter to Fred Brown, May 20, 1984, Box 2, FLIC Papers; John Evans, letter to Roland Riechmann, May 27, 1964, Box 2, FLIC Papers; John Evans, letter to Joseph Bistowish, April 15, 1964, Box 2, FLIC Papers.

296   **making pre-Xerox-technology**: John Evans, letter to Vermont Citizens for Decent Literature, July 2, 1964, Box 2, FLIC Papers.

296   **Robert Delaney**: John Evans, letter to Paul Welch, April 6, 1964, Box 2, FLIC Papers.

296   **pamphlet to Paul Welsh**: Evans, letter to Welch, April 6, 1964.

296   **Washington, D.C., a mail-order distributor**: Jim Strothman, "That 'Purple Pamphlet' Still a Saleable Item," *Miami Herald*, September 6, 1965, James T. Sears Papers.

296   price of $2: Strothman, "That 'Purple Pamphlet' Still a Saleable Item."
297   "smut market": "State's 'Purple Pamphlet' Costly in Smut Market," *Miami Herald*, April 22, 1967, 8C.
297   "A Potomac News Co.": "State's 'Purple Pamphlet' Costly in Smut Market."

CHAPTER 28. PURPLE PANIC

298   "The war to protect the people": Robert H. Williams, "Sex, Tallahassee," *New Republic*, May 23, 1964, 5, Box 19, FLIC Papers.
298   "I would like to join": Hal Call, "Open Letter to the Florida Legislature's 'Johns Committee,'" *Mattachine Review* 10, no. 11 (November–December 1964): 5.
299   "irresponsible": Paul Welch, "Homosexuality in America," *Life*, June 26, 1964, accessed online, https://mudcub.com/homophobia/homosexuality_in _america.htm.
299   Evans gave a keynote address: John Evans, "Remarks . . . to the Annual Convention of the Florida Federation of Women's Clubs," April 15, 1964, #10-31, Box 1, FLIC Papers.
299   "You may have heard": Evans, "Remarks . . . to the Annual Convention of the Florida Federation of Women's Clubs."
300   "Gentlemen of the Legislature": Richard Mitchell, letter to Gentlemen of the Legislature, April 15, 1964, Box 2, FLIC Papers.
300   cited figure of 123: "Sex Charges Unchecked, Official Says," *Miami Herald*, April 16, 1965, Section C.
300   "Gentlemen of the Committee": Richard Mitchell, letter to Gentlemen of the Committee, April 15, 1964, #11-69, Box 2, FLIC Papers.
300   quoted the estimate: "Board Due Perversion Details," *Orlando Sentinel*, April 19, 1964, 18A.
300   memo labeled "10-45": "Florida Legislature Investigation Committee," 1961, #10-45, Bonnie Stark Papers.
301   "I did not say that 123": John Evans, letter to Stanford Witwer, April 27, 1964, Box 2, FLIC Papers.
301   because "other commitments": FLIC Meeting Minutes for June 5, 1964, Clerk of the House Papers.
301   one-man gay political movement: "Perverts' Lobby Lashed," *Miami News*, July 21, 1964, 6B; Jim Giltmier, "Homosexual Law Deletions Asked," *Miami Herald*, December 15, 1964, 2C; Maurice Labelle, "Miami Cabbie Leads Drive to Relax State Homo Laws," *Coral Gables Times*, March 11, 1965, 2, James T. Sears Papers.
301   letter-writing campaign: Richard Inman, letter to Richard Mitchell, May 24, 1965, James T. Sears Papers.
301   "A figure closer to 200,000": Richard Inman, "Blueprint For?," *Atheneum Review* 1, no. 4 (December 1964): 7.
301   Pettigrew's office responded: Richard Pettigrew, letter to Richard Inman, June 21, 1965, James T. Sears Papers.
301   "seems that the Johns Committee": Richard Inman, letter to Warren D. Adkins, April 21, 1965, James T. Sears Papers.

301   **as Florida Mattachine:** Richard Inman, "Viewpoint" newsletter, August 1965, James T. Sears Papers.

301   **civil rights impulse:** Craig Loftin, *Masked Voices: Gay Men and Lesbians in Cold War America* (SUNY Press, 2012), 7–8.

301   **"Prejudices of the era":** Loftin, *Masked Voices*, 7, 9.

301   **came to Orlando:** "Martin Luther King Visits Orlando," *Orlando Evening Star*, March 7, 1964, 4B; David D. Porter, "Living 'in Two Different Worlds,'" *Orlando Sentinel*, August 10, 2003, G5.

301   **"wind of change":** "Martin Luther King Visits Orlando"; Porter, "Living 'in Two Different Worlds.'"

301   **"how expensive its funeral":** "Martin Luther King Visits Orlando"; Porter, "Living 'in Two Different Worlds.'"

302   **freeing of the "St. Augustine Four":** "Florida Frees 4 Youths Held 5 Months for Sit-in," *New York Times*, January 15, 1964; "Negro Leaders Here Say They Are Arming in the Event of Race Trouble," *St. Augustine Record*, Appendix 1 to "Racial and Civil Disorders in St. Augustine," FLIC, 1964.

302   **"keep our kids white":** Paul Wills, "St. Augustine's Hoss Manucy Heads Big Segregation Army," *Sarasota Herald-Tribune*, June 30, 1964, Clerk of the House Papers.

302   **a "long, hot summer":** "King Promises Long, Hot Summer," *Fort Pierce Tribune*, March 19, 1964, 1.

302   **May 18, 1964:** "Racial and Civil Disorders in St. Augustine," FLIC, February 1965, 9.

302   **"flooding the jails":** "Racial and Civil Disorders in St. Augustine," 10–11.

302   **"the most lawless city":** "Racial and Civil Disorders in St. Augustine," 11.

302   **June 10, the U.S. Senate broke:** E. W. Kenworthy, "Senate Invokes Closure on Rights Bill, 71 to 29, Ending 75-Day Filibuster," *New York Times*, June 11, 1964, 1.

302   **Monson Motor Lodge:** "King Jailed in St. Augustine Mix Try," *Orlando Sentinel*, June 12, 1964, 1.

302   **Farris Bryant invoked emergency powers:** "Racial and Civil Disorders in St. Augustine," FLIC, February 1965, 15, Appendix II; "St. Augustine Control Taken by the State," *Tallahassee Democrat*, June 16, 1964, 1; "Bryant's Police Guard St. Augustine Marchers," *Tampa Bay Times*, June 16, 1964, 1.

302   **"Letter from the St. Augustine Jail":** Taylor Branch, *Pillar of Fire: America in the King Years, 1963–1965* (Simon & Schuster, 1998), 340.

302   **"dictating this letter":** Branch, *Pillar of Fire*, 340.

302   **"Do not be a spectator":** Theodore Gibson, "Sermon of the Week," *Miami News*, June 13, 1964, 8.

302   **June 12, the Ku Klux Klan:** "Racial and Civil Disorders in St. Augustine," FLIC, February 1965, 14.

303   **"The Kluxers were":** Neale J. Pearson, "It Happened in St. Augustine," *Florida Alligator*, June 17, 1964, 1.

303   **"If you marched with":** Pearson, "It Happened in St. Augustine."

303   **Charley Johns hired private agents:** Martin Waldron, "Saga of the Johns Committee," *Tampa Bay Times*, September 13, 1964, 4D.

303   **"Lynch location":** JB, memo to SM, July 23, 1964, Box 6, FLIC Papers.

303   offered protection: JB, memo to SM, July 23, 1964.

303   "the cliff's edge of a crisis": Clarence Jones and Gene Miller,
      "How Will White Leaders Solve Race Crisis?" *Miami Herald*, June 14,
      1964, 14A.

303   That June 18: John Herbers, "16 Rabbis Arrested as Pool Dive-In Sets Off St.
      Augustine Rights Clash," *New York Times*, June 19, 1964, 1, 16; "Why We
      Went: A Joint Letter from the Rabbis Arrested in St. Augustine," June 19,
      1964, accessed via RAC, https://rac.org/why-we-went-joint-letter
      -rabbis-arrested-st-augustine.

303   nearby Chimes Restaurant: Herbers, "16 Rabbis Arrested as Pool Dive-In
      Sets Off St. Augustine Rights Clash."

303   mass arrest of rabbis: "Why They Went: The Forgotten Story of the St.
      Augustine 17," *Tablet*, June 18, 2019, https://www.tabletmag.com
      /sections/news/articles/the-st-augustine-17.

303   restore "racial harmony": "Racial and Civil Disorders in St. Augustine,"
      FLIC, February 1965, Appendix 14.

303   "immoral": Branch, *Pillar of Fire*, 355.

303   passed the Civil Rights Act: "73 to 27, Historic Rights Vote," *New York
      Times*, June 21, 1964, 134; "Senate Passes Civil Rights Bill," *Orlando
      Sentinel*, June 20, 1964, 1.

303   of a biracial committee: "Biracial Council Named by Bryant," *Miami
      Herald*, July 1, 1964, 1; "Racial and Civil Disorders in St. Augustine," FLIC,
      February 1965, 45.

303   "The purpose of our": "Racial Peace Returns to Augustine," *Pensacola News
      Journal*, July 1, 1964, 3.

303   Gibson abided by: Jack Oswald, "Integration Pace Hit Here," *Miami News*,
      June 2, 1963, 14A.

304   biracial committee was not staffed: "Governor Hits Critics on St. Augustine,"
      Orlando Sentinel, September 11, 1964, 5.

304   July 2, 1964, the U.S. House: "President Signs Civil Rights Bill; Bids All Back
      It," *New York Times*, July 3, 1964, 1, 9.

304   Johnson administration planned: Branch, *Pillar of Fire*, 387–90.

304   "My fellow citizens": Branch, *Pillar of Fire*, 387–90; "President
      Signs Civil Rights Bill; Bids All Back It," 19.

304   won the Nobel Peace Prize: "Martin Luther King Wins the Nobel Prize for
      Peace," *New York Times*, October 15, 1964, 1.

304   "biggest jokes of the year": "St. Augustine Police Chief Says King Award Is
      'Joke,'" *Tampa Tribune*, October 15, 1964, 1.

304   "The New South is here": Amanda Regan and Eric Gonzaba, "Mapping the
      New Gay South: Queer Space and Southern Life, 1965–1980," *Southern
      Quarterly* 58, nos. 1–2 (Fall 2020/Winter 2021): 11.

304   iconic anti-Reconstructionist phrase: Henry Louis Gates, Jr., *Stony the
      Road: Reconstruction, White Supremacy, and the Rise of Jim Crow*
      (Penguin Books, 2019).

304   symbolize a resurgent Dixie: Amanda Bryan, "Henry Grady's Vision of the
      New South," *Teaching American History* (blog), January 6, 2022, https://
      teachingamericanhistory.org/blog/henry-gradys-vision-of-the-new-south/.

304   "Teacher 'Morals' Case": Robert Sherrill, "Teacher 'Morals' Case List Said to Be Nonexistent," *Tampa Bay Times*, June 1, 1964, 2.

304   "I don't know": Sherrill, "Teacher 'Morals' Case List Said to Be Nonexistent."

304   "remaining lead sheets": Karen L. Graves, *And They Were Wonderful Teachers: Florida's Purge of Gay and Lesbian Teachers* (University of Illinois Press, 2009), 116.

304   diagnosed with cancer: Bonnie Stark, "McCarthyism in Florida: Charley Johns and the Florida Legislative Investigation Committee July, 1956 to July, 1965" (master's thesis, University of South Florida, 1985), 97, https://palmm.digital.flvc.org/islandora/object/usf%3A49370#page/title/mode/1up, 221–22; "Probe United Director Won't Reconsider Quitting Post," *Tampa Tribune*, September 22, 1964, 4.

305   he largely ignored the commotion: "State Prober 'Won't Resign,'" *Miami News*, September 29, 1964, 14A.

305   began to meet independently: FLIC Meeting Minutes for September 3, 1964, Clerk of the House Papers.

305   reconvened FLIC: FLIC Meeting Minutes for September 3, 1964.

305   Mitchell "advised the staff": FLIC Meeting Minutes for September 3, 1964.

305   "an appearance subpoena": FLIC Meeting Minutes for September 3, 1964.

305   "he doubted it would": FLIC Meeting Minutes for September 3, 1964.

305   "ride herd on this project": FLIC Meeting Minutes for September 3, 1964.

305   September 8, Evans, along with: Martin Waldron, "Sen. Charley Johns Resigns Committee Named After Him," *Tampa Bay Times*, October 1, 1964, 1; Stark, "McCarthyism in Florida," 222.

306   *"Dear Dick"*: John Evans, resignation letter to Richard Mitchell, September 8, 1964, Box 82, Bryant Papers.

306   "great regret": Richard Mitchell, statement on resignations, September 9, 1964, Box 82, Bryant Papers.

306   "not so much what": Robert Sherrill, "State Investigators Told 'Probe Bryant,' They Quit," *Miami Herald*, September 10, 1964, 1.

306   "When a staff is": Sherrill, "State Investigators Told 'Probe Bryant,' They Quit."

306   "inside dope": Martin Waldron, "Saga of the Johns Committee," *Tampa Bay Times*, September 13, 1964, 4D.

306   "Staff members learned": "No Communists in Florida Universities, Says Bryant," *Tampa Tribune*, September 11, 1964, 12A.

307   Johns announced his sudden: Vernon Bradford, "Williams, Johns Quit Probe Unit," *Tampa Tribune*, 1, 4A; "Future of Probe Up in Air," *Tallahassee Democrat*, October 1, 1964, 17.

307   "close the office": "Resignations of 2 Senators Spell End of Legislative Probing Committee," *Fort Lauderdale News*, October 1, 1964, 22.

307   "I disagree that": "Legislators Quit Probe Committee," *News-Press*, October 1, 1964, 3.

307   "The only thing the Committee": Martin Waldron, "Sen. Charley Johns Resigns Committee Named After Him," *Tampa Bay Times*, October 1, 1964, 1.

307 **"Charley Johns is":** "Still Want St. Augustine Probe, Johns Says," *Miami Herald*, October 6, 1964, 2-B; "Legislators Quit Probe Committee."

CHAPTER 29. DEATH STROKE

311 **Chairman Mitchell emerged:** "Mitchell Says State Probers Still Have Things to Say," *Palm Beach Post*, October 2, 1964, 8s; "Proposal with Staff Director, January 1, 1964–June 30, 1965," Clerk of the House Papers.

311 **"Racial and Civil Disorders":** "Racial and Civil Disorders in St. Augustine," FLIC, February 1965; Richard Mitchell, letter to "To Whom It May Concern," October 13, 1964, Clerk of the House Papers.

311 **"The sooner it":** "Hefty Report Submitted by Legislative Probers," *Tallahassee Democrat*, May 22, 1965, 2.

311 **not sponsor an extension bill:** Bonnie Stark, "McCarthyism in Florida: Charley Johns and the Florida Legislative Investigation Committee July, 1956 to July, 1965" (master's thesis, University of South Florida, 1985), 97, https://palmm.digital.flvc.org/islandora/object/usf%3A49370#page/title/mode/1up, 226.

311 **enabling statute expired:** Stark, "McCarthyism in Florida."

312 **($497,150):** Calculation arrived at by tallying legislative appropriations already cited: (1956) $50,000 + (1957) $75,000 + (1959) $75,000 + (1961) $75,000 + (1962) $67,150 + (1963) $155,000 = $512,150.

312 **"executive session":** Stephen Kahn, letter to Bonnie Stark, June 26, 1980, Bonnie Stark Papers; Constitution of 1885, State of Florida, https://library.law.fsu.edu/Digital-Collections/CRC/CRC-1998/conhist/1885con.html.

312 **"doors of each House":** Constitution of 1885, State of Florida.

312 **Department of Law Enforcement:** Department of Law Enforcement, "Agreement for Transfer of Records to Florida State Archives," April 24, 1972, Bonnie Stark Papers.

312 **greater pension payments:** "Lower on the Hog for Charley Johns," *Tampa Times*, May 20, 1965, 12.

312 **"He proposed":** "Lower on the Hog for Charley Johns."

313 ***Swann v. Adams:*** *Swann v. Adams*, June 22, 1964, https://supreme.justia.com/cases/federal/us/378/553/; "Happy State Leaders Plan for Election," *Orlando Sentinel*, February 8, 1963, 1.

313 **beloved 15th senatorial district:** "Two Members of Senate Majority Bloc Bumped," *News-Press*, May 5, 1960, 1.

313 **brand-new 5th District:** Stark, "McCarthyism in Florida," 228; "Keep Senator Charley Johns 5th District," *Tallahassee Democrat*, May 22, 1966, 7D; "Candidates in Accord Second District Too Big," *Tallahassee Democrat*, April 27, 1966, 4.

313 **tamper with his new boundaries:** "Choppers All but Kill One Plan to Block Foes," *Tampa Tribune*, June 19, 1965, 4.

313 **His gallbladder condition:** "Sen. Johns 'Good' After Operation," *Miami Herald*, December 29, 1965, 2A.

313 **"good":** "Sen. Johns 'Good' After Operation."

313   **"We can't quite":** "For Senate, with Misgivings," *Tallahassee Democrat*, May 22, 1966, 4.

313   **Class of 1958:** Seminole 1958 yearbook, University of Florida.

313   **Charley won the May:** "Some Old-Time Senators Jobless," *Orlando Evening Star*, May 4, 1966, 2.

314   **Charley lost:** "First Victory Hard One for Lawyer Who Defeated Johns," *Tampa Tribune*, May 27, 1966, 1B; "Davis Edges Johns by 282 Votes," *Bradford County Telegraph*, May 26, 1966, 1.

314   **"Johns Beaten":** "Charley Johns Beaten After 32 Years," *Pensacola News Journal*, May 29, 1966, 6D.

314   **"some discrepancies":** "Charley Johns Beaten After 32 Years."

314   **"'Pork Choppers' Fall":** "'Pork Choppers' Fall by Wayside in State," *Pensacola News Journal*, May 4, 1966, 21.

314   **held on to just seven seats:** Berkeley Miller and William Canak, "From 'Porkchoppers' to 'Lambchoppers': The Passage of Florida's Public Employee Relations Act," *ILR Review* 44, no. 2 (1991): 353; Robert McKnight, "Reapportionment in 1960s Led to State's Transformation," *Gainesville Sun*, September 6, 2013, https://www.gainesville.com/story/news/2013/09/08/robert-mcknight-reapportionment-in-1960s-led-to-states-transformation/31852640007/.

314   **Kirk Jr. was elected governor:** "Kirk Pledges Harmony with Cabinet, Legislators," *Tampa Times*, November 9, 1966, 1.

314   **sowed further uncertainty:** Vernon Bradford and Tom O'Connor, "The Peaceful Legislature May Not Stay That Way," *Tampa Tribune*, May 16, 1965, 4B.

314   **"I'm going to leave":** "Johns Says He Won't Contest His Defeat," *Tampa Bay Times*, May 28, 1966, 3B.

314   **Government in the Sunshine:** "Kirk Signs 'Sunshine' Meeting Bill into Law," *Tampa Tribune*, July 13, 1967, 10.

314   **Emory Cross:** "Kirk Signs 'Sunshine' Meeting Bill into Law."

315   **and a fine of $500:** "Government in Sunshine Passed Along to Senate," *Tampa Tribune*, June 28, 1967, 8.

315   **revisited *Swann v. Adams*:** *Swann v. Adams*, 1967, https://supreme.justia.com/cases/federal/us/385/440/.

315   **1968 constitution:** George Hanna, "New Charter's Main Changes," *Miami News*, November 1, 1968, 56.

315   **Florida's eighty-three-year experiment:** Frank Caperton, "Revision Erases Color Line in State," *Florida Today*, October 8, 1968, 12C.

315   **1968, Gibson mediated:** Carita Swanson Vonk, *Theodore R. Gibson: Priest, Prophet, and Politician* (Little River Press, 1997), 81–82; "'The Community Is Involved Now,' Student Says," *Miami Herald*, May 15, 1968, 8.

315   **police station and joined:** "'The Community Is Involved Now,' Student Says."

315   **"died in vain":** "Negro Pastor Sees Hope in King's Death," *Miami Herald*, April 9, 1968, 2B.

315   **led an opening prayer:** Journal of the House, April 20, 1970, 234.

315   **"As they engage":** Journal of the House, April 20, 1970, 234.

316   **nominated Father Theodore:** Vonk, *Theodore R. Gibson*, 85; "City Commission Appoints Gibson," *Miami Herald*, April 19, 1972, 1B.

316   **"Politics is not my":** Ed Taylor, "Crusader Gibson Now in City Hall," *Miami News*, April 19, 1972, 1.

316   **1973, Gibson became the vice-mayor:** Vonk, *Theodore R. Gibson*, 85; Louis Salome, "Reboso, Gibson Win in Runoff," *Miami News*, November 14, 1973, 5.

316   **Park was renamed:** "Park to Honor Gibson," *Miami Herald*, November 27, 1980, 20.

316   **prostate cancer:** "Gibson's Illness Delays City Votes," *Miami Herald*, January 21, 1981, 29.

316   **announced soon afterward:** Bill Gjebre, "Where Is Theo Gibson's Successor?" *Miami News*, January 20, 1981, 9.

316   **Gibson took his final:** "Theodore Gibson Helped Free Us All," *Miami News*, September 22, 1982, 12.

316   **hundreds filed by his:** Michael Browning, "Tears, Smiles Express 'Goodby' to Gibson," *Miami Herald*, September 24, 1982, 1C.

316   **"In 1959, he was sentenced":** "Rev. T. R. Gibson Dies: Rights Activist Was 67," *New York Times*, September 22, 1982, D25.

316   **"He was beloved":** Congressional Record, House of Representatives, September 21, 1982; Vonk, *Theodore R. Gibson*, 131.

316   **continued to hold court:** "Proud Porkchopper Denies Running Raiford as Fiefdom," *Palm Beach Post*, April 20, 1972, 10; Ray Washington, "The Porkchopper," *Fort Pierce Tribune*, May 27, 1979, 5.

317   **"Charley E. Johns":** "'Porkchopper' Charley Johns: Didn't Like Job," *Playground Daily News*, December 19, 1977, 15.

317   **"The Johns Committee":** Mike Fowler, "Charley Johns: From Flour Sacks to the Statehouse," *Tampa Tribune*, May 7, 1972, 4–5.

317   **"We went investigating":** Charles Johns, oral history interview, Ray Washington, 1979, Samuel Proctor Oral History Program, University of Florida Archives.

317   **"naïve":** Fowler, "Charley Johns: From Flour Sacks to the Statehouse."

317   **"I tell you, I don't get":** Fowler, "Charley Johns: From Flour Sacks to the Statehouse."

317   **he rebuffed her request:** Stark, "McCarthyism in Florida," 229.

CHAPTER 30. DAYS OF FUTURE, PASSED

318   **Tampa's state senate seat:** "Johns Committee-Type Investigations Hit," *Tampa Tribune*, April 8, 1966, 21.

318   **"From my experience":** "Johns Committee-Type Investigations Hit," B.

318   **thumping at the ballot:** "Legislative Races Spotlight Education," *Tampa Tribune*, May 1, 1966, 14B; "District 34," *Tampa Tribune*, May 6, 1966, 27.

318   **his "big switch":** David Watson, "McClain Beams as He Bags Big One," *Tampa Tribune*, November 15, 1968, 2B.

319   **Hillsborough County solicitor:** Ron Hutchinson, "Solicitor Bill Up for Talk," *Tampa Times*, April 24, 1967, 8.

319   **office again in 1972:** "Mark Hawes," *Tampa Bay Times*, September 10, 1972, 14I.

319   **omitted his nearly seven years:** "Vote for Mark Hawes," *Tampa Tribune*, September 11, 1972, 5B.

319   **lost his bid:** "Lester, Simmons in Oct. 3 Run-off," *Tampa Times*, September 13, 1972, 11.

319   **debilitating stroke:** Bonnie Stark, "McCarthyism in Florida: Charley Johns and the Florida Legislative Investigation Committee July, 1956 to July, 1965" (master's thesis, University of South Florida, 1985), 97, https://palmm.digital .flvc.org/islandora/object/usf%3A49370#page/title/mode/1up, 231–32; Bonnie Stark, interview with Robert Fieseler, August 22, 2021.

319   **their Tampa residence:** Mark Hawes, letter on letterhead to Remus Strickland, February 10, 1960, Box 3, FLIC Papers; Bonnie Stark, "McCarthyism in Florida," 231; "Ex-Hillsborough Prosecutor Dies," *Tampa Tribune*, April 25, 1985, 11B.

319   **kept scrapbooks:** Bonnie Stark, interview with Robert Fieseler, August 22, 2021.

319   **wear prison stripes:** "Floyd Christian, Ex-Education Chief," *Tallahassee Democrat*, May 14, 1998, 9C; "Turlington Needs Letterhead," *Orlando Sentinel*, December 21, 1975, 54.

319   **awarding $1.5 million:** "Floyd T. Christian After Federal Sentencing— Tallahassee, Florida," Florida Memory, 1975, https://www.floridamemory .com/items/show/103391.

319   **died on April 24, 1985:** "Ex-Hillsborough Prosecutor Dies"; Stark, "McCarthyism in Florida," 231–32.

319   **Born in 1954:** Florida Voter Registration Records, Ancestry.com; "Bonnie S. Stark—Florida Personal Injury Lawyer, Attorneys," Searcy Law, accessed December 3, 2024, https://www.searcylaw.com/paralegals/bonnie-s-stark/.

319   **public school kid active:** Miami Norland Senior High School 1971 yearbook, Ancestry.com; Miami Norland Senior High School 1972 yearbook, Ancestry.com.

320   **she graduated with dual:** "Bonnie S. Stark—Florida Personal Injury Lawyer, Attorneys," Searcy Law.

320   **civil rights history:** Bonnie Stark, interview with Robert Fieseler, August 22, 2021; Steven F. Lawson, "The Florida Legislative Investigation Committee and the Constitutional Adjustment of Race Relations, 1956–1963," in *An Uncertain Tradition: Constitutionalism and the History of the South*, ed. Kermit L. Hall and James W. Ely Jr. (University of Georgia Press, 1989).

320   **"I was sitting":** Bonnie Stark, interview with Robert Fieseler, August 22, 2021.

320   **an institutional memory:** Stephen Lawson, interview with Robert Fieseler, September 5, 2024.

320   **"There were colleagues":** Stephen Lawson, interview with Robert Fieseler, September 5, 2024.

320 **"She was a prodigious":** Stephen Lawson, interview with Robert Fieseler, September 5, 2024.

320 **January 1977, the Dade County:** "Bias Against Homosexuals Is Outlawed in Miami," *New York Times*, January 19, 1977, 14; Dudley Clendinen and Adam Nagourney, *Out for Good: The Struggle to Build a Gay Rights Movement in America* (Simon & Schuster, 1999), Location 5770, Kindle.

320 **singer and spokesperson:** Byron O. Parvis, "Singer Anita Bryant Uses 'Christ's Strength,'" *Journal and Courier* (Lafayette, Indiana), October 27, 1973, 10; "'Citrus Songstress' Plans Appearance," *Tampa Tribune*, November 5, 1969; "Spotlighting 2 Baptists: Lillian Carter, Anita Bryant," *Philadelphia Inquirer*, June 17, 1978, 11; Lillian Faderman, *The Gay Revolution: The Story of the Struggle* (Simon & Schuster, 2015), 330.

321 **"resident of Florida for 16 years":** Transcript of Dade County Commission Meeting, January 17, 1977, 17–18, Bryant Papers, National Stonewall Archives.

321 **ordinance passed:** "Bias Against Homosexuals Is Outlawed in Miami," *New York Times*, January 19, 1977.

321 **"just the beginning":** "Gay Measure Passes at Heated Metro Session," *Miami Herald*, January 19, 1977, 4A.

321 **revision to the RSV Bible:** Kathy Baldock, "As a 21-Year-Old Seminarian, David Fearon Challenged the RSV Translators on the Word 'Homosexual,'" *Baptist News Global*, January 11, 2023, https://baptistnews.com/article /as-a-21-year-old-seminarian-david-fearon-challenged-the-rsv-translators -on-the-word-homosexual/.

321 **made to the second edition:** American Psychiatric Association Reference Committee, "Homosexuality and Sexual Orientation Disturbance: Proposed Change in DSM-11, 6th Printing, page 44," November 1973.

321 **they would "be removing":** American Psychiatric Association, "Homosexuality and Sexual Orientation Disturbance."

321 **Save Our Children campaign:** Clendinen and Nagourney, *Out for Good*, Location 5789, Kindle; "Archbishop to Defy Gay Ordinance," *News-Press*, January 28, 1977, 26.

321 **"trying to recruit our children":** "Anita Bryant Pledges to Fight Gay Rights," *Tampa Tribune*, February 16, 1977, 3B; "Friend Day '78 with Anita Bryant," *Florence Morning News*, October 28, 1978, 5.

321 **was a Florida resident:** "Anita Bryant Marries Florida Disc Jockey," *Ada Evening News*, June 26, 1960, 12.

322 **former Miss Oklahoma:** "Anita Bryant Weds Florida Disk Jockey," *Stillwater News-Press*, June 26, 1960, 12.

322 **small army of followers:** "Gay Rights Meeting Criticized," *Palm Beach Post*, March 28, 1977, 25.

322 **had been sealed:** Department of Law Enforcement, "Agreement for Transfer of Records to Florida State Archives," April 24, 1972, Bonnie Stark Papers.

322 **"Records shall":** Department of Law Enforcement, "Agreement for Transfer of Records to Florida State Archives," April 24, 1972.

322   **Bryant embodied the voice:** Robert W. Fieseler, *Tinderbox: The Untold Story of the Up Stairs Lounge Fire and the Rise of Gay Liberation* (Liveright, 2018), 229.

322   **"As a mother, I know that":** "Rites of Lauderdale Take on Gay Tinge," *Palm Beach Post*, April 17, 1977, C4.

322   **record 64,304 signatures:** "Gay-Rights Foes Get Enough Signatures for Repeal or Referendum," *Miami News*, March 14, 1977, 3P.

322   **"The problem is homosexuals":** "Homo Bill Is Enacted," *Panama City News-Herald*, June 1, 1977, 3; "Gov. Askew Gets Bills Outlawing Homosexual Marriages, Adoptions," *News-Press*, June 1, 1977, 8B.

323   **69 percent to 31:** "Gay-Rights Law Is Crushed," *Miami Herald*, June 8, 1977, 1; "Dade Voters Repeal Gay Rights Law," *News-Press,* June 8, 1977, 1; Clendinen and Nagourney, *Out for Good*, Location 5827, Kindle.

323   **"We won 2 to 1":** B. Drummond Ayres Jr., "Miami Vote Increases Activism on Homosexual Rights," *New York Times*, June 9, 1977, 48.

323   **"With God's continued":** B. Drummond Ayres Jr., "Miami Votes 2 to 1 to Repeal Law Barring Bias Against Homosexuals," *New York Times*, June 8, 1977, 1.

323   **Similar legislative campaigns:** Fieseler, *Tinderbox*, 229; "Gay Rights Ordinance Defeated by a Margin Greater Than 2-to-1," *Miami Herald*, June 8, 1977, 18A.

323   **Florida governor signed:** "Gov. Askew Gets Bills Outlawing Homosexual Marriages, Adoptions," 8B; "Florida Moves to Crack Down on Gays," *Wisconsin State Journal*, June 1, 1977, 12.

323   **a drop in popularity:** "Anita Bryant Says She's Been Blacklisted," *Bradenton Herald*, February 25, 1977, 16; "Bryant Receives Ovation," *Word and Way*, June 22, 1978, 5.

323   **Citrus Commission allowed:** "Helping Out Anita Bryant," *New York Times*, September 16, 1980, C8; "Orange Juice Contract Runs Dry for Anita Bryant," *New York Times*, September 2, 1980, 30.

323   **she wrote the Florida:** Stephen Kahn, letter to Bonnie Stark, June 26, 1980, Bonnie Stark Papers.

323   **"I was very naïve":** Bonnie Stark, interview with Robert Fieseler, August 22, 2021.

324   **"Dear Ms. Stark":** Stephen Kahn, letter to Bonnie Stark, June 26, 1980.

324   **ways to complete her thesis:** Bonnie Stark, interview with Robert Fieseler, August 22, 2021.

324   **Stark moved from Tampa to Tallahassee:** Tallahassee City Index, Ancestry .com, https://www.ancestry.com/search/collections/1732/records/321171742 ?tid=&pid=&queryId=0893de86-005f-4516-8048-c73ec20efa2f&_phsrc =Pmf1088&_phstart=successSource.

324   **declined to speak:** Bonnie Stark, "McCarthyism in Florida: Charley Johns and the Florida Legislative Investigation Committee July, 1956 to July, 1965" (master's thesis, University of South Florida, 1985), 97, https://palmm.digital .flvc.org/islandora/object/usf%3A49370#page/title/mode/1up, 229.

324   "confined to his home": Ron Word, "Ex-Governor Didn't Expect Post; Didn't
        Enjoy It Either," *News-Press*, January 27, 1985, 16B.

324   his eightieth-birthday reception: "Sen. Charley Johns Celebrates 80th
        Birthday at Reception," *Bradford County Telegraph*, February 28, 1985, 5A.

324   "He died a horrible": Cliff Herrell, interview with Bonnie Stark, August 3,
        1993, Bonnie Stark Papers.

324   April 1984, Bonnie Stark met: Remus Strickland, transcript of interview
        with Bonnie Stark, April 1984, Bonnie Stark Papers; Stark, "McCarthyism
        in Florida," 231; Bonnie Stark, interview with Robert Fieseler, August 22,
        2021.

325   he got hired by DNR: "DNR Official R. J. Strickland Cleared of Lying to
        Grand Jury," *Palm Beach Post*, July 6, 1980, B12.

325   came under fire on May 6, 1980: Peter Racher, "Natural Resources
        Investigator Indicted," *Tallahassee Democrat*, May 7, 1980, C; "DNR
        Inspector Charged with Perjury," *Tampa Tribune*, May 7, 1980, 22.

325   twenty-page indictment: Racher, "Natural Resources Investigator Indicted";
        "DNR Inspector Charged with Perjury."

325   Unaware of the audio evidence: Racher, "Natural Resources Investigator
        Indicted"; "DNR Inspector Charged with Perjury."

325   arrested, perp-walked: "DNR Inspector Charged with Perjury"; "Inspector
        Suspended," *Tampa Times*, May 8, 1980, 10.

325   "forgotten": "DNR Official R. J. Strickland Cleared of Lying to Grand Jury,"
        Palm Beach Post, July 6, 1980, B12.

325   at 2:15 a.m.: "DNR Official R. J. Strickland Cleared of Lying to Grand
        Jury."

325   "It [the committee] deserves a role": Remus Strickland, transcript of
        interview with Bonnie Stark, April 1984.

326   "heart of gold": Remus Strickland, transcript of interview with Bonnie Stark,
        April 1984.

326   Strickland died: "Remus James Strickland," *Tallahassee Democrat*,
        November 3, 1992, 3B.

326   thesis, "McCarthyism in": Stark, "McCarthyism in Florida," page called
        "Certificate of Approval."

Chapter 31. Truth Will Out

327   In 1971, Copleston quit: Art Copleston, interview with Robert Fieseler, May
        3, 2020.

327   Belmont Psychiatric Hospital: Art Copleston, interview with Robert Fieseler,
        May 3, 2020.

328   June 2, 1972: Art Copleston, interview with Robert Fieseler, July 11, 2021;
        Art Copleston, *Demons and Deliverance* (published by author, 2014),
        Kindle, 197.

328   1270 Panorama Drive: Art Copleston, interview with Robert Fieseler, May 3,
        2020.

328   "You never enjoy anything": Art Copleston, interview with Robert Fieseler,
        May 3, 2020.

328   **"I am a tarnished"**: Art Copleston, outtakes of interview with Allyson Beutke for *Behind Closed Doors*, 1999, Allyson Beutke Papers.

328   **"It became clear that"**: Art Copleston, interview with Robert Fieseler, July 11, 2021.

328   **"Honey, I can't do this"**: Art Copleston, interview with Robert Fieseler, July 11, 2021.

329   **Thus, an unspoken**: Art Copleston, interview with Robert Fieseler, July 11, 2021.

329   **"I'm HIV positive!"**: Art Copleston, interviews with Robert Fieseler, May 3, 2020, and July 11, 2021.

329   **When he passed in 2002**: Art Copleston, interview with Robert Fieseler, July 12, 2021; "Dennis A. Fillmore," Find a Grave, https://www.findagrave.com /memorial/94378178/flora_fillmore#view-photo=146852359.

329   **lost his emotional connection**: Art Copleston, interview with Robert Fieseler, June 14, 2021.

330   **"Had the demeaning"**: Copleston, *Demons and Deliverance*, 265.

330   **Then in 1999**: Allyson Beutke Devito, interview with Robert Fieseler, January 28, 2020.

330   **He flew down**: Art Copleston, outtakes of interview with Allyson Beutke for *Behind Closed Doors*, 1999; Allyson Beutke Devito, interview with Robert Fieseler, February 13, 2023.

330   *Behind Closed Doors*: *Behind Closed Doors: The Dark Legacy of the Johns Committee*, 2000, produced by Allyson Beutke.

330   **"I can't say that"**: John Tileston, transcript of interview with Allyson Beutke, 1999, Allyson Beutke Papers.

330   **"flimsy and self-serving"**: Art Copleston, email to Robert Fieseler, January 19, 2023.

330   **Beutke guessed that**: Allyson Beutke Devito, interview with Robert Fieseler, February 13, 2023.

330   **"He was looking"**: Art Copleston, interview with Robert Fieseler, May 3, 2020.

331   **Tileston passed away**: "John Stanton Tileston Sr.," *Gainesville Sun*, July 23, 2014, https://www.legacy.com/us/obituaries/gainesville/name/john-tileston -obituary?id=16966982.

331   **Johns closed his eyes**: "Charley E. Johns, Ex-Florida Official, 84," *New York Times*, January 25, 1990, D25.

331   **"last of the old"**: "Charley Johns: End of an Era," *Orlando Sentinel*, January 26, 1990, A14.

331   **"He was always very personable"**: "Charley Eugene Johns, 84, Dies; Served as Governor and Lawmaker," *Miami Herald*, January 24, 1990, 2B.

331   **"In 1961, he was"**: "Services Set Today for Former Gov. Johns," *Bradford County Telegraph*, January 25, 1990, 1.

331   **"sometimes controversial figure"**: "From Railroad Conductor to Governor's Mansion, Charley Johns Carved Out Self-Made Career," *Bradford County Telegraph*, January 25, 1990, 4A.

331   **"Floridians undoubtedly felt"**: "Abuser of Power; II," *Miami Herald*, January 26, 1990, 16A.

331   **family held the funeral:** "Funeral Rites Held for Charley Johns Attended by Many State Officials," *Bradford County Telegraph*, February 1, 1990.

331   **"Should death wipe":** "Should Death Wipe the Slate Clean?," letter to the editor, *Miami Herald*, February 10, 1990, 30A.

332   **"Some reporter asked":** Cliff Herrell, interview with Bonnie Stark, August 3, 1993, Bonnie Stark Papers.

332   **Gwen Margolis:** Ellen McGarrahan, "Florida's Secret Shame," *Miami Herald*, December 8, 1991, 9–16.

332   **June 26, 1992:** Stephen Kahn, letter to Bonnie Stark, June 26, 1992, Bonnie Stark Papers.

332   **"grant public access":** Sample ballot, "No. 2 Constitutional Amendment Article I, Section 24, Article XII, Action 20: Access to Public Records and Meetings," November 1992, Bonnie Stark Papers; Karen Branch, "Putting Government in Sunshine," *Miami Herald*, November 1, 1992, 6M.

332   **"Any we're in doubt":** Charlotte Sutton, "Senate Bill Opens More Records," *Tampa Bay Times*, April 3, 1993, 14.

333   **strong veto message:** "Chiles Vetoes Reporter Source Bill," *News-Press*, May 15, 1993, 8B.

333   **more modest bill:** Kahn draft S.B. 20-B, Bonnie Stark Papers.

333   **"This language could":** Bonnie Stark, letter to Toni Jennings, May 25, 1993, Bonnie Stark Papers.

333   **"I believe that when":** Transcript of Bonnie Stark testimony to Senate Committee on Rules and Calendar, May 26, 1993, Bonnie Stark Papers.

334   **"So in other":** Transcript of Bonnie Stark testimony to Senate Committee on Rules and Calendar, May 26, 1993.

334   **"When the Johns":** Transcript of Stephen Kahn testimony to Senate Committee on Rules and Calendar, May 26, 1993.

334   **"forever":** Transcript of Stephen Kahn testimony to Senate Committee on Rules and Calendar, May 26, 1993, Bonnie Stark Papers.

334   **thirty-one legislators voted yea:** Journal of the Senate, May 27, 1993, 83.

Chapter 32. The Great Erasure

336   **estimated 30,000 pages:** Booth Gunter, "State Releases Once-Secret Johns Records," *Tampa Tribune*, July 2, 1993, 1; "They Tried, but Some Names No Longer Secret," *Tampa Tribune*, July 2, 1993, 7; "Records of State's 'Spy' Committee to Be Made Public," *Stuart News*, June 14, 1993, 13.

336   **line-by-line deletions:** Bonnie Stark, interview with Robert Fieseler, August 22, 2021.

337   **"They were just kids":** Bonnie Stark, interview with Robert Fieseler, August 22, 2021; "They Tried, but Some Names No Longer Secret."

337   **"You could track":** "They Tried, but Some Names No Longer Secret."

337   **"incinerated" in 1963:** Michael Browning, "Light of Day to Finally Shine on Sordid State Secrets," *Miami Herald*, June 30, 1993, 17A.

337   **July 1, 1993, when:** Bill Cotterell and Dana Peck, "Opening a Window to a Different Time," *Tallahassee Democrat*, July 1, 1991, 1; Bonnie Stark, interview with Robert Fieseler, August 22, 2021.

337   **into three large piles:** Browning, "Light of Day to Finally Shine on Sordid State Secrets."

337   ***The Philadelphia Inquirer***: Curt Anderson, "Ex-Florida Panel Believed Klan Was Peaceful Group," *Philadelphia Inquirer*, July 4, 1993, A8; Curt Anderson, "McCarthy-Era Panel Was an Anti-Gay Witch Hunt," *San Francisco Examiner*, July 5, 1993, A7.

337   ***The New York Times***: "Florida Examines Era of Suspicion," *New York Times*, July 4, 1993, 14.

338   **Bonnie Stark recalls:** Bonnie Stark, interview with Robert Fieseler, August 22, 2021.

338   **"professional work first":** Bonnie Stark, email to Robert Fieseler, December 16, 2024.

338   **unprecedented records:** Bonnie Stark, interview with Robert Fieseler, August 22, 2021.

338   **"My friends knew":** Bonnie Stark, email to Robert Fieseler, December 16, 2024.

338   **Lawson was taken aback:** Stephen Lawson, interview with Robert Fieseler, September 5, 2024.

338   **"additional":** Ellen Debenport, "Crenshaw Says He Would Not Hire Gays," *Tampa Bay Times*, June 17, 1994, 5A.

338   **"I don't think":** Debenport, "Crenshaw Says He Would Not Hire Gays."

338   **rigorously defended:** Nick Driver, "Florida Is the Odd State Out on Gay Adoptions," *San Francisco Examiner*, July 11, 2002, 6A.

338   **Bush recused himself:** Dana Milbank, "Bush Quietly Slips into Florida," *Kenosha News*, December 27, 2000, A8; Fred Grimm, "Forget It, Jake; It's S. Florida," *Miami Herald*, March 16, 2001, B1.

339   **amended the state constitution:** "Drive to Enshrine Bias Marches On," *Tampa Bay Times*, November 28, 2008, 16A; "Advocates, Opponents Argue Effect on Partner Benefits," *Palm Beach Post*, June 23, 2008, 6A.

339   **summer 2005 issue:** "Charley Johns' Florida Legacy," *The Ledger*, July 2, 2005, https://www.theledger.com/story/news/2005/07/02/charley-johns -florida-legacy/26163542007/; Craig Pittman, "Should the State Now Apologize for Targeting Gay People as a Threat in the 1950s?," *Tampa Bay Times*, February 19, 2019, https://www.tampabay.com/florida-politics/buzz /2019/02/19/florida-had-a-committee-that-targeted-civil-rights-activists-and -homosexuals-can-it-now-apologize/.

339   **magazine *UF Today*:** "Gators You Should Know," *UF Today*, Summer 2005, 27.

339   **UF student union:** "Student Unions at the University of Florida," Reitz Union Division of Student Life, University of Florida, accessed December 2024, https://union.ufl.edu/AboutUs/UnionHistory/; "Johns Building at 725 South Bronough Street—Tallahassee, Florida," Florida Memory, June 1969, https:// www.floridamemory.com/items/show/16375.

339   **2008 that the official song:** Shannon Colavecchio-Van Sickler, "A Dance on State Song," *Tampa Bay Times*, April 11, 2008, 1B, 8B.

339   **2010, when it was struck:** Yolanne Almanzar, "Florida Gay Adoption Ban Is Ruled Unconstitutional," *New York Times*, November 25, 2008; "In Re: Gill," *American Civil Liberties Union* (blog), accessed December 3, 2024,

https://www.aclu.org/cases/re-gill; Steve Rothaus, "Amendment Would Back Gay Adoption Ban," *Naples Daily News*, March 21, 2015, 6A.

CHAPTER 33. ARC OF HISTORY

340 **decided it was past due:** Craig Pittman, "Half a Century Later, Regret for a Witch Hunt," *Tampa Bay Times*, February 21, 2019, 54.

340 **"pointed it out":** Evan Jenne, interview with Robert Fieseler, March 27, 2023.

340 **Stacy Braukman:** Stacy Braukman, interview with Robert Fieseler, February 17, 2023; "Communists and Perverts Under the Palms: The Johns Committee in Florida, 1956–1965," UPF.com, accessed December 2024, https://upf.com/book.asp?id=BRAUK001.

340 **"A concurrent resolution":** Stacy Braukman, "House Concurrent Resolution" draft, January 8, 2019, Stacy Braukman Papers.

341 **February 18, 2019:** "HCR 893 (2019)—Florida Legislative Investigation Committee," accessed December 3, 2024, https://www.myfloridahouse.gov/Sections/Bills/billsdetail.aspx?BillId=65314.

341 **submitted the same resolution:** Lauren Book, interview with Robert Fieseler, March 9, 2023.

341 **"I couldn't get":** Evan Jenne, interview with Robert Fieseler, March 27, 2023.

341 **March 14, 2022:** Patricia Mazzei, "DeSantis Signs Florida Bill That Opponents Call 'Don't Say Gay,'" *New York Times*, March 28, 2022, sec. U.S., https://www.nytimes.com/2022/03/28/us/desantis-florida-dont-say-gay-bill.html; "House Bill 151 (2022)—The Florida Senate," accessed December 3, 2024, https://www.flsenate.gov/Session/Bill/2022/151/ByCategory.

341 **Individual Freedom Act:** "House Bill 7 (2022)—The Florida Senate," accessed December 3, 2024, https://www.flsenate.gov/Session/Bill/2022/7.

342 **"indoctrination masquerading":** Eliza Fawcett and Anemona Hartocollis, "Florida Gives Reasons for Rejecting A.P. African American Studies Class," *New York Times*, January 22, 2023, sec. U.S., https://www.nytimes.com/2023/01/21/us/florida-ap-african-american-studies.html.

342 **the Florida Heritage website:** Margaret Doherty, letter to Bonnie Stark, May 5, 2000, Bonnie Stark Papers.

343 **I composed an email:** Robert Fieseler, email to Beth Golding, August 21, 2021.

344 **I've lugged these around:** Bonnie Stark, interview with Robert Fieseler, August 22, 2021.

EPILOGUE: CLOUD READING

345 **box came back:** Beth Golding, email to Robert Fieseler, November 5, 2021.

INDEX

Note: Italicized page numbers indicate material in photographs or illustrations.

ABOUT THE AUTHOR

Robert W. Fieseler is a journalist investigating marginalized groups and a scholar excavating forgotten histories. A Journalist of the Year with NLGJA: The Association of LGBTQ+ Journalists and recipient of the Pulitzer Traveling Fellowship, his debut book, *Tinderbox*, won seven awards, including the Edgar Award, and his reporting has appeared in *Slate*, *Commonweal*, and *River Teeth*, among others. Fieseler graduated as covaledictorian from the Columbia Journalism School and is pursuing a PhD at Tulane University as a Mellon Fellow. He lives with his husband on the gayest street in New Orleans.